EXAM✓CRAM

CompTIA® A+
220-901 and 220-902

David L. Prowse

Pearson
800 East 96th Street
Indianapolis, Indiana 46240 USA

CompTIA® A+ 220-901 and 220-902 Exam Cram

Copyright © 2016 by Pearson Education, Inc.

ISBN-13: 978-0-7897-5631-2
ISBN-10: 0-7897-5631-5

Library of Congress Control Number: 2015956432

Printed in the United States of America

3   16

Trademarks

All terms mentioned in this book that are known to be trademarks, or service marks have been appropriately capitalized. Pearson IT Certification cannot attest to the accuracy of this information. Use of a term in this book should not be regarded as affecting the validity of any trademark or service mark.

Warning and Disclaimer

Every effort has been made to make this book as complete and as accurate as possible, but no warranty or fitness is implied. The information provided is on an "as is" basis. The author and the publisher shall have neither liability nor responsibility to any person or entity with respect to any loss or damages arising from the information contained in this book or from the use of the DVD or programs accompanying it.

Special Sales

For information about buying this title in bulk quantities, or for special sales opportunities (which may include electronic versions; custom cover designs; and content particular to your business, training goals, marketing focus, or branding interests), please contact our corporate sales department at corpsales@pearsoned.com or (800) 382-3419.

For government sales inquiries, please contact governmentsales@pearsoned.com.

For questions about sales outside the U.S., please contact international@pearsoned.com.

Associate Publisher
Dave Dusthimer

Acquisitions Editor
Betsy Brown

Development Editor
Eleanor C. Bru

Managing Editor
Sandra Schroeder

Senior Project Editor
Tonya Simpson

Copy Editor
Box Twelve Communications

Indexer
Lisa Stumpf

Proofreader
Chuck Hutchinson

Technical Editor
Chris Crayton

Publishing Coordinator
Vanessa Evans

Media Producer
Lisa Matthews

Cover Designer
Alan Clements

Compositor
Studio Galou

Contents at a Glance

DVD Only:

Table of Contents

DVD Only:

About the Author

David L. Prowse is the author of more than a dozen computer training books and video products. He has worked in the computer field for 20 years and loves to share his experience through teaching and writing. He runs the website www.davidlprowse.com, where he gladly answers questions from readers and students.

Acknowledgments

Thanks to David Dusthimer, Betsy Brown, Eleanor Bru, and everyone else at Pearson who was involved in this project.

Special thanks to Chris Crayton, the best technical editor a person could ask for!

About the Technical Reviewer

Chris Crayton (MCSE) is an author, technical consultant, and trainer. Formerly, he worked as a computer technology and networking instructor, information security director, network administrator, network engineer, and PC specialist. Chris has authored several print and online books on PC repair, CompTIA A+, CompTIA Security+, and Microsoft Windows. He also has served as technical editor and content contributor on numerous technical titles for several of the leading publishing companies. Chris holds numerous industry certifications, has been recognized with many professional teaching awards, and has served as a state-level SkillsUSA competition judge.

We Want to Hear from You!

As the reader of this book, *you* are our most important critic and commentator. We value your opinion and want to know what we're doing right, what we could do better, what areas you'd like to see us publish in, and any other words of wisdom you're willing to pass our way.

We welcome your comments. You can email or write to let us know what you did or didn't like about this book—as well as what we can do to make our books better.

Please note that we cannot help you with technical problems related to the topic of this book.

When you write, please be sure to include this book's title and author as well as your name and email address. We will carefully review your comments and share them with the author and editors who worked on the book.

Email: feedback@pearsonitcertification.com

Mail: Pearson IT Certification
           ATTN: Reader Feedback
           800 East 96th Street
           Indianapolis, IN 46240 USA

Reader Services

Register your copy of *CompTIA A+ 220-901 and 220-902 Exam Cram* at www.pearsonitcertification.com for convenient access to downloads, updates, and corrections as they become available. To start the registration process, go to www.pearsonitcertification.com/register and log in or create an account*. Enter the product ISBN 9780789756312 and click Submit. Once the process is complete, you will find any available bonus content under Registered Products.

Be sure to check the box that you would like to hear from us to receive exclusive discounts on future editions of this product.

CompTIA.

Becoming a CompTIA Certified IT Professional is Easy

It's also the best way to reach greater professional opportunities and rewards.

Why Get CompTIA Certified?

Growing Demand

Labor estimates predict some technology fields will experience growth of over 20% by the year 2020.* CompTIA certification qualifies the skills required to join this workforce.

Higher Salaries

IT professionals with certifications on their resume command better jobs, earn higher salaries and have more doors open to new multi-industry opportunities.

Verified Strengths

91% of hiring managers indicate CompTIA certifications are valuable in validating IT expertise, making certification the best way to demonstrate your competency and knowledge to employers.**

Universal Skills

CompTIA certifications are vendor neutral—which means that certified professionals can proficiently work with an extensive variety of hardware and software found in most organizations.

 Learn　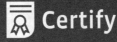 Certify　Work

Learn more about what the exam covers by reviewing the following:

- Exam objectives for key study points.

- Sample questions for a general overview of what to expect on the exam and examples of question format.

- Visit online forums, like LinkedIn, to see what other IT professionals say about CompTIA exams.

Purchase a voucher at a Pearson VUE testing center or at CompTIAstore.com.

- Register for your exam at a Pearson VUE testing center:

- Visit pearsonvue.com/CompTIA to find the closest testing center to you.

- Schedule the exam online. You will be required to enter your voucher number or provide payment information at registration.

- Take your certification exam.

Congratulations on your CompTIA certification!

- Make sure to add your certification to your resume.

- Check out the CompTIA Certification Roadmap to plan your next career move.

Learn more: **Certification.CompTIA.org/aplus**

Introduction

Welcome to the *CompTIA A+ Exam Cram*, Seventh Edition. This book prepares you for the CompTIA A+ 220-901 and 220-902 certification exams. Imagine that you are at a testing center and have just been handed the passing scores for these exams. The goal of this book is to make that scenario a reality. My name is David L. Prowse, and I am happy to have the opportunity to serve you in this endeavor. Together, we can accomplish your goal to attain the CompTIA A+ certification.

Target Audience

The CompTIA A+ exams measure the necessary competencies for an entry-level IT professional with the equivalent knowledge of at least 12 months of hands-on experience in the lab or field.

This book is for persons who have experience working with desktop computers and mobile devices and want to cram for the A+ certification exam—*cram* being the key word. This book does not cover everything in the computing world; how could you in such a concise package? However, this guide is fairly thorough and should offer you a lot of insight...and a whole lot of test preparation.

If you do not feel that you have the required experience, have never attempted to troubleshoot a computer, or are new to the field, then I recommend the following:

▶ Attend a hands-on A+ class with a knowledgeable instructor.

▶ Consider purchasing the *CompTIA A+ Cert Guide*, which goes into much more depth than this text. On a side note, another great reference book that should be on every computer technician's shelf is the latest edition of *Upgrading and Repairing PCs* by Scott Mueller.

Essentially, three types of people will read this book: those who want a job in the IT field, those who want to keep their job, and those who simply want a basic knowledge of computers and want to validate that knowledge. For those of you in the first group, the new CompTIA A+ certification can have a positive career impact, increasing the chances of securing a position in the IT world. It also acts as a stepping stone to more advanced certifications. For those in the second group, preparing for the exams serves to keep your skills sharp and your knowledge up-to-date, helping you to remain a well-sought-after technician. For those of you in the third group, the knowledge within this book can be very beneficial to just about any organization you might work for—as long as that organization uses computers!

Regardless of your situation, one thing to keep in mind is that I write my books to teach you how to be a well-rounded computer technician. While the main goal for this book is to help you become A+ certified, I also want to share my experience with you so that you can grow as an individual.

A person might be tempted to purchase this book solely for the practice exams, but I recommend against studying the practice questions *only*. This book was designed from the ground up to build your knowledge in such a way that when you get to the practice exams, they can act as the final key to passing the real exams. The knowledge in the chapters is the cornerstone, whereas the practice exam questions are the battlements. Complete the entire book and you will have built yourself an impenetrable castle of knowledge.

About the CompTIA A+ 220-901 and 220-902 Exams

This book covers the CompTIA A+ 220-901 and 220-902 exams. There are quite a few changes and additions to these versions of the A+ exams including the following:

▶ Increased content concerning the troubleshooting of hardware and software.

▶ Troubleshooting questions are to be found in *both* exams.

▶ Addition of Windows 8 and 8.1 content.

▶ Windows XP operating system has been removed.

▶ OS X and Linux operating system basics have been added.

▶ Content on mobile devices, such as tablets and smartphones, has been increased.

▶ Increased performance-based questions where you will be required to answer questions within simulated computer environments, drag-and-drop scenarios, and other performance-related settings.

This book covers all these changes and more within its covers.

For more information about how the A+ certification can help your career, or to download the latest official objectives, access CompTIA's web page at http://certification.comptia.org/.

About This Book

This book is organized into 20 chapters, each pertaining to particular objectives on the exam. Because the official CompTIA objectives can have long names that sometimes deal with multiple subjects, the chapters are divided into more manageable (and memorable) topics. All the questions in this book refer to these topics. Chapter topics and the corresponding CompTIA objectives are listed in the beginning of each chapter.

For the most part, the exam topics in this book are structured to build on one another. Because of this, you should read this entire book in order to best prepare for the CompTIA A+ exams. If you want to review a particular topic, those topics are listed at the end of this introduction. In addition, you can use the index or the table of contents to quickly find the concept you are after.

Chapter Format and Conventions

Every Exam Cram chapter follows a standard structure and contains graphical clues about important information. The structure of each chapter includes the following:

▶ **Opening topics list:** This defines the topics to be covered in the chapter; it also lists the corresponding CompTIA A+ objective numbers.

▶ **Topical coverage:** The heart of the chapter, this explains the topics from a hands-on and a theory-based standpoint. This includes in-depth descriptions, tables, and figures geared to build your knowledge so that you can pass the exam. The chapters are broken down into between two and five topics each.

▶ **Cram Quiz questions:** At the end of each topic is a quiz. The quizzes, and ensuing explanations, are meant to gauge your knowledge of the subjects. If the answers to the questions don't come readily to you, consider reviewing individual topics or the entire chapter. In addition to being in the chapters, you can find the Cram Quiz questions on the disc. The questions are separated into their respective 220-901 and 220-902 categories for easier studying when you approach the exam.

▶ **Exam Alerts, Sidebars, and Notes:** These are interspersed throughout the book. Watch out for them!

> **ExamAlert**
>
> This is what an Exam Alert looks like. An alert stresses concepts, terms, hardware, software, or activities that are likely to relate to one or more questions on the exam.

Additional Elements

Beyond the chapters, there are a few more elements that I've thrown in for you. They include

▶ **Practice Exams:** These are located directly after Chapter 20 within the book. There is one for each CompTIA A+ exam. These exams (and additional exams) are available on the disc as well. They are designed to prepare you for the multiple-choice questions that you will find on the real CompTIA A+ exams.

▶ **Real-World Scenarios:** These are located after the two practice exams. They describe actual situations with questions that you must answer. Their solutions can be found on the disc in the form of videos and computer simulations. They are designed to help prepare you for the performance-based questions within the real CompTIA A+ exams.

▶ **Cram Sheet:** The tear-out Cram Sheet is located in the beginning of the book. This is designed to jam some of the most important facts you need to know for the exam into one small sheet, allowing for easy memorization. It is also in PDF format on the disc. If you have an e-book version, this might be located at the end of the e-book.

The Hands-On Approach

This book refers to two different computers as the following:

▶ *AV Editor*: I built this desktop computer for this seventh edition in July of 2015. It is an Intel Core i7 system and is designed to act as a powerful audio/video editing workstation.

▶ *Media PC*: I built this desktop computer for the previous edition in January 2012. It is an Intel Core i5 system.

> **Note**
>
> Previous editions of this book included a computer known as *Tower PC*. It was built in 2009 and, as such, is based on older technologies. It has been removed from this edition of the book, but information about it can be found at my website: www.davidlprowse.com.

I built both *A/V editor* and *Media PC* using components that are a good example of what you will see in the field today and for a while to come. These components are representative of the types of technologies that will be covered in the exams. I refer to the components in these systems from Chapter 2, "Motherboards," onward. I like to put things into context whenever possible. By referencing the parts in the computer during each chapter, I hope to infuse some real-world knowledge and to solidify the concepts you need to learn for the exam. This more hands-on approach can help you to visualize concepts better. I recommend that every computer technician build their own PC at some point (if you haven't already). This can help to reinforce the ideas and concepts expressed in the book.

You should also work with multiple systems while going through this book: one with Windows 8, one with Windows 7, and one with Windows Vista. (Not to mention OS X, Linux, Android, and iOS.) Or you might attempt to create a dual-boot or three-way-boot on a single hard drive. Another option is to run one computer with one of the operating systems mentioned and virtual machines running the other operating systems. However, if at all possible, the best way to learn is to run individual computers. This will ensure that you discover as much as possible about the hardware and software of each computer system and how they interact with each other.

This book frequently refers to various ancillary websites, most notably:

- ▶ **Microsoft TechNet:** http://technet.microsoft.com
- ▶ **Microsoft Support:** http://support.microsoft.com
- ▶ **Android OS Help:** https://support.google.com/android
- ▶ **Apple Support:** https://www.apple.com/support

As an IT technician, you will be visiting these sites often; they serve to further illustrate and explain concepts covered in this text.

Goals for This Book

I have three main goals in mind while preparing you for the CompTIA A+ exams.

My first goal is to help you understand A+ topics and concepts quickly and efficiently. To do this, I try to get right to the facts necessary for the exam. To drive these facts home, the book incorporates figures, tables, real-world scenarios, and simple, to-the-point explanations. Also, in Chapter 20, you can find test-taking tips and a preparation checklist that gives you an orderly, step-by-step approach to taking the exam. Be sure to complete every item on the checklist! For students of mine who truly complete every item, there is an extremely high pass rate for the exams.

My second goal for this book is to provide you with an abundance of *unique* questions to prepare you for the exam. Between the Cram Quizzes and the practice exams, that goal has been met, and I think it will benefit you greatly. Because CompTIA reserves the right to change test questions at any time, it is difficult to foresee exactly what you will be asked on the exam. However, to become a good technician, you must know the *concept*; you can't just memorize questions. To this effect, each question has an explanation and maps back to the topic (and chapter) covered in the text. I've been using this method for more than a decade with my students (more than 2,000 of them) and with great results.

My final goal is to provide support for this and all my titles, completing the life cycle of learning. I do this through my personal website (www.davidlprowse.com), which has additional resources for you, including an errata page (which you should check as soon as possible), and is set up to take questions from you about this book. I'll try my best to get to your questions ASAP. All personal information is kept strictly confidential.

Good luck in your certification endeavors. I hope you benefit from this book. Enjoy!

Sincerely,

David L. Prowse

www.davidlprowse.com

Exam Topics

Table I.1 lists the exam topics covered in each chapter of the book.

TABLE I.1 **Exam Cram CompTIA A+ Exam Topics**

Exam Topic	Chapter
The Six-Step A+ Troubleshooting Process	1
Troubleshooting Examples and PC Tools	
Motherboard Components and Form Factors	2
The BIOS/UEFI	
Installing and Troubleshooting Motherboards	
CPU 101	3
Installing and Troubleshooting CPUs	
RAM Basics and Types of RAM	4
Installing and Troubleshooting DRAM	
Understanding and Testing Power	5
Power Devices	
Power Supplies	
Hard Drives	6
RAID	
Optical Storage Media	
Solid State Storage Media	
Installing, Configuring, and Troubleshooting Visible Laptop Components	7
Installing, Configuring, and Troubleshooting Internal Laptop Components	
Understanding Tablet and Smartphone Hardware	
Installing and Upgrading to Windows 8	8
Installing and Upgrading to Windows 7	
Installing Windows Vista	
Windows User Interfaces	9
System Tools and Utilities	
Files, File Systems, and Drives	
Updating Windows	10
Maintaining Hard Drives	
Repair Environments and Boot Errors	11
Windows Tools and Errors	
Command-Line Tools	

CHAPTER 1

Introduction to Troubleshooting

This chapter covers the following A+ exam topics:

▶ The Six-Step A+ Troubleshooting Process

▶ Troubleshooting Examples and PC Tools

You can find a master list of A+ exam topics in the "Introduction."

This chapter covers CompTIA A+ 220-902 objectives 5.1 and 5.5.

Let's begin this book by talking about troubleshooting. Excellent troubleshooting ability is vital; it's probably the most important skill for a computer technician to possess. It's what we do—troubleshoot and repair problems! So it makes sense that an ever-increasing number of questions about this subject are on the A+ exams. Every chapter of this book deals with troubleshooting to some extent; therefore, each chapter in a way is based off of this chapter. To be a good technician, and to pass the exams, you need to know how to troubleshoot hardware *and* software-related issues. The key is to do it methodically. That's why CompTIA has incorporated a six-step troubleshooting process within the exam objectives. This chapter covers the six-step process and gives a few basic examples of troubleshooting within this methodology. Because troubleshooting makes up a large portion of the CompTIA A+ objectives, you should apply this troubleshooting process throughout the rest of the chapters and also apply it whenever you attempt to solve a computer problem.

The Six-Step A+ Troubleshooting Process

It is necessary to approach computer problems from a logical standpoint, and to best do this, we use a troubleshooting process. Several different trouble-shooting methodologies are out there; this book focuses on the CompTIA A+ six-step troubleshooting theory.

This six-step process included within the A+ objectives is designed to increase the computer technician's problem-solving ability. CompTIA expects the technician to take an organized, methodical route to a solution by memorizing and implementing these steps. Incorporate this six-step process into your line of thinking as you read through this book and whenever you troubleshoot a desktop computer, mobile device, or networking issue.

Step 1: Identify the problem.

Step 2: Establish a theory of probable cause. (Question the obvious.)

Step 3: Test the theory to determine cause.

Step 4: Establish a plan of action to resolve the problem and implement the solution.

Step 5: Verify full system functionality and if applicable implement preventative measures.

Step 6: Document findings, actions, and outcomes.

Let's talk about each of these six steps in a little more depth.

Step 1: Identify the Problem

In this first step, you already know that there is a problem; now you have to identify exactly what it is. This means gathering information. You do this in a few ways:

▶ **Question the user.** Ask the person who reported the problem detailed questions about the issue. You want to find out about symptoms, unusual behavior, or anything that the user might have done of late that could have inadvertently or directly caused the problem. Of course, do this without accusing the user. If the user cannot properly explain a computer's problem, ask simple questions to further identify the issue.

► **Identify any changes made to the computer.** Look at the computer. See if any new hardware has been installed or plugged in. Look around for anything that might seem out of place. Listen to the computer— even smell it! For example, a hard drive might make a peculiar noise or a power supply might smell like something is burning. Use all your senses to help identify what the problem is. Define if any new software has been installed or if any system settings have been changed. In some cases you might need to inspect the environment around the computer. Perhaps something has changed outside the computer that is related to the problem.

► **Review documentation.** Your company might have electronic or written documentation that logs past problems and solutions. Perhaps the issue at hand has happened before. Or perhaps other related issues can aid you in your pursuit to find out what is wrong. Maybe another technician listed in the documentation can be of assistance if he or she has seen the problem before. Perhaps the user has documentation about a specific process or has a manual concerning the computer, individual component, software, or other device that has failed.

Keep in mind that you're not taking any direct action at this point to solve the problem. Instead, you are gleaning as much information as you can to help in your analysis. However, in this stage it is important to back up any critical data before you do make any changes in the following steps.

> **ExamAlert**
>
> Perform backups before making changes!

Step 2: Establish a Theory of Probable Cause (Question the Obvious)

In Step 2, you theorize as to what the most likely cause of the problem is. Start with the most probable or obvious cause. For example, if a computer won't turn on, your theory of probable cause would be that the computer is not plugged in! This step differs from other troubleshooting processes in that you are not making a list of causes but instead are choosing one probable cause as a starting point. In this step, you also need to define whether it is a hardware or software-related issue.

If necessary, conduct external or internal research based on symptoms. This means that you might need to consult your organization's documentation (or your own personal documentation), research technical websites, and make calls to various tech support lines—all depending on the severity of the situation. It also means that you might inspect the inside of a computer or the software of the computer more thoroughly than in the previous step.

The ultimate goal is to come up with a logical theory explaining the root of the problem.

Step 3: Test the Theory to Determine Cause

In Step 3, test your theory from Step 2. Back to the example, go ahead and plug in the computer. If the computer starts, you know that your theory has been confirmed. At that point move on to Step 4. But what if the computer *is* plugged in? Or what if you plug in the computer and it still doesn't start? An experienced troubleshooter can often figure out the problem on the first theory but not always. If the first theory fails during testing, go back to Step 2 to establish a new theory and continue until you have a theory that tests positive. If you can't figure out what the problem is from any of your theories, it's time to escalate. Bring the problem to your supervisor so that additional theories can be established.

Step 4: Establish a Plan of Action to Resolve the Problem and Implement the Solution

Step 4 might at first seem a bit redundant, but delve in a little further. When a theory has been tested and works, you can establish a plan of action. In the previous scenario, it's simple: plug in the computer. However, in other situations, the plan of action will be more complicated; you might need to repair other issues that occurred due to the first issue. In other cases, an issue might affect multiple computers, and the plan of action would include repairing all those systems. Whatever the plan of action, after it is established, have the appropriate people sign off on it (if necessary), and then immediately implement it.

ExamAlert

Always consider corporate policies, procedures, and impacts before implementing changes!

Step 5: Verify Full System Functionality and, If Applicable, Implement Preventative Measures

At this point, verify whether the computer works properly. This might require a restart or two, opening applications, accessing the Internet, or actually using a hardware device, thus proving it works. As part of Step 5, you want to prevent the problem from happening again if possible. Yes, of course, you plugged in the computer and it worked. But why was the computer unplugged? The computer being unplugged (or whatever the particular issue) could be the result of a bigger problem that you would want to prevent in the future. Whatever your preventative measures, make sure they won't affect any other systems or policies; if they do, get permission for those measures first.

Step 6: Document Findings, Actions, and Outcomes

In this last step, document what happened. Depending on the company you work for, you might have been documenting the entire time (for example, by using a trouble-ticketing system). In this step, finalize the documentation, including the issue, cause, solution, preventative measures, and any other steps taken.

Documentation is extremely important and helps in two ways. First, it provides you and the user with closure to the problem; it solidifies the problem and the solution, making you a better troubleshooter in the future. Second, if you or anyone on your team encounters a similar issue in the future, the history of the issue will be at your fingertips. Most technicians don't remember specific solutions to problems that happened several months ago or more. Plus, having a written account of what transpired can help to protect all parties involved in case there is an investigation and/or legal proceeding.

Note

Try to incorporate this methodology into your thinking when covering the chapters in this book. In the upcoming chapters, apply it to any of the components (for example, motherboards, adapter cards, and power supplies). In later chapters, apply it to mobile devices, Windows, and network computing.

Cram Quiz

Answer these questions. The answers follow the last question. If you cannot answer these questions correctly, consider reading this section again until you can. Each Cram Quiz is divided into sections for the 220-901 and 220-902 exams to better organize your studies when you are doing final review for the exams. Chapter 1 has questions pertaining to the 220-902 exam only.

1. What is the second step of the A+ troubleshooting methodology?

    ○ **A.** Identify the problem.

    ○ **B.** Establish a theory of probable cause.

    ○ **C.** Test the theory.

    ○ **D.** Document.

2. When you run out of possible theories for the cause of a problem, what should you do?

    ○ **A.** Escalate the problem.

    ○ **B.** Document your actions so far.

    ○ **C.** Establish a plan of action.

    ○ **D.** Question the user.

3. What should you do before making any changes to the computer? (Select the best answer.)

    ○ **A.** Identify the problem.

    ○ **B.** Establish a plan of action.

    ○ **C.** Perform a backup.

    ○ **D.** Escalate the problem.

4. Which of the following is part of Step 5 in the six-step troubleshooting process?

    ○ **A.** Identify the problem.

    ○ **B.** Document findings.

    ○ **C.** Establish a new theory.

    ○ **D.** Implement preventative measures.

5. What should you do next after testing the theory to determine cause?

    ○ **A.** Establish a plan of action to resolve the problem.

    ○ **B.** Verify full system functionality.

    ○ **C.** Document findings, actions, and outcomes.

    ○ **D.** Implement the solution.

Cram Quiz Answers

1. **B.** The second step is to establish a theory of probable cause. You need to look for the obvious or most probable cause for the problem.

2. **A.** If you can't figure out why a problem occurred, it's time to get someone else involved. Escalate the problem to your supervisor.

3. **C.** Always perform a backup of critical data before making any changes to the computer.

4. **D.** Implement preventative measures as part of Step 5 to ensure that the problem will not happen again.

5. **A.** After testing the theory to determine cause (Step 3), you should establish a plan of action to resolve the problem (Step 4).

Troubleshooting Examples and PC Tools

The purpose of this section is to familiarize you with some introductory troubleshooting. As we progress through the book, we demonstrate more in-depth troubleshooting of problems that might occur. Let's go ahead and give a few basic examples of troubleshooting utilizing the methodology we just covered.

Troubleshooting Example 1—Basic: Display Issue

In this scenario, you are a computer technician working for the technical services department of a mid-sized company. During the morning you get a call from a member of the Graphics department. Apparently, he can't see anything on his screen. Troubleshoot!

Identify the Problem

While questioning the user, you discover the computer worked fine yesterday, but when the user came in today and started the computer, the display was blank.

While examining the computer, you can tell that it is turned on due to the power LED and can tell it is working due to the activity of the hard drive LED. The monitor has an amber LED lit next to the power button. As the user mentions, restarting the computer and turning the monitor on and off have no effect.

Establish a Theory of Probable Cause (Question the Obvious)

Again, look for the obvious or most probable cause. In this case you surmise that the monitor is not connected to the computer.

ExamAlert

Check the connections first! They are a common culprit outside and inside the computer.

You guess the monitor is not connected to the computer because the computer appears to be working normally and the monitor seems to get power (due to the amber LED). The theory is that the video signal is not getting to the monitor from the computer.

Test the Theory to Determine Cause

To test this theory, simply go to the back of the computer and check the video connection; then check the connection on the monitor to see whether it has screw terminals. If either is loose or disconnected, firmly connect them and then see whether the monitor displays anything.

If the monitor now displays video, the theory is confirmed; however, if it does not, you need to construct a new theory. Maybe the monitor's backlight source (lamp) has burned out. Or maybe there is a problem with its inverter. Or maybe the video card has some kind of issue. Perhaps the user neglected to tell you that he set the video resolution to a higher setting than the monitor could handle! Start with the next most likely cause and test it, moving down the line until the cause is discovered. If you can't find the cause, escalate the problem and get others involved.

Establish a Plan of Action to Resolve the Problem and Implement the Solution

Your plan of action should include connecting the monitor to the computer securely. Maybe the plug was never screwed in, making it an easy target to get disconnected. Make sure that the plug is firmly seated and screw it in tightly. Do the same if the other end of the cable screws into the monitor. As part of your plan of action, you might want to explain what the problem was to the user and show him how to reconnect the monitor in the future.

Verify Full System Functionality and if Applicable Implement Preventative Measures

At this point, verify that the computer works properly. This might require a restart or two as proof or might require you to open applications that the user utilizes. Also, as part of Step 5, you want to prevent the problem from happening again if possible. Maybe the user inadvertently kicked the connector loose, or a member of the cleaning crew ran over the cable with a vacuum, disconnecting it from the computer. In either case, rerouting or tie-wrapping the video cable (and any other cables) might be a good solution to preventing future problems with these connections. You should also inspect the cable for any type of wear. Any possible irresponsibility on the part of the cleaning crew should be escalated to your supervisor.

Document Findings, Actions, and Outcomes

Document according to your company's policies. This might mean using an online ticketing system or just writing things down on paper. In this scenario, you should document the user and computer that had the issue, the cause of the issue, how you repaired it, and any type of preventative measures and training of the user you implemented.

Troubleshooting Example 2—Intermediate: Power Issue

In this scenario, you are a network support specialist within an IT department that supports 500 computers. First thing in the morning, you get a call from the Marketing department alerting you to the fact that several computers will not start. Troubleshoot!

Identify the Problem

While questioning the manager of the Marketing department, you find out that the computers worked fine yesterday, but when everyone came in this morning, four of the computers grouped in one area wouldn't start.

While examining the computers, you do indeed see that none of the four computers will turn on. Not only that, but the monitors at the employees' desks are also off. So the problem is that four computers and their monitors will not turn on.

Establish a Theory of Probable Cause (Question the Obvious)

Don't forget, you are looking for the most probable cause. In this case, it would appear that there is a power issue because all four computers and their monitors are not turning on. A possible theory is that a circuit breaker tripped, causing all the electronic equipment on that circuit to fail.

Test the Theory to Determine Cause

To test this theory, plug in another device to any of the outlets that are part of the supposed problem. You can also use a receptacle tester to test the affected outlets.

If the outlets test negative for power and your electrician confirms that a circuit has tripped at the main panel, you know that your theory is correct. However, if the outlets test positive or have some other kind of erroneous reading, you need to troubleshoot further and most likely escalate the problem to a licensed electrician.

> **ExamAlert**
>
> If a problem is electrical, contact your building supervisor or manager so that they can contact a licensed electrician to fix the problem.

Establish a Plan of Action to Resolve the Problem and Implement the Solution

If the circuit is tripped, the plan of action would simply be to reset the breaker and verify that the computers and monitors receive power.

Verify Full System Functionality and if Applicable Implement Preventative Measures

At this point, verify that the computers and other equipment work properly. This might require a restart or two as proof as well as turning the monitors on and off. Also, as part of Step 5, you want to prevent the problem from happening again if possible. Chances are that the circuit was overloaded, and that's why it tripped. Consider moving one of the computer systems to another circuit, or possibly having the electrician add a new circuit to that area.

Document Findings, Actions, and Outcomes

Again, document according to your company's policies. In this scenario, you would document this as an issue that affected several computers. Include names of the people dealt with, including any Marketing staff, electricians, and perhaps building supervisors.

Power issues are fairly common with computers. For more information on power, power supplies, and the problems you might encounter, see Chapter 5, "Power."

Troubleshooting Example 3—Advanced: Wireless Issue

In this scenario, you have been contracted by a growing organization that currently has 50 employees and one IT person. You are called in on Tuesday morning to fix a connectivity problem. Approximately 25 percent of the users in the organization are not able to connect to the wireless network. Troubleshoot!

Identify the Problem

The first thing you do is talk to the in-house IT person to learn more about the problem. The IT person tells you that the wireless router was updated last night and rebooted after the update. This morning, 12 of the 50 computers were not able to connect to the wireless network. The IT person mentions that those are older computers that the company was thinking of replacing. The IT person says that no changes were made to any of the client computers.

At this point, you realize that you have to dig further. After more questioning, you find out that the IT person also reconfigured the wireless settings because some of them had been automatically set to the defaults during the update. Next, you confirm that nothing else has been changed, and you restate the problem back to the IT person for additional confirmation. For example, you state, "The problem is that 12 of the 50 computers cannot connect to the wireless network. Is this correct?" Always restate the problem as you understand it so you can make sure that all parties are in agreement.

You ask for all network documentation from the IT person. You then make a backup of the router configuration and begin studying the logs and the current configuration. The router is currently configured for 5 GHz 802.11ac and 802.11n connections only. Move on to Step 2.

Establish a Theory of Probable Cause (Question the Obvious)

The most obvious possibilities in this scenario are that either the IT person misconfigured the router or the update caused the router to fail. Regardless, the router is in a different state than it was in yesterday, and because of that, 12 computers cannot connect.

Next, you need to delve a bit deeper and conduct some additional research based on the symptoms that have been discovered. The best way to do this is to test an actual client connection. You decide to go to one of the affected computers and attempt to connect to the wireless network. The connection fails. You then analyze the wireless adapter settings in the computer and note that the wireless adapter can make only 802.11g and 802.11b connections. Bingo! The cause of the problem should now become clear. The wireless router is configured only for 5 GHz connections (802.11ac and 802.11n). It is not configured for 2.4 GHz connections (such as 802.11g or 802.11b).

So, your theory of probable cause should be that, after the reconfiguration, the wireless router is configured incorrectly, accepting 5 GHz network connections only. The result is that any computers using 2.4 GHz connections only (such as 802.11g or 802.11b) will no longer be able to connect to the wireless router. It is most likely that the router was previously configured for 5 GHz *and* 2.4 GHz wireless networks. Because the problem affects 12 computers, this is the most likely cause. If only one computer was affected, it might be a different problem, but in this case, this is the most likely scenario.

Test the Theory to Determine Cause

To test your theory, you would need to reconfigure the router so that it accepts 2.4 GHz connections in addition to the 5 GHz connections, and then run a test connection from one of the affected computers. Of course, you should first get approval and then back up the current configuration again (just in case any changes were made during Step 2). You will also need to make sure you are using the same 2.4 GHz wireless network name (SSID), the same wireless channel, and the same encryption settings that were used previously. Refer to the network documentation (and the IT person) for this information. Notify the IT person that the router will need to be rebooted and that the wireless network will be down for a minute or two.

You reconfigure the router to accept 2.4 GHz connections (802.11g, b, and n) and then reboot the router. (Note that 802.11n can run on 5 GHz *or* 2.4 GHz.) Then you go to that same affected computer as before and simply reboot it—and voilà, there it is: the 802.11g connection to the wireless network that you wanted. Your theory has been proven.

Establish a Plan of Action to Resolve the Problem and Implement the Solution

Often, this step is fairly easy and you might find that half of the solution has already been accomplished. In this case, your plan of action should be to reconfigure the router (which you have already done) and reboot all affected computers so that they can connect to the 2.4 GHz wireless network.

Remember to automate if at all possible. There are 11 more computers that need to be rebooted. If you were to physically walk to each system and reboot each one, it would be quite time-consuming. A better solution is to collaborate with the IT person by sending out a mass communication to the users with the affected computers, telling them to save their work and reboot their systems. It could be done via voicemail or by using the intercom system. Or, if the organization embraces a bring your own device (BYOD) policy, consider sending out an e-mail to the employees' mobile devices. Also explain that users should attempt to access the Internet and let you know whether they experience any problems. If anyone is absent that day, physically go to the corresponding computer and reboot it yourself.

> **Note**
>
> Of course, it would be great if you could simply reboot the systems remotely, but this is most likely impossible because the only network connection the client computers use is currently not functioning!

Verify Full System Functionality and if Applicable Implement Preventative Measures

Always test! I can't stress this enough! You need to make sure that all the wireless clients that were affected can now connect to the 2.4 GHz wireless network. Verify that all systems have connected by viewing the logs within the wireless router or by running command-line tests. Sometimes, encryption can pose problems, and you might actually have to reconnect manually from one or more of the clients (or possibly all of them if you are using a new encryption key or password). You also need to make sure that there are no problems with the 5 GHz wireless network after the router reboot. Verify that systems are still connecting on that wireless network as well. For future reference and documentation purposes, save the router configuration and make sure the IT person knows where that information is. You could also print out the configuration and add that to the IT person's network documentation. The problem shouldn't happen again, but if the router needs to be reset to the factory defaults, you can prevent this same issue from occurring by writing a step-by-step procedure on how to configure the router, including the current router configuration and printed documentation.

Document Findings, Actions, and Outcomes

Keep a record of the problem and solution for the IT person and for the organization that you work for. Define what the problem was, how you came up with your theory, how you tested the theory, how you implemented the solution, and especially how you tested all systems for functionality. Have the appropriate people at the organization sign off (on paper or digitally), and be on your merry way!

PC Tools

Every technician needs to use tools when troubleshooting a computer. Field replaceable units (FRUs)—such as power supplies, hard drives, and RAM—will be difficult to remove without them. Remember, the best tools are your hands, eyes, and ears—though it could be debated whether these are actually "tools." But when it comes to tools that you hold in your hands, there are several you should definitely have in your toolkit. Table 1.1 lists some common personal computer (PC) tools and their descriptions.

TABLE 1.1 **Common PC Tools**

PC Tool	Description
Antistatic strap	Protects from electrostatic discharge (more on ESD in the next section).
Demagnetized Phillips head screwdriver	For assembling/disassembling PCs.
Multimeter	For testing wires in a PC as well as AC outlets.
Power Supply Tester	For testing a PC's power supply. Also known as a PSU tester.
Torx screwdriver	For assembling/disassembling computers that use the less common Torx screw. Size T10 and T8 for PCs and smaller sizes for laptops.
Hex screwdriver	For cases and other components that do not use Phillips screws.
Plastic tweezer	For grabbing screws that fall into difficult-to-reach areas and for removing jumper shunts. A parts grabber is also good for this.
Compressed air	Cleans dust from a computer. (Do this outside!)
Penlight	Helps to illuminate when working inside the computer case and when making connections on the back of a computer when working under a dark desk.
Magnifying glass	Helps to read small writing on components and locate damage to circuits or chips.

ExamAlert

Know the basic set of PC tools and their purpose!

This is just a basic list of items that you should know for the A+ exams. As we progress through the book, we'll incorporate more tools that you should consider adding to your toolkit.

More Troubleshooting Tidbits

When working on the inside of a computer, it is imperative to protect against electrostatic discharge (ESD), which occurs when two objects of different voltages come into contact with each other. For example, when you walk across carpeting, your body gathers a lot of static electricity—more than enough to damage a computer component. If you touch the component, the static electricity would discharge from you to the component, damaging the computer part. There are several ways to protect against this, including wearing an antistatic wrist strap and connecting it to the chassis of the computer, touching the chassis of the computer before handling any components, and using an antistatic mat.

Self-grounding should always be on your mind. Other more indirect ways to prevent ESD are to keep your feet stationary when working on a computer, work in a noncarpeted area, keep the humidity raised to approximately 50 percent (if possible), and use antistatic sprays. You can find more information about protecting against ESD in Chapter 19, "Safety, Procedures, and Professionalism."

ExamAlert

To prevent ESD, use an antistatic wrist strap and other antistatic methods.

If a computer won't start, you should check the power cable. But what if the computer and monitor are getting power and the display is still blank? You can narrow this down to four components: the video card, RAM, processor, and motherboard. From a hardware standpoint, the first thing to check is whether the monitor is securely connected to the computer's video card. Next, you want to make sure that all the other components connect properly. It's not unheard of for a connector, an adapter card, or even a processor to get jarred loose. If the video card, processor, or RAM is not connected properly, they can stop the computer from booting, whereby nothing shows up on the screen. Also, if the motherboard has a loose main power connector, the computer will not boot. When troubleshooting a no-display issue, and you know that the computer and monitor are receiving power, remember the *big 4*: video, RAM, processor, and motherboard.

Another key concept that you need to remember is that a large percentage of the issues you troubleshoot are due to user error. From a customer service standpoint, this is not something you want the user to pick up from your demeanor. You don't want to accuse or blame a user; but it is something to keep in mind when questioning the user.

On a final note, when troubleshooting, try to keep a level head. Think logically about a solution to the problem. I like to tell my students to think like Mr. Spock; try not to let emotion cloud your judgment. It is understandable that at times the number of trouble tickets might be a bit overwhelming. Just remember that you can only do what you can do. By clearing everything from your mind except for a methodical troubleshooting approach, you can obtain solutions much more efficiently—live long, and prosper.

Cram Quiz

Answer these questions. The answers follow the last question. If you cannot answer these questions correctly, consider reading this section again until you can. Chapter 1 has questions pertaining to the 220-902 exam only.

1. There is a problem with the power supplied to a group of computers and you do not know how to fix the problem. What should you do first?

   ○ **A.** Establish a theory of why you can't figure out the problem.

   ○ **B.** Contact the building supervisor or your manager.

   ○ **C.** Test the theory to determine cause.

   ○ **D.** Document findings, actions, and outcomes.

2. You have confirmed your theory that a video card is bad and needs to be replaced. What should you do next?

   ○ **A.** Escalate the problem.

   ○ **B.** Document your actions so far.

   ○ **C.** Establish a plan of action.

   ○ **D.** Question the user.

3. A computer won't turn on when you press the Power button. What should you check first?

   ○ **A.** If an operating system is installed.

   ○ **B.** Documentation.

   ○ **C.** If the monitor is plugged in.

   ○ **D.** If the computer is plugged in.

4. Which of these is contained within Step 1 of the six-step troubleshooting theory?

   ○ **A.** Question the user.

   ○ **B.** Document findings.

   ○ **C.** Establish a new theory.

   ○ **D.** Escalate the problem.

5. Which of the following are possible faulty components when nothing appears on the display? (Select all that apply.)

   ○ **A.** Sound card

   ○ **B.** Video card

   ○ **C.** Processor

   ○ **D.** Network card

6. You dropped a screw in the case of a PC. What is the best tool to use to retrieve the screw?

  ○ **A.** Compressed air

  ○ **B.** Computer vacuum

  ○ **C.** Plastic tweezers

  ○ **D.** Screwdriver with magnetized tip

7. What is the last step of the six-step troubleshooting process?

  ○ **A.** Question the user.

  ○ **B.** Verify full system functionality.

  ○ **C.** Establish a plan of action.

  ○ **D.** Document findings.

Cram Quiz Answers

1. **B.** If you can't figure out a cause to a problem and have exhausted all possible theories, escalate the problem to the appropriate persons.

2. **C.** After you confirm a theory, move to Step 4 to establish a plan of action, and then implement the solution.

3. **D.** Connections are quite often the culprit outside and inside the computer. If a computer won't turn on, make sure it is plugged securely into an AC outlet.

4. **A.** Questioning the user is important when gathering information to identify the problem.

5. **B and C.** The big 4 (as I like to call them) are the video card, RAM, processor, and motherboard. If your computer is definitely getting power and there is still nothing on the display, you want to check these, most likely in order.

6. **C.** Plastic tweezers is the best answer. You don't want to damage any internal components with a metal tool or a magnetized tool. If plastic tweezers are not available, most basic PC toolkits include a three-pronged grabber tool. If that is not available, you can use small pliers with the tips wrapped in electrical tape. In some cases, you can turn the computer upside down to loosen the screw. A magnetized screwdriver or extension magnet is your final resort. Just remember that, if at all possible, keep metal away from components—touch only the screw. Using your hands to grab the screw in this scenario is not an option, even if you think you are protected from ESD.

7. **D.** Document findings, actions, and outcomes is the sixth and last step of the CompTIA A+ troubleshooting theory. Remember this process for the exam!

CHAPTER 2
Motherboards

This chapter covers the following A+ exam topics:

▶ Motherboard Components and Form Factors

▶ The BIOS/UEFI

▶ Installing and Troubleshooting Motherboards

You can find a master list of A+ exam topics in the "Introduction."

This chapter covers CompTIA A+ 220-901 objectives 1.1, 1.2, and 4.1.

Without a doubt, the motherboard is the foundation of the computer. Everything connects to the motherboard and all data is transferred through this matrix of circuitry.

In this chapter, we delve into the components that make up the motherboard, the various types of motherboard form factors, the ports and interfaces you find on the face and the side of the motherboard, the Basic Input Output System (BIOS) and Unified Extensible Firmware Interface (UEFI), and we show the proper methods for installing and troubleshooting motherboards.

Motherboard Components and Form Factors

Over the years I have found that if a student is going to lack knowledge in one area, it's quite often going to be the motherboard. Unfortunately, this is one of the key elements in a computer system. It's the starting point for a quick and efficient computer. Because it connects to everything in the computer system, you need to know many concepts concerning it. Let's begin with the parts that make up the motherboard.

Motherboard Components

You don't need to know every single chip and circuit that resides on the motherboard. Generally, if a motherboard fails—which is uncommon—the entire board needs to be replaced. However, you do need to know the main components, interfaces, and ports of a motherboard and have some knowledge of how it transmits data. This ensures compatibility of components when you design your own system and when you add or replace devices to a motherboard. It also enhances your troubleshooting skills—when the time comes... muhahahah!

Main Components

As mentioned in the "Introduction," I decided to build a new computer for this book (and for me, I suppose) and wanted to use fairly new components. Not the very latest or most expensive components, mind you, but still current, decent parts that reflect the type of components you will see in the field now and for a few years to come. Within this book, I refer to this computer as *AV Editor*. For the motherboard, I chose the ASUS X99-A. Its name tells you that it incorporates the Intel X99 chipset, which we discuss in more detail later. Figure 2.1 shows this motherboard with callouts to the main components you need to know for the exam.

You might have noticed that this motherboard has the characteristics of the ATX form factor, which is discussed later in this chapter. And don't worry if you are confused about one or two of the components; each is covered as you progress through this book. Processors are covered in more depth in Chapter 3, "The CPU," RAM is covered in Chapter 4, "RAM," power connections are covered in more depth in Chapter 5, "Power," and SATA is covered in Chapter 6, "Storage." The remainder of the listed components are discussed within this chapter.

FIGURE 2.1   **ASUS X99-A motherboard components**

ExamAlert

Identify motherboard components for the exam.

Product documentation usually accompanies a device. But if you didn't receive any, or you want more information about the components of this or any motherboard, consider grabbing a technical document from the manufacturer's website. "Go to the source!"—that's what I always tell my students. For example, for this motherboard, you would go to the ASUS website, locate the X99-A board, and then look for its associated technical documentation. You will find a manual in PDF format that contains the motherboard specifications. A manual such as this has all the information you can possibly want about a motherboard. It includes diagrams, descriptions, installation procedures...the whole nine yards. Now I know you have seen a lot of acronyms (and there are a slew more coming), but here's a vital one for you: RTM (Read The Manual!). It helps when installing, configuring, and troubleshooting a device.

ExamAlert

Go to the manufacturer's website for technical documentation.

Chipsets and Buses

In a general sense, the chipset *is* the motherboard, incorporating all the controllers on the motherboard; many technicians refer to it in this way. But in the more specific sense, the chipset is one or two specific chips. How many chips will depend on the design and the manufacturer of the board. If you refer to Figure 2.1, you see the chipset is the Intel X99, which is a Platform Controller Hub (PCH), a name Intel uses. This chipset is composed of a single chip.

You can download the technical specification PDF for this chipset from Intel's website (www.intel.com). This PDF is in depth, even bordering on the hyper-technical! It goes far beyond what you will need to know for the A+ exams, but you should at least understand the basic connections. You can often find more simplified information within the chipset's product brief PDF. Figure 2.2 illustrates the basic connections between the X99 chipset and the rest of the motherboard.

Starting clockwise at 3 o'clock, you can see connections for high-definition audio, PCI Express 2.0 (x1 slots), SATA 3.0, Serial Peripheral Interface (called SPI in the figure; used for connecting to the BIOS), USB, and the network connection. You've probably heard of most of these, but each will be covered in depth as you continue through this book. The point for now is that the chipset is the central meeting point for many devices. It also has a high-speed, point-to-point interconnection to the processor called the Direct Media Interface (DMI) link, also known as the DMI bus.

Intel X99 Chipset Block Diagram

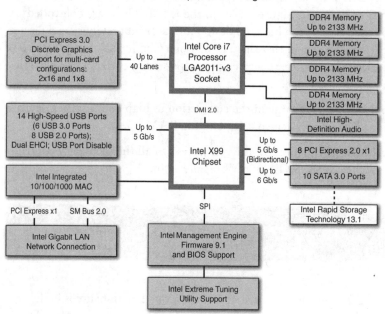

FIGURE 2.2 **Intel X99 chipset connections**

> **Note**
>
> A quick word on buses and lanes: A bus can be one wire (serial) or a group of wires working in unison (parallel) that carries data from one place to another. DMI and PCI Express make use of *lanes*. A lane is composed of two serial wires that enable the sending and receiving of data simultaneously. Parallel buses, on the other hand, are normally designed in multiples of eight wires that can send 1 byte of data (8 bits) at a time in one direction. Parallel technologies are far less common nowadays; they have been overshadowed by SATA, PCIe, DMI, and so on.

The DMI carries all the traffic from the previous list of controllers to the processor. You can imagine that the DMI needs to be powerful. The original DMI provided a data transfer rate of 10 gigabits per second (10 Gb/s) in each direction. (Note the lowercase 'b' indicating bits.) The X99 chipset makes use of a DMI 2.0 connection and can handle 20 Gb/s in each direction. For the sake of comparison, this is equal to approximately 2.5 gigabytes per second (2.5 GB/s; note the uppercase 'B' for bytes.)

The chipset does *not* connect directly to any PCI Express x16 slots (the longer expansion slots shown in Figure 2.1) or to the RAM. These are controlled directly by the processor. This Intel design differs from previous Intel designs and some AMD designs in that there is only one chip in the chipset instead of two. Historically, the motherboard chipset consisted of two chips: the northbridge and the southbridge.

▶ **Northbridge:** In charge of the connection to high data transfer devices, such as PCI Express video cards and the RAM.

▶ **Southbridge:** In charge of the connection to all the secondary controllers, such as USB, SATA, FireWire, and so on.

ExamAlert

Know the concept of the northbridge and southbridge for the exam!

On our ASUS X99-A motherboard, the northbridge functionality is built directly into the processor; some refer to this as an on-die northbridge. The southbridge functionality is all within the X99 chipset. However, AMD designs such as the AMD 990FX chipset make use of a northbridge and southbridge. In this scenario, the northbridge controls the PCI Express connections and connects directly to the processor and the southbridge connects to just about everything else. But the RAM is still controlled directly by the processor, a technique started by AMD.

The AMD connection between the northbridge and the processor is called HyperTransport, similar to Intel's DMI. Version 3.1 of HyperTransport has a maximum transfer rate of 25.6 or 51.2 GB/s, depending on whether it is unidirectional or bidirectional. You might note that this is a lot more than Intel's DMI. The reason is that HyperTransport also moves all the PCI Express video data, which accounts for a large chunk.

There is a more powerful version of Intel's DMI called Quick Path Interconnect (QPI), which can also transfer 25.6 GB/s, similar to HyperTransport. It is used by more powerful workstations and server motherboards, such as the ones found in Xeon-based systems using multiple CPUs.

Older Intel motherboard designs used the northbridge/southbridge concept, but Intel gave names to each chip. The northbridge was known as the Memory Controller Hub (MCH). It was connected to the CPU by way of the front side bus (FSB). The southbridge was known as the I/O Controller Hub (ICH).

> **Note**
>
> For more information about this older Intel design, go to the A+ archive on my website: www.davidlprowse.com.

A last word about chipsets: Certain applications prefer or even require specific chipsets (and CPUs, for that matter). Graphics, music, engineering, and even gaming applications might recommend specific chipsets. So before designing your computer, think about which applications you will use and whether they prefer certain chipsets.

Drive Technologies

The main type of drive technology on motherboards is Serial ATA (SATA). This always connects to the southbridge or simply the chipset (if there is only *one* chip). SATA supports the connection of hard drives and optical drives.

The first generation of SATA is rated at 1.5 Gb/s (once again, note the lower-case b indicating bits), equal to roughly 150 MB/s. Second-generation SATA offers a 3.0 Gb/s data rate. Third-generation SATA runs at either 6 Gb/s (revision 3.0) or 16 Gb/s (revision 3.2). Most of today's motherboards are compatible with second- and third-generation SATA. Again, hard drives, CD-ROMs, DVDs, and Blu-ray drives can be connected to an SATA port. SATA is covered in greater depth in Chapter 6, "Storage."

> **Note**
>
> The older Integrated Drive Electronics (IDE) technology has been completely eclipsed by SATA. It utilizes the Parallel ATA (PATA) standard that commonly has a maximum data transfer rate of 133 MB/s. For more information on IDE, see the A+ Archive on my website: www.davidlprowse.com.

Expansion Buses

There are two main expansion buses and their corresponding adapter card slots that you need to know for the exam. They include PCI Express (PCIe) and PCI:

▶ **PCIe:** Currently the king of expansion buses, PCI Express is the high-speed serial replacement of the older parallel PCI standard and the deprecated AGP standard. The most powerful PCIe slots with the highest data transfer rates connect directly to the northbridge or directly to the processor; the lesser PCIe slots connect to the southbridge or simply to the main chipset. This expansion bus sends and receives data within *lanes*. These lanes are full-duplex, meaning they can send and receive data simultaneously. PCIe version 1 has a data rate of 2 Gb/s (250 MB/s) per lane; version 2 is 4 Gb/s (500 MB/s); version 3 is approximately 8 Gb/s (1 GB/s); and version 4 is approximately 16 Gb/s (2 GB/s). Remember, those numbers are for each direction, so PCIe version 4 can send 16 Gb/s and receive 16 Gb/s at the same time. The number of lanes a PCIe bus uses is indicated with an x and a number—for example, x1 (pronounced "by one") or one lane. Commonly, PCIe video cards are x16 (16 lanes). Let's give an example using bytes. A version 3 PCIe x16 video card can transfer approximately 16 gigabytes of data per second (1 GB × 16 = 16 GB). And version 4 PCIe x16 video cards take it even further, doubling that to approximately 32 GB/s. Most other PCIe adapter cards are x1, but you might find some x4 cards as well. Of course, compatibility is key. A x1 card can go in a x1 slot or larger, but a x16 card currently fits only in a x16 slot. So, for example, a PCIe x4 card won't fit in a x1 slot, but it will fit in a x4 slot. It also fits in a x16 slot but with no increase in performance. Figure 2.3 displays three x16 slots and one x1 slot. Keep in mind that x16 slots are controlled by the northbridge, or processor, whereas x1 slots are controlled by the southbridge, or the main chipset (refer to Figure 2.2). Table 2.1 shows a comparison of PCIe and PCI.

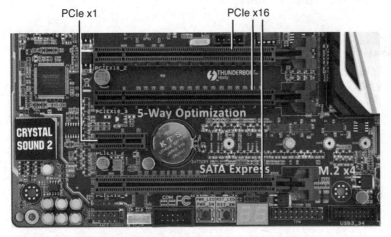

FIGURE 2.3   **PCIe x16 and PCIe x1**

> **Note**
>
> As of the publishing of this book, a x32 slot is also defined in the PCIe specification, but x16 slots are the most common in motherboards.

▶ **PCI:** The Peripheral Component Interconnect bus was developed in the '90s by Intel as a faster, more compatible alternative to the deprecated ISA bus. It allows for connections to modems and to video, sound, and network adapters; however, PCI connects exclusively to the southbridge, or main chipset. Because of this, other high-speed video alternatives were developed that could connect directly to the northbridge, or directly to the processor. The PCI bus is used not only by devices that fit into the PCI slot but by devices that take the form of an integrated circuit on the motherboard. PCI version 2.1 cards are rated at 66 MHz, and their corresponding PCI bus is 32-bits wide, allowing for a maximum data transfer rate of 266 MB/s. Derivatives of PCI include PCI-X, which was designed for servers using a 64-bit bus and rated for 133 MHz/266 MHz, and Mini PCI, which is used by laptops. PCI slots are seldom found on today's motherboards. For the most part, they have been overtaken by PCIe technology. An example of PCI is shown in Figure 2.4 along with PCIe x16 and PCIe x1 for comparison.

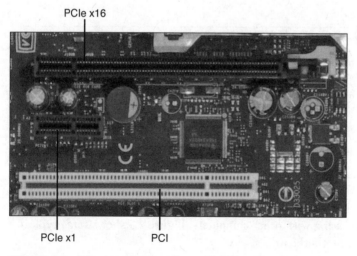

FIGURE 2.4   **PCI expansion bus along with PCIe x16 and x1**

TABLE 2.1   **Comparison of PCIe and PCI**

Expansion Bus	Bus Width	Frequency	Max. Data Rate
PCIe	Serial, consists of between 1 and 16 full-duplex lanes	Version 1 = 2.5 GHz* Version 2 = 5 GHz Version 3 = 8 GHz Version 4 = 16 GHz	2 Gb/s (250 MB/s) per lane 4 Gb/s (500 MB/s) per lane 8 Gb/s** (1 GB/s) per lane 16 Gb/s** (2 GB/s) per lane
PCI	32-bit	33 MHz 66 MHz	133 MB/s 266 MB/s
PCI-X	64-bit	133 MHz (v 1.0) 266 MHz (v 2.0) 533 MHz (v 2.0)	1066 MB/s (1 GB/s) 2133 MB/s (2 GB/s) 4266 MB/s (4 GB/s)

* This is also measured in transfers per second referring to the number of operations that send and receive data per second. It is often closely related to frequency. For example, PCIe v1 is 2.5 gigatransfers per second (2.5 GT/s) and PCIe v4 is 16 GT/s.

** These numbers are approximate.

Note

Maximum data transfer rates are never attained, even in a lab environment. You can expect actual throughput to be substantially lower, but professionals use the maximum data rate as a point of reference and as a way of comparison.

I/O Ports and Front Panel Connectors

Without input and output ports, you could not communicate with the computer (unless it was through telepathy, and I don't think that technology has developed yet). These ports also take care of displaying information, printing it, and communicating with other computers. Figure 2.5 shows some typical ports found on a motherboard.

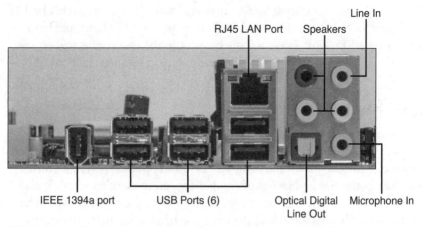

FIGURE 2.5   I/O port cluster on the back panel of the motherboard

Starting at the left and continuing counter-clockwise, you see the following in the figure:

▶ **IEEE 1394:** Also known as FireWire, this port is used for devices that demand the low-latency serial transfer of data, usually concerning music or video.

▶ **USB:** Universal Serial Bus ports are used by many devices, including keyboards, mice, printers, cameras, and much more. Most of today's motherboards come with at least a couple USB 3.0 ports that have a maximum data transfer rate of 5 Gb/s (or even faster USB ports) but will also come with several USB 2.0 ports that have a maximum data rate of 480 Mb/s.

▶ **Audio cluster:** There are six ports in this audio cluster, including an optical digital output, microphone in, line in, and speaker outs.

▶ **RJ45 LAN port:** This is the wired network connection. On this partic-ular motherboard, it is a Gigabit Ethernet LAN controller and is rated for 10/100/1000 Mb/s. This means that it can connect to any of those speed networks and function properly.

ExamAlert

Identify back-panel connectors (I/O ports) for the exam.

Quite often, cases come with front (or top) panel ports that might be wired to the motherboard or to an adapter card. These include USB ports, audio ports, memory card readers, external SATA ports, and more. The front panel also has connections for the Power button, reset button, power LED light, and hard drive activity LED light. These usually connect to the case connectors on the edge of the motherboard, which we'll discuss more in Chapter 5, "Power."

Form Factors

A computer form factor specifies the physical dimensions of some of the components of a computer system. It pertains mainly to the motherboard but also specifies compatibility with the computer case and power supply. The form factor defines the size and layout of components on the motherboard. It also specifies the power outputs from the power supply to the motherboard. The most common form factors—and the ones you need to know for the exam— are ATX, microATX, and ITX. Let's discuss these a little further now.

ATX

Advanced Technology Extended (ATX) was originally designed by Intel in the mid-'90s to overcome the limitations of the now-deprecated AT form factor. It has been the standard ever since. The motherboard in Figure 2.1 is ATX. Full-size ATX motherboards measure 12 inches × 9.6 inches (305 mm × 244 mm). ATX motherboards have an integrated port cluster on the back and normally ship with an I/O plate that snaps into the back of the case, filling the gaps between ports and keeping airflow to a minimum. One identifying characteristic of ATX is that the RAM slots and expansion bus slots are perpendicular to each other. The ATX specification calls for the power supply to produce +3.3 V, +5 V, +12 V, and –12 V outputs and a 5 V standby output. These are known as "rails" (for example, the +12 V rail). The original ATX specification calls for a 20-pin power connector (often referred to as P1); the newer ATX12V Version 2.x specification calls for a 24-pin power connector. The additional four pins are rated at +12 V, +3.3 V, +5 V, and ground, as shown in Table 2.2. Those pins are numbered 11, 12, 23, and 24.

TABLE 2.2 **ATX Pin Specification of the Main Power Connector**

Pin	Color	Signal	Pin	Color	Signal
1	Orange	+3.3 V	13	Orange	+3.3 V
				Brown	+3.3 V sense
2	Orange	+3.3 V	14	Blue	–12 V
3	Black	Ground	15	Black	Ground

Pin	Color	Signal	Pin	Color	Signal
4	Red	+5 V	16	Green	Power on
5	Black	Ground	17	Black	Ground
6	Red	+5 V	18	Black	Ground
7	Black	Ground	19	Black	Ground
8	Gray	Power good	20	White	−5 V (optional)
9	Purple	+5 V standby	21	Red	+5 V
10	Yellow	+12 V	22	Red	+5 V
11	Yellow	+12 V	23	Red	+5 V
12	Orange	+3.3 V	24	Black	Ground

ExamAlert

Know the voltages supplied to an ATX motherboard by a power supply: +3.3 V, +5 V, +12 V, −12 V outputs and +5 V standby output.

Now you might say: "Why should I memorize these? I can just look them up on the Internet!" To which I reply: you never know where you will be working on a computer and whether you will have access to the Internet. Plus, memorization (or at least some handy documentation) will help you to troubleshoot faster and more efficiently.

microATX

microATX (or mATX) was introduced as a smaller version of ATX; these motherboards can be a maximum size of 9.6 inches × 9.6 inches (244 mm × 244 mm) but can be as small as 6.75 inches × 6.75 inches (171.45 mm × 171.45 mm). In comparison, microATX boards are usually square, whereas full-size ATX boards are rectangular. microATX is backward compatible with ATX, meaning that most microATX boards can be installed within an ATX form-factor case and they use the same power connectors as ATX. Often, they have the same chipsets as ATX as well. Figure 2.6 shows an example of microATX. Note how this unit is square in comparison to the rectangular motherboard shown in Figure 2.1. (This figure also shows its main components for further reinforcement.)

Expansion Bus Slots   Port Cluster

4-pin CPU Power

Processor Socket
LGA1155

SATA   CR2032   24-pin ATX
Connectors Lithium   Power Connector
            Battery
P67 Express
Chipset (PCH)

FIGURE 2.6   **microATX motherboard (Intel DP67DE)**

I used this motherboard in the *Media PC* computer referenced in the Introduction of this book. I selected this board because its smaller form factor is common for multimedia PCs and home theater PCs (HTPCs) using desktop cases.

ITX

ITX is a group of form factors developed by VIA Technologies, Inc., between 2001 and now for use in small, low-power motherboards. The ITX group includes the following:

▶ **Mini-ITX:** Originally designed in 2001, this 6.7 × 6.7-inch (17 × 17 cm) motherboard is a bit smaller than microATX and is screw-compatible, enabling it to be used in microATX and ATX cases if so desired. The original version used passive cooling to keep it quiet and to conserve power, making it ideal for HTPCs; newer versions use active cooling due to the more powerful processors involved. The first version of these boards came with one expansion slot: PCI. The second version comes with a single PCIe x16 slot.

▶ **Nano-ITX:** Released in 2005, this measures 4.7 × 4.7 inches (120 × 120 mm). It boasts low power consumption and is used in media centers, automotive PCs, set-top boxes (STBs), and personal video recorders (PVRs).

▶ **Pico-ITX:** Designed and released in 2007, this is half the area of Nano-ITX, measuring 3.9 × 2.8 inches (10 × 7.2 cm). It uses powerful processors and RAM, thus requiring active cooling. It is used in extremely small PCs and ultra-mobile PCs (UMPCs).

▶ **Mobile-ITX:** Released in 2010, this is the smallest of the four ITX form factors, measuring 60 mm × 60 mm. There are no ports and it requires a secondary I/O board. It is intended for military use, surveying, transportation, and medical markets and is used in UMPCs and smartphones.

Table 2.3 compares the ATX, microATX, and ITX form factors, supplying the sizes of these motherboards and some of the characteristics that set them apart.

TABLE 2.3 **Comparison of Motherboard Form Factors**

Form Factor	Width	Depth	Identifying Characteristic
ATX	12 inches	9.6 inches	RAM slots and expansion slots are perpendicular to each other (90-degree angle).
microATX	9.6 inches	9.6 inches	Smaller than ATX but backward compatible to it.
ITX family	From 60 mm to 6.7 inches, depending on the type	From 60 mm to 6.7 inches, depending on type	Designed for HTPCs, UMPCs, and smartphones.

ExamAlert

Know the basics of ATX, microATX, ITX, and BTX for the exam.

Note

Though not listed in the CompTIA A+ bulleted objectives, the BTX (Balanced Technology Extended) form factor can be found in the CompTIA objectives acronym list. For more on this older form factor, see the A+ Archive page on my website: www.davidlprowse.com.

Cram Quiz

Answer these questions. The answers follow the last question. If you cannot answer these questions correctly, consider reading this section again until you can.

220-901 Questions

1. What voltage does an orange pin indicate?

   ○ **A.** +12 V

   ○ **B.** +5 V

   ○ **C.** −5 V

   ○ **D.** +3.3 V

2. Which motherboard form factor measures 12 inches × 9.6 inches?

   ○ **A.** microATX

   ○ **B.** BTX

   ○ **C.** ATX

   ○ **D.** ITX

3. Which expansion bus uses lanes to transfer data?

   ○ **A.** PCI

   ○ **B.** PCI-X

   ○ **C.** PCIe

   ○ **D.** Mini PCI

4. Which of the following does a PCIe x16 slot connect to? (Select the two best answers.)

   ○ **A.** RAM

   ○ **B.** Southbridge

   ○ **C.** USB 3.0 controller

   ○ **D.** Northbridge

   ○ **E.** Processor

5. Which of the following are serial technologies? (Select all that apply.)

   ○ **A.** USB

   ○ **B.** IEEE 1394

   ○ **C.** PCIe

   ○ **D.** PCI

6. Which of the following is used by the CPU to communicate with system memory?

   ○ **A.** Southbridge

   ○ **B.** BIOS

   ○ **C.** Northbridge

   ○ **D.** PCIe

Cram Quiz Answers

220-901 Answers

1. **D.** Orange signifies +3.3 volts. Red indicates +5 volts; yellow is +12 volts; and –5 volts would be the white optional wire.

2. **C.** ATX boards measure 12 inches × 9.6 inches.

3. **C.** PCIe (PCI Express) uses serial lanes to send and receive data.

4. **D** and **E.** PCIe x16 connects to the northbridge on AMD systems and older Intel systems. On newer Intel systems, it connects to the processor.

5. **A, B,** and **C.** The only one listed that is not a serial technology is PCI, which is a 32-bit parallel technology.

6. **C.** The northbridge is used by the CPU to communicate with system memory (RAM). Remember that on newer Intel motherboards, the northbridge functionality is built into the CPU.

The BIOS/UEFI

Historically, the Basic Input Output System (BIOS) has been the firmware
loaded on most desktop and laptop computers. However, since 2005 the
Unified Extensible Firmware Interface (UEFI) has gained in popularity to
the point where in 2014 it became the predominant type of firmware shipped
with motherboards. UEFI is often pronounced similar to "unify" or the
acronym is simply spelled out: U-E-F-I. But many technicians (and even
some manufacturers) will still just refer to it as "BIOS" or possibly as "UEFI
BIOS." For the most part in this chapter, the two terms "BIOS" and "UEFI"
can be used interchangeably. For simplicity during the course of the book, I
often refer to a motherboard's firmware simply as BIOS.

BIOS, CMOS, and the Lithium Battery

The BIOS, CMOS, and the lithium battery have a nice little relationship with
each other. In a way, the BIOS relies on the CMOS and the CMOS relies on
the lithium battery, as shown in Figure 2.7.

FIGURE 2.7   **The BIOS, CMOS, and lithium battery**

The BIOS is the first thing that runs when you boot a PC. The BIOS's job
is to identify, test, and initialize components of the system. It then points
the way to the operating system so that the OS can load up and take over.
Collectively, this process is known as *bootstrapping*. Originally, the BIOS
was stored on a Read-Only Memory (ROM) chip. It later progressed to
Programmable ROM (PROM), enabling the user to modify settings in the
BIOS. Finally, today's system BIOS resides on an EEPROM chip on the
motherboard. EEPROM stands for Electrically Erasable Programmable ROM
and means that not only can you modify settings, you can fully update the
BIOS by erasing it and rewriting it in a process known as *flashing*.

Most motherboards take advantage of the Unified Extensible Firmware
Interface (UEFI). This is code that is ultimately meant to replace the BIOS,
and on some systems it has already done so. On other systems, it can be run
in conjunction with the BIOS, and on still other systems, it isn't included at
all. But expect to see it more as time goes by.

UEFI allows for a mouse-driven firmware-based setup program (instead of the menu-based BIOS setup program) and advanced system diagnosis (except for the worst of errors, such as the CPU failing). It also has a built-in secure boot mode, which prevents digitally unsigned drivers from being loaded and helps prevent rootkits from manifesting themselves. It has faster startup times than the BIOS and supports more partitions (128) and larger drive sizes. As far as the firmware setup program, it behaves in essentially the same manner as the typical BIOS setup program (and might even work alongside it), but the manner in which it can boot to hardware—and the type of hardware it can boot to—is different. Regardless, many technicians still refer to this firmware collectively as the BIOS, and for the purposes of this book, we will do so as we progress through the chapters.

The complementary metal-oxide semiconductor (CMOS) stores the contents of the BIOS's findings (for example, the type and speed of the processor, the capacity of the hard drive, and the current time and date). It uses little power, which makes it a good choice for storing these settings. When the computer is on, the CMOS chip is powered by the power supply. However, the CMOS by nature is volatile, so if it is not receiving power, it loses its stored contents.

Lithium battery to the rescue! The lithium battery powers the CMOS when the computer is shut off. The most common battery used on today's motherboards is the CR2032, a nickel-sized battery that snaps into the motherboard and has a shelf life of anywhere from 2 to 10 years, depending on usage. The more you leave the computer on, the longer the battery lasts. The lithium battery is sometimes referred to simply as the CMOS battery. It is most commonly found in desktop and tower computers.

The POST

The power-on self-test (POST) is the first step in bootstrapping. The POST is essentially a piece of code that the BIOS runs to find out which type of processor is on the motherboard and verifies the amount of RAM. It also identifies buses on the motherboard (and other devices) as well as which devices are available for booting.

The BIOS indicates any system problems that the POST finds by either on-screen display codes or beep codes. For example, a displayed 301 Error would most likely be a keyboard issue. Or one beep might indicate a memory error. This all depends on the type of BIOS used. Some common vendors of BIOS are American Megatrends (AMI) and Phoenix Technologies. Your motherboard should come with documentation about any possible BIOS error codes. If not, the documentation can usually be downloaded from the manufacturer's website; you just need to know the model number of the board. In the case of a proprietary computer (Dell, HP, and such), you need the model number of the computer to download any necessary documentation from its website.

But what happens if the display is blank? You might see repetitive flashing lights on the keyboard that indicate a hardware error, or there might be other more subtle indications of a problem. But to really analyze an issue when there is a blank display, you want to do a POST analysis. Some motherboards come with built-in troubleshooting LEDs and perhaps even a two-digit hexadecimal display that shows error codes you can look up. You might also use a POST adapter card, which is inserted into an adapter card slot (usually PCI but possibly PCIe), or perhaps a USB-based POST tester. All of these can read the system while it is booting. If the display on the motherboard or POST card shows 00 or FF after the system finishes booting, everything is probably okay. However, any other number would indicate a problem that can be cross-referenced in the accompanying booklet, disc, or online documentation.

Accessing and Configuring the BIOS

Accessing the BIOS must be done before the operating system boots. This can be accomplished by pressing a key on the keyboard. It can be F2 or DEL (the most common), or F1, F10, and so on—depending on the manufacturer and type/age of system. Sometimes, the correct key displays on the bottom of the screen when you first start the computer. If there is only a splash screen, you can press Esc to remove it and hopefully the BIOS key displays. When you press the appropriate key, the system enters the BIOS Setup Utility or UEFI BIOS Utility (sometimes also referred to as CMOS) and then displays a screen, as shown in Figure 2.8.

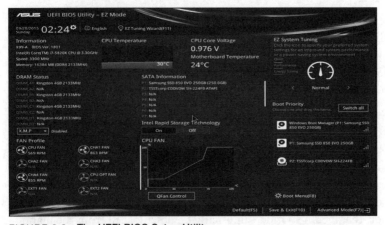

FIGURE 2.8 The UEFI BIOS Setup Utility

From here you can modify many things, several of which are important for the exam:

▶ **Time and Date:** These are normally set on the main screen. By default, operating systems retain their time and date from this, unless they synchronize to a time server.

▶ **Boot Device Priority:** Also known as BIOS boot order, this setting enables you to select which media will be booted: hard drive, optical drive, USB, over-the-network, and so on. Usually, this should be set to hard drive first. But if you install an operating system (OS) from a disc, you would want to configure this as the optical drive first. For a secure and trouble-free system, it is recommended that you set this to hard drive first, as shown in Figure 2.9. If the system is set to optical drive first, and there is a disc in the drive, it could cause Windows to fail to load properly and could pose a security risk. You'll note that the first boot device in the figure says: "Windows Boot Manager," P1, and the name of the device—a 250 GB Samsung solid-state drive. Windows Boot Manager is the primary boot file in Windows and it is the first file on the hard drive that the BIOS looks for when it starts up. P1 means the first physical SATA port connection.

FIGURE 2.9 **BIOS Boot Order**

ExamAlert

If you boot a PC and see a black screen with a white blinking underscore on the top left, the issue could be the boot order.

▶ **Passwords:** Two passwords are available on most BIOS: User and Supervisor (or administrator). The User password (also known as a power-on password) authenticates a user before it enables the operating system to boot. The Supervisor password authenticates a user to the BIOS Setup Utility itself. For a secure system, enter a strong Supervisor password.

▶ **Power Management:** This enables you to select if power management is running and which type is used. The older Advanced Power Management (APM) enables the OS to work with the BIOS to achieve power management. This has been supplanted by the Advanced Configuration and Power Interface (ACPI), enabling the OS to take full control of power management.

▶ **Wake-on-LAN (WoL):** This is a tool that enables you to wake up the computer remotely by sending data to it through the network adapter.

▶ **Monitoring:** Several items can be monitored in the BIOS (for example, processor temperature). An acceptable operating range is between 60 and 75 degrees Celsius (140 to 167 degrees Fahrenheit). Thresholds can be set to increase or decrease the maximum operating temperature of the processor before automatic system shutdown. Processor fan and case fan speeds can also be monitored and changed if need be. For example, if the processor keeps tripping the temperature threshold, you should consider increasing the fan speed. Voltage can also be monitored; this ensures that your system isn't damaged when overclocking or if incompatible components are used. Speaking of overclocking, if you do decide to do this, you should definitely monitor the CPU and RAM clock speeds and any other appropriate bus speeds. Finally, some motherboards can detect whether the computer case has been opened; this is known as intrusion detection/notification. The BIOS can notify you of this and log it for future reference.

▶ **Virtualization Support:** To support virtual computing, the BIOS must be configured properly. This setting is often buried within the BIOS in a CPU submenu. For Intel CPUs, the Intel Virtualization Technology (Intel VT) option should be enabled. For AMD CPUs, enable AMD-V. We'll talk more about virtualization in Chapter 13, "Peripherals and Custom Computing."

You can also enable or disable USB ports and legacy devices. Plus, you can load BIOS defaults if you configure something in the BIOS that stops the system from booting.

Did you ever know someone who forgot a password? Technicians remember their passwords like the backs of their hands, but many users don't fare quite as well. And for some reason, users love to set supervisory passwords in the BIOS—and then forget them. To fix this, you need to turn off the computer, disconnect it, open it, and remove the lithium battery. By doing so, the CMOS forgets what it stored. The time and date probably revert to a date in the past (such as January 1, 2000), and all passwords will be erased. In some cases, you might also need to modify a BIOS configuration jumper block solely or in addition to removing the battery. Sometimes referred to as the CMOS jumper, this is a 3-pin jumper, usually near the lithium battery, that has three possibilities: Normal, Configuration, and Recovery. If necessary, move the 2-pin jumper shunt from Normal to Configuration; at that point you can access the BIOS without a password. Recovery mode is normally accomplished by removing the jumper altogether. So you know, motherboards are usually shipped in the Normal state.

Flashing the BIOS

Flashing the BIOS is the term given to the process of erasing the BIOS firmware and rewriting it with a new version of the BIOS. It is sometimes referred to as *updating* the BIOS. It is important to check for updates to the BIOS, just like you would update an OS. However, only flash the BIOS if your system needs it (for example, if your motherboard "sees" the processor but doesn't know specifically what type it is or at what speed it runs). Motherboard manufacturers release these updates quite often, and their descriptions can tell you exactly what they fix. If you build a new computer, you should check for a BIOS update before you even install an OS. BIOS updates close security holes, identify new devices (or identify them better), and are sometimes released simply to fix some incorrect code. There are several ways to update the BIOS, but generally you would either do it from within Windows or by using some kind of bootable media (CD-ROM or USB flash drive) to boot the system and rewrite the BIOS. Because the process varies from motherboard to motherboard, the following lists a few of the most common steps:

1. **Identify what BIOS you are running:** To do this, access the BIOS and check the main menu. There is usually some kind of code that you can check against the latest BIOS download on the manufacturer's website. If it is the same code, there is no need to update the BIOS. BIOS updates are cumulative, so you need to download and install only the newest version.

2. **Download the BIOS from the Web:** The file format could be a .zip, .exe, or .iso file. Usually, you need to extract the actual BIOS update file. There is normally an instruction file you can download as well, explaining exactly how to flash the BIOS step by step. Or that documentation can be found on the motherboard (or PC) manufacturer's website.

3. **Select your method of BIOS updating:** For example, an Express BIOS Update would be done within Windows; simply download the file and double-click it to begin the process. Or a flash update could be performed within the BIOS from a USB device. You could also create your own bootable media if you have the wherewithal and a lot of time on your hands. With some manufacturers, you can download an ISO image to be burned to a CD-ROM. After this is done, boot the computer with the CD and continue to the BIOS update. If the BIOS update is interrupted for some reason or does not complete properly, it might be necessary to recover the BIOS. To do this, you need the recovery file and might need to remove the BIOS configuration jumper from the motherboard.

4. **Flash the BIOS:** Run the BIOS flash update from the appropriate media. If the media is a CD-ROM, restart the computer and boot to that media. Otherwise, run the BIOS update from within the BIOS or from within Windows. Some BIOS programs may appear unresponsive but be careful; they are probably updating the BIOS even though it might look like nothing is happening. Let the system do its "thing" for several minutes. Do not run a BIOS update during a lightning storm. Never turn off the computer during a BIOS update, and if you use a laptop, make sure that it is plugged in before starting the update.

ExamAlert

Know how to flash the BIOS for the exam!

Cram Quiz

Answer these questions. The answers follow the last question. If you cannot answer these questions correctly, consider reading this section again until you can.

220-901 Questions

1. Which component supplies power to the CMOS when the computer is off?

   ○ **A.** Lithium battery

   ○ **B.** POST

   ○ **C.** Power supply

   ○ **D.** BIOS

2. To implement a secure boot process, which device should be listed first in the Boot Device Priority screen?

   ○ **A.** Network

   ○ **B.** CD-ROM

   ○ **C.** USB

   ○ **D.** Hard drive

3. What is the term for how the BIOS readies the computer for and initiates the booting of the operating system?

   ○ **A.** Bootlegging

   ○ **B.** Booting

   ○ **C.** Bootstrapping

   ○ **D.** POST

4. How can you reset a forgotten BIOS supervisor/administrator password?

   ○ **A.** Access the BIOS by pressing F2.

   ○ **B.** Remove the battery.

   ○ **C.** Extract the .EXE contents to removable media.

   ○ **D.** Remove the main 24-pin power connector.

5. You just rebooted a PC and it displays a black screen with a white blinking underscore on the top left. What is the most likely problem?

   ○ **A.** BIOS needs to be flashed.

   ○ **B.** Windows Recovery Environment is running.

   ○ **C.** PC is in Safe Mode.

   ○ **D.** Incorrect boot order.

Cram Quiz Answers

220-901 Answers

1. **A.** The lithium battery supplies power to the CMOS when the computer is off. This is because the CMOS is volatile and would otherwise lose the stored settings when the computer is turned off.

2. **D.** To ensure that other users cannot boot the computer from removable media, set the first device in the Boot Device Priority screen to hard drive.

3. **C.** Bootstrapping is accomplished by the BIOS. It is defined as one system readying the computer and leading to another larger system.

4. **B.** Removing the battery (and possibly moving the BIOS configuration jumper) resets the BIOS passwords. You might also need to configure the BIOS configuration jumper.

5. **D.** When you see a black screen with a white blinking underscore, there is a good chance that the BIOS boot order is incorrect.

Installing and Troubleshooting Motherboards

Installing Motherboards

You might ask, "Haven't we talked enough about motherboards?" Not quite. But installing them is easy when you know how, so this section shouldn't take too long. We'll break it down into some simple steps:

1. **Select a motherboard:** If you build a new computer, it should be designed with a compatible case and processor in mind. Also, make sure that it has the expansion ports that you need for audio, video, and so on, and verify that it has the necessary I/O ports. Also, give a thought to the applications you will use and if they require or prefer a specific chipset. If you replace a motherboard, make sure that it is compatible with the system you put it in and that all the components can connect to it. If it is a proprietary computer (HP, Dell, and such), your choice of motherboards might be limited; see the computer manufacturer's website for details.

2. **Employ ESD prevention methods:** Use an antistatic strap and mat. And before touching the motherboard, place both hands on an unpainted portion of the case chassis as a means of self-grounding. For more information on ESD preventative measures, see Chapter 19, "Safety, Procedures, and Professionalism."

3. **Ready the case:** Most cases come with brass standoffs that are already screwed directly into the case. Additional standoffs usually accompany the motherboard. Line up the motherboard's predrilled holes with the standoffs. Add more standoffs as necessary so that the motherboard is supported properly. Some motherboards come with additional rubber standoffs that provide additional support and protection from ESD.

4. **Install the motherboard:** Carefully place the motherboard into the case so that the holes meet and line up with the brass standoffs. Secure the motherboard by screwing it in wherever there is a standoff. You might prefer to install the processor and RAM first before installing the motherboard. This allows you to ultimately perform breadboarding, (testing/troubleshooting of the system) while it is outside the case. Some people prefer to install the CPU, RAM, and video card last, after the rest of the system has been built, because they are very expensive components and can be easily damaged. Of course, in some cases (pun

intended), you have no choice in the matter, but in general, if you are concerned about damaging these components, then install them last.

5. **Connect cables:** Now it's time to connect the 24-pin power cable from the power supply to the motherboard. This connector is tabbed; make sure that the tabs match up. When connected, it should lock into place. Case connectors can be fitted to the motherboard as well. These wires start at the inside front of the case and have thin 2-, 3-, or 4-pin plugs on the other end. They are labeled POWER LED, POWER SW (for power switch), HDD LED, and so on. These plugs connect to items such as the Power button, reset button, and LED lights. Connect them to the corresponding ports on the edge of the motherboard closest to the front of the case. There might also be front panel ports (USB, audio), external SATA connectors, and more that need to be connected from the case to the motherboard. You can usually find documentation for all these connections with the motherboard. If not, download the technical manual from the motherboard manufacturer's website.

6. **Install or reinstall components:** Now it's time to install the rest of the components, such as the hard drives, optical drives, and any other components. Installation of these additional components is covered in their corresponding chapters.

7. **Test the installation:** Finally, after you install anything, test it! Make sure it works. Boot the computer and access the BIOS or UEFI. Tool around awhile until you are satisfied the motherboard is functional and that the BIOS is identifying the components of the system correctly. If there is an issue, troubleshoot the problem using the techniques discussed in the next section.

Troubleshooting Motherboards

That time has come. Remember the "big four" mentioned in Chapter 1, "Introduction to Troubleshooting." The motherboard is one of them. Here's a common scenario: You boot the computer, don't get anything on the display, you are sure that power is not an issue, and you are certain that the computer is actually booting. When this happens, you should check all connections. Chances are, it isn't the motherboard. A loose video card can cause these types of issues; make sure it is firmly pressed into its slot. Check the processor, RAM, and any connectors and other adapter cards in an attempt to rule out the motherboard as the culprit. You see, it is rare that the motherboard fails, and checking these connections doesn't take long; however, removing the motherboard can be time-consuming. If you suspect a particular component has failed (for example, the video card), attempt to swap out the video card with a known good device. Do the same with the RAM and even the processor. Finally, if you rule out the rest of the devices, continue troubleshooting the motherboard. If necessary, use built-in POST analysis (or a POST card) to help find the culprit. Also, as mentioned previously, consider breadboarding the system: Remove all of the components from the case and reassemble them on an antistatic mat. This way, you can easily test components individually. Or you can utilize the half-split method, whereby you make an educated guess as to the source of the problem and then move forward or backward as necessary. This half-split (or divide and conquer) method is for more experienced technicians, but it can be quite time-saving compared to "easter-egging" for the guilty party. Finally, if worst comes to worst, swap the motherboard with a known good one to verify if it is indeed the motherboard that is causing the problem.

Let's run through a quick troubleshooting scenario using the CompTIA six-step troubleshooting methodology outlined in Chapter 1.

Motherboard Issue

In this scenario you are a PC technician working for the PC repair department of an electronics store. You are given a PC that supposedly reverts back to 12:00 AM, January 1, 2000, every time it starts. Troubleshoot!

1. **Identify the problem:** While viewing the work order, you see some of the customer comments: "PC worked fine until a few days ago. Now, every time it starts, it shows the date as Jan. 1, 2000. After changing the time and date in Windows, it reverts back to Jan. 1, 2000 when restarted. The latest operating system update must have messed the computer up; I had updated and that is when the problem started. Now, in my Outlook application, the calendar and meetings are not synchronized to my employees' Outlook! Please fix right away!"

   A co-worker tells you the motherboard should be replaced and says your manager just wants the job done as quickly as possible.

   Remember to respect the user/customer, but don't always take the user's word for it. Test the computer yourself; you might find something entirely different is causing the problem, and you can save yourself a lot of time. Also, don't rush, regardless of how fast the manager wants the work done. When you rush, you risk the chance of overlooking the obvious, simple solution.

> **Note**
>
> This concept applies to questions on the actual CompTIA A+ exams as well!

So, while examining the computer, you notice it runs Windows and that Windows does indeed revert to January 1, 2000, even after you reconfigured the Date and Time Properties window. Otherwise, the computer seems to work fine, aside from Outlook synchronization issues, which is understandable because the system can't synchronize properly if time isn't being kept correctly. The computer doesn't display anything peculiar or make any strange sounds. The latest service pack seems to have been installed correctly and is operating properly without any errors in the Event Viewer.

2. **Establish a theory of probable cause (question the obvious):** Again, look for the obvious or most probable cause. Remembering your training, you surmise that the lithium battery in the motherboard has discharged, causing the CMOS to lose its contents. If this happens, the BIOS has no recourse but to revert back to its earliest known time, which in this case is January 1, 2000. It sounds logical, so you move onto the next step.

3. **Test the theory to determine cause:** To test this theory, you decide to restart the computer and access the BIOS. When in the BIOS, you change the time to the current time and date and then you save the settings and shut down the computer. After turning it back on, you access the BIOS again and note that the time has once again reverted back to Jan. 1, 2000. You never accessed Windows in this procedure, so it would seem that the theory is correct. Now, if the time and date you had configured remained in the BIOS without reverting, your theory would probably be incorrect, and you would need to go back to Step 2 to formulate a new theory. Although you try to establish and test theories without opening the PC, you can also test the lithium battery with a multimeter. The CR2032 lithium battery has a nominal voltage of 3.0 V. If it measures below 2.0 volts, you know the battery has discharged to such a state that it cannot power the CMOS any longer.

4. **Establish a plan of action to resolve the problem and implement the solution:** Your plan of action should be to replace the CR2032 lithium battery with a new one. Implementing this requires you to shut down the PC and unplug it, open the PC, employ ESD prevention methods, and remove the CR2032 battery. This battery is easy to spot;

it is shiny and is about the size of a nickel. They are usually labeled as CR2032 as well. Removing it entails pushing on a tab and gently prying the battery out. Use something nonmetallic to do this. Then, find or requisition a new lithium battery. Next, test the new battery with your trusty multimeter to make sure it is within proper voltage range (the closer to 3.0 volts, the better). Remember that batteries slowly discharge, even when they sit on the shelf. Finally, install the battery into the motherboard.

5. **Verify full system functionality and if applicable implement preventative measures:** Now you need to make sure it works, so you boot the PC and access the BIOS. From there, you update the time and date, save the settings to the BIOS, and shut down the computer. Next, boot the system again, and again access the BIOS. At this point, you verify that the time and date have not reverted back to Jan. 1, 2000. If the time is correct, boot to Windows. Check the time in Windows after several "full cycles" (shutting the computer off and turning it back on) and warm boots to ensure that it works properly. As a preventative measure, you might want to recommend that the user synchronize Windows to a time server. This can be done by opening the Date and Time Properties window, selecting the Internet Time tab, and configuring the system to automatically synchronize with an Internet time server. (Most versions of Windows are set this way by default.) This way, even if the lithium battery fails, Windows resynchronizes to the time server every time it boots. This also creates a more consistent meeting time for the user and other employees when meetings are set in Outlook. Another way to prevent synchronization problems such as this is to use a web-based calendar from companies such as Google, Microsoft, or Yahoo. These services obtain the time from the Internet as well.

6. **Document findings, actions, and outcomes:** Document according to your company's policies. Complete the work order and any other paperwork necessary. Additional documentation might be required in a trouble-ticketing software program—and make a mental note of who the person was that said to replace the motherboard; be careful of that person's suggestions in the future!

ExamAlert

If the time and date have reset on a system, there is a good chance that the rest of the settings have also reset to defaults. You should always review the UEFI/BIOS configuration settings, compare them with your organization's documentation, and make any modifications necessary. Always remember to save your work!

Again, it is uncommon to see a motherboard fail, but if it does, it can be because of a few different things. Let's discuss several of these now.

First and probably the most common of these rarities are BIOS issues. Remember that you might need to flash the BIOS to the latest version. For example, a new CPU or RAM might not be recognized at the correct clock speeds (such as 3.1 GHz for the CPU or 1600 MHz for the RAM) or might not be recognized at all. An adapter card might not be seen properly. Or perhaps Windows isn't working as it should be with the hardware in the system. Updating the BIOS should fix many of these issues. On a separate note, you might encounter a PC that instead of booting normally accesses the BIOS instead. A faulty CMOS battery is the most common culprit of this. Change out the battery and the system should boot normally.

Second are ESD and other electrical issues. These might present themselves intermittently. If you find some intermittent issues (for example, the computer reboots out of nowhere) or you receive random Blue Screens of Death, ESD could be the culprit. Or a surge could cause the problem. A particular wire, circuit, or capacitor on the motherboard could have been damaged. Document when failures occur. Swap out the motherboard with a known good one to see if the issue happens again when running through the same processes. If the issue doesn't recur, chances are the original motherboard is headed for the bit bucket. There are lots of circuits on a motherboard; electrical damage to any one could cause the system to behave "irrationally" at best. Other computers don't fare so well; electrical damage can go right through the power supply to the motherboard, disabling it permanently. Be sure to use a surge suppressor or UPS to protect your equipment and, of course, implement antistatic measures whenever you work inside a system.

Third are component failures. It is possible that a single component of the motherboard (for example, the SATA controller) can fail, but the rest of the motherboard works fine. This can also be verified by doing a POST analysis. To fix this, a separate PCIe (or PCI) SATA controller card can be purchased. Then you can connect the hard drives to the new controller and disable the original integrated SATA controller in the BIOS. Be wary, however; sometimes these add-on cards can be pricey—perhaps more pricey than a new motherboard.

And last are manufacturing defects and failed motherboard components. Printed circuit boards (PCBs), such as motherboards, are mass-produced at high speeds. Problems might be found immediately when receiving a motherboard. In general, defects are uncommon but can occur due to mechanical problems in the machinery or due to an engineering error. If you suspect a manufacturing defect, you should return the motherboard. Motherboard component failure can also manifest itself over time, such as in the form of distended capacitors. This is when a capacitor becomes swollen and possibly leaks electrolytic material; this bulging can cause the system to restart/ shut down, cause a BSOD, or cause other errors. If possible, the affected capacitor(s) should be replaced right away. If that does not work, the motherboard should be replaced. In the early 2000s, swollen caps were somewhat prevalent due to raw material issues—the problem was even dubbed the "capacitor plague." However, the problem is much less common today.

Cram Quiz

Answer these questions. The answers follow the last question. If you cannot answer these questions correctly, consider reading this section again until you can.

220-901 Questions

1. Before installing a motherboard, what should you do? (Select the best answer.)

   ○ **A.** Install the processor.

   ○ **B.** Verify that it is compatible with the case.

   ○ **C.** Employ ESD prevention methods.

   ○ **D.** Test the motherboard with a multimeter.

2. Which of the following are possible reasons for motherboard failure? (Select all that apply.)

   ○ **A.** Power surges

   ○ **B.** Manufacturer defects

   ○ **C.** CD-ROM failures

   ○ **D.** Incorrect USB devices

3. How can you tell if a lithium battery has been discharged? (Select the best answer.)

   ○ **A.** Use a power supply tester.

   ○ **B.** Check within Windows.

   ○ **C.** Use a multimeter.

   ○ **D.** Plug it into another motherboard.

4. A PC reboots without any warning. You ruled out any chance of viruses. When you look at the motherboard, you see that some of the capacitors appear distended and out of shape. What should you do?

   ○ **A.** Replace the motherboard.

   ○ **B.** Replace the hard drive.

   ○ **C.** Remove and replace the capacitors.

   ○ **D.** Reconfigure the BIOS.

5. A computer you are troubleshooting won't boot properly. When you power on the computer, the video display is blank and you hear a series of beeps. What should you do?

   ○ **A.** Check power supply connections.

   ○ **B.** Consult the vendor documentation for the motherboard.

   ○ **C.** Remove all memory and replace it.

   ○ **D.** Unplug the speakers because they are causing a conflict.

Cram Quiz Answers

220-901 Answers

1. **C.** Always employ ESD prevention methods before working with any components inside the computer. Although A and B are correct, they are not the best answers. You might decide to install the CPU to the motherboard before installing the motherboard in the case or you might not—it depends on the scenario. Verification of compatibility should have happened prior to *purchase*, not just before the installation.

2. **A** and **B.** Power surges and manufacturing defects are possible reasons for motherboard failure. If a CD-ROM fails, it should not affect the motherboard. Any USB device can connect to a USB port (if it has the right connector). There is no such thing as an "incorrect" USB device.

3. **C.** Although there might be a Windows application that monitors the battery, the surefire way is to test the voltage of the lithium battery with a multimeter.

4. **A.** You should replace the motherboard if it is damaged. It would be much too time-consuming to even attempt replacing the capacitors and probably not cost-effective for your company.

5. **B.** You should check the BIOS version and consult the documentation that accompanies the motherboard. You might need to go online for this information. You can also try performing a POST analysis to discern the problem.

CHAPTER 3

The CPU

This chapter covers the following A+ exam topics:

▶ CPU 101

▶ Installing and Troubleshooting CPUs

You can find a master list of A+ exam topics in the "Introduction."

This chapter covers CompTIA A+ 220-901 objectives 1.6 and 4.1.

The central processing unit, or CPU, is quite often referred to as the "brain" of the computer. Today's CPUs are like superbrains! A typical CPU today runs between 2 and 3.5 GHz or higher, uses multiple cores, and some can easily process 100 billion operations per second. That's a good deal more than you would have seen just five years ago. Some mornings I have trouble processing the thought: *Need coffee!* Of course, we know that the human brain is much more sophisticated and functional than a CPU, but the CPU wins out when it comes to sheer calculating power.

You might hear the CPU referred to as a microprocessor; technically, it is. It's a much smaller version of the processors that were used 50 years ago. And although microprocessor might be a more accurate term, it has become more acceptable to refer to it as CPU, which this chapter does. However, you also see CPU manufacturers such as Intel refer to them as processors, so for all intents and purposes, the three terms mean the same thing. A computer has other processors used by video cards and elsewhere, but know that the CPU is the main processor.

To start, this chapter discusses some CPU technologies and cooling methods. Then the chapter demonstrates how to install and troubleshoot the CPU.

CPU 101

The CPU is often the most-expensive component in the computer; it's also one of the, if not *the*, most important. The CPU's main function is to execute instructions or programs. Its speed, or *clock rate*, is measured in Hertz. For example, at 3.1 GHz, a CPU operates at 3.1 billion cycles per second; we will speak more to this concept in a moment. Although the speed of the CPU might be important, other factors should also play into your decision when choosing a CPU, including the chipset on the motherboard, *CPU technology*, and cooling. Chapter 2, "Motherboards," covers chipsets, but let's go ahead and talk about the various CPU technologies and brands of CPUs now.

CPU Technology

CPU technology is a key factor when considering a CPU. It all comes back to the motherboard; the CPU must be compatible with the motherboard in a number of ways. It is important to think about the speed (clock rate) of the CPU you want to use and whether that speed can be supported by the motherboard and whether the CPU fits in the motherboard's socket. Also, a decision must be made as to whether to use a 64-bit or 32-bit CPU and how many cores the CPU will contain. This decision will be determined by the motherboard, the type of operating system you plan to install, and whether this is a new install or an upgrade of an older computer. Getting deeper into the technical side of the CPU, you might want to know the amount of cache included with the CPU and the amount of power it requires.

Clock Rate

The *clock rate* is the frequency (or speed) of a component. It is rated in cycles per second and measured in hertz (Hz). For all practical purposes, the term clock rate is the same as the more commonly used term: *clock speed*.

Components are sold to consumers with a *maximum* clock rate, but they don't always run at that maximum number. To explain, let me use a car analogy. The CPU is often called the "engine" of the computer, like a car engine. Well, your car's speedometer might go up to 120 MPH, but you'll probably never drive at that maximum—for a variety of reasons! When it comes to CPUs, the stated clock rate is the *maximum* clock rate, and the CPU usually runs at a speed less than that. In fact, it can run at any speed below the maximum, but there are only several plateaus that it will usually hover around.

Now, we're all familiar with speeds such as 2.4 GHz, 3.0 GHz, or 3.5 GHz. But what is the basis of these speeds? Speed can be divided into two categories that are interrelated:

▶ **Motherboard bus speed:** This is the base clock of the motherboard and is often referred to simply as "bus speed." This is generated by a quartz oscillating crystal soldered directly to the motherboard. For example, the base clock on the X99-A motherboard used in *AV Editor* in Chapter 2 is 100 MHz.

▶ **Internal clock speed:** This is the internal frequency of the CPU and is the well-known number that CPUs are associated with. For the X99-A motherboard, I purchased the Intel Core i7-5820K, which is rated at 3.3 GHz. The CPU uses an internal multiplier based off the motherboard base clock. The multiplier for this particular CPU is 33. The math is as follows: base clock × multiplier = internal clock speed. In our example, that would be 100 MHz × 33 = 3.3 GHz. This motherboard can support faster and slower CPUs from a variety of CPU families, but the math works in the same way. To see the specifications for the i7-5820k CPU, go to http://ark.intel.com/products/82932/Intel-Core-i7-5820K-Processor-15M-Cache-up-to-3_60-GHz.

Some motherboards allow for overclocking, which enables the user to increase the multiplier within the BIOS/UEFI, thereby increasing the internal clock speed of the CPU. For example, our X99-A can perform overclocking, taking advantage of Intel's CPU Turbo Boost technology, going from 3.3 GHz to 3.6 GHz, a 10 percent increase. It is also possible on many motherboards to increase the base clock, for example from 100 MHz to as much as 300 MHz. This not only increases the speed of the CPU, it increases the speed of RAM, which Chapter 4, "RAM," discusses. Either of these overclocking methods increases the voltage, creates more heat, and could possibly cause damage to the system—analogous to blowing the engine of a car when attempting to run a 10-second 1/4 mile. So approach overclocking with extreme caution!

ExamAlert

For today's CPUs, two of the most commonly used terms are *bus speed* (the base clock of the motherboard) and *clock speed* (the frequency of the CPU). They might not be completely accurate, technically, but you will see and hear them often and you could see them on the exam as well.

> **Note**
>
> Older systems use a term known as external clock speed—the frequency at which
> the front side bus (FSB) connects the CPU to the RAM. I discuss this more on my
> A+ Archive page at www.davidlprowse.com.

32-Bit Versus 64-Bit

Almost all of today's PC-based CPUs are 64-bit; it's a type of CPU architecture that incorporates registers that are 64 bits wide. These registers, or
temporary storage areas, allow the CPU to work with and process 64-bit data
types and provide support for address space in the terabytes. 64-bit CPUs
have been available for PCs since 2003. Examples of 64-bit CPUs include the
AMD FX and Intel Core series of CPUs.

A little history: The predecessor to the 64-bit CPU was the 32-bit CPU. Intel
started developing well-known 32-bit CPUs as early as 1985 with the 386DX
CPU (which ran at a whopping 33 MHz!) and AMD did likewise in 1991 with
the Am386. A 32-bit CPU can't support nearly as much address space as a
64-bit CPU; 32-bit is limited to 4 GB. Most editions of Windows are available in both 32-bit and 64-bit versions.

You still see 32-bit CPU technologies in the field. However, due to applications' ever-increasing need for resources, these older CPUs continue to
diminish, whereas 64-bit technologies (such as the Core i5 and Core i7) have
become more prevalent. In addition, you will find that some applications are
still written for the 32-bit platform. 32-bit technologies are still common in
the mobile device market but 64-bit technologies are also available.

You might hear of the terms x86 and x64. x86 refers to older CPU names that
ended in an 86—for example, the 80386 (shortened to just 386), 486, 586, and
so on. Generally, when people use the term x86, they refer to 32-bit CPUs
that enable 4 GB of address space. On the other hand, x64 (or x86-64) refers
to newer, 64-bit CPUs that are a superset of the x86 architecture. This technology has a wider data path to handle program execution; it can run 64-bit
software and 32-bit software and can address a default maximum of 256 terabytes (TB) of RAM. This can optionally be extended to 4 petabytes (PB), but
that extension isn't currently used on PCs. As of the writing of this book, only
a true supercomputer would need more than 256 TB of RAM. The real limitation right now is the operating system. For example, Windows Vista 64-bit is
"limited" to 128 GB max depending on the edition. Some Windows 7 64-bit
editions can go as high as 192 GB, and Windows 8.1 Pro 64-bit can handle
512 GB. To put this into perspective, the X99-A motherboard supports only a

maximum of 64 GB of RAM. This is far less than Windows 7 or Windows 8 can handle, which in itself is just a tiny slice of what a 64-bit CPU can address.

Windows 8, 7, and Vista come in 64-bit (x64) and 32-bit (x86) versions so that users from both generations of computers can run the software efficiently.

> **ExamAlert**
>
> Know the differences between 32-bit and 64-bit architectures. For example, remember that 32-bit CPUs can only address a maximum of 4 GB of RAM.

Sockets

The *socket* is the electrical interface between the CPU and the motherboard. It attaches directly to the motherboard and houses the CPU. It also physically supports the CPU and heat sink and enables easy replacement of the CPU.

The socket is made of either plastic or metal and uses metal contacts for connectivity to each of the pins/lands of the CPU. One or more metal levers (retaining arms) lock the CPU in place. Figure 3.1 shows an example of an unlocked LGA socket from the X99-A motherboard.

FIGURE 3.1 **An unlocked LGA 2011 socket**

Historically, the socket has been considered a ZIF, short for zero insertion force. This means that the CPU should connect easily into the socket, with no pressure or force involved during the installation. The socket will have many pin inserts, or lands, for the CPU to connect to. Pin 1 can be found in one of the corners and can be identified by either a white corner drawn on the motherboard or one or more missing pins or pinholes. This helps you to orient the CPU, which also has the arrow, or missing pin(s), in the corresponding corner. Here are two types of sockets you should know for the exam:

▶ **PGA:** Pin Grid Array sockets accept CPUs that have pins covering the majority of their underside. The pins on the CPU are placed in the pinholes of the socket and the CPU is locked into place by a retaining arm. PGA has been in use since the late '80s and is still in use on some motherboards today. Many AMD CPUs use PGA sockets. Examples of AMD sockets include the AM and FM series.

▶ **LGA:** Land Grid Array sockets use lands that protrude out and touch the CPU's contact points. This newer type of socket (also known as Socket T) offers better power distribution and less chance to damage the CPU compared to PGA. LGA has been used since the later versions of Pentium 4 and is commonly used today on Intel motherboards. Examples of Intel sockets include the LGA 1150 and the LGA 2011.

The CPU and socket must be compatible. For example, the X99-A motherboard used in the *AV Editor* computer has an LGA 2011 socket, which is common but not the only socket that Intel uses on its motherboards. The Core i7-5820K CPU used on that motherboard is designed to fit into the LGA 2011 socket and several other CPUs—but not all CPUs—can fit into this socket as well. For example, the Intel Core i5-2400 (used in *Media PC*) needs to be installed into an LGA 1155 socket, which means purchasing a completely different motherboard. Table 3.1 shows the Intel and AMD sockets you should know for the A+ exam and the CPUs that can be installed to them. Keep in mind this is not a finite list; there are lots of other sockets, both older and newer.

TABLE 3.1 **Common Sockets and Corresponding CPUs**

Intel Sockets	Intel CPUs	AMD Sockets	AMD CPUs
LGA 775	Core 2 Duo	AM3	Phenom II
	Core 2 Quad		Athlon II
	Xeon		Sempron
	Pentium, Celeron		

Intel Sockets	Intel CPUs	AMD Sockets	AMD CPUs
LGA 1155 (replaces the LGA 1156)	Core i7, i5, i3 Xeon Pentium, Celeron	AM3+	FX Vishera FX Zambezi Phenom II Athlon II Sempron
LGA 1156	Core i7, i5, i3 Xeon Pentium, Celeron	FM1	Athlon II Llano
LGA 1366	Core i7 Xeon	FM2	Trinity
LGA 1150 (replacement for the LGA 1155)	Haswell Broadwell	FM2+	Kaveri Godavari A8/A10 series
LGA 2011 (replacement for the LGA 1366)	Core i7 Xeon		

ExamAlert

Know the socket types used with common Intel and AMD CPUs.

CPU Cache

Several types of cache are used in computers, but CPU cache is a special high-speed memory that reduces the time the CPU takes to access data. By using high-speed static RAM (SRAM) and because the cache is often located directly on—or even in—the CPU, CPU cache can be faster than accessing information from dynamic RAM (DRAM) modules. However, it will be limited in storage capacity when compared to DRAM. Cache is divided into levels:

▶ **Level 1:** L1 cache is built into the CPU and gives fast access to *the most frequently* used data. This level of cache is the first one accessed by the CPU and is usually found in small amounts. However, it is the fastest cache to be found, offering the lowest latency of any of the types of cache. One of the reasons for this is that it resides within the CPU core. The Core i7-5820K (used in *AV Editor*) has 6 × 64 KB of L1 cache—64 KB for each of its six cores. You can find more information about multi-core technology later in this chapter. In comparison, the Core i5-2400 CPU (used in *Media PC*) has 4 × 32 KB of L1 cache—32 KB for each of its four cores.

2422

▶ **Level 2:** L2 cache is usually built on to the CPU (on-die). It is accessed after L1 cache and it serves the CPU with less frequently used data in comparison to L1 but it is still more frequently used data than the data that comes from typical DRAM. L2 cache feeds the L1 cache, which in turn feeds the CPU. L2 cache is not as fast as L1 cache but is far superior to DRAM. This and L3 cache take up the majority of the CPU's real estate. The Core i5-5820K has 256 KB per core, for a total of 1.5 MB of L2 cache. The Core i5-2400 CPU also has 256 KB per core, for a total of 1 MB L2 cache.

▶ **Level 3:** L3 cache comes in the largest capacities of the three types of cache and has the most latency; therefore, it is the slowest. If the CPU can't find what it needs in L1, it moves to L2 and finally to L3. Or you could think of it this way: L3 cache feeds L2 cache, which feeds L1 cache, which in turn feeds the CPU with data. If the CPU can't find the data it is seeking within cache, it moves on to the DRAM sticks. L3 cache could be on-die or on-board, but most of today's CPUs have it on-die; however, it is shared among the cores of the CPU. The Core i7-5820K has 15 MB of L3 cache. The Core i5-2400 has 6 MB of L3 cache.

ExamAlert

Know the difference between L1, L2, and L3 cache for the exam.

Generally, the more cache, the better. The less the CPU needs to access DRAM, the faster it can calculate data.

Note

You might hear of L4 cache. This is not as common in PCs but is sometimes used on more powerful workstation and server computers. Although it's not accurate, some people might refer to main memory as L4 cache.

Hyper-Threading

Intel's Hyper-Threading (HT) enables a single CPU to accept and calculate two independent sets of instructions simultaneously, thereby simulating two CPUs. The technology was designed so that single CPUs can compete better with true multi-CPU systems but without the cost involved. In an HT environment, only one CPU is present, but the operating system sees two virtual CPUs and divides the workload, or threads, between the two.

> **Note**
>
> Don't confuse Hyper-Threading with HyperTransport used by AMD. HyperTransport is a high-speed, low-latency, point-to-point link that increases communication speeds between various devices (such as the CPU and the northbridge).

Multicore Technologies

Whereas HT technology simulates multiple CPUs, *multicore* CPUs physically contain two or more actual processor cores in one CPU package. These newer CPUs can have 2, 4, 6, or even 8 cores, each acting as a single entity but in some cases sharing the CPU cache. This enables more-efficient processing of data. Not only is less heat generated, but a lower-frequency, multicore CPU (for example, 2.0 GHz) can process more data per second than a higher-frequency, single-core CPU (for example, 3.2 GHz).

Current examples of multicore CPUs include Intel's various Core series and AMD's FX CPUs. Today's CPUs combine multicore technology with Hyper-Threading, enabling for as many as 12 or 16 simultaneous threads in a single CPU package. It just goes on and on!

> **ExamAlert**
>
> Know the differences between Hyper-Threading and multicore technologies for the exam. Hyper-Threading enables a single-core CPU to calculate two instruction sets simultaneously, whereas multicore CPUs calculate two or more instruction sets simultaneously—one instruction set per core.

Power Consumption

Power consumption of CPUs is normally rated in watts. For example, the Core i7-5820K is rated as a 140 watt-hour CPU. The Core i5-2400 is rated as a 95 watt-hour CPU. This rating is known as *thermal design power* (*TDP*) and it signifies the amount of heat generated by the CPU, which the cooling system is required to dissipate when operating with a complex workload. This number is nominal; it could be more or it could be less, depending on CPU usage, and does not take into account overclocking. The measurement should play into your decision when planning which power supply to use and which kind of cooling system. For more information on power supplies, see Chapter 5, "Power." 100 to 150 watts (or thereabouts) is a common TDP rating for multicore CPUs. They are more efficient than their predecessor single-core CPUs, which could dissipate as much as 200–250 watts.

Because we are talking electricity, another important factor is voltage. CPUs are associated with a voltage range; for example, the Core i7-5820K runs at about .7 V and the Core i5-2400 runs at about 1 V by default. However, a CPU's voltage will increase as applications demand more processing power. It is important to monitor the voltage that is received by the CPU; you can do this in the BIOS or, better yet, with applications within Windows. If the CPU goes beyond the specified voltage range for any extended length of time, it *will* damage the CPU. This becomes especially important for overclockers.

Brands of CPUs

For the average user, it doesn't matter too much which CPU you go with. However, for the developer, designer, gamer, video editor, or musician, it can make or break your computer's performance. Although the CompTIA A+ objectives cover only Intel and AMD (Advanced Micro Devices), you should be aware that there are others in the market. Intel and AMD dominate the PC and laptop arena, but other companies such as VIA Technologies have made great inroads into niche markets and are moving deeper into the laptop/mobile markets as well.

CPU manufacturers use the make/model system. For example, the CPU used in *AV Editor* is the Intel (make) Core i7-5820K (model). An example of an AMD CPU is the AMD (make) FX 8-Core Processor Black Edition (model).

Some CPUs come with a built-in graphics processing unit (GPU). This means that with a compatible motherboard, no separate video card is necessary and the monitor can be plugged directly into the video port on the motherboard. Both Intel and AMD have many CPUs that incorporate a GPU. AMD refers to this as the Accelerated Processing Unit (APU). Built-in GPUs have come a long way, but for power-users (gamers, graphics designers, and so on), a separate video card is usually required for best functionality.

Intel and AMD are both good companies that make quality products, which leads to great competition. Which is better? In all honestly, it varies and depends on how you use the CPU. You can find advocates for both (albeit subjective advocates), and the scales are constantly tipping back and forth. On any given day, a specific Intel CPU might outperform AMD; three months later, a different AMD CPU can outperform an Intel. It's been that way for many years now. Whichever CPU you choose, make sure that you get a compatible motherboard. A few things to watch for are compatibility with the chipset, socket type, and voltage. However, Intel and AMD have tools on their websites that make it easy for you to find compatible motherboards. Again, the most important compatibility concern is that the CPU is the right one for the user.

Note

Periodically visit the Intel and AMD websites for the latest and greatest CPUs.

Cooling

Now that you know a CPU can effectively use as much electricity as a light bulb, you can understand why it gets so hot. Hundreds of millions of transistors are hammering away in these powerhouses, so you need to keep it and other devices in the computer cool. This is done in a few ways, as outlined in this section.

Heat Sinks

The *heat sink* is a block of metal made to sit right on top of the CPU, with metal fins stretching away from the CPU. It uses conduction to direct heat away from the CPU and out through the fins. With a passive heat sink, that's all there is to it; it dissipates heat and requires no moving parts—it is "fanless." But with an active heat sink, a fan is attached to the top of the heat sink. The fan plugs into the motherboard for power and usually blows air into the heat sink and toward the CPU, helping to dissipate heat through the heat sink fins. More powerful aftermarket CPU fans can be installed as well; just make sure that your power supply can handle the increased power requirements and that you have the space needed, because some CPU fans are *big*.

In PC-based motherboards, the chipset's northbridge and southbridge usually have passive heat sinks, but all new CPUs come with active heat sinks. Traditionally, heat sinks have been made of aluminum, but now you also see copper heat sinks used due to their superior conductivity. An important point about heat sinks: If they come loose, they could adversely affect the performance of the CPU or cause overheating, which could lead to random reboots. Make double sure that the heat sink is attached securely.

Thermal Compound

The CPU cap and the bottom of the heat sink have slight imperfections in the metal. Surface area is key; the best heat dissipation from CPU to heat sink would occur if the metal faces on each were completely and perfectly straight and flat, but...we live in the real world. So, to fill the tiny gaps and imperfections, thermal compound is used. (This is also known as thermal paste or thermal interface material.) One example of thermal compound is Arctic Silver, available online and at various electronics stores.

Now, if this is a new installation, thermal compound is probably not needed. Most new CPUs' heat sinks have factory applied thermal compound that spreads and fills the gaps automatically after you install the heat sink and boot the computer. However, if you need to remove the heat sink for any reason (for example, to clean it, or when upgrading, or if the CPU did not come with a heat sink), then thermal compound should be applied to the CPU cap before installing or upgrading the heat sink.

To do this, first clean any old thermal compound off of the CPU cap and the heat sink with thermal compound remover. Then apply new thermal compound to the CPU cap. The application method will vary depending on the CPU used, but it could require the traditional surface spread method (have an old, clean credit card handy for spreading), the middle dot method, or the increasingly common vertical line method (no credit card required!). There are other methods as well; review your CPU's documentation to find out which method is recommended. Another great resource is www.articsilver. com, where you will find a variety of application methods and in-depth, step-by-step guides for a host of CPU families. Finally, install the heat sink. Try to do so in one shot, without jostling the heat sink excessively.

ExamAlert

Reapply thermal compound whenever removing and reinstalling a heat sink.

Fans

Case fans are also needed to get the heat out of the case. The power supply has a built-in fan that is adequate for lesser systems. However, more powerful systems should have at least one extra exhaust fan mounted to the back of the case, and many cases today come with one for this purpose. An additional fan on the front of the case can be used as an intake of cool air. If you aren't sure which way the fan blows, connect its power cable to the computer but don't mount it; then hold a piece of paper against the fan. The side that pulls the paper toward it should be the side facing the front of the computer when it is mounted. Some cases come with fans that are mounted to the top, which is also ingenious because heat rises.

Another thing to consider is where the heat goes after it leaves the case. If the computer is in an enclosed area, the heat has a hard time escaping and might end up back in the computer. Make sure there is an area for air flow around the computer case. I have seen some people point the front of their computer toward an AC vent in the summer and even use special exhaust fans (such as bathroom fans) that butt up against the power supply or secondary exhaust fan on the case and lead hot air directly out of the house, but I digress.

Of course, three or four fans can make a decent amount of noise, and they still might not be enough for the most powerful computers, especially the overclocked ones, which leads us to our next option.

Liquid Cooling Systems

Although this method is not as common as the typical CPU/heat sink/fan combination, liquid-cooled systems are looked at as more of a viable option than they would have been 10 years ago. And newer water-cooling kits can be used to not only cool the CPU, but cool the chipset, hard drives, video cards, and more. A kit often comes with a CPU water block, pump, radiator/fan, PVC tubing, and, of course, coolant; although there are more simplified versions of liquid cooling systems as well. The advantages are improved heat dissipation (if installed properly), potential for higher overclocking rates, and support for the latest, hottest CPUs. Some of the disadvantages include the risk of a leak that can damage components; water pumps becoming faulty over time; air being trapped in the lines, which can cause the system to overheat; and maintenance in the form of inspecting the lines and replacing the coolant every few years. Due to the complexity of the installation and the fact that most computers do not need this level of heat dissipation, liquid cooling is usually employed by enthusiasts (such as gamers). But you might see it in other CPU-intensive systems, such as virtualization computers, CAD/CAM systems, audio/video editing systems, and possibly server systems. Regardless of cost, installation complexity, and maintenance, liquid cooling systems can help dissipate heat the most efficiently.

> **ExamAlert**
>
> Of all PC cooling methods, liquid cooling systems can dissipate heat the most efficiently.

Cram Quiz

Answer these questions. The answers follow the last question. If you cannot answer these questions correctly, consider reading this section again until you can.

220-901 Questions

1. Which of the following represents the speed of the CPU?

   ○ **A.** TDP

   ○ **B.** Cache

   ○ **C.** Internal clock speed

   ○ **D.** Bus speed

2. Which of the following sockets work with a Core i7 processor?

   ○ **A.** AM3

   ○ **B.** 1366

   ○ **C.** FM2+

   ○ **D.** 775

3. Which of the following is the fastest cache memory?

   ○ **A.** L2

   ○ **B.** L3

   ○ **C.** DRAM

   ○ **D.** L1

4. What does Hyper-Threading do?

   ○ **A.** It gives you multiple cores within the CPU.

   ○ **B.** It enables four simultaneous threads to be processed by one CPU core.

   ○ **C.** It enables two simultaneous threads to be processed by one CPU core.

   ○ **D.** It is a high-speed connection from the CPU to RAM.

5. What seals the tiny gaps between the CPU cap and the heat sink?

   ○ **A.** Grape jelly

   ○ **B.** Plumber's putty

   ○ **C.** 3-in-1 house oil

   ○ **D.** Thermal compound

6. Which of the following can be defined as the amount of heat generated by the CPU, which the cooling system is required to dissipate?

   ○ **A.** GPU

   ○ **B.** TDP

   ○ **C.** PSU

   ○ **D.** 140 watts

7. Which kind of socket incorporates "lands" to ensure connectivity to a CPU?

   ○ **A.** PGA

   ○ **B.** Chipset

   ○ **C.** LGA

   ○ **D.** Copper

8. Which of the following describes the difference between clock speed and bus speed?

   ○ **A.** The clock speed is the external speed of the CPU; it is the same as the bus speed.

   ○ **B.** The clock speed matches the RAM speed.

   ○ **C.** The clock speed is the internal speed of the CPU.

   ○ **D.** The bus speed is the speed of the CPU.

9. A customer's liquid-cooled system is intermittently overheating. What are the possible reasons for this? (Select the two best answers.)

   ○ **A.** Memory is overheating.

   ○ **B.** Air is trapped in the lines.

   ○ **C.** Power supply has failed.

   ○ **D.** Water pump is becoming faulty.

   ○ **E.** Hard drive is getting too much voltage.

10. Which of the following represent valid Intel socket types?

   ○ **A.** FM3, FM4, 1367, 2012+

   ○ **B.** AM3, AM3+, FM1, FM2, FM2+

   ○ **C.** 775, 1155, 1156, 1366, 1150, 2011

   ○ **D.** Core i3, Core i5, Core i7

Cram Quiz Answers

220-901 Answers

1. **C.** The internal clock speed is the speed of the CPU (for example, 3.3 GHz). TDP stands for thermal design power, a rating of CPU heat generated. CPU cache is a special high-speed memory that reduces the time the CPU takes to access data. The bus speed (base clock) is what the internal clock speed is based off. An example of a base clock system bus speed would be 100 MHz.

2. **B.** Intel's LGA 1366 socket can house a Core i7 CPU. (So could others, such as the LGA 2011.) LGA 775 is an older Intel socket. AM3 and FM2+ are AMD sockets.

3. **D.** L1 is the fastest cache memory and is located within the CPU's core. L2 is not as fast as L1 cache but is far superior to DRAM. L3 cache comes in the largest capacities of the three types of cache and has the most latency; therefore, it is the slowest. Dynamic RAM (DRAM) is not a type of cache memory. If the CPU can't find the data it is seeking within cache, it moves on to the DRAM sticks.

4. **C.** Hyper-Threading allows for an operating system to send two simultaneous threads to be processed by a single CPU core. The OS views the CPU core as two virtual processors. Multiple cores would imply multicore technology, which means there are two physical processing cores within the CPU package. The high-speed connection used by AMD from the CPU to RAM is HyperTransport.

5. **D.** Thermal compound is used to seal the small gaps between the CPU and heat sink. It is sometimes referred to as thermal gel or jelly (among a variety of other names), but not *grape* jelly. (Did I ever tell you about the time I found grape jelly inside a customer's computer? Fun times.) Note: Never use petroleum-based products (such as 3-in-1 oil or WD-40) inside a computer; the oils can damage the components over time.

6. **B.** TDP (thermal design power) is the amount of power required to cool a computer and is linked directly to the amount of heat a CPU creates. Some CPUs come with a built-in graphics processing unit (GPU). This means that with a compatible moth-erboard, no separate video card is necessary. PSU stands for power supply unit. 140 watts is a potential TDP rating but does not define what TDP is.

7. **C.** LGA (Land Grid Array) is the type of socket that uses "lands" to connect the socket to the CPU. PGA sockets have pinholes that make for connectivity to the CPU's copper pins.

8. **C.** The clock speed (also known as clock rate) is the internal speed of the CPU (for example, the Core i7-5820K runs at 3.3 GHz by default).

9. **B and D.** The water-cooled system could be caused to overheat due to a faulty water pump and air being trapped in the coolant lines. If the memory or hard drive receives too much voltage and overheats, they should stop working but probably won't overheat the entire system. If the power supply fails, the system will shut off.

10. **C.** Valid Intel socket types include 775, 1155, 1156, 1366, 1150, and 2011. Valid AMD socket types include AM3, AM3+, FM1, FM2, and FM2+. Core i3, Core i5, and Core i7 are Intel CPU brand names, not socket types.

Installing and Troubleshooting CPUs

This section delves into the hands-on steps involved when installing or troubleshooting a CPU. Installation of CPUs has actually become easier over time, especially with the advent of LGA sockets. However, troubleshooting a CPU can be just as much of a challenge as ever. It's important to note that proper installation of a CPU can reduce the number of CPU failures and the ensuing amount of CPU troubleshooting necessary.

Installing CPUs

As with most computer components, installing a CPU is easy. But you must be careful because it can be easily damaged. Take it slow and employ proper safety measures. Let's break it down into some simple steps:

1. **Select a CPU:** If you build a new computer, the CPU needs to be compatible with the motherboard for the type of CPU, speed, socket type, and voltage. If you upgrade a CPU, be sure that it is on the manufacturer's compatible list (which can be found on its website). You would usually go to the motherboard manufacturer, but in some cases, you might have to go to the proprietary computer manufacturer (such as HP or Dell).

    Power down the PC, disconnect the power cable (or turn off the kill switch), open the PC, and get your boxes of components ready!

2. **Employ ESD prevention methods:** Use an antistatic strap and mat. Remove the CPU and heat sink from the package, inspect them, and then place the CPU inside an antistatic bag until you are ready to install it. (An antistatic bag usually comes with the motherboard, but you should have extra ones handy.) To prevent damage, make sure that the CPU's lands (or pins) are facing up. Never touch the lands or pins of a CPU. Before touching any components, place both hands on an unpainted portion of the case chassis. For more information on ESD preventative measures, see Chapter 19, "Safety, Procedures, and Professionalism."

3. **Ready the motherboard:** Some technicians prefer to install the CPU into the motherboard and then install the motherboard into the case. If so, place the motherboard on the antistatic mat. (The mat should be on a hard, flat surface.) If you install the CPU directly into an already installed motherboard, clear away any cables or other equipment that might get in the way or could possibly damage the CPU, heat sink, or fan.

4. **Install the CPU:** Be careful with the CPU! It is extremely delicate! Always touch the case chassis before picking up the CPU. Hold it by the edges and do not touch any pins, lands, or other circuitry on the CPU. If you need to put it down, put it down in an antistatic mat with the pins/lands facing up. Most of the time, a CPU will be installed to either an LGA socket or a PGA socket. The following two bullets show how to install a CPU into each type of socket. Be sure to refer to the installation guide that comes with your particular CPU and motherboard.

   ▶ If you install to an LGA socket, unlock the socket by releasing the retaining arm(s) and swinging it open as far as it can go. Open the socket hatch, unhook it if necessary, and remove any plastic cover. Next, place the CPU into the socket. One corner of the CPU has an arrow that should be oriented with either a white corner or other similar marking on the motherboard or the socket's missing pin(s); both of these corresponding corners indicate pin 1, as shown in Figure 3.2. Carefully place the CPU into the socket. If it is oriented correctly, the lands on the CPU match up with the lands on the socket. Make sure it is flush and flat within the socket. Close the cap and secure the retaining arm underneath the tab that is connected to the socket, thus securing the CPU. Install thermal compound if necessary. Next, install the heat sink/ fan assembly. (If the heat sink came with the CPU, it might have thermal compound applied already.) LGA sockets usually have four plastic snap-in anchors. Carefully press each of these into and through the corresponding motherboard holes. Don't use too much force! Then turn each of them to lock the heat sink in place. Make sure that the heat sink is installed flush with the CPU by inspecting the assembly from the side. You want to be positive of this before turning on the computer because the thermal compound will begin to expand and fill the imperfections right away. Plug the fan into the appropriate motherboard power connector, as shown in Figure 3.3. (These are usually labeled directly on the motherboard; if not, see your motherboard documentation for details on where to plug in the fan.) Install the entire motherboard assembly into the case (if that is your method of choice).

Pin 1

Pin 1

FIGURE 3.2   Orientation markings on a CPU and LGA socket

Fan Power Connector   Plastic Anchor

FIGURE 3.3   An installed multicore CPU with connected fan

▶ If you install to a PGA socket, unlock the socket by moving the retaining arm(s) out and upward until it is open as far as it will go, without forcing it. Then gently place the CPU into the ZIF socket. There will be an arrow on one corner of the CPU that should correspond to a missing pin (or arrow) on the socket. Don't use force; slide the CPU around until it slips into the socket. Look at the CPU from the side and make sure it is flush with the socket. Lock down the retaining arm to keep the CPU in place. Then attach the heat sink/fan assembly to the metal clips that are on the sides of the socket. Make sure that the heat sink is installed flush with the CPU by inspecting the assembly from the side. You want to be positive of this before turning on the computer because the thermal compound will begin to expand and fill the imperfections right away. Attach the fan's power cable to the motherboard. (See your motherboard documentation for details on where to plug in the fan.) Install the entire motherboard assembly into the case (if that is your method of choice).

5. **Test the installation:** With the case still open, boot the computer to make sure that the BIOS POST recognizes the CPU as the right type and speed. Enter the BIOS and view the CPU information to verify this. If the BIOS doesn't recognize the CPU properly, check if a BIOS upgrade is necessary for the motherboard. Also make sure that the CPU fan is functional. Then view the details of the CPU within the BIOS. Be sure that the voltage reported by the BIOS is within tolerance. Then access the operating system (after it is installed) and make sure it boots correctly. Complete several full cycles and warm boots. Finally, view the CPU(s) within Windows and with CPU-Z:

▶ **Within Windows:** Check in Device Manager to make sure that the CPU is identified correctly. This can be accessed within the Control Panel, within Computer Management, or by pressing Windows+R to open the Run prompt and typing `devmgmt.msc` and pressing Enter. Once opened, you should see a category named Processors; expand it and the CPU that is installed should be listed. In Figure 3.4 you can see the system I am running has the Core i7-5820K; the CPU shows up as six separate CPUs running at 3.3 GHz. You can view similar information in Windows at the System Information window, which can be accessed by opening the Run prompt and typing `msinfo32`.

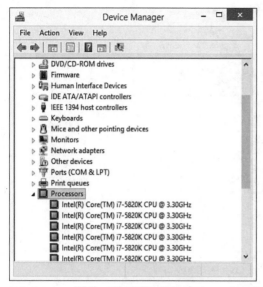

FIGURE 3.4   **A Core i7-5820K CPU as shown in Device Manager**

▶ **With CPU-Z:** The CPU-Z program can be downloaded from
http://www.cpuid.com/softwares/cpu-z.html; it is freeware that
gathers all the information you just saw in Device Manager and
also identifies the voltage, clock speeds, cache memory, and much
more. This is a great program to use when analyzing and monitoring your CPU. When installed (which is easy), simply run it
to analyze your CPU. You can see the CPU in Figure 3.5; this
program ties in everything talked about in this chapter in a more
real-world way. It shows a real-time look at the socket, cache, TDP,
voltage, and so on. For example, near the bottom left, you see the
core speed is 1199.29 MHz (1.2 GHz). Remember that the CPU
can run at any clock rate below the maximum. With Windows
8 running with no applications open, this CPU sits at 1.2 GHz,
multiplying the bus speed by 12 times. However, if you open additional CPU-intensive programs, this number can go up (as shown
in Figure 3.6). Notice the core speed has risen to 2.4 GHz, now a
multiplier of 24. The voltage hasn't increased from an initial reading of .7 V, but if we ran more programs with even bigger files,
the CPU would eventually go high enough where the CPU voltage would also go up, ultimately creating additional heat that the
system would need to dissipate. With a powerful CPU such as this,
I wouldn't be concerned about over-voltage unless I was overclocking the system, but I would still monitor the voltage every now and
again in the BIOS/UEFI and within a program such as CPU-Z.

86

CHAPTER 3: The CPU

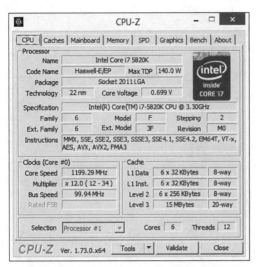

FIGURE 3.5 CPU-Z showing the same Core i7-5820K CPU

FIGURE 3.6 CPU-Z showing the same Core i7-5820K CPU at a higher clock rate

6. **Close the case and monitor the system:** Finally, if everything looks okay, close the case and consider monitoring the clock rate, voltage, and heat during the first few hours of operation. Voltage and heat can usually be monitored within the BIOS. All three can be monitored within Windows using third-party applications (such as CPU-Z) or by using monitoring utilities that accompany the motherboard. If all went well, congratulate yourself on a job well done!

Troubleshooting CPUs

The most common issue with a CPU is when it isn't installed properly or securely. This could possibly cause a complete failure when trying to turn on the system. This failure could be accompanied by a series of beeps from the POST. If this happens, always check the power first, just in case. Another possibility is that the system will turn on and power will be supplied to the system, but nothing else will happen: no POST, no display, and no hard drive activity. In any of these situations, after checking power, make sure of the following:

▶ **Check the big four:** Remember that the CPU is part of the big four, including the video card, RAM, and motherboard. Be sure to check these other components for simple connectivity problems, which could be the actual culprit here. Always check connections first before taking the CPU assembly apart.

▶ **Fan is connected and functional:** Some motherboards have a safeguard that disables booting if the fan is defective or not plugged in. Or you might get a message on the screen or other type warning depending on the motherboard. Be sure that the fan is plugged in to the correct power connector on the motherboard (or elsewhere), and verify whether it turns when the computer is on. If the fan has failed, replacement fans can be purchased; just make sure that the new fan is compatible with the heat sink and motherboard.

▶ **Heat sink is connected properly:** Make sure that the heat sink is flush with the CPU cap and that it is securely fastened to the motherboard (or socket housing).

▶ **CPU is installed properly:** Make sure it was installed flush into the socket and that it was oriented correctly. Of course, this means removing the heat sink. If you do so, you should clean off excess thermal compound and reapply thermal compound to the CPU cap before reinstalling the heat sink.

ExamAlert

When troubleshooting the CPU, be sure to first check all connections and then make sure the fan, heat sink, and CPU are secure and installed properly.

> **Note**
>
> As always, turn off the computer, unplug it, and employ ESD measures before working on the inside of the computer.

Following are a few more possible symptoms of a failing CPU:

▶ Unexplained crashes during boot up or during use.

▶ The computer locks after only a short time of use.

▶ Voltage is near, at, or above the top end of the allowable range.

Sometimes, the CPU is just plain defective. It could have been received this way, or maybe it overheated. Perhaps there was a surge that damaged it, or maybe someone overclocked it too far and it was the victim of overvoltage (and subsequent overheating). Regardless of these reasons, the CPU needs to be replaced. Now, by default, CPUs come with a heat sink and fan; if that is the case, install the CPU as you normally would. But in some cases, you can save money by purchasing only the CPU and using the existing heat sink. In this case, remember to clean excess thermal compound and then reapply thermal compound; but reapply to the CPU cap, not to the heat sink. If the CPU were installed properly, users don't usually have many problems with it (aside from the overclockers). Keep this in mind when troubleshooting the CPU or when troubleshooting an issue that *might* appear to be a CPU issue but is actually something else altogether.

On a lighter note, sometimes you might get reports from customers about strange noises coming from inside a PC, almost a buzzing of sorts. The noise could be caused by a wire or cable that is brushing up against the CPU fan (or other case fan). Be sure to reroute cables inside the computer so that they are clear of the CPU and any other devices. This will also aid with airflow within the PC, keeping the PC cooler. The CPU fan might also make noise due to it being clogged with dust, especially in dirtier environmental conditions. If the fan is still functional, you can take the computer outside and use compressed air to clean it out. Keep a computer vacuum handy to clean up the mess if necessary; I've seen computers that had so much dust and dirt inside, it could fill a garden.

Cram Quiz

Answer these questions. The answers follow the last question. If you cannot answer these questions correctly, consider reading this section again until you can.

220-901 Questions

1. When deciding on a CPU for use with a specific motherboard, what does it need to be compatible with?

   ○ **A.** Case

   ○ **B.** Socket

   ○ **C.** Wattage range

   ○ **D.** PCIe slots

2. You are troubleshooting a CPU and have already cut power, disconnected the power cable, opened the case, and put on your antistatic strap. What should you do next?

   ○ **A.** Check the BIOS.

   ○ **B.** Check connections.

   ○ **C.** Remove the CPU.

   ○ **D.** Test the motherboard with a multimeter.

3. You have installed the CPU and heat sink/fan assembly. What should you do next?

   ○ **A.** Apply thermal compound.

   ○ **B.** Boot the computer.

   ○ **C.** Plug in the fan.

   ○ **D.** Replace the BIOS jumper shunt.

4. What is a possible symptom of a failing CPU?

   ○ **A.** CPU is beyond the recommended voltage range.

   ○ **B.** Computer won't boot.

   ○ **C.** BIOS reports low temperatures within the case.

   ○ **D.** Spyware is installed into the browser.

5. You just completed a CPU installation. However, when you turn on the computer, the POST sounds a series of beeps and the system won't boot. What is the most likely cause?

    ○ **A.** The mouse is not plugged in.

    ○ **B.** The operating system is corrupted.

    ○ **C.** The CPU is not properly seated.

    ○ **D.** The fan is running too fast.

Cram Quiz Answers

220-901 Answers

1. **B.** The CPU needs to be compatible with the socket of the motherboard. The case doesn't actually make much of a difference when it comes to the CPU. (Just make sure it's large enough!) There is no wattage range, but you should be concerned with the voltage range of the CPU. PCI Express (PCIe) slots don't actually play into this at all because there is no direct connectivity between the two.

2. **B.** Check connections first; it is quick, easy, and a common culprit.

3. **C.** After installing the heat sink/fan assembly, plug in the fan to the appropriate connector on the motherboard.

4. **A.** If the CPU is running beyond the recommended voltage range for extended periods of time, it can be a sign of a failing CPU. If the computer won't boot at all, another problem might have occurred or the CPU might have already failed. Low case temperatures are a good thing (if they aren't below freezing!). Spyware is unrelated, but we talk about it plenty in Chapter 17, "Security."

5. **C.** The most likely cause is that the CPU needs to be reseated or there is a RAM problem. No other answer choice would cause the POST to issue a series of beeps. Also, the POST doesn't look for operating system corruption; it is relegated to hardware only.

CHAPTER 4

RAM

This chapter covers the following A+ exam topics:

▶ RAM Basics and Types of RAM

▶ Installing and Troubleshooting DRAM

You can find a master list of A+ exam topics in the "Introduction."

This chapter covers CompTIA A+ 220-901 objectives 1.3 and 4.1.

When people talk about the RAM in their computer, they are almost always referring to the "sticks" of memory that are installed into the motherboard. This is known as Dynamic Random Access Memory (DRAM), or main memory, and often comes in capacities of 1, 2, 4, 8 GB, or more. This type of RAM has its own clock speed and must be compatible with the motherboard's RAM slots. It's not the only type of RAM, but it's the one you should be most concerned with for the exam. For all practical purposes, the terms stick, DIMM, and memory module mean the same thing; they refer to the RAM installed into a motherboard's RAM slots.

The most important concept in this chapter is compatibility. There are a lot of RAM technologies to know, but the bottom line is, "Will it be compatible with my motherboard?" The best way to find out is to go to the RAM manufacturer's website and search for your motherboard. They usually list the matching RAM.

This chapter concentrates on SRAM (static random-access memory) and DRAM; however, there are other types—for example, NVRAM, which is covered in Chapter 6, "Storage." This chapter discusses SRAM, DRAM, and DRAM types and demonstrates how to install and troubleshoot DRAM memory modules.

RAM Basics and Types of RAM

RAM Basics

Memory is the workspace for the CPU. Random-access memory (RAM) is the main memory that the CPU uses to store or retrieve data, which can be done in any order, regardless of whatever the CPU last accessed. The beauty of RAM is that the CPU can access any piece of memory it needs from anywhere in RAM and each access takes an equal amount of time. You often hear people associate RAM with a person's memory. But a person might take more time to recall certain memories in comparison to other memories. Conversely, the CPU has *equal* access to *all* contents of RAM. It's fast and efficient, but the drawback is that RAM is typically cleared when the computer is shut off. To store data permanently, it would need to be written to a hard drive or other device, which is slower and less uniform in its storage and delivery of data. An example of this is when you work on a Word document; as you work, the contents of that file are stored in RAM, but when you save the file, the contents are then stored on a hard drive (or other media of your choice), which is done at a substantially slower rate.

The CPU, however, is sort of closed off from memory—and the rest of the computer, for that matter. It's kind of like the wizard behind the curtain. But someone does indeed pay attention to it—and that "someone" is the memory controller chip. The memory controller is the go-between; basically, information is stored in and retrieved from RAM with the help of the memory controller. When the CPU wants to store or retrieve data to and from RAM, the memory controller is the chip responsible for getting the job done. It does this by moving the data along the address bus, which connects the memory controller to RAM. Figure 4.1 shows the two possible locations for the memory controller.

As you can see in the figure, the memory controller can be in one of two places:

▶ **Within the chipset:** In older systems, the memory controller is within the northbridge. Refer to the left side of Figure 4.1 to see this deprecated design.

▶ **Integrated to the CPU:** In most of today's systems, the memory controller is part of the CPU (known as "on-die"), as shown in the right side of Figure 4.1. It does the same job, but it can do that job faster than a northbridge memory controller.

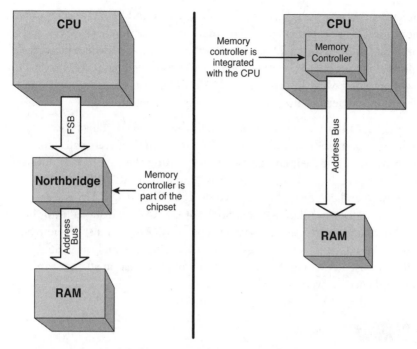

FIGURE 4.1   **Comparison of the two memory controller designs**

RAM discussed in this chapter is considered *volatile* (unless otherwise noted). This means that it loses any stored contents when it stops receiving power (for example, when you shut off the computer). However, not all RAM is volatile. Chapter 6 talks about nonvolatile types of RAM (for example, NVRAM).

Today's RAM is a set of integrated circuits (ICs) that works at high speed. These ICs could be on the motherboard, on adapter cards, within or on the processor, and of course, on those RAM sticks installed into the motherboard.

Types of RAM

Let's start by discussing the two main categories of RAM. Afterward, we'll move on to the types of RAM sticks that a technician might install in a computer.

SRAM Versus DRAM

SRAM is RAM that does not need to be periodically refreshed. Memory refreshing is common to other types of RAM and is basically the act of reading information from a specific area of memory and immediately rewriting that information back to the same area without modifying it. Due to SRAM's architecture, it does not require this refresh. You can find SRAM used as cache memory for CPUs, as buffers on the motherboard or within hard drives, and as temporary storage for LCD screens. Normally, SRAM is soldered directly to a printed circuit board (PCB) or integrated directly to a chip. This means that you probably won't be replacing SRAM. SRAM is faster than—and is usually found in smaller quantities than—its distant cousin, DRAM.

DRAM is RAM that *does* need to be periodically refreshed. This is because every bit of information stored in DRAM is stored in a separate capacitor. These capacitors lose their charge over time, causing the data to fade unless the capacitor is recharged or *refreshed*. It is slower than SRAM but is of simple design and can reach high capacities. Like SRAM, DRAM is volatile and requires power to retain its data. Sticks of DRAM are installed into the motherboard and are the most common type of DRAM you install and troubleshoot. Many technicians refer to these DRAM sticks simply as memory modules, or just RAM. However, DRAM might also exist on adapter cards and other devices as well.

> **Note**
>
> Another type of memory you should know for the exam is ROM or Read-Only Memory. Unlike the RAM types discussed in this chapter, ROM is nonvolatile, meaning that it retains its contents, even if it is not supplied with power. Historically, ROM chips could be read from but not written to. But now you have ROM chips that can do both (for example, EEPROM implemented as a BIOS chip). For more information on EEPROM and the BIOS, see Chapter 2, "Motherboards."

Let's talk about the different types of DRAM sticks you see in computers and how fast they can go!

SDRAM

Synchronous DRAM (SDRAM) is DRAM that is synchronized to the base clock of the motherboard (also referred to simply as "bus speed"). The original SDRAM had a bus width of 64 bits (8 bytes) and ran at speeds such as 100 MHz. It is unlikely that you will see the original SDRAM in the field but the concept of SDRAM lays the foundation for DDR.

> **Note**
>
> For more information about SDRAM, see the A+ Archive on my website: www.davidlprowse.com.

DDR

Let's talk about today's RAM—Double Data Rate (DDR) is by far the most commonly used RAM on the planet. DDR is synchronized to the memory clock just like SDRAM; it's also called DDR SDRAM. The original DDR (also known as DDR1) is actually SDRAM that has been double-pumped, meaning that twice the data is transferred but at the same clock speed. It does this by transferring data on the rising *and* falling edges of each clock signal (every cycle). So let's use DDR-200 as an example. A 100 MHz system bus's transfers are doubled, so instead of 100 million transfers, it can now do 200 million transfers per second. (That's where the 200 comes from in DDR-200.) DDR also has a 64-bit wide bus, allowing for 8 bytes of data per cycle. A 100-MHz DDR bus can, therefore, transfer 8 bytes of data, 100 million times per second, *times* 2, equaling 1600 MB/s. The equation for this data transfer rate (also known as bandwidth) is

Clock speed × bytes × 2 = Data Transfer Rate

Example: 100 MHz × 8 × 2 = 1,600 MB/s

Whenever you do these types of equations, be interested in solving for bytes because that is what these data rates measure.

People, and even manufacturers, sometimes refer to transfers per second as MHz. Although this is not completely accurate, it is common terminology. For example, DDR-200 can do 200 million transfers per second, but it is also referred to as 200 MHz. DDR-200 is the standard, whereas the module name for DDR-200 is known as PC1600 (the 1600 specifies the transfer rate). All types of DDR1 RAM run at 2.5 V.

Now, an easier way to solve the data transfer rate equation for *all* types of DDR is to simply multiply the megatransfers per second (MT/s) by 8. Why 8? Because DDR sends 8 bytes per transfer. Now solve for DDR-200 once again.

Equation: 200 MT/s × 8 = 1,600 MB/s.

Boom, simple. Just remember that you are solving for bytes. If you know you are using DDR-200 RAM, then you know it is capable of 200 MT/s. (The numbers match up.) And because you know that DDR sends 8 bytes of data per transfer, you can easily find the total data transfer rate per second.

ExamAlert

Know how to calculate the data transfer rate of DDR RAM for the exam.

The DDR DIMM has 184 pins and a specifically placed notch; this notch prevents you from using the wrong memory module in a DDR RAM slot.

DDR2

DDR2 builds on the original DDR specification by decreasing voltage (to 1.8 V) and by increasing speed. It increases speed through faster signaling, which requires additional pins. Standard DDR2 DIMMs have 240 pins and cannot be used in DDR1 memory slots.

Now calculate the data transfer rate for a typical stick of DDR2 RAM (also known as PC2-6400). Remember that it is MT/s × 8. Solve for DDR2-800.

Equation: 800 MT/s × 8 = 6,400 MB/s.

Easy! Just remember to solve for bytes.

DDR3

DDR3 was designed for lower power consumption and higher reliability while enabling higher levels of performance. 240-pin DDR3 DIMMs are similar to DDR2 DIMMs but are *not* backward compatible. At the writing of this book, DDR3 is very popular due to its capability to transfer twice as much data, use less voltage (1.2 to 1.5 V), and ultimately work faster and more efficiently.

Table 4.1 gives a comparison of the various types of DDR3, their speeds, and their transfer rates. Note that the transfers per second measurement is often counted in millions. For example, DDR3-800 can do 800 million transfers per second, which is the same as 800 *mega*transfers per second (MT/s). Figure 4.2 shows a DDR3-1333 memory module.

TABLE 4.1 **Comparison of DDR3 Types**

DDR3 Standard	I/O Clock Speed	Transfers per Second	Transfer Rate	Module Name
DDR3-800	400 MHz	800 Million (800 MT/s)	6400 MB/s	PC3-6400
DDR3-1066	533 MHz	1.066 Billion (1066 MT/s)	8533 MB/s	PC3-8500
DDR3-1333	667 MHz	1.333 Billion (1333 MT/s)	10667 MB/s	PC3-10600
DDR3-1600	800 MHz	1.600 Billion (1600 MT/s)	12800 MB/s	PC3-12800
DDR3-1866	933 MHz	1.866 Billion (1866 MT/s)	14933 MB/s	PC3-14900
DDR3-2133	1066 MHz	2.133 Billion (2133 MT/s)	17066 MB/s	PC3-17000
DDR3-2400	1200 MHz	2.400 Billion (2400 MT/s)	19200 MB/s	PC3-19200

Note

The standards listed in Table 4.1 are based on the JEDEC standards (www.jedec.org). JEDEC develops various open standards for the microelectronics industry.

ExamAlert

Know the various DDR3 standards for the exam.

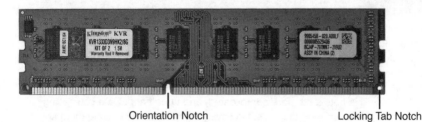

Orientation Notch   Locking Tab Notch

FIGURE 4.2   **A 240-pin PC3-10600 4 GB DIMM (DDR3-1333)**

The DDR3 module in Figure 4.2 has a sticker on the left that shows an identification code. You might not be able to read it, but it says KVR1333D3N9HK2/8G and Kit of 2, 1.5 V. The 1333 and D3 in the code tell you that this is DDR3-1333 RAM. The 8G tells you the capacity (8 GB) but only when installed as a kit of two memory modules—as the label goes on to say. Finally, it tells you that the memory runs at 1.5 volts. Leave the sticker on the memory module so that the warranty is not voided and you can find out important characteristics of the RAM later. Often you will come across sticks of RAM just lying about and you might not remember what they are—the code on the sticker tells you everything you need to know.

Now calculate the data transfer for DDR3-800. Remember that you can solve this by multiplying the MT/s × 8.

Equation: 800 MT/s × 8 = 6,400 MB/s

Does this look familiar? It should; you used the same equation for a typical DDR2 module. Although the end result is the same as far as transfer rate, remember that DDR3 is more efficient, uses less voltage, and gives off less heat. Because of this, you can ultimately attain higher levels of transfer that wouldn't be possible with DDR2.

Now, you should be able to figure out the data transfer rate of DDR3 given any one of the following pieces of information:

▶ **DDR standard, such as DDR3-1333:** The 1333 in the name is the same number as the megatransfers per second.

▶ **I/O clock speed for DDR3, such as 667 MHz:** This is always half the megatransfers.

▶ **Module name, such as PC3-10600:** The data transfer rate is in the name itself! PC3-10600 can transfer 10,600 MB/s.

Note

If you have heard of the term *base memory clock* (or just *memory clock*) and won-der about it, well, it is simply the initial frequency of a given type of DDR before being multiplied to get the I/O clock speed. For DDR3, it is one-quarter of the I/O clock speed. So, for example, DDR3-1600 has a 200 MHz base memory clock and an 800 MHz I/O clock. However, for DDR2, the base memory clock is only half of the I/O clock. This gets a bit more complicated, and I don't anticipate you seeing questions on the exam regarding this. However, if you have an inquiring mind and want to learn more, feel free to contact me at my website.

DDR4

When is enough, enough? Never! Make way for DDR4. At 1.2 to 1.35 V, it has a lower voltage range than most DDR3 (and there is the possibility of it going as low as 1.05 V). It also has a higher module density and a higher data transfer rate. Of course, like previous versions of DDR, it is not backward-compatible—this type of RAM has 288 pins and has a different physical configuration. Table 4.2 compares some typical DDR4 types, and Figure 4.3 shows an example of DDR4.

TABLE 4.2 **Comparison of DDR4 Types**

DDR4 Standard	I/O Clock Speed	Transfers per Second	Transfer Rate	Module Name
DDR4-2133	1066 MHz	2.133 Billion	17,000 MB/s	PC4-17000
DDR4-2400	1200 MHz	2.4 Billion	19,200 MB/s	PC4-19200
DDR4-2666	1333 MHz	2.666 Billion	21,300 MB/s	PC4-21300
DDR4-3200	1600 MHz	3.2 Billion	25,600 MB/s	PC4-25600

FIGURE 4.3   **A 288-pin PC4-17000 4 GB DIMM (DDR4-2133)**

I actually used the memory module in Figure 4.3 within the *AV Editor* computer. Or more accurately, I used four of them in a quad-channel configuration that we will speak of more later. Note how both connectors are slightly angled. This, and the number of pins (among other things), make it incompatible with DDR3 slots. As of the writing of this book, DDR4 is the fastest type of RAM module you can get for your motherboard, but DDR5 is available on video cards, which we will discuss more in Chapter 12, "Video and Audio."

RAM Technologies

When you decide on the type of RAM to use, you must decide on more technical details; for example, the configuration of channels, which will be dictated for the most part by the motherboard. Your particular environment might need RAM that doesn't lag, so memory latency should be another consideration. There are several other lesser considerations, such as whether to use single-sided or double-sided RAM, parity, ECC RAM, and whether to use buffered RAM. For the most part, these additional factors don't play into the decision much. Your motherboard dictates whether the RAM is single-sided or double-sided, and parity and ECC RAM are more rare nowadays. So let's concentrate on the different channel architectures for RAM.

Single-Channel Versus Multichannel Architectures

Single-channel is the original RAM architecture. In modern computers, there is a 64-bit bus (or data channel) between the memory and the memory controller. One or more sticks of RAM can be installed into the motherboard, but they share the same channel.

Dual-channel is a common technology that essentially doubles the data throughput. Two separate 64-bit channels are employed together, resulting in a 128-bit bus. To incorporate this, the proper motherboard will have color-coded matching banks. See Figure 4.4 for an example of this.

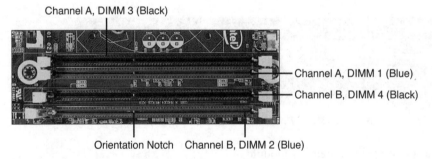

FIGURE 4.4 **A motherboard's dual-channel memory slots**

In Figure 4.4 you can see four RAM slots. The top slot (labeled DIMM 3) is black. Underneath that, you see a blue slot (which might appear as gray in some versions of this book) labeled DIMM 1. Collectively, they are known as Channel A. Then you see other black and blue slots, labeled DIMM 4 and DIMM 2. These are known as Channel B. To use dual-channel architecture, a kit of two RAM sticks would be installed to the matching color (matching bank). For example, they could be installed to both blue slots: one in Channel A and one in Channel B, collectively forming the first bank of RAM. For best performance, both DIMMs should be identical. This means the capacity, speed, and number of chips must be the same on both DIMMs. However, if you access a website such as www.kingston.com, you can find a user-friendly memory database that tells you exactly which kits of RAM will be compatible with your motherboard. This is the easiest way to ensure a harmonious system. As a final note, you should install to banks sequentially, meaning that you install two memory sticks to the blue bank and then (optionally) install two memory sticks to the black bank. These colors might vary depending on the motherboard; Intel uses blue and black. Another simple method is to look at the motherboard (or documentation) and identify DIMM 1 and DIMM 2. Use those first!

Triple-channel architecture accesses three memory modules at the same time, in effect a 192-bit bus. In this less common setup, a motherboard would have one of two configurations. The first would be three channels of two different color memory slots each. A bank of RAM would include Channel A DIMM 0, Channel B DIMM 0, and Channel C DIMM 0. The first bank is usually blue and the second bank is black. The other configuration would have three blue slots, each its own channel, and a separate black slot that can be used for single channel mode if the triple-channel option is not used. Normally the black slot would be left unused. One example of triple-channel can be found with Intel Core i7-900 series processors and the LGA 1366 socket.

Quadruple-channel (or simply quad-channel) architecture takes this idea to the next level. It works only when four identical memory modules are placed in the correct slots. Quad-channel is common in computers that use DDR4. Now we have four 64-bit wide buses working together, but for it to work properly, a module of RAM must be installed to each of the four banks. If only three modules are installed (thus only three banks used), the architecture downgrades to triple-channel automatically. Likewise, if only two are used, the motherboard scales back to dual-channel architecture. Platforms that are compatible with quad-channel include Intel LGA 2011 and AMD G34.

Figure 4.5 shows an example of a motherboard's RAM slots making use of quad-channel technology.

As you can see in the figure, there are four banks, each with two slots (one of which is black and one of which is gray). By installing a memory module into each of the gray slots (known as A1, B1, C1, and D1), we can harness the collective power of the quad-channel technology.

Channel B, DIMM B1 and B2

Channel A, DIMM A1 and A2

Channel C, DIMM C2 and C1

Channel D, DIMM D2 and D1

FIGURE 4.5   **A motherboard with quad-channel capable RAM slots**

This is the configuration used in *AV Editor*, as we'll show later in the chapter. Of course, we have the ability to add another four memory modules if we wish (those would be added to the black slots). The ASUS X99-A motherboard used in this computer can handle 64 GB of RAM total. To take advantage of this, we could install eight 8 GB RAM modules, but at this point we would want to really think about whether that much RAM is necessary. Will we be running applications that will need to access that much RAM? For example, at times I will concurrently run Microsoft Word and PowerPoint, Adobe Premiere Pro, Pro Tools, Camtasia, and a couple of virtual machines for good measure, and only end up utilizing 4 to 5 GB of RAM total.

Sometimes it's better to upgrade other parts of the computer before the RAM or consider using faster RAM (quality as opposed to quantity), if your motherboard can handle it.

ExamAlert

Know the difference between single-, dual-, triple-, and quad-channel for the exam.

Note

New memory technologies are constantly being developed. One of these next-generation technologies is point-to-point technology (or single-ended signaling), in which more efficient signal integrity ultimately enables faster data transfer rates. Always try to keep informed of the latest emerging technologies.

Memory Latency

Memory latency or Column Address Strobe (CAS) latency happens when a memory controller tries to access data from a memory module. It is a slight delay (usually measured in nanoseconds) while the memory module responds to the memory controller. It is given a rating of CAS (or more commonly referred to as CL). The higher the CL number, the longer the delay. As an example, the DDR3 RAM used in *Media PC* is CL9. The general range of DDR3 memory is between CL5 and CL10, so I'm near the slowest end of the spectrum. However, the difference between the ratings is small, so it usually has an effect only on users that run powerful memory-intensive applications (for example, graphics rendering). Video editors, graphic designers, and gamers beware! Otherwise CL9 is fine for *Media PC's* purposes. DDR4 RAM commonly has a latency of CL14 or CL15.

Single-Sided Versus Double-Sided

The terms single-sided and double-sided are not quite literal. Use your motherboard's documentation or a memory manufacturer's database to verify whether your motherboard accepts single-sided or double-sided memory modules, and then acquire the compatible RAM from a reputable vendor. Single-sided refers to a memory module with a single "bank" of chips. The computer's memory controller can access all the chips at once. The memory module might have chips on both physical sides or only on one side, but it is known as single-sided because the computer can address all the chips at once.

Double-sided memory modules have their chips divided into two "sides" known as banks. Only one "side" can be seen by the computer at any time. To use the second half of the storage available, the computer must switch to the second bank and can no longer read or write to the first half until it switches back again.

> **Note**
>
> Don't confuse double-sided memory and dual-channel memory when it comes to banks. An individual stick of RAM that is double-sided is divided into two banks, but this has no bearing on the installation of the RAM. A bank of dual-channel RAM is two sticks of RAM that must be installed as a pair to matching color-coded slots. More often you will be concerned with dual-channel banks as opposed to double-sided memory.

Parity Versus Nonparity

There are several types of parity in computing; RAM parity is when memory stores an extra bit (known as a parity bit) used for error *detection*. This means that the memory module can store 9 bits instead of 8 bits for every byte of data. So parity RAM includes this extra bit and the more common nonparity RAM does not. Parity RAM might be required when data integrity is a necessity.

ECC Versus Non-ECC

Error Correction Code (ECC) in RAM can detect and correct errors. Real-time applications might use ECC RAM. Like parity RAM, additional information needs to be stored, and more resources are used in general. This RAM is the slowest and most expensive of RAM types. DDR3 ECC modules are identified with either the letter E or as ECC (for example, PC3-10600E).

> **Note**
>
> Most new PCs do not need or support parity or ECC RAM due to the low possibility of data corruption. If it is supported, but not necessary, these options can be disabled in the BIOS.

Registered and Fully Buffered

Registered memory (also known as buffered memory) improves the integrity of the signal between RAM and the memory controller by electrically buffering the signals using an extra register. This is done for stability, especially when using multiple memory modules; however, this could cause additional latency. An example of DDR3 registered memory would be PC3-10600R. Typically, consumer-grade RAM is unbuffered.

Fully buffered memory goes beyond this and introduces an advanced memory buffer between the memory controller and the memory module. For this to work, a completely different memory module must be used, with the notch in a different location, making it incompatible with motherboards that support regular DDR or registered DDR. This kind of memory module is known as a FB-DIMM; an example would be PC3-10600F or PC3-10600FB.

The terms "registered" and "fully buffered" are not listed in the A+ objectives, but you never know if you will see mention of these terms on the exam, and you might see them in the field, especially in systems that require a lot of RAM while keeping signal integrity.

One Final Note About RAM

The main thing to "remember" when working with RAM is that it needs to be compatible with the motherboard. Check your motherboard's documentation regarding capacity per slot (or channel), maximum capacity, speed, and whether it accepts single- or multichannel RAM. The best thing to do is to run a search on your particular motherboard at the RAM manufacturer's website to attain a complete list of a compatible RAM.

Cram Quiz

Answer these questions. The answers follow the last question. If you cannot answer these questions correctly, consider reading this section again until you can.

220-901 Questions

1. Which technology divides the RAM slots into colors?
   - ○ **A.** ECC
   - ○ **B.** Parity
   - ○ **C.** Double-sided
   - ○ **D.** Dual-channel

2. Which of the following is the delay it takes for a memory module to start sending data to the memory controller?
   - ○ **A.** DDR
   - ○ **B.** Propagation
   - ○ **C.** Latency
   - ○ **D.** FSB

3. What is the transfer rate of DDR2-800?
   - ○ **A.** 6,400 MB/s
   - ○ **B.** 8,533 MB/s
   - ○ **C.** 5,333 MB/s
   - ○ **D.** 800 MHz

4. Which of the following would you find internal to the CPU?
   - ○ **A.** DRAM
   - ○ **B.** DIMM
   - ○ **C.** SDRAM
   - ○ **D.** SRAM

5. What is the transfer rate of DDR3-1600?
   - ○ **A.** 6,400 MB/s
   - ○ **B.** 12,800 MB/s
   - ○ **C.** 14,933 MB/s
   - ○ **D.** 17,066 MB/s

6. Which chip designates where data will be stored in RAM?
   - ○ **A.** Southbridge
   - ○ **B.** Northbridge
   - ○ **C.** CPU
   - ○ **D.** DRAM

7. How many pins are on a DDR3 memory module?
   - ○ **A.** 288
   - ○ **B.** 184
   - ○ **C.** 240
   - ○ **D.** 200

Cram Quiz Answers

220-901 Answers

1. **D.** Dual-channel memory configurations have two RAM slots of a particular color, each of which is placed in a different channel; these are collectively known as banks.

2. **C.** Latency is the delay between the memory module and the memory controller, usually rated as CL and a number.

3. **A.** DDR2-800 can transfer 6,400 MB/s; DDR2-1066 transfers 8,533 MB/s. DDR2-667 transfers 5,333 MB/s. MHz is sometimes used to refer to the amount of megatransfers per second; in this case, the RAM can do 800 MT/s.

4. **D.** One function of SRAM is to act as CPU cache. For example, L1 and L2 cache memory as mentioned in Chapter 3, "The CPU"

5. **B.** The transfer rate of DDR3-1600 is 12,800 MB/s. DDR3-800 is 6,400 MB/s. DDR3-1866 is 14,933 MB/s. DDR3-2133 is 17,066 MB/s.

6. **B.** The northbridge, specifically the memory controller chip, is in charge of storing and retrieving data to and from RAM. Even though new systems use a memory controller that is part of the CPU, it is not the CPU that is in charge of this. The CPU knows what bytes it wants but not the location of those bytes.

7. **C.** DDR3 is a 240-pin architecture. 288-pin is DDR4, 184-pin is the first version of DDR (DDR1), and you can find 200-pin architectures in laptops; they are known as SODIMMs. To review, Table 4.3 shows the pin configurations for PC-based DDR 1 through 4.

TABLE 4.3 **Comparison of DDR Pinouts**

DDR Standard	Number of Pins
DDR1	184 pins
DDR2	240 pins
DDR3	240 pins
DDR4	288 pins

Installing and Troubleshooting DRAM

In this section, we'll briefly discuss how to install DRAM, namely DDR memory modules, from a hands-on perspective. Installing the physical RAM doesn't take much time, but testing it and making sure it is identified properly in the BIOS/UEFI and in the operating system is a bit more time consuming. Testing is an important part of any installation, so we'll discuss that as well.

Then we'll talk about some of the things that can go wrong with RAM and how to troubleshoot those problems quickly and efficiently. This is where you can really spend some time as a technician, so I've included some tips that can help you easily get to the solution for most RAM issues.

Installing DRAM

Installing DRAM is fun and easy. Simply stated, it can be broken down into these steps: Orient the RAM properly, insert the RAM into the slot, and press down with both thumbs until the ears lock. Then test. Easy! But let's take it a little further. Remember that some people refer to memory modules as DIMMs, DRAM, RAM sticks, or just plain RAM, and you could get any of these terms on the exam as well. The following describes the steps involved when installing RAM:

1. **Select the correct memory module:** The memory module must be compatible with the motherboard. Again, this means it must be the correct standard, the right pin configuration, the correct speed, the proper capacity, and within voltage parameters. Don't forget to use the memory manufacturer's website. It has a search engine that enables you to input the motherboard you have, by make and model, and then the search displays all the different RAM configurations compatible with the motherboard. If you have a proprietary computer such as an HP or Dell, the website asks for the make and model of the computer instead of the motherboard. How much simpler could it be? Be wary of websites that don't have searchable databases like these.

   Let's talk about each of the computer builds I have been referring to. For each step along the way, we'll start with DDR3 and then describe DDR4.

   For *Media PC*, I used Kingston RAM. I went to its website, plugged in the make (Intel) and the model (DP67DE) of the motherboard, and it came up with a whole slew of different DDR3 RAM stick configurations; from 2 GB configs all the way up to 8 GB. As you might have guessed, I chose the 8 GB configuration, which is actually a kit of two 4 GB sticks running at 1,333 MHz, which work in a dual-channel configuration (as we display in a minute). To be sure, I checked Intel's website to verify how much RAM I could use per slot and what speeds would run. The documentation shows that I could use up to 32 GB maximum of DDR3 RAM, a maximum of 8 GB per slot, and at a top speed of 1,333 MHz. Well, for now, I don't need more than 8 GB, but I can always upgrade or add an identical kit later if I want; otherwise, everything sounds compatible. When the RAM is added, the BIOS should find it automatically; however, it is wise to check if any BIOS upgrades are available on the motherboard's website that deal with the latest types of RAM.

For *AV Editor* I again used Kingston, plugged in the make (ASUS) and the model (X99-A), and found a couple DDR4 options. I chose the 16 GB kit, which contains four 4 GB sticks. This allows me to take advantage of the quad-channel architecture of the motherboard. Later, I could add another four 4 GB sticks (or use RAM with higher capacities, as the motherboard can handle 64 GB) but I don't foresee that happening in the near future given the fact that I don't expect the operating system and applications to actually use more than 5 or 6 GB of RAM at a time.

When the RAM arrives, you are ready to install. Power down the PC, disconnect the power cable (or turn off the kill switch), open the PC, and get ready!

2. **Employ ESD prevention methods:** Use an antistatic strap and mat. Before touching any components, place both hands on an unpainted portion of the case chassis. For more information on ESD preventative measures, see Chapter 19, "Safety, Procedures, and Professionalism." Never touch any of the pins or chips on the memory module; instead, grab the module from the side edges. Remove the memory modules (could be one or more) from the package and place them on an antistatic bag.

3. **Ready the motherboard:** Some technicians prefer to install the RAM into the motherboard and then install the motherboard into the case; this can also depend on whether you are building a new computer or upgrading one. If you do choose to install the RAM to the motherboard separately, place the motherboard on the antistatic mat. (The mat should be on a hard, flat surface.) If you install the RAM directly into an already installed motherboard, clear away any cables or other equipment that might get in the way or could possibly damage the RAM during installation.

You will see a plastic tab (ear) on each side of the RAM slot in the motherboard (for DDR3 and earlier) or you will see a single tab (for DDR4). Carefully swing them out from the slots you plan to use so that they end up at an angle from the slot; this enables room for the memory module to be inserted.

4. **Install the RAM:** Be careful with the RAM and the RAM slot! They are delicate! Always touch the case chassis before picking up the RAM. Hold it by the edges and do not touch any pins or other circuitry on the memory module. If you need to put it down, put it down on an antistatic mat.

Take a look at the slot; there should be a break in the slot somewhere near the middle (but not the exact middle). This is where the notch in the memory module will go. Gently place the memory module in the slot, pins down. If the notch does not line up with the break in the slot, you might need to turn the module around. When it appears that the RAM is oriented correctly, press down with both thumbs on the top of the memory module. Keep your thumbs as close to the edge as you can so that you can distribute even pressure to the memory module. Press down with both thumbs at the same time until the "ears" on the edge of the RAM slot close and lock on to the memory module. You might hear a click or two when it is done. You might also have to push both of the ears toward the RAM to completely lock them into place. (For DDR4, look for a single ear.) Take a look at the memory module from the side or compare them to other ears in unused slots; the plastic ears should be standing straight up now. You might need a bit of force to fully insert the RAM, but don't go overboard! If the motherboard is bending excessively, you are using too much force. If this is the case, make sure that the RAM is oriented correctly; the notches should match up and the RAM should be straight within the slot. Figure 4.6 shows a bank of DDR3 memory modules installed into the blue DIMM slots in a dual-channel configuration. Figure 4.7 shows a bank of DDR4 memory modules installed into the gray DIMM slots in a quad-channel configuration. Each of these is 4 GB, giving us a total of 16 GB of RAM.

Channel A, DIMM 1 (Blue)

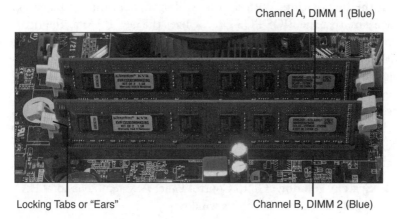

Locking Tabs or "Ears"   Channel B, DIMM 2 (Blue)

FIGURE 4.6   **Installed bank of DDR3 memory modules**

Channel A, DIMM A1   Channel B, DIMM B1

Channel D, DIMM D1   Channel C, DIMM C1

FIGURE 4.7   **Installed bank of DDR4 memory modules**

Install the entire motherboard assembly into the case if that was your
method of choice.

5. **Test the installation:** With the case still open, boot the computer and make sure that the BIOS POST recognizes the new RAM as the right type and speed. Next, enter the BIOS and view the details of the RAM within the BIOS setup program. The amount is often on the main page, but you might need to look deeper for the exact configuration, depending on the motherboard. Next, access the operating system (after it is installed) and make sure it boots correctly. Complete several full cycles and warm boots. Also, at some point, you should view the RAM within Windows or in CPU-Z to verify that the operating system sees the correct capacity of RAM:

> ▶ **System Window:** Go to Control Panel > System. The total RAM should be listed within this window.

> ▶ **Task Manager:** As mentioned before, you can view the Task Manager by right-clicking the taskbar and selecting Task Manager. There are several other ways to open this; I like this one: Press Windows+R to bring up the Run prompt and type `taskmgr`. When it is open, go to the Performance tab and view the memory section. It should show the total physical memory as well as the memory that is in use. Keep in mind that this might show the amount of RAM in megabytes (depending on the version of Windows) and that 1024 MB is roughly 1 GB. Figure 4.8 shows *Media PC* running Windows 7, displaying 8 GB of RAM in the Task Manager.

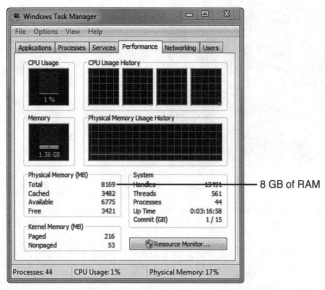

FIGURE 4.8   **Windows 7 Task Manager displaying 8 GB of RAM**

▶ **CPU-Z:** Simply open CPU-Z and click the Memory tab, as shown in Figure 4.9. This shows the type and total amount of RAM used by *Media PC* (8192 MB or 8 GB of Dual-Channel DDR3), the DRAM Frequency (666 MHz approximately), and the latency (CL9).

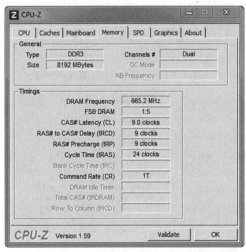

FIGURE 4.9 **CPU-Z showing Total RAM, Frequency, and CL Rating**

Consider testing the RAM by seeing if you can open several applications at once without any issues or delays.

ExamAlert

Know how to select, install, and verify RAM for the exam.

Finally, if everything looks okay, close up the case, and if all went well, congratulate yourself on another job well done!

A couple important things to mention here: First, if you were for some reason to install two different types of RAM (for example, one stick of DDR3-1333 and one stick of DDR3-1066 and the motherboard supported both; then the system would run at the lower speed of 1066. This is an example of under-clocking; the DDR3-1333 would act as a DDR3-1066 stick of RAM. However, in a multichannel system, this could cause the system to fail, if the motherboard insists that the modules be identical. Also, if you install the latest type of RAM that is supposed to be compatible with the motherboard, be prepared to flash the BIOS so that the system can recognize the new RAM, especially in multichannel environments.

Troubleshooting DRAM

It's not common, but RAM memory modules can cause intermittent issues or they can fail altogether. Always make sure that the RAM is fully seated within the RAM slot and that the plastic ears are locking the RAM into place. An unstable system can be caused by several components including RAM. Remember to check the big four: video card, CPU, RAM, and motherboard.

A lot of the issues you see are because a user has purchased and installed a memory stick that is not compatible, or is semi-compatible, with the motherboard: wrong speed, incorrect capacity, improper configuration, and so on. Be ready for this; check the RAM compatibility against the motherboard, even if the user swears it has been checked already. A good technician has documentation available and has access to the Internet. This can help to ensure that the correct RAM has been installed originally and that it is configured properly. Some RAM manufacturers (www.kingston.com, www.crucial.com) have tools to check compatibility issues.

> **ExamAlert**
>
> Verify compatibility of RAM when troubleshooting!

Perhaps there was some kind of surge inside the computer; maybe the computer is not protected by a surge suppressor/protector or UPS. Another possibility is that the RAM was damaged by ESD, and this damage manifests itself as intermittent problems. There are expensive hardware-based RAM testers that can tell you if the RAM is electrically sound and if it can process data correctly. If your company owns one, or if you can get your hands on one for a short time, you might narrow the problem. However, from personal experience, I have rarely needed to use these.

Here are some possible symptoms of a RAM issue and corresponding troubleshooting techniques:

▶ **Computer will not boot/intermittently shuts down:** If there is no RAM in the computer, or if the RAM is damaged or not installed securely, it can prevent the computer from doing anything at all (aside from draining electricity from your AC outlet). For example, the power supply fan turns but nothing else—no beeps and no displays. First, if the RAM were just installed, make sure that the RAM is compatible. Next, and in general, try reseating the RAM before you attempt to troubleshoot a CPU or motherboard. Add RAM if none exists. (Sounds silly but I've seen it!) If you suspect faulty RAM, corroded contacts, or a faulty RAM slot, you can try taking the RAM out, cleaning the RAM and RAM slot if necessary, and putting the RAM back in, being sure to seat the memory module properly. (For cleaning, use Stabilant 22 or similar cleaner on the RAM contacts and use compressed air on the slot.) Next, if the computer has two memory modules, try booting it with just one (if the motherboard allows it) or try moving memory modules to different slots—check your motherboard documentation for proper orientation. As mentioned in previous chapters, a POST analysis can be helpful in these situations as well. If necessary, replace the memory module with an identical one (if you have an extra one handy), or at worst, purchase a new one if you have identified the memory module as the source of the problem. In some cases, RAM can overheat and cause intermittent shutdowns. Heat sinks can be purchased for RAM. These are made of aluminum or copper just like CPU heat sinks and are sometimes referred to as heatspreaders. RAM can also be purchased with heat sinks preinstalled. This type of RAM might be necessary for high-end systems, such as virtualization systems, computer-aided design workstations, and gaming systems.

▶ **BIOS indicates a memory error:** The BIOS can indicate a memory error through a gray message on the screen and a flashing cursor or by beeping. If it beeps, you need to reference your motherboard documentation for the specific beep codes. Sometimes a BIOS setting can be incorrect. For example, maybe the RAM's latency setting or some other setting needs to be modified. If the computer has a saved version of the BIOS settings, you can try reverting to them or you can try loading the BIOS defaults; I can't tell you how many times this has worked for me! Sometimes the BIOS indicates the wrong amount of RAM. If this is the case, check the RAM as explained in the first bullet. Finally, a BIOS update can be the cure; perhaps the BIOS just doesn't have the programming necessary to identify the latest type of RAM that was installed.

▶ **Memory errors occur:** Several types of memory errors are initiated by the operating system:

  ▶ **Stop error, aka BSOD or Blue Screen of Death:** This is a critical system error that causes the operating system to shut down. Most of the time, these are due to device driver errors (poor code), but they can be associated with a physical fault in memory. One example of this would be a nonmaskable interrupt (NMI). An NMI can interrupt the processor to gain its attention regarding nonrecoverable hardware errors, resulting in a BSOD. The BSOD usually dumps the contents of memory to a file (for later analysis) and restarts the computer. If you don't encounter another BSOD, it's probably not much to worry about. But if the BSOD happens repeatedly, you want to write down the information you see on the screen and cross-reference it to the Microsoft Support website at http://support.microsoft.com. Again, if you suspect faulty RAM, try the troubleshooting methods in the first bullet ("Computer will not boot").

▶ **Page faults (hard faults), out-of-memory or low-on-virtual memory errors:** These are usually issues with the operating system or application that was running. However, you see less and less of these with each new Windows version. If a particular application keeps failing, or if you get a particular message listing a specific memory location over and over again, it can indicate a physical problem with RAM. Be sure to document error messages and any error codes or memory locations that display on the screen.

▶ **General protection fault (GPF):** This can cause a program to fail, and in older versions of Windows, it would cause the entire OS to shut down and display a black screen. Today, these errors are uncommon and are usually related to the OS, running applications, and CPU. It is also possible that memory errors can cause a GPF (for example, writing to a read-only portion of memory) or a conflict in a particular part of memory, but again, these are rare.

Chapter 11, "Troubleshooting Windows," troubleshoots these BSODs, page faults, and other Windows issues.

Chances are you won't need them often, but memory testing programs such as MemTest86 (http://www.memtest86.com/) are available online. Plus, you can use the Windows Memory Diagnostics Tool, which can be accessed by typing **mdsched.exe** in the Run prompt or from the Windows Recovery Environment (more on that in Chapter 11, "Troubleshooting Windows"). These can help diagnose whether a memory module needs to be replaced. But in general, trust in your senses; look at and listen to the computer to help diagnose any RAM issues that might occur.

Cram Quiz

Answer these questions. The answers follow the last question. If you cannot answer these questions correctly, consider reading this section again until you can.

220-901 Questions

1. Where can you view how much RAM you have in the computer? (Select all that apply.)

   ○ **A.** Task Manager

   ○ **B.** Computer window

   ○ **C.** System window

   ○ **D.** BIOS

2. How should you hold RAM when installing it?

   ○ **A.** By the edges

   ○ **B.** By the front and back

   ○ **C.** With tweezers

   ○ **D.** With an Integrated Circuit (IC) puller

3. You are repairing a computer that has been used in a warehouse for several years. You suspect a problem with a memory module. What should you do first?

   ○ **A.** Replace the module with a new one.

   ○ **B.** Install more RAM.

   ○ **C.** Clean the RAM slot.

   ○ **D.** Install RAM heat sinks.

4. If a BSOD occurs, what should you do?

   ○ **A.** Replace all the RAM.

   ○ **B.** Reinstall the operating system.

   ○ **C.** Check the RAM settings in the BIOS.

   ○ **D.** Wait for it to happen again.

5. You just upgraded a PC's motherboard and CPU. However, when you turn the computer on, it will not POST. What should you do first?

   ○ **A.** Check that the system hasn't overheated.

   ○ **B.** Check whether the RAM is properly seated.

   ○ **C.** Check that the OS was installed properly.

   ○ **D.** Check whether the mouse and keyboard are connected properly.

6. You just investigated a computer that is suffering from intermittent shutdowns. You note that the RAM modules are overheating. What is the best solution?

   ○ **A.** Install a heat sink on the memory controller.

   ○ **B.** Install more CPU fans.

   ○ **C.** Install heat sinks on the RAM modules.

   ○ **D.** Install a heat sink on the chipset.

7. You just installed new, compatible RAM into a motherboard, but when you boot the computer, it does not recognize the memory. What should you do?

   ○ **A.** Flash the BIOS.

   ○ **B.** Replace the RAM.

   ○ **C.** Upgrade the CPU.

   ○ **D.** Add more RAM.

Cram Quiz Answers

220-901 Answers

1. **A, C,** and **D.** The BIOS displays what type of RAM you have and the amount. Windows has several locations in which you can discern how much RAM there is, including the Task Manager, System window, and System Information (accessible from Run > msinfo32). The Computer window is simply a window within Windows Explorer (or File Explorer).

2. **A.** Hold RAM by the edges to avoid contact with the pins, chips, and circuitry.

3. **C.** Because the computer is being used in a warehouse (which is often a fairly dirty environment), you should clean the RAM slot and memory module. Consider using compressed air or the proper spray (such as Stabilant 22). Clean out all of the dust bunnies within the entire computer. Using MemTest86 or another memory diagnostic tool is another good answer.

4. **D.** A singular BSOD doesn't necessarily mean that the RAM or any other components have gone bad. Often, a single BSOD occurs, but you never see it again. You want to see two or more of the same errors before starting into a lengthy troubleshooting session!

5. **B.** The first thing you should do is check if the RAM is seated properly. This is easier than troubleshooting the CPU or motherboard and is a more common culprit due to the amount of force it takes to install DIMMs. A system will not have enough time to overheat before it gets to the POST. The OS hasn't even started yet, so you can rule that out. Mice and keyboards don't play a part in a system not posting.

6. **C.** The best thing to do in this situation is to install heat sinks on the RAM modules. On older computers, the memory controller in a northbridge doesn't usually overheat because it already has a heat sink; on newer computers, it is within the CPU. A CPU can have only one fan. You can't install more (although an additional case fan might help). The chipset also usually has a heat sink.

7. **A.** If you are sure that the RAM is compatible and the system doesn't recognize it during POST, try flashing the BIOS. It could be that the RAM is so new that the motherboard doesn't have the required firmware to identify the new RAM.

CHAPTER 5

Power

This chapter covers the following A+ exam topics:

▶ Understanding and Testing Power

▶ Power Devices

▶ Power Supplies

You can find a master list of A+ exam topics in the "Introduction."

This chapter covers CompTIA A+ 220-901 objectives 1.2, 1.8, and 4.1, and part of 220-902 objective 5.2.

Everything relies on power. Clean, well-planned power is imperative in a computer system. It's so important that I almost made this the first chapter of the book. I can't tell you how many power-related issues I have trouble-shot in the past. Many of the issues that you see concerning power are due to lack of protection and improper planning, and as such you will see several questions (if not more) on the A+ exams regarding this subject.

Imagine a scenario in which you work for a technical services division of a company. You are required to install a new, more powerful power supply in a computer that contains many devices and requires a lot of electricity. You need to install the computer in a new area of the company's building. This requires you to plug the computer into an AC receptacle that has never been used or tested.

What kind of power supply should you select? How can you verify that the AC outlet is properly wired? And how can you protect the computer? This chapter answers all those questions and furnishes you with the knowledge you need to install, test, and troubleshoot power supplies and test power that comes from the wall outlet.

Understanding and Testing Power

The power for your computer is derived from electricity, which is basically the flow of electric charge. Electricity is defined and measured in several ways, most commonly as the following:

▶ **Voltage:** A representation of potential energy. Sometimes it's more simply referred to as pressure; its unit of measurement is volts (V).

▶ **Wattage or electric power:** The rate of electric energy in a circuit, measured in watts (W).

▶ **Amperage or electric current:** The movement of electric charge, measured in amperes or amps (A).

▶ **Impedance:** The amount of resistance to electricity, measured in ohms (Ω).

This chapter covers each of these, but by far the most common of these that you will be testing is voltage. Following are two examples of voltages you are probably familiar with:

▶ 120 Volts AC (the voltage associated with many U.S. homes)

▶ 5 Volts DC (the voltage associated with some of the internal power connections in your PC)

The difference in these two examples (aside from the number of volts) is that a house's outlets use alternating current (AC), in which the flow of electrons alternate; your computer (again, internally) uses direct current (DC), in which the flow of electrons is one way.

Back to our scenario. Because you can't control who wired the AC outlet that you will be connecting the computer to or how clean the power is that comes from your municipality, you should test the outlet prior to plugging in the computer. Two good tools to use when testing are a receptacle tester and a multimeter.

> **Note**
>
> Warning: Read through these sections carefully before attempting to test a live AC outlet. If you still feel unsure, contact a qualified electrician to test and make repairs to an AC outlet.

Testing an AC Outlet with a Receptacle Tester

Type B AC outlets are the most common and might also be referred to as wall sockets, electric receptacles, or power points. It is type B that you need to be concerned with for the A+ exam. If any of the hot, neutral, or ground wires are connected improperly, the computer connected to the outlet is a sitting duck, just waiting for irreparable damage. To ensure that the AC outlet is wired properly, you can use a receptacle tester, like the one shown in Figure 5.1. These are inexpensive and are available at most home-improvement stores and electrical supply shops. When you plug in the receptacle tester, it tells you if the receptacle is wired properly or indicates which wires are incorrect.

FIGURE 5.1   A common receptacle tester and labeled receptacle

In Figure 5.1 the test has passed. With this particular tester, two yellow lights tell you that the outlet is wired correctly. Any other combination of lights tells you that there is a wiring error. The different combinations are usually labeled on the tester itself; for example, an open ground error is displayed by one single, yellow light on this tester. Important: If you receive any erroneous readings or if there are no lights at all, *do not use the outlet* and contact your supervisor and/or building management so a licensed electrician can be brought in to fix the problem.

> **ExamAlert**
>
> If you find an AC outlet is improperly wired, contact your supervisor and/or building management to resolve the problem.

Testing an AC Outlet with a Multimeter

Every PC technician should own a multimeter, which we will use throughout this chapter. A multimeter is a handheld device that, among other things, can be used to measure amps and impedance and to test voltage inside a computer and from AC outlets. It has two leads: one black and one red. Whenever using the multimeter, try to hold both of the multimeter leads with one hand and hold them by the plastic handles; don't touch the metal ends. It will be like holding chopsticks but is a safer method, reducing the severity of electric shock in the uncommon chance that one occurs. To test an AC outlet with a multimeter, perform the following steps:

1. Place the multimeter's black lead in the outlet's ground. (The parts of the outlet are labeled in Figure 5.1.)

2. Place the red lead in the hot opening.

3. Turn on the multimeter to test for volts AC (sometimes labeled as VAC). Hold the leads steady and check for readings. Optimally, the reading will hover around 115 volts or 120 volts, depending on where you are in the United States. Watch the readings for a minute or so. Remember the reading or range of readings that display. A common reading is shown in Figure 5.2.

4. Turn off the multimeter.

5. Remove the red lead.

6. Remove the black lead.

What was your reading? A steady reading closest to 120 volts is desirable. It might be less in some areas, but the key is that it's steady at one voltage; this is also known as *clean power*. If the reading fluctuates a lot (for example, it fluctuates between 113 volts and 121 volts), you have one of the varieties of *dirty power*. This could be because too many devices use the same circuit or because power coming from the electrical panel or from the municipal grid fluctuates—maybe because the panel or the entire grid is under/overloaded. A quick call to your company's electrician can result in an answer and possibly a long-term fix. However, you would like an immediate solution, which in this case is to install an uninterruptible power supply (UPS) or other line-conditioning device between the computer and the AC outlet. This can regulate the output of AC to the computer.

Red Lead to Hot

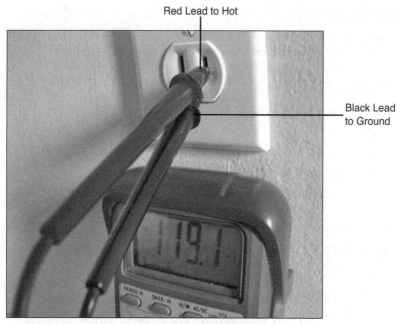

Black Lead
to Ground

FIGURE 5.2   **A receptacle tested with a multimeter**

You can also test the neutral and ground wires in this manner. You should
be especially concerned with whether the ground wire is connected properly.
Previously, you saw how to test this with the receptacle tester, but to test this
with the multimeter, connect the black lead to ground and the red lead to
neutral. This should result in a reading of 0 volts. Any other reading means
that the outlet is not grounded properly, which can result in damage to a
computer that connects to it. You can also use a voltage detector, which is a
pen-shaped device that beeps when it comes into contact with voltage. On a
properly grounded outlet, the only part that should give audible beeps is the
hot lead. Everything else, including the screw and outlet plate, should not
register any sounds. If sounds do register by simply touching the outlet plate
with the voltage detector, the outlet is not grounded properly. If this is the
case, or if you got any other reading besides 0 volts on the multimeter, contact an electrician right away.

Cram Quiz

Answer these questions. The answers follow the last question. If you cannot answer these questions correctly, consider reading this section again until you can.

220-901 Questions

1. Which tool is used to test the amount of voltage that comes from an AC outlet?

   ○ **A.** Multimeter

   ○ **B.** Voltage detector

   ○ **C.** Receptacle tester

   ○ **D.** Impedance tester

2. Which of the following is a representation of potential energy?

   ○ **A.** Wattage

   ○ **B.** Voltage

   ○ **C.** Impedance

   ○ **D.** Amperage

3. Which wire, when tested, should display zero volts on a multimeter?

   ○ **A.** Black

   ○ **B.** Hot

   ○ **C.** Ground

   ○ **D.** Red

Cram Quiz Answers

220-901 Answers

1. **A.** The multimeter is the only testing tool that can display voltage numerically.

2. **B.** Voltage is a representation of potential energy; an analogy for voltage would be water pressure in a pipe.

3. **C.** When testing the ground wire with a multimeter, it should display a reading of zero volts. (The neutral wire could also display zero volts, but that is not what we were testing for in the chapter.)

Power Devices

Utilizing proper power devices is part of a good preventative maintenance plan and helps to protect a computer. You need to protect against several things:

▶ Surges

▶ Spikes

▶ Sags

▶ Brownouts

▶ Blackouts

A *surge* in electrical power means that there is an unexpected increase in the amount of voltage provided. This can be a small increase or a larger increase known as a spike. A *spike* is a short transient in voltage that can be due to a short circuit, tripped circuit breaker, power outage, or lightning strike.

A *sag* is an unexpected decrease in the amount of voltage provided. Typically, sags are limited in time and in the decrease in voltage. However, when voltage reduces further, a brownout could ensue. During a *brownout* the voltage drops to such an extent that it typically causes the lights to dim and causes computers to shut off.

A *blackout* is when a total loss of power for a prolonged period occurs. Another problem associated with blackouts is the spike that can occur when power is restored. In the New York area, it is common to have an increased number of tech support calls during July; this is attributed to lightning storms! Quite often this is due to improper protection.

ExamAlert

A power surge is an unexpected increase in voltage. A brownout is a drop in voltage that can cause computers to shut off. A blackout is a total loss of power for a prolonged time.

Some devices have specific purposes and others can protect against more than one of these electrical issues. Let's describe a few of these devices.

Power Strips

A *power strip* is a group of sockets, usually in-line, that includes a flexible cable that plugs into an AC outlet. It allows multiple devices to share a single receptacle in that outlet. Due to this, a maximum wattage rating can be applied to the power strip (for example, 3,000 watts is a decent amount). A computer might have a 300-watt power supply, but on the average, it might use less than that while running. A monitor might use between 35 watts and 100 watts, depending on the type of monitor. You can check the wattage rating on the back or side of most devices. Add the total for all devices connected to the power strip and remember not to exceed the maximum rating. This concept applies to other devices in this section, including surge protectors and UPS devices.

Power strips might not have surge protection functionality. If they don't have surge protection capabilities, they cannot protect from any of the electrical issues (surges and spikes) listed in the previous section.

A power strip has a master on/off switch and usually has a 15-amp circuit breaker to prevent overloading. If an overload occurs, the circuit breaker trips, cutting power, and the device can usually be reset by pressing a black button normally located somewhere near the power button. Overloads occur because the power strip tries to pull too much current (amps) from the wall outlet or because too much current is supplied to the power strip. As a rule of thumb, no more than three or four computers (and monitors) should use the same power strip and, therefore, the same circuit. This calls into question whether any other AC outlets connect to the same circuit. To find this out, a qualified electrician can use a circuit-testing tool to locate all the outlets on the circuit in question, or this information might be included in your building's electrical diagram. By the way, you can also calculate the number of computers and monitors that can connect to a circuit by their amperage rating. For example, at AC (wall-outlet level), a typical computer would draw 2 to 3 amps and perhaps another 2 amps for the monitor maximum. (Keep in mind that these are estimates.) So on a standard 15-amp circuit, it would be wise to have no more than three computers and three monitors running simultaneously.

Surge Protectors

A *surge protector* or *surge suppressor* is a power strip that also incorporates a metal-oxide varistor (MOV) to protect against surges and spikes. Most power strips that you find in an office supply store or home improvement store have surge protection capability. The word *varistor* (sometimes spelled varsistor) is a blend of the terms *variable* and *resistor*.

> **ExamAlert**
>
> To protect against surges and spikes, use a surge protector!

Surge protectors are usually rated in joules, which are a way to measure energy; essentially, the more joules, the better. For computer systems, 1,000 joules or more is recommended. This joule rating gives you a sense of how long the device can protect against surges and spikes. Surges happen more often than you might think, and every time a surge happens, part of the varistor is burned out. The higher the joule rating, the longer the varistor (and therefore the device) should last. Most of today's surge protectors have an indicator light that informs you if the varistor has failed.

Because surges can occur over telephone lines, RG-6 cable lines, and network lines, it is common to see input and output ports for any or all these on a decent surge protector. Higher-quality surge protectors have multiple MOVs not only for the different connections (such as AC and phones), but for the individual wires in an AC connection.

Uninterruptible Power Supplies

An *uninterruptible power supply* (*UPS*) takes the functionality of a surge suppressor and combines that with a *battery backup*. So now, our computer is protected not only from surges and spikes, but also from sags, brownouts, and blackouts.

> **ExamAlert**
>
> Use a UPS/battery backup to protect your computer from power outages!

But the battery backup can't last indefinitely! It is considered emergency power and typically keeps your computer system running for 5 to 30 minutes, depending on the model you purchase. Figure 5.3 shows an example of a typical inexpensive UPS. Notice that some of the outlets on the device are marked for battery backup and surge protection, whereas others are for surge protection only.

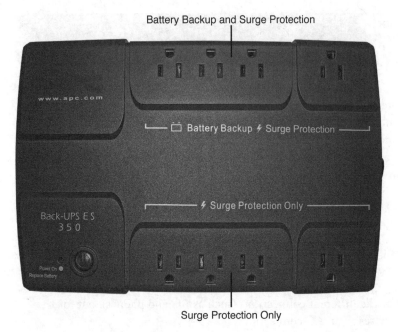

Battery Backup and Surge Protection

Battery Backup ⏹ Surge Protection

⚡ Surge Protection Only

Surge Protection Only

FIGURE 5.3   **A common UPS**

Most UPS devices also act as line conditioners, protecting from over- and under-voltage; they condition (or regulate) the voltage sent to the computer. If you happen to see a customer's lights flickering, this could indicate dirty power, and you should consider recommending a UPS for the customer's computers and networking equipment. The device shown in the figure, and most UPS devices today, has a USB connection (not displayed) so that your computer can communicate with the UPS. When there is a power outage, the UPS sends a signal to the computer telling it to shut down, suspend, or stand-by before the battery discharges completely. Most UPSs come with software that you can install that enables you to configure the computer with these options.

UPS devices' output power capacity is rated in volt-amps (VA) and watts. Although you might have heard that volt-amps and watts are essentially the same, this is one of those times that they are somewhat different. The volt-amp rating is slightly higher due to the difference between apparent power (when in battery backup mode) and real power (when pulling regular power from the AC outlet). For example, the device in Figure 5.3 has a volt-amp rating of 350 VA but a wattage rating of 200 watts. Generally, this is enough for a computer, monitor, and a few other devices, but a second computer might be pushing it given the wattage rating. The more devices that connect to the UPS, the shorter the battery lasts if a power outage occurs; if too many devices are connected, there might be inconsistencies when the battery needs to take over. Thus, many UPS manufacturers limit the amount of battery backup-protected receptacles. Connecting a laser printer to the UPS is not recommended due to the high current draw of the laser printer; also, to protect the UPS from being overloaded, never connect a surge protector or power strip to one of the receptacles in the UPS.

ExamAlert

Do *not* connect laser printers to UPS devices.

The UPS normally has a lead-acid battery that, when discharged, requires 10 to 20 hours to recharge. This battery is usually shipped in a disconnected state. Before charging the device for use, you must first make sure that the battery leads connect to the UPS. If the battery ever needs to be replaced, a red light usually appears and is accompanied by a beeping sound. Beeping can also occur if power is no longer supplied to the UPS by the AC outlet.

Cram Quiz

Answer these questions. The answers follow the last question. If you cannot answer these questions correctly, consider reading this section again until you can.

220-902 Questions

1. Which device should be used to protect against power outages?

   ○ **A.** Multimeter

   ○ **B.** UPS

   ○ **C.** FedEx

   ○ **D.** Surge protector

2. You want a *cost-effective* solution to the common surges that can affect your computer. Which device offers the best solution?

   ○ **A.** UPS

   ○ **B.** Surge suppressor

   ○ **C.** Power strip

   ○ **D.** Line conditioner

3. Which of the following is an unexpected increase in voltage?

   ○ **A.** Sag

   ○ **B.** Blackout

   ○ **C.** Spike

   ○ **D.** Whiteout

4. You are fixing a computer for a customer when you notice a few of the fluorescent lights flickering every now and then. Which of the following should be recommended to the customer to protect his equipment?

   ○ **A.** To get an electrician

   ○ **B.** To install a UPS

   ○ **C.** To get an extra power supply

   ○ **D.** To buy a generator

Cram Quiz Answers

220-902 Answers

1. **B.** The UPS is the only item listed that protects the computer from power outages like blackouts and brownouts.

2. **B.** A surge suppressor (or surge protector) is the right solution at the right price. A UPS is a possible solution but costs more than a surge protector. A line conditioner also would be a viable solution but, again, is overkill. And a power strip doesn't necessarily have surge protection functionality.

3. **C.** A spike (or a surge) is an unexpected increase in voltage. A sag is a decrease in voltage, a blackout is a power outage, and a whiteout is actually a blizzard, which could result in a blackout!

4. **B.** You should recommend that the customer install a UPS for computer equipment. Flickering lights could be a sign of voltage fluctuations (dirty power), which could also affect the computers. The UPS can combat dirty power by conditioning it.

Power Supplies

Okay, now that you've tested your AC outlet and put some protective power devices into play, let's talk power supplies. The power supply unit (PSU) in a PC is in charge of converting the alternating current (AC) drawn from the wall outlet into direct current (DC) to be used internally by the computer. The power supply makes use of a transformer and a rectifier, working together to convert AC over to DC. The power supply feeds the motherboard, hard drives, optical drives, and any other devices inside of the computer. Talk about a single point of failure! That is why many higher-end workstations and servers have redundant power supplies.

Planning Which Power Supply to Use

It is important to use a reliable brand of power supply that is certified; for example, in the United States, power supplies can be certified by Underwriter Laboratories (known as UL listed).

You also must take into account the following factors when planning which power supply to use in your computer:

▶ Type of power supply and compatibility

▶ Wattage and capacity requirements

▶ Number and type of connectors

Now, in the scenario mentioned in the beginning of the chapter, you need a power supply that can support several devices in your workstation—one that can output a lot of power. In this scenario, the computer has two SATA hard drives, a Blu-ray drive, a DVD-ROM, and a PCIe video card. In addition, let's say that you use an ATX 12V 2.x motherboard. So you need to look for a high-capacity, compatible ATX power supply with a decent number of connectors for your devices. Let's discuss planning now.

Types of Power Supplies and Compatibility

The most common form factor used in PCs today is Advanced Technology Extended (ATX). Depending on the type of ATX, the main power connector to the motherboard will usually have 24 pins or, for older systems, 20 pins. Generally, today's systems use power supplies that adhere to one of the ATX 12V 2.x standards. The key is compatibility. In this scenario, you have a previously built computer, which means that the case and motherboard are already compatible. If this computer were *proprietary*, you could go to the computer manufacturer's website to find out the exact form factor and possibly a replacement power supply for that model computer. Some third-party power supply manufacturers also offer replacement power supplies for proprietary systems. However, if this computer were custom built, you would need to find out the form factor used by the motherboard and/or case, and you should open the computer to take a look at all the necessary power connections. Then you need to find a compatible power supply (according to those specifications) from a third-party power supply manufacturer.

> **ExamAlert**
>
> Original ATX power supplies connect to the motherboard with a 20-pin connector. Newer ATX 12V 2.x power supplies connect with a 24-pin connector.

Most of today's motherboards have an additional 4-pin or 8-pin 12 V power connector for the CPU (referred to as EATX12V). A typical power supply offers one or two 4-pin connectors or one 8-pin connector for this extra power. If the motherboard and power supply don't match up, there are 4- to 8-pin adapters available. Among other things, Figure 5.4 shows a motherboard's main 24-pin and additional 4-pin CPU power connections.

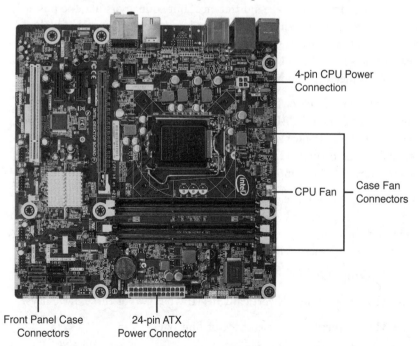

FIGURE 5.4   **Main power, 4-pin CPU power, case fan, CPU fan, and case connections**

A quick word about *dual-rail* power. You might have heard of dual-rail or multirail power supplies, for example multiple 12 V rails. This technology is important in systems that draw a lot of power. It is a way of monitoring power circuits individually instead of collectively (single-rail) and helps to prevent overheating and possible fire by shutting down the PSU if a certain point is reached (for example, more than 18 amps on a single 12 V wire). If you plan to run a CPU-intensive system, such as a gaming system or multimedia system, you should look into a multirail PSU.

> **ExamAlert**
>
> The purpose of "dual-rail" PSUs is to separate and limit the current through each wire to avoid overheating.

Also, remember about case fans. Some case fans must connect directly to the power supply feeds. However, if they have 4-pin connectors, they can connect directly to the motherboard, as shown in Figure 5.4. Finally, case connectors for the Power button and the reset button are usually located toward the front of the motherboard. When connecting these, the colored wire normally goes to positive (+) if necessary. Some of the case connectors can be connected either way and it won't make a difference. But connectors like the power LED and the hard-drive activity LED need to be connected properly for the LEDs to display. Quite often the motherboard will be color-coded; the fold-out instruction sheet will show exactly where to plug in each case connector and the case connectors themselves are normally labeled.

There are other types of form factors, such as microATX (mATX) and ITX (covered in Chapter 2, "Motherboards"); however, the ATX form factor is the important one to know regarding power supplies for the A+ exam. For any other form factors, just remember that the power supply, case, and motherboard all need to be compatible.

Another important piece to consider is the type of case used. Larger cases require longer power cables to reach the devices. You can find the measurements for the cables on the power supply manufacturer's website. There are several types of cases that you need to be familiar with:

▶ **Desktop:** Lies horizontally; usually has one or two 5 1/4-inch drive bays.

▶ **Mini-tower:** Stands vertically; usually has two or three drive bays.

▶ **Mid-tower:** Usually has three or four bays.

▶ **Full tower:** Usually has six bays.

▶ **Slim line:** Usually stands vertically; small form factor. For example, mini-ITX systems and microATX.

▶ **All-in-one (AOC):** The computer case and components are integrated into the monitor. This could be a monitor that is meant to sit on a desktop or a handheld device with touchscreen.

Many power supply manufacturers also make computer cases and often sell them as a package or to be purchased separately.

Wattage and Capacity Requirements

Power supplies are usually rated in watts. They are rated at a maximum amount that they can draw from the wall outlet and pass on to the computer's devices. Remember that the computer will not always use all that power the way in which a light bulb does. And the amount of power used depends on how many devices work and how much number-crunching your processor does! In addition, when computers sleep or suspend, they use less electricity. What you need to be concerned with is the maximum amount of power all the devices need collectively. Most power-supply manufacturers today offer models that range from 300 watts all the way up to 1,500 watts. Although 300 watts is a decent amount of power for many computers, it might not suffice in our scenario. Devices use a certain amount of power defined in amps and/or watts. By adding all the devices' power consumption together, you can get a clearer picture of how powerful a power supply you need. Consult the manufacturer's web page of the device for exact requirements. In this scenario, the computer has two SATA hard drives, a Blu-ray drive, a DVD-ROM, and a PCIe video card. It also has a quad-core processor and 8 GB of RAM (in two sticks).

After doing the math, it appears that the computer in the scenario needs approximately 400 watts or so to run smoothly. The power supply you purchase should be rated slightly higher, just in case. So in this scenario, you would obtain a 450-watt or 500-watt power supply. Most power supplies are rated for 15 amps, so it is important to connect the computer to a 15-amp circuit or higher.

Number and Type of Power Connectors

It is important to know how many of each type of power connector you need when planning which power supply to use. In this scenario, you need four SATA power connectors (for the two hard drives, the Blu-ray drive, and the DVD-ROM). You also need a 6-pin power connection for your video card and you have two case fans that require power. You must be familiar with each type of power connector for the A+ exams. Be prepared to identify them by name and by sight. Table 5.1 defines the usage and voltages for the most common power connectors (Molex, SATA, and PCIe), which are shown in Figures 5.5 through 5.7.

TABLE 5.1   **Power Connectors**

Power Connector	Usage	Pins and Voltages
Molex	Case fans, IDE hard drives, and optical drives	Red (5 V), black (G), black (G), and yellow (12 V)
SATA	Serial ATA hard drives and optical drives	15-pin, 3.3 V, 5 V, and 12 V
PCIe	PCI Express video cards	6-pin, 12 V (ATX12V version 2.1)
		8-pin, 12 V (ATX12V version 2.2 and higher)

Note

Some power supplies come with 6-pin PCIe power. Before purchasing a power supply, be sure that it has the proper video power you require (6-pin or 8-pin).

FIGURE 5.5   **Molex power connector**

FIGURE 5.6   **SATA 15-pin power connector**

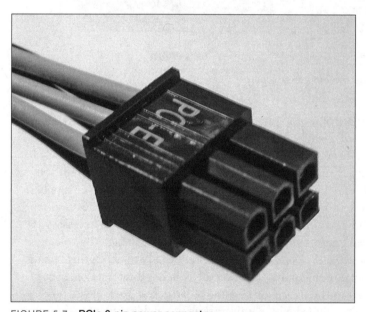

FIGURE 5.7   **PCIe 6-pin power connector**

ExamAlert

Be able to identify power connectors and know their associated voltages.

Installing the Power Supply

When the power supply arrives, you can install it. But first take a look at the back of the power supply to identify the components you see, as shown in Figure 5.8.

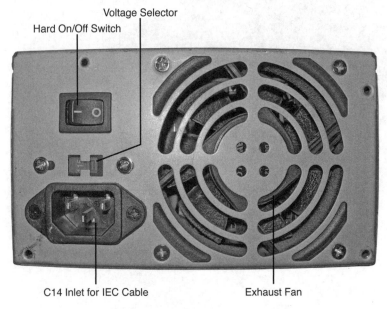

FIGURE 5.8 **Rear view of power supply**

On the top-left portion of Figure 5.8, you see a hard on/off switch, sometimes referred to as a kill switch. This is a helpful feature when troubleshooting PCs. Instead of disconnecting the power cable, you can shut off this switch. It works effectively in emergencies as well. Below that, you see a (red) voltage selector switch. This indicates that this is a dual voltage power supply. This should be set to 115 V in the United States. It also has a 230 V option to be used in other countries. (An additional adapter might be necessary for the different wall outlets you might encounter.) Never change the voltage selector switch while the computer is running. Be sure to check this setting before using the power supply. This selector switch indicates an older power supply—I used it in the figure for illustrative purposes. Most newer power supplies are now equipped with a universal input, enabling you to connect the power supply to any AC outlet between 100 V and 240 V without having to set a voltage switch. To determine if a PSU without a voltage switch is truly dual-voltage, look for the phrase: "100-240 V input" or something similar.

Back to the figure, below the voltage selector, you see the power cable inlet; this is known as a C14 inlet and is where you attach your power cord to the power supply. These inlets and cables that connect to them are defined by the IEC 60320 specification (previously the IEC 320 spec) and because of this, some techs refer to the power cord as an "IEC cable" (which, by the way, stands for International Electrotechnical Commission). This cord actually has a standard three-prong connector suitable for an AC outlet on one end and a C13 line socket on the other to connect to the power supply. To the right, you see the power supply fan that is of great importance when troubleshooting power supplies.

If there is a power supply connected to the computer, turn off the computer and unplug the power supply. ATX motherboards are always receiving 5 volts even when they are off (if the computer is plugged in). Be sure that you use antistatic methods. Remove the old power supply and prepare to install the new one.

You might want to test the new power supply before installing it. This can be done by connecting a power supply tester (described in the next section), plugging in the power supply to the AC outlet and turning on the hard on/off switch. Or you can test the power supply after it is installed by simply turning the computer on.

The power supply is placed inside the case and is often mounted with four standard screws that are screwed in from the back of the case. In some instances, a plastic housing inside the case might need to be removed. In addition, the power supply might not fit without the removal of other devices, such as the processor and such, but in most cases (pun intended) you should install the power supply without too much trouble. Next, connect the main power connector to the motherboard and attach the Molex, SATA, and PCIe as necessary to their corresponding devices. The main 24-pin connector can be plugged in only in one way: A locking tab prevents a wrong connection and keeps the plug in place. Also, most other connectors are molded in such a way as to make it difficult to connect them backward. If you need a lot of strength to plug in the connector, make sure that it is oriented correctly. Don't force the connection. Afterward, remove any antistatic protection and, finally, plug in the power supply to the AC outlet, turn on the hard on/off switch (if the power supply has one), and turn on the computer. Check to see if the fan in the power supply is working and if the computer boots correctly.

Troubleshooting Power Supply Issues

Installation of the power supply is easy, and usually there aren't many issues when doing so, but power supplies don't last forever. Moreover, many issues that occur with power supplies are intermittent, making the troubleshooting process a little tougher. Your best friends when troubleshooting power supplies are going to be a multimeter, a power supply tester, and your eyes and ears. Of course, always make sure that the power supply connects to the AC outlet properly before troubleshooting further. Here are a couple of the issues you might encounter with power supplies:

▶ Fan failure

▶ Fuse failure

▶ Quick death

▶ Slow death

Fan failure can be due to the fact that the power supply is old, extremely clogged with dirt, or the fan was of a cheaper design (without ball bearings). However, for the A+ exam, it doesn't make a difference. As far as A+ is concerned, if the fan fails, the power supply needs to be replaced (and that strategy makes sense). Chances are, if the fan has failed, other components of the power supply are on their way out also. It is more cost-effective to a company to simply replace the power supply than to have a technician spend the time opening it and trying to repair it. More important, although it is possible to remove and replace the fan by opening the power supply, this can be a dangerous venture because the power supply holds an electric charge. So the A+ rule is to never open the power supply.

> **ExamAlert**
>
> Do not open a power supply! If it has failed, replace it with a working unit.

Fan failure can sometimes cause a loud noise to emanate from the power supply; it might even sound like it is coming from inside the computer. Any fan in the computer (power supply fan, case fan, and CPU fan) can make some strange noises over time. If a customer reports a loud noise coming from the inside of a PC, consider the power supply fan.

On the other hand, sometimes the fans spin but no other devices receive power and the computer doesn't boot. This could be due to improper installation (or failure) of the motherboard, CPU, or RAM. See Chapters 2–4 for more information on how to troubleshoot those.

Fuse failure can occur due to an overload or due to the power supply malfunctioning. Either way, the proper course of action is to replace the power supply. Do not attempt to replace the fuse. Chances are that the power supply is faulty if the fuse is blown.

If the power supply dies a quick death and provides no power, it might be because of several reasons, ranging from an electrical spike to hardware malfunction. First, make sure that the IEC cable is connected properly to the power supply and to the AC outlet. Sometimes it can be difficult to tell whether the power supply has failed or if it's something else inside or outside the computer system. You should check the AC outlet with your trusty receptacle tester, make sure that a circuit hasn't tripped, and verify that any surge protectors and/or UPS devices work properly. Depending on what you sense about the problem, you might decide to just swap out the power supply with a known good one. Otherwise, move to the following numbered steps.

If the power supply is dying a slow death and is causing intermittent errors or frequent failure of hard drives and other devices, it could be tough to troubleshoot. If you suspect intermittent issues, first make sure that the power cord is connected securely and then try swapping out the power supply with a known good one. Boot the computer and watch it for a while to see if the same errors occur.

> **Note**
>
> If a system were recently upgraded, the power supply could cause the system to reboot intermittently because the new components are causing too much of a power drain. When upgrading components, be sure to check if you need to upgrade the power supply as well!

Whether the power supply has apparently failed completely or is possibly causing intermittent errors, and you can't figure out the cause to this point, continue through the following steps:

1. Remove the computer case.

2. Connect a PSU tester, as shown in Figure 5.9, to the main power connector and look at the results. These PSU testers normally test for +12 V, –12 V, +5 V, –5 V, and 3.3 V, but they might not test every individual pin. If there are error lights, no lights, or missing lights for specific voltages on the tester, replace the power supply. If all the lights are green, move to the next step.

FIGURE 5.9 **Testing a 24-pin power connector with a PSU tester**

> **Note**
>
> The –5 V light in Figure 5.9 is not lit. This is because the –5 V wire (white) is optional. See Chapter 2 for more information on the individual pins in an ATX connection.

3. Use a multimeter to test the power supply. Use the same methodology for testing with a multimeter as described in the beginning of this chapter.

   a. Turn off the hard on/off switch. (If there is one; if not, unplug the IEC cord.)

   b. With the main motherboard connector inserted into the motherboard, connect the black lead to a ground wire (or other source of ground) and insert the red lead to a colored voltage wire in the main power connector, as shown in Figure 5.10. You need to dig a little bit to get the lead in there, but don't press too hard. When the leads are stationary, move to the next step.

   c. Turn on the hard on/off switch (or plug the IEC cord back in) and turn on the computer.

   d. Turn on the multimeter to volts DC and view the results. In Figure 5.10, you notice that we test an orange wire (which is rated for +3.3 volts). Generally, supply voltages should be within +/– 5 percent of the nominal value. The result was +3.43 volts, which is within tolerance.

FIGURE 5.10   Testing the 3.3 V wire with a multimeter set to volts DC

Note

If you have an analog multimeter, you would usually set this to 20 or higher. Just remember to move the decimal point in the reading for every increment higher than 20!

    e. Shut off the multimeter and computer every time before moving to another wire. Check each wire for proper voltage. A chart of all the voltages for the 24-pin connector is available in Chapter 2.

    f. If a wire fails or gives intermittent results, first verify whether you have a decent connection with the multimeter leads; then see whether the wire just needs to be inserted into the main motherboard connector better. If it continues to fail, replace the power supply. If all wires are fine (which is doubtful), move to the next step.

4. Swap the power supply with a known good power supply. Boot the computer and watch it for several minutes or longer to see if there are any strange and intermittent occurrences.

Remember that connections sometimes can be jarred loose inside and outside the computer. Check the IEC cord on both ends and all power connections inside the computer. This includes the main motherboard connector as well as the Molex, SATA, and PCIe connectors. Any single loose connector can have interesting results on your computer!

Heating and Cooling

Another thing to watch for is system overheating. This can happen for several reasons:

▶ Power supply fan failure

▶ Auxiliary case fan failure

▶ Inadequate number of fans

▶ Missing or open slot covers

▶ Case isn't tightly closed and screwed in

▶ Location of computer

Air flow is important on today's personal computers because their processors can often operate at 100 billion instructions per second or more (referred to as 100 giga-instructions per second or GIPS). That creates a lot of heat! Add to that the video card and other cards that have their own on-board processors and you quickly realize it can get hot inside the computer case. Plus, environmental factors and higher temperature areas (such as warehouses and cafeterias) can cause heat to be trapped in the case, producing intermittent shutdowns. Circulation is the key word here. Air should flow in the case from the front and be exhausted out the back. Any openings in the case or missing slot covers can cause circulation to diminish. If you have a computer that has a lot of devices, does a lot of processing, or runs hot for any other reason, your best bet is to install a case fan in the front of the case (which pulls air into the case) and a second case fan in the back of the case (which, with the power supply fan, helps to exhaust hot air out the back). Standard sizes for case fans are 80 and 120 mm. Also, try to keep the computer in a relatively cool area and leave space for the computer to expel its hot air! Of course, there are other special considerations and options, such as liquid cooling and special processor cooling methods. For more on these, see Chapter 3, "The CPU."

You should also train your nose smells and watch for smoke. If a power supply starts to emit a burning smell, or you see any smoke emanating from it, you should turn off the computer and disconnect the power right away. The power supply is probably about to fail, and it could short out, trip the circuit, or worse yet, start a fire. Be sure to replace it. In some cases, a power supply has a burn-in period of 24 to 48 hours, during which time you might smell some oils burning off, but it's best to be safe and check/test the power supply if you smell something that seems wrong.

Cram Quiz

Answer these questions. The answers follow the last question. If you cannot answer these questions correctly, consider reading this section again until you can.

220-901 Questions

1. Which device tests multiple wires of a power supply at the same time?

   ○ **A.** Multimeter

   ○ **B.** Power supply tester

   ○ **C.** Line conditioner

   ○ **D.** Surge protector

2. Which power connector should be used to power an SATA hard drive?

   ○ **A.** Molex

   ○ **B.** 6-pin

   ○ **C.** 24-pin

   ○ **D.** 15-pin

3. Which voltages are supplied by a Molex power connector?

   ○ **A.** 12 V and 5 V

   ○ **B.** 5 V and 3.3 V

   ○ **C.** 3.3 V and 1.5 V

   ○ **D.** 24 V and 12 V

4. A company salesperson just returned to the United States after three months in Europe. Now the salesperson tells you that her PC, which worked fine in Europe, won't turn on. What is the best solution?

   ○ **A.** Install a new power supply.

   ○ **B.** The computer will not work in the United States due to European licensing.

   ○ **C.** Install a power inverter to the power supply.

   ○ **D.** Change the voltage from 230 to 115.

5. You are troubleshooting a computer that won't power on. You have already checked the AC outlet and the power cord, which appear to be functioning properly. What should you do next?

    ○ **A.** Test the computer with a PSU tester.

    ○ **B.** Plug the computer into a different outlet.

    ○ **C.** Check that the RAM is seated correctly.

    ○ **D.** Install a UPS.

6. You suspect that incorrect voltage is provided to a power supply. What tool should you use to test this?

    ○ **A.** PSU tester

    ○ **B.** Loopback adapter

    ○ **C.** Multimeter

    ○ **D.** Voltage detector

7. You just upgraded a motherboard in a computer and put the system back together. It boots, but the power LED on the front of the computer case doesn't light when the system is on. The rest of the computer seems to work fine. What should you do first?

    ○ **A.** Check the power supply.

    ○ **B.** Check the power LED pinout.

    ○ **C.** Replace the LED.

    ○ **D.** Replace the power button.

8. A computer you are troubleshooting shuts down without warning. After a few minutes, it boots back up fine, but after running for a short time, it shuts down again. Which of the following components could be the cause? (Select the two best answers.)

    ○ **A.** Power supply

    ○ **B.** SATA hard drive

    ○ **C.** RAM

    ○ **D.** CPU fan

    ○ **E.** Video card

Cram Quiz Answers

220-901 Answers

1. **B.** The power supply tester tests 3.3 V, 5 V, −5 V, 12 V, and −12 V simultaneously. A multimeter tests only one wire at a time. Line conditioners and surge
   protectors are preventative devices, not testing devices.

2. **D.** 15-pin connectors power SATA hard drives and other SATA devices (such as
   optical drives). Molex connectors power fans, older IDE devices, and other secondary devices. 6-pin power connectors are used for video cards (as are 8-pin
   connectors). 24-pin refers to the main power connection for the motherboard.

3. **A.** Molex connectors provide 12 volts and 5 volts. There are four wires: Yellow is
   12 V, red is 5 V, and the two blacks are grounds.

4. **D.** Most likely, the voltage selector was set to 230 V so that it could function
   properly in Europe (for example, in the UK). It needs to be changed to 115 V so
   that the power supply can work properly in the United States. Make sure to do
   this while the computer is off and unplugged.

5. **A.** You should test the computer with a PSU tester. This can tell you whether the
   power supply functions properly. You already know that the AC outlet is functional, so there is no reason to use another outlet. The computer would still turn
   on if the RAM wasn't seated properly. A UPS won't help the situation because it
   is part of the power flow before the power supply.

6. **C.** In this scenario, you should test the AC outlet with a multimeter because you
   suspected incorrect voltage. The multimeter can tell you exactly which voltage is supplied. A voltage detector and PSU Tester tell you only if voltage is
   present on a given wire; they don't tell you the exact amount. Plus, you don't
   want to test the power supply. However, the multimeter is the right tool to use
   if you wanted to find exactly which voltages were supplied to the motherboard.
   Loopback adapters are used to test network cards and serial ports.

7. **B.** You should check the power LED pinout. The case connector that goes to
   the motherboard is probably installed backward. Motherboards are usually
   labeled. If not, check your documentation for the computer. If the Power button
   works, there is no reason to replace it. The rest of the computer works fine and
   other case connectors are getting power, so the power supply can be ruled out.
   Replacing the LED can be difficult and time-consuming; plus LEDs almost never
   need to be replaced.

8. **A** and **D.** The two components that could cause the system to shut down are
   the power supply and the CPU fan. Check the CPU fan settings and temperature
   in the BIOS first before opening the computer. If those are fine, you most likely
   need to replace the power supply. The RAM, video card, and hard drive should
   not cause the system to suddenly shut down.

CHAPTER 6

Storage

This chapter covers the following A+ exam topics:

▶ Hard Drives

▶ RAID

▶ Optical Storage Media

▶ Solid-State Storage Media

You can find a master list of A+ exam topics in the "Introduction."

This chapter covers CompTIA A+ 220-901 objectives 1.4, 1.5, 1.7, 1.9, 1.11, and 4.2.

Everyone needs a place to store data. Whether it's business documents, audio/video files, or data backups, users must decide on the right storage medium. This can be magnetic media, solid-state media, or optical media. Devices include hard drives, DVD/CD-ROM drives, and USB flash drives among others. It all depends on what is stored and how often and where it is needed. This chapter concentrates on those three categories of media and how to identify, install, and troubleshoot them. We begin with the most typical storage place—the hard drive.

Hard Drives

By far the most common type of storage used in a computer is the hard drive; this is where the operating system is normally stored. Users also store frequently accessed data on the hard drive as well, such as Word documents, music, pictures, and so on. The two main types of hard drives are magnetic (the hard disk drive) and solid-state (which contains no disk). Let's discuss these and the most common standard for hard drive storage—SATA.

Hard Disk Drives

Hard disk drives (HDDs) are the most common of magnetic media. They are nonvolatile, which means that any information stored on them cannot be lost when the computer is turned off. This makes them a good choice to store permanent data that is accessed frequently.

Let's discuss some hard disk drive basics. A hard disk drive contains one or more platters with a magnetic surface. Data is recorded to the disk by magnetizing ferromagnetic material directionally, basically as 0s and 1s. The disk is usually made of a cobalt-based alloy. As the platters rotate at high speed, read/write heads store and read information to and from the disk. The heads are located on an actuator arm that arcs across the disk. Together, the arm and read/write heads are similar to the arm and needle combination of a record player. Figure 6.1 shows some of the components inside and outside of the magnetic disk drive.

The hard drive depicted in Figure 6.1 is a typical Serial ATA 3.5-inch wide drive. This hard drive, like all internal hard drives, has a data connector and power connector. On this particular drive, the data connector attaches to the motherboard (or expansion card) by way of a 7-pin cable. The power connector attaches to the power supply by way of a 15-pin power cable. Regardless of the type of hard drive, always make sure that the data and power cables are firmly connected to it.

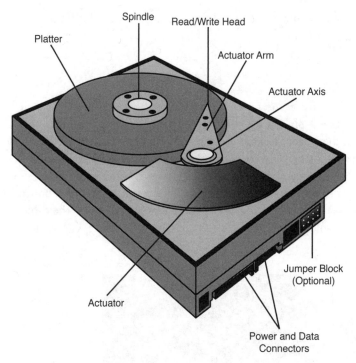

FIGURE 6.1   Components of a typical magnetic hard disk drive

Solid-State Drives

Solid-state drives (SSD) are used to store operating systems and files, similar to a magnetic hard disk drive. However, they don't use spinning disks or read/write heads; they instead write data to nonvolatile microchips or to DRAM. Because of this, they are silent, more resistant to physical shock, and have lower access time and less latency. Because there are no moving parts, you are not concerned with rotation speed.

SSD drives normally measure 2.5 inches in width. Installation requires either a 2.5-inch internal bay, special screw holes drilled directly into the computer case, or an adapter kit to install it to a 3.5-inch internal bay.

> **Note**
>
> SSD drive technology can be combined with magnetic disk technology—this is known as a hybrid drive. This could be accomplished in a dual-drive fashion or more likely as a single drive that incorporates NAND flash memory (for caching of data and speed) and a magnetic disk (for increased capacity).

Usually, SSDs (as well as magnetic disk drives) connect via the SATA interface. Let's discuss SATA now.

SATA

SATA drives are the most-common hard drives in use today. To transmit data,
the SATA drive uses a 7-pin flat (or right-angle) cable, as shown in Figure 6.2.
Obviously, the motherboard should be equipped with one or more SATA
connectors to use SATA hard drives. The other option would be to install a
SATA PCIe or PCI expansion card. Most motherboards come with one or
more SATA data cables. These cables are easily connected to the drive, but to
remove them, press down on the top of the connector at the end of the cable
before pulling the cable out. Only one drive can connect to the SATA cable.

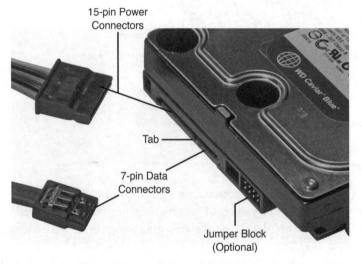

FIGURE 6.2 **SATA data and power connectors**

For power, the SATA drive utilizes a 15-pin power connector, as shown in
Figure 6.2. The hard drive's power connector has a vertical tab at the right
side, making for easier orientation when connecting the power cable. Power
supplies send 3.3 V, 5 V, and 12 V to the SATA drive via orange, red, and yellow cables, respectively.

SATA revision 1.0 (transferring data at 1.5 Gb/s) was the first generation of
SATA devices. Table 6.1 shows the different SATA versions you need to know
for the exam.

TABLE 6.1   **Comparison of SATA Standards**

Standard	Maximum Data Transfer Rate	
SATA Revision 1.0	1.5 Gb/s	150 MB/s
SATA Revision 2.0	3 Gb/s	300 MB/s
SATA Revision 3.0	6 Gb/s	600 MB/s
SATA Revision 3.2	16 Gb/s	1969 MB/s

Actual data transfer rates can be less when you take encoding into account. For example, SATA revision 1.0 goes from 1.5 Gb/s to 1.2 Gb/s (which comes to about 150 MB/s). Rev 2 goes from 3.0 to 2.4 Gb/s (about 300 MB/s.) Rev 3.0 goes from 6.0 to 4.8 Gb/s (about 600 MB/s.)

Note

You might also see some organizations refer to SATA measurements as Gbit/s or Gbps, instead of Gb/s, but they mean the same thing.

ExamAlert

Know the maximum data transfer rates for SATA Revisions 1, 2, 3, and 3.2.

SSDs cost more per GB than their magnetic disk counterparts, so you often see computers using smaller SSDs than they would magnetic drives. As an example, *AV Editor* uses a Samsung 250 GB 6 Gb/s SSD. *Media PC* only uses a Western Digital 128 GB 3 Gb/s solid-state drive (SSD). That houses the operating system. The bulk of the data is stored on a 2 TB disk drive, which at the time of the computer build cost the same amount as the 128 GB SSD. But because SSDs are small, quiet drives with no moving parts and can work very quickly and efficiently, they have become very common in today's computers.

Older SATA drives can run on a newer SATA controller; however, data transfer will be limited to the speed of the drive, not the controller. For example, *Media PC's* DP67DE motherboard has two SATA 6 Gb/s interfaces and four 3 Gb/s interfaces (including one internal and one external eSATA port). Drives can be installed to any of the ports, but to take full advantage of a SATA revision 3.0 (6 Gb/s) controller, you would need a 6 Gb/s drive. Likewise, to take advantage of a SATA revision 3.2 controller, you would need a SATA 3.2 16 Gb/s drive.

ExamAlert

Remember that older SATA drives installed to newer SATA controllers can run only at the speed of the drive.

Note

You might still see a Parallel ATA (PATA) drive in the field. These use the older interface technology known as Integrated Drive Electronics (IDE); an example would be the Ultra ATA/133, which can transfer 133 MB/s over a 40-pin ribbon cable. This technology has been all but wiped out by SATA, but if you want to learn more about it and other less common technologies—such as older parallel versions of the Small Computer System Interface (SCSI) and floppy drives—go to the A+ archive on my website: www.davidlprowse.com.

Hard Drive Specifications

The specifications that you should be interested in when purchasing a hard drive (be it magnetic disk or solid-state), and should know for the A+ exams, include the following:

▶ **Capacity:** A hard drive might be marketed as a 500 GB drive, but accessible capacity can vary depending on the environment the hard drive is used in. For example, after being formatted, this drive might hold a number slightly higher, such as 500,107 MB. But in a RAID 1 mirrored environment, it can hold 490,402 MB.

Note

Going beyond this, a typical operating system such as Windows 7 will display the same 500 GB drive as 465 GB. This is due to a difference in numbering systems used to measure the drive. A hard drive manufacturer (such as Western Digital) will use the $base^{10}$ system, whereas Windows will use the $base^2$ system, resulting in a lower number. No actual space was lost during the conversion!

▶ **Data transfer rate:** A SATA revision 3.0 drive has a theoretical maximum of 600 MB/s, which is considered the maximum data transfer rate, but these numbers are not usually achieved. A drive will usually transfer less; this number is sometimes referred to as *data throughput*. The actual number will depend on several factors—the best way to find out your hard drive's data throughput is to use a benchmarking application.

▶ **Cache:** A drive also has cache memory, which is also known as a buffer. The cache on most hard drives is on-board DRAM. Compare this with CPUs that use SRAM cache that is significantly faster. Like CPUs, the hard drive's cache helps to access frequently used information faster than if it were to get the information from the disk. As an example, the SSD hard drive in *AV Editor* has 512 MB of DDR3 cache memory. Usually, the larger the capacity drive, the more cache it comes equipped with.

▶ **Rotational speed:** (magnetic disks only) The platters in the example hard drive can rotate at a maximum of 7,200 RPM, which is common; other typical speeds for hard drives include 5,400 RPM (slower access time) and 10,000 RPM (faster access time).

▶ **Latency:** (magnetic disks only) After a track has been reached by the read head, latency is the delay in time before a particular sector on the platter can be read. It is directly related to rotational speed and is usually half the time it takes for the disk to rotate once. For example, our 7,200 RPM drive has an average latency of 4.2 ms (milliseconds), but a 10,000 RPM drive has an average latency of 3.0 ms. Though there is latency associated with all devices, we are not overly concerned with it when it comes to SSDs and the A+ exam.

ExamAlert

Understand hard drive specifications, including capacity, data transfer rate, and cache. And for magnetic disk drives specifically, know rotational speed and latency.

Installing Hard Drives

Installing hard drives is quite easy. First, make sure you employ antistatic measures and verify that the computer is off and unplugged.

Next, the drive will either need to be screwed into a drive bay or placed in a drive tray. In some cases, the drive bay or tray might need to be removed before attaching the drive. Some cases have a latching screwless system. However, if you need to screw in the drive, make sure you use all the screws (usually four), and turn the screws with a screwdriver until they are tight; but don't go any further. Try to stay away from motorized screwdrivers or other tools that might have too much torque and can possibly damage the hard drive.

After the drive is screwed in or attached to the case chassis, connect the data and power connectors. For SATA drives, attach the data connector with the exposed metal or Serial ATA label facing up. Orient the power connector according to the tab on the right side of the hard drive's port. Verify that both the data and power connectors are firmly secured to the drive and to the motherboard. A loose connector can cause a boot failure in the operating system. However, don't force the connection, especially the data connection. If SATA data cable is upside down and forced into the port, it could cause damage to the port.

Finally, test the drive and make sure it is recognized by the BIOS at the correct capacity. If, for some reason, the BIOS doesn't see the full capacity, check for any possible BIOS updates. Then either install an operating system to the drive or verify that a current operating system (on another existing disk) can see the new drive at its correct capacity. Remember that a drive might show up as slightly less than its marketed amount within the operating system, depending on the environment the drive is used in.

Preventative Maintenance and Troubleshooting Hard Drives

Hard drives will fail. It's not a matter of if; it's a matter of when, especially when it comes to mechanical drives. The moving parts are bound to fail at some point. Hard drives have an average warranty of 3 years, as is the case with the SATA drives used in this book. It is interesting to note that most drives last around 3 years before failing. Of course, by implementing good practices, you can extend the lifespan of any hard drive, for example:

▶ **Turn the computer off when not in use:** By doing this, the hard drive is told by the operating system to spin down and enter a "parked" state. It's kind of like parking a car or placing a record player's arm on its holder. Turning the computer off when not in use increases the lifespan of just about all its devices (except for the lithium battery). You can also set the computer to hibernate, stand by, or simply set your operating system's power scheme to turn off hard disks after a certain amount of inactivity, such as 5 minutes. The less the drive is in motion, the longer lifespan it will have. Of course, if you want to take the moving parts out of the equation, you could opt for a solid-state drive, as discussed later in this chapter.

▶ **Clean up the disk:** Use a hard drive cleanup program to remove temporary files, clean out the Recycle Bin, and so on. Microsoft includes the Disk Cleanup program in Windows. Another free program is CleanUp!, which you can download from the Internet after a quick Google search. By removing the "junk" from the hard drive, there is less data that the drive must sift through, which makes it easier on the drive when it is time to defragment.

▶ **Defragment the disk:** Defragmenting, also known as defragging, rearranges the data on a partition or volume so that it is laid out in a contiguous, orderly fashion. You should attempt to defragment the disk every month, maybe more often if you are a power user. Don't worry: the operating system tells you if defragging is not necessary during the analysis stage. Over time, data is written to the drive, and subsequently erased, over and over again, leaving gaps in the drivespace. New data will sometimes be written to multiple areas of the drive, in a broken or fragmented fashion, filling in any blank areas it can find. When this happens, the hard drive has to work much harder to find the data it needs. Logically, data access time is increased. Physically, the drive will be spinning more, starting and stopping more—in general, more mechanical movement. It's kind of like changing gears excessively with the automatic transmission in your car. The more the drive has to access this fragmented data, the shorter its lifespan becomes due to mechanical wear and tear. But before the drive fails altogether, fragmentation can cause intermittent read/write failures. Defragmenting the drive can be done with Microsoft's Disk Defragmenter, with the command-line `defrag`, or with other third-party programs. If using the Disk Defragmenter program, you need 15 percent free space on the volume you want to defrag. If you have less than that, you need to use the command-line option `defrag -f`. To summarize, the more contiguous the data, the less the hard drive has to work to access that data, thus decreasing the data access time and increasing the lifespan of the drive.

ExamAlert

Know the tools available to defragment a hard drive.

▶ **Scan the drive with antimalware:** Make sure the computer has an antimalware program installed, which includes antivirus and antispyware. Verify that the software is scheduled to scan the drive at least twice a week. (Manufacturers' default is usually every day.) The quicker the software finds and quarantines threats, the less chance of physical damage to the hard drive.

You might find several issues when troubleshooting hard drives:

▶ **BIOS does not "see" the drive:** If the BIOS doesn't recognize the drive you have installed, you can check a few things. First, make sure the power cable is firmly connected and oriented properly. Next, make sure SATA data cables weren't accidentally installed upside down; if you find one that was, consider replacing it because it might be damaged due to incorrect installation. An OS Not Found error message, or other boot failure, could also be caused by improperly connected drives. Finally, check if there is a motherboard BIOS update to see the drive; sometimes newer drives require new BIOS code to access the drive.

▶ **Windows does not "see" a second drive:** There are several reasons why Windows might not see a second drive. Maybe a driver needs to be installed for the drive or for its controller (for example, a PCIe SATA card). Perhaps the secondary drive needs to be initialized within Disk Management. Or it can be that the drive was not partitioned or formatted. Also try the methods listed in the first bullet.

▶ **Slow reaction time:** If the system runs slow, it can be because the drive has become fragmented or has been infected with a virus or spyware. Analyze and defragment the drive. If it is heavily fragmented, the drive can take longer to access the data needed, resulting in slow reaction time. You might be amazed at the difference in performance! If you think the drive might be infected, scan the disk with your antivirus/antispyware software to quarantine any possible threats. It's wise to schedule deep scans of the drive at least twice a week. You will learn more about viruses and spyware in Chapter 17, "Security." In extreme cases, you might want to move all the data from the affected drive to another drive, being sure to verify the data that was moved. Then format the affected drive and, finally, move the data back. This is common in audio/video environments and when dealing with data drives, but it should not be done to a system drive (meaning a drive that contains the operating system).

▶ **Missing files at startup:** If you get a message such as BOOTMGR Is Missing, the file needs to be written back to the hard drive. For more on how to do this, see Chapter 11, "Troubleshooting Windows." In severe cases, this can mean that the drive is physically damaged and needs to be replaced. If this happens, the drive needs to be removed from the computer and slaved off to another drive on another system. Then the data must be copied from the damaged drive to a known good drive (which might require a third-party program), and a new drive must be installed to the affected computer. Afterward, the recovered data can be copied on the new drive.

▶ **Other missing/corrupted files:** Missing or corrupted files could be the result of hard drive failure, operating system failure, malware infection, user error, and so on. If this happens more than once, be sure to back up the rest of the data on the drive, and then use the preventative methods mentioned previously, especially defragmenting and scanning for malware. You can also analyze the drive's S.M.A.R.T. data. S.M.A.R.T. stands for Self-Monitoring, Analysis, and Reporting Technology—it is a monitoring system included with almost all hard drives that creates reporting data which, when enabled in the BIOS, can be accessed within the operating system. OS X and some versions of Linux have built-in tools to view this data. Windows does not, but there are plenty of third-party tools available (HD Tune, SpinRite, and so on) that can be downloaded from the Internet and are very easy to use. The problem with S.M.A.R.T. data is that it can be unreliable at times due to lack of hardware and driver support within the third-party S.M.A.R.T. application, lack of common interpretation, and incorrectly diagnosed data. Also, a hard drive might be diagnosed as a failing drive when in reality the problem is power surges.

> **Note**
>
> If a file is written during a power surge (whether originating internally or externally), that file will most likely be placed on the drive in a corrupted fashion—the associated sector being affected by the power surge. In this case, you should find out two things: 1, if the power supply has the right capacity for the equipment in the computer, and 2, if the proper power suppressing/conditioning equipment is being used. If a drive is making clicking sounds or other strange noises, analysis with S.M.A.R.T. data is not recommended. See the following bullet for more information.

▶ **Noisy drive/lockups:** If your SATA magnetic disk drive starts getting noisy, it's a sure sign of impending drive failure. You might also hear a scratching or grating sound, akin to scratching a record with the record player's needle. Or the drive might intermittently just stop or lock up with one or more audible clicks. You can't wait in these situations; you need to slave off the drive to another computer immediately and copy the data to a good drive. Even then, it might be too late. However, there are some third-party programs available on the Internet that might help recover the data.

As I mentioned, hard drives *will* fail, so it is important to make backups of your data. The backup media of choice will vary depending on the organization. It could be the cloud, a secondary system, DVD-ROM discs, even USB flash drives. It differs based on the scenario. In some cases, an organization might decide to back up to tape. Let's briefly discuss tape drives now.

Tape Drives

Tape drives are devices primarily used for archival or backup of data. These devices use removable media in the form of magnetic tape cartridges, which are inserted into the tape drive. Usage of tape drives has declined greatly in recent years due to the advent of cloud storage and writable optical media, but you might still see some devices in use.

The tape drive is rated in one of two ways: native capacity (for example, 800 GB) or compressed capacity (for example, 1600 GB). As you can see, compressed capacity will normally be at a 2:1 ratio compared to native capacity. Examples of magnetic tapes include Linear Tape-Open (LTO) and the older Digital Linear Tape (DLT).

The tape drive can be internal or external. It might connect via SCSI, SATA, USB, IEEE 1394, or Fibre Channel. For example, the typical connectivity for LTO drives is *Serial Attached SCSI (SAS)*. This provides for high-speed data transfer: SAS-1 = 3.0 Gb/s; SAS-2 = 6.0 Gb/s; SAS-3 = 12.0 Gb/s. The driver for the tape drive must be installed and a tape drive must be used with backup software. Some drives come with their own third-party software, or you can use Windows backup programs. Be careful with these programs. Quite often, they back up all the data into one big compressed file. Be sure to use the verify option when backing up data, and consider running a test backup and restore when you first start using a tape drive to verify it works properly.

Network Attached Storage

Another type of hard drive storage is network attached storage (NAS). This is when one or more hard drives are installed into a device known as a NAS box or NAS server that connects directly to the network. The device can then be accessed via browsing or as a mapped network drive from any computer on the network. For example, a typical two-bay NAS box can hold two SATA drives to be used together as one large capacity or in a RAID 1 mirrored configuration for fault tolerance. RAID 1 mirroring means that two drives are used in unison and all data is written to both drives, giving you a mirror or extra copy of the data if one drive fails. We'll discuss RAID later in this chapter.

These devices connect to the network by way of an RJ45 port (often at 1000 Mb/s) or directly to a computer via USB. Of course, there are much more advanced versions of NAS boxes that would be used by larger companies. These often have *hot-swappable* drives that can be removed and replaced while the device is on. Usually, they are mounted to a plastic enclosure or tray that is slid into the NAS device. But watch out: Not every hard drive in a plastic hard drive enclosure is hot-swappable. There are cheaper versions of this for PCs that can be swapped in and out but not while the computer is on. These devices might work in conjunction with cloud storage and, in some cases, act as cloud storage themselves. It all depends on their usage. The ultimate goal of the NAS box is to allow accessibility of data to multiple users in one or more locations.

Cram Quiz

Answer these questions. The answers follow the last question. If you cannot answer these questions correctly, consider reading this section again until you can.

220-901 Questions

1. What is the maximum data transfer rate of SATA revision 2.0?

   ○ **A.** 3.0 Mb/s

   ○ **B.** 600 MB/s

   ○ **C.** 300 MB/s

   ○ **D.** 1.5 GB/s

2. Which of the following is the delay it takes for the hard drive to access a particular sector on the disk?

   ○ **A.** Actuator

   ○ **B.** Latency

   ○ **C.** Lag

   ○ **D.** Propagation

3. What should you do first to repair a drive that is acting sluggish?

   ○ **A.** Remove the drive and recover the data.

   ○ **B.** Run Disk Cleanup.

   ○ **C.** Run Disk Defragmenter.

   ○ **D.** Scan for viruses.

4. How much data can a SATA revision 3.0 drive transfer per second?

   ○ **A.** 1.5 Gb/s

   ○ **B.** 3.0 Gb/s

   ○ **C.** 4.5 Gb/s

   ○ **D.** 6.0 Gb/s

   ○ **E.** 16.0 Gb/s

5. Which of the following devices is hot-swappable?

   ○ **A.** RAID

   ○ **B.** Tape drive

   ○ **C.** Hard drive

   ○ **D.** DVD drive

6. Which of the following are possible symptoms of hard drive failure? (Select the two best answers.)

○ **A.** System lockup

○ **B.** Antivirus alerts

○ **C.** Failing bootup files

○ **D.** Network drive errors

○ **E.** BIOS doesn't recognize the drive

7. You just replaced a SATA hard drive that you suspected had failed. You also replaced the data cable between the hard drive and the motherboard. When you reboot the computer, you notice that the SATA drive is not recognized by the BIOS. What most likely happened to cause this?

○ **A.** The drive has not been formatted yet.

○ **B.** The BIOS does not support SATA.

○ **C.** The SATA port is faulty.

○ **D.** The drive is not jumpered properly.

8. You are troubleshooting a SATA hard drive that doesn't function on a PC. When you try it on another computer, it works fine. You suspect a power issue and decide to take voltage readings from the SATA power connector coming from the power supply. Which of the following readings should you find?

○ **A.** 5 V and 12 V

○ **B.** 5 V, 12 V, and 24 V

○ **C.** 3.3 V, 5 V, and 12 V

○ **D.** 3.3 V and 12 V

Cram Quiz Answers

220-901 Answers

1. **C.** SATA Revision 2.0 can transfer a maximum of 300 MB/s (but most devices won't ever attain that maximum). The standard specifies the transmission of 3 Gb/s (notice the lowercase 'b' for bits); 600 MB/s is the data transfer rate of SATA Revision 3.0.

2. **B.** Latency is the delay it takes for a magnetic hard disk drive to access the data; it is directly related to the rotational speed (RPM) of the disk.

3. **C.** Attempt to defragment the disk. If it is not necessary, Windows lets you know. Then you can move to other options, such as scanning the drive for viruses.

4. **D.** SATA Revision 3.0 drives can transfer 6.0 Gb/s. Revision 1.0 does 1.5 Gb/s. Revision 2.0 does 3.0 Gb/s. Revision 3.2 is 16 Gb/s.

5. **C.** Hard drives can be hot-swappable. This is common in NAS devices and advanced servers. It is not common in PCs. Tape drives and DVD drives are not hot-swappable. However, they use media that can be inserted and removed while the computer is on. Tricky, eh? Be ready for these types of questions. RAID is not a device, per se, but a technology that can potentially employ hot-swappable drives.

6. **A** and **C.** System lockups and failed boot files or other failing file operations are possible symptoms of hard drive failure. Antivirus alerts tell you that the operating system has been compromised, viruses should be quarantined, and a full scan should be initiated. Sometimes hard drives can fail due to heavy virus activity, but usually if the malware is caught quickly enough, the hard drive should survive. Network drives are separate from the local hard drive; inability to connect to a network drive suggests a network configuration issue. If the BIOS doesn't recognize the drive, consider a BIOS update.

7. **C.** Most likely, the SATA port is faulty. It might have been damaged during the upgrade. To test the theory, you would plug the SATA data cable into another port on the motherboard. We can't format the drive until it has been recognized by the BIOS, which, by the way, should recognize SATA drives if the motherboard has SATA ports! SATA drives don't use jumpers unless they need to coexist with older IDE drives.

8. **C.** If you test a SATA power cable, you should find 3.3 V (orange wire), 5 V (red wire), and 12 V (yellow wire). If any of these don't test properly, try another SATA power connector.

RAID

RAID stands for Redundant Array of Independent (or Inexpensive) Disks. RAID technologies are designed to increase the speed of reading and writing data, to create one of several types of fault-tolerant volumes, or both. Fault tolerance is the capability of the hard drive system to continue working after there is a problem with one of the drives. The exam requires you to know RAID levels 0, 1, 5, and 10. Table 6.2 describes each of these.

TABLE 6.2 **RAID 0, 1, 5, and 10 Descriptions**

RAID Level	Description	Fault Tolerant?	Minimum Number of Disks
RAID 0	Striping. Data is striped across multiple disks in an effort to increase performance.	No	2
RAID 1	Mirroring. Data is copied to two identical disks. If one disk fails, the other continues to operate. When each disk is connected to a separate controller, this is known as Disk Duplexing. See Figure 6.3 for an illustration. RAID 1 is not available in Windows Vista but is available in Windows 7 Professional and Ultimate and Windows 8/8.1.	Yes	2 (and 2 only)
RAID 5	Striping with Parity. Data is striped across multiple disks; fault-tolerant parity data is also written to each disk. If one disk fails, the array can reconstruct the data from the parity information. See Figure 6.4 for an illustration.	Yes	3
RAID 10	Combines the advantages of RAID 1 and RAID 0. Requires a minimum of two disks but will usually have four or more. The system contains at least two mirrored disks that are then striped.	Yes	2 (usually 4)

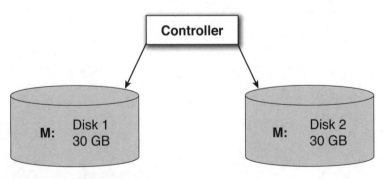

FIGURE 6.3 **RAID 1 illustration**

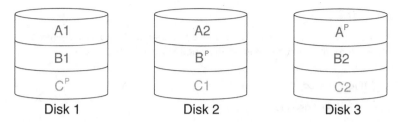

FIGURE 6.4   **RAID 5 illustration**

Even though Windows Vista cannot support RAID 1 from within the operating system, it *can* support hardware controllers that can create RAID arrays. Of course, newer versions of Windows also support hardware-based RAID controllers. Some motherboards have built-in RAID functionality as well. Figure 6.3 shows an illustration of RAID 1; you can see that data is written to both disks and that both disks collectively are known as the M: drive or M: volume. Figure 6.4 displays an illustration of RAID 5. In a RAID 5 array, blocks of data are distributed to the disks (A1 and A2 are a block, B1 and B2 are a block, and so on) and parity information is written for each block of data. This is written to each disk in an alternating fashion (Ap, Bp, and such) so that the parity is also distributed. If one disk fails, the parity information from the other disks will reconstruct the data.

Remember that hard drive arrays should be built using identical drives. That means using a group of the same magnetic disk drives or a group of the same solid-state drives. Deviate from this suggestion at your own risk!

It is important to make the distinction between fault tolerance and backup. Fault tolerance means that the hard drives can continue to function (with little or no downtime) even if there is a problem with one of the drives. Backup means that you are copying the data (and possibly compressing it) to another location for archival in the event of a disaster. An example of a disaster would be if two drives in a RAID 5 array were to fail.

Sometimes, hardware RAID arrays will fail. They might stop working or the OS could have trouble finding them. If you see an issue like this, check whether the hard drives are securely connected to the controller and that the controller (if an adapter card) is securely connected to the motherboard. Also, if you use a RAID adapter card or external enclosure, and the motherboard also has built-in RAID functionality of its own, make sure you disable the motherboard RAID within the BIOS—it could cause a conflict. Verify that the driver for the RAID device is installed and updated. Finally, check if any of the hard drives or the RAID controller has failed. If a RAID controller built into a motherboard fails, you will have to purchase a RAID adapter card.

Cram Quiz

Answer these questions. The answers follow the last question. If you cannot answer these questions correctly, consider reading this section again until you can.

220-901 Questions

1. Which level of RAID uses two disks only?

   ○ **A.** RAID 0

   ○ **B.** RAID 1

   ○ **C.** RAID 5

   ○ **D.** Striping

2. Which level of RAID stripes data and parity across three or more disks?

   ○ **A.** RAID 0

   ○ **B.** RAID 1

   ○ **C.** RAID 5

   ○ **D.** Striping

3. Which level of RAID contains two sets of mirrored disks that are then striped?

   ○ **A.** RAID 0

   ○ **B.** RAID 1

   ○ **C.** RAID 5

   ○ **D.** RAID 10

Cram Quiz Answers

220-901 Answers

1. **B.** RAID 1 (mirroring) uses two disks only. RAID 0 (striping) can use two disks or more. RAID 5 (striping with parity) can use three disks or more.

2. **C.** RAID 5 stripes data and parity across three or more disks. RAID 0 does not stripe parity; it stripes data only and can use two disks or more. RAID 1 uses two disks only. Striping is another name for RAID 0.

3. **D.** RAID 10 contains two sets of mirrored disks that are then striped. RAID 0 is a set of two or more disks that stripe data. RAID 1 is a mirror. RAID 5 is striping with parity.

Optical Storage Media

The three main types of optical media in use today are compact discs (CDs), digital versatile discs (DVDs), and Blu-ray discs. These discs have a variety of functions, including audio, video, application, data, and so on. Some discs can be read from and some can also be written to. Finally, some discs can be rewritten to as well. It all depends on which media you use. Now there are a lot of different versions of optical media; let's try to organize them so that they will be easier to remember. We start with the most familiar: the compact disc.

> **ExamAlert**
>
> You've probably noticed by now that most magnetic media is known as "disk" and optical media is known as "disc." Keep this in mind for the exam.

Compact Disc (CD)

A CD is a flat, round, optical disc used to store music, sounds, or other data. It can be read from a compact disc player. For example, audio CDs can be played on a compact disc player that is part of a stereo or a computer. However, data CDs can be read only from CD-ROM drives that are part of, or externally connected to, a computer. The A+ exam focuses on data CDs, so let's talk about some of the different data CD technologies.

Data CD Technologies

The most common acronym that comes to mind is the CD-ROM (compact disc-read-only memory). Data is written to a CD-ROM in a similar way that audio is written to a music CD; a laser shines on the reflective surface of the CD and stores data as a plethora of microscopic indentations known as lands and pits. These are the types of CDs you get when you purchase a computer program or game. They can be read from but not written to and can be read only from a compatible CD-ROM drive. CD-ROM drives are rated in read speeds (for example, 48x). The x equals 150 KB/s. So to calculate a CD-ROM drive's maximum read speed, you multiply the number preceding the x by 150 KB. In this example, this would be 48 × 150 KB = 7.2 MB/s.

Over time, the technology to write to CDs was developed, enabling users to store information to CD that they would previously store on outdated technologies, such as floppy disks or Zip drives. A typical CD can hold up to 700 MB of data, but there are 650 MB, 800 MB, and 900 MB versions available as well. Table 6.3 describes the two most common recordable technologies.

TABLE 6.3 **Comparison of CD Recording Technologies**

Technology	Full Name	Typical Maximum Recording Speed
CD-R	Compact Disc-Recordable	48x (7.2 MB/s) or 52x (7.8 MB/s)
CD-RW	Compact Disc-ReWritable	24x (3.6 MB/s) or 32x (4.8 MB/s)

Most optical drives that you can purchase for a computer today have all three compact disc functions. They can read from CD-ROMs, write to CD-Rs, and write/rewrite to CD-RWs. Usually, the read speed and CD-R speed are the same.

> **ExamAlert**
>
> Know the difference between CD-ROM, CD-R, and CD-RW.

SATA CD-ROM drives connect the same way as their hard drive counterparts: a 7-pin data cable and a 15-pin power cable. SATA CD-ROMs send stereo music information directly through the data cable, unlike older technologies (such as IDE) that utilized a separate stereo audio cable.

CD-ROM discs are known as removable media; however, the drive is normally fixed in the computer. It installs much like a SATA hard drive. One notable exception is that most CD-ROM drives are 5.25 inches wide (instead of 3.5 or 2.5 inches). So they must be installed to one of the larger bays in a case that has an opening on the front; this way, the drive tray is accessible. Most CD-ROM drives can also play audio CDs and they have a volume knob on the front. In addition, many drives have a pinhole near the volume knob. This small hole is for when a CD (or the tray) gets jammed. Insert a paper clip into the hole to attempt to free the tray and CD. Most other optical drives have this feature as well.

> **ExamAlert**
>
> The paper clip should be added to your toolkit; it dislodges jammed optical trays.

Digital Versatile Disc (DVD)

For data, Digital Versatile Discs, also known as Digital Video Discs, are the successor to CDs for a variety of reasons. First, they can be used to play and record video. Second, they have a much greater capacity than CDs. This is because the pits etched into the surface of the DVD are smaller than CD pits (.74 micrometers compared to 1.6 micrometers). Also, DVDs can be written to faster than CDs. There are read-only DVDs and writable DVDs; however, there are a lot more variations of DVDs than there are CDs. Table 6.4 describes some of the DVD-ROM (Digital Versatile Disc-Read-Only Memory) versions, specifications, and differences starting with the common DVD-5 version.

TABLE 6.4 **Comparison of DVD Technologies**

DVD-ROM Technology	Sides	Total Layers	Capacity
DVD-5	1	1	4.7 GB
DVD-9	1	2	8.5 GB
DVD-10	2	2	9.4 GB
DVD-14	2	3	13.2 GB
DVD-18	2	4	17 GB

The most common DVD is currently the single-sided, single-layer (SS, SL) DVD-5 technology that can store 4.7 GB of data. But some DVDs can be written to two sides (known as dual-sided or DS); simply flip the DVD to access the information on the other side. Layers however work differently. A DVD with two layers (known as dual layer or DL) incorporates both layers onto a single side of the disc. The second layer is actually underneath the first one; the DVD laser reads this second layer by shining through the first semi-transparent layer. By combining dual-sided and dual-layer technologies, you end up with a DVD that can store up to 17 GB of data (known as DVD-18) at 8.5 GB per side.

ExamAlert

Know the capacity of DVD-5 and DVD-18 for the exam.

Once again, for DVD-ROMs and recordable DVDs, the most common is DVD-5. Typically, a DVD drive reads these discs at 16x. However, the x in DVD speeds is different than the x in CD-ROM speeds. For DVDs, the x means approximately 1.32 MB/s or about nine times the core CD speed. So a typical 16x DVD is equal to 21 MB/s. Typically, a DVD drive reads at 16x, records once at 22x or 24x, and rewrites at 6x or 8x. Table 6.5 provides a description of the different types of recordable DVDs.

TABLE 6.5   **Comparison of DVD Recordable Technologies**

DVD Recordable Technology	Capacity	Typical Write Speed*
DVD–R SL	4.707 GB	22x or 24x
DVD+R SL	4.700 GB	22x or 24x
DVD–R DL	8.544 GB	12x
DVD+R DL	8.548 GB	16x
DVD–RW SL or DL	4.707 or 8.544 GB	6x
DVD+RW SL or DL	4.700 or 8.548 GB	8x

* The write speeds vary from drive to drive. The stated typical speeds are the write speeds of a Samsung combo drive (DVD/CD) used for this book.

As you can see in Table 6.5, there is a slight difference in capacity between DVD– and DVD+. DVD– was developed by Pioneer and approved by the DVD Forum; DVD+ was developed by a group of corporations headed up by Sony. Likewise, DVD–RW was developed by Pioneer and approved by the DVD Forum; DVD+RW was developed by the same group of corporations that developed DVD+R. This group is now known as the DVD+RW Alliance. It's probably not important to know this for the exam, because most DVD drives support all these formats. However, always check your drive to be sure before purchasing recordable DVDs.

Like most CD-ROM drives, the bulk of DVD drives connect via SATA. Most DVD drives are known as combo drives, meaning they can read and write to CDs and read DVDs (DVD-ROM drive), write DVDs (DVDR), and rewrite DVDs (DVDRW). Some drives also include features such as LightScribe technology, which can create labels by etching text and graphics onto specially coated CDs and DVDs.

Because they are relatively cheap, DVD drives—like CD-ROM drives—are usually replaced if they fail. It could easily cost a company more money to try to repair a DVD drive than to simply purchase one for $10 to $20. However, if a problem does occur, remember to check the obvious; it takes only a few minutes. For example, if a DVD (or CD) drive tray won't open, press the eject button one time and wait. It can take a few moments for the DVD to spin down before opening. Then press it a few more times, waiting a couple of moments after each time. You can also try to eject the disc from within the operating system. To do this, go to Windows Explorer (or File Explorer), right-click the drive in question, and then select Eject. If this doesn't work, you can try to restart the computer and try the eject options again. Don't forget the pinhole near the open button. You can slide a paper clip in there to get the tray to open. Sometimes, DVD drives have been installed with incorrect screws that are too long. This can cause damage to the drive tray. Finally, make sure that the drive is getting power! A loose SATA power connector results in the tray not opening or closing.

DVD and CD Usage

DVDs are used as much or more than CDs in computers nowadays. The only place where DVDs haven't taken off is in the music arena. Although DVD-Audio (DVD-A) discs arguably have superior audio quality compared to audio CDs (DVD-A boasts a 24-bit rate and up to 192 kHz sampling compared to a CD's 16-bit/44 kHz), not many people have DVD-Audio players, so the audio CD is still the most common of the two.

Blu-ray

Currently, Blu-ray is *the* standard for high-definition video. It is used by high-def movies, console games, and for storing data (up to 50 GB per disc, 10 times the amount of a typical DVD-5 disc). The standard disc is 12 cm (the same size as a standard DVD or CD) and the mini-disc is 8 cm. Table 6.6 shows some of the Blu-ray specs.

TABLE 6.6 **Comparison of Blu-ray Specifications**

Blu-ray Type	Layers	Capacity
Standard disc, single-layer	1	25 GB
Standard disc, dual-layer	2	50 GB
Standard disc, XL 3 layer	3	100 GB
Standard disc, XL 4 layer	4	128 GB
Mini-disc, single-layer	1	7.8 GB
Mini-disc, dual-layer	2	15.6 GB

> **Note**
>
> Triple- and quadruple-layer discs can be accessed by BD-XL drives.

Drive speeds range from 1x to 16x (with more undoubtedly on the way). 1x is equal to 36 Mb/s or 4.5 MB/s. A 16x would be 16 times that core amount, which is 576 Mb/s or 72 MB/s, which is superior to DVD write speeds. Single-layer discs, though their capacity is half, can be written to in half the time of dual-layer discs.

To play movies, games, or read the data from a Blu-ray disc, the computer must have a compatible Blu-ray drive. Currently, there are combo drives on the market that can read Blu-ray discs (but not write to them; these are known as BD-ROMs), read/write DVDs, and read/write CDs.

Like CD and DVD drives, Blu-ray drives for the PC are installed into a 5.25-inch bay in the computer case. If you upgrade a computer, the power supply needs an extra 15-pin SATA power connector and the motherboard (or SATA card) needs to have one free SATA data port.

I just had to install Blu-ray drives to the *AV Editor* and *Media PC* computers. These computers wouldn't be complete without the ability to watch Blu-ray movies! Typically, these drives read Blu-ray discs as well as DVD and CD and can write to DVD-ROMs and CD-ROMs. However, if I wanted to burn a lot of data to a single disc (for example, 20 GB or more), I would have to upgrade to a Blu-ray burner, which often comes with disc encryption methods as well. (Refer to Chapter 17 for more about encryption.) There are two methods of burning Blu-ray discs: Blu-ray Disc Recordable (BD-R), which can write to a disc once, and Blu-ray Disc Recordable Erasable (BD-RE), which can be erased and re-recorded multiple times. Burning speed depends on the drive, but as of the writing of this book, there are some that can go as high as 16x. To burn discs in Blu-ray format, you must either install the drivers and software that came with the drive or utilize a third-party program.

ExamAlert

Know the differences between BD-R and BD-RE for the exam.

Cram Quiz

Answer these questions. The answers follow the last question. If you cannot answer these questions correctly, consider reading this section again until you can.

220-901 Questions

1. What does the x refer to in Compact Disc technology?

   ○ **A.** 150 KB/s

   ○ **B.** 1.32 MB/s

   ○ **C.** 150 MB/s

   ○ **D.** 4.5 MB/s

2. Which of the following has the largest potential for storage capacity?

   ○ **A.** CD-R

   ○ **B.** CD-RW

   ○ **C.** DVD-RW

   ○ **D.** Blu-ray

3. What is the maximum capacity of a standard size, dual-layer Blu-ray disc?

   ○ **A.** 700 MB

   ○ **B.** 4.7 GB

   ○ **C.** 17 GB

   ○ **D.** 50 GB

4. If a user wants to write information more than one time to a DVD, which type should you recommend? (Select all that apply.)

   ○ **A.** DVD-R

   ○ **B.** DVD–RW

   ○ **C.** DVD+RW

   ○ **D.** DVD+R

5. A customer complains that an important disc is stuck in the computer's DVD-ROM drive. What should you recommend to the customer?

   ○ **A.** To get a screwdriver and disassemble the drive

   ○ **B.** To format the disc

   ○ **C.** To use a paper clip to eject the tray

   ○ **D.** To dispose of the drive and replace the media

6. A marketing kiosk requires a CD-ROM to be in the drive for the program to work correctly. However, the kiosk fails to boot when restarted. What should you do?

- ○ **A.** Change the drive letter assignments.
- ○ **B.** Defrag the hard drive.
- ○ **C.** Replace the CD-ROM with rewritable media.
- ○ **D.** Configure the BIOS settings.

7. One of your customers attempts to copy a DVD with a third-party application. It reads the source DVD fine, but when a blank disc is inserted, the program keeps asking the customer to insert blank media. What are some possible reasons for this? (Select the three best answers.)

- ○ **A.** The customer is using the wrong DVD type.
- ○ **B.** The program cannot copy the DVD due to copyright laws.
- ○ **C.** There isn't enough free space on the hard drive.
- ○ **D.** A CD was inserted into the drive.
- ○ **E.** The drive is a CD-RW drive.
- ○ **F.** The DVD was inserted upside down.

Cram Quiz Answers

220-901 Answers

1. **A.** The x in CD technology is equal to 150 KB/s. A 1x drive can read or write 150 KB/s, a 2x drive can read or write 300 KB/s, and so on. 1.32 MB/s is the 1x speed of a DVD. 150 MB/s is the maximum data transfer rate of a SATA revision 1.0 drive. 4.5 MB/s is the 1x speed of a Blu-ray disc.

2. **D.** Blu-ray, at a maximum of 50 GB, has the largest storage capacity. CDs top out just under 1 GB. DVDs have a maximum of 17 GB.

3. **D.** Standard size (12 cm) dual-layer Blu-ray discs have a maximum capacity of 50 GB. A typical CD capacity is 700 MB. 4.7 GB is the capacity of the common DVD-5. 17 GB is the capacity of a DVD-18 (using both sides).

4. **B and C.** DVD–RW and DVD+RW are the rewritable versions of DVDs. DVD-R and DVD+R are write-once formats.

5. **C.** Tell the customer to use a paper clip to eject the DVD-ROM tray. Disassembling the drive is not necessary; the customer shouldn't be told to do this. If the disc is rewritable, formatting it would erase the contents, even if you could format in this scenario. Never tell a customer to dispose of a DVD-ROM drive; they rarely fail.

6. **D.** You should configure the BIOS boot order so that the CD-ROM is first; then the kiosk computer will boot to that drive. Changing drive letter assignments in the operating system will have no effect on the boot order. The hard drive has nothing to do with this scenario. And if you replace the CD-ROM, you lose the program that the kiosk needs to boot to.

7. **A, D, and F.** If the source DVD was read fine, there are three possible correct answers: A blank CD was inserted into the drive; an incorrect DVD type was inserted into the drive; or the DVD was inserted upside down. The hard drive doesn't play into this scenario because the program's message is simply to insert blank media. The drive can't be a CD-RW if it accepted the source DVD.

Solid-State Storage Media

There are many types of solid-state media. Solid-state media, by definition, is media with no moving parts; it is based on the semiconductor. Most of these are implemented as large amounts of nonvolatile memory, known as flash memory, and are located on a card or drive. Remember that *nonvolatile* means any data on the device is retained, even if the device is not receiving power. Examples of cards include SD cards and CompactFlash cards. Examples of solid-state drives (SSDs) include the SATA solid-state drive, USB flash drives, and even PCIe drives (which are integrated into a PCIe storage card for extreme speed—heads up for you gamers and media enthusiasts). This section focuses on three types of solid-state media: USB flash drives, SD cards, and CompactFlash.

USB Flash Drives

The USB flash drive is probably the most familiar of all flash media. Also known as USB thumb drives, they are often retractable and can be carried on a keychain. Figure 6.5 shows an example of a USB flash drive connected to a laptop's USB port.

FIGURE 6.5   A typical USB flash drive in a laptop's USB port

Notice that the USB flash drive is lit, indicating that it is connected to the laptop's USB port and ready to transfer data. In this scenario, the drive shows up as a volume within Windows Explorer (or File Explorer), usually named Removable Disk. Connecting the drive is easy; just find an open USB port. But remember that you should safely remove hardware in the operating system before disconnecting the drive physically. If you don't, it can cause electrical irregularities that can damage the data on the drive. In Windows, right-click the "Safely Remove Hardware and Eject Media" icon in the Notification Area, and then click Eject to shut down power to the selected USB device. Then it can be safely removed from the physical USB port. The icon appears as a USB cable with a check mark. If your USB device has a light, make sure that light is off before physically removing the device. You can also "eject" optical drives and virtual drives in this manner.

ExamAlert

Remember to *safely remove* USB flash drives in the operating system before physically disconnecting them.

Tip

Sometimes a USB or other flash-based, solid-state device can't be removed with the Safely Remove Hardware option in Windows. If this happens, consider shutting down the computer before physically disconnecting the device to avoid data corruption or loss.

The advantages of a USB flash drive are obvious. For example, the drive in Figure 6.5 is an 8 GB flash drive that cost approximately $6. That is a good cost-to-MB ratio for an instantly rewritable media. It would take 2 standard DVD-RWs or 10 standard CD-RWs to match that capacity. The best part is that no special setup is necessary; data can simply be dragged and dropped to the drive (unlike CDs and DVDs, which need to be burned). In addition, a USB flash drive's read/write speed is comparable to DVD technology, averaging about 30 MB/s reads and 15 MB/s writes. Finally, it's *small*, so it has a little footprint. What I used to carry around in a CD case is now on one flash drive on my keychain. Plus, newer flash drives range in size to 256 GB and beyond and have a much longer lifespan than just a few years ago. They can also be used to boot or install operating systems.

Let's talk about the type of memory used in this solid-state device: NAND flash memory is the core of a USB flash drive. This memory is divided into blocks that are generally between 16 KB and 512 KB. Know that a USB flash drive's blocks can be written to only so many times before failures occur.

With some flash drives, manufacturers estimate this limit is 1 million write/ erase cycles or 10 years of use. However, just like hard drives will never attain their maximum data transfer rate, it is doubtful that a flash drive will ever attain that maximum number of write/erase cycles. In addition, the number of years is subjective; it all depends on how often a user works with the flash drive. Basically, if you take the number given by the manufacturer and cut it in half, you should be in good shape, unless you are an extreme power user. Now back to NAND flash failures: Because this type of memory incurs a small amount of faults over time (as opposed to NOR flash, which should remain free of faults), a method known as Bad Block Management is implemented. Bad Block Management maintains a table of the faulty blocks within the USB flash device, making sure not to save data to those blocks. Blocks are divided into pages, which can be between 512 bytes and 4 KB. Each page has error detection and correction information associated with it. All this is done to prolong the lifespan of devices that use NAND memory.

Normally, USB flash drives are shipped in a formatted state, usually FAT32. This enables the drive to be accessed by just about any computer on the market and makes for easy repair of corrupted files with Windows utilities. If the user so chooses, these drives can also be formatted as NTFS. Sometimes NAND flash devices (such as USB flash drives) act up intermittently. Unless the device has failed completely, a quick reformat usually cures the flash drive of its woes. Just be sure to back up your data first! This method applies to other forms of solid-state, NAND-based media.

Troubleshooting of these devices is not usually necessary, but you might see a couple of issues:

▶ Sometimes USB flash drives and other solid-state media can conflict with each other, prompting you to change the drive letter of one or more devices within Disk Management.

▶ USB flash drives might intermittently fail when writing or reading data. As this occurs more often, consider reformatting the drive. After reformatting, test the drive by moving files to it and then opening them. Of course, after a certain point, the drive will fail and will need to be replaced.

In general, make sure that your operating system has the latest updates installed. For more information on USB, see Chapter 13, "Peripherals and Custom Computing."

Some USB flash drives are preloaded with software that can restore data and possibly secure transferred data. The only problem with USB flash drives is that although they are small, they can't fit inside most digital cameras, smartphones, and other handheld devices. For that, you need something even smaller: Enter the SD card.

Secure Digital Cards

Secure Digital cards (SD cards), for the most part, are technically the same type of device as a USB flash drive. They are solid-state, they use NAND memory, and they have most of the same pros and cons as a USB flash drive. The difference is the form factor of the SD device; because of this, SDs are used differently. Instead of connecting an SD card to a USB port of a computer, it slides into a Memory Card Reader. There are specialized Memory Card Readers for SD cards only and other readers that can read multiple formats of cards. Like USB flash drives, be sure to use the Safely Remove Hardware icon in Windows before physically removing the SD card. There are three sizes of SD cards, each smaller than the last: standard (32 mm × 24 mm), miniSD (21.5 mm × 20 mm), and microSD (15 mm × 11 mm). You can still find many standard-sized SD cards used in cameras and some other devices but note that most cell phones and smartphones use microSD cards for additional memory. Figure 6.6 shows a full-size SD card and a microSD card. Figure 6.7 shows the standard SD card inserted into a laptop's Memory Card Reader slot. Note that this slot can accommodate SD cards or smaller but nothing bigger than an SD card.

FIGURE 6.6   A typical microSD card (left) and a standard SD card (right)

FIGURE 6.7   A standard SD card inserted in a laptop's Memory Card Reader.

> **Note**
>
> You might run across an xD-Picture Card. This is a flash memory technology similar to SD that is used in some older digital cameras.

Standard SD cards have capacities up to 4 GB. High-capacity (SDHC) cards range up to 32 GB. The newer eXtended Capacity (SDXC) has a maximum capacity of 2 TB, but as of the writing of this book, typical capacities include 64, 128, 256, and 512 GB. When it comes to data transfer rate, SD cards are divided into a variety of classes: SD Class 2, 4, 6, and 10 as well as UHS 1 and 3, each with a different range of speeds. For example, Class 10, required for Full HD video recording (1080p), has a minimum data writing speed of 10 MB/s. To record 4K video, you would need at least UHS 3, which has a minimum data writing speed of 30 MB/s.

> **ExamAlert**
>
> Know the different capacities of standard SD, SDHC, and SDXC.

Another difference between USB flash drives and SD cards is that many typical SD cards today (such as SDXC cards) are formatted by the manufacturer as exFAT instead of FAT32. (For more information on file systems, see Chapter 9, "Configuring Windows."

Some SD cards, like the one shown in Figure 6.6, have a write-protect tab within the notch on the left side of the card. Sliding the tab down "locks" the card so that it can be read from but not written to.

You might encounter an issue where a newer SDHC or SDXC card will not work in a PC or laptop card reader, but older standard SD cards work fine. This suggests that the card reader needs the latest firmware and drivers.

SD Cards were introduced in 1999 as an improvement over the MultiMediaCard (MMC) standard. Though you will normally use an SD card for portable devices such as camcorders and cameras, your smartphone or tablet will probably use embedded MMC (eMMC) instead for its main storage. eMMC can typically transfer data at 400 MB/s (as of the writing of this book).

CompactFlash Cards

CompactFlash (CF) is another kind of solid-state memory that can be used in a variety of formats, the most common of which is the CompactFlash card. These are categorized as either Type I cards that are 3.3 mm thick or Type II cards that are 5 mm thick. These cards are larger than SD cards and are often used in handheld computers, high-end cameras (Type I), and Microdrives (Type II).

Common capacities for CF cards max out at about 32 GB; however, the technology can go as high as 137 GB. The cards are formatted by the manufacturer as either the FAT32 or FAT file system; the formatting is done in the same manner as USB flash drives and SD cards. Like USB flash drives and SD cards, CF cards have a built-in ATA controller that makes them appear as a hard drive to the operating system; they show up as a volume within Windows Explorer. In the past, CompactFlash cards used NOR memory; today, they are typically NAND-based, again like USB flash drives and SD cards. The data transfer rate ranges from 6 to 133 MB/s. CF speeds have increased with each new version, starting with the original CF and moving on to CF High Speed, CF 3.0, and so on. For example, CF 4.0 allows for a maximum data transfer rate of 133 MB/s. CF 6.0 brings this number up to 167 MB/s. Newer versions allow for larger block transfers of data (up to 32 MB) and higher capacities.

Cram Quiz

Answer these questions. The answers follow the last question. If you cannot answer these questions correctly, consider reading this section again until you can.

220-901 Questions

1. What should you do before physically removing a USB flash drive? (Select the best answer.)

   ○ **A.** Turn it off.

   ○ **B.** Shut down Windows.

   ○ **C.** Format the drive.

   ○ **D.** Use the Safely Remove Hardware icon.

2. How are most SD cards formatted by the manufacturer?

   ○ **A.** As FAT32

   ○ **B.** As NTFS

   ○ **C.** As exFAT

   ○ **D.** As FAT16

3. Which type of controller is built into a CF card?

   ○ **A.** SATA

   ○ **B.** IDE

   ○ **C.** ATA

   ○ **D.** SCSI

4. You discover that a newer SDXC card won't work in the card reader of a user's PC. It works fine in another computer's card reader and standard SD cards work fine in the user's PC. What should you do to fix the problem?

   ○ **A.** Format the card.

   ○ **B.** Install the latest firmware and drivers.

   ○ **C.** Purchase a new external USB card reader.

   ○ **D.** Use a CF card instead.

Cram Quiz Answers

220-901 Answers

1. **D.** In Windows, right-click the Safely Remove Hardware icon in the Notification Area and then click Eject to shut down power to the device. Shutting off Windows is another possibility, but it's not the best answer because it is time-consuming.

2. **C.** exFAT is the most common file system used by SD cards (especially SDXC). FAT32 is the standard for USB flash drives. NTFS is the file system used by Windows. If they want to, users can reformat most solid-state devices as NTFS. FAT16 is an older file system (simply known as FAT) used in legacy Windows systems.

3. **C.** An ATA controller is built into the CF card. ATA (for example, Ultra ATA/133) is SATA's predecessor. This technology was used by the now-deprecated IDE drive. SCSI is another less used technology meant for servers and power workstations.

4. **B.** If older SD cards work but new ones don't, install the latest firmware and/or drivers for the card reader. Do this before trying other technologies or making purchases. No reason to try formatting the card if it works fine on another computer.

CHAPTER 7

Mobile Device Hardware

This chapter covers the following A+ exam topics:

▶ Installing, Configuring, and Troubleshooting Visible Laptop Components

▶ Installing, Configuring, and Troubleshooting Internal Laptop Components

▶ Understanding Tablet and Smartphone Hardware

You can find a master list of A+ exam topics in the "Introduction."

This chapter covers CompTIA A+ 220-901 objectives 3.1 through 3.5, and 4.5.

Now we move away from the stationary computer and move into the realm of the mobile computer. For the purposes of simplicity, I refer to laptops as mobile devices but I also include smartphones and tablets in the mobile computing category. Let's face it, they are all computers, and they are all portable or mobile. In your travels, you might encounter different terminology in this regard, but for this book, the term *mobile devices* includes any portable computers (laptops, tablets, and smartphones).

We begin the chapter with laptops and discuss their visible and internal components. For the exams, it is important to identify the components of a laptop and the ports that surround the machine, how to install and configure hardware, and how to take care of and troubleshoot the laptop. In many respects, laptops work the same way as desktop computers. This chapter focuses on the differences that make a laptop stand out from the desktop PC.

Then we move on to smartphones and tablet PCs. Know that the A+ exams require only that you know the basics of these devices' hardware. Due to warranties, the amount of repair you perform on these devices will be limited. If the warranty has expired or if you work for a mobile device manufacturer or repair shop, you will need to learn more. But for the A+ exams, the content covered in this chapter will suffice.

In this chapter, we focus on hardware only. Software will be covered later in the book. This way we can keep hardware and software separate. Let's get to it.

Installing, Configuring, and Troubleshooting Visible Laptop Components

Ah, the laptop. The beauty of laptops is that they are portable, and all the connections are right at your fingertips. However, quite often there is a trade-off in performance and in price—that is, in comparison to PCs. This chapter assumes a basic knowledge of laptops and jumps straight into how to install, configure, and troubleshoot laptop devices.

Laptops were originally designed for niche markets but today are often used in businesses and at home. Laptops (also known as notebooks or portable computers) have integrated displays, keyboards, and pointing devices, making them easy to transport and easy to use in confined spaces.

In this section, we discuss the visible components of the laptop, such as the keyboard and the display. These two devices are probably the most prone to failure, so we discuss some methods and step by steps on how to repair them. In addition, we talk about a laptop's audio, power, expansion buses, and optical disc drives.

Laptop 101

For the exam, it is important to identify the main components of a laptop and its ports. Figure 7.1 shows some of the main components of the laptop.

The main components of the laptop include the liquid crystal display (LCD), keyboard (with the special Fn key), touchpad, the Power button, and extra buttons. The extra buttons offer additional functionality (for example, enabling and disabling wireless, turning the sound on or off, and opening applications such as web browsers and e-mail applications).

A laptop manufacturer needs to squeeze in ports wherever it can find space, so quite often you find ports on various sides of the laptop. These can include (but are not limited to) the following:

▶ USB, for keyboards, mice, and so on

▶ RJ45, for network connections

▶ HDMI, for external video monitors and projectors

Power and Extra Buttons   LCD

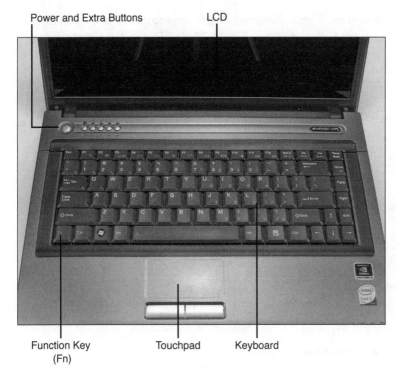

Function Key   Touchpad   Keyboard
(Fn)

FIGURE 7.1   **A typical laptop's main components**

You might also see other video and audio ports. We'll talk about all of these ports and technologies in more depth in Chapter 12, "Video and Audio," and Chapter 13, "Peripherals and Custom Computing."

Input Devices

Inputting information to a laptop is just like inputting information to a PC, except all of the devices are miniaturized. Laptops have a few different input devices, such as keyboards, pointing devices, and the stylus.

Keyboards and Function Keys

Some laptops have keyboards similar to the 101-key keyboard found on a PC and include a numeric keypad; these laptops are larger than most and are known as desktop replacements. However, most laptops are designed with a small form factor in mind, and this means a smaller keyboard. For example, the keyboard in Figure 7.2 has 86 keys. But as shown in the figure, a user has the option of using the Fn key. The Fn key (Function key) is a modifier key used on most laptops. This is designed to activate secondary or special functions of other keys. For example, in Figure 7.2, the F8 key has the secondary function of "volume up" but only if you press the Fn key at the same time you press the F8 key.

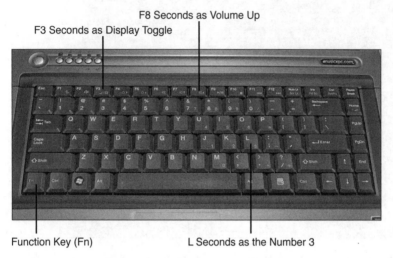

FIGURE 7.2 **A typical laptop keyboard**

Using this method, much more functionality can be incorporated into the keyboard without the need for additional keys. This idea has since grown to include all kinds of controls (for example, using media player controls; putting the computer to sleep; and enabling Bluetooth, the keyboard backlight, the touchpad, GPS, and a variety of other functions, including enabling an external monitor). On this laptop, the F3 key seconds as a display toggle between the built-in LCD and an external monitor. In addition, the entire numeric keypad is added to the keyboard as secondary keys. For example, in Figure 7.2, the L key seconds as the number 3, but this works only if the Number Lock (Num Lock) key has been enabled. (The Fn key is not necessary for the numeric keypad to work.) Quite often, users forget about the Num Lock key, and when they try to type, strange garbled code comes out! Simply press the Num Lock key once to fix the problem. This is also common if the user works with an external keyboard at the office and disconnects it when leaving the office.

ExamAlert

Press the Num Lock key to enable/disable the numeric keypad on a laptop. If the Num Lock indicator light is on, then the numeric key is enabled.

I have had a dozen people I know approach me telling me that their laptop's keyboard wasn't working properly. Over time I've noticed several culprits: overuse, loose ribbon cables, spilled coffee, or users simply pounding the tar out of the keyboard! Here are a couple of problems you might encounter:

▶ **Stuck keys:** Sticking keys could be a result of overuse, damage to the individual key's switch, or liquid spilled on the keyboard. (And if a stuck key is the worst that happens due to a liquid spill, consider yourself lucky!) A stuck key can be identified by the key failing to work in the operating system or the BIOS reporting a 3xx error. (It might say something similar to Keyboard Stuck Key Failure.) If there is a BIOS error, look for a two-digit hexadecimal code just before the 3xx error. This code identifies which key(s) is stuck. Of course, you have to access your BIOS documentation to find out which key a particular hexadecimal code refers to. (In some cases, this will be based off of the standard ASCII printable character code.) By removing the keycap and cleaning the keyswitch underneath, you can usually fix the problem. If not, the entire keyboard will probably have to be replaced. See Table 7.1 for more information.

▶ **Loose connection:** If the laptop is moved around and jostled a lot, as many laptops are, it could possibly cause loose connections. One of these is the ribbon cable that connects the keyboard to the motherboard. To fix this, the keyboard must be lifted away from the laptop and the ribbon cable attached securely. Follow the steps listed in Table 7.1 to accomplish this.

▶ **Damaged keyboard:** Users who inadvertently drop heavy items onto the keyboard or operate the keyboard with a heavy hand might cause a warped or bent keyboard. Some brands of laptops suffer from this more than others. This is usually impossible to repair; the keyboard often needs to be replaced, as shown in Table 7.1.

TABLE 7.1 **Steps Involved in Replacing a Laptop Keyboard**

Step	Procedure
1. Prepare the laptop for surgery!	Shut down the laptop, unplug it, and disconnect the battery. Then employ ESD prevention measures. Because there is nowhere on a laptop to connect an antistatic strap or mat, you need to connect these to the chassis of a nearby unplugged desktop computer or to a proper earth bonding point of some sort.

Step	Procedure
2. Remove the trim or cover.	The keyboard might be accessed from underneath the laptop, in which case the entire cover must be removed, and a lot of components must be removed as well. Or, it might be accessed by removing a piece of plastic trim from the top near the keyboard. The trim might be between the keyboard and the monitor, or it might surround the keyboard. The plastic trim might have to be pried out with a thin, flat tool, which can be a little tricky. You can use wooden trim sticks, which are thin, cylindrical pieces of wood that have an angled edge (available at drug stores, craft stores, and some hardware stores), to get underneath plastic housings, or you can use a fine flathead screwdriver (though wood or plastic is preferred). In addition, some laptops come with a special tool to remove trim, bezels, and hinge covers. Go slow and be gentle with the plastic parts that snap in and out of the laptop case.
3. Remove the screws.	When the trim or cover is removed, you should see two screws. You might need a small Phillips head screwdriver or a small Torx screwdriver. (Some laptops require smaller Torx screwdrivers than PCs do—as low as T8 or even T6—something to add to your computer repair toolkit!)
4. Disconnect the keyboard.	When the keyboard can be lifted up, you can see it is connected to the system board by a ribbon cable, also known as a flex cable. Figure 7.3 shows the keyboard lifted up and the back displaying the flex cable connector. Be gentle with this cable and its connection. The connector usually has two locking tabs, one on each end of the flex cable connector. Unlocking this is a delicate procedure; the locks need to be pulled out only slightly to unlock the flex cable. Some technicians use an extremely small screwdriver or a toothpick to move these tabs into the unlocked position. On many systems, this also provides you with access to the hinges that can remove the display.
5. Replace the keyboard.	A new keyboard can sometimes be purchased from the manufacturer, but you might not find out the part number you need from the manufacturer by giving them the model number of the laptop. If you can't find the part number, or if the manufacturer will not supply the component you need, look for the part number on the bottom of the keyboard and search for that part on the Internet. After you acquire the correct part (always check the part number of the new keyboard against the old one), connect the flex ribbon cable, lock it on both sides with those tiny locking tabs, screw in the keyboard, and replace the plastic trim.
6. Test the keyboard.	Verify that the new keyboard works by testing every key using a word processor like WordPad and by testing Fn enabled keys as well.

> **Note**
>
> Step 1 should be employed whenever you replace parts in the laptop.

> **ExamAlert**
>
> Understand the steps involved when replacing keyboards for the exam.

FIGURE 7.3 **Keyboard flex cable connector**

If a user needs access to a laptop right away (before it can be repaired), a temporary solution would be to connect a USB external keyboard. This should be recognized automatically by the operating system.

> **Note**
>
> When repairing a laptop, try to document the process as you go. Write down what you see and how and where cables and screws were attached. Also make note of how devices were oriented before they were removed. Label any parts that you remove for easier identification later on. If available, refer to the manufacturer's documentation that came with the laptop.

Pointing Devices

Whereas a PC uses a mouse, the laptop uses a pointing device. The bulk of laptops come with a pointing device known as a touchpad. By gliding a finger across the touchpad surface, a user can move the cursor on the screen. Touchpads might also come with two buttons that take the place of a mouse's buttons. In portable computing lingo, the word "click" is replaced with the word "tap." In addition to using the buttons, most touchpad surfaces can also be tapped or double-tapped upon, just by tapping with the finger. The buttons are oriented in such a way as to be used with the thumb. Touchpads can be replaced, though it is uncommon to do so; they are connected by two cables similar to the flex cable that connects the keyboard. However, you might have to remove other devices first to get at the touchpad. You might also have to work from the bottom and from the top of the laptop; this depends on the brand of laptop. Some touchpad buttons can be replaced the way keys on the keypads are. Touchpads are sometimes referred to as track pads as well.

Now and again you will encounter users reporting that when they type on the keyboard, the mouse pointer scrolls across the screen. This is sometimes referred to as a "ghost cursor" or "pointer drift." It could be because a part of the user's hand, or even the user's sleeve, is brushing against the touchpad. To remedy this, pointing devices can be turned off within the operating system, usually through the laptop manufacturer's software. Watch out for situations in which the entire device might have been disabled or perhaps just the pad portion of the touchpad was disabled. It's also possible to disable tapping capability of the touchpad while still allowing movement of the cursor. In rarer cases, a ghost cursor occurring while working in the operating system or in an application can be caused by a bad driver or the OS itself. If this happens, reinstall or update the mouse/touchpad driver, the video driver, and update the OS as well.

Another common type of pointing device is the pointing stick, known within IBM/Lenovo laptops as the TrackPoint. This device manifests itself as a smaller rubber cap (that looks like an eraser head) just above the B key or as two buttons that work essentially the same as a touchpad's buttons. External keyboards are also sold with integrated TrackPoint devices.

Of course, external mice can be connected to the laptop or its docking station as well. These would be connected to USB ports or could be wireless devices that connect via Bluetooth.

Stylus/Digitizer

A *stylus* is a writing tool, usually a thin plastic "pen" type of device used to take the place of a mouse; it enables you to tap and "write" on a touchscreen (also known as a *digitizer* screen). This method is widely used in tablet PCs, smartphones, and handheld computers and it has become more common with laptops over recent years. Usually, whenever you sign for a package from a shipping company, you sign with a stylus on a touchscreen. This takes the place of pencil and paper.

Video

A laptop's video subsystem is composed of an LCD and a graphics processing unit (GPU):

▶ **LCD:** The LCD is a flat-panel display that consists of two sheets of polarizing material surrounding a layer of liquid crystal solution. It connects to the motherboard by way of a flex ribbon cable and gets its power from an inverter board. Some laptops offer rotating touchscreens that allow a user to use the laptop as a tablet as well. A few laptops now use LED displays. More information on the different types of displays can be found in Chapter 12.

▶ **GPU:** The GPU is the processor for video. On a laptop, it is usually integrated with the motherboard. In some cases, it is part of the chipset and utilizes RAM as shared video memory. In other scenarios, namely more powerful laptops, it is a separate processor that has its own memory and possibly is situated upon its own circuit board.

Most of today's LCD screens are thin-film transistor (TFT) active-matrix displays, meaning they have multiple transistors for each pixel. These transistors are contained within a flexible material and are located directly behind the liquid crystal material. In general, LCDs use low amounts of power, generate a small amount of heat, and cause little in the way of interference and emissions.

Display Controls

Brightness can be adjusted from the keyboard on most laptops. On the laptop keyboard shown previously in Figure 7.2, pressing and holding the Fn key while pressing the F4 key decreases brightness, and pressing Fn + F5 increases brightness. Unlike typical standalone LCD monitors, there usually aren't contrast controls on a laptop.

Resolution is the number of pixels, measured horizontal by vertical, on the display; it is user selectable. The higher the resolution, the more that can be fit on the screen, which is beneficial to a certain point, especially if the laptop's screen isn't big. Table 7.2 shows some of the common resolutions that laptops use currently.

TABLE 7.2 **Common Laptop Resolutions**

Resolution Standard	Full Name	Pixels (HxV)	Aspect Ratio
WXGA	Widescreen Extended Graphics Array	1280×800	16:10 (1.6:1)
HD Ready	High-Definition display similar to WXGA	1366×768	16:9 (1.78:1)
WSXGA+	Widescreen Super Extended Graphics Array Plus	1680×1050	16:10 (1.6:1)
Full HD (1080p)	Full High-Definition	1920×1080	16:9 (1.78:1)

Laptops' active-matrix screens are sometimes set to run at one specific resolution (for example, 1920×1080). If the resolution is changed to something else, the laptop usually scales the resolution, making the picture unclear and perhaps not even fitting on the screen correctly. Or, in the worst-case scenario, the laptop displays a blank screen. Because of this, you're pretty much stuck with the default resolution. Sometimes this default resolution can be a bit tough on the eyes (for example, when the laptop's display runs at Full HD 1920×1080 but the screen size is only 14 inches). When users plan to use laptops for long periods of time, they should consider using laptops that have larger displays or external displays.

That brings us to the capability of sending video signals to an external monitor. Some people refer to this technology as *screen switching* and/or extending the display. Most laptops come with an external connection (for example, HDMI or DisplayPort) for a second monitor or for a projector. When this monitor is plugged in, it can be enabled by pressing the display toggle key (otherwise known as the secondary monitor button). On the laptop used in this chapter, this can be done by pressing Fn + F3 simultaneously; however, on other brands of laptops, this key might be a different key than F3. The icon on the key usually looks like an open laptop viewed from the side with a monitor to its right. Normally, you have several options: display the desktop to the laptop, display the desktop to the external monitor, display a copy of the desktop to both screens, or "extend" the desktop across both monitors. In addition to using the display toggle key, in Windows you can configure your video for any of these scenarios by going to the Screen Resolution window in the Control

Panel and modifying the "Multiple displays" setting (also referred to as dual displays). This is also available by right-clicking on the desktop. Try it on your system now!

If the external monitor won't display anything, make sure that the cable is firmly connected to the external port, verify that the external monitor is plugged in and on, and then try cycling through the various video options by pressing the button several times, waiting a few seconds each time. Make sure you are holding down the Fn key while doing so. Finally, restart the computer if necessary. This can get a little trickier when you are using a projector as the second display. Sometimes, the projector might need time to warm up or might need to be configured via its on-screen display (OSD). You might also need a video adapter if your laptop and projector's ports don't match up. Locate the projector's documentation for more details.

Troubleshooting Video Issues

The video display in laptops is integrated; however, while being a main feature of the portability of laptops, that can be a point of failure as well. Minor issues such as intermittent lines on the screen suggest that the display cable needs to be reconnected or replaced. However, complete display failures suggest a worse problem that will take longer to repair. Display failures can be broken down into a few categories:

▶ **Damaged inverter:** On a laptop with an LCD type of screen, the LCD is lit by a Cold Cathode Fluorescent Lamp (basically a bulb); it is the LCD backlight. The backlight is driven by a high-voltage inverter circuit. Because the inverter runs at high voltage, and possibly at high temperatures, it is prone to failure. If the inverter fails, the display will go dark; however, an external monitor should work properly. Another possibility is that the backlight has failed. You can verify if it is an inverter/backlight issue by shining a flashlight directly at the screen. When you do this, you should be able to make out Windows! This means that the display is getting the video signal from the motherboard and the problem, most likely, is indeed the inverter or the backlight. If the display's flex cable that connects the LCD to the motherboard was loose or disconnected, nothing would show up on the screen at all. The inverter circuit is usually situated on its own circuit board. To replace this circuit board, follow the steps in Table 7.3.

▶ **Damaged LCD screen:** An LCD could be damaged in a variety of ways. Sometimes, the damage could be minor, perhaps caused by the keyboard scratching against the display due to worn or missing rubber bumpers or rubber screw cover inserts. Simply attach new ones with adhesive or by snapping them into place. But the damage could be more extensive. For example, you might see a crack in the screen or you might notice a portion of the screen doesn't display properly. Or you might notice dark, irregular lines that run the width of the display in all video modes. If any of these are the case, the LCD will have to be replaced. Follow steps 1–3 in Table 7.3 to open the display assembly.

▶ **Worn-out backlight:** A laptop's backlight usually lasts a long time. However, at some point the lamp starts to wear out. You might notice a dimmer screen than before, or a reddish/pinkish hue to the screen, or maybe a loss of color. All these things indicate the possibility of a worn-out lamp. To replace the backlight, follow the steps in Table 7.3 but during steps 4 and 5, instead of replacing the inverter, replace the backlight.

TABLE 7.3 **Steps to Replace a Damaged Inverter Board**

Step	Procedure
1. Prepare the laptop for surgery!	Shut down the laptop, unplug it, and disconnect the battery. Then employ ESD prevention measures.
2. Remove the display.	To remove the display, the keyboard must be removed first. (Depending on the brand of laptop, there might be a few other items to unscrew and remove.) Then remove the screws holding the hinges down to the base of the laptop. Finally, disconnect the flex cable and any other connectors from the display to the system board.
3. Open the display.	Several screws hold the display together located on the plastic bezel that surrounds the display. These screws are covered with either tape or plastic domes. Remove the tape/domes and then remove the screws. Pry the plastic bezel open (carefully!) and remove the display.
	Note: Sometimes the display case needs to be opened with a plastic shim or similar tool. Insert the shim between the two pieces of plastic and slowly pry around the case until it is opened.
4. Remove the inverter.	The inverter often has two connectors: one for the high-voltage connection that leads to the power source and one for a flex cable that connects to the display. Disconnect these and remove the inverter. As always, hold circuit boards by the edges and try not to touch any actual circuits or chips.
	Note: At this stage, the bulb could be replaced (if it failed) on some laptops. It is usually located on the back of the display at the bottom. However, some displays have nonremovable bulbs. If this is the case, the entire display must be replaced.
5. Install the new inverter.	Inverters can be purchased from a variety of places online, including the manufacturer of the laptop or of the display. Verify that you are getting the correct part number. Connect the flex cable and the other connector to the inverter board.

Step	Procedure
6. Rebuild the display.	Now the tough part. The display must be put back into the bezel. Then the bezel needs to be snapped together and screwed in. Replace the tape or domes that covered the screws. Then reconnect the display assembly to the rest of the laptop; the hinges normally connect with a few screws. Next, reconnect the flex cable and any other connectors from the display to the system board. Finally, reconnect and screw in other components like the keyboard.

ExamAlert

Warning! The inverter should not be handled if the laptop is on! Be sure to turn off and unplug the laptop and remove the battery before removing an inverter.

Note

Table 7.3 details how to replace an inverter in a laptop using an LCD, but the process is similar for other types of displays as well.

Audio

Almost all laptops have an integrated sound card (often a Mini PCI card) and speakers. These work in the same manner as a PC's sound card and speakers, just on a smaller scale. Quite often, a laptop comes equipped with USB ports that can be used for audio. Also, it might have a speaker out/headphone out connector, line in connector, microphone connector, and perhaps an IEEE 1394 (FireWire) connector. For more information on audio, see the section titled "The Audio Subsystem" in Chapter 12.

A laptop's volume can be adjusted in one of two ways:

▶ **Volume knob/button:** Older laptops have a knob, which can sometimes be a little hard to find. This can be the culprit when users inform you that they cannot hear anything from their speakers. Newer laptops use a button, usually one that is activated with the Fn key (refer to Figure 7.2). Most new laptops have an on-screen display that shows the volume level as you adjust it.

▶ **Software adjustment:** Volume can be adjusted within Windows by accessing the speaker icon in the notification area or by navigating to the Sound applet in the Control Panel and then accessing the Speakers Properties window and the Levels tab. Most sound cards come with their own software as well in which a user can adjust volume, the equalizer, and more. This software might place an icon within the Notification Area as well in which a user can access the third-party software directly.

Optical Drives

Due to the amount of abuse a typical laptop receives, it is not uncommon to see an optical drive fail. However, optical disc drives are usually easy to replace on a laptop—easier than on a desktop PC, in fact. Most of the time there will be a couple screws on the bottom of the laptop that hold the optical drive in place. When removed, the drive can be slid out of the side of the laptop. Drives that can be installed simply by sliding them into a slot are becoming more and more commonplace; most laptops incorporate them—that is, if the laptop has an optical drive at all. Check your laptop's documentation for a compatible replacement (or upgrade), or check the bottom of the drive for part numbers that you can use to find a replacement drive online.

Some laptops don't have an optical drive whatsoever. But sometimes you might need one. Enter the USB optical drive, an external drive that gets its power from the USB port. There are several manufacturers of these for laptops/PCs, and Apple has the USB SuperDrive that can be used with its MacBooks as well.

Fans

Laptops need to exhaust hot air just like PCs do. To accomplish this, a laptop might have fans on the side or bottom. These can get clogged easily—more easily than PC fans, given the abuse that laptops receive. Indicators of a clogged fan include a clicking sound or worse: an unusually high-pitched noise. The first thing to do in this case is to use a vacuum to suck dust and debris out of the fan slots. Be sure not to blow air into the system, and I recommend doing this outside; you never know what will come out. If this doesn't work, consider checking whether something is obstructing the fan. Use a penlight to look through the fan and inside the system if possible. If not, you'll have to open the system to see what is causing the problem. If necessary, while the laptop is open, blow compressed air through the fan slot and out of the computer. Be careful not to touch the compressed air canister against anything in the laptop, and do not use a vacuum inside the laptop. The worst case scenario is that you would have to replace the fan.

ExamAlert
If the fan makes a high-pitched noise, try using a vacuum (from the outside) or blowing compressed air (from the inside).

Power

Laptops are designed to run on battery power, but laptops can run only between 2 and 5 hours on these batteries. So the laptop comes with an AC power adapter to plug into an AC outlet; these adapters should always be carried with the laptop. How many times have I heard users who forgot their power bricks! Recommend to users that they always put the AC adapter back in the laptop case.

The worst is when a laptop won't turn on! Without power, a user can't do anything. When troubleshooting power problems, envision the entire chain of power in your mind (or write it on paper); from the AC outlet to the AC adapter and all the way to the Power button. There are a few things you can check if it appears that the laptop is not getting any power.

▶ **Check the power LED:** Check the power light on the AC adapter. If this is off, not only will the laptop not get power, but the battery won't charge as well. Most laptops also have a power LED just above the keyboard. If this lights up, then maybe it isn't a power problem at all. For example, the user might start the laptop, see nothing on the display, and determine that the laptop has no power—when, in reality, it is a display issue. Many laptops also have hard drive and wireless LEDs, which can tell you more about the status of the laptop without seeing anything on the screen.

▶ **Check connections:** Verify that the laptop is firmly connected to the AC adapter and that the AC adapter is firmly connected to the AC outlet. Sometimes a user presses the Power button expecting the laptop to start without realizing that the battery is discharged and that the AC adapter is not connected. Also, check for damage. Inspect the DC jack that is soldered onto the motherboard of the laptop. Make sure it isn't loose or damaged. Sometimes the battery only charges if the output cord of the AC adapter is held at an angle—probably because the laptop was transported while the output cord was plugged into the laptop, causing damage to the DC jack.

▶ **Make sure the user uses the right power adapter:** Swapping power adapters between two different laptops is not recommended, but users try to do it all the time. Two different laptop models made by the same manufacturer might use what appear to be similar power adapters, with only one or two volts separating them; however, the laptop usually won't power on with that "slightly" different power adapter. Laptop AC adapters are known as fixed-input power supplies, meaning they work at a specific voltage. The adapter is not meant to be used on another model laptop. Unfortunately, a user might have plugged in the incorrect power adapter; the laptop then worked fine for 4 or 5 hours because it was actually running on battery power, but the user might not have noticed the laptop wasn't charging, even though the system should have notified the user when the battery was low (and critical). If you do suspect that an AC power adapter is faulty, consider testing your theory by swapping it out with an *identical* power adapter. Chances are, a company will have extra power adapters or will have several laptops of the same make and model. Another power adapter-related issue could be that the user is trying to work in another country. To do this, the user needs an auto-switching AC adapter, meaning that it can switch from 120 to 240 VAC automatically. Some laptops do not come with auto-switching AC adapters, but after-market versions can be purchased for many models of laptops. Remember that an additional adapter might be necessary to make the actual connection to the AC outlet in foreign countries.

▶ **Check the battery and voltage:** It might sound silly, but check if the battery hasn't been removed for some odd reason. Also, check if the battery is fully inserted into the battery compartment. There is usually a locking mechanism that should hold the battery in place. Finally, test the battery's voltage. Batteries last a finite amount of time. They can be recharged (known as cycles) by the laptop only so many times before failure. After a few to several years, the battery won't hold a charge any longer or will lose charge quickly. In some cases, you can try discharging and recharging the battery a few times to "stimulate" it, but in most scenarios, an extremely short battery life means that the battery must to be replaced. An old or failing battery can cause the system to overheat or could cause operating system freeze-ups or slow performance. In general, lithium-ion batteries last longer when the laptop is operated and stored at the right temperature ranges. Acceptable operating range for laptops is from 50–95°F (10–35°C), and acceptable storage ranges are from –4 to 140°F (–20 to 60°C). Watch out for swollen batteries, which could be caused by age, overcharging, or manufacturer defect. If it is user-removable, use great caution in attempting to remove it and be sure not to puncture it. Store it in a dark, cool container until you can recycle it. If it is a non-user-serviceable battery, bring the device to the nearest authorized repair center and, as before, keep the entire device within a cool container that light cannot get to.

> **Note**
>
> For more information on how to prolong lithium-ion batteries (the most common laptop battery), visit http://batteryuniversity.com/learn/article/how_to_prolong_lithium_based_batteries. Great site by the way if you work with mobile devices on a regular basis.

▶ **Check whether standby, sleep/suspend, or hibernate mode has failed:** If users regularly put their laptops into standby or hibernate modes, they could encounter issues once in a while. In some cases, the Power button needs to be held down for several seconds to reboot the machine out of a failed power-down state. This might have to be done with the battery removed. If either of these modes failed, check the Event Viewer for any relative information and possibly turn off hibernation and/or standby mode until the situation has been rectified. (On a slightly different note, sometimes laptops take a long time to come out of standby mode and it's not necessarily an issue with standby, it's a case of the lid switch being stuck. It looks like a power issue, but it's a simple hardware fix.)

▶ **Reconnect the Power button:** In rare cases, the Power button might have been disconnected from the system board. To fix this, the laptop must be opened; usually removing the keyboard and laptop housing provides you with access to the buttons.

▶ **Check the AC outlet:** Make sure the AC outlet that the user has plugged the laptop into is supplying power. A simple test would be to plug a lamp, clock, or other device into the outlet, but a more discerning and safer test would be to use a receptacle tester. For more information on testing AC outlets, see Chapter 5, "Power."

There are a few different types of batteries that a laptop or other mobile device might use, including lithium-ion (Li-ion), nickel-metal hydride (NiMH), and nickel-cadmium (NiCd), but Li-ion is by far the most common. They have the best energy-to-weight ratio and don't suffer from "memory effect" like NiCd batteries. They also discharge slowly when they are not used.

However, you can't run on batteries forever! So Windows includes alarms that can be set to notify the user when the battery is getting low and real low (known as critical). These alarms are set in Power Options.

Power options on portable systems running Windows 8/7/Vista can be modified by going to the Power Options applet in the Control Panel or by right-clicking the battery icon in the Notification Area. You might see plans such as Balanced, Power saver, eco, and High performance; however, users can create their own power plans as well. Each plan can be modified by clicking the Change plan settings link. There are a lot of settings in this window; following is one example. In Balanced, click Change plan settings. The Display can be set to turn off as quickly as 1 minute or as long as 5 hours; it also can be set to never. If you click the Change advanced power settings link, the Power Options button appears. From here, you can specify how long before the hard disk turns off and set power savings for devices such as the processor, wireless, USB, and PCI Express. To configure alarms in 8/7/Vista, go to the Battery Area and Low Battery Notification. Take a few minutes to look through these options and the options for the other power plans. Almost all of today's laptops use the Advanced Configuration and Power Interface (ACPI), which enables Windows to control the device power management instead of the BIOS controlling it.

ExamAlert

Know where to modify battery alarms in Windows.

Expansion Devices

There are several ways to expand upon your laptop, including external and internal expansion slots and docking stations. Let's talk about each of these briefly.

▶ **External expansion buses:** The most common type of external expansion bus is ExpressCard; I'm talking about that 2-inch-wide slot on the side of the laptop. This expansion bus accepts credit card-size devices that can be added to a laptop to increase memory or to add functionality in the form of wireless networking, 4G support, hard drives, and more. They are hot-swappable, meaning they support hot plugging into the expansion slot while the computer is powered on. There are two form factors of ExpressCard: /34, which is 34 mm wide, and /54, which is 54 mm wide and can be identified by a cutout in one corner of the card.

It has a 26-pin connector. A manufacturer of ExpressCard devices can select to design them using the PCI Express technology or USB technology, depending on which type of card they make. For example, an ExpressCard sound card wouldn't need the speed of PCI Express, so it would probably be designed from a USB standpoint.

▶ **Internal expansion buses:** As far as internal expansion buses go, laptops use Mini PCI Express or the older Mini PCI. These are about a quarter the size of their desktop computer counterparts and work essentially the same, although there might be less performance in the laptop versions. For example, Mini PCI has a maximum data transfer rate of 133 MB/s, which is one-half of some PCI cards in desktops. However, Mini PCIe (also known as PCI Express x1 Mini Card) can increase this speed; it can be used in laptops for solid-state drives, Wi-Fi, and video cards. If you find that a laptop will not display video through the laptop screen or an external monitor, or it doesn't connect to the wireless network, you might have to replace the mini video adapter. Replacing them can be a bit of a chore on some laptops. You will first need to remove either the back cover, back hatch, or the keyboard, then disconnect three power connections from the card, remove two screws, and remove the card from the slot. By the way, when replacing components like this, be sure to put the keyboard upside down on an antistatic bag and put the cards in an antistatic bag as well until you are ready for them. Note: A newer form factor as of the writing of this book is called M.2. It's similar to Mini PCIe but smaller and with only two power connectors.

▶ **Docking stations:** The docking station expands the laptop so that it can behave more like a desktop computer. By connecting the laptop to the docking station and adding a full-size keyboard, mouse, and monitor, the user doesn't actually touch the laptop any more except perhaps to turn it on. Most laptops can *hot dock*, meaning they can connect to the docking station while powered on. The docking station recharges the laptop's battery, and possibly a second battery, and has connections for video, audio, networking, and expansion cards. Docking stations might even have an optical disc drive or additional hard drive; it all depends on the brand and model. If all these extras aren't necessary, a user might require only a *port replicator*, which is a similar device but it has only ports (for example, video, sound, network, and so on). Sometimes these are just referred to as docking stations as well.

▶ **USB port adapters:** USB port adapters or "dongles" such as USB to RJ45, USB to Wi-Fi, and USB to Bluetooth are commonly used for laptop communication.

> **Note**
>
> Of course, you can also expand your laptop by using the integrated USB and
> IEEE 1394 ports, built-in memory card readers, and smart card readers. For more
> information on USB and IEEE 1394, see Chapter 13, "Peripherals and Custom
> Computing." For more information on memory cards, see Chapter 6, "Storage."

Communications

Communicating quickly and efficiently is key in business environments. To
do so, laptops use a variety of different devices, including the following:

▶ **Ethernet:** Most laptops today come equipped with wired and wireless Ethernet adapters to connect to a local area network (LAN) or a
wireless local area network (WLAN). The wired connection presents
itself as an RJ45 port and can typically transfer data at 1000 Mb/s or
100 Mb/s, auto-negotiating its speed to the network it is connected to.
Wireless connections are made with an internal Mini PCIe or Mini
PCI card that can potentially connect to 802.11ac, n, g, and b networks. It is also possible to connect wired or wireless network adapters
to USB ports or to ExpressCard slots. Otherwise, these technologies
work the same on a laptop as they do on a desktop computer. For more
information on wired and wireless LAN technologies, see Chapter 15
and Chapter 16. There is usually a WLAN button (located near the
Power button) that can enable/disable the wireless adapter. Keep this in
mind when troubleshooting. If this is disabled, the laptop cannot connect wirelessly, even if the device is enabled in the Device Manager. If
a wireless adapter is enabled but is detecting a weak signal even though
it is in close proximity to the wireless access point, check the antenna
and make sure it is connected and/or screwed in properly. Many laptops
use proprietary software for the configuration of wireless network connections instead of using the built-in Windows WLAN AutoConfig
program. In some cases, it might be easier to disable the proprietary
application and use Windows instead.

> **ExamAlert**
>
> If the laptop can't connect to the wireless network, try pressing the Wi-Fi button
> near the Power button, or press the associated function key.

▶ **Bluetooth:** Bluetooth adapters enable a laptop to connect to other Bluetooth devices over short distances, thus joining or creating a personal area network (PAN). A Bluetooth adapter might be included inside the laptop as an individual card or as a combo Bluetooth/WLAN card. External USB and ExpressCard Bluetooth adapters and remote controls are also available. For more information on Bluetooth, see Chapter 13. Many laptops come with WLAN and Bluetooth capabilities; however, the two technologies compete over frequencies. It is recommended that a user make use of only one at a time if possible. Buttons are usually available on the laptop (near the Power button) for enabling/disabling Wi-Fi and Bluetooth.

▶ **Infrared:** Infrared (IR) wireless ports can be used to transfer data between the laptop and another computer, smartphone, or other mobile device over a short distance. Unlike Bluetooth, IR connections must be line-of-sight. Built-in IR ports are not seen as often on laptops as Bluetooth but can be purchased in USB format if necessary.

▶ **Cellular WAN:** Connecting to the Internet through cellular WAN cards has become more popular over the past few years. Telecommunications providers offer cellular WAN ExpressCards (also known as wireless WAN cards) and USB-based travel routers. Some laptops are designed with built-in Mini PCIe cellular devices (sometimes called modems).

▶ **Modem:** The standard traditional dial-up modem is less common in today's laptops. If available, this circuitry is often built into the motherboard but can also be a Mini PCI card or a separate card altogether. If the modem fails and it is integrated into the motherboard, the entire motherboard would either have to be replaced (which would be costly and time consuming) or more likely an ExpressCard or USB version could be purchased.

ExamAlert

For the exam, know the various ways that a laptop could communicate with other computers, including wired and wireless Ethernet, Bluetooth, IR, cellular WAN, and dial-up modems.

Cram Quiz

Answer these questions. The answers follow the last question. If you cannot answer
these questions correctly, consider reading this section again until you can.

220-901 Questions

1. Which kinds of ports are typically found on a laptop? (Select all that apply.)

   ○ **A.** RJ45

   ○ **B.** USB

   ○ **C.** RJ11

   ○ **D.** HDMI

2. Which kind of video technology do most laptops incorporate?

   ○ **A.** TFT Active Matrix

   ○ **B.** Passive Matrix

   ○ **C.** OLED

   ○ **D.** TFT Passive Matrix

3. Which of the following is a common resolution on today's laptops?

   ○ **A.** 640×480

   ○ **B.** 800×600

   ○ **C.** 1280×800

   ○ **D.** 1920×1080

4. Which of the following is the most common battery used by today's laptops?

   ○ **A.** AA batteries

   ○ **B.** Lithium-ion (Li-ion)

   ○ **C.** Nickel-metal hydride (NiMH)

   ○ **D.** Nickel-cadmium (NiCd)

5. In which of the following locations are battery alarms modified in Windows?

   ○ **A.** Display Properties window

   ○ **B.** Power Properties window

   ○ **C.** BIOS

   ○ **D.** Power Options window

6. Which of the following are ways that a laptop can communicate with other computers? (Select all that apply.)

   ○ **A.** Bluetooth

   ○ **B.** WLAN

   ○ **C.** Ultraviolet

   ○ **D.** Cellular WAN

7. When a user types, a laptop's screen displays letters and numbers instead of only letters. What should you check first?

   ○ **A.** Fn key

   ○ **B.** LCD cutoff switch

   ○ **C.** Num Lock key

   ○ **D.** Scroll Lock key

8. Which of the following are possible reasons that a laptop's keyboard might fail completely? (Select the best two answers.)

   ○ **A.** A stuck key.

   ○ **B.** A disconnected ribbon cable.

   ○ **C.** The user spilled coffee on the laptop.

   ○ **D.** The keyboard was disabled in the Device Manager.

9. Which of the following are two possible reasons why a laptop's display suddenly went blank with no user intervention? (Select the two best answers.)

   ○ **A.** Damaged inverter

   ○ **B.** Damaged LCD

   ○ **C.** Burned-out backlight

   ○ **D.** Incorrect resolution setting

10. A user doesn't see anything on his laptop's screen. He tries to use AC power and thinks that the laptop is not receiving any. Which of the following are two possible reasons for this? (Select the two best answers.)

    ○ **A.** He is using an incorrect AC adapter.

    ○ **B.** The AC adapter is not connected to the laptop.

    ○ **C.** Windows won't boot.

    ○ **D.** The battery is dead.

11. One of your customers reports that she walked away from her laptop for 30 minutes. When she returned, the display was very dim. She increased the brightness
setting and moved the mouse but to no effect. What should you do first?

○ **A.** Replace the LCD screen.

○ **B.** Check the operating system for corruption.

○ **C.** Connect an external monitor to verify that the video card works.

○ **D.** Check whether the laptop is now on battery power.

Cram Quiz Answers

220-901 Answers

1. **A, B, and D.** RJ45, USB, and HDMI ports are all common on a laptop. However,
the older RJ11 dial-up port is not common.

2. **A.** TFT active-matrix LCDs are the most common in laptops today. Passive-
matrix screens have been discontinued, but you might see an older laptop that
utilizes this technology. There is no TFT passive matrix. OLED technology is up
and coming and could possibly displace the standard LCD screen, but LCD is
still the most common for laptops built between 2000 and 2015.

3. **C.** 1920x1080 (Full HD or 1080P) is a common video resolution on laptops.
640x480 and 800x600 are older VGA modes that can't fit much on the screen.
1280x800 (WXGA) is a resolution used by older laptops that you may still see
in the field. 2048x1536 (QXGA) is a higher resolution than most laptops' video
adapters can display, but it's not outside the realm of possibility. For more information on video resolutions, see Chapter 12.

4. **B.** There are a few different types of batteries that a laptop might use, including
lithium-ion (Li-ion), nickel-metal hydride (NiMH), and nickel-cadmium (NiCd), but
lithium-ion is by far the most common. Believe it or not, some laptops (namely
children's laptops) can run on four AA batteries, but it is not common or feasible
in today's business environments.

5. **D.** To change the thresholds for battery alarms, a user would access the Power
Options window.

6. **A, B, and D.** Laptops can communicate with other computers through
Bluetooth, WLAN, IR, and cellular WAN wireless connections, plus wired connections like Ethernet (RJ45) and dial-up (RJ11).

7. **C.** The Number Lock key (Num Lock) can enable or disable the numeric keypad. This might be necessary if the user inadvertently turned it on or disconnected an external keyboard from the laptop. Some laptops require you to press
Ctrl+Num Lock to enable or disable the numeric keypad. Laptops are usually
color-coded (for example, white options might require the Ctrl key and blue
options might require the Fn key). In this scenario, pressing the Function (Fn)
key is not necessary when pressing the Num Lock key. The LCD cutoff switch
is used to turn off the bulb that lights the LCD. The Scroll Lock key is used little
but is meant to lock any scrolling done with the arrow keys.

8. **B and C.** A laptop's keyboard could fail due to a disconnected or loose keyboard ribbon cable. It could also fail if a user spilled coffee on the laptop, by being dropped on the ground, and so on. One stuck key will not cause the entire keyboard to fail, and on most laptops, the keyboard cannot be disabled in the Device Manager.

9. **A and C.** A damaged inverter or burned-out bulb could cause a laptop's display to go blank. You can verify whether the LCD is still getting a signal by shining a flashlight at the screen. A damaged LCD usually works to a certain extent and will either be cracked, have areas of Windows missing, or show other signs of damage. An incorrect resolution setting can indeed make the screen suddenly go blank (or look garbled), but that scenario will most likely occur only if the user has changed the resolution setting—the question specifies with no user intervention.

10. **A and B.** An incorrect adapter will usually not power a laptop. The adapter used must be exact. And of course, if the laptop is not plugged in properly to the adapter, it won't get power. Windows doesn't play into this scenario. And if the battery was dead, it could cause the laptop to not power up, but only if the AC adapter was also disconnected; the scenario states that the user is trying to use AC power.

11. **D.** It could be that the laptop is now on battery power, which is usually set to a dimmer display and shorter sleep configuration. This indicates that the laptop is not getting AC power from the AC outlet for some reason. The battery power setting is the first thing you should check; afterward, start troubleshooting the AC adapter, cable, AC outlet, and so on. It's too early to try replacing the display; try not to replace something until you have ruled out all other possibilities. A dim screen is not caused by OS corruption. No need to plug in an external monitor; you know the video adapter is working, it's just dim.

Installing, Configuring, and Troubleshooting Internal Laptop Components

Now that you know how to troubleshoot the visible components of a laptop, let's discuss the internal components a little bit. Because they are not exposed, these devices won't fail as often as components such as the keyboard and the display, but sometimes failures still occur. You might need to replace a hard drive (and possibly recover the drive's data) or add or swap out memory. Hard drives and memory are known as field replaceable units (FRUs). This means that the part can be quickly removed from the system and that you can do it at the customer location. On a laptop, the component is accessed by opening a hatch or unlatching and sliding it out. Other items such as the CPU and motherboard are not usually field replaceable. If one of these fails, the repair process will be longer and will usually require bringing the laptop to the shop. Dealing with hard drive trouble and working with RAM is more common, so let's begin with those.

Hard Drives

So far, we mentioned a few times that hard drives will fail; it's just a matter of when. And laptop hard drives are more susceptible to failure than desktop computers due to their mobility and the bumps and bruises that laptops regularly sustain. The majority of new laptops come with SATA hard disks (magnetic-based), but you will also see many laptops with SSDs in the field. The bulk of the hard drives in laptops are 2.5 inches wide; the smaller form factor is necessary in today's laptops. Ultra-small laptops and other small portable devices might use a hard disk as small as 1.8 inches.

One of the ways to make a laptop run faster is to replace the hard drive. For example, if the laptop comes with an SATA magnetic disk, you might opt to replace it with an SSD or perhaps a hybrid drive, which combines the capacity of a magnetic disk with the performance of an SSD. These can offer greater data transfer rates as well as improvements in overall system efficiency. Upgrades such as these might also need to be performed if the original drive fails. At that point, you'll probably need to rescue some data from the original drive.

ExamAlert

Know that laptop hard drive types include magnetic disk, SSD, and hybrid. Also be aware they have either 2.5- or 1.8-inch form factors.

Of course, to rescue data from a hard drive, you first must remove it. Laptop hard drives can be accessed from one of three places. The first, and maybe the most common, is from an access panel on the bottom of the laptop. The second is from underneath the keyboard. And the third is from the side of the laptop. In this last scenario, the hard drive is inside a caddy that has a handle for easy removal; it should slide directly out of the side of the laptop. In this scenario, the hard drive has to be removed from the caddy, and in any of the three scenarios, there is usually some kind of bracket that has to be unscrewed from the drive when replacing it. Hold on to this bracket for the new hard drive. In any case, I recommend employing antistatic measures and using care when working around any connections inside the laptop—they are more fragile than their PC counterparts.

Memory

Most of today's laptops use DDR SDRAM, just as desktop computers do. But again, you are dealing with a much smaller device, so the memory is also smaller; it is known as a small outline dual in-line memory module (SODIMM). Table 7.4 shows the four types of SODIMMs and their pin formats—information you should know for the exam. As with desktop RAM, different versions of memory in laptops are not compatible; for example, you can't put a DDR3 SODIMM into a DDR2 SODIMM slot. SODIMM DDR speeds are similar to their PC equivalents.

TABLE 7.4 **SODIMM Versions**

Memory Type	Module Format
DDR	200-pin
DDR2	200-pin
DDR3	204-pin
DDR4	260-pin

ExamAlert

Memorize the types of SODIMMs and understand the pin format differences between them and DIMMs.

> **Note**
>
> For more information on RAM types, see Chapter 4, "RAM."

RAM has a center notch that helps to orient the RAM during installation. This notch will usually be in a different location depending on the SODIMM version.

Before installing any new RAM, check compatibility. Remember to consult the laptop's documentation to find out exactly how much RAM and which type of RAM the laptop will accept. When you have purchased compatible RAM, installing it to a laptop is usually quite simple. RAM is often located on the bottom of the laptop, underneath an access cover. In other laptops, it might be underneath the keyboard or there could be one stick of RAM under the keyboard and a second (usually for add-ons) under an access cover underneath the laptop. Consult your laptop's documentation for the exact location of the RAM compartment. Sometimes the compartment has a small icon identifying it as the location for memory. Table 7.5 shows the steps involved in adding RAM to a laptop. Keep in mind that SODIMMs, and their corresponding memory boards, are much more delicate than their counterparts in a desktop computer.

TABLE 7.5 **Installing a SODIMM to a Laptop**

Step	Procedure
1. Prepare the laptop for surgery!	Shut down the laptop, unplug it, and disconnect the battery. Then employ ESD prevention measures.
2. Review your documentation.	Review your documentation to find out where RAM is located. For this step, assume that the RAM can be added to a compartment underneath the laptop.
3. Open the memory compartment.	Usually there will be two screws that you need to remove to open the memory compartment door. Often, these are captive screws and will stay in the door. But if they are not, store them in a safe place and label them.

Step	Procedure
4. Insert the RAM.	There could be one or two slots for RAM. One of them might already be in use. Some laptops support dual-channel memory. If this is the case and you install a second memory module, make sure it is identical to the first.
	Insert the memory module at a 45-degree angle into the memory slot, aligning the notch with the keyed area of the memory slot. Press the module into the slot; then press the module down toward the circuit board until it snaps into place (GENTLY!). Two clips (one on either side) lock into the notches in the side of the memory module. Press down again to make sure it is in place. See Figure 7.4 for an example of an installed SODIMM. There are actually two SODIMMs on top of each other; the one on top is farther to the left. Note the locking clips holding the memory module into place.
5. Close the compartment and then test.	Screw the compartment door back on to the laptop. Then boot the computer into the BIOS and make sure it sees the new memory module. Finally, boot into Windows and make sure that the operating system sees the new total amount of RAM, and then verify whether applications work properly.

Memory Slot   Locking Clip

Notch   Locking Clip

FIGURE 7.4   Installed SODIMM

Sometimes upgraded memory fails to be identified by the BIOS. This usually means that the memory was not installed properly. Turn off the computer, reseat the RAM modules, and then reboot. This usually fixes the problem.

Occasionally a laptop fails to boot, emitting a series of continuous beeps. This could be due to faulty memory. However, it could simply be that the memory contacts are dirty. As mentioned before, laptops are often mistreated and are used in a variety of environments. Pop the memory hatch and inspect the RAM modules. If they require cleaning, use compressed air or try Stabilant 22 or similar cleaners. Plug the modules back in and verify functionality by rebooting the system several times. If they still don't work, try swapping out the RAM with known good modules.

System Board and CPU

As mentioned before, the worst thing that could happen to a laptop is that it doesn't start. Let me rephrase: That would be the worst thing that could happen to a *user*. The worst thing for a tech would be if the system board failed. This is because it would require almost a complete disassembly of the unit to repair it, a process that is is time-consuming and requires heavy documentation to get all the parts back together properly when done. CPU replacement (and upgrading) is not quite as difficult but still requires removing at least the keyboard and likely a few other components that will be in the way. Documentation is still important when replacing a CPU.

Sometimes a system board's lithium battery needs replacement. This is done in the same manner as it is within a desktop computer; however, you need to remove the keyboard, and perhaps other devices and connections, to gain access to the battery. Some laptops come with the same CR2032 battery that desktop models use; however, a few laptops (and other handheld devices) come with a rechargeable system board lithium battery that has a shelf life of up to 10 years. Other laptops simply make use of the main lithium-ion battery.

Before you do decide to take this type of plunge into a laptop, one thing to keep in mind is that a lot of companies will purchase 1- to 3-year warranties for the laptops they use. Even though there is a cost involved in purchasing warranties, it is usually the wise choice. If the laptop did fail, the alternative would be to have a technician spend several hours (at least) disassembling, testing, replacing, and reassembling the laptop—all of which could cost the company more money in man hours than it would have cost to just purchase the warranty. Warranties are a type of insurance, and this type of insurance is usually acceptable to a company. So check your company's policies and procedures first before doing these types of repairs.

Before removing a CPU or other internal components, employ ESD prevention measures. If the CPU is surface-mounted, you cannot remove it. If it has failed, the entire system board would need to be removed. But if it is socketed (which is more likely on newer laptops) with either a Pin Grid Array (PGA) or Ball Grid Array (BGA), it can be removed. Usually there is some kind of locking arm mechanism that must be unlocked to remove the CPU from the socket. Common sockets for mobile Intel CPUs include the Socket M (for several CPUs, including the Core 2 Duo), Socket P (the replacement for Socket M), and the newer Socket G1, G2, and G3 for Core i3, i5, and i7 CPUs. Upgrade ranges for laptop CPUs are usually quite narrow. If a CPU fails, it is usually best to install an identical CPU. If you do plan to upgrade a CPU, check the documentation carefully to make sure that the exact model laptop (and its motherboard) can support the faster CPU. After removing the CPU, be sure to place it in an antistatic bag with the pins facing up. When installing CPUs, employ the same delicate procedure as you would with a desktop PC. These CPUs require no force to insert them into the socket.

> **Note**
>
> For more information on installing motherboards and CPUs into desktops, see Chapter 2, "Motherboards," and Chapter 3, "The CPU."

Cram Quiz

Answer these questions. The answers follow the last question. If you cannot answer
these questions correctly, consider reading this section again until you can.

220-901 Questions

1. What is the module format for a stick of SODIMM DDR RAM?

   - ○ A. 200-pin
   - ○ B. 168-pin
   - ○ C. 144-pin
   - ○ D. 204-pin

2. How are SODIMMs installed to a laptop?

   - ○ A. By pressing straight down
   - ○ B. Into a ZIF socket
   - ○ C. On a 45-degree angle
   - ○ D. On a 90-degree angle

3. What should you do when upgrading a CPU in a laptop? (Select all that apply.)

   - ○ A. Check documentation to see if the CPU is supported.
   - ○ B. Install more RAM.
   - ○ C. Employ antistatic measures.
   - ○ D. Remove the system board.

4. You need to replace the CMOS battery in a laptop. Which of the following is a
   common location for the battery?

   - ○ A. Under the DVD-ROM
   - ○ B. Behind the laptop battery
   - ○ C. Under the keyboard
   - ○ D. Behind the hard drive

5. You just added a second memory module to a laptop. However, after rebooting
   the system, the OS reports the same amount of memory as before. What should
   you do next?

   - ○ A. Replace both memory modules.
   - ○ B. Run Windows Update.
   - ○ C. Replace the motherboard.
   - ○ D. Reseat the laptop memory.

6. You are required to add a second memory module to a laptop. You open the hatch on the bottom of the laptop to reveal only a single memory module installed to the only slot. Where should you look for a second memory slot?

   ○ **A.** Behind the removable hard drive

   ○ **B.** Underneath the keyboard

   ○ **C.** Under the battery

   ○ **D.** Behind the DVD-ROM drive

Cram Exam Answers

220-901 Answers

1. **A.** DDR SODIMM modules have 200 pins. Desktop SDRAM has 168 pins. SODIMM SDRAM has 144 pins. DDR3 SODIMMs have 204 pins. DDR4 SODIMMs have 260 pins.

2. **C.** SODIMMs are installed to a laptop at a 45-degree angle, unlike a desktop's DDR memory, which is installed by pressing straight down. ZIF sockets refer to CPUs.

3. **A and C.** When upgrading a CPU in a laptop, check for laptop documentation to see if the faster CPU is supported and then employ ESD prevention measures. More RAM is not necessary when upgrading a CPU, but it could help the laptop get the best out of the CPU when an open memory slot is available. Usually the system board does not have to be removed to replace or upgrade a CPU.

4. **C.** The CMOS battery is usually underneath the keyboard. Once you locate it, it is usually removed and replaced in the same manner as in a PC.

5. **D.** The next step you should take is to reseat the memory. SODIMM can be a bit tricky to install. They must be firmly installed, but you don't want to press too hard and damage any components. If the laptop worked fine before the upgrade, you shouldn't have to replace the modules or the motherboard. Windows Update will not find additional RAM.

6. **B.** Memory modules are either located inside a hatch on the bottom of the laptop (optimally) or underneath the keyboard (not quite so optimal). Sometimes one is accessed via the hatch. For add-ons or upgrades, the second goes underneath the keyboard.

Understanding Tablet and Smartphone Hardware

Mobile devices are computers—smaller and lighter than desktops and laptops, but computers nonetheless. There are similarities and differences in hardware between the two. You will find there are new players on the software side and these, too, have similarities and differences compared to PCs and laptops. But remember that at their core, mobile devices are still computers, and many of the principles and rules that you have learned earlier in this book regarding hardware still apply.

Mobile Hardware Examples

In this section, we'll give examples of a tablet computer and a smartphone and discuss the hardware that these devices use. Then we'll talk briefly about how mobile devices can be made compliant with dust-tight and water-tight code.

Tablet Example

A common device as of the writing of this book is the Apple iPad Air 2. It is known as a tablet computer and is manufactured by Foxconn, which also makes the iPhone, Kindle, and popular gaming consoles. Table 7.6 provides a list of the hardware the iPad Air 2 uses.

TABLE 7.6 **Apple iPad Air 2 Hardware**

Hardware Component	Description
1.5 GHz ARMv8 CPU	▶ Called the Apple A8X ▶ 64-bit system on a chip (SoC)
2 GB LPDDR3 RAM	▶ Mobile DDR—similar DDR standard to what PCs use, but a much smaller form factor
16, 64, or 128 GB Flash Memory	▶ Similar to solid-state flash memory in a USB flash drive ▶ Used for permanent storage instead of an SATA hard drive
Multitouch touchscreen	▶ Capacitive touchscreen that responds to fingers and stylus devices

Hardware Component	Description
Lithium-ion polymer battery	▶ Similar to lithium-ion batteries in laptops ▶ Can be made into any shape ▶ 7,340 mAh (milliamp hours). Lasts for 10 hours on a full charge (typical usage)
9.7-inch display (diagonal) LED-backlit widescreen multi-touch display with in-plane switching (IPS) technology	▶ Quad Extended Graphics Array (QXGA), 2048x1536 resolution ▶ 4:3 aspect ratio

ExamAlert

Memorize the basic types of hardware used by a tablet computer.

As you can see from the table, the basic components of CPU, RAM, and so on are the same as desktop/laptop computers. But the *types* of components are different. The whole concept of this hardware configuration is based on portability and ease of use. Therefore, tablet computers are less powerful than desktop computers and laptops but the hardware is matched to the type of applications the device will be used for.

Similar tablets (but with different software) include devices from Motorola, Samsung, and ASUS. These will often be less proprietary than an Apple device; for example, they might use micro-USB ports for charging and synchronization of data, whereas the iPad has a proprietary charging port (as of the writing of this book, it's known as the Lightning connector). You might also see different names for the touch interface of a device, but most tablets (and smartphones for that matter) feature some kind of multitouch touchscreen.

The iPad we discussed has a 64-bit CPU. However, for some time yet, you will support older mobile devices that use 32-bit CPUs. Be prepared for them, and realize that they often cannot run the latest mobile operating systems; in some cases, they cannot run the latest versions of some apps. These older, 32-bit-based devices frequently need to be streamlined to work efficiently. We'll discuss that more in Chapter 18, "Android, iOS, OS X, and Linux."

Smartphone Example

Now that we've discussed a typical tablet, let's talk about the common smartphone—we'll use the Samsung Galaxy S6 as our example. Unlike many companies that use Foxconn or another manufacturer to make their products,

Samsung manufactures its own. Table 7.7 provides a list of the hardware the S6 uses.

TABLE 7.7 **Samsung Galaxy S6 Hardware**

Hardware Component	Description
2.1 GHz ARMv8 CPU	▶ Called Exynos 7 Octa ▶ 64-bit system on a chip (SoC)
3 GB LPDDR4 RAM	▶ Mobile DDR version 4
32, 64, or 128 GB Flash Memory	▶ Similar to solid-state drives' flash memory
Multitouch touchscreen	▶ Capacitive touchscreen
Lithium-ion polymer battery	▶ 2,550 mAh
5.1-inch display	▶ Quad HD (QHD), 2560x1440 resolution ▶ 16:9 aspect ratio

ExamAlert

Memorize the basic types of hardware used by a smartphone.

When you analyze the CPU and RAM, you'll note some small differences between the iPad Air 2 tablet and the Samsung Galaxy S6 smartphone. For example, the S6 has a faster CPU and uses DDR4 RAM instead of DDR3. These variations are common among tablets and smartphones—manufacturers are constantly releasing new devices, each faster than the last. So these disparities are minor. However, the difference between the batteries is much greater—and much more important. A typical smartphone's battery will not last nearly as long as a typical tablet and this is important to many users. Most smartphones need to be charged every day. However, a tablet needs to be charged only every couple of days, perhaps every week, depending on usage. But some users want the best of both worlds, and it is available to them—enter the *phablet* (a combination of the words "phone" and "tablet"). An example of this is the Samsung Galaxy Note series of phablets. This product has a larger screen than a typical smartphone, more battery power (typically around 3,000 mAh), and often has a powerful CPU. But keep in mind that a phablet is usually more similar to a smartphone than a tablet—in screen size as well as battery power.

IP Compliance

Some smartphones and other handheld computers are certified as being ingress protection (IP) compliant. For example, the Samsung Galaxy S5 is certified as IP67 compliant. Ingress protection means protection against dust and water, which are tested separately. For the S5, the "6" deals with dust and means that the device is dust tight and that no ingress of dust can occur. The "7" concerns water and means that the device can be immersed in water up to 1 meter for as long as 30 minutes. Other devices might be listed as IP65 compliant, which means they are dust tight and can protect from water jets for up to 3 minutes. The number associated with water protection is not cumulative, so if a device needs to be protected from water jets *and* immersion in water, it would have to be tested for IP65 *and* IP67 compliance. Many specialized handheld computers in the military (as well as in the medical, transportation, and surveying markets) meet these requirements. However, as mentioned, a device such as the S5 is IP67 compliant only. What does this mean to you? Don't bring it in the shower or spray it with a hose! It might survive, but it probably won't because it isn't tested for that type of abuse. You should also remember that many consumer smartphones do not meet any IP requirements and must be treated accordingly. If a device is damaged during use in a dusty environment or sprayed with or immersed in water, the warranty might become void.

Hardware Differences Between Tablets/ Smartphones and Laptops

One of the big distinctions between tablets/smartphones and laptops is the lack of field-serviceable parts. Another difference is that tablets and other similar devices are usually not upgradable. Some smartphones might have upgradable memory cards and/or batteries, as shown in Figure 7.5, but the trend is moving toward nonremovable batteries); these upgradable memory cards and/or batteries are sometimes not serviceable in the field because it is difficult to protect yourself from ESD. (Though that doesn't mean it isn't done!) Many organizations recommend that you bring the device back to the lab for upgrades or parts swaps. Other devices (such as iPads) are not user-serviceable whatsoever; any attempt at doing so voids the warranty. If a repair, upgrade, or replacement is necessary, most organizations utilize the warranties built in to these products instead of trying to do the work in-house.

FIGURE 7.5 **Typical smartphone with removed battery and memory card**

ExamAlert

Know the basic differences between tablets, smartphones, and laptops.

A laptop is actually just a smaller, portable version of a desktop computer. Like the desktop computer, it contains a similar processor; similar DDR RAM; and a hard drive that could possibly be solid-state, but regardless, the hard drive will most likely be plugged in to an SATA port. It also has a keyboard, and a touchpad similar to a mouse. All this hardware is designed to make the best use of operating systems that you would normally find on a desktop computer. Tablets and smartphones, on the other hand, use ARM-based processors and nonvolatile flash memory that is hard-wired to the system instead of being stored to a magnetic or solid-state hard drive. So, as you can imagine, tablets and smartphones often suffer a lack of performance compared to laptops. In addition, these devices utilize an on-screen keyboard and thus don't require any type of mouse or touchpad. All this hardware is designed to work with software such as Android or iOS. Compare this with a laptop, which will most likely run Windows. Of course, there are some devices that blur the lines a bit, such as the Microsoft Surface. It is a tablet that uses a keyboard, but the keyboard can be removed (or you could say it has a removable screen, depending on your point of view). Plus its OS is the same that a PC or laptop would use. So now we have devices that are tougher to classify, but you can always just call it a mobile computer, because it definitely falls into that category.

Tablet/Smartphone Ports and Accessories

The types of ports and accessories available with mobile devices will vary depending on the manufacturer of the device, the type of device (tablet, smartphone, and so on), and the version of that device. There are quite a few types of connections and accessories that you need to know for the exam. Let's briefly describe some of those now.

Mobile Device Ports and Connection Types

When it comes to tablets and smartphones, there are two types of connections—wired and wireless. Wired connections are frequently used for charging and synchronization; wireless connections are used to access the Internet, make phone calls, connect to GPS, and quickly move data from one device to another.

A whole lot of the tablets and smartphones out there use micro-USB wired connections for charging and synchronization. That's the little USB connector on Samsung phones and lots of other devices; you've most definitely seen them (unless you've been living under a rock). The bulk of these devices run the Android OS. However, there is another side of the mobile device world— the world of Apple and iOS—in which these devices have always used proprietary ports (for example, the Lightning connector) that aren't compatible with micro-USB. These work only on Apple products.

> **ExamAlert**
>
> Understand the types of ports used by Android-based and iOS-based mobile devices.

Another purpose of the wired port is to tether the mobile device to a desktop or laptop computer (usually via the computer's USB port). This tethering allows the mobile device to use the desktop computer's Internet connection. Tethering functionality can be very useful in areas with a weak cellular or 4G signal and no Wi-Fi yet where PCs have access to the Internet over cable Internet or another wired Internet service provider. On some devices, you need to specifically select tethering once you connect via USB; on others, you can set a configuration where the device can automatically sense the tethered connection and allow Internet access through the PC or other computer. For example, on a typical Samsung device, this would be accomplished in Settings > Tethering and Wi-Fi (Mobile) HotSpot. On an Apple iPhone 6, this would be accomplished in Settings > Personal Hotspot.

Given the inherent mobility of smartphones and tablets, most technologies regarding communications and control are wireless. Wireless connections offer ease of use, efficiency, and even great speed. We'll discuss Wi-Fi, 4G, GPS, and similar data-related wireless technologies later in the book. For now, let's focus on wireless connections used by mobile devices to communicate with accessories and other mobile devices.

One of the most common is Bluetooth. This is a technology that allows users to incorporate wearable technology (such as headsets, earpieces, earbuds, and smartwatches) with their existing mobile devices. But the technology goes much farther, allowing for the streaming of music to an automobile's music system and even the creation of basic PANs.

Another commonly used wireless technology is the mobile hotspot. When enabled on a properly equipped smartphone or tablet (with 4G connection), it allows a user to connect desktops, laptops, and other mobile devices (wirelessly, of course) through the device running the hotspot, ultimately allowing access to the Internet. It is effectively the reverse of tethering, done in a wireless fashion. This can be a great way to connect your laptop or other computer if Wi-Fi goes down, often with speeds rivaling cable Internet access. But there's usually a catch! Many providers charge a pretty penny for data usage (unless you have a corporate plan). Because of this, it is often used as a secondary connection or as a backup plan. In addition, the further the hotspot-enabled mobile device is from a 4G tower, the lower the data transfer rate. So know the pros and cons of running a hotspot on your mobile device.

ExamAlert

Understand the difference between configuring tethering and creating a mobile hotspot.

Next on the list is near field communication (NFC). This allows smartphones to communicate with each other via radio frequency by touching the devices together or, in some cases, by simply having them in close proximity to each other. NFC uses the radio frequency 13.56 MHz and can transmit 100 to 400 kb/s. It doesn't sound like much, but it's usually plenty for sending and receiving contact information, MP3s, and even photos. Besides working in peer-to-peer mode (also known as adhoc mode), a full NFC device can also act like a smart card performing payment transactions and reading NFC tags. If you are not sure whether your device supports NFC, check the settings in the mobile OS or open the case and look for the words "near field communication." For example, in Figure 7.5, this is listed directly on the battery.

Another wireless technology used in many smartphones and tablets is infrared (IR). For example, newer mobile devices come with an IR blaster that can take control of televisions and some other devices (given they have the proper app installed). Infrared works on a different (and higher) frequency range than Wi-Fi, Bluetooth, and cellular connections, so it does not interfere with those technologies when it is used. Table 7.8 summarizes the wired and wireless connections we just discussed.

TABLE 7.8   **Mobile Device Wired and Wireless Technologies**

Technology	Usage
Micro-USB	▶ Charging connector ▶ Synchronization with desktops/laptops ▶ Tethering
Lightning	▶ Proprietary charging and synchronization connector for Apple devices
Bluetooth	▶ Allows for usage of headsets ▶ Personal area networks (PANs)
Mobile hotspot	▶ Creates a wireless network allowing other computers to share the mobile device's Internet connection
NFC	▶ Near field communication ▶ Allows communication by touching mobile devices together (or in close proximity)
IR	▶ Infrared blaster/sensor allows for control of TVs and other equipment

Mobile Device Accessories

Well, a person has to accessorize, right? It almost seems a requirement with today's mobile devices. Probably the number one thing that people do to augment their device is to protect it. That means using protective cases, plastic- or glass-based screen protectors, waterproofing, car mounts, and so on. Then there's the battery to think about. Most mobile devices come with a charger, but you might want a second one for your car or for the workplace, especially if your organization embraces a bring your own device (BYOD) policy. If you are on the road a lot, a second (and possibly third) battery becomes paramount.

Then there's add-on memory. You can never have enough memory, right? The device shown in Figure 7.5 comes with 32 GB of storage built in—an amount that is fairly common for smartphones—but you might want to add more memory to the memory slot. This is usually accomplished with the addition of a microSD card. It is common for people who shoot a lot of videos (or a whole lot of photos) to need more memory than the mobile device comes with when purchased.

Next on the list are audio accessories. The 3.5 mm audio jack allows a user to connect headsets, earbuds, or small speakers. Or you can connect a 3.5 mm to 3.5 mm cable from your phone to the auxiliary port of your car radio or your all-in-one music device. When it comes to music, you can connect a mobile device to anything (given the right cable or adapter): stereos or TVs, and you can even use the device when performing live. The possibilities are endless. And today's mobile device audio ports can be programmed in such a way as to accept special credit-card readers and a host of other devices. Appliance repair persons and other maintenance workers that need to be paid onsite will often make use of this technology.

Speaking of programming ports to do what you want, the micro-USB port is another example. From a more basic perspective, there are dozens of docking station and cradle products available for most smartphones and some tablets. These allow you to place the device into a cradle that automatically makes a connection between the cradle and the device's micro-USB port. This ultimately enables charging and synchronization via an included USB cable. Getting a bit more advanced, you will also see devices such as game pads that can connect to the micro-USB port using on-the-go (OTG) USB technology. However, a lot of game pads will connect wirelessly, either via Bluetooth or through Wi-Fi.

We could go on for days about the accessories available for mobile devices, but that should be enough for the exams. Remember, having enough battery power and memory capacity is crucial. The rest of the products we discussed enable a user to protect a device, increase functionality, or just plain make it more fun, but these products are usually not essential to the device performing its job.

Other Types of Mobile Devices and Wearable Technology

Nowadays there are lots of other types of mobile devices. Many combine the functionality of multiple devices into a single device (for example, the Kindle reading device has a built-in web browser). In this section, we'll focus on these devices' primary functions.

Let's start with the e-reader. By far the most common e-reader is the Kindle, but there is also the Nook, Kobo, Boox, and so on. These use electronic paper technology, making longer-term reading easier on the eyes when compared to reading on a tablet or a smartphone. However, they are not great when it comes to surfing the Web, though most do have Internet access. For some, the trade-off is worth it because of the inherent efficiency of the e-reader. They display text well in both dark environments and in sunlight. Plus, battery life is far superior to tablets and smartphones. Most manufacturers of these devices allow users to read their digital libraries by installing a reader app to their tablets or smartphones (or PCs) and synchronizing between the devices. Most e-readers are charged via micro-USB, and many can connect via Wi-Fi or with a cellular connection to facilitate the downloading of book files.

Next is the smart camera (or intelligent digital camera). While a smartphone or tablet usually includes a "decent" camera, a smart camera is much better at photography and video but acts as a limited mobile computing device as well. Smart cameras can use Wi-Fi connections to transfer photos to other mobile devices and PCs. Some can post photos directly to social media sites and even surf the Web. You can safely assume that smart cameras will include more smartphone and tablet-like functionality as time goes on.

> **Note**
>
> I put the word *decent* in quotation marks because it is a relative concept—professional photographers who use $5,000 cameras probably won't consider a mobile device's camera decent!

If you have a smartphone, you probably use some kind of GPS app (Google Maps, MapQuest, Scout, and so on); there are also dedicated smart GPS systems for your car that can integrate with your smartphone and social media via Wi-Fi and Bluetooth. The beauty of these is that the bulk of the CPU in the device is dedicated to GPS. If you have ever run GPS on a smartphone while other apps are running—and you experience slow performance—then you can understand why a dedicated GPS system might be a valid option for delivery drivers, those in the transportation industry, or those who simply want more accurate and efficiently presented GPS data.

Moving outside of mobile devices, let's briefly discuss wearable technology. This concept has become quite the trend in recent years. The most common (as of the writing of this book) is the smartwatch. Initial product offerings required that a smartphone be nearby (with the watch connecting via Bluetooth), but newer versions are network-ready, meaning that you can use the smartwatch on Wi-Fi networks, increasing the usability (and range) of the device. Most of these allow a user to answer calls and communicate by e-mail and text. (If you like obscure references, you could say that Dick Tracy technology has finally arrived!)

Another example of wearable technology is a fitness monitor, which is worn on the wrist or elsewhere and used by people who want to track their exercise routines and for physical rehabilitation purposes. They connect to compatible smartphones. However, most smartwatches also include fitness monitoring apps. Other wearable technology includes enhanced glasses (which can take photos and send them to your mobile device), specialized Bluetooth earpieces and headsets, and virtual reality headsets (for gaming and so forth). The list keeps going when it comes to how you can add on to your mobile device. As a technician, you should understand that many of these connect via Bluetooth (which might require a PIN code) and that Bluetooth has a limited range—usually about 30 feet. Some can work independently of the mobile device but you would need to configure it to connect to Wi-Fi. This would be done by either setting up a connection profile and/or by allowing automatic connections to "open," which means using unsecured Wi-Fi networks. We discuss Bluetooth and Wi-Fi in more depth later in the book, but for now, remember that wearable devices' wireless connections can fail and at times need to be troubleshot like any other wireless device.

Collectively, tablets, smartphones, e-readers, and other mobile devices—not to mention their wearable counterparts—make up a portion of the "Internet of Things" (IoT). The IoT is the global network of physical objects which have embedded processors (of some sort) that can communicate with computers across the Internet. I've simplified the concept greatly, but for the purposes of this book, it should suffice. This is a buzz term that you will no doubt encounter more and more. But know that it isn't limited to just personal devices; it also includes devices used in the medical, manufacturing, and transportation industries, among others. Depending on the organization you work for, you will need to install, configure, and troubleshoot a specific subset of IoT devices. Regardless, if you apply the methods and techniques in this book, you will be able to work with any device—in any market.

ExamAlert

Be able to define the Internet of Things (IoT).

Cram Quiz

Answer these questions. The answers follow the last question. If you cannot answer these questions correctly, consider reading this section again until you can.

220-901 Questions

1. Which of the following is *not* a mobile device?

   ○ **A.** Tablet

   ○ **B.** Smartphone

   ○ **C.** Desktop PC

   ○ **D.** E-reader

2. Which type of memory do most mobile devices store long-term data to?

   ○ **A.** LPDDR3

   ○ **B.** SATA magnetic disk

   ○ **C.** SATA SSD

   ○ **D.** Solid-state flash memory

3. Which type of charging connector would you find on an iPad?

   ○ **A.** micro-USB

   ○ **B.** Lightning

   ○ **C.** Thunderbolt

   ○ **D.** IP67

4. You are required to add memory to a smartphone. Which type of memory would you most likely add?

   ○ **A.** DDR3

   ○ **B.** microSD

   ○ **C.** eMMC

   ○ **D.** Compact Flash

5. You have been tasked with connecting a wireless earpiece to a smartphone. Which technology would you most likely use?

   ○ **A.** Wi-Fi

   ○ **B.** NFC

   ○ **C.** 3.5 mm

   ○ **D.** Bluetooth

6. The organization you work for allows users to work from their own mobile devices. What is this referred to as?

- ○ **A.** Mobile hotspot
- ○ **B.** IoT
- ○ **C.** BYOD
- ○ **D.** IR

Cram Quiz Answers

220-901 Answers

1. **C.** The desktop PC is not a mobile device. It is a stationary computer that is meant to stay at a person's desk. Tablets, smartphones, and e-readers are all examples of mobile devices.

2. **D.** Most mobile devices store their long-term data to solid-state flash memory. They do not use SATA as the method of connectivity. LPDDR3 is a common type of RAM used in mobile devices for short-term storage.

3. **B.** The Lightning connector is Apple's proprietary charging and synchronization connector. Micro-USB is used by most other mobile devices. Thunderbolt is a high-speed hardware interface used in desktop computers, which we will discuss more in Chapter 13. IP67 deals with ingress protection from dust and water jets.

4. **B.** You would most likely add a microSD card (if the smartphone has a slot available for add-on or upgrading). This is the most common method. DDR3 is a type of RAM; it is not used for adding long-term memory storage. eMMC is used internally on many mobile devices, but microSD is by far more common for add-on storage. Compact Flash (CF) is used by some mobile devices, but it is used much less frequently than microSD and is almost never used on a smartphone.

5. **D.** When connecting an earpiece (those little cricket-looking devices) to a smartphone, you would most likely use Bluetooth—just remember that most of them have a 30-foot range (10 meters). Wi-Fi is less likely to be used; it is more likely to be used to connect the smartphone to the LAN and ultimately to the Internet. NFC is used to transmit data between mobile devices in close proximity to each other. 3.5 mm refers to the audio port on a mobile device. It is quite possible that a user will utilize a wired headset, but the question focuses on wireless.

6. **C.** When an organization allows users to work from their own mobile devices, the organization is embracing a bring your own device (BYOD) policy. A mobile hotspot enables a smartphone or tablet to act as an Internet gateway for other mobile devices and computers. IoT stands for the Internet of Things. IR stands for infrared.

CHAPTER 8

Installing and Upgrading Windows

This chapter covers the following A+ exam topics:

▶ Installing and Upgrading to Windows 8

▶ Installing and Upgrading to Windows 7

▶ Installing Windows Vista

You can find a master list of A+ exam topics in the "Introduction."

This chapter covers CompTIA A+ 220-902 objectives 1.1 and 1.2.

Now that we have discussed the "guts" of desktop and mobile computers, it's time to talk about installing operating systems. Over the next four chapters the focus will be on Windows 8 and Windows 7, but Windows Vista is also briefly discussed.

For the CompTIA A+ 220-902 exam, you must know how to

▶ Install Windows 8, 7, and Vista

▶ Upgrade to Windows 8 and 7

▶ Troubleshoot Windows 8/7/Vista installations and upgrades

> **Note**
>
> I recommend that you get your hands on full-version copies of Windows 8 and
> Windows 7 (8.1 Pro and 7 Ultimate or Professional are preferred) and a test com-
> puter to run clean installations and upgrades of the operating systems. If you have
> been building a computer as you progress through this book, install to that one.
> This hands-on approach can help you to better visualize how operating system
> installs and upgrades perform.

I've broken this chapter into three main sections so that we can focus on
everything to do with Windows 8, then Windows 7, and finally Windows
Vista. Let's start by talking about how to install and upgrade to Windows 8.

Installing and Upgrading to Windows 8

Before you can install Windows 8 or upgrade to it, you first need to decide
which edition you will use. Then you should check the computer's hardware
to make sure it is compatible with Windows 8. Next, you need to decide on an
installation method: from DVD, from USB, as an image, or over the network.
Finally, start the installation. New installations are known as "clean" installs;
the other option is to upgrade. Upgrades to Windows 8 can be done directly
from Windows 7 and Vista (depending on hardware and the current edition of
Vista); you will learn more about upgrades to Windows 8 later in this chapter.
If it is a clean installation, Windows 8.1 is recommended from the very start. If
you are dealing with a computer that already has Windows 8, or if you cannot
get access to media with 8.1, you should upgrade the computer to 8.1 as soon
as possible. This can be done from the Start screen; the update is downloaded
from the Internet. For more details, visit the following site:

http://windows.microsoft.com/en-us/windows-8/update-from-
windows-8-tutorial

For the sake of simplicity, I often use the term "Windows 8" in various locations throughout the book, but I highly recommend updating to the latest
point release of Windows 8.

Windows 8 Editions

Windows 8 is a group of Microsoft operating systems designed for desktop
PCs, laptops, and tablet computers. The editions include Windows 8 (known

as "Core"), Windows 8 Pro, Windows 8 Enterprise, and Windows 8 RT. While Windows 8 has the core features necessary to the average user, Windows 8 Pro includes more features, such as encryption and virtualization, and optional features, such as Windows Media Center. The Enterprise edition has almost everything from the Pro edition plus additional network services for large-scale IT infrastructures. Windows RT (which is being phased out as of the writing of this book) is designed for tablet PCs that use 32-bit ARM-based CPUs; we will discuss that OS more in Chapter 18, "Android, iOS, OS X, and Linux." The rest of the Windows editions are available for 32-bit and 64-bit architectures—x86 (also known as IA-32) and x64 platforms, respectively. In Table 8.1, the check marks indicate some of the components that are included in these various editions of Windows 8. Chapter 9, "Configuring Windows," talks more about these components.

TABLE 8.1 **Comparison of Windows 8 Editions**

Component	Windows 8	Windows 8 Pro	Windows 8 Enterprise*
Internet Explorer 10	✓	✓	✓
Remote Desktop	✓ but client only	✓	✓
Domain Join	—	✓	✓
BitLocker Encryption and EFS	—	✓	✓
Hyper-V	—	✓ but 64-bit edition only	✓ but 64-bit edition only
Windows To Go	—	—	✓

* Windows 8 Enterprise is not sold through retail or OEM channels.

> **ExamAlert**
>
> Know the differences between the various editions of Windows 8.

Windows 8 Minimum Requirements and Compatibility

After you have planned out which edition of Windows 8 you will use, and before installing that operating system, you should find out more about the computer you plan to install to. The components in the computer need to meet the minimum requirements for installing Windows 8—and really should exceed them if you want good performance. Table 8.2 shows the minimum hardware requirements for Windows 8.1. (Sorry for the somewhat confusing numbers, it just worked out that way!)

TABLE 8.2 **Windows 8.1 Minimum Requirements**

Component	Requirement
Processor	1 GHz (support for PAE, NX, and SSE2). 64-bit is recommended.
RAM	1 GB (32-bit) or 2 GB (64-bit). 4 GB is recommended.
Free drive space	16 GB free space (32-bit) or 20 GB (64-bit).
Video	DirectX 9 with WDDM 1.0 or higher driver. DirectX 10 is recommended.

ExamAlert

Memorize the *minimum* requirements for Windows 8.

In general, you can use several websites and system analysis tools to check whether a system's hardware is compatible with Windows. If you check a computer that already has an operating system installed, you can make use of the System window in the Control Panel within the current version of Windows, or you can use the System Information tool (Run > msinfo32.exe). Alternatively, you can access Microsoft's website for detailed information about requirements or use third-party analysis tools such as Belarc Advisor.

For computers without an installed operating system, go to the BIOS/UEFI to find out what's running in the system. This is what I do first and most often. Or consider looking at the actual components inside the computer. A quick glance should tell you whether the computer is compatible or not. Finally, you can use one of the many free, self-booting diagnostic programs available on the Internet, and we'll discuss a few of these later in the book.

Windows 8 Installation Methods

Windows 8 can be installed in a variety of ways. The most typical is from installation media: either DVD or a bootable USB flash drive. These are known as local installations and they work great for installing Windows 8 to a single computer. The steps involved in a local installation are not difficult, but if you want more information, visit the following Microsoft site:

http://windows.microsoft.com/en-us/windows-8/clean-install

You can also install Windows 8 over the network. This can be done using a Windows Server and the Windows Deployment Services and/or System Center Configuration Manager (SCCM) or by accessing any Windows or Linux server acting as a repository of the Windows installation files. (Those servers will also operate as DHCP and TFTP servers.) If you do need to perform an over-the-network installation, be sure that the target computer has a Preboot Execution Environment (PXE)-compliant network adapter. This allows the computer to boot to the network and locate the DHCP server and ultimately perform the installation (as long as the server is configured properly).

You can also "image" the computer with a premade OS image. Do this with the Microsoft Deployment Toolkit or with third-party tools such as Symantec Ghost. In addition, you can install from a recovery disc that you created or that was supplied by the vendor of the computer. To learn more about Windows 8 deployment, visit the following TechNet site:

https://technet.microsoft.com/en-us/windows/hh974336.aspx

We'll discuss some of these installation methods in more detail in the Windows 7 section.

Upgrading to Windows 8

If a computer is running Windows 7 or Windows Vista, the upgrade to Windows 8 is fairly painless. As with clean installations, you will need to check the compatibility of the system and make sure it meets the minimum requirements. The Windows Upgrade Assistant can be helpful in this regard. This can be downloaded from the following website. You will also find additional information on upgrading to Windows 8.

http://windows.microsoft.com/en-us/windows-8/upgrade-from-windows-7-tutorial

The Upgrade Assistant will provide a report of the computer and what you need to review. In some cases, a portion of the devices and applications need to be reinstalled once the Windows 8 installation is complete. The Upgrade Assistant asks what you want to keep; for example, personal files. The installation can then be done by USB flash drive, DVD-based media, or from an .ISO file (if purchased as a download over the Internet) that will need to be burned to a DVD or copied to a USB flash drive.

> **Note**
>
> You can also download the Windows Installation Media Creation Tool to create Windows 8.1 operating system media: http://windows.microsoft.com/en-us/windows-8/create-reset-refresh-media.

Finally, choose settings and sign in, and Windows 8 is installed and running. It is wise to then update the computer to Windows 8.1 or install any additional updates. Remember to install antimalware software before going any further with the system.

> **Note**
>
> As always, any important files and settings should be backed up to an external source before beginning the installation. That source could be a secondary hard drive, DVD(s), or USB flash drive.

Another consideration when upgrading is the upgrade path. By upgrade path, we mean the path from the edition of Windows that is currently running on the computer to the edition of Windows 8 that is desired. Table 8.3 gives some examples of upgrade paths for Windows 7 to Windows 8. For more information, visit the following TechNet site:

https://technet.microsoft.com/en-us/library/JJ203353.aspx

TABLE 8.3 **Windows 7 to 8 Upgrade Paths**

From Windows 7	To Windows 8
Starter	Windows 8, Windows 8 Pro
Home Basic	Windows 8, Windows 8 Pro
Home Premium	Windows 8, Windows 8 Pro
Professional	Windows 8 Pro, Windows 8 Enterprise
Ultimate	Windows 8 Pro
Enterprise	Windows 8 Enterprise

Know that this is not a finite list. There are a lot of potential permutations when it comes to upgrading so be sure to research whether or not the target computer is actually upgradeable and, if so, what the exact process will be. Also know that older operating systems, such as Windows Vista and Windows XP, that are to be upgraded to Windows 8 require installation media. I give more upgrade considerations in the Windows 7 section.

Cram Quiz

Answer these questions. The answers follow the last question. If you cannot answer these questions correctly, consider reading this section again until you can.

220-902 Questions

1. Of the following, which media can be used for a local installation of Windows 8? (Select the two best answers.)

   ○ **A.** USB flash drive

   ○ **B.** PXE network adapter

   ○ **C.** DVD-ROM

   ○ **D.** CD-ROM

2. Which editions of Windows 8 offer Hyper-V? (Select the two best answers.)

   ○ **A.** Windows 8 Core

   ○ **B.** Windows 8 Pro

   ○ **C.** Windows 8 Enterprise

   ○ **D.** Windows RT

3. What is the minimum CPU required for Windows 8?

   ○ **A.** 1 GB

   ○ **B.** 1 GHz

   ○ **C.** 16 GB

   ○ **D.** 2 GHz

4. Which edition of Windows 8 can Windows 7 Ultimate be upgraded to?

   ○ **A.** Windows 8

   ○ **B.** Windows 8 Pro

   ○ **C.** Windows 8 Enterprise

   ○ **D.** Windows 8 Ultimate

Cram Quiz Answers

220-902 Answers

1. **A and C.** You can use a DVD or a USB flash drive. A PXE-compliant network adapter is necessary if you wish to install Windows 8 over the network. Microsoft does not offer Windows 8 installation media in CD-ROM format, nor can you burn a Windows 8 .ISO file to a CD (the installation media is too small).

2. **B and C.** Windows 8 Pro and Enterprise offer Hyper-V virtualization functionality. Windows 8 Core (or simply Windows 8) does not, nor does Windows RT for tablet PCs.

3. **B.** The minimum requirement is 1 GHz for the CPU. The minimum RAM requirement for 32-bit systems is 1 GB (2 GB for 64-bit systems). 16 GB is the minimum free drive space required in 32-bit systems (20 GB for 64-bit systems).

4. **B.** Windows 7 Ultimate can be upgraded to Windows 8 Pro only. There is no Windows 8 Ultimate.

Installing and Upgrading to Windows 7

Windows 7 is similar to Windows 8 in many ways. From a more generalized perspective, you perform essentially the same tasks when planning, installing, and upgrading Windows 7. You should check for hardware compatibility and make sure that hardware meets the minimum requirements for Windows 7. Then decide on your installation method, be it DVD, USB, over the network, or from an image. As before, brand-new installations are known as clean installs. On the other hand, upgrades to Windows 7 can be done directly from Windows Vista (depending on hardware and the current edition of Vista), but they require more effort from older versions of Windows (such as Windows XP); we will cover more about upgrades to Windows 7 later in this chapter.

> **Note**
>
> Some of the topics in the Windows 7 section can be applied to Windows 8 as well. Keep in mind that architecturally, the two operating systems are quite similar.

Windows 7 Editions

Windows 7 is an entire line of Microsoft operating systems designed for desktop PCs and laptops. Within the Windows 7 group are the editions Starter, Home Premium, Professional, Ultimate, and Enterprise. Starter is only available through original equipment manufacturers (OEMs) and is common among laptops. In addition, Starter is only available in a 32-bit version. However, the other editions are all available in 64-bit and 32-bit versions. In Table 8.4, the check marks indicate the components that are included in these various editions of Win7. Chapter 9, "Configuring Windows," talks more about these components.

TABLE 8.4   **Comparison of Windows 7 Editions**

Component	Starter	Home Premium	Professional	Ultimate	Enterprise*
Internet Explorer 8	✓	✓	✓	✓	✓
Create Home Group	—	✓	✓	✓	✓
Domain Join	—	—	✓	✓	✓

Component	Starter	Home Premium	Professional	Ultimate	Enterprise*
Windows XP Mode	—	—	✓	✓	✓
Backup to home or business network	—	—	✓	✓	✓
BitLocker Encryption	—	—	—	✓	✓

* Windows 7 Enterprise is not sold through retail or OEM channels.

> **ExamAlert**
>
> Know the differences between the various editions of Windows 7.

Windows 7 Minimum Requirements and Compatibility

When you decide on the edition of Win7 you want to use, and before installing that operating system, you should learn as much as you can about the computer you plan to install to. Components in a computer should meet Windows 7 minimum requirements and should be listed on Microsoft's website as compatible with Windows 7. Table 8.5 shows the minimum hardware requirements for Windows 7.

TABLE 8.5 **Windows 7 Minimum Requirements**

Component	Requirement
Processor	1 GHz 32-bit (x86) or 64-bit (x64)
RAM	1 GB (32-bit) or 2 GB (64-bit)
Free drive space	16 GB free space (32-bit) or 20 GB (64-bit)
Video	DirectX 9 with WDDM 1.0 or higher driver

> **ExamAlert**
>
> Memorize the *minimum* requirements for Windows 7.
>
> An important consideration is the CPU. Not only must it be fast enough, it must also be the right type: 32-bit or 64-bit.

As mentioned in the Windows 8 section, you can use several websites and system analysis tools to check whether a system's hardware is compatible with Windows 7. These include the System window, System Information tool, Microsoft online tools, and third-party analysis tools.

Windows 7 Installation Methods

There are several types of installation methods for Windows 7 (many of them apply to other Windows versions as well):

▶ **Local installation from DVD-ROM:** Installation by DVD-ROM is the most common installation method for Windows 7. A "local" installation is the default type. It means that you insert the DVD-ROM into the DVD-ROM drive of the computer you are sitting at, known as the local computer. When you sit at the computer and answer all the questions it asks you, it is known as an Attended Installation; you are attending to the computer as the install progresses.

▶ **Local installation from USB:** Installation by USB is much easier than it used to be. Images of Windows operating systems can be purchased and downloaded from the Microsoft website in .ISO format and then copied to a USB flash drive. After this, the image can be made bootable by downloading, installing, and running the Windows USB/DVD Download Tool. This can be obtained from https://www.microsoft.com/en-us/download/windows-usb-dvd-download-tool. To run this program and install from USB, the user must be an administrator and the computer must have the .NET Framework 2.0 or higher installed. This process makes things a lot easier for users with compact laptops or other small form-factor devices that might not have optical drives.

> **Note**
>
> If you are interested in step-by-step instructions for a standard local installation of Windows 7, go to the A+ archive page on my website: www.davidlprowse.com.

▶ **Network installation:** You can install Windows over the network in a variety of ways. To automate the process, Windows 7 can be installed from a server automatically by using Windows Deployment Services, which can be installed on Windows Server. This server-based program works with the Windows System Image Manager program in Win7. This program can be used to create an answer file that is used during an

Unattended Installation. The answer file provides the responses needed for the installation, with no user intervention necessary. In Windows 7, there is a single XML-based answer file called Unattend.xml.

> **Note**
>
> The Windows System Image Manager (SIM) for Win7 is part of the Windows Automated Installation Kit (AIK), which can be downloaded from www.microsoft.com; just search for Windows Automated Installation Kit (AIK). For detailed instructions on how to use SIM, visit the following site:
>
> http://technet.microsoft.com/en-us/library/dd744394(WS.10).aspx
>
> The Windows Preinstallation Environment, known as Windows PE or simply WinPE, is also available as part of the Windows AIK. It can be booted from optical disc, USB flash drive, over the network via PXE, or from the hard drive. Windows 7 uses WinPE version 3.0 and 3.1. It can be used to run recovery tools such as the Windows Recovery Environment (Windows RE) and Winternals as well as for running drive-cloning utilities.
>
> For general information about Windows 7 deployment, visit the following site:
>
> http://technet.microsoft.com/en-us/library/dd744519(WS.10).aspx

▶ **Drive image:** Windows can also be installed from a previously made System Restore image (for more information on System Restore, see Chapter 11, "Troubleshooting Windows") or by cloning the entire drive image of another installation. This can be done by using programs such as Acronis True Image or Symantec Ghost. When cloning a drive image, both computers must be identical, or as close to identical as possible. The hard drive of the target for a cloned installation must be at least as large as the original system. To avoid Security Identifier (SID) conflicts, use the Sysprep utility. The Sysprep utility for Windows 7 is installed with the operating system and can be found by navigating to C:\Windows\System32\Sysprep. Sysprep uses an answer file created with the SIM. It creates a unique SID and makes other changes as needed to the network configuration of the system.

> **Note**
>
> If installing an OS over the network from a drive image or through deployment, your network adapter needs to be PXE-compliant. PXE needs to be enabled in the BIOS.

▶ **Installing from a recovery disc:** Computers with Windows preinstalled use a recovery disc, hidden partition, or both. This disc and/or
partition contains a factory image of Windows. The purpose of this is
to enable users to return their computers back to the state when they
were first received. This means that the system partition (usually the
C: drive) will be properly formatted and reimaged with Windows. This
works well in a two partition system, in which the operating system is
on C: and data is stored on D: or another drive letter. In this scenario,
when the operating system fails and cannot be repaired, the computer
can be returned to its original "factory" state, but the data won't be
compromised. Whenever buying a computer from a company such as
HP, Dell, and so on, make sure that they offer some kind of factory
recovery partition, recovery disc, or other recovery option.

> **ExamAlert**
>
> Know the difference between a local, network, drive image, and recovery disc
> installation.

▶ **Multiboots:** Since the 1990s, technicians have been setting up two or
more operating systems on the same hard drive; this is known as dual-
booting, tri-booting, and so on. This is easier than it used to be back
in the 1990s; nowadays you can usually get away with using built-in
tools in Windows. For example, if you have Windows 7 installed, you
can modify the partition structure with Disk Management, create an
additional partition, and install Windows 8 to that partition. If successful, both operating systems display in a menu when the computer
is booted. The information pertaining to these operating systems is
stored in the Boot Configuration Data (BCD) store in Windows 7. You
might also want to dual-boot different types of operating systems, such
as Windows and Linux. This requires additional planning, and might be
easier done with tools such as GParted or KDE Partition Manager.

> **ExamAlert**
>
> Understand that multiboots allow two or more operating systems to inhabit one
> hard drive.

Upgrading to Windows 7

Upgrades are done in essentially the same manner as clean installs. The difference is that all the settings, applications, and user files will ultimately be kept in place if the upgrade is successful (and if it is the right type of upgrade). However, it is recommended that those files and settings are backed up before you begin the upgrade—just in case. Before starting the upgrade, you should first check to see if your computer (and operating system) is compatible and if it will survive the process. Refer to Table 8.5 for the Windows 7 minimum requirements. You can also use the following utilities and websites to do this:

▶ **Windows Upgrade Advisor:** This is a website that is accessed by clicking on the Check compatibility online button when you first insert the Windows 7 DVD. Of course, the computer that you are upgrading must have Internet access. You can also download the Windows 7 Upgrade Advisor from Microsoft's website.

▶ **Windows Compatibility Center:** http://www.microsoft.com/windows/compatibility/.

ExamAlert

Remember that the Upgrade Advisor can be used to check if a system meets Windows 7 requirements.

Only Windows Vista can be upgraded directly to Windows 7. To upgrade Windows Vista to Windows 7, make sure that service pack 1 or 2 is installed to Vista prior to the upgrade, insert the DVD, and then select the Upgrade option. The steps to complete the upgrade are similar to the clean installation steps. Table 8.6 shows which editions of Windows 7 can be upgraded from the various editions of Windows Vista.

TABLE 8.6 **Windows Vista to 7 Upgrade Paths**

From Windows Vista (SP1, SP2)	To Windows 7
Business	Professional, Enterprise, Ultimate
Enterprise	Enterprise
Home Basic	Home Basic, Home Premium, Ultimate
Home Premium	Home Premium, Ultimate
Ultimate	Ultimate

Any other combinations of upgrades from Vista to Win7 would require

► Backing up all data prior to the upgrade

► A Custom (advanced) installation (basically wipes the hard drive)

► The reinstallation of any applications post-upgrade

► The restoration of all data files

Microsoft recommends the Windows Easy Transfer program for the backup and restoration of files.

Here are a couple of important points concerning 32-bit and 64-bit versions of Windows:

► 32-bit versions of Windows *cannot* be directly upgraded to 64-bit versions.

► 32-bit or 64-bit versions of Windows can be installed to a computer with a 64-bit processor.

► However, 32-bit processors accept only 32-bit versions of Windows.

Okay, let's all take a deep breath!

Moving on! Let's talk about Anytime Upgrades and Repair-In-Place Upgrades.

An *Anytime Upgrade* is when a person upgrades one edition of Windows 7 to a more advanced edition of Windows 7. For example, say that a user working with Home Premium needs access to the BitLocker functionality. That user would have to upgrade to Windows 7 Ultimate. Anytime Upgrades do not require a physical disc or a download because all the Windows 7 software is preloaded to the disc. A user simply needs to purchase an upgrade key online. Table 8.7 shows what the various editions of Windows 7 can be upgraded to.

TABLE 8.7 **Windows 7 Anytime Upgrades**

From Windows 7	Anytime Upgrade to Windows 7
Home Basic	Home Premium, Professional, Ultimate
Home Premium	Professional, Ultimate
Professional	Ultimate
Starter	Home Premium, Professional, Ultimate

When troubleshooting a system, a *Repair-In-Place Upgrade* is your last resort before doing a complete reinstall of the OS. It's also known as a repair installation. Say there was an issue with Windows 7 Ultimate and you could not fix it. You could close all applications, insert the Windows 7 Ultimate DVD, and start the upgrade, being sure to select Upgrade when the time comes. This type of repair installation is not supposed to damage files and applications that are currently installed to the computer. However, it can copy original system files and reset certain settings. A lot can go wrong with these repair installations, so again, try to solve any issues in another way; use this option as your last hope (and be sure to back up important data). You learn more about this in Chapter 11.

Verifying and Troubleshooting Windows 7 Installations

When you complete the clean installation or upgrade, test your installation to verify it has gone smoothly. For example, attempt to navigate through Windows, access administrative functions, connect to the Internet, and so on.

ExamAlert

Be sure you know where tools and settings are located within the various operating systems mentioned. You will encounter performance-based exam questions that will expect you to navigate through Windows and complete specific tasks.

If you have confirmed that Windows 7 is working normally, update the system. Install the service pack and additional updates as necessary. It is possible that the service pack was included on your installation media, but if not, download it and install it before going any further. Then download any other necessary updates by utilizing the Windows Update feature. More information about service packs and updates can be found in Chapter 9.

Installations usually go smoothly, but not always. If an installation fails for any reason, or if the installation completed but Windows doesn't seem to be behaving properly, consider reviewing the log files to find out more about the problem and why it occurred. Table 8.8 describes the important log files you should know and their locations.

TABLE 8.8 Windows 7 Setup Log Files and Locations

Log File Location	Description
$windows.~bt\Sources\Panther	Location of the log before Setup can access the drive.
$windows.~bt\Sources\Rollback	Location of the log when setup rolls back in the event of a fatal error.
%WINDIR%\Panther	Location of the log containing setup actions after drive configuration.
%WINDIR%\Panther\setuperr.log	Contains information about setup errors during the installation. Start with this log file when troubleshooting. A file size of 0 bytes indicates no errors during installation.
%WINDIR%\Panther\setupact.log	Contains information about setup actions during the installation.
%WINDIR%\Inf\Setupapi*.log	Used to log Plug and Play device installations. setupapi*.log can refer to multiple files (the asterisk is wild), including setupapi.offline.log (as on a Win7 computer) and Online configuration phase files setupapi.dev.log and setupapi.app.log. This applies to any other references in the book to setupapi*.log. Visit the following site for more information on Windows setup log files: http://support.microsoft.com/kb/927521
%WINDIR%\Panther\Setup.etl	Location of Windows Setup performance events.
%WINDIR%\Memory.dmp	Location of memory dump to use for bug checks.
%WINDIR%\Minidump*.dmp	Location of mini-memory dumps to use for bug checks.
%WINDIR%\System32\Sysprep\	Location of logs generated by Sysprep Panther.

Table 8.8 shows the variable directory called %WINDIR%. By default, the name of this folder in Windows 7 will be Windows. %WINDIR% is the newer name of the variable previously called %systemroot%. Also, $windows.~bt is a temporary boot folder created during setup. It remains if the installation was not successful, allowing you to analyze the log files, but should be automatically deleted when the installation completes properly.

Windows includes the capability to review Setup events within the Event Viewer, or by way of a script. Visit the following site for details:

http://technet.microsoft.com/en-us/library/dd744583(WS.10).aspx

If the system won't start, you can still view these files. However, this depends on the type of installation and how far the installation got. If it was a clean installation, you should boot to the Windows 7 DVD, select Repair your computer, access the System Recovery Options menu (in the Windows Recovery Environment), and then select the Command Prompt. If it was an upgrade that didn't get far, and if Windows Vista was previously installed on an NTFS drive, you can boot to the System Recovery Options and view the log files from there. For more information about System Recovery Options and the Windows Recovery Environment, see Chapter 11.

> **ExamAlert**
>
> Know that you can view the log files to aid in troubleshooting Windows installation issues. Use the Windows Recovery Environment if necessary.

If you cannot start the clean installation or upgrade, check the following:

- ▶ **Processor speed and memory size:** Verify that your computer meets the minimum requirements for Windows 7. Refer to Table 8.5 for more information.

- ▶ **Windows type and edition:** Make sure you are installing the correct type (32-bit or 64-bit) and edition of Windows 7 (Starter, Home Premium, and so on).

- ▶ **Free drive space:** Make sure you have at least 16 GB/20 GB free for Windows 7 (for 32-bit and 64-bit editions respectively); the more space available, the better.

- ▶ **Hardware conflicts or hardware issues:** Use Device Manager to ensure that all hardware works correctly before you start an upgrade.

- ▶ **Installation media:** Make sure that your DVD-ROM or USB media is not scratched or damaged in any way. Verify that it is genuine Microsoft software and that you have the right type of media for your installation (for example, Windows 7 Full Version License or Upgrade DVD or a properly configured USB flash drive).

> **ExamAlert**
>
> Know your Windows 7 installation troubleshooting techniques for the exam.

Cram Quiz

Answer these questions. The answers follow the last question. If you cannot answer these questions correctly, consider reading this section again until you can.

220-902 Questions

1. What is the minimum RAM requirement for Windows 7 (64-bit)?

   ○ **A.** 2 GB

   ○ **B.** 256 MB

   ○ **C.** 1536 MB

   ○ **D.** 768 MB

2. Which log file contains information regarding Windows 7 Setup performance events?

   ○ **A.** Setupapi*.log

   ○ **B.** Setupact.log

   ○ **C.** Setup.etl

   ○ **D.** Event Viewer

3. Where can you go to find out if your current operating system can be upgraded to Windows 7?

   ○ **A.** MSKB

   ○ **B.** Windows Upgrade Advisor

   ○ **C.** HAL

   ○ **D.** Belarc Advisor

4. Which editions of Windows 7 have the capability to back up to a home or business network? (Select the best two answers.)

   ○ **A.** Starter

   ○ **B.** Home Premium

   ○ **C.** Professional

   ○ **D.** Ultimate

5. What is the minimum hard drive requirement for Windows 7?

   ○ **A.** 16 GB free space

   ○ **B.** 15 GB partition

   ○ **C.** 25 GB free space

   ○ **D.** 16 GB partition

6. To avoid SID conflicts when drive imaging, which program should you use in Windows 7?

   ○ **A.** Sysprep

   ○ **B.** Setup Manager

   ○ **C.** SIM

   ○ **D.** Windows Deployment Services

7. Which of the following are possible ways to install Windows 7? (Select all that apply.)

   ○ **A.** From DVD

   ○ **B.** From CD

   ○ **C.** Over the network

   ○ **D.** Using Symantec Ghost

8. You want to perform a network installation of Windows. Which of the following must be supported by the client computer?

   ○ **A.** PCIe

   ○ **B.** PXE

   ○ **C.** BitLocker

   ○ **D.** Multiboot

9. Which of the following is available in Windows 7 Professional but *not* in Windows 7 Home Premium? (Select the two best answers.)

   ○ **A.** Windows XP Mode

   ○ **B.** IE 8

   ○ **C.** BitLocker

   ○ **D.** Home Group

10. Which of the following can be used to install a manufacturer's recovery image on a computer? (Select the two best answers.)

    ○ **A.** Data backup

    ○ **B.** Recovery CD

    ○ **C.** Recovery Agent

    ○ **D.** System Restore utility

Cram Quiz Answers

220-902 Answers

1. **A.** The minimum RAM requirement for Windows 7 is 2 GB for 64-bit versions and 1 GB for 32-bit versions.

2. **C.** Setup.etl contains information regarding Windows 7 Setup performance events. Setupapi*.log is used for events about Windows 7 Plug and Play device installations. Setupact.log is a log file that contains information regarding actions during installation. The Event Viewer is an application, not a file.

3. **B.** The Windows Upgrade Advisor can tell you if your current operating system can be upgraded to Win7. This, and other tools like it, is located at www.microsoft.com, not at the MSKB (http://support.microsoft.com). HAL is a file in Windows; it stands for hardware abstraction layer. Belarc Advisor is a third-party offering that analyzes your computer but does not determine whether it can be upgraded.

4. **C and D.** Windows 7 Professional and Ultimate include the capability to back up to a home or business network easily.

5. **A.** Windows 7 (32-bit) requires a minimum 16 GB of free space. 64-bit versions require 20 GB.

6. **A.** Sysprep can modify unattended installations so that every computer gets a unique SID (and other unique information). Windows SIM creates the answer files for unattended installations. Setup Manager (setupmgr.exe) is the now deprecated program that Windows XP/2000 used to create answer files. Windows Deployment Services is run on Windows Server and is used to deploy operating systems across the network.

7. **A, C, and D.** Windows 7 can be installed from DVD, USB, over the network, and by using programs such as Symantec Ghost.

8. **B.** To perform a network installation, a network adapter in a computer must be PXE-compliant. PCIe is an expansion bus. BitLocker is a full drive encryption feature included with select editions of Windows, such as Windows 7 Ultimate and Enterprise. Multiboot technology means that the computer can boot to two or more operating systems.

9. **A and C.** Windows XP Mode is available in Windows 7 Professional, Ultimate, and Enterprise. This mode can be helpful if you need to run older programs that won't work in Windows 7. It is not included in Home Premium or Starter. BitLocker is not included in Home Premium either (or Starter or Professional, for that matter). Internet Explorer 8 and Home Group are all components included in both Windows 7 Professional and Home Premium.

10. **B and D.** A recovery CD and an image previously made with System Restore can be used to install an image to a computer. Data backups are the files that must be recovered after the OS is installed or recovered. The Recovery Agent is used in Windows to recover encryption keys from deleted or unavailable user accounts to gain access to lost data.

CHAPTER 8: Installing and Upgrading Windows

Installing Windows Vista

Before you can install Windows Vista or upgrade to it, you need to decide which edition of Vista to use. Then you should check the computer's hardware to make sure it is compatible with Windows Vista. Next, you need to decide on an installation method: from DVD, CD, as an image, or over the network. Finally, start the installation. New installations are known as "clean" installs; the other option is to upgrade from Windows XP or earlier. However, I don't cover upgrades from previous operating systems because Windows XP (and earlier) is not in the 220-901/220-902 objectives. Also, Microsoft support of Windows XP has ended. So I will limit the discussion to the clean installation.

Windows Vista Editions

Windows Vista is an entire line of Microsoft operating systems designed for desktop PCs and laptops. Within the Windows Vista group are the editions Home Basic, Home Premium, Business, and Ultimate, available in 64-bit and 32-bit versions. In Table 8.9, the check marks indicate the components that are included in these various editions of Vista. We talk more about these components in Chapter 9.

TABLE 8.9 **Comparison of Windows Vista Editions**

Component	Home Basic	Home Premium	Business	Ultimate	Enterprise*
Windows Aero	—	✓	✓	✓	✓
Share Documents	—	✓	✓	✓	✓
Media Center Functionality	—	✓	—	✓	—
Windows Complete PC Backup	—	—	✓	✓	✓
Remote Desktop Connection	—	—	✓	✓	✓
BitLocker Encryption	—	—	—	✓	✓

* Vista Enterprise is not sold through retail or OEM channels.

> **Note**
>
> There is an additional edition of Vista called Vista Starter (sold in underdeveloped technology markets).

ExamAlert

Know the main differences between the Vista editions Home Premium, Business, and Ultimate for the exam.

Windows Vista Minimum Requirements and Compatibility

When you decide on the edition of Vista you want to use, and before installing that operating system, you should learn as much as you can about the computer you plan to install to. Components in a computer should meet Windows Vista's minimum requirements and should be listed on Microsoft's website as compatible with Vista. Table 8.10 shows the minimum hardware requirements for Windows Vista.

TABLE 8.10   Windows Vista Minimum Requirements

Component	Requirement
Processor	800 MHz
RAM	512 MB
Free drive space	15 GB free space (Within 20 GB partition)
Other	DVD-ROM or CD-ROM drive

ExamAlert

Memorize the *minimum* requirements for Windows Vista.

You can use several websites and system analysis tools to check whether a system's hardware will be compatible with Windows Vista, including the System Information tool, Belarc Advisor, and PC diagnostic tools, as mentioned previously in the chapter. However, nowadays it will be uncommon for you to find a computer that can't run Windows Vista.

Note

The Windows Vista DVD has a Check compatibility online option, but this is meant more for upgrades rather than clean installations.

Windows Vista Installation Methods

Windows Vista can be installed in the same ways as Windows 7, with the addition of a local installation from CD-ROM. Microsoft recommends that the DVD-ROM be used for installations of Windows Vista; however, you can order a CD-ROM version if you can provide proof of purchase.

The installation of Vista is pretty straightforward and is similar to Windows 7. For a written step-by-step and video of the process, access my website at http://www.davidlprowse.com and go to the A+ videos section.

Verifying and Troubleshooting Windows Vista Installations

When you complete the clean installation or upgrade, *test it*. If you have confirmed that Windows is working normally, update the system. The latest (and last) service pack (SP) for Windows Vista is SP2. It is possible that the service pack was included on your installation media, but if not, download it and install it before going any further. Then download any other necessary updates by utilizing the Windows Update feature. More information about service packs and updates can be found in Chapter 10.

> **Note**
>
> You can also learn about all of the latest Windows operating systems service packs and updates at the Windows Service Pack and Update Center by visiting the following site:
>
> http://windows.microsoft.com/en-us/windows/service-packs-download# sptabs=vista

Installations usually go smoothly, but not always. If an installation fails for any reason, or if the installation completed but Windows doesn't seem to be behaving properly, consider reviewing the log files to learn more about the problem and why it occurred. Windows Vista is a bit more complicated than older Windows systems when it comes to log files. Vista's log files might vary slightly and have different locations depending on the phase of the installation when they were logged. The Vista installation process is broken into four phases:

▶ **Downlevel phase:** This is the phase that is run from within the previous operating system (meaning when you start the installation from the DVD in Windows XP, for example).

▶ **Windows Preinstallation Environment phase:** Also known as Windows PE, this phase occurs after the restart at the end of the down-level phase. If you are installing to a new hard drive, this phase occurs when you first boot the computer to the Windows Vista DVD.

▶ **Online configuration phase:** The online configuration phase starts when a user receives the following message: Please wait a moment while Windows prepares to start for the first time. Hardware support is installed during this phase.

▶ **Windows Welcome phase:** During this phase, a computer name is selected for the computer and the Windows System Assessment Tool (Winsat.exe) checks the performance of the computer. This is the final phase before the user first logs on.

There are log files for each phase (as shown previously in Table 8.8). To review, these are located in one of several locations. For example, C:\Windows\Panther houses setuperr.log, a file that contains errors regarding the installation of Windows, and setupact.log, which contains information about setup actions taken. Another example is C:\Windows\Inf, where setupapi.dev.log resides. A third location is C:\Windows\Performance\Winsat, where the Winsat.log file can be found. For a list of all log files within all phases of the Windows Vista installation, visit the following site:

http://support.microsoft.com/kb/927521

If you cannot start the clean installation or upgrade, check the following:

▶ **Processor speed and memory size:** Verify that your computer meets the minimum requirements for Windows Vista. Refer to Table 8.10 for more information.

▶ **Free drive space:** Make sure you have at least 15 GB free for Windows Vista; the more space available, the better.

▶ **Hardware conflicts or hardware issues:** Use Device Manager to ensure that all hardware works correctly before you start an upgrade.

▶ **Installation media:** Make sure that your DVD-ROM (or CD-ROM) media is not scratched or damaged in any way. Verify that it is genuine Microsoft software and that you have the right type of media for your installation (for example, Vista Full Version License or Upgrade DVD).

Upgrades to Windows Vista can be especially troublesome. You might experience problems connecting to a LAN or the Internet, or certain hardware might not work properly. Be sure to access the Microsoft Knowledge Base (MSKB) at http://support.microsoft.com for clues as to why these errors occur. Because Windows XP is not supported any longer, most organizations will simply back up all important data and do a clean installation of Vista (or newer version of Windows) instead of going through the trouble of an upgrade. For a list of specific errors concerning a Windows Vista upgrade, visit http://support.microsoft.com/kb/930743.

Cram Quiz

Answer these questions. The answers follow the last question. If you cannot answer these questions correctly, consider reading this section again until you can.

220-902 Questions

1. What is the minimum RAM requirement for Windows Vista?
   - ○ **A.** 2 GB
   - ○ **B.** 256 MB
   - ○ **C.** 512 MB
   - ○ **D.** 768 MB

2. Which file contains information regarding errors during a Windows Vista installation?
   - ○ **A.** Setuperr.log
   - ○ **B.** Setupact.log
   - ○ **C.** Event Viewer
   - ○ **D.** Unattend.xml

3. Which editions of Vista have media center functionality? (Select the best two answers.)
   - ○ **A.** Home Basic
   - ○ **B.** Home Premium
   - ○ **C.** Business
   - ○ **D.** Ultimate

4. Which of the following is the hard drive requirement for Windows Vista?
   - ○ **A.** 15 GB free space
   - ○ **B.** 15 GB partition
   - ○ **C.** 20 GB free space
   - ○ **D.** 25 GB partition

Cram Quiz Answers

220-902 Answers

1. **C.** The minimum RAM requirement for Windows Vista is 512 MB. Microsoft recommends 1 GB of RAM for Home Premium, Business, and Ultimate.

2. **A.** Setuperr.log contains information regarding errors during installation. Setupact.log contains information regarding *actions* during installation. The Event Viewer is an application, not a file, and might not contain installation details. Unattend.xml is the answer file generated by Windows SIM for unattended installations.

3. **B and D.** Windows Vista Home Premium and Ultimate include media center functionality; the others do not.

4. **A.** Vista requires 15 GB of free space within a 20 GB partition.

CHAPTER 9

Configuring Windows

This chapter covers the following A+ exam topics:

▶ Windows User Interfaces

▶ System Tools and Utilities

▶ Files, File Systems, and Drives

You can find a master list of A+ exam topics in the "Introduction."

This chapter covers CompTIA A+ 220-902 objectives 1.1 through 1.5.

So the computer is built and Windows is installed; now it's time to configure the operating system! This chapter covers Windows user interfaces, system tools, and utilities, and describes how to manage files and drives. Our focus is on Windows 7 and Windows 8 and 8.1 (which I simply refer to as Windows 8), but we also discuss Windows Vista. However, instead of breaking the sections up by the operating system (like we did in Chapter 8), this chapter merges Windows 8, 7, and Vista together by topic. Because these operating systems are similar, you will find that many of the configurations work the same way. You will also note that operating system navigation might be slightly different from one version to the next when you are trying to access the same feature. The learning curve is small, however. In addition, there are slight differences in some of the application names. Keep this in mind as we progress through the chapter. Also, make note of the fact that a particular setting in Windows might be arrived at from several different routes. This chapter tries to show alternative routes but doesn't cover all of them. Use the route that is the fastest and easiest for you, but try to remember as many routes as possible for the exam.

> **Note**
>
> I recommend that you run through all the configurations in this chapter on your computer(s). If you don't have computers available for Windows 8, 7, and Vista, consider running virtual machines to act as the additional computers. Microsoft offers Windows Virtual PC for free; it can be downloaded from Microsoft's website. There is also Hyper-V for Windows 8.1 (see http://windows.microsoft.com/en-us/windows-8/hyper-v-run-virtual-machines). Or you could use third-party virtualization programs such as VirtualBox. This hands-on approach can help you to better visualize how operating systems are configured.

Windows User Interfaces

The essence of Windows is the graphical user interface (GUI), which is what Windows employs to interact with the user. Normally, a keyboard, a mouse, a touchpad, or a touchscreen are used to input information to the operating system's GUI, and that input is shown on the screen. Basically, everything you see on the display (including windows, icons, menus, and other visual indicators) is part of the GUI, but remember that the GUI also governs how the user interacts with the OS.

The Windows GUI has many parts, including the desktop with all its pieces, the Start screen, applications such as File Explorer, Windows Explorer and the Control Panel, and Administrative Tools such as Computer Management and the Device Manager. To master Windows, you need to learn how to navigate quickly through the GUI to the application or tool that you need. The GUI can be customized for a particular user, or it can be customized to optimize the system. Let's begin this section by talking about the various components of Windows.

Windows Components

What do you see when you start Windows? Some of the components that make up Windows include

▶ **Start screen:** In Windows 8, the Start screen is displayed by default. An example is shown in Figure 9.1. This is the initial environment that a user can work in. It includes clickable (or tappable) elements, known as "tiles," which link to applications. It also contains *live* tiles, which can display real-time updated information. This interface is also referred to by some technicians as "Metro," though Microsoft doesn't use that term in their documentation. You can search the system and access tools within the Control Panel as well as perform other functions by navigating to the Charms toolbar (also known as the Charms bar), which is a vertical toolbar that appears when you point the mouse at the right corner or when you swipe from the right edge of a touchscreen or touchpad.

FIGURE 9.1   The Windows 8 Start screen

▶ **Desktop:** In Windows 7 and earlier, the desktop environment is basically what you see on the screen—essentially, it *is* Windows, from a cosmetic standpoint. An example is shown in Figure 9.2, which displays the Start menu in the open position. The desktop is a key component of the GUI; it includes icons, wallpapers, windows, toolbars, and so on. It is meant to take the place of a person's physical desktop, at least to a certain extent, replacing calculators, calendars, and so on. The desktop is also accessible in Windows 8 by clicking the Desktop tile on the Start screen; by clicking the Start button on the Start screen, Charms bar, and elsewhere; or by pressing the Windows key + D on the keyboard. If the desktop was started previously, you can also point the mouse to the top-left corner of the Start screen to reveal an icon of it. Though this dual-interface design in Windows 8 has caused some confusion, it does offer users the option to work in whatever interface they are most comfortable in (or they can use both options). The desktop was originally designed to be a user-friendly environment in which the user can easily save and retrieve files, make changes to the OS, and modify features. The same can be said of the Start screen. However, for more control of the OS, a user might still need to use advanced programs, such as the command line or the registry.

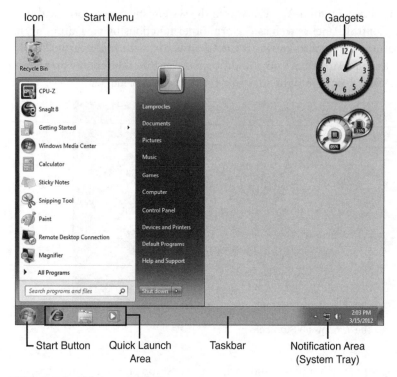

Icon   Start Menu   Gadgets

Start Button   Quick Launch   Taskbar   Notification Area
                 Area   (System Tray)

FIGURE 9.2   **Windows 7 Desktop**

▶ **Icons:** Icons are the little, clickable pictures you see on the desktop.
   They can be entire programs that run directly from the desktop, files
   that are stored directly on the desktop, or *shortcuts* that redirect to a
   program or file that is stored elsewhere in Windows. You can often tell
   if it's a shortcut by the little arrow in the lower-left corner of the icon.
   Shortcuts are small, usually around 1 KB to 4 KB in size, which store
   well on the desktop. However, storing actual files and programs on the
   desktop is not recommended because it can adversely affect the performance of the computer—and can quickly get really unorganized!

▶ **Taskbar:** This is the bar that spans the bottom of the desktop. It
   houses the Start button, Quick Launch, any open applications, and the
   Notification Area (where applicable). It can be moved to the top or to
   any sides of the desktop and can be resized to fill as much as 40 percent
   of the screen.

▶ **Start menu:** In Windows 7 and earlier, this is the main menu that is
   launched from the Start button. It contains a listing of all the tools
   within Windows and any Microsoft or third-party applications. From

here, you can search for files and access the Control Panel—you can get anywhere in Windows from the Start menu. It shows who is currently logged on to the system and also enables you to log off, restart, shut down, or place the computer in sleep mode. (Windows 8 does away with this Start menu, but in Windows 8.1, you can right-click the Start button to bring up many Windows utilities. Also, a similar utility that emulates the older Start menu can be added with third-party software, such as Classic Shell, though Microsoft does not support this type of software.)

▶ **Quick Launch:** In Windows 7 and earlier, the Quick Launch is directly to the right of the Start button. It contains shortcuts to applications or files. The beauty of the Quick Launch is that, by default, it is always visible, whereas shortcuts on the desktop background are covered up by open applications. Initially, the Quick Launch is enabled in Windows 7/Vista. This feature is effectively merged into Windows 8; users can "pin" frequently used applications directly to the taskbar.

▶ **Notification Area:** To the far right of the taskbar is the Notification Area, previously known as the System Tray. This houses the clock and shows the icons of applications that are running in the background. The more icons you see in the Notification Area, the more resources are used (in the form of memory and CPU power), possibly making the computer less responsive. In Windows 8, this presents itself in the Desktop environment but not in the Start screen.

▶ **Sidebar and gadgets:** The Windows Sidebar is a window pane on the side of the desktop used exclusively in Windows Vista. It was primarily used to house gadgets (mini-applications offering a variety of services). Windows 7 did away with the Sidebar, and although you can use the built-in gadgets, you can no longer download them from Microsoft due to vulnerabilities in the technology. If you refer back to Figure 9.2, you will see it displays two gadgets: a clock and a CPU meter. However, if you find that gadgets (or the sidebar in Windows Vista) are running, you should disable them because they pose a serious security threat. You should also update the operating system.

▶ **Application windows and dialog boxes:** Application windows are the windows that are opened by programs such as Microsoft WordPad, as shown in Figure 9.3. The window consists primarily of a Title bar (which says Document — WordPad), a Menu bar (with the File, Edit, and other menus), a toolbar (with icons for opening, saving, and printing documents), and a work area. This program runs as an actual process known as wordpad.exe. Dialog boxes are windows that open from within another window, usually an application window. For example, Figure 9.3 shows the Computer Name/Domain Changes dialog box, which was opened from the System Properties window. System Properties (not shown) runs as a process, but the Computer Name dialog box is just part of that overall process. The dialog box prompts a user for information (in this case, for the name of the computer) and the name of the network the computer is a member of.

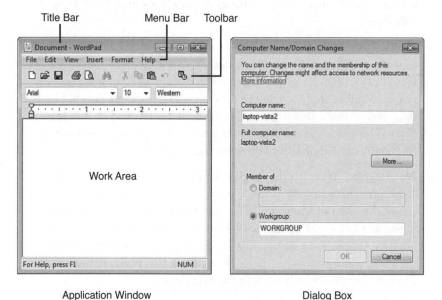

FIGURE 9.3 **An application window and a dialog box**

ExamAlert

Be able to identify the various Windows components by name.

Today's versions of Windows can run side-by-side apps with the use of Snap technology. This means that you can drag an application to an edge of the screen and it will snap in place, inhabiting that half of the display. A second application can be dragged in the same manner to the other side of the screen. It's an easy way to run two apps on the same screen without having to resize them manually. This becomes a bit more complex when you have multiple monitors, but, essentially, only the outer edges of the collective group of monitors can be used with Snap.

Configuring the Taskbar and Start Menu

The taskbar and Start menu can be customized to just about any user's liking. To make modifications to these, right-click the taskbar and select Properties. This brings up the Taskbar and Start Menu Properties window (Taskbar and Navigation properties window in Windows 8). The default tab is called Taskbar; from here, you can unlock/lock the taskbar, auto-hide it, and so on. In Windows 7/Vista, the next tab is Start Menu; from here, you can customize the menu by adding or removing items, by selecting secondary menus, or by selecting to show items as a link. Figure 9.4 shows a default Windows 7 Start menu, a customized Start menu, and the classic menu.

Original Start Menu   Customized Menu   Classic Menu

FIGURE 9.4   A standard Win7 Start menu, a customized menu, and the classic menu

As you can see, the customized menu has smaller program icons and I added the Run command (which is *always* accessible on any version of Windows by pressing Windows+R on the keyboard—even if you can't see it). The classic menu is a more basic graphic representation of the menu that uses fewer computer resources. This is a smart option to select when your computer needs every ounce of power it can muster.

Windows 8/7/Vista can also modify the Notification Area. For example, in Windows 7, if you were to access the Taskbar and Start Menu Properties window and then click the Customize button, a window would display with the option to hide the icons or hide the icons and their notifications. This can also be accessed by right-clicking the clock and selecting Customize notification icons.

ExamAlert

Know how to modify notification icons for the exam.

Windows Aero

Windows Aero is a Windows 7/Vista visual experience featuring translucent windows, window animations, three-dimensional viewing of windows, and a modified taskbar. You can make modifications to the look of Aero by right-clicking the desktop and selecting Personalize; from here, you can select themes, desktop background colors, and Windows colors. However, Windows Aero uses a lot of resources and can be taxing on the computer. To improve system performance (especially on older systems), you have the option to disable Aero. To do so, go back to the Personalize window and select Theme. At the Theme drop-down menu, select Windows 7 Basic—or, even better, select Windows Classic and watch the transformation!

To make more specific changes to the look of Aero, go to Start, right-click Computer, and select Properties; this opens the System window. Then click the Advanced system settings link; this opens the System Properties dialog box. Click the Advanced tab and then click Settings in the Performance box. This displays the Performance Options dialog box, where you can change various visual effects (for example, enabling/disabling sliding menus or removing drop shadows from icon labels). You might have to restart the system for these changes to take effect. A quicker way to get to the Performance Options dialog box is to click Start, in the Search area type `Adjust the`, and then press Enter. And the hypertechnical way would be to open the Run prompt and type `SystemPropertiesPerformance.exe`. (Capital letters are not necessary.)

Note

Windows 7/Vista Starter editions are not configured to run Aero. Windows 8 did away with the Aero look and instead runs a very flat theme that is designed to be user-friendly and save on computer resources.

Windows Applications

There are a lot of built-in applications within Windows. The following is a description of some of the programs you will use frequently:

▶ **Computer/This PC:** In Windows 7/Vista, the Computer window can be accessed by clicking Start and selecting Computer. That opens the Windows Explorer application to the Computer location. From here, you can browse through your computer to access data on the hard drive, optical drives, and other removable media (such as USB flash drives). You can also right-click Computer on the Start menu, which gives you access to things such as System Properties and Computer Management. Figure 9.5 shows an example of the Windows 7 Computer window within Windows Explorer. Note the functionality included in this window, such as the Organize feature and the Uninstall or change a program feature.

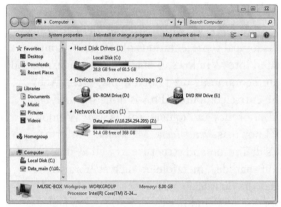

Windows 7
Computer Window

FIGURE 9.5   **The Windows 7 Computer window**

In Windows 8, Windows Explorer is renamed File Explorer and the location Computer is now listed as This PC. This PC can be accessed by right-clicking the Start button (in either the Start screen or the Desktop) and selecting File Explorer.

▶ **Windows Explorer/File Explorer:** As mentioned, Windows 8 calls this File Explorer, and it is accessed by right-clicking the Start button. In Windows 7/Vista, Windows Explorer can be accessed by clicking Start > All Programs > Accessories and clicking Windows Explorer. Regardless of the OS, this application can also be accessed by going to Run and typing **Explorer** or by pressing the Windows key + E on the keyboard. (Think "E" for Explorer!) However, different ways of accessing Explorer will bring you to different locations within it. For example, the Windows+E keys bring you to the root of the computer (which is This PC in Windows 8 and Computer in Windows 7/Vista), but going to Run and typing **Explorer** brings you to the Libraries view.

Actually, any folder that you access will open in the Windows Explorer or File Explorer interface; the difference will be the amount of functionality given to you in the toolbar. These folders show up as different applications in Task Manager, but they are all controlled by one process: explorer.exe. To see for yourself, open Computer and Windows Explorer. Then open Task Manager by right-clicking the taskbar and selecting Task Manager. Click the Applications tab. From there, you should see the various windows that are running. Next, view the process called explorer.exe within the Processes tab. Try an experiment in Windows 7: Watch explorer.exe's memory size go down as you close the Windows Explorer window and the Computer window. This should drive the point home.

Windows 7 and 8 incorporate *Libraries*, which are user-defined collections of folders that act as logical representations of the user's content. This has been incorporated into Windows to enable faster indexing and searching of important and commonly used documents, even if they are spread out among the entire computer. This is done by analyzing file properties and *metadata* of files and folders; this is why Windows Libraries are commonly known as *metafolders*. Metadata is information that describes a file's definition and structure as well as how it is administered. Building on that idea, metafolders such as libraries have information that describes the definition and structure of the contents within. The Libraries portion of Windows Explorer is the default view in Windows 7, but it might have to be enabled in the Windows 8 Navigation pane in order to be seen. Normally, you see the Documents, Music, Pictures, and Videos libraries when opening Windows Explorer. Double-clicking a library shows all the folders and documents that are part of it, regardless of the location of the folder they are stored in. For example, the Documents library includes two locations by default: My Documents and Public Documents. This can be discerned by clicking the two locations' links. (The number of actual locations may vary from computer to computer.) You can add locations by clicking the link and then clicking the Add button. This allows users to organize their documents and media by category, even if the files are scattered throughout the computer and beyond (such as locations on a network). You can also add new libraries within the main Libraries window by right-clicking Libraries (or right-clicking the work area) and selecting New > Libraries. After a library has been created, you can add folders to it by right-clicking it and selecting Properties. From there, you can also specify the default folder location to save files in a library and you can optimize the library. The concept of libraries has been in use for some time, especially in media players, but Windows 7 is the first Microsoft operating system to incorporate it for use with any and all files. Some third-party applications might not integrate properly with Windows libraries due to programming inadequacies. If this is the case, a user must store the files created in that application by navigating to the actual folder where they are to be stored, bypassing the library. Always check for updates to third-party applications that might make them library-compatible.

▶ **Control Panel:** The Control Panel (CP) is where a user would go to make system configuration changes; for example, changing the color scheme, making connections to networks, installing or modifying new hardware, and so on. The Control Panel can be opened in a variety of ways. For example, in Windows 8, you can use the Charms bar or right-click Start. In Windows 7/Vista, you can click Start > Control Panel. Or in any Windows OS, you can type `control` in the Search field or Run prompt. By default, the Control Panel shows up in Category view. For example, in Windows 8 and 7, System and Security is a category. To see all the individual Control Panel icons, click the drop-down arrow next to View by: Category, and then select either Large icons or Small icons. (In Windows Vista, click the Classic View link on the left side.) Within the Taskbar and Start Menu Properties window in Windows 7, the Control Panel option in the Start menu can be configured to show up as a submenu, composed of the individual icons.

ExamAlert

The CompTIA A+ exams expect you to know the individual icons in the Control Panel. In Windows, this is also referred to as All Control Panel Items. Study them!

▶ **Network:** The Network window shows computers and other devices on the network. It can be opened in Windows Vista by clicking Start > Network. (In Windows 7 and 8, you would have to open Windows Explorer or File Explorer first and then select Network.) It runs in an Explorer window and might take a few moments to register the devices on the network. The address bar at the top of the window shows the status of the registration of devices as a bar that extends from left to right. The Network window should automatically find other computers, routers, wireless access points, and network attached devices (if you are configured as a member of the network). You can also add printers and wireless devices from here.

▶ **Command Prompt:** Microsoft's Command Prompt is its command-line interface (CLI). This is the text-based interface in which you can issue commands concerning files and folders, networking, services, and so on. You can open it in several ways, including the following:

    ▶ In Windows 8: Right-click the Start button and select Command Prompt.

    ▶ In Windows 7/Vista: Navigate to Start > All Programs > Accessories > Command Prompt.

    ▶ For all versions of Windows: Open the Search tool and type CMD (or search for a variety of words/phrases associated with the Command Prompt). The Search tool can be found in Windows 8 on the Start screen or by bringing up the Charms bar. The Search tool can be found in Windows 7/Vista by simply clicking Start.

    ▶ For all versions of Windows: Press Windows+R to open the Run prompt and type CMD (my personal favorite).

In Windows, some commands need to be run as an administrator; to open the Command Prompt as an administrator, do one of the following:

    ▶ In Windows 8: Right-click the Start button and select Command Prompt (Admin).

    ▶ In Windows 7/Vista: Click Start > All Programs > Accessories; then right-click Command Prompt and select Run as Administrator.

    ▶ In all versions of Windows: Open the search tool and type CMD in the Search field; instead of pressing Enter, press Ctrl+Shift+Enter.

Running the Command Prompt as an administrator is also known as running it in *elevated mode*.

ExamAlert

Know how to open programs from the Search tool, the Start menu, and from the Run prompt.

An additional command line called the PowerShell is integrated into Windows 7 and Windows 8 and can be downloaded for use with older versions of Windows. PowerShell is a combination of the Command

Prompt and a scripting language. (It is the successor to the Windows Script Host.) It enables administrators to perform administrative tasks that integrate scripts and executables. This can be opened using the Search tool; in Windows 7, you can open it by navigating to Start > All Programs > Accessories > Windows PowerShell. It should be noted that if you use PowerShell in place of the Command Prompt, you should remember to always use a space after a command; otherwise the shell will not recognize the command. For example, typing `ipconfig /all` is correct, whereas `ipconfig/all` would not function. For administrators who run scripts often, there is also the Windows PowerShell ISE (Integrated Scripting Environment); this color codes the syntax and is generally a friendlier environment to work in.

This is just the tip of the iceberg when it comes to programs you will be working with. There are many more available in Windows—and even more third-party programs. Windows 8 and 7 can run 32-bit and 64-bit applications as long as the CPU is 64-bit, which is typical. 64-bit programs are installed to C:\Program Files by default. However, 32-bit programs are installed to C:\Program Files (x86) by default. There will come a time when you need to uninstall programs, change programs, and repair them. This can be done by going to Control Panel and selecting Programs and Features. As your hard drive gets filled up with applications, you might realize that you don't need all of them. Uninstalling unused applications can save hard drive space and make the system more secure. However, if you remove a lot of programs, you might consider defragmenting the hard drive. More on that in Chapter 10, "Maintaining Windows."

Administrative Tools and the MMC

The administrator (that's you) of a computer or network can access Administrative Tools from the Control Panel and in Windows 7/Vista by going to Start > All Programs > Administrative Tools. There are several tools here used to configure advanced options for the computer. We cover each of them as we go through this chapter as well as Chapter 10, "Maintaining Windows," and Chapter 11, "Troubleshooting Windows." One example is Computer Management, which you will use quite often. It has many utilities loaded into one nice, little console window. An example of Computer Management is shown in Figure 9.6.

FIGURE 9.6   The Windows 7 Computer Management window

Note this is a three-pane window. The left pane has all the modules that you might work on, such as the Event Viewer, Device Manager, and Disk Management. The middle pane shows the details of whatever you click in the left pane. The right pane provides additional actions, which are also available on the Menu bar. There are a few other ways to open this window, including

▶ In Windows 7/Vista: Click Start, right-click Computer, and then select Manage.

▶ In Windows 8: Right-click Start and then click Computer Management.

▶ In Windows 8/7/Vista: Access the Run prompt and type compmgmt.msc. The extension .msc defines the file type as a Microsoft Management Console Snap-in Control file, also known as Microsoft Console.

Computer Management and other console windows can be grouped into one master console window known as the Microsoft Management Console (MMC) window. MMC acts as a shell for these other console windows. You can also use it to control remote computers in addition to the local computer. And you can control what particular users see by changing the Console Mode. Finally, part of the beauty of MMC is that it saves everything you added and remembers the last place you worked. To create an MMC window, open the Run prompt and type MMC. By default, the MMC window is empty.

> **Note**
>
> You will learn quickly that administrative functions should be carried out only by users who have administrative privileges. Even if you have administrative privileges, a pop-up User Account Control (UAC) window displays every time you try to access tools such as the MMC. Simply click Yes or Continue to open the program. If users don't have administrative capabilities, they will be blocked altogether or when the UAC window pops up, they won't be able to continue. For more information on UAC, see Chapter 17, "Security."

To add consoles (known as snap-ins), do the following:

1. On the Menu bar, click File and then click Add/Remove Snap-in. The Add/Remove Snap-ins window should appear.

2. Select the components you want from the left by highlighting them one at a time and clicking the Add button. You need to select the local computer or a remote computer. Click OK when finished. These snap-ins should now be shown inside of the Console Root. An example MMC is shown in Figure 9.7.

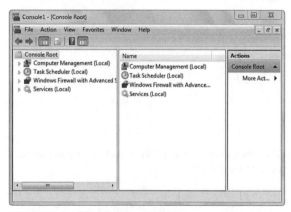

FIGURE 9.7 **The Windows 7 MMC**

3. Save the MMC. By default, this window prompts you to save to the Administrative Tools folder of the user who is currently logged on.

> **ExamAlert**
>
> Know how to add snap-ins to an MMC.

Cram Quiz

Answer these questions. The answers follow the last question. If you cannot answer these questions correctly, consider reading this section again until you can.

220-902 Questions

1. A small arrow at the lower-left corner of an icon identifies it as what?
   - ○ **A.** A super icon
   - ○ **B.** An icon headed for the Recycle Bin
   - ○ **C.** A shortcut
   - ○ **D.** A large file

2. What can a user do to cut back on the amount of resources that Windows 7 uses? (Select the two best answers.)
   - ○ **A.** Increase RAM.
   - ○ **B.** Use the Classic theme.
   - ○ **C.** Disable some of the Performance Options.
   - ○ **D.** Use the computer less.

3. Which utility groups snap-ins into one window?
   - ○ **A.** Computer Management
   - ○ **B.** MSC
   - ○ **C.** MCC
   - ○ **D.** MMC

4. You open File Explorer in Windows 8 by pressing Windows+E on the keyboard. Which folder does it bring you to by default?
   - ○ **A.** Computer
   - ○ **B.** Network
   - ○ **C.** This PC
   - ○ **D.** Recycle Bin

5. How can the Run prompt be opened in Windows 7? (Select the two best answers.)
   - ○ **A.** By pressing Windows+R
   - ○ **B.** By pressing Windows+Run
   - ○ **C.** By clicking Start and typing **Run**
   - ○ **D.** By pressing Ctrl+Shift+Esc

Cram Quiz Answers

220-902 Answers

1. **C.** An icon with an arrow is a shortcut, redirecting to a file or program in another location in Windows. The file size is actually very small, from 1 KB to 4 KB.

2. **B and C.** By using the Classic theme or by disabling some or all of the Performance Options, the operating system will not need as much graphics computing power. Increasing RAM increases the amount of resources your computer has, but it doesn't decrease the amount of resources that Windows uses.

3. **D.** The MMC can have one or more snap-ins, such as Computer Management and so on. MSC is the extension that MMC and individual console windows use. MCC stands for memory controller chip.

4. **C.** When opening File Explorer in Windows 8 by pressing Windows+E, the folder that is displayed is This PC. Other options for opening File Explorer in Windows 8 (such as going to Run and typing `Explorer`) will bring you to the Libraries folder. Windows 7 displays either Computer or Libraries, depending on how you open the program. The Network location and the Recycle Bin location in File Explorer/Windows Explorer can be accessed from other areas of Windows (for example, by right-clicking the Recycle Bin icon on the desktop and selecting Open).

5. **A and C.** By pressing Windows+R on the keyboard, you can open the Run prompt; you can also click Start and type `run` in the Search field. There is no Run key, so there is no Windows+Run shortcut, and pressing Ctrl+Shift+Esc would usually bring up Task Manager. In Windows 8, you can right-click the Start button and select Run to open the Run prompt.

System Tools and Utilities

Windows 8, 7, and Vista have a cornucopia of system tools and utilities. There are tools that help you to analyze and manage devices, such as Device Manager and System Information. There are also tools that can aid in optimizing the operating system and customizing the user environment. And there are advanced utilities that enable you to edit the registry and connect remotely to other computers. Knowledge of these types of tools and utilities separates the good technician from the "okay" technician. In this portion of the chapter, we'll give a more generalized overview of these system tools and utilities that you can apply to most versions and editions of Windows. Let's discuss how to manage devices first.

Managing Devices

A computer probably has a dozen or more devices that all need love and attention. Taking care of a computer means managing these devices. The primary tool with which a technician does this is Device Manager.

Device Manager

There are a few ways to open Device Manager, for example:

▶ Open it from the Control Panel (in icons mode).

▶ Open Computer Management, expand System Tools, and then select Device Manager. (You can also open Computer Management as a snap-in within an MMC.)

▶ Open the System Properties window, click the Hardware tab, and then click the Device Manager button. To get to the System Properties window in Windows 7/Vista, click Start, right-click Computer, select Properties, and then click Advanced system settings. (Note that Device Manager is also listed.) You can also open the Run prompt and type `systempropertieshardware.exe` to directly access the Hardware tab of the System Properties window in Windows 8/7/Vista.

▶ Open the Run prompt and type `devmgmt.msc`.

When Device Manager opens, you will notice that there are categories for each type of device. By expanding any one of these categories, you will see the specific devices that reside in your computer. Figure 9.8 shows Device Manager.

FIGURE 9.8 **Device Manager in Windows 7**

By right-clicking a specific device, you can update its driver, enable or disable it, uninstall it altogether, check for any hardware changes, or access additional properties, such as the driver details and resources used by the device. Figure 9.8 shows the resulting menu when right-clicking an Intel network adapter. These are the standard options, but your options might be more or less, depending on the device you have right-clicked.

ExamAlert

Know how to access the properties of a device, install drivers, and enable/disable devices in Device Manager.

Some drivers are installed/updated through .exe files that are downloaded from the manufacturer's website. Others are installed from within Device Manager. Device Manager can search for drivers automatically, or you can manually install the driver by browsing for the correct file (often, it's a file with an .inf extension). Windows attempts to install drivers automatically when it recognizes that a device has been added to the system. Usually, however, it is recommended that you use the driver disc that came with the device or that you download the latest version of the driver from the manufacturer's website, especially when dealing with video, audio, and hard drive controller drivers.

Driver Signing

Windows device driver files are digitally signed by Microsoft to ensure quality. The digital signature ensures that the file has met a certain level of testing and that the file has not been altered. By default in Windows, driver signing is configured automatically, and only administrators can install unsigned drivers. Driver signing can be turned off (for example, in the Windows 8 Startup Settings) but it is not recommended because it can pose a tremendous security risk.

System Information

Another tool that Windows offers for device analysis is the System Information tool. This can be accessed in Windows 7/Vista by navigating to Start > All Programs > Accessories > System Tools and then clicking System Information, or in all versions of Windows, you can access this tool by opening the Run prompt and typing **msinfo32.exe**. (Typing **.exe** actually isn't necessary.) From here, you can view and analyze information about the hardware components, the software environment, and the hardware resources used; for example, hardware conflicts, IRQ settings, and Input/Output (I/O) settings. An Interrupt ReQuest (IRQ) is the circuit that a device uses to "interrupt" the CPU and get its attention in an attempt to send data to it. However, it is rare that IRQ conflicts occur; therefore, you won't be making changes to IRQ settings often (if ever), so the chance of a question about this on the exams is unlikely. You might have to configure an I/O setting at some point, but this is uncommon. The I/O setting is the range of memory that is used by a particular device to transmit the data to the CPU. If a certain range of memory fails, a new range needs to be selected. Reconfiguring I/O ranges and IRQs is done in Device Manager.

DxDiag

When it comes to making sure your devices work properly, one of the most important devices is the video card; a utility you can use to analyze and diagnose the video card is DxDiag. To run the DxDiag program, open the Run prompt and type **dxdiag**. First, the utility asks if you want it to check whether the corresponding drivers are digitally signed. A digitally signed driver means it is one that has been verified by Microsoft as compatible with the operating system. After the utility opens, you can find out what version of DirectX you are running. DirectX is a group of multimedia programs that enhance video and audio, including Direct3D, DirectDraw, DirectSound, and so on. With the DxDiag tool, you can view all the DirectX files that have been loaded, check their date, and discern whether any problems were found with any files. You can also find out information about your video and sound card, what level of acceleration they are set to, and you can test DirectX components such as DirectDraw and Direct3D. Windows 8/7 ship with DirectX version 11, as shown in Figure 9.9. Windows Vista ships with DirectX version 10. The DirectX feature is important to video gamers and other multimedia professionals.

FIGURE 9.9   The Windows 7 DxDiag window showing the Display tab

Removing Hot-Swappable Devices

When it comes to removing devices, some devices can be physically removed only if the computer has first been shut down. However, other devices can be hot-swapped, meaning they can be removed while the power to the computer is on; no reboot is necessary. USB flash drives are an example of this; however, you should first "Safely Remove" them within the operating system. This can be done by right-clicking or double-clicking the Safely Remove Hardware and Eject Media icon in the Notification Area and stopping the device. Other devices that can be hot-swapped include smartphones and tablets, printers, digital cameras, scanners, webcams, microphones, and so on.

Operating System Optimization

A fresh installation of Windows will probably not work exactly the way you want it to right from the start. It might take some tweaking and some optimization to get it just right. You will also find that systems running Windows for a while have of late suffered performance setbacks. These systems also need to be optimized. But to optimize, you first need to do some analysis of the system.

Task Manager

One simple, yet effective, tool to use when analyzing the computer is Task Manager. There are several ways to open Task Manager, including

▶ Right-click on the taskbar and select Task Manager.

▶ Press Ctrl+Alt+Del and select Task Manager.

▶ Open the Run prompt and type `taskmgr`.

▶ Press Ctrl+Shift+Esc.

Task Manager gives you the ability to analyze your processor and memory performance in real time; this can be done from the Performance tab, as shown in Figure 9.10.

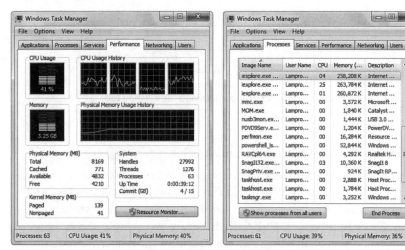

FIGURE 9.10 Windows 7 Task Manager showing the Performance tab and the Processes tab

As you can see, the processor in Figure 9.10 hovers at 41 percent usage. Something is gobbling up a big portion of the processing power! You also note that nearly 3.25 GB of memory is used; that's quite a bit for a Windows 7 computer. If this system were simply browsing the Web, the CPU would be hovering at approximately 2 to 5 percent and the memory would be at only 1 GB or so. What could be the reason for this jump in resource usage? Was the processor not recognized by the BIOS properly? Is a powerful application using all those resources? Maybe the computer, unbeknownst to the user, is used as a zombie to send attacks to various organizations, or the user has turned the computer into an MP3 file server for friends. These are the types of things you would want to investigate. In reality, the reason for the 41 percent processor and 3.25 GB memory usage is because I am receiving multiple video feeds in Internet Explorer and am running a Windows Vista virtual machine at full power (among other things). Audio, video, and virtual machines can be quite a drain on the system. Now we are crossing over into the realm of troubleshooting, but then again, sometimes the lines between configuration, optimization, and troubleshooting can be blurred.

For the sake of comparison, take a look at Figure 9.11. This shows the same Performance tab and Processes tab but in Windows 8. The information is the same, but it's presented in a slightly different format. You can see from the figure that the Firefox and Chrome browsers are using the bulk of the memory on that system.

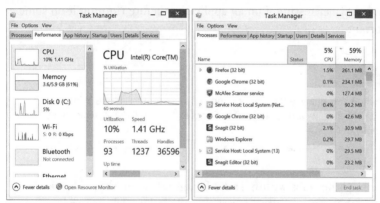

FIGURE 9.11   Windows 8 Task Manager showing the Performance tab and the Processes tab

Optimizing the system can be as simple as shutting down programs. In Windows 8, "Apps" are shut down in the Processes tab. In Windows 7 and Vista, programs can be shut down in the Applications tab. But sometimes you need to shut down the underlying process. For example, the Processes tab in Figures 9.10 and 9.11 show all the processes that are running and the amount of CPU and RAM resources they are using individually. A process that is hording resources can be stopped by clicking it and then clicking End Process in Windows 7/Vista and End Task in Windows 8. (This can also be done in the Details tab of Windows 8.) Keep in mind that this shuts down only the process or application temporarily. If it is designated to do so, it will turn back on when the computer is rebooted. Later in this section, we discuss the programs that can be used to permanently disable programs, processes, and services.

ExamAlert

Understand how to open Task Manager, how to read its Performance tab, and how to end processes and applications.

Optimizing the system can also mean temporarily boosting the power to a particular process. For example, if you were working within an important application that was crunching some heavy-duty numbers and you needed to increase that one process's performance, you could do so by right-clicking the process, highlighting Set Priority, and then selecting an option that is higher than Normal. In Windows 8, this can be done from the Details tab. The higher the option on the list, the more processing power that process gets. Be wary, however; changing a process's priority can have undesired effects, such as system lockups or other errors. Be sure to save your work before attempting this, and consider testing it on an application before running it on something important.

Note

Other tools that can analyze the performance of a computer include Windows Performance Monitor, which is covered in Chapter 11, and CPU-Z, which was covered briefly in Chapter 3.

There are some other tabs within Task Manager that you should know about. The Services tab is one of several locations in Windows where services can be started and stopped. The Users tab shows the active logged-in users on the system; users can be disconnected from here if necessary. In Windows 8, it also shows resource utilization by the user. The Networking tab in Windows 7 is where the network adapter's utilization can be viewed; it is integrated into the Performance tab in Windows 8. Windows 8 also includes the App history tab, which shows the resources used by all apps that were run over the course of the past month. Finally, Windows 8 incorporates the Startup tab, where you can enable or disable applications, a feature that was previously included in the msconfig application.

Msconfig

Msconfig.exe (Microsoft System Configuration Utility) is one of the programs mentioned in the previous section that can permanently disable programs and services that are designed to run when the computer starts up, thus optimizing the system. To open this program, open the Run prompt and type **msconfig**. To disable programs from starting in Windows 7/Vista, click the Startup tab, and deselect the desired entries. (In Windows 8, this is done in the Startup tab of the Task Manager.) Msconfig also lets you select different boot options and can enable/disable services. We will revisit msconfig in Chapter 11.

> **ExamAlert**
>
> If you need to disable programs from starting at bootup, use Msconfig.

Virtual Memory

Virtual memory makes a program think that it has contiguous address space, when in reality the address space can be fragmented and often spills over to a hard drive. RAM is a limited resource, whereas virtual memory is, for most practical purposes, unlimited.

There can be a large number of processes, each with its own virtual address space. When the memory in use by all the existing processes exceeds the amount of RAM available, the operating system moves pages of information to the computer's hard drive, freeing RAM for other uses. In Windows, virtual memory is known as the paging file, specifically, pagefile.sys, which exists in the root of C:. To view this file, you need to unhide it. This can be done within the Folder Options dialog box in the View tab. Select the radio button called Show hidden files, folders, and drives. Then, a few lines below, deselect the check mark next to Hide protected operating system files. While you're at it, deselect Hide extensions for known file types. This allows you to not only see the filename but the three-letter extension as well. Finally, pagefile.sys should now show up in the root of C:, where pagefile is the filename and .sys is the extension.

Take a look at the size of your page file and jot down what you find. To modify the size and location of the page file, open the System Properties dialog box and click the Advanced tab (or try using Run and typing **systempropertiesadvanced.exe**). Next, click the Settings button within the Performance box; this brings up the Performance Options window. Now click the Advanced tab and then click Change in the Virtual memory box. From here, you can let Windows manage the virtual memory for you or select a custom size for the page file. The paging file has the capability to increase in size as needed. If a user runs a lot of programs simultaneously, then increasing the page file size might resolve performance issues. Another option would be to move the page file to another volume on the hard drive or to another hard drive altogether. It is also possible to create multiple paging files or stripe a paging file across multiple drives to increase performance. Of course, nothing beats adding physical RAM to the computer, but when this is not an option, possibly because the motherboard has reached its capacity for RAM, optimizing the page file might be the solution. For more information about configuring virtual memory in Windows, visit http://technet.microsoft.com/en-us/magazine/ff382717.aspx.

> **ExamAlert**
>
> Know where to configure virtual memory, and know the location of pagefile.sys.

Working with Services

Services control particular functions in Windows, such as printing, wireless networking, and so on. If a service is stopped or disabled, its corresponding program or utility will not run. You can start or stop services in the GUI or in the command line.

▶ **Start and stop services in the Services console window:** You can open the Services console from Administrative Tools by typing `services.msc` in the Run or Search fields, and you can find it within the Computer Management console window. Scroll in the right window pane until you find the service you want. To start a stopped service, right-click it and click Start, as shown in Figure 9.12. Alternatively, you can click the Start button on the toolbar or double-click the service and then click the Start button from the Properties window. The Properties window of the service also enables you to change the startup type (refer to Figure 9.12). There are four startup types. You might need to set a service to Automatic so that the service starts automatically every time the computer boots; many services are set this way by default. (There is also a delayed start option, if necessary.) Or you might want to set a service to Manual so that you have control over it. In other cases, you might want to set it to Disabled when it is not necessary or when it is a security concern.

Status of Service

FIGURE 9.12   The Firewall Service in the Computer Management window and its Properties window

▶ **Start and stop services in the Command Prompt:** In Windows 8/7/ Vista, you need to run these commands as an administrator. When the Command Prompt is open, you can start a service by typing **net start [service]**; for example, net start spooler starts the Print Spooler service. net stop spooler stops the service. You can also use the sc start and sc stop commands. To enable or disable a service in the Command Prompt, use the sc config command.

ExamAlert

Know how to start and stop services within the Services console and in the Command Prompt.

Note

You can also start/stop services in Task Manager, and you can enable/disable services with msconfig.

Power Management

Part of optimizing an operating system is to manage power wisely. You can manage power for hard drives, the display, and other devices; you can even manage power for the entire operating system.

To turn off devices in Windows after a specified amount of time, navigate to the Control Panel. Then select Large icons for Windows 8/7, or Classic view for Windows Vista. (From now on, I will assume you know how to use the individual icons in the Control Panel.) Next, open the Power Options icon. From here, you can select a power plan such as Balanced, eco, Power Saver, or High Performance—it will vary from one computer to the next. There are a lot of settings within these power plans; here's one example. In Balanced, click Change plan settings. The Display is set to turn off after a certain amount of time; it can be set from 1 minute to 5 hours, or it can be set to never. Going a little further, if you click the Change Advanced Power Settings link, the Power Options dialog box appears. From here, you can specify how long before the hard drive turns off and set power savings for devices such as the processor, wireless, USB, PCI Express, and so on. Take a few minutes looking through these options and the options for the other power plans.

Some users confuse the terms standby and hibernate; let's try to eliminate that confusion now. Standby means that the computer goes into a low power mode, shutting off the display and hard drives. Information that you were working on and the state of the computer are stored in RAM. The processor still functions but has been throttled down and uses less power. Taking the computer out of standby mode is a quick process; it usually requires the user to press the power button or a key on the keyboard. It takes only a few seconds for the CPU to process the standby information in RAM and return the computer to the previous working state. Hard drives and other peripherals might take a few more seconds to get up to speed. Keep in mind that when there is a loss of power, the computer will turn off and the contents of RAM will be erased, unless it is a laptop (which has a built-in battery) or if the computer is connected to a UPS; but either way, uptime will be limited. Note that some laptops still use a fair amount of power when in standby mode. Hibernate is different than standby in that it effectively shuts down the computer. Hibernation consumes the least amount of power of any power state except for when the computer is turned off. All data that was worked on is stored to the hard drive in a file called hiberfil.sys in the root of C:. This will usually be a large file. Because RAM is volatile and the hard drive is not, hibernate is a safer option when it comes to protecting the data and the session that you were working on, especially if you plan to leave the computer on for an extended period of time. However, because the hard drive is so much slower than RAM, coming out of hibernation will take longer than coming out of standby mode. Hibernation has also been known to fail in some cases and cause various issues in Windows.

Standby is known as "Sleep" in Windows and is accessible from the Start button (click Start in Windows 7/Vista; right-click Start in Windows 8) or by pressing Alt+F4 on the keyboard (after all other programs have been closed).

Hibernation, however, might need to be turned on before it can be used. To enable hibernation in Windows, open the Command Prompt as an administrator. Then type `powercfg.exe/hibernate on`. Next, you need to turn off Hybrid sleep in the Power Options dialog box that we accessed previously. Expand Sleep, expand Allow Hybrid Sleep, and then set it to off. Finally, set the Hibernate After option to the number of minutes you desire. Now check the Start menu again; the Hibernate option should be there just below Sleep.

> **ExamAlert**
>
> Know the differences between standby, sleep, and hibernate.

User Migrations and Customizations

Users often customize their own computer to a certain extent; they modify colors, auto-hide the taskbar, add shortcuts, and so on. But some customizations, modifications, and migrations can be done only by an administrator.

Migrating User Data

If a user will be using a new operating system, either on the same computer or on a new computer, you might need to move his files and settings to the new system. When doing so, make sure that the destination computer has the latest service packs and updates and also has the same programs that are currently running on the original computer. There are a few options for migrating data:

▶ **Windows Easy Transfer:** This program enables you to copy files, photos, music, e-mail, and settings from one Windows computer to another; all of this information is collectively referred to as user state. Files and settings can be migrated over the network or by USB cable. The data can also be stored on media like a CD, DVD, or USB flash drive until the destination computer is ready. Normally, you would start with the computer that has the files and settings that you want to transfer (the source computer). You can transfer the files and settings for one user account or all the accounts on the computer. All the files and settings will be saved as a single .MIG file (Migration Store). Then you would move to the computer to which you want to transfer the files (destination computer) and either load the .MIG file from CD, DVD, or USB flash drive or locate the file on the source computer through the use of a USB cable or network connection.

▶ **User State Migration Tool (USMT):** This is a command-line tool that can be used to migrate user files and settings for one *or more* computers. The program can be downloaded from www.microsoft. com. It is also included in the Windows Assessment and Deployment Kit (Windows ADK) for Windows 8. When installed, two different tools are used: Scanstate.exe saves all the files and settings of the user (or users) on a computer, known as the user state; loadstate.exe transfers that data to the destination computer(s). There are many options when using the `scanstate` and `loadstate` commands, including the ability to select which users are migrated and whether the store of data is uncompressed, compressed, or compressed and encrypted. By utilizing scripting programs, the transfer of files to multiple computers can be automated over the network. For more information on how to transfer files and settings with USMT in Windows 8, visit https:// technet.microsoft.com/en-us/library/Hh825256.aspx. In Windows 7, visit http://technet.microsoft.com/en-us/library/dd560801(v=ws.10).aspx. For Windows Vista, visit http://technet.microsoft.com/en-us/library/ cc722032(WS.10).aspx.

ExamAlert

Understand the tools that can be used to migrate user data.

Customizing the User Environment

A user might not be completely comfortable using Windows, or perhaps the user's computer is not the newest or most powerful system and the Windows operating system is making it crawl due to the resources required to run it. To create a more enjoyable user experience, and to make the best use of the resources a computer has, you might need to customize the user's environment. There are a couple ways to do this:

▶ **Disable visual effects:** Any special graphic effects will put a strain on the computer's performance. Open the System Properties window to the

Advanced tab and then click the Settings button in the Performance box. This brings up the Performance Options dialog box. (Don't forget, you can quickly get here by typing `SystemPropertiesPerformance.exe` in the Run prompt.) Select the Adjust for Best Performance radio button. This will remove all the jazzy effects that slow down the computer!

▶ **Revert to Classic mode:** By reverting to the original Windows look, the user might feel more comfortable and you can free up additional resources on the computer. There are two ways to accomplish this in Windows 7/Vista. First, turn off Windows Aero by right-clicking the desktop wallpaper and selecting Personalize, and then selecting the Windows Classic theme. This removes the glassy translucent windows and lets the video card and processor in a lesser computer breathe a sigh of relief. Second, in Windows Vista, revert to the classic Start menu by right-clicking the taskbar, selecting Properties, clicking the Start Menu tab, and then selecting the Classic Start menu radio button. (This is not necessary in Windows 7.) Even if you are a power user who runs intensive applications, this might be a smart solution, effectively trading style for performance. Classic mode is not available in Windows 8. By default, Windows 8 does not use Aero; it has a more basic look to its windows.

You can also customize a user's experience by using the Task Scheduler tool and Region and Language Options.

Task Scheduler can run particular programs, send e-mails, or display messages at a scheduled time (or times) designated by the user. Search for this utility by typing `schedule tasks`. Aside from basic scheduling, you can specify certain conditions and triggers that cause a task to run, and you can tell the scheduler which actions to take when the task starts. Plus, there are a slew of built-in preprogrammed tasks in the Task Scheduler Library—from memory diagnostics to registry backups. Instead of re-creating the wheel, consider using one of these tasks to help automate the process. Some of these built-in tasks are enabled by default. For example, if two computers mistakenly get the same IP address, an IP conflict occurs and the IpAddressConflict1 task (located in Tcpip) logs the event and places a notification on the screen and in the System log of the Event Viewer. You can run any task in the library at any time. To see the IpAddressConflict1 task in action, go to Task Scheduler Library > Microsoft > Windows > and then click Tcpip. Then go to Action on the Menu bar and click Run. This should display the IP conflict notification. Try creating some tasks yourself, such as memory diagnostic, registry backup, and time synchronization.

Region and Language Options are available in the Control Panel. These enable the user to modify the format of numbers, currency, time, and date.

The user can also change how programs service the computer based on its location; also, different keyboards, keyboard layouts, and languages can be installed for users who spend most of their time working in other countries or for users who work with documents in different languages.

Advanced System Tools

Several tools can affect advanced configuration changes in Windows. This section describes a few of those: the Registry Editor, Remote Desktop, and Windows Compatibility.

The Windows Registry

The Windows Registry is a database that stores the settings for Windows. It contains hardware and software information and user settings. If you cannot make the modifications that you want in the Windows GUI, the registry is the place to go. To modify settings in the registry, use the Registry Editor, which can be opened by typing `regedit.exe` at the Run prompt. This displays a window like the one shown in Figure 9.13.

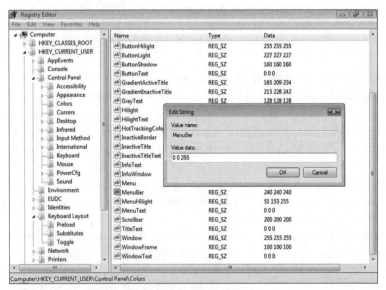

FIGURE 9.13   **The Registry Editor in Windows**

The registry is divided into several sections, known as hives, and these hives begin with the letters HKEY. Table 9.1 describes the five visible hives in the Registry Editor.

TABLE 9.1   **Description of Registry Hives in Windows**

Registry Hive	Description
HKEY_CLASSES_ROOT	Stores information about applications' file associations and Object Linking and Embedding (OLE).
HKEY_CURRENT_USER	Stores settings that concern the currently logged-on user. It is common to make changes in this hive.
HKEY_LOCAL_MACHINE	Stores hardware and software settings that are specific to the computer. This is where the bulk of a PC technician's registry edits are made. One example of data stored here are the programs that run when the OS starts.
HKEY_USERS	Stores data corresponding to all users who have ever logged on to the computer.
HKEY_CURRENT_CONFIG	Contains information that is gathered every time the computer starts up.

Hives are also known as keys that contain other keys and subkeys. This forms the organizational system for the registry. It is similar to folders and subfolders within Windows Explorer or File Explorer. However, the registry does not store actual data files; it stores settings. Inside the keys and subkeys are registration entries that contain the actual settings. These can be edited or new entries can be created. The types of entries include

▶ String values, which are used for decimal numbers

▶ Binary values, which are used for binary entries

▶ DWORD and QWORD entries, which are used for binary and hexadecimal entries

▶ Multistring values, which can have a variety of information

Registry hives are stored in \%systemroot%\System32\Config.

Many users fear the registry, but the technician need not. Just follow a couple simple rules: 1) Back up the registry before making changes and 2) don't make modifications or additions until you have a thorough understanding of the entry you are trying to modify or add. Figure 9.13 shows a registry entry called MenuBar within HKEY_CURRENT_USER\Control Panel\Colors. By double-clicking the MenuBar entry, an Edit String window appears (as shown). Again, the beauty of the registry is that you can make modifications to things that normally can't be modified in the Windows GUI. MenuBar is one of these examples. In the figure, the entry's string value has been changed to 0 0 255, which means the color blue. To effect this change, click OK, close the Registry Editor (no saving necessary), and then log off and log back on. Some registry changes require a reboot of the system.

As previously mentioned, you need to know how to back up the registry. You can back up any individual key or the entire registry. Say a user wanted to back up the Colors subkey before making changes to the MenuBar entry. The proper procedure would be to highlight the Colors subkey, click File on the Menu bar, and then select Export. Then it's as simple as selecting a location to save the registry entry and naming it. It exports as a .reg file. A typical subkey like this is about 2 KB in size. Backing up the entire registry can be done in two ways. First, you can do this by highlighting Computer, selecting Export, and saving the file. The other option is to select any registry key, select Export, and in the Export Registry File window, select the All radio button in the Export range box. Later, individual keys or the entire registry can be imported with the Import option on the File menu. You might need to do this if a registry modification caused a problem with the system. For example, certain changes to the registry could cause the GUI to fail to load. Or audio could become disabled. Again, be sure to make a backup before playing around with the registry. To repair a missing graphical interface or audio issue that is registry-related, attempt a System Repair from the Windows DVD or, if possible, restore an older version of a backed-up registry. (You will learn more about System Repair in Chapter 11.)

Finally, you can connect to remote computers to gain partial access to their respective registries. To do this, select File and then select Connect Network Registry. You can then browse for computers that are members of the same network your computer is a member of, connect to them, and then make modifications to those remote registries. Of course, you need to have administrative privileges on the remote computer.

> **ExamAlert**
>
> Know how to open the Registry Editor, modify entries, export the registry, and connect to remote registries.

Remote Desktop

Ever want to control a computer remotely? Remote Desktop software, included with Windows, enables a user to see and control the GUI of a remote computer. This enables users to control other computers on the network or over the Internet without leaving their seats; this aids technicians in their attempts to repair computers because they don't have to go to the system that needs repair. But first, to have a remote desktop session, you need to configure the software. To do so, open the System Properties window and select the Remote tab. From here, there are two boxes of information:

▶ **Remote Assistance:** This is selected by default. This means that connections can be made via Remote Assistance invitations, by e-mail, or via instant messaging. These invitations can ask for help or offer help. This is often implemented in help-desk scenarios in which a user invites a technician to take control of her computer so that it can be repaired. Invitations are made by accessing the Windows Remote Assistance program (simply type it into the Search field). For this to function, the Remote Assistance option Allow Remote Assistance connections to this computer must be selected in the System Properties/Remote tab; also, Remote Control must be selected, which can be enabled by clicking the Advanced button. When the proper settings are enabled, Remote Assistance calls flow right through the Windows Firewall.

▶ **Remote Desktop Connection:** This is where you can select whether other users can connect to, and control, your computer at any time without an invitation from you. There are options to disable remote connections, enable connections with any version of Remote Desktop, and enable connections running Remote Desktop with Network-level Authentication for security. This is disabled by default, but if enabled, the remote users can make connections to your computer by computer name or by IP address. Finally, you can select the users who are allowed to connect to your computer. If your network is a workgroup, then the local user account(s) you select is just that: local. For the remote user to connect, the remote computer must have an identical account (the same username and password) as the one you selected on your computer and the remote user must know the username/password. If the network is a domain, this is not an issue due to centralized administration of accounts.

ExamAlert

Be able to explain the difference between Remote Assistance and Remote Desktop.

To make a Remote Desktop connection to a remote computer, first make sure that the remote computer has Remote Desktop enabled. Next, open the program. In any version of Windows, simply type `remote` in the Search field and select Remote Desktop Connection. In Windows 7/Vista, you can also click

Start > All Programs > Accessories and Remote Desktop Connection. Either method opens the program. Click Options for more logon settings, as shown in Figure 9.14. To make the connection, you need to supply a computer name or the IP address of the remote computer and a username and password of an account on the remote computer.

FIGURE 9.14   The Remote Desktop Connection window

Click Connect and the screen of the other computer should show up on your local display. At this point, you can control the remote computer as if you were sitting locally at it. By default, the remote computer's screen locks; it can be unlocked only with a username/password.

> **Note**
>
> Remote Desktop is based off the Remote Desktop Protocol (RDP). When Remote Desktop is enabled, this protocol is allowed through the Windows Firewall using TCP port 3389 (by default). Give strong consideration to using Network Level Authentication when allowing Remote Desktop connections.

You can also use the `mstsc` command in the Command Prompt to make Remote Desktop connections, edit existing Remote Desktop configuration files, and migrate old connection files to newer systems. This command can be used in the Command Prompt or in the Run prompt. For example, if you wanted to remotely control another system with the `mstsc` command in full-screen mode, you would type

```
Mstsc.exe /v:computername /f
```

For more information on the `mstsc` command, visit http://technet.microsoft.com/en-us/library/cc753907(v=ws.10).aspx.

Program Compatibility

Most applications run properly on Windows. However, some applications that were designed for older versions of Windows might not run properly on Windows 8, 7, or Vista. To make applications written for older versions of Windows compatible with Windows 8/7/Vista, use the Program Compatibility utility or the Compatibility tab of a file's Properties window.

To start the wizard in Windows, open the Control Panel and then click the Programs icon (this time in Category mode). Then, under Programs and Features, click the link called Run Programs Made for Previous Versions of Windows (in Windows 8/7) or click Use an Older Program with This Version of Windows (in Windows Vista). This program asks you which programs you want to make compatible, which OS it should be compatible with, and inquires as to the resolution and colors that the program should run in.

To use the Compatibility tab, right-click the program you want to make compatible from within Windows Explorer or File Explorer and then click Properties. From there, click the Compatibility tab. From there, you can select which OS compatibility mode you want to run the program in and define settings such as resolution, colors, and so on.

Windows 8 incorporates the Program Compatibility Assistant (PCA), which automatically helps end users to run applications that were designed for earlier versions of Windows. It generally applies one of three compatibility modes: Windows XP SP3, Windows Vista SP2, or Windows 7. For more information on some common PCA scenarios for Windows 8, visit https://msdn.microsoft.com/en-us/library/windows/desktop/hh994464(v=vs.85).aspx.

ExamAlert

Know how to use the Program Compatibility utility and the Compatibility tab in a program's Properties window.

Windows XP Mode

Windows 7 can emulate the entire Windows XP OS if you so desire. This is done to help with program compatibility—meaning older programs that run or perform better with Windows XP or perhaps will only run with Windows XP. Because Microsoft support of Windows XP has ended, it is wise (more secure) to run these programs in Windows XP Mode as opposed to running them within an actual Windows XP system. To do this, you must first have Windows 7 Professional or Ultimate installed. Then additional components must be installed to emulate Windows XP. First, install Windows XP Mode, then Virtual PC, and, finally, the Windows XP Mode update. These additional components can be downloaded for free (as long as you have a valid copy of Windows 7) starting at http://www.microsoft.com/windows/virtual-pc/download.aspx.

Windows 8/8.1 does away with Windows Virtual PC in favor of Hyper-V. As such, Windows XP Mode is not available in Windows 8.

ExamAlert
Understand what XP Mode does.

Component Services

Component Services is a snap-in you can add to the MMC. It allows you to configure and administer three types of components: the Component Object Model (COM), COM+ Applications, and the Distributed Transaction Coordinator (DTC).

COM is a software interface used to allow interprocess communications and dynamic object creation by using different programming languages. The term COM includes the following technologies: ActiveX controls (such as the real-time charts found in Task Manager), Object Linking and Embedding (OLE databases), COM+ (an extension to COM, providing better memory and processor management), and DCOM (programming as it relates to networked computers).

The Microsoft Distributed Transaction Coordinator (MSDTC) is a relatively newer component of Windows that uses a transaction manager to coordinate information between databases, file systems, and other resources. It works in conjunction with COM and .NET architectures.

For more information on Component Services administration, visit http://technet.microsoft.com/en-us/library/cc731901.aspx.

If certain Dynamic-Link Libraries (DLLs) or ActiveX controls need to be troubleshot (for example, ones that work with Internet Explorer), they can be manipulated with the REGSVR32 command. Controls can be registered or unregistered in the Command Prompt. For example, to register a sample ActiveX control, you would type `regsvr32 sample.ocx`. Unregistering requires the /u parameter. To register a .DLL file, you would type `regsvr32 msi.dll`, replacing msi with whatever DLL you wish to register or unregister. To use the REGSVR32 command, you must run the Command Prompt as an administrator. More information on REGSVR32 can be found at http://support.microsoft.com/kb/249873.

Data Sources (ODBC)

Open Database Connectivity (ODBC) is an interface used within the C programming language to access database management systems. It is primarily used by Microsoft for its SQL database systems but can also be utilized by Microsoft Access Databases, dBASE, or Excel files. Different applications within Windows and from third-party vendors might make use of one of these technologies and will, therefore, need ODBC. If you want to make configuration changes to ODBC, you can access it by going to Administrative Tools and then clicking ODBC Data Sources in Windows 8 or clicking Data Sources (ODBC) in Windows 7/Vista. That opens the ODBC Data Source Administrator. From here, you can add or remove Database Source Names (DSNs), which are data structures that describe a connection to a data source. DSNs include the name of the data source, the folder it is located in, the driver used to access the data source, and so on. For example, if you wanted to run a program in Windows 7 that was reliant on a SQL Server database, or if you just wanted to make a connection to a SQL database, you would need to add the Microsoft SQL Server data source to the User DSN list. The name of the SQL Server would be required to complete the connection. For more information on ODBC in Windows, visit https://technet.microsoft.com/en-US/library/ms187039(v=sql.105).aspx.

> **Note**
>
> The previous two sections (COM and ODBC) and REGSVR32 deal with in-depth system configuration and application developing within Windows, going a bit beyond what a PC technician will usually be required to perform. However, they are listed on the CompTIA A+ objectives, so you should at least know what they are and how to access them in Windows.

Cram Quiz

Answer these questions. The answers follow the last question. If you cannot answer these questions correctly, consider reading this section again until you can.

220-902 Questions

1. Which of the following should be typed in the Run prompt to open Device Manager?

   ○ **A.** MMC

   ○ **B.** secpol.msc

   ○ **C.** CMD

   ○ **D.** devmgmt.msc

2. Where is the best place to get a driver for a video card?

   ○ **A.** CD-ROM

   ○ **B.** USB flash drive

   ○ **C.** Manufacturer's website

   ○ **D.** Microsoft's website

3. Which command opens the System Information tool?

   ○ **A.** devmgmt.msc

   ○ **B.** compmgmt.msc

   ○ **C.** systempropertiesadvanced.exe

   ○ **D.** msinfo32.exe

4. Which tab of Task Manager informs you of the total usage of the CPU?

   ○ **A.** Performance

   ○ **B.** Processes

   ○ **C.** Networking

   ○ **D.** Processing

   ○ **E.** App History

5. Where can a user go to start and stop services in Windows? (Select all that apply.)

   ○ **A.** msconfig

   ○ **B.** Task Manager

   ○ **C.** Computer Management

   ○ **D.** Command Prompt

6. Which window would you navigate to in order to modify the virtual memory settings in Windows 8? (Select the best answer.)

   ○ **A.** Device Manager

   ○ **B.** Performance Options

   ○ **C.** System

   ○ **D.** Folder Options

   ○ **E.** System Properties

7. Which of the following commands stops a service in the Command Prompt?

   ○ **A.** `spooler stop`

   ○ **B.** `network stop`

   ○ **C.** `net stop`

   ○ **D.** `stop`

8. Which power management mode stores data on the hard drive?

   ○ **A.** Sleep

   ○ **B.** Hibernate

   ○ **C.** Standby

   ○ **D.** Pillow.exe

9. Which tool enables a technician to move user state data from within the command line?

   ○ **A.** Windows Easy Transfer

   ○ **B.** Elevated mode

   ○ **C.** USMT

   ○ **D.** FAST

10. What is HKEY_LOCAL_MACHINE considered to be?

   ○ **A.** A registry entry

   ○ **B.** A subkey

   ○ **C.** A string value

   ○ **D.** A hive

11. When users invite a technician to help repair their computers, what is this called?

   ○ **A.** Remote Desktop Connection

   ○ **B.** Remote Assistance

   ○ **C.** RDP

   ○ **D.** Remote connectivity

Cram Quiz Answers

220-902 Answers

1. **D.** `Devmgmt.msc` is the Microsoft console window known as Device Manager. MMC opens up a new blank Microsoft Management Console. `Secpol.msc` opens the Local Security Policy window. CMD opens the Command Prompt.

2. **C.** The manufacturer's website is the best place to get the latest driver for your device; next on the list would be the CD-ROM that came with the device, and last, attempt to have Microsoft automatically install its version of the driver.

3. **D.** `Msinfo32.exe` opens the System Information tool. `Devmgmt.msc` opens the Device Manager. `Compmgmt.msc` opens Computer Management. `Systempropertiesadvanced.exe` (if typed in the Run prompt or Command Prompt) opens the System Properties dialog box to the Advanced tab.

4. **A.** The Performance tab shows the percentage of processing power used in real time. The Processes tab shows the individual processes that are running, the amount of processing power each of them is using, and the amount of memory they are utilizing. The Networking tab shows the percentage of network utilization for each network adapter. There is no Processing tab. The App History tab in Windows 8 shows the resources used per application over the last month.

5. **B, C, and D.** Task Manager, Computer Management, and the Command Prompt. Msconfig is not a correct answer because it lets you enable/disable services but does not start/stop them.

6. **B.** Navigate to the Performance Options window and then click the Advanced tab to modify virtual memory in Windows. You access that window from the System Properties window, clicking the Advanced tab, selecting the Performance section, and then clicking the Settings button. Although System Properties is essentially correct, it is not the best, or most accurate, answer.

7. **C.** `Net stop` (and the service name) stops the service in the Command Prompt (for example, `net stop spooler)`.

8. **B.** When a computer hibernates, all the information in RAM is written to a file called hiberfil.sys in the root of C: within the hard drive.

9. **C.** USMT is a migration tool that can be used from the command line that can move any user states to and from multiple computers. Windows Easy Transfer is the successor to FAST (Files and Settings Transfer Wizard), a program that was used in the deprecated Windows XP operating system. Elevated mode is what you need to be in when running administrative-level functions from within the Command Prompt.

10. **D.** HKEY_LOCAL_MACHINE is one of the five visible hives that can be modified from within the Registry Editor.

11. **B.** Remote Assistance calls can be made from users to invite other users to help fix a problem for them. Remote Desktop Connections are the connections that a computer makes to a remote computer to control it.

Files, File Systems, and Drives

This section covers file structures, file locations, ways of manipulating files, and file systems. It also delves into how to manage drives, including how to partition and format drives, create mount points, and identify drive status. Plus, we'll demonstrate some commands in the command line that are used to manipulate directories and files. Let's start by talking about files and file systems.

Working with Files and File Systems

Files are what makes the world go round, it seems. But because there are so many of them, you need to organize them efficiently. To do so, operating systems use a directory structure. It all starts with the root of the operating system and moves on from there, as detailed in Table 9.2.

TABLE 9.2 **Directory Structure in Windows 8/7/Vista**

Directory	Usage
C:\	This is the root of the C: drive, which is the drive in which the OS is usually installed. Boot files such as bootmgr are stored here.
C:\Windows	This folder is the %systemroot%, in which the operating system is actually installed to, folder by folder and file by file. This is also known as %WINDIR%.
C:\Windows\System32	This folder contains the critical Windows system files (for example, NTOSKRNL.EXE) and many applications (such as cmd.exe and dxdiag.exe).
C:\Windows\SysWOW64	This folder also contains critical 32-bit Windows system files. Used when a 64-bit system runs 32-bit processes; those processes are redirected to this folder.
C:\Boot	This folder contains the Boot Configuration Data (BCD) store. Note: This folder might be in a different partition depending on which partition is the system partition. In Windows 8/7, this will default to a hidden, 100 MB system partition that you can remove during the partitioning process.
C:\Program Files	This is where the bulk of applications are installed to (for example, Microsoft Office or Adobe Acrobat Reader). ▶ 64-bit applications are installed to Program Files. ▶ 32-bit applications are installed to Program Files (x86).
C:\Users	This is where all user account information is stored in Windows. It is redirected from the protected \Documents and Settings folder. (This is also known as a junction.)
C:\Windows\Temp	This is where temporary files are stored.

Directory	Usage
C:\Windows\CSC	This is where offline files are stored. Offline files are files that you have previously selected from the network to be available to you even when the network is not available.
C:\Windows\Fonts	This is the default location for fonts used by Windows and installed applications. When additional fonts are downloaded from the Internet, they should be placed in this folder.

> **Note**
>
> If the operating system were installed to another volume (for example, D:), all the paths shown in Table 9.2 would be modified to reflect this. If the operating system were installed in a different folder than %systemroot%, that would affect all sub-folders of the systemroot as well.

Windows 8/7/Vista Boot Files

After the BIOS is done bootstrapping and the master boot record (MBR) and boot sector of the hard drive have been located and accessed, a loader file is accessed on the hard drive. In Windows 8/7/Vista, this is the Windows Boot Manager. The following files are required to start Windows 8/7/Vista:

▶ **Bootmgr (Windows Boot Manager):** Bootmgr is the first file to load on the hard drive and is initiated by the BIOS. It takes care of reading the BCD and displaying the OS menu (if you have one). So it is responsible for starting a particular OS. It is outside of the OS (as it would have to be) so it can call on one of multiple versions of Windows. It can be shared among various versions of Windows and even other operating systems if configured properly (with the use of the Unified Extensible Firmware Interface or UEFI). Bootmgr switches CPU operation from real mode to protected mode, which could be 32-bit or 64-bit, depending on which version of the OS you installed. Among other things, this allows the Bootmgr to access all memory (and is not just limited to 1 MB).

▶ **BCD (Boot Configuration Data):** This is located in \boot\bcd; it furnishes the Windows Boot Manager with information about the operating system(s) to be booted. It is the successor to boot.ini and can be modified with msconfig or with the bcdedit.exe program. BCD was developed to provide an improved mechanism for describing boot configuration data and to work better with newer firmware models (such as UEFI). If you want to modify your dual-boot menu configuration manually, this is what you would go to.

▶ **Winload.exe:** Winload.exe is the Windows Boot Loader program and is within the OS. This program loads the kernel file (ntoskrnl.exe) of the particular OS that was selected from the Bootmgr program. Bootmgr invokes winload.exe for the OS that was selected. This file is located in \%systemroot%\System32.

Note

If a system is in hibernate mode, Winresume.exe is initiated by the Bootmgr/BCD instead of Winload.exe being initiated by Bootmgr.

ExamAlert

Memorize the required Windows 8/7/Vista boot files and their functions.

File Associations

File associations are the relationships between files and the applications that are used to open them. The extension of the file is what determines this. Take, for example, a file named sales-report.docx. The filename is sales-report and the extension is .docx. This extension is important because it tells you it is a Microsoft Word document; the relationship is such that Microsoft Word will be launched automatically when the file is opened.

In Windows 8/7/Vista, these associations are stored in Control Panel > Default Programs and can be modified by clicking the Set your default programs link. For example, if you wanted Windows Media Player to open additional types of files by default, you would highlight a media file (for example, a file with the .mp3 extension) and then select Choose Defaults for This Program. From there you can check the various audio and video file formats you want associated with Windows Media Player. Conversely, from the same Default Programs window, you can also click the link called Associate a file type or protocol with a program, which makes a specific file type always open with the same program.

ExamAlert

It is common for multimedia applications to attempt to become the default program of audio and video file formats. Be prepared to add or remove file associations for these types of applications.

Indexing

Because there are so many files, Windows offers the Indexing service to help you more quickly find the files you want. However, indexing too much content can lead to poor operating system performance.

To adjust the indexing settings in Windows, go to Control Panel > Indexing Options (show individual icons in the Control Panel). From here, you can modify whether folders are indexed by clicking the Modify button and selecting or deselecting the folders you want. It is not recommended to select an entire volume (like C:) because it can cause poor performance. Use indexing for specific folders in which you store important data that you search for on a regular basis. If you don't want indexing at all, you can either deselect all folders that are selected or disable indexing in general. To disable indexing altogether:

1. Open the Computer Management window.

2. Expand Services and Applications in the left window pane, and then click Services. (Alternatively, you could skip Step 1 and simply go to Run and type `services.msc`.)

3. In the right window pane, scroll down to Windows Search, right-click it, and then select Stop. You can start the stopped service at any time by right-clicking the service and selecting Start. Or you can simply select Restart to stop and start the service. Check the startup type by right-clicking the service and selecting Properties. If the startup type is set to Automatic, you should change it to manual or disabled; otherwise, the service starts back up again when you restart the computer.

You can also turn off indexing for individual drives. To do so:

1. Open File Explorer/Windows Explorer.

2. Right-click the volume you want to stop indexing on (for example, C:) and then select Properties.

3. At the bottom of the window, deselect the indexing option.

Working with Directories and Files in the Command Prompt

Have I mentioned yet that just about anything you can do in Windows can also be done in the Command Prompt? It's true. And sometimes the Command Prompt is faster (if you can type quickly) than the GUI. There are three commands used to work with directories in the Command Prompt. By the way, *directory* is the original name for *folder*. They are more accurately called directories when working in any command line (such as the Windows Command Prompt) and folders when working in the GUI, but the two terms can be used interchangeably.

▶ **CD:** Change Directory. This command enables you to move from one directory to another. Actually, you can go from any one directory to any other using just one CD command.

▶ **MD:** Make Directory. This command creates directories.

▶ **RD:** Remove Directory. This command enables you to remove directories. You can also remove directories that contain files by utilizing the /S switch.

All these commands can be used such that their functions affect any folder you choose within the directory structure (which used to be known as the DOS tree, but I digress). Figure 9.15 provides a sample directory structure.

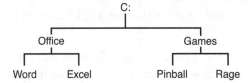

FIGURE 9.15 **A sample directory structure**

For example, let's say that your current position is C:\Office. From here or any other location, you can do anything to any folder in the entire directory tree. Let's give a couple examples:

▶ Change the current position to the Pinball folder. To do this, the command would be either cd c:\games\pinball or just cd \games\ pinball.

▶ Make a directory called "documents" within Word. To do this, the command syntax would be md c:\office\word\documents.

▶ Delete the directory Excel. To do this, the command would be rd c:\ office\excel.

> **Note**
>
> Making directories can be quick in the Command Prompt. If you need to create several subdirectories, using the MD command can be quicker than clicking with the mouse in Explorer. For example, to make four folders with one command, you could type: **md folder1; folder2; folder3; folder4**.

> **ExamAlert**
>
> Know the difference between CD, MD, and RD.

Some other commands you might use when working with directories and files include DIR, TREE, COPY, and DEL.

▶ **DIR:** This is the directory command. When used alone, it displays the contents of the current directory. But it can be configured to show information in any other directory. For example, DIR \office\excel will show the contents of the Excel directory regardless of what directory you are currently in. You can also use the DIR command to customize how content is listed. For example, /p will show information by the page, /w is wide list format, and so on. To find out more about the DIR command (or any other command, for that matter), type **DIR /?**. The /? is the switch that tells the Command Prompt to display the help file for that command. It can be placed on the end of any valid Command Prompt command.

▶ **TREE:** This command shows all the directories and subdirectories within your current position. Be careful where you run this because it could list information for quite a while and cause some stress on the hard drive. For example, stay away from big directories, such as the root, which is C:\, \Windows, and \Windows\System32.

▶ **COPY:** This command allows you to copy one or more files to another location. If I wanted to copy a file named test.txt from the office directory to the Excel directory, I would type **copy \office\test.txt \office\excel**. Now the original is in \office and the copy is in \excel. There are more powerful versions of this command—known as xcopy and robocopy—that we will talk about in Chapter 11.

▶ **DEL:** When you are done with a file and are ready to delete it, use DEL. For example, if you want to delete the test.txt file that you just copied to the Excel folder, type **del \office\excel\test.txt**.

> **Note**
>
> By the way, I created the test.txt text file within Notepad, which is available via the search tool or by going to Run and typing **notepad**. Notepad is Windows' default graphical text editor that you can use for editing text and batch files. However, you might opt to use third-party text editors, such as Notepad++ or TextPad, especially if you plan to create batch files or do any coding (for example, in HTML or PHP).

These are some of the basic commands you can make use of in the Command Prompt. We'll get into some more advanced commands in Chapter 11.

Managing Drives

Okay, so you have three 5 TB SATA hard drives. Now what do you do with them? You manage them. The main tool with which to do this is called Disk Management. It can be accessed either by opening Computer Management and expanding Storage or by typing **disk management** in the Search field.

Partitioning, Formatting, and Drive Status

The proper order for drive preparation is to partition the drive, format it, and then copy files to your heart's delight. However, sometimes you might also need to initialize additional drives within Windows; this would be done before partitioning. All of these things can be done within the Disk Management program. The Disk Management tool within Computer Management is the GUI-based application for analyzing and configuring hard drives. You can do a lot from here, including the following:

▶ **Initialize a new drive:** A secondary hard drive installed in a computer might not be seen by File/Windows Explorer immediately. To make it accessible, locate the drive (for example, it might be referred to as Disk 1), right-click where it says Disk 1, Disk 2, and such, and then select Initialize Disk. When you install an OS to the only drive in the system, it is initialized automatically.

▶ **Create volumes, partitions, and logical drives:** When creating these, Windows 8/7 refers to them simply as volumes. Windows Vista and earlier use the terms *partition* and *logical drive*. Regardless, you must right-click the area with the black header named unallocated. Figure 9.16 shows an example of creating a new simple volume by right-clicking that area.

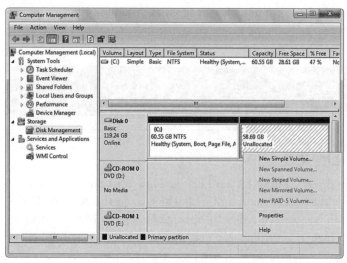

FIGURE 9.16　Creating a volume within unallocated disk space

▶ **Format volumes:** When formatting, select the file system (NTFS usually) and whether to do a quick format. If it is a new drive, quick formats are okay, but if the drive was used previously, you should leave this option unchecked so that you are left with a properly formatted boot drive.

> **Note**
>
> WARNING: ALL DATA WILL BE ERASED during the format procedure.

▶ **Make partitions active:** Partitions need to be set to active if you want to install an operating system to them.

▶ **Convert basic disks to dynamic:** Basic disks can have only simple volumes or regular partitions/logical drives. If you want to create a spanned, striped, mirrored, or RAID-5 volume, you need to convert the disk to dynamic. This is done by right-clicking the drive where it says Disk 0 or Disk 1, for example, and selecting Convert to Dynamic Disk. It's highly recommended that you back up your data before attempting this configuration.

▶ **Extend and shrink volumes:** A volume can also be extended or shrunk. Any volume can be shrunk, but to extend a volume, you need available unallocated space on the drive. By shrinking a volume that takes up the entire hard drive, you can also ultimately split that partition into two pieces, allowing you to better organize where the OS is stored and where the data files are stored.

You might ask: What is the difference between a partition and a volume? The partitions are physical (and logical) divisions of the drive. A volume is actually any space among one or more drives that receives a drive letter.

Disk 0 has a C: drive that is a primary partition. In the typical system that uses the master boot record (MBR) partitioning system, the first partition you create on a drive must be a primary partition. This primary partition gets a letter; for example C:. Afterward, you can create more primary partitions or an extended partition. The extended partition starts as free space but can be divided into logical drives. Logical drives are also given letter assignments. You can have up to four primary partitions or three primary partitions and an extended partition. The purpose of the extended partition is to allow you to logically divide the hard drive into more than just four parts. For example, Figure 9.17 shows a drive divided into three primary partitions and an extended partition with two logical drives.

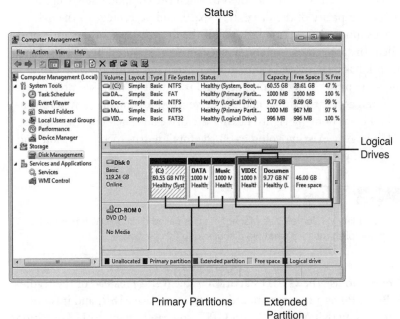

FIGURE 9.17 **A drive with three primary partitions, one extended partition, and two logical drives**

Although you might not see the colors, the color key in Figure 9.17 shows that you have three primary partitions. These are named C: (where your OS is installed), Data (the F: drive), and Music (the G: drive). Dark blue headers equate to primary partitions. The letters D: and E: were skipped because those letters are used by the DVD-ROM and Blu-ray drives. Furthermore, there is a dark green boxed area that contains three other items. Dark green means it is an extended partition. The extended partition does not get a drive letter. But the two medium blue logical drives inside, named Video and Documents, do get drive letters, H: and I:.

> **ExamAlert**
>
> Understand the differences between basic and dynamic disks, primary partitions, extended partitions, logical drives, and volumes.

These volumes were given a variety of file system types: NTFS (the most common), FAT, and FAT32. We'll talk more about these in a little bit.

You can also see the drives at the top of the window shown in Figure 9.17 and their status. For example, the C: partition is healthy. You see it is a System partition, which tells you that the OS is housed there. Plus, it is a Boot partition; this is the partition that is booted to when the computer starts up. It also shows the capacity of the drive, free space, and percentage of the drive used. What's more, this section tells you if the drive is basic or dynamic or if it has failed. In some cases, you might see "foreign" status. This means that a dynamic disk has been moved from another computer (with another Windows operating system) to the local computer and it cannot be accessed properly. To fix this and access the drive, add the drive to your computer's system configuration. This is done by right-clicking the drive and then clicking Import Foreign Disks. Any existing volumes on the foreign drive become visible and accessible when you import the drive.

> **Note**
>
> The command-line version of Disk Management is called diskpart. With this tool, you can accomplish most of what we discussed in this section.

You might opt to use the GUID Partition Table (GPT) instead of the traditional MBR. GPT is a newer standard meant to replace MBR, and it is not limited in the way that MBR is. With GPT, you can have up to 128 partitions and no extended partition is necessary. Also, you are not limited to the MBR's maximum partition size of 2 TB. In addition, the GPT is stored in multiple locations, so it is harder to corrupt the partition table data.

GPT is used heavily in Linux systems and Windows has supported it since 2005. It forms a part of the UEFI standard, so your system needs to have a UEFI-compliant motherboard. It uses globally unique identifiers (secure 128-bit numbers) to reference each partition, making it virtually impossible for any two computers to have two partitions with the same ID.

It is, however, dependent on the version of Windows used. For example, 64-bit versions of Windows Vista and newer have read and write support for GPT and can boot from a GPT-based system (it requires UEFI), but 32-bit systems such as Windows 7 and older cannot boot from GPT-based partitions. This means that those OSes cannot be installed on a GPT-based drive.

In essence, GPT is meant to replace MBR in the way that UEFI is meant to replace BIOS. As of the writing of this book, you might need to use one or the other (or a hybrid of the two), depending on the scenario. It's important to remember that you need to select your method (MBR or GPT) when you first add a new drive or start an installation. You can, however, convert a drive, but the drive will be wiped. For more information on how to do this, visit https://technet.microsoft.com/en-us/library/dn336946.aspx.

Mount Points and Mounting a Drive

You can also "mount" drives in Disk Management. A mounted drive is a drive that is mapped to an empty folder within a volume that has been formatted as NTFS. Instead of using drive letters, mounted drives use drive paths. This is a good solution for when you need more than 26 drives in your computer because you are not limited to the letters in the alphabet. Mounted drives can also provide more space for temporary files and can allow you to move folders to different drives if space runs low on the current drive. To mount a drive:

1. Right-click the partition or volume you want to mount and select Change Drive Letters and Paths.

2. In the displayed window, click Add.

3. Then browse to the *empty* folder you want to mount the volume to, and click OK for both windows.

As shown in Figure 9.18, the DVD-ROM drive has been mounted within the Data folder on the F: volume on the hard drive. It shows that it is a mounted volume and shows the location of the folder (which is the mount point) and the target of the mount point, which is the DVD drive containing a Windows 7 DVD. To remove the mount point, just go back to Disk Management,

314

CHAPTER 9: Configuring Windows

right-click the mounted volume, select Change Drive Letters and Paths, and then select Remove. Remember that the folder you want to use as a mount point must be empty, and it must be within an NTFS volume.

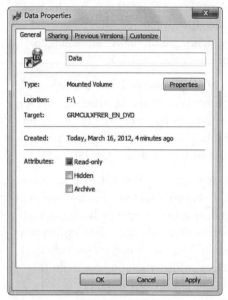

FIGURE 9.18 An empty NTFS folder acting as a mount point

Storage Spaces

Windows 8 and newer, as well as Windows Server 2012 and newer, incorporate a technology called storage spaces. This enables the Windows user to virtualize storage by grouping physical hard drives into storage pools and then creating virtual drives called storage spaces from the available capacity in the storage pools. The physical drives need to be SATA or Serial Attached SCSI (SAS). This tool can be accessed by typing **spaces** in the Search field or by going to Control Panel > System and Security > Storage Spaces. From here, multiple drives can be selected and used collectively as a "pool." There are four main types of pools that can be selected: Simple, which is similar to RAID 0 and has no fault tolerance; two-way mirror, which is similar to RAID 1 mirroring; three-way mirror, which is similar to RAID 10; and parity, which is similar to RAID 5.

File System Basics

When formatting a hard drive, you have the option to format it as NTFS (recommended), FAT32, or FAT. NTFS is a more secure and stable platform and can support larger volume sizes. It also supports encryption with the

Encrypting File System (EFS) and works better with backups. FAT32 and FAT should be used only to interact with older versions of Windows and to format devices such as USB flash drives. Depending on the cluster size used, NTFS can support up to 16 TB (4 KB clusters) or 256 TB (64 KB cluster) partitions, but some systems will be limited to 2 TB due to the limitations of partition tables on MBR-based drives. This hardware limitation applies to maximum FAT32 partition sizes of 2 TB as well (aside from the installation maximum of 32 GB). To go beyond this, a set of striped or spanned dynamic drives would have to be employed, creating a multidrive volume.

FAT (specifically known as FAT16) was the predecessor to FAT32 and is not available within extended partitions. It is recommended to stay away from FAT16 in general because it is deprecated.

Another file system introduced by Microsoft is called the Extended File Allocation Table (exFAT), which is suited specifically for USB flash drives but addresses the needs of many other mobile storage solutions. The successor to FAT32, it can handle large file sizes and can format media that is larger than 32 GB with a single partition. In fact, exFAT (also known as FAT64) has a recommended maximum of 512 TB for partitions, with a theoretical maximum of 64 ZB (zettabytes). The file size limit when using exFAT is 16 EB (exabytes). This file system can be used in many versions of Windows. If NTFS is not a plausible solution and the partition size needed is larger than 32 GB, exFAT might be the best option.

As of the writing of this book, exFAT is not used for internal SATA hard drives; it is used for flash memory storage and other external storage devices. exFAT is considered to be a more efficient file system than NTFS when it comes to flash memory storage; it has less fragmentation, leading to more possible read/write cycles over the life of the flash memory device.

Another file system you should understand is the Compact Disc File System (CDFS). This is the ISO 9660 standard, which defines how information is written to optical discs and is used by Windows and OS X. A CD-ROM consists of frames, which can each hold 24 bytes. Ninety-eight frames put together creates a sector. Those bytes are divided up; the majority of them are used for data and others are used for error detection and correction. How they are divided is determined by the mode used. CD-ROM Mode 1 and Mode 2 Form 1 are usually used for computer data. CD-ROM Mode 2 Form 2 is more tolerant of errors and is used by audio and video data.

ExamAlert

Know the differences between NTFS, FAT32, exFAT, and CDFS.

Cram Quiz

Answer these questions. The answers follow the last question. If you cannot answer these questions correctly, consider reading this section again until you can.

220-902 Questions

1. Where is NTOSKRNL.EXE located?

   ○ **A.** C:\Window

   ○ **B.** C:\Boot

   ○ **C.** C:\Windows\System

   ○ **D.** C:\Windows\System32

2. Which of these is the boot loader for Windows?

   ○ **A.** BCD

   ○ **B.** Winload.exe

   ○ **C.** NTLDR

   ○ **D.** Boot Manager

3. Which command creates a directory?

   ○ **A.** CD

   ○ **B.** MD

   ○ **C.** RD

   ○ **D.** Chdir

4. Where would you go to mount a drive in Windows?

   ○ **A.** Device Manager

   ○ **B.** Services.msc

   ○ **C.** Disk Management

   ○ **D.** Control Panel

Cram Quiz Answers

220-902 Answers

1. **D.** NTOSKRNL.EXE is located in C:\Windows\System32, otherwise referred to as \%systemroot%\System32.

2. **B.** Winload.exe (Windows Boot *Loader*) is the boot loader for Windows 8/7/ Vista. BCD is the Boot Configuration Data store in those OSes. NTLDR is the boot loader for the now unsupported (and therefore deprecated) Windows XP. Bootmgr is the Windows Boot *Manager* file in Windows 8/7/Vista, which is the first file to load when Windows starts. Don't confuse the Windows Boot Manager with the Windows Boot Loader!

3. **B.** MD (Make Directory) creates directories. CD is change directory, RD is remove directory, and chdir is the older version of CD.

4. **C.** Use the Disk Management program (Run > **diskmgmt.msc**) to mount drives in Windows. Device Manager is used to enable/disable and configure the hardware components of the computer. Services.msc can be used to start and stop services. The Control Panel houses many of the configuration utilities in Windows and although you could get to Disk Management indirectly through the Control Panel, it is not the best answer.

CHAPTER 10

Maintaining Windows

This chapter covers the following A+ exam topics:

▶ Updating Windows

▶ Maintaining Hard Drives

You can find a master list of A+ exam topics in the "Introduction."

This chapter covers CompTIA A+ 220-902 objectives 1.4, 1.5, and 1.7.

Windows maintenance is important as a security precaution and as a way to prevent any strange and unforeseen issues that might occur. Bad guys are always finding ways to exploit Windows code, and as these exploits are discovered, Microsoft releases updates (also known as patches) to fix those issues.

Keeping up maintenance on hard drives is one of the best things you can do for your computer. By maintaining the hard drive, you increase its lifespan and reduce the chance of corrupted files.

This chapter shows how to update Windows and how to configure the Windows Update program. It also shows how to maintain the hard drive with cleanup and defragmenting programs. This chapter is a little less intense than the last one, but it still contains some important information for the exams and for the IT field in general.

Updating Windows

Updating Windows can be done in two ways: by using the Windows Update program and by installing the latest service pack. Let's begin by discussing Windows Update.

Windows Update

As with any OS, Windows should be updated regularly. Microsoft recognizes deficiencies in the OS—and possible exploits that could occur—and releases patches to increase OS performance and protect the system. These patches can be downloaded and installed automatically or manually depending on the user's needs and are controlled via the Windows Update program. Updates are broken down into three types: important, recommended, and optional.

Important updates offer significant benefits, such as improved security, privacy, and reliability. They should be installed as they become available, and they can be installed automatically with Windows Update.

Recommended updates address noncritical problems or help enhance your computing experience. While these updates do not address fundamental issues with your computer or Windows software, they can offer meaningful improvements. These can be installed automatically.

Optional updates can include updates, drivers, or new software from Microsoft to enhance your computing experience. You can only install these manually.

To install updates for Windows through the Windows Update program, do the following:

1. Launch Windows Update from the Control Panel or from the search field. In Windows 7/Vista you can also click Start > All Programs > Windows Update.

2. This displays the Windows Update window in which you can check for updates or modify the Windows Update settings. Follow the prompts to install the latest version of the Windows Update software, if necessary.

> **Note**
>
> Do not let Microsoft automatically install all updates if you do not want to use newer applications; for example, the latest version of Internet Explorer.

3. (Optional) Depending on the configuration, the system might auto-matically scan for updates. Depending on the type of update, Windows Update can deliver one or more of the following:

▶ **Security updates:** A broadly released fix for a product-specific security-related vulnerability. Security vulnerabilities are rated based on their severity, which is indicated in the Microsoft secu-rity bulletin as critical, important, moderate, or low.

▶ **Critical updates:** A broadly released fix for a specific problem addressing a critical, nonsecurity-related bug.

▶ **Service packs:** A tested, cumulative set of hotfixes, security updates, critical updates, and updates, as well as additional fixes for problems found internally since the release of the product. Service packs might also contain a limited number of customer-requested design changes or features.

▶ **Windows updates:** Recommended updates to fix noncritical problems certain users might encounter; also adds features and updates to features bundled into Windows.

▶ **Driver updates:** Updated device drivers for installed hardware.

To modify how you are alerted to updates, click the Change Settings link. From here there will be four options:

▶ **Install updates automatically (recommended):** This is the recom-mended option by Microsoft. You can schedule when and how often the updates should be downloaded and installed.

▶ **Download updates but let me choose whether to install them:** This automatically downloads updates when they become available, but Windows prompts you to install them instead of installing them automatically. Each update has a checkbox, so you can select individual updates to install.

▶ **Check for updates but let me choose whether to download and install them:** This lets you know when updates are available, but you are in control as to when they are downloaded and installed.

▶ **Never check for updates:** This is not recommended by Microsoft because it can be a security risk but might be necessary in some envi-ronments in which updates could cause conflicts over the network. In some networks, the administrator takes care of updates from a server and sets the local computers to this option.

ExamAlert

Know how to install Windows updates and how to modify how they are downloaded and installed.

Larger organizations with a lot of computers will be concerned with *patch management*, which is the patching of many systems from a central location. Microsoft updates can be pushed out to multiple clients from a Windows Server system with System Center Configuration Manager (SCCM) or Windows Server Update Services (WSUS). Third-party tools can be used as well. The patch management process should be considered thoughtfully. Typically a patch management strategy will consist of four steps: planning, testing, implementing, and auditing. So before actually pushing the updates out, you should carefully consider what you will be updating and test it thoroughly on a couple of systems on a separate test network. After you implement the patch across the network, you should analyze whether the patch took to the systems. By using this four-step process, you can minimize errors in Windows updating.

Service Packs

A service pack (SP) is a group of updates, bug fixes, updated drivers, and security fixes that are installed from one downloadable package or from one disc. Service packs are numbered (for example, SP1, SP2, and so on). Installing an SP is relatively easy and requires answers to only a few basic questions. When those questions are answered, it takes several minutes or more to complete the update; then a restart will be required. While the service pack is installed, it rewrites many files and copies new ones to the hard drive as well.

Historically, some service packs have been cumulative, meaning that they also contain previous service packs. However, others are incremental. An example of an incremental SP is Windows Vista SP2; SP1 must be installed first before updating to SP2 in Windows Vista.

Windows 8 has moved away from the term "service pack" and instead has returned to the concept of the point release. For example, Windows 8.1 is the eighth version of Windows with the first point release installed. This is sometimes referred to by techs as SP1, but Microsoft simply refers to it as the Windows 8.1 update. However, it is important to know the service pack level of Windows 7 and Vista because that terminology is still used by Microsoft.

To find out which service pack is installed to Windows 7/Vista, access the System window from the Control Panel. Alternatively, you can click Start, then right-click Computer, and select Properties to open the System window.

In the Windows Edition section, you should see system information, including the operating system version and the SP that is installed. If the words "service pack" do not appear, there is no SP installed. This is informally known as SP0. You can also find out your SP level by going to the Run prompt and typing **winver**. Plus, you can discern SP levels directly in the Command Prompt. For example, if you open the Command Prompt in Windows 7 and see on the top line Microsoft Windows [Version 6.1.7600], then no SP is installed. But if you do this on Windows 7 with SP1, you will see Microsoft Windows [Version 6.1.7601]. Note the difference in the last digit of the build number—7600 means no service pack and 7601 means SP1.

Typing **ver** in the Command Prompt also gives this information. Finally, you can also open the System Information tool. (Open the Run prompt and type **msinfo32.exe**.) It will be listed directly in the system summary.

These methods also allow you to find out what point release of Windows 8 you are using. As an example, Windows 8.1 might be shown as 6.3.9600, which is Windows 8.1 with Update 1. The default version number for Windows 8 without any updates is 6.2.9200. If you see that build number, you should most definitely update Windows 8.

ExamAlert

Know where to check the SP level of Windows.

For the individual user, the SP can be automatically downloaded and installed if you have configured Automatic Updates within the Windows Update program; this is the easiest way for the average user to install service packs.

You can also download the SP in .exe, .msi, or .iso format. For example, Windows 7 SP1 can be downloaded from http://www.microsoft.com/download/en/details.aspx?id=5842.

These various packages can be helpful if you need to deploy SP1 to multiple computers. Your particular environment will dictate which file you should download. Before downloading, I recommend reading the article at http://support.microsoft.com/kb/2505743.

Service packs can also be acquired through a Microsoft Developer Network (MSDN) subscription. A SP might have been incorporated into the original operating system distribution media. This is known as *slipstreaming*. This method enables the user to install the OS and the SP at the same time in a seamless manner. It is also possible for system administrators to create slipstreamed images of the OS and SP by using the Windows Automated Installation Kit (AIK). The Win7 version of this is available at http://www.microsoft.com/download/en/details.aspx?displaylang=en&id=5753.

To summarize: Service packs are groups of updates that are installed to Windows 7 and Vista. As of the writing of this book, Windows 7 has a single service pack (SP1) and Vista has two service packs (SP1 and SP2). Windows 8 and 8.1 simply use updates instead of service packs.

Cram Quiz

Answer these questions. The answers follow the last question. If you cannot answer these questions correctly, consider reading this section again until you can.

220-902 Questions

1. Which Windows Update option is not recommended?

   ○ **A.** Download Updates but Let Me Choose Whether to Install Them

   ○ **B.** Install Updates Automatically

   ○ **C.** Never Check for Updates

   ○ **D.** Check for Updates but Let Me Choose Whether to Download and Install Them

2. Where can you find out the latest service pack that is used by Windows? (Select all that apply.)

   ○ **A.** System window

   ○ **B.** Windows Update

   ○ **C.** System Information

   ○ **D.** System Tools

3. In Windows 7, where would you go to modify how you are alerted to updates?

   ○ **A.** Click Start > Windows Update; then click the Change settings link.

   ○ **B.** Click Start > Control Panel; then select Classic view and double-click Automatic Updates.

   ○ **C.** Click Start; then right-click My Computer and select Properties.

   ○ **D.** Click Start > All Programs > Windows Update; then click the Check for updates link.

4. Where can you launch Windows Update in Windows 8? (Select the two best answers.)

   ○ **A.** Click Start and then click Windows Update

   ○ **B.** Control Panel

   ○ **C.** System window

   ○ **D.** Msinfo32.exe

Cram Quiz Answers

220-902 Answers

1. **C.** It is not recommended that you set Windows Update to Never Check for Updates because it is a security risk.

2. **A and C.** You can find out the latest SP in use by Windows within the System window and the System Information tool.

3. **D.** To modify how you are alerted to updates and how they are downloaded and installed in Window 7, click Start > All Programs > Windows Update and then click the Change settings link. In all versions of Windows, the Windows Update program can also be accessed from the Control Panel or with the search tool.

4. **B and C.** You can launch Windows Update in Window 8 from the Control Panel and from the System window (the link on the bottom left of the screen). In fact, these options can be used in other versions of Windows as well. Of course, you could also use the search option, and you might also open it from the Run prompt (or command-line) by typing **wuapp**. The answer "Click Start and then click Windows Update" works for Windows 7 and Vista, but it does not work in Windows 8 because of the change to the user interface. Msinfo32.exe gives system information but does not provide a link to Windows Update.

Maintaining Hard Drives

In Chapter 6, "Storage," I made a bold statement: "Hard drives will fail." But it's all too true; it's not a matter of *if*; it's a matter of *when*. By maintaining the hard drive with various utilities, you attempt to stave off that dark day as long as possible. To further protect data, you can back it up using programs that Windows provides to you or by using third-party programs. And to protect operating system files, Windows offers the System Restore utility. Let's start with some of the hard drive utilities that you will use in the field.

Hard Drive Utilities

To keep that hard drive running clean, I recommend that you remove temporary files, check the drive periodically, and defragment the drive when necessary. Let's talk about these three now.

Removing Temporary Files

Temporary files and older files can clog up a hard drive and cause a decrease in performance. You can view and delete a user's temporary files by going to Run and typing `%temp%`. However, you might want to use a program that deletes information from multiple locations in one shot. One program used to remove these files is called Disk Cleanup. Within this program, users can select which volume they want to clean up; it then scans the volume and calculates how much space you can save. It can clean away temporary files and downloaded program files, offline web pages, Office setup files, and older files; it can also empty the Recycle Bin. This program can be accessed by going to Run (or Search) and typing `cleanmgr.exe`. In Windows 7/Vista it can also be accessed by clicking Start > All Programs > Accessories > System Tools > Disk Cleanup. It is recommended that all programs are closed prior to running Disk Cleanup.

> **Note**
>
> You can find third-party cleanup programs on the Internet, such as CleanUp! and CCleaner.

You can also delete temporary files and Internet files manually. To remove temporary files manually, navigate to C:\Windows\Temp and remove any temp files and Internet files necessary. (You will need administrator access to do this.) There are also various folders within the user profile folder (for example, the Recent folder) that have temporary files. However, it is easier to remove these files with one of the programs mentioned previously. Temporary Internet files and cookies can be removed by accessing the Internet Properties window within Internet Explorer, selecting the General tab, locating the Browsing History section, and clicking Delete. This offers you the option to remove a variety of information, including temporary Internet files, cookies, history, form data, and passwords. The same method can be used in Firefox and Chrome by accessing the History setting.

> **ExamAlert**
>
> Know how to remove temporary files from the operating system and from the browser.

Checking the Drive

Windows provides a program that checks for basic errors on the hard drive. You can check any volume in this manner. Simply right-click the volume in Windows/File Explorer, select Properties, and then click the Tools tab. From here, you can click the Check (now) button. This can check for and fix basic errors on the drive. You can also run a thorough check of the drive by selecting Scan for and attempt recovery of bad sectors. You cannot check a drive while it is in use, so remember to close all files before checking a volume. If you need to check the C: drive, you should schedule the check. You can schedule one check, or you can schedule recurring Check Disks by opening the Task Scheduler, creating a basic task, and telling it to run chkdsk.exe with whatever parameters you wish. We'll talk more about this command in Chapter 11, "Troubleshooting Windows."

Removing Unnecessary Applications

As a computer is used more and more, the number of applications that are loaded onto it can pile up. Chances are, the typical user needs only a few applications; the rest are either hardly used or have been completely forgotten.

You can remove these unnecessary applications by going to the Control Panel and selecting the Programs and Features option. From here, you can view a list of installed programs and remove those that are no longer necessary.

In Windows 8, you can also remove programs (and increase drive space in other ways) by opening the Charms bar, selecting the Settings icon, selecting Change PC settings, PC and devices, and then selecting Disk space.

Removing unwanted programs saves space on the hard drive and typically makes the system run a bit more efficiently. However, the more you install and remove applications, the more likely the files on the drive will become fragmented. That leads us to our next method of maintaining the drive.

Defragmenting the Drive

Over time, data is written to the drive and subsequently erased, over and over again, leaving gaps in the drive space. New data will sometimes be written to multiple areas of the drive in a broken or fragmented fashion by filling in any blank areas it can find. When this happens, the hard drive must work much harder to find the data it needs—spinning more and starting and stopping more (in general, more mechanical movement). The more the drive has to access this fragmented data, the shorter its lifespan becomes due to mechanical wear and tear. Also, the computer will run slower and continually get worse until the problem is fixed. A common indicator of this is when the hard drive LED light constantly shows activity. When this happens, you need to rearrange the file sectors so that they are contiguous—you need to defragment!

Defragmenting the drive can be done with Microsoft's Disk Defragmenter, with the command-line utility defrag.exe, or with third-party programs. In Windows 8/8.1, you can open the Disk Defragmenter by doing one of the following:

▶ Using the search tool, type **defragment** and then select the correct application (for example, in Windows 8, select Defragment and optimize your drives).

▶ Open the Run prompt and enter **dfrgui.exe**.

In addition to the options mentioned in the previous bullets, in Windows 7/ Vista, you can click Start > All Programs > Accessories > System Tools > Disk Defragmenter.

The program automatically analyzes volumes and lets you know if a volume needs to be defragmented. (You can also access this by right-clicking the volume in Windows/File Explorer, selecting Properties, and then clicking the Tools tab.)

If you are using the Disk Defragmenter program, you need 15 percent free space on the volume you want to defrag. If you have less than that, you need to use the command-line option defrag -f.

ExamAlert

Know how to access the disk defragmenter in Windows, and know the `defrag` command in the Command Prompt.

Figure 10.1 shows the Windows 7 Disk Defragmenter. Before clicking the Defragment disk button, it's recommended that you first click the Analyze disk button to find out whether the drive needs to be defragmented. If the drive requires defragmentation, Windows will tell you so; otherwise, the program simply shows the amount that is currently fragmented. As you can see in Figure 10.1, the C: is 1 percent fragmented. Although a drive such as this doesn't need a defrag just yet, it's a good idea to keep an eye on it and recheck it periodically. Or better yet, you could turn on the Task Scheduler directly within the window in Figure 10.1 and schedule when you want analysis and possible defragmentation to occur.

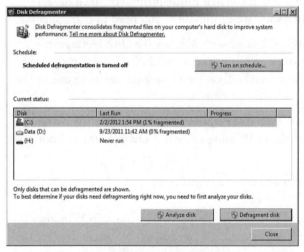

FIGURE 10.1   Windows 7 Disk Defragmenter

If you do initiate a defrag, it could take a while, so it's best to do this off-hours. After it completes, a restart is recommended.

Backups

Backing up data is critical for a company. It is not enough to rely on a fault-tolerant array. Individual files or the entire system can be backed up to another set of hard drives, or to optical discs, or to tape. Windows 8, Windows 7, and Windows Vista use three separate programs for backing up data. They are each accessed differently, but they work in similar ways.

Using Windows 8's File History and Recovery

File History is a file backup program that can be accessed from the Control Panel. When opened, it automatically searches for accessible drives on the network that are potential candidates for backups. By default, it copies files from the Libraries location, Desktop, Contacts, and Favorites. You can select the copy destination that the File History program will use. You can also restore personal files from here as well. To initiate a file copy within the File History program:

1. Start File History by accessing Control Panel > File History. (If in category mode of the Control Panel, go to System and Security > File History.)

2. Enable File History by clicking the Turn on button. That will automatically initiate a backup. Or click the Select a drive link to select or add a network location to back up to. Click OK when finished. This returns you to the main File History window and initiates the backup.

3. Subsequent backups can be made by clicking the Run now link or by selecting the Advanced Settings link and configuring when the files are to be saved.

If File History is no longer needed or desired, click the Turn off button.

In some cases, you might want to back up more than just personal files from specific locations, and you might want to back up the entire system. A good way to do this is to use the System Image Backup option (linked to the bottom-left corner of the File History window). This creates an image of your entire drive(s), from which you can restore later on. There are third-party imaging products as well (for example, Symantec Ghost). Some organizations prefer to use these.

Using Windows 7's Backup and Restore

Backup and Restore can back up individual files, create an image of the system, and create a system repair disc. You might have to set up the backup program prior to use, depending on your configuration. To create a backup with Windows 7's Backup and Restore:

1. Start Backup and Restore by accessing Start > Control Panel > Backup and Restore. (In category mode of the Control Panel, go to System and Security > Backup and Restore.) You can access this program (and Windows 8's File History) with the sdclt executable as well, as long as you have administrative permissions.

2. Click the Set Up Backup link (if necessary) or the Back Up Now button if a backup device has already been set up. You need to have an external storage device, second hard drive, or second partition to back up to. If no device or media can be found, the only other option is to back up to the network.

3. Select the media or partition you want to back up to, and then click Next.

4. Select whether Windows will automatically back up data or choose your own files to be backed up, and then click Next.

5. Select the folders and files you want to back up and whether to include a system image of each drive. Then click Next.

6. Review the settings and then click the Save Settings and Backup button. This initiates the backup. Backups can be restored using this program as well.

After you have set up what you want to back up, scheduled backups are automatically configured to run every week. You can disable this by clicking the Turn Off Schedule link. You can modify when the automatic backups occur by clicking the Change Settings link. Go through the backup questions again until you get to the Review your backup settings page. From there, click the Change Schedule link to tell the system when to automatically back up.

> **Note**
>
> You can also initiate backups of volumes in Windows Vista and Windows 7 by right-clicking the volume in Windows Explorer, clicking Properties, and then clicking the Tools tab.

Using Windows Vista's Backup Status and Configuration

Backup Status and Configuration is name of the backup program in Windows Vista. It can back up individual files or an entire image of your system (using Complete PC Backup) to the removable media of your choice (for example, a DVD). To create a complete backup of your PC with Vista's Complete PC Backup:

1. Start the Complete PC Backup by going to Start > All Programs > Accessories > System Tools > Backup Status and Configuration.

2. Click the Complete PC Backup button.

3. Select Create a backup now and then follow the directions. Have media ready that can hold an image of your operating system (for example, a DVD-R). Be ready; this will be a sizeable image!

ExamAlert

Be able to demonstrate how to back up data in Windows 8, 7, and Vista.

Creating Restore Points

System Restore can fix issues caused by defective hardware or software by reverting back to an earlier point in time. Registry changes made by hardware or software are reversed in an attempt to force the computer to work the way it did previously. Restore points can be created manually and are also created automatically by the operating system before new updates, applications, or hardware is installed.

To create a restore point in Windows 8/7/Vista:

1. Open the System window and then click the System Protection link. This displays the System Protection tab of the System Properties dialog box, as shown in Figure 10.2.

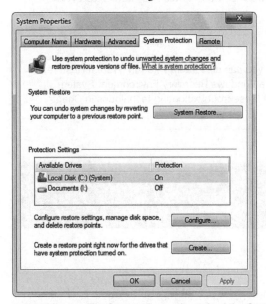

FIGURE 10.2 **The System Protection tab of the System Properties dialog box in Windows 7**

2. Click the Create button. This opens the System Protection dialog box.

3. Type a name for the restore point, and then click Create.

If System Restore is not available, it might be turned off. There are several reasons why a person might turn it off (for example, if the system had been scanned for viruses recently).

To enable or disable System Restore in Windows, click the Configure button within the System Protection tab of the System Properties dialog box. From here you would click the radio button for Turn on system protection in Windows 8. In Windows 7/Vista, you would click Restore system settings and previous versions of files (on the system drive, usually C:) or you would click Restore previous versions of files (on other drives containing data only).

System Restore is kind of like using a time machine (if one actually existed). It allows you to reset the computer to an earlier configuration—hopefully, one that functioned properly. To actually restore the computer to an earlier point in time, just click the System Restore button on the System Properties/System Protection dialog box and then follow the instructions. But beware, some applications might be removed and drivers might be uninstalled.

Alternatively, in Windows 7/Vista, you can create a restore point by going to Start > All Programs > Accessories > System Tools > System Restore.

> **Note**
>
> If the system won't boot normally, you can also attempt to run System Restore from Safe Mode or you can use the Windows Recovery Environment/System Recovery Options. We'll talk about those troubleshooting techniques in Chapter 11, "Troubleshooting Windows."

> **ExamAlert**
>
> Understand how to enable and disable System Restore, how to create restore points, and how to restore the system to an earlier point in time.

Shadow Copy

Shadow Copy is a Windows technology that enables you to make backup copies of data known as snapshots. It is dependent on the Volume Shadow Copy service. The data can be backed up manually or automatically and is reliant on restore points.

To use this service, you first need to enable System Restore on one or more volumes (as mentioned in the previous section). After that is complete, Windows automatically creates shadow copies of files whenever a restore point is created. You can find out if a file has been shadow copied by right-clicking the file, selecting Properties, and then clicking the Previous Versions tab.

Figure 10.3 shows an example of a text file that is stored on a drive with System Restore enabled.

FIGURE 10.3   The Previous Versions tab of a text file in Windows 7

System Restore was configured for the I: drive of the computer. This means that any files within that drive will be shadow copied. As you can see in the figure, a restore point was created on 3/16/2012. When that happened, the file Shadow Copy Test1.txt was shadow copied. If the file were somehow modified and the user wanted an older version, you could open or restore that older version from here.

> **Note**
>
> The Previous Versions tab (which displays any shadow copies of the file) does not exist in Windows 8, though the Volume Shadow Copy service still runs. In Windows 8, this functionality is incorporated into File History.

There are a few caveats to all this. First, Shadow Copy does not take the place of an actual file backup. Second, restored files that were Shadow Copied can at times have missing data or other errors. Lastly, System Restore and Shadow Copy work decently on the system partition where the OS is stored, but they can seriously slow down a system when used on data volumes, especially because additional shadow copies of the files will be made each time they are modified.

Users should be encouraged to back up data with one of the programs previously mentioned in the "Backups" section. Shadow Copy does not take the place of a backup; it should be treated as a supplement to a regular file backup and used only as a last resort. A final word on this: Due to the drawbacks of Shadow Copy, newer versions of Windows (including Windows 8) move away from any user intervention of shadow copying.

ExamAlert

Know what Shadow Copy is and where to find shadow copies of files.

Cram Quiz

Answer these questions. The answers follow the last question. If you cannot answer these questions correctly, consider reading this section again until you can.

220-902 Questions

1. Which program removes temporary files?

   ○ **A.** Backup and Restore

   ○ **B.** Disk Cleanup

   ○ **C.** System Restore

   ○ **D.** Disk Defragmenter

2. If there is less than 15 percent free space within a volume, how would a user defragment that volume in Windows?

   ○ **A.** By using Disk Defragmenter

   ○ **B.** By using the command `defragment -f`

   ○ **C.** By using the command `defrag -f`

   ○ **D.** By using a third-party tool

3. Which program in Windows Vista creates a Complete PC Backup?

   ○ **A.** Backup Status and Configuration

   ○ **B.** File History

   ○ **C.** Backup and Restore

   ○ **D.** System Restore

4. Where would you go in Windows to enable System Restore? (Select the best answer.)

   ○ **A.** The System Properties window

   ○ **B.** The Advanced Protection tab of the System Properties window

   ○ **C.** Task Manager

   ○ **D.** The System Protection tab of the System Properties window

5. Which program in Windows 7 allows you to back up files?

   ○ **A.** Backup Status and Configuration

   ○ **B.** Backup and Restore

   ○ **C.** File History

   ○ **D.** System Restore

6. Which program in Windows 7 should not be used to back up data?

   ○ **A.** Backup Status and Configuration

   ○ **B.** Backup and Restore

   ○ **C.** Shadow Copy

   ○ **D.** File History

7. One of your customers complains that applications take a long time to load and that the LED light on the front of the computer is constantly blinking. What is the most likely cause?

   ○ **A.** The power supply is faulty.

   ○ **B.** The processor is faulty.

   ○ **C.** The motherboard is sending faulty signals to the LED.

   ○ **D.** The file system is fragmented.

8. Which program in Windows 8 backs up Documents, Music, Pictures, Videos, and Desktop folders and the OneDrive files available offline on your PC?

   ○ **A.** Backup Status and Configuration

   ○ **B.** Backup and Restore

   ○ **C.** Shadow Copy

   ○ **D.** File History

9. Which of the following is accomplished by defragging a drive?

   ○ **A.** File sectors are made contiguous.

   ○ **B.** The drive is checked for errors.

   ○ **C.** The MBR is rewritten.

   ○ **D.** The pagefile size is increased.

Cram Quiz Answers

220-902 Answers

1. **B.** Disk Cleanup removes temporary files and other types of files and clears the Recycle Bin.

2. **C.** `defrag –f` defragments the drive even if free space is low. However, be prepared to use a lot of system resources to complete the defrag. Close any open windows before starting the process.

3. **A.** Backup Status and Configuration has an option called Complete PC Backup within Windows Vista. File History is the backup program used in Windows 8. Backup and Restore is the name of the Windows 7 backup program. System Restore creates restore points, which deals more with settings than it does data.

4. **D.** To enable (or disable) System Restore in Windows, go to the System Protection tab of the System Properties window.

5. **B.** The Backup and Restore program allows you to back up files in Windows 7. Backup Status and Configuration is used in Windows Vista. File History is used in Windows 8. System Restore is available on all three operating systems.

6. **C.** Shadow Copy should not be used to *back up* data. It should be used to *restore* data only in the chance that a real backup is not available. It is a last resort. Always use a real backup program. The title of the program will vary with the OS: The Backup and Restore program enables you to back up files in Windows 7; Backup Status and Configuration is used in Windows Vista; and File History is a Windows 8 program.

7. **D.** If applications are loading slowly and the hard drive LED light is constantly active, the hard drive is most likely fragmented. A defrag is in order. The other answers are hardware-based and should not be the cause of those symptoms.

8. **D.** File History is the backup program used in Windows 8.

9. **A.** When you defrag the drive, all the file sectors are straightened out and made contiguous. This makes the drive more efficient. CHKDSK or SFC checks a drive for errors. The pagefile can be increased by the user in the System Properties dialog box. The master boot record would be updated if the `bootrec /fixmbr` command were issued (more on that and the CHKDSK and SFC commands in Chapter 11).

CHAPTER 11

Troubleshooting Windows

This chapter covers the following A+ exam topics:

▶ Repair Environments and Boot Errors

▶ Windows Tools and Errors

▶ Command-Line Tools

You can find a master list of A+ exam topics in the "Introduction."

This chapter covers CompTIA A+ 220-902 objectives 1.3, 1.4, and 4.1.

Now for the toughest part of working with Windows: troubleshooting. Before beginning this chapter, I recommend that you review the six-step troubleshooting process in Chapter 1, "Introduction to Troubleshooting." As I mentioned in Chapter 1, troubleshooting is the most important skill for a computer technician to possess. There are many different things that can go wrong in a computer; the majority of them are software-related. This chapter endeavors to give you the tools, utilities, and skills necessary to troubleshoot the various boot errors, stop errors, and other Windows errors that you might encounter.

Repair Environments and Boot Errors

Windows startup errors prevent you from accessing the operating system. Because of this, Windows 8, 7, and Vista have various startup tools, menus, and repair environments that you can use to troubleshoot these startup and boot errors.

ExamAlert

The CompTIA 220-902 exam will present performance-based questions requiring you to know where the various troubleshooting tools are located within Windows and how to use them to resolve a given problem. Pay very close attention to the details in this chapter!

Windows Recovery Environments

There are many tools included with Windows 8, 7, and Vista designed to help you troubleshoot and repair just about any issue that might come up. Before getting into the exact issues you might face, let's discuss some of these advanced repair and preinstallation environment repair tools, what they do, and where you can access them. We'll start with the Windows Recovery Environment.

Windows Recovery Environment (Windows RE)

Windows RE (or WinRE) is a set of tools included in Windows whose purpose is to recover Windows from errors that prevent it from booting; these tools can also be instrumental in fixing issues that cause a computer to "freeze up." There are several possible ways to access Windows RE; each method varies according to the version of Windows being used.

In Windows 8, Windows RE is accessed through the Boot Options menu. You can get to Boot Options in a variety of ways, including the following:

▶ Right-click the Start button, select Shut down or sign out, and while holding the Shift key, select Restart. You can access Restart from several other places as well, mostly within the Charms bar.

▶ Open the Charms bar and go to Settings > Change PC settings > General. Then under Advanced startup, select Restart now. (No Shift key necessary.)

▶ In the Command Prompt, type **shutdown /r /o** and then press Enter.

Note

These options are based on Windows 8 or higher. For more information on gaining access to Windows RE in Windows 8 or 8.1, visit https://technet.microsoft.com/ en-us/library/hh825173.aspx.

Once the system has rebooted, you should see the "Choose an option" screen. Selecting Troubleshoot will present several options, including Refresh your PC (which saves personal files but removes all programs installed to the desktop and resets PC settings), Reset your PC (which removes all files and essentially performs a factory reset), and Advanced Options. Selecting Advanced Options brings up the main tools that a technician will use to troubleshoot a system. However, if the system won't boot, you will have to press F8 when the system boots, boot from the installation disc, or use the recovery media that came from the manufacturer of the computer.

In Windows 7/Vista, you either boot from the installation media or boot to a special partition on the hard drive that had Windows RE installed. The first option is more common with an individual computer that had Windows installed (for example, if you performed a clean installation with the standard Windows DVD and made no modifications to it). To start Windows RE, make sure that the DVD drive is first in the boot order of the BIOS, boot to the Windows DVD (as if you were starting the installation), choose your language settings and click Next, and then select Repair Your Computer (which is located at the lower-left corner of the screen). Select the Use Recovery Tools radio button and then click Next.

Note

Important! Do not select Install Now because that begins the process of reinstalling Windows on your hard drive.

The second option of booting to a special partition in Windows 7/Vista is used by OEMs (original equipment manufacturers) so that users can access Windows RE without having to search for and boot from a Windows DVD. These OEMs (computer builders and system integrators) will preinstall Windows RE into a special partition on the hard drive, separate from the operating system, so the user can boot into it at any time. To access WinRE that has been preinstalled, press F8 to bring up the Advanced Boot Options menu, highlight Repair Your Computer, and then press Enter. However, there is no way to access these options from *within* Windows 7/Vista the way they can be from Windows 8.

Figure 11.1 shows the Advanced options screen in Windows 8, where the main recovery tools are available. Figure 11.2 shows the Windows 7/Vista equivalent (that screen is named System Recovery Options). Table 11.1 describes these options in more depth.

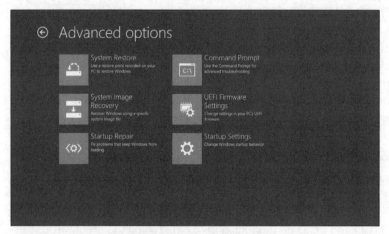

FIGURE 11.1   The Windows 8 Advanced options screen

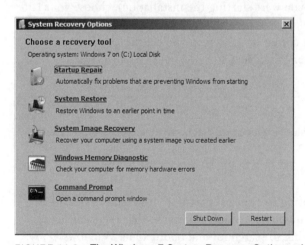

FIGURE 11.2   The Windows 7 System Recovery Options window

TABLE 11.1 **Description of the Windows 8 and 7/Vista Recovery Options**

Recovery Option	Description
System Restore	Restores the computer's system files to an earlier point in time. It's a way to undo system changes to your computer without affecting your personal files, such as e-mail, documents, or photos. Note: If you use System Restore when the computer is in Safe Mode, you cannot undo the restore operation. However, you can run System Restore again and choose a different restore point, if one exists.
System Image Recovery (Windows 8/7) Windows Complete PC Restore (Vista)	These programs are used to restore a hard drive from a backup in select editions of Windows.
Startup Repair	When clicked, this automatically fixes certain problems, such as missing or damaged system files that might prevent Windows from starting correctly. When you run Startup Repair, it scans your computer for the problem and then tries to fix it so your computer can start correctly.
Command Prompt	Advanced users can use Command Prompt to perform recovery-related operations and also run other command-line tools for diagnosing and troubleshooting problems. This option puts the user into a directory called X:\Sources.
UEFI Firmware Settings	(Windows 8 only.) Allows a user to access the UEFI from the OS to make changes. (Requires UEFI compatible BIOS.)
Startup Settings	(Windows 8 only.) Enables booting to a variety of modes that are explained later in the chapter. This was previously known as the Advanced Boot Options menu in Windows 7/Vista.
Windows Memory Diagnostic	(Windows 7/Vista only.) Scans the computer's memory for errors.

ExamAlert

Memorize the different Windows RE options in Windows 8 and Windows 7/Vista.

One thing to keep in mind is that Windows will attempt to do a self-repair if it senses a boot issue. This will occur first when you start, or restart, the system. If this automatic repair does not fix the problem, the Windows Recovery Environment is your next stop. But in some cases, you need to boot the system in a different *way* in order to fix a problem. Let's discuss advanced booting now.

Advanced Booting

If Windows 8/7/Vista is not functioning properly, the culprit might be a video driver, new configuration, or other system issues. There are several startup options that can aid in fixing these problems. Historically, these options were accessed by pressing the F8 key immediately after the computer starts up. In Windows 7/Vista, this brings up the Windows Advanced Boot Options menu (also known as the ABOM), as shown in Figure 11.3. However, in Windows 8, this is known as "Startup Settings." In comparison, it becomes a bit more complicated to access this, albeit less necessary due to Windows 8's ability to repair many problems automatically. While the F8 (and Shift+F8) keypresses are still supported by Microsoft, they might not work for one of two reasons. First, if the system uses a UEFI/BIOS, the F8 options may be disabled. To enable the ABOM in Windows 8, type the following into the Command Prompt (as an admin):

```
bcdedit /set {default} bootmenupolicy legacy
```

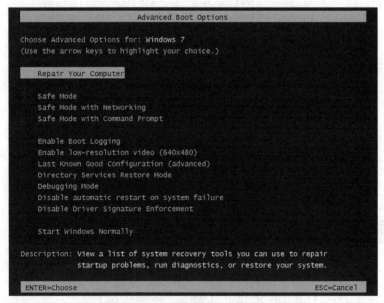

FIGURE 11.3 **The Windows 7 Advanced Boot Options menu**

To disable the ABOM (also known as F8/legacy boot options), use the same command but replace "legacy" with "standard." Secondly, Windows 8 boots through that stage very quickly (especially in a system using SATA drives and UEFI), sometimes too quickly to register the keypress. However, there are several other ways to access this, including the following:

▶ Access the Windows RE Advanced options screen (shown previously in Figure 11.1) and select Startup Settings. This then lists ways to restart Windows. Press Restart and the system restarts into a basic mode, giving the user the boot options listed in Figure 11.4. If necessary, you can also boot the system to a system recovery disc or flash drive to access Windows RE.

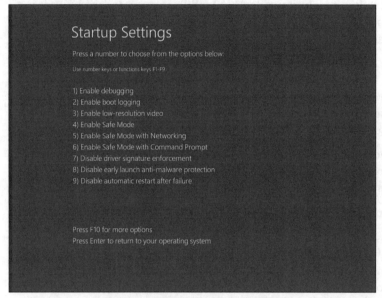

FIGURE 11.4   **The Windows 8 Startup Settings screen**

▶ Use the System Configuration Tool (msconfig) and click the Boot tab. Then select Safe boot in the Boot options area. Click OK and restart the computer.

The following options are included in the Advanced Boot Options menu/ Startup Settings screen. I've listed them according to how Windows 7/Vista displays them because I believe it is more likely that you will access them in Windows 7/Vista than in Windows 8. Keep in mind that Windows 8's list is rearranged (as shown in Figure 11.4), the names are slightly different, and there is one addition to the list.

▶ **Safe Mode:** Starts system with a minimal set of drivers; used in case one of the drivers fails. Safe Mode is a good option when attempting to use System Restore and when scanning systems for viruses. It is also a good option if you encounter a Blue Screen of Death (BSOD) error, and you need to roll back a driver.

▶ **Safe Mode with Networking:** Starts system with a minimal set of drivers and enables network support.

▶ **Safe Mode with Command Prompt:** Starts system with a minimal set of drivers but loads Command Prompt instead of the Windows GUI.

▶ **Enable Boot Logging:** Creates a ntbtlog.txt file.

▶ **Enable low-resolution video (640x480):** Uses a standard VGA driver in place of a GPU-specific display driver but uses all other drivers as normal.

▶ **Last Known Good Configuration (advanced):** Starts the system with the last configuration known to work; useful for solving problems caused by newly installed hardware or software. The last known good configuration (also known as LKG) is derived from the most recent successful login.

▶ **Directory Services Restore Mode:** This is used to restore a domain controller's Active Directory (Windows Server). Even though it is listed, it is not used in Windows 7/Vista.

▶ **Debugging Mode:** Enables the use of a debug program to examine the system kernel for troubleshooting.

▶ **Disable automatic restart on system failure:** Prevents Windows from automatically restarting, if an error causes Windows to fail. Choose this option only if Windows is stuck in a loop in which Windows fails, attempts to restart, and fails again repeatedly.

▶ **Disable driver signature enforcement:** Enables drivers containing improper signatures to be installed.

▶ **Start Windows Normally (Windows 7/Vista):** This can be used to boot to regular Windows. This option is listed in case a person inadvertently pressed F8 but did not want to use any of the Advanced Boot Options. In Windows 8, simply press Enter to return to the operating system in normal mode.

▶ **Disable early launch antimalware protection (Windows 8 only):** Rootkits can infect a system early on as it boots and some antimalware programs are designed to check for these early on in the boot process. But in some cases, you need to disable these antimalware programs to diagnose and fix the system; for example, when using System Restore.

ExamAlert

Know the Advanced Boot Options/Startup Settings for the exam.

If Windows 7/Vista fails to start properly and then restarts automatically, it normally displays the Windows Error Recovery screen and gives you the following options: Safe Mode, Safe Mode with Networking, Safe Mode with Command Prompt, Last Known Good Configuration, and Start Windows Normally. This means that Windows has acknowledged some sort of error or improper shutdown and offers a truncated version of the Advanced Options Boot menu.

Other Repair Installations

If all the previous methods don't fix the problems you are experiencing, there is one more thing you can try before wiping the drive and doing a clean installation: a repair installation. There are several ways to do this—these will depend on the version of Windows that you are running.

First, you could try advanced recovery. Go to Control Panel > Recovery. Windows 8 allows you to create a recovery USB drive from here and run or configure System Restore, but you can't actually repair an issue directly from this window. However, there is also a link to the Update and recovery window, where you can refresh or reset the computer or access the Advanced startup options.

In Windows 7, once in the Recovery window, click the Advanced recovery methods link. From here, you have two options. The first option is the Use a system image that you created earlier to recover the computer (similar to some of the image restore options mentioned earlier). The second option is to Reinstall Windows. The second option requires you to back up your files and then reinstall applications and restore the files when the reinstall of the OS is complete. Existing files might remain in a folder named Windows.old. This method can also be done by simply inserting the OS DVD and starting setup, making sure to select Upgrade when the time comes. This is known as a Repair/In-Place Upgrade.

These can be tricky, time-consuming solutions, plus they might not work correctly; therefore they should be your last resort for repairing Windows.

Boot Errors

There are various reasons why a computer will fail to boot. If it is operating system-related, you usually get some type of message that can help you to troubleshoot the problem.

Windows 8/7/Vista Boot Errors

Windows 8, 7, and Vista use the bootmgr and BCD files during the startup process. If these files are corrupted or missing, you will get a corresponding error message. The two most common are "Bootmgr is missing" and "The Windows Boot Configuration Data file is missing required information." Let's talk about each of these now.

BOOTMGR is missing: This message displays if the Windows Boot Manager file (bootmgr) is missing or corrupt. This black screen probably also says Press Ctrl+Alt+Del to Restart; however, doing so will probably produce the same results.

There are a few methods to repair this error. The first is to boot to the Windows Recovery Environment and select the Startup Repair option. This should automatically repair the system and require you to reboot. If this doesn't work, try the second method, which is to rebuild the Boot Configuration Data (BCD) store. Again, boot to the Windows RE, select the Command Prompt option, and then type the command **bootrec /rebuildbcd**. That rebuilds the data store and might fix the problem. You might also need to run System Restore from the Windows Recovery Environment to fix the problem.

Sometimes, you might find that the C: partition needs to be set to active. Or the 100 MB special partition (which houses important boot information) is missing. Check these as well when troubleshooting this error.

Finally, in some cases the commands bootrec /fixboot and bootrec /fixmbr can help. These rewrite the boot sector and master boot record, respectively. (One scenario in which you might need to do this is when the Windows 7 or Windows 8 computer was configured to dual-boot with an older version of Windows.) Note that bootrec /fixmbr is not required for GPT-based systems because they do not use a master boot record.

For more information about fixing this error, visit https://support.microsoft.com/en-us/kb/2622803.

> **ExamAlert**
>
> Make sure you understand that bootrec can be used to troubleshoot and repair a master boot record, a boot sector, or a Boot Configuration Data store.

For more information on how to use bootrec, visit https://support.microsoft.com/en-us/kb/927392.

The Windows Boot Configuration Data file is missing required information: This message means that either the Windows Boot Manager (bootmgr) entry is not present in the BCD store or the Boot\BCD file on the active partition is damaged or missing. Additional information you might see on the screen includes File: \Boot\BCD and Status: 0xc0000034. Unfortunately, this means that the BCD store needs to be repaired or rebuilt. Hold on to your hat; there are three methods of repair for this error. The first two are the same as with our "bootmgr is missing" error. Let's review those again. Chances are you'll be called on to perform these in the field or perhaps on the exam, so know them well.

The first method of repair is to boot to the System Recovery Options and select the Startup Repair option. This should automatically repair the system and require you to reboot. If not, move on to the second method.

The second method of repair is to boot to the System Recovery Options and select the Command Prompt option. Type **bootrec /rebuildbcd**. At this point, the bootrec.exe tool either succeeds or fails. If the Bootrec.exe tool runs successfully, it displays an installation path to a Windows directory. To add this entry to the BCD store, type **Yes**. A confirmation message appears that indicates the entry was added successfully.

If the Bootrec.exe tool can't locate any missing Windows installations, you have to remove the BCD store and then re-create it. To do this, type the following commands:

```
Bcdedit /export C:\BCD_Backup
ren c:\boot\bcd bcd.old
Bootrec /rebuildbcd
```

These methods usually work, but if not, there is another method that is more in depth and requires rebuilding the BCD store manually. For more information, you can find this step-by-step process and learn more about fixing BCD store issues at http://support.microsoft.com/kb/927391.

ExamAlert

Know how to recover from Windows boot errors.

Cram Quiz

Answer these questions. The answers follow the last question. If you cannot answer these questions correctly, consider reading this section again until you can.

220-902 Questions

1. Which option starts the system with a minimal set of drivers?

   - ○ **A.** Last Known Good Configuration
   - ○ **B.** System Restore
   - ○ **C.** Safe Mode
   - ○ **D.** Debugging Mode

2. Which tool should be used if you want to do Startup Repair in Windows?

   - ○ **A.** File Recovery
   - ○ **B.** Windows RE
   - ○ **C.** System Restore
   - ○ **D.** Safe Mode

3. Which command repairs the bootmgr file in Windows 8/7/Vista? (Select the best answer.)

   - ○ **A.** `msconfig`
   - ○ **B.** `bootrec /fixmbr`
   - ○ **C.** `bootrec /rebuildbcd`
   - ○ **D.** `boot\bcd`

4. One of your customers updated the software for a wireless adapter on a PC. After rebooting, the user logged in and the computer displayed a blue screen. What should you do?

   - ○ **A.** Install the device on a known good computer.
   - ○ **B.** Reboot the computer and use the Last Known Good Configuration.
   - ○ **C.** Purchase a new wireless adapter.
   - ○ **D.** Roll back the device drivers in Safe Mode.

5. You are running Windows 8.1 and want to save personal files and remove all programs installed to the desktop while resetting PC settings. Which of the following should you select?

○ **A.** Reset your PC

○ **B.** Refresh your PC

○ **C.** System Recovery Options

○ **D.** Command Prompt

Cram Quiz Answers

220-902 Answers

1. **C.** Safe Mode starts the operating system with a minimal set of drivers.

2. **B.** Windows RE includes Startup Repair. File Recovery is the backup and restore feature of Windows 8. Safe Mode is part of the Startup Settings screen (Windows 8) and the Advanced Boot Options menu (Windows 7/Vista). System Restore is a different tool that is also available in Windows RE; it can be used to restore the computer's settings to a previous point in time.

3. **C.** `bootrec /rebuildbcd` is one of the methods you can try to repair bootmgr in Windows 8/7/Vista. (The full filename is bootmgr.exe.) `Msconfig` is used to modify how the OS starts up but cannot repair bootmgr.exe. `Bootrec /fixboot` is used to repair the boot sector. In rare cases, it might be able to fix the bootmgr file. `Boot\bcd` is where the boot configuration store is located.

4. **D.** You should boot into Safe Mode and roll back the drivers of the device in Device Manager. The drivers that the customer installed were probably corrupt and caused the Stop error. No need to remove the device and install it anywhere just yet. Last Known Good Configuration won't work because the user has already logged in. Never purchase new equipment until you have exhausted all other ideas!

5. **B.** You should select Refresh your PC. This removes programs that were installed and resets PC settings but it saves personal files. When you select Reset your PC, all files are removed and the system is reset to the original state. System Recovery Options in Windows 7/Vista is where the Windows Recovery Environment tools are found. The Command Prompt is used to run specific commands (either from within the OS or from Windows RE) and isn't the best answer for this scenario.

Windows Tools and Errors

Windows could fail while you work within the operating system. Quite often, error messages accompany these failures. There are various Windows repair tools you can use to troubleshoot these issues. The worst possible scenario is when Windows fails and cannot be repaired. In these cases, a restoration is necessary. There are several types of restoration techniques available to you in Windows as well. But before restoring the system—because it can be time-consuming and possibly unnecessary—you should first attempt to trouble-shoot with Windows repair tools.

Troubleshooting Within Windows

If there are not any boot errors, Windows should start and operate properly. However, errors (recoverable ones) can occur while Windows runs. Devices can fail, applications can terminate for various reasons, and hardware can suffer performance issues.

Troubleshooting Tool

The Windows Troubleshooting tool (within the Control Panel) is your first step to troubleshoot errors that happen while Windows is running. It is an automated program that tries to figure out what has gone wrong and fix it while you sit there sipping Earl Grey tea (or whatever it is you kids do these days). From this tool you can have Windows troubleshoot program issues, hardware problems, network and Internet connectivity difficulties, and security glitches. If you do not want Windows to automatically troubleshoot errors that occur, click the Change settings link and then, in Computer Maintenance, click the Off radio button.

If you are lucky, Windows will fix the problem for you. However, the majority of problems you face need to be fixed manually...by you. Let's get into the tools you will be using for troubleshooting within Windows.

Device Manager

Device Manager can detect if a device is malfunctioning, if it has the wrong driver installed, if it has a conflicting resource (like an IRQ or I/O setting, which is rare), or if it has been disabled. Figure 11.5 shows a malfunctioning PCI Simple Communications Controller (highlighted). You know it's malfunctioning because of the exclamation mark (!) within a yellow triangle. If a device is disabled, this will be displayed as a down arrow in Windows, as shown in the AMD device in the figure. These devices won't work properly until they are fixed.

FIGURE 11.5 **The Device Manager window in Windows 7 showing a malfunctioning device and a disabled device**

ExamAlert

Know what the exclamation point and down arrow indicate in Device Manager.

Of course, we can't just leave these devices this way! A clean Device Manager is a good sign of a healthy computer. When a user opens this program, he should see nothing but collapsed categories; none should be open. Conflicting resources like IRQs and I/O settings are, for the most part, a thing of the past and are controlled automatically. But it is certainly possible for a device driver issue. Perhaps the driver failed, the wrong one was installed initially, or a device was updated with the wrong type of driver. In any case, you would need to repair it by opening Control Panel > Device Manager, right-clicking on the device with the exclamation point, and then selecting Properties. Look at Figure 11.6. Notice in the Device status area that it says The Drivers for this Device Are Not Installed (Code 28). Well, the solution is obvious; you need to install the driver! In reality, I neglected to install this driver for demonstration purposes. The PCI Simple Communications Controller is part of the motherboard in one of my systems. These controllers are sometimes used for HD audio or for internal modems or similar devices.

FIGURE 11.6   **The PCI Simple Communications Controller Properties window**

To repair this, you have a few options. Your first instinct might tell you to click the Update Driver button. In some cases, this might locate and install the correct driver automatically. But you might remember me saying previously to "Get the driver from the manufacturer's disc or website." In fact, I probably sound like a broken record. But that is the right solution for this situation.

In this case, I neglected to install the Intel Management Engine driver. It is located on the disc, but I could—and probably would—search for the latest version on the Intel website.

Internet installs are usually quite easy; download the .exe (or .zip, or similar) file and double-click it to install. But if the driver is already on the computer, it might be a bit more complicated. For example, you might need to find a specific .inf file or you might need to search for the driver within Windows' driver database (a manual install). If you install the driver within Device Manager, do the following:

1. In the Properties window of the device, click the Driver tab.

2. Click Update Driver. (You can also click the Update Driver button on the General tab.)

3. Select whether you would like Windows to search for the driver or whether you will manually do it.

If Windows fails in its search, you have to manually find the driver. You need to specify the manufacturer and model of the device and either find the driver file on the hard drive or supply your own media. If this fails, you are back to square one and must locate the correct driver on the Internet. But I'll let you in on a secret: *Every* driver is on the Internet...somewhere. And if you download the driver from the manufacturer, you don't have to risk a Microsoft version of the driver being installed.

As mentioned, a down arrow on a device means it has been disabled. To enable it, simply right-click it and select Enable. You can also enable/disable it on the Driver tab of its Properties sheet. Enabling some devices requires a restart.

Codes (such as the code 28 mentioned previously) can be helpful when troubleshooting issues with devices. If a device is malfunctioning or is configured incorrectly, it should show a code number within its Properties sheet on the General tab. For a list of these Device Manager codes, visit https://support.microsoft.com/en-us/kb/310123.

Event Viewer

Applications are a boon and a bane to mankind. They serve a purpose, but sometimes they are prone to failure. The operating system itself can cause you grief as well by underperforming, locking up, or causing other intermittent issues. One good tool for analyzing applications and the system is Event Viewer.

Event Viewer tells a technician a lot about the status of the operating system and programs. It notifies of any informational events or audits, warns about possible issues, and displays errors as they occur. It can be accessed from the Control Panel in Administrative Tools, through the System Tools node in the Computer Management console window, by right-clicking the Start button in Windows 8, or by typing `eventvwr.msc` in the Run or Search prompts. Information, auditing entries, warnings, and errors are stored in log files. In Windows 8/7/Vista, they are inside the Windows Logs folder. There are three main log files located inside the Event Viewer that you should know for the exam:

- ▶ **System:** The System log contains information, warnings, and errors about hardware, device drivers, system files, and so on. This log deals primarily with the operating system.

- ▶ **Application:** The Application log contains events about programs that are built into Windows, such as the Command Prompt or File/Windows Explorer, and might contain information about applications that have been loaded after the operating system was installed.

▶ **Security:** The Security log holds information that was gathered for auditing and security purposes; for example, it might log who logged on to the computer or who tried to gain access to a particular file.

An event can be viewed by double-clicking it. Events are organized into four categories:

▶ **Information:** Indicated by an "i" in a circle. This tells you basic information about a service starting or an application that ran successfully. The log files are usually chock-full of these as part of the normal operation of the system.

▶ **Warning:** Indicated by an exclamation point "!" within a yellow triangle. This might be a message telling you an installation did not complete or a service timed out. You should check for these now and again and investigate them if nothing else is pressing.

▶ **Error:** Indicated by an exclamation point "!" in a red circle. This means that something failed or has been corrupted, a service failed to start, and so on. Errors should be investigated right away.

▶ **Audit Success:** Indicated by a gold colored key; these entries are located within the Security log file. They track what a user attempts to accomplish within the operating system. For example, if auditing was turned on for a specific folder and a person attempted to access that folder, a security event would be written to the log, especially if the person was denied access. Auditing entries are maintained by organizations so that they can trace what happened to deleted or modified data.

You can find more information about a specific error code by either typing the code number for the event or typing the description into Microsoft Help and Support: http://support.microsoft.com. Sometimes you can find out information about these types of services just by running a search, but it is best to go to the source: Microsoft. You never know when an error can occur, so the Event Viewer logs should be reviewed regularly. Entire logs can be erased by right-clicking the log file (for example, System) and selecting Clear Log. The system asks if you want to save the log for future viewing. By right-clicking a log and selecting Properties, you can modify the maximum size of the log and disable logging altogether.

ExamAlert

Be able to describe the System, Application, and Security log files as well as the information, warning, error, and audit success events.

Problem Reports and Solutions and the Action Center

Problem Reports and Solutions is a program in Windows Vista that can be accessed directly within the Classic view of the Control Panel. Problem Reports and Solutions enables you to check for solutions to hardware and software problems. Windows can be set to report problems and check for solutions automatically or solutions can be checked for manually when a problem occurs. To modify how problems will be reported, click the Change settings link. Problem descriptions and solutions are saved, for later viewing.

In Windows 8/7, this functionality is built into the Action Center, which can be accessed by clicking its icon in the Notification Area of the taskbar or by navigating to the Control Panel and Action Center. Chapter 17, "Security," talks more about the Action Center.

Performance

There are several tools you can use to track the performance of a Windows-based computer. Windows 8 and 7 use the Performance Monitor and Resource Monitor. Windows Vista uses the Reliability and Performance Monitor. These programs track how much your devices are utilized; for example, what percentage of the processor is used or how much RAM is currently being accessed.

These utilities are accessed from Administrative Tools. The Resource Monitor tracks the usage of the CPU, drives, network, and memory; these are ActiveX graphs like the ones used in the Performance tab of the Task Manager. They are done in real time but are not stored. To customize what you want to track and save the information, use the Performance Monitor, as shown in Figure 11.7.

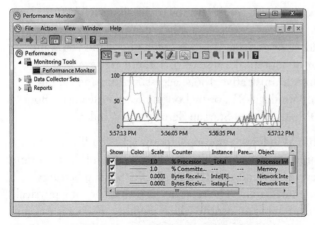

FIGURE 11.7 **Performance Monitor in Windows 7**

By working with Performance Monitor, you can track the usage of any device in the computer (known as objects) and you can track it using a variety of measurements (known as counters). By default, this screen tracks only the CPU. By clicking the + sign toward the top of the window, you can add devices to track—and in myriad ways. In Figure 11.7, I added the default counters for memory and the network adapter card. The highest spikes are from the network adapter; at the time of this monitor, it is sending and receiving a lot of data over the Internet. The second highest levels are from the processor, which is running about seven real-time applications simultaneously.

Information can be viewed in different formats, such as line charts and histograms, and can also be viewed and saved in Report view. They can be exported as well. However, any objects that are added in this program are not saved when you close the window. But you can configure the program so that it saves your additions; enter the MMC. From an MMC, a user in Windows can add the Performance Monitor. You can also use the System Monitor Control snap-in, which effectively *is* the Performance Monitor; it is one of the ActiveX Controls that can be added to the MMC. In addition, you can add Performance Logs and Alerts to log your findings and alert you to any changes or tripped thresholds. The MMC saves its contents and remembers the last place you were working in, which works great if you will be analyzing the same things day in and day out.

The Performance Monitor (and similar Windows applications) can tell you a lot about the functionality of your computer. When troubleshooting why a certain piece of hardware isn't living up to its reputation, it can be invaluable.

Windows Memory Diagnostics

Chapter 4, "RAM," talked about several ways to troubleshoot RAM. One way is to use Windows Memory Diagnostics. You might need to check your memory while within Windows, or perhaps Windows won't boot and you want to check the memory from bootup. Because of this, there are several ways to open this tool: within Administrative Tools, accessing Run and typing **mdsched**, by booting to Windows RE, or by booting to the Advanced Boot Options menu (or ABOM; also called Startup Settings in Windows 8).

If you do this from within Windows, a pop-up window asks you if you want to restart the computer immediately and run the check or wait until the next time the computer is restarted. The Windows RE and ABOM/Startup Settings methods start the check immediately. The test checks if there are any physical issues with the RAM and attempts to identify which memory module is causing the problem. When done, it restarts the computer auto-matically. If an error is found, it displays after you log back on. You can also view errors in the System log of the Event Viewer. To find results quickly, right-click the System log, click Find, and enter `MemoryDiagnostics-Results`. If there are errors with a particular stick of memory, try removing it, cleaning it and the RAM slot, and reseating it. Run the test again; if you get the same results, replace the RAM.

Msconfig

Msconfig is the System Configuration tool. It can help troubleshoot various things, from operating system startup issues to application and service problems. To open Msconfig, open the Run prompt and type `msconfig.exe` (or simply `msconfig`). A program similar to Figure 11.8 should display.

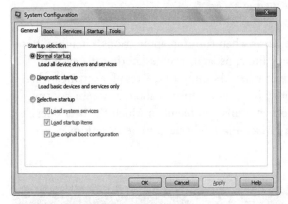

FIGURE 11.8   **Msconfig application**

This is an excellent troubleshooting tool that has multiple tabs that do the following:

▶ **General:** You can configure the system for diagnostic or selective start-up. This helps to troubleshoot devices or services that are failing.

▶ **Boot:** You can modify OS bootup settings, such as using Safe boot, logging the boot process, and booting without video. If you have multiple operating systems, you can change the order and choose which to set as default (instead of configuring the BCD file). Also, the advanced options let you choose things such as how much memory you want to use and what port to use if you need to output debugging information.

▶ **Services:** This tab lists the services and their current status. You can enable or disable them from here (it requires a computer restart). However, you can't start or stop them. To do that, you would need to go to the Services section of Computer Management or do it from within the Command Prompt. The beauty of this tab is the speed at which you can enable/disable services compared to other options in Windows.

▶ **Startup:** This tab lists the various applications that start when the computer boots up. You can disable and enable these here to aid you in troubleshooting slow applications, failures, and lock-ups. In Windows 8, the Startup tab still exists but displays "To manage Startup items, use the Startup section of Task Manager" and it provides a link to open Task Manager.

▶ **Tools:** This tab lists a lot of the common utilities you might use in Windows and allows you to launch them from there. As a launching point for programs we have used a lot (Computer Management, System Properties, Task Manager, Command Prompt, and so on), this section of Msconfig can be a real time-saver.

Consider Msconfig as a time-saver when running applications, changing boot settings, working with services and apps, and troubleshooting the system. One word of caution: Be sure to reset Msconfig to the regular settings when you finish using it. For example, if a user complains about a system booting to Safe Mode every time or other similar problems in which the user doesn't have full access to the system, Msconfig might need to be reconfigured to Normal Startup.

> **ExamAlert**
>
> Know the reasons to use Msconfig.

Stop Errors

A stop error (also known as a Blue Screen of Death or BSOD) is the worst type of error that can happen while Windows is operating. It completely halts the operating system and displays a blue screen with various text and code. Anything you were working on is, for the most part, lost. In some cases, it reboots the computer after a memory dump has been initiated. (This is also known as auto-restart.) If not, you need to physically turn the computer off at the Power button and turn it back on. Some BSODs happen only once, and if that is the case, you need not worry too much. But if they happen two or three times or more, you should investigate. Quite often they are due to a hardware issue, such as improperly seated memory or a corrupt driver file. If you see two columns of information with a list of drivers and other files, a driver issue could be the culprit. Look at the bottom of the second (or last) column and identify the driver that has failed (for example, ntfs.sys). These drivers can become corrupt for a variety of reasons and would need to be replaced when you boot into Windows. Or if you can't boot into Windows and Windows does not auto-repair the file, you can replace them from within Windows RE's Command Prompt. Less commonly, a BSOD might be caused by a memory error that will have additional code that you can research on Microsoft's websites (Microsoft support and TechNet).

By default, three things happen when a Stop error occurs:

1. An event will usually be written to the System log within Event Viewer, if that option has been selected in the Startup and Recovery window, as shown in Figure 11.9. When a STOP error is written to the System log, it is listed as an Information entry, not as an Error entry. The STOP error will be listed as The System Has Rebooted from a Bugcheck. The Bugcheck was (Error Number). Use the error number to look up the problem—and hopefully find a solution—on Microsoft Support and/or TechNet.

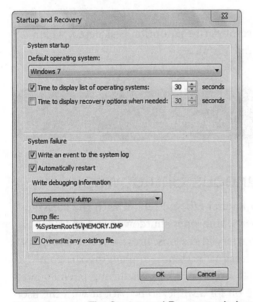

FIGURE 11.9 **The Startup and Recovery window**

The settings shown in Figure 11.9 can be accessed on the Advanced tab in the System Properties dialog box. (You could also open the Run prompt and type **SystemPropertiesAdvanced.exe**). Click the Settings button in the Startup and Recovery area to access the Startup and Recovery window.

2. Windows will write debugging information to the hard drive for later analysis with memory dump debugging programs; this debugging information is essentially the contents of RAM. The default setting in Windows is to only write a portion of the contents of RAM, known as a Kernel memory dump. The Kernel memory dump is saved as the file %systemroot\MEMORY.DMP. You can also select a Small Memory Dump; this is written to %systemroot%\Minidump. Windows 8, 7, and Vista operating systems all support the option for a Complete Memory Dump, which dumps the entire contents of RAM to a file again named MEMORY.DMP. To support the Complete Memory Dump, the paging file must be large enough to hold all the physical RAM plus 1 megabyte. For more information on how to analyze the debugging information resulting from these stop errors, and to learn about various dump files, visit http://support.microsoft.com/kb/254649 and https://msdn.microsoft.com/en-us/library/windows/hardware/ff556895(v=vs.85).aspx.

3. The computer automatically restarts (if that option is selected, which is the default in Windows 8, 7 and Vista).

ExamAlert

Know how Stop errors occur and how memory dumps function.

Improper and Spontaneous Shutdowns

You've probably seen a Windows computer fail and reboot with the message Windows Was Shut Down Improperly. Improper shutdowns and spontaneous shutdowns could happen for a variety of reasons: brownouts or blackouts, power surges, hardware failures, a user inadvertently unplugging the computer, or perhaps a virus or other malware. It can be a disturbing phenomenon to users and one that could be going on for a while, so be patient with the user (and the computer) when troubleshooting this problem.

Some of the methods you can use to troubleshoot these issues include:

▶ **Check Event Viewer:** Look in the System log to see if there are any alerts about hardware failures, service failures, and so on. If there are, consider upgrading the driver for the affected hardware or upgrading the software that the service is dependent on. Ensure the computer is running the latest SP (Windows Vista/7) and updates (all OSes).

▶ **Use Msconfig:** On the General tab, select the Selective Startup checkbox and the Load startup items checkbox. To weed out third-party program issues, click the Services tab, click the Hide All Microsoft Services checkbox, and then click Disable All. Restart the system and see if the same issues return or if events are still written to Event Viewer. Remember to restore Normal startup in Msconfig when finished troubleshooting.

▶ **Boot into Safe Mode:** Use Safe Mode to further investigate the problem. Safe Mode uses only the most basic drivers, so if it is a driver issue, this could help you find out about it.

▶ **Run a virus scan:** Run a scan for malware and quarantine anything unusual. Update the antivirus software when you are finished.

▶ **Check power:** Make sure the AC outlet is wired properly and is supplying clean power. Verify that the power plug is firmly secured to the computer. If necessary, you might have to check the power supply. Intermittent and unexplainable shutdowns can sometimes be linked to power supplies or other hardware failures.

▶ **Use Windows RE:** If necessary, use the Windows Recovery Environment to troubleshoot spontaneous shutdowns. See the section, "Repair Environments and Boot Errors" earlier in this chapter for more information.

Additional Windows Errors and Error Reporting

Windows errors less serious than Stop errors might display a pop-up window after the application has closed. You might get similar pop-up windows if a device or service fails to start or if there is a missing Dynamic-Link Library (DLL). DLLs provide much of the functionality of a Windows operating system. They can be used by more than one program at a time, which could lead to conflicts. A missing DLL can cause a program or a device to fail. However, the OS usually continues to function when any of these errors occur.

Windows 8/7/Vista can recover from these types of errors and continue to function. You can learn more about the error in Event Viewer. You also have the option to send an error report to Microsoft, in the hopes of acquiring a solution or fix. To have Windows 8/7 automatically check for solutions to problems, go to the Action Center, click the Change Action Center settings link, and then click the Problem reporting settings link. You can also select programs to exclude from error reporting here. To enable/disable error reporting in Windows Vista, navigate to Control Panel > System and Maintenance > Problem Reports and Solutions > Change settings > Advanced settings. To find out if any new solutions are available, click the Check for New Solutions link within Problem Reports and Solutions.

If you have a program compatibility issue and a particular program (perhaps an older one) won't run or won't install properly in your version of Windows, do the following. First, try installing or running the program as an administrator. Also, check out events in the Reliability Monitor. (Go to the Search field and type the name to open it; it's also available from the Action Center.) Finally, attempt to run the program in compatibility mode. To do this, locate and right-click the program and then select Properties. Click the Compatibility tab and select which OS the program should be compatible with. Also, modify any settings, such as colors or resolution, if necessary. This is common for older games and applications written for previous versions of Windows. Finally, check with the manufacturer to see if there is an update to the program that can make it compatible with your version of Windows.

If a file fails to open every time you double-click it, you might be the victim of a virus. Scan the system with antivirus software and consider downloading the Microsoft Safety Scanner to scan the system as well at http://www.microsoft.com/security/scanner/en-us/default.aspx.

Restoring Windows

Beyond even Stop errors, a complete system failure is when a system cannot be repaired. When this happens, the only options are to reinstall or to restore Windows. There are several methods for restoring Windows, including

▶ **Windows 7:** Boot to the DVD, click the repair option, and at the first System Recovery Options window (with the possible list of operating systems), select the Restore Your Computer Using a System Image That You Created Earlier. (You will be required to provide the backup media.)

▶ **Windows 8/7/Vista:** Boot to the DVD and click the repair option. At the main Windows RE (or System Recovery Options) window, select System Image Recovery (Windows 8/7) or Windows Complete PC Restore (Vista). Provide backup media.

▶ **All Windows:** Reset the system to a factory image stored on a separate partition of the hard drive. This is common on laptops, especially ones that do not have optical drives. Or use third-party tools such as Symantec Ghost or Acronis True Image. Remember, the image needs to be created before the disaster!

There are various other ways to access the utilities mentioned. Refer to earlier parts of this chapter for details or refer to the documentation that came with your third-party software. For more support with Windows troubleshooting in general, visit the Microsoft support site (https://support.microsoft.com) and the Microsoft TechNet (https://technet.microsoft.com).

Cram Quiz

Answer these questions. The answers follow the last question. If you cannot answer these questions correctly, consider reading this section again until you can.

220-902 Questions

1. What could a yellow exclamation point in the Device Manager indicate?

   - ○ **A.** Disabled device
   - ○ **B.** Event Viewer error
   - ○ **C.** Incorrect driver
   - ○ **D.** Device is not installed

2. Which log file in the Event Viewer contains information concerning auditing?

   - ○ **A.** System
   - ○ **B.** Application
   - ○ **C.** Internet Explorer
   - ○ **D.** Security

3. A Stop error could manifest itself as what?

   - ○ **A.** A BSOD
   - ○ **B.** An Event Viewer error
   - ○ **C.** An Action Center notification
   - ○ **D.** An Internet Explorer error

4. Which tools can be used to restore a computer? (Select all that apply.)

   - ○ **A.** Windows Complete PC Restore
   - ○ **B.** System Restore
   - ○ **C.** System Image Recovery
   - ○ **D.** Msconfig

5. In Windows Vista and Windows 7, which of the following *cannot* be performed in Msconfig?

   - ○ **A.** Enabling services
   - ○ **B.** Disabling applications
   - ○ **C.** Stopping services
   - ○ **D.** Enabling applications

6. You try to install a program on a Windows 7 laptop but the installation fails. What should you do next?

    ○ **A.** Run the installer as an administrator.

    ○ **B.** Reinstall Windows 7.

    ○ **C.** Contact the manufacturer of the program.

    ○ **D.** Restore from an earlier restore point.

7. Which tool should first be used when troubleshooting software installation issues and application failures in Windows?

    ○ **A.** Task Manager

    ○ **B.** System Information

    ○ **C.** System Restore

    ○ **D.** Reliability Monitor

8. Which of the following might cause a blue screen?

    ○ **A.** A faulty DVD-ROM

    ○ **B.** A CPU without a fan

    ○ **C.** Bad drivers

    ○ **D.** A program compatibility issue

Cram Quiz Answers

220-902 Answers

1. **C.** A yellow exclamation point could indicate an incorrect device driver or other malfunction of a device. A disabled device would be indicated by a down arrow. If the device is not installed, it will either not show up on the list at all or it will show up in a category named Unknown devices.

2. **D.** The Security log contains information about auditing and other security events.

3. **A.** A BSOD is what results from a Stop error in Windows.

4. **A, B, and C.** Windows Complete PC Restore is the Windows Vista solution for restoring an image. System Restore is the tool used to restore a computer to an earlier point in time. While this doesn't completely restore from an image, it is still a form of restoration. System Image Recovery is the Windows 7 solution for restoring an image. Msconfig is used to modify how Windows boots and which services are run.

5. **C.** Msconfig cannot start or stop services. However, it can enable/disable them and report on the status of those services. It can also enable/disable applications in Windows Vista and Windows 7. Note that in Windows 8, the Msconfig Startup tab directs you to "Open Task Manager." From there, you can enable/disable Startup applications.

6. **A.** If a program won't install on Windows 8/7/Vista, try installing it as an administrator. Administrative privileges are usually needed to install programs to Windows. Afterward, you can check the Windows Compatibility Center at the Microsoft website and attempt to install the program in compatibility mode. If all else fails, contact the manufacturer of the program for help. Restoring the computer or reinstalling Windows should not be necessary in this scenario.

7. **D.** The Reliability Monitor is the first of the listed tools you should use when troubleshooting software installs and application failures. You should also try running the install or program as an administrator, check compatibility, and use the Event Viewer to find out more about errors.

8. **C.** Bad drivers could cause a blue screen error (Stop error). Blue screens could also be caused by improperly seated RAM, among other hardware issues. A faulty DVD-ROM drive would not cause a blue screen. A CPU installed without a fan would overheat, causing the system to shut down. Incompatible programs simply don't run.

Command-Line Tools

Let's face it; the command-line interface (CLI) is where the extreme techs live. Some things are just easier to do in the command line or the functionality needed might be accessible only in the command line. This section covers two groups of commands: First, commands that run from within Windows; second, commands that should be run within the Command Prompt option in the Windows Recovery Environment.

Commands use switches, sometimes also referred to as options or parameters; for the most part, I refer to them as switches. They modify how a command works or they modify how a command's results are displayed. For example, when you type **DIR /?**, the switch is /?. That brings up the help file for the DIR command, defining what the command does and listing additional switches you could use with the command. Be ready to type commands, type switches, and to access the help file for any given command.

Windows Command Prompt

Microsoft's name for the command line is the Command Prompt. The Command Prompt can be found in a variety of places, such as by right-clicking Start in Windows 8, by going to Start > All Programs > Accessories in Windows 7/Vista, or by simply accessing it from the Search field or Run prompt. However, as you troubleshoot Windows, you will find that you often need to run the Command Prompt in elevated mode (as an administrator), which can be done in several ways:

1. In all versions of Windows: Type **cmd** in the Search field and instead of pressing Enter, press Ctrl+Shift+Enter.

2. In Windows 8: Right-click Start and select Command Prompt (Admin).

3. In Windows 7/Vista: Click Start > All Programs > Accessories; then right-click Command Prompt and select Run as Administrator.

4. In many cases, you can simply right-click the Command Prompt icon (wherever it is located—for example, pinned to the taskbar) and select Run as Administrator.

Let's show some of the commands that you might be tested on and that you will most likely use in the field.

> **ExamAlert**
>
> Learn by doing! Practice every command discussed on your own computers! Learn more about each by accessing their help files—type **/?** after each command.

Chkdsk

Chkdsk checks a drive, fixes basic issues like lost files, and displays a status report; it can also fix some errors on the drive by using the /F switch. Here's an example of the three stages of results when running the chkdsk command:

```
The type of the file system is NTFS.
Volume label is WinXPC.
WARNING!  F parameter not specified.
Running CHKDSK in read-only mode.
CHKDSK is verifying files (stage 1 of 3)...
File verification completed.
CHKDSK is verifying indexes (stage 2 of 3)...
Index verification completed.
CHKDSK is recovering lost files.
Recovering orphaned file ~WRL3090.tmp (59880) into directory file
  28570.
Recovering orphaned file ~DFA188.tmp (59881) into directory file
  28138.
CHKDSK is verifying security descriptors (stage 3 of 3)...
Security descriptor verification completed.
Correcting errors in the master file table's (MFT) BITMAP attribute.
Correcting errors in the Volume Bitmap.
Windows found problems with the file system.
Run CHKDSK with the /F (fix) option to correct these.
  31471300 KB total disk space.
  13053492 KB in 56091 files.
     16340 KB in 4576 indexes.
         0 KB in bad sectors.
    133116 KB in use by the system.
     65536 KB occupied by the log file.
  18268352 KB available on disk.
      4096 bytes in each allocation unit.
   7867825 total allocation units on disk.
   4567088 allocation units available on disk.
```

Notice that the utility warned that the /F switch was not specified and, because of this, it ran in read-only mode. Also notice that the orphaned files were recovered, although they are just .tmp files and most likely not necessary for the functionality of Windows. Finally, the program found issues with the file system; to repair these, you would have to use the /F option. Be sure that you actually need to run chkdsk with the /F parameter before doing so. For example, if the system seems to function properly, but the standard chkdsk command gave an error, it might not be absolutely necessary to run chkdsk with the /F parameter.

One issue that plagues users is the infamous Missing Operating System message. If you get this, it usually means that either the drive has a few small errors or the master boot record has been damaged. But even though the system won't boot, you can still run chkdsk to find and fix problems on the drive. Boot to the Windows media, access Windows RE, and then open the Command Prompt. From there, run chkdsk with either the /F switch (which fixes errors on the drive) or the /R switch (which locates bad sectors and recovers data)—or run both. This procedure can also help with Invalid Boot Disk errors. (Of course, first check that the BIOS is booting to the correct drive in the boot priority menu.)

SFC

System File Checker (SFC) is a Windows utility that checks protected system files. It replaces incorrect versions or missing files with the correct files. SFC can be used to fix problems with Internet Explorer or other Windows applications. To run SFC, open the Command Prompt and type **SFC** with the appropriate switch. A typical option is SFC /scannow, which scans all protected files immediately and repairs files. Another is SFC /verifyonly, which scans the integrity of files but does not perform a repair. If SFC finds that some files are missing, you might be prompted to reinsert the original operating system disc so the files can be copied to the DLL cache.

Format

Format is a command used to format magnetic media such as hard drives and solid-state media (such as USB flash drives) to the FAT, FAT32, or NTFS file systems. An example of formatting a USB flash drive in the command line would be format F:. The type of file system that the media will be formatted to can be specified with the switch /FS:filesystem, where file system will equal FAT32 or NTFS, and so on.

Convert

The convert command enables you to convert a volume that was previously formatted as FAT32 over to NTFS without losing any data. An example of the convert command would be convert d: /FS:NTFS, which would convert the hard drive volume D: to NTFS. Sometimes you might encounter older computers' hard drives (or flash media) that require being formatted as NTFS for compatibility with other devices and networked computers.

Diskpart

The `diskpart` utility is the command-line counterpart of Windows' Disk Management program. This program needs to be run by typing **diskpart** before any of the `diskpart` actions can be implemented. This brings the user into the DISKPART> prompt. From here, you can create, delete, and extend volumes, assign drive letters, make a partition active, and so on. Essentially, everything that was covered in the Disk Management portion of Chapter 9 can be done with `diskpart`. When you are in the DISKPART> prompt, press the question mark (?) key on the keyboard to learn about the various options within the Diskpart program. When you finish using `diskpart`, type **exit** to return back to the standard Command Prompt.

Defrag

`Defrag` is the command-line version of the Disk Defragmenter. To analyze a drive, type **defrag -a**. If a volume needs to be defragmented, but has less than 15 percent free space, use the -f parameter.

Xcopy

The `xcopy` command is meant to copy large amounts of data from one location to another; it even makes exact copies of entire directory trees. One example of its usage would be to copy the contents of a Windows DVD-ROM over to a USB flash drive so that you can use the USB flash drive as installation media. The command for this would be `xcopy d:\*.* /E/F e:\`. This is assuming that D: is the DVD-ROM drive and E: is the USB flash drive. *.* means all files with all extensions within the D: drive. /E indicates that all folders and subfolders will be copied including empty ones. /F displays full source and destination files while copying. For more information about xcopy, type **xcopy /?**.

Robocopy

`Robocopy` (Robust File Copy) is a directory replication tool. It is meant to copy directories that contain lots of data; it can even mirror complete directory trees from one computer to another. `Robocopy` is the successor to `xcopy`. Some of the advantages of this tool are that it can tolerate network interruptions, skip past junctions (such as the \Documents and Settings to \Users junction), and preserve data attributes and time stamps. `Robocopy` does not copy individual files; it copies only directories (for example, `Robocopy c:\office c:\games`). This will copy all the information within the \office directory to the \games directory. It also gives in-depth results of its actions. You can also use Robocopy to copy information to other computers by using the \\computername\share universal naming convention, which we speak more about in Chapter 16, "Computer Networking Part II."

Tasklist

Tasklist shows all the processes running similar to the Processes tab of the Task Manager. Each process is assigned a Process Identification number or PID. These are assigned dynamically and won't use the same number for an application twice. Tasklist also shows the memory usage of each process. An example of a process would be excel.exe (Microsoft Excel) or winword.exe (Microsoft Word).

Taskkill

Just as you can shut processes down in the Task Manager, you can also use the command-line tool taskkill. Perhaps you run into a situation where certain applications or processes are frozen and you cannot open the Task Manager. If you can get to the Command Prompt, you can end these processes without restarting the computer. For example, if Microsoft Excel has stopped responding, you can find out its process ID with tasklist (say it was 4548) and close it by either typing **taskkill /IM excel.exe** or **taskkill /PID 4548**. Tasklist and taskkill are not available in the recovery environment Command Prompt in Windows 8/7/Vista.

Shutdown

The shutdown command is used to turn off the computer, restart it, send it to hibernate mode, log a person off, and so on. For example, if you want to shut down the computer after a short delay, you can type **shutdown /s**. For an immediate shutdown, you can type **shutdown /p**. The command can also be used programmatically to shut down systems at specific times while providing a pop-up window explaining the reason for the shutdown.

ExamAlert

Memorize as many of the commands mentioned in this section as you can! Try them on your computer, and write them down to force those little gray cells into action.

Recovery Command Prompt

The Windows RE Command Prompt in Windows 8, 7, and Vista is used to repair issues with the operating system. For example, a system file causing the system to fail at startup can be copied from installation media. This environment can also be used to edit files and run commands that can fix the boot sector (for GPT and MBR systems) as well as the master boot record (if you are not using GPT).

Copy

As we mentioned previously in the book, the copy command copies files from one location to another. An example of its usage in a recovery Command Prompt would be to replace a file that was missing or corrupt, such as the bootmgr file, or any other file that you need to replace that was not repaired automatically by Windows. The file can be found on the installation media (optical disc or flash drive) and copied to the hard drive to fix the problem file.

> **Note**
>
> Another example is a missing NTLDR file, the Windows loader program in Windows XP. Though Windows XP is no longer supported by Microsoft, you never know if you might find a system that has to run it or a system that dual-boots to it. To fix this problem, the file would have to be copied from the installation disc to the hard drive. Assuming that all drive letters are standard (the hard drive is C: and the installation drive is D:), the syntax for this would be copy d:\i386\ntldr c:\. This copies the NTLDR file from the I386 folder on the disc to the root of C: on the hard drive.

Expand

Sometimes you can't just *copy* files from installation media to the hard drive. Many of these files are compressed. If a file ends with an underscore (for example, ntoskrnl.ex_), it is a compressed file that has to be expanded. Let's say that it's a dark day and that ntoskrnl.exe fails. You can't do much without that core operating system file. To fix the problem in a recovery environment Command Prompt, you would expand the file from installation media to the hard drive. In a standard environment (where the hard drive is C: and the installation media drive is D:), the syntax would be

```
expand D:\i386\ntoskrnl.ex_ C:\Windows\System32\ntoskrnl.exe.
```

This decompresses the file and places a copy of the decompressed version on the hard drive. Be sure to type the entire name of the file in the destination; otherwise, you need to rename the file.

> **Note**
>
> The copy and expand commands can also be used within Windows in the
> Command Prompt.

Other Recovery Environment Commands

If Windows 8/7/Vista has startup issues, you can use several commands, the
first three of which are review:

- ▶ **bootrec /fixboot:** Replaces the bootmgr file and writes a new compatible boot sector to the system partition.

- ▶ **bootrec /fixmbr:** Rewrites the Windows compatible master boot record to the system partition. This can also repair boot sector blocks after a virus has been removed. This is not necessary in a system using GPT.

- ▶ **bootrec /rebuildbcd:** Repairs the BCD store.

- ▶ **bootrec /ScanOs:** Scans all drives for installations compatible with Windows. This option also displays the entries that are currently not included in the BCD store. Use this command if there are Windows installations that the Boot Manager menu does not list.

> **ExamAlert**
>
> Know your bootrec command and options! I can't stress it enough!

Cram Quiz

Answer these questions. The answers follow the last question. If you cannot answer these questions correctly, consider reading this section again until you can.

220-902 Questions

1. Which commands can fix lost files? (Select the two best answers.)
   - ○ **A.** chkdsk
   - ○ **B.** diskpart
   - ○ **C.** chkdsk /R
   - ○ **D.** bootrec /fixmbr

2. Which command can decompress a file as it copies it to the hard drive?
   - ○ **A.** extract
   - ○ **B.** expand
   - ○ **C.** compress
   - ○ **D.** encrypt

3. Which command can copy multiple files and entire directory trees?
   - ○ **A.** copy
   - ○ **B.** cut
   - ○ **C.** paste
   - ○ **D.** xcopy

4. Which command can write a new boot sector and replace the bootmgr file in Windows?
   - ○ **A.** bootrec /fixboot
   - ○ **B.** bootrec /fixmbr
   - ○ **C.** bootrec /rebuildbcd
   - ○ **D.** bootrec /ScanOs

5. Which command will determine if protected system files have been overwritten and replace those files with the original version?
   - ○ **A.** chkdsk
   - ○ **B.** msconfig
   - ○ **C.** SFC
   - ○ **D.** xcopy

6. An application is frozen and cannot be closed. However, the rest of the operating system works fine. Which tool can be used to close the application?

○ **A.** tasklist

○ **B.** taskkill

○ **C.** shutdown

○ **D.** convert

Cram Quiz Answers

220-902 Answers

1. **A and C.** Chkdsk can recover some lost files (such as orphaned files). chkdsk /R verifies the integrity of a drive, fixes errors on the drive, and can fix lost (or orphaned) files.

2. **B.** The expand command decompresses files that are compressed on installation media, such as ntoskrnl.ex_.

3. **D.** Xcopy can copy an entire drive of information with just one command (including switches).

4. **A.** Bootrec /fixboot replaces the bootmgr file and writes a new Windows compatible boot sector to the system partition.

5. **C.** SFC determines whether system files have been overwritten and replaces those files with the original versions. Chkdsk can check for errors and fix some errors but not when it concerns system files. msconfig is used to boot the system in a selective way and disable services and applications. Xcopy is used to copy large amounts of data exactly to a new location.

6. **B.** Taskkill ends the underlying process of an application, closing the application. Tasklist is used to view which processes are running, their process IDs, and the memory used by each. Shutdown is a command used to turn off the computer in a variety of ways. Convert is used to alter a FAT32 partition to NTFS.

CHAPTER 12

Video and Audio

This chapter covers the following A+ exam topics:

▶ The Video Subsystem

▶ The Audio Subsystem

You can find a master list of A+ exam topics in the "Introduction."

This chapter covers CompTIA A+ 220-901 objectives 1.4, 1.7, 1.10, 1.11, 3.2, and 4.3, and 220-902 objective 1.5.

Video makes a computer sparkle, and audio makes it rock. This chapter describes the technologies and devices that transform the computer from a boring block of metal to a multimedia juggernaut. We could talk about video and audio for days, but lucky for you this chapter has a page limit! So we'll stick to what you need to know for the exam.

This chapter is broken down into two sections: first, the video subsystem, which includes the video card and display; second, the audio subsystem, which includes the sound card and speakers. However, the bulk of the information in this chapter pertains to video, so let's begin with that first.

The Video Subsystem

The computer can be broken down into several subsystems, with the video subsystem being one of the most important. The video subsystem includes the video card (or integrated video), the card's expansion bus, internal connections, external connections between the video card and the display, the display itself, and the video driver. This section details those portions of the video subsystem. Of course, it's also vital to know how to install and configure video cards and how to troubleshoot any issues that might occur.

Video Cards

Today's video cards are like little self-contained computers! They have a processor, known as a graphics processing unit (GPU), and a substantial amount of RAM. When choosing a video card, there are several things to take into account, including the expansion bus that the card connects to, the card's GPU speed and amount of memory, the connectors it offers, whether there is an expansion slot available for it on the motherboard, whether the video card can fit in the case, and whether the case has adequate power and cooling capabilities for the card.

Expansion Buses: PCI and PCIe

Before purchasing and installing a video card, make sure that the motherboard in the computer has a corresponding open expansion slot for the card. As we discussed in Chapter 2, "Motherboards," the two main expansion slots you need to know are PCI Express (PCIe) and Peripheral Component Interconnect (PCI), with PCIe easily being the most common expansion bus slot in today's motherboards. Because PCIe slots have high data transfer rates, those expansion slots connect directly to the northbridge of a motherboard's chipset (or directly to the CPU on newer Intel designs). PCI, however, has lower data transfer rates; therefore, PCI slots connect to the southbridge. Because of this, you won't see many PCI video cards. (In fact, you don't see many PCI slots anymore either.)

Installing a video card to a PCI slot is easy: just press the card straight down into the slot and screw it into the chassis. However, PCI Express cards require a little bit more work, which is discussed later. For more information on expansion buses, see Chapter 2.

Connector Types

Your choice of video card will probably dictate the connector that you
will use. Most of today's PCIe video cards come with either DVI, HDMI,
DisplayPort, or Mini DisplayPort outputs, but there are several other connectors that you see in the field. Table 12.1 details these. Figure 12.1 shows some
of the typical video ports you will see.

TABLE 12.1 **Video Card Connectors**

Connector Type	Full Name	Description
VGA (also known as SVGA)	Video Graphics Array	15-pin, usually blue, known as DE15 (also sold as DB15 or HD15). Used for older monitors that display VGA, SVGA, and XGA resolutions.
DVI	Digital Visual Interface	High-quality connections used with LCD displays. Carries uncompressed digital video; is partially compatible with HDMI. Types include ▶ **DVI-D:** Digital-only connections. ▶ **DVI-A:** Analog-only connections. ▶ **DVI-I:** Digital and analog connections. ▶ **DVI-DL:** Dual-link connections. (There are dual-link versions for DVI-I and DVI-D.) ▶ **M1-DA:** Digital, analog, and USB connections.
HDMI	High-Definition (HD) Multimedia Interface	Used mainly for high-definition television. Can carry video and audio signals. Some video cards do not offer HDMI; they instead offer DVI: ▶ **Type A:** Supports all HD modes, compatible with DVI-D connectors. ▶ **Type B:** Double-video bandwidth, supports higher resolutions. ▶ **Type C:** Mini-HDMI, used in portable devices. ▶ **Type D:** Micro-HDMI; smallest connector, also used in portable devices.
DisplayPort	DisplayPort	▶ Royalty-free interface similar to HDMI; designed to be the replacement for HDMI and DVI. ▶ Uses packet transmission similar to Ethernet connector. Looks similar to USB. ▶ Not as common as DVI and HDMI.
S-Video	Separate Video	Used for standard-definition video; no audio signal. Uses a mini-DIN 4-, 6-, 7-, or 9-pin connector.

Connector Type	Full Name	Description
Component/ RGB	Component Video	Used to send analog or digital signal over three wires (red, green, and blue), with each wire ending with an RCA plug. Can send high-definition signals digitally.
BNC/RCA	Composite Video	▶ Uses either A single RCA port (yellow), often used with white and red RCA ports for audio. A single BNC port (for example, with a video switcher); uses a coaxial cable. ▶ Standard definition only.

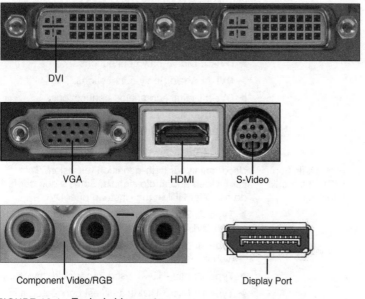

FIGURE 12.1 **Typical video ports**

Many DVI connectors on a video card look the same; however, it is the monitor's cable and plug that define which type of DVI it can support. Figure 12.2 shows an illustration of the various DVI plugs and the associated pins you might see on the end of a monitor cable.

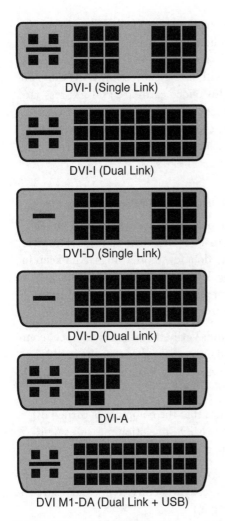

DVI-I (Single Link)

DVI-I (Dual Link)

DVI-D (Single Link)

DVI-D (Dual Link)

DVI-A

DVI M1-DA (Dual Link + USB)

FIGURE 12.2   Various DVI plug connector pins

A computer's DVI connector is usually compatible with HDMI and VGA. Adapters and adapter cables are available if a user wants to connect a VGA monitor or HDMI television to the DVI port of a computer.

Video Card Chipset, GPU, and Memory

As previously mentioned, today's video cards are like computers unto themselves. To a certain extent, this is true. These cards have a chipset that is similar to a motherboard's chipset but more simplified; it takes care of the connection between the GPU and the RAM on the card. The GPU of a video card is measured much like a CPU. For example, the GPU in a video card might run at 1100 MHz; this is known as its core clock. Likewise, a video card's RAM is measured like a motherboard's RAM. Many video cards use DDR4 or DDR5. Video card RAM is also known as GDDR or Graphics Double Data Rate. A typical video card will have gigabytes of RAM that run within the gigahertz frequency range. Most video cards are PCI Express x16, meaning they use 16 lanes and can connect only to a PCIe x16 slot. Because today's video cards have powerful GPUs, the GPU might have its own heat sink and fan or the entire card will be enclosed and have its own exhaust fan, thus cooling the GPU, chipset, and RAM.

Installing and Troubleshooting Video Cards

Video cards, like other adapter cards, are inserted into an expansion bus slot and then screwed into the chassis of the case to keep them in place. However, PCI Express cards require the installer to do a few more things. And keep in mind that some newer PCIe cards are *big*. When deciding on a video card, make sure it fits in the computer case first and doesn't cover any important ports! The following steps describe how to install a PCIe video card:

Step 1. **Check if the card is compatible:** Verify that there is an open, compatible slot on the motherboard. Also, make sure that the card is compatible with the operating system. For more information on OS compatibility, see Chapter 8, "Installing and Upgrading Windows."

Step 2. **Ready the computer:** Make sure that the computer is turned off and unplugged. Then implement ESD prevention measures (antistatic mat, antistatic wrist strap, and so on).

Step 3. **Ready the video card:** Remove the card from the package and keep it in the antistatic bag until it is ready to be inserted. (Make sure the card is sealed when first opening it.)

Step 4. **Document:** If the computer had a video card already, document how and where it was connected. Otherwise, review the documentation that came with the motherboard and video card so a plan can be put into place as to where to install the card and what cables need to be connected to the card (and how they should be routed through the case).

Step 5. **Prepare the slot:** Use a Phillips head screwdriver to remove the slot cover (or covers) where the card will be installed. Bigger PCIe cards inhabit the space used by two slot covers. On most PCIe slots there will be a thumb lever. Open this gently. When the card is inserted, the lever locks the card into place. In some cases, this lever isn't necessary.

Step 6. **Install the card to the slot:** Insert the card using both thumbs, applying equal pressure straight down into the slot. Try not to wiggle the card in any direction. Press down until the card snaps into place and you can't see any of the gold edge connectors. If it doesn't seem to be going in, don't force it. There might be something in the way (for example, one of the slot covers hasn't been removed or the thumb lever isn't in the correct position).

Step 7. **Connect cables:** PCIe cards need their own power connection (or two). These are 6- or 8-pin PCIe power connectors. Most cases come with PCIe power connectors, but if not, you can use a PCIe to Molex adapter (or two), which will work with older cases and power supplies. Next, make any Scalable Link Interface (SLI) connections necessary, in case you have two or three video cards (which is less common but popular in high-end gaming systems). Then connect optional cables (for example, connect an S/PDIF header cable to the motherboard) and any other ancillary cables. When complete, it should look similar to Figure 12.3.

FIGURE 12.3 **An installed PCIe video card**

Step 8. **Test:** Testing is simple: plug in the monitor to the video card's port and boot the computer. If you don't get anything on the display, it's time to troubleshoot. Make sure that the monitor is connected securely to the correct port. Then (after shutting down the PC) make sure that the card is seated properly and that the power connections and any other connections are connected firmly. Listen for any beep codes that might be issued by the BIOS/UEFI POST. Check if the computer is booting without video; this can be done by watching the LED lights on the front of the case and listening for the power supply fan and hard drive activity.

Step 9. **Install the driver:** When the system boots properly, install the driver from the manufacturer's disc. If no disc was supplied with the device or it is missing, or if you don't have an optical drive on the computer in question, go to the manufacturer's website and download the latest version of the driver for the exact model of the video card.

Step 10. **Test again:** Now that the driver is installed, test again. Verify whether the card is shown as the correct make and model in Device Manager. Then make sure the display can output the desired resolution. Keep in mind that some video cards can output a higher resolution than a monitor can support. If the computer is used for graphics or gaming, open the appropriate application and verify that it works as expected. For example, check for fluidity, quick response, frame rate, and so on.

ExamAlert

Know how to install and test a video card.

When troubleshooting video issues, there are a number of things to check, including the following:

▶ **Connections:** If nothing is showing up on the display, first make sure that the monitor is plugged into the video card properly (and to the correct video port), and then verify whether the monitor is connected to the AC outlet and is powered on. If the image on the display is scrambled, check that it is connected to the correct port on the video card. If necessary, try removing the video card and reseating it carefully.

▶ **Power cycle the computer, display, and any power protection equipment:** Power cycling the equipment can fix all kinds of problems and is an easy solution to implement. Problems such as video memory (image retention) and stuck pixels might be easily repaired by a power cycle of the display, the computer, and any surge suppressor that the equipment is plugged into. You might also need to leave the display off for a couple of hours to fix a video memory problem. The video memory/image retention issue is sometimes referred to as burn-in, but that is actually a symptom of a problem that occurs in the older cathode ray tube (CRT) type of monitor.

▶ **Check for an onboard video setting in the UEFI/BIOS:** If you install a new video card to a computer that previously used onboard video, always check that the onboard video setting is disabled in the UEFI or BIOS. It can conflict with the new video card. And, of course, be sure to plug the monitor into the new video card—not the old onboard connection.

▶ **Resolution setting:** If the resolution was set too high or was set to a resolution not supported by the monitor, you might get a distorted image or no image at all. Boot into low-resolution VGA mode or Safe Mode. This starts the computer with a resolution of 640×480. Then modify the resolution setting in the Screen Resolution window. Lower resolutions will result in oversized icons and images that might be preferable to some but will make it difficult for the typical user to view all the information required on one screen (for example, within a spreadsheet or A/V editing program). Simply increase the resolution to "resolve" the problem! More on resolution later in this chapter.

▶ **Check the driver:** Maybe the driver failed, or perhaps the wrong driver was installed during installation, or maybe an update is necessary. If there is nothing on the display, or if the image is distorted, or if the monitor only displays a lower resolution, boot into low res mode or Safe Mode and update the driver from within Device Manager. Driver failures could also be the cause of BSODs.

▶ **Check the version of DirectX:** DirectX is a Windows technology that includes video, animation, and sound components. It helps a computer get more performance out of multimedia, games, and movies. As mentioned in Chapter 9, "Configuring Windows," the DirectX Diagnostic Tool (DxDiag) helps to troubleshoot DirectX-related issues. This tool gives information about the installed version of DirectX and whether it is operating correctly, among other things. The DirectX Diagnostic Tool can be started by opening the Run prompt and typing **dxdiag**. By default, Windows Vista uses DirectX 10 and Windows 7 and 8 use DirectX 11. However, these systems can be updated to newer versions of DirectX if necessary.

▶ **Check the temperature threshold of the video card:** High-end video cards are intensely used by gamers and designers. If the temperature surpasses the safeguards in place, it might cause the card to throttle back the GPU speed or the video card might stop working altogether, causing the current application to close or, at worst, the display could go blank. If this happens more than once or twice, consider additional cooling fans or a liquid cooling system.

▶ **Use software to check and repair stuck or dead pixels:** When a single pixel fails, it can be irritating. But there are third-party software programs that can be used to identify stuck pixels and possible dead pixels and attempt to fix them (search "LCD repair," "dead pixel repair," or similar terms). Always try power-cycling the device as well. If you can't repair the stuck or dead pixel, you might have to bring the display in for repair or for replacement.

▶ **Calibrate the monitor:** If you see artifacts (image distortions) or you notice incorrect color patterns, or the display just doesn't seem to look quite as good as it used to, try calibrating the monitor by either resetting it with the on-screen display (OSD) or by adjusting the contrast, brightness, and color level. Also try adjusting the color depth in Windows, and check the screen resolution. Try to limit reflections on the screen. If using an older CRT monitor and the artifacts still appear, consider upgrading to an LCD display! Dim images could also be caused by misconfiguring the brightness and contrast. Always configure the brightness first, and once the optimal brightness level has been found, then configure the contrast.

▶ **Use a filter on the monitor:** Sometimes a user will complain of eye strain. This might not be a video issue at all; it could be due to glare. Consider using an antiglare filter. Companies such as 3M make these specifically for individual models of monitors. They help to reduce glare from fluorescent lights, sunlight, and so on. In a more secure environment, consider also using privacy filters. These reduce the viewing angle of the screen—only the person sitting directly in front of the screen can read it, helping to reduce the chance of shoulder surfing. Privacy filters often reduce glare as well.

▶ **Check for newly installed applications:** New applications could cause the display to malfunction or stop working altogether. Check the application manufacturer's website for any known hardware compatibility issues.

▶ **Check inside the computer:** I usually leave this for last because it is time-consuming to open the system, unless I have a sneaky suspicion that one of the connections inside the computer is loose. Check whether the card is seated properly. In areas in which the temperature and humidity change quickly, the card could be unseated due to thermal expansion and contraction. (Some refer to this as chip creep or card creep!) Also, if the computer was moved recently, it could cause the card to come out of the slot slightly. Verify that the power connections and other cables are not loose. Check all other connections inside the PC to make sure it isn't a video problem. For example, if the system makes use of an onboard video controller and you start seeing garbled images, strange colors, or cursor trails, you might have defective RAM (or maybe you have been working on computers too long). Remember that onboard video controllers rely on the sticks of RAM in the motherboard, as opposed to individual video cards that have their own RAM.

> **ExamAlert**
>
> The previous 12 bullets are all very important troubleshooting techniques that you should know for the 220-901 exam. Study them carefully!

Again, verify that it is actually a video problem. Don't forget about the "big four." When you can't see anything on the display and you know the computer is receiving power, you can narrow it down to video, RAM, processor, and the motherboard. But if the system appears to boot, you can hear the hard drive accessing data, and you can see hard drive activity from the LED light on the front of the case, it is most likely a video problem. Go back to the basics: check power and connections. Try substituting a known-good monitor in place of the current one. When it comes to video, the simple answers are the most common.

Video Displays

Regardless of what type of video card (or cards) is in a computer, it means nothing if the computer doesn't have an output device. The most common video output device in a computer system is the liquid crystal display (LCD).

LCD

A liquid crystal display (LCD) is a flat panel display that consists of two sheets of polarizing material surrounding a layer of liquid crystal solution. Most of today's LCD screens are thin-film transistor (TFT) active-matrix displays, meaning they have one or more powered transistors for each pixel; the transistors are contained within a flexible material. The transistors store the electrical state of each pixel, while all the other pixels are updated. These transistors are located directly behind the liquid crystal material. Here are two types of active-matrix LCD technologies you should know for the exam:

▶ **Twisted nematic (TN):** This technology uses liquid crystals that actually twist and untwist at varying angles, letting certain amounts of light through. Less expensive LCD monitors will often use TN technology.

▶ **In-plane switching (IPS):** This technology aligns the liquid crystals on a plane that is parallel to the glass. Because of this, an additional transistor is required for each picture element (pixel). This means that it uses more power than a TN-based LCD. However, it allows for better color reproduction and wider viewing angles. All this comes at a higher cost, of course.

LCD displays use a Cold Cathode Fluorescent Lamp (CCFL) as the lighting source. The CCFL develops ultraviolet light by discharging mercury into the lamp. The lamp's inner fluorescent coating then allows for the emitting of visible light, which is sent to the actual display panel. LCDs typically have DVI, HDMI, and/or DisplayPort connections but might also be equipped with VGA for backward compatibility. In general, LCDs use low amounts of power, generate a small amount of heat, and cause little in the way of interference and emissions.

One measurement of an LCD screen is resolution (for example, 1920×1080, which is known as high-definition 1080p). Generally, an LCD will be designed for one resolution, known as the *native resolution*; it's the resolution that the LCD works best at. If this is the case, any other resolution selected will be scaled and will usually appear stretched or compressed. If a user complains of these symptoms, check the LCD documentation to find its native resolution and then switch to that resolution in the Screen Resolution window. More on video resolution later in this chapter.

Another measure of an LCD is contrast ratio. Contrast ratio is a comparison of the brightest and darkest colors (white and black) that can be generated on a display. It can be measured statically or dynamically (known as DC). Generally, the higher the contrast ratio, the better. Dynamic will always be a higher number than static. For example, one of the monitors used with the *AV Editor* computer (an IPS monitor) has a static contrast ratio of 1000:1 and a dynamic contrast ratio of 2,000,000:1. Many TN-based LCDs have inferior contrast compared to IPS and cannot be measured dynamically.

When it comes to cleaning displays, be careful. Liquid can possibly get between the bezel and the screen; when it infiltrates the display assembly, bad things can happen! To avoid this, conservatively spray the cleaner on to a soft, clean, lint-free cloth first; then carefully clean the display with the cloth. Many manufacturers of displays recommend using isopropyl alcohol diluted with water. Basically, no more than 50 percent of the solution should be alcohol; the rest should be water. Isopropyl alcohol can be found in most supermarkets and drug stores; the higher the purity level, the better (for example, 90 percent purity is acceptable; this purity level will be printed directly on the label of the bottle). Again, use the solution conservatively, apply it to the cloth first, and try not to get any on the plastic bezel—apply it to the screen only. It usually isn't necessary to clean the screen often; once every 3 to 6 months is fine unless you work in a dirty environment. Instead of cleaning the screen, you can also try wiping the dust (which can affect visibility) with a soft lint-free cloth or a canister of compressed air. This might help as an added step before cleaning the screen, so you can avoid streaking. There are also various spray cleaners available at electronics stores and online; some of them are simply expensive isopropyl alcohol/water solutions! Personally, for more than a decade, I have simply mixed my own isopropyl/water solution for use on LCDs, laptop LCDs, handheld computers, smartphones, and cell phones and I have never had a problem.

LED Monitors

LED monitors utilize light-emitting diodes to display images. LED display technology is used in computer monitors, televisions, billboards, and storefront signs. LED monitors can use two different kinds of technologies: conventional discrete LEDs and surface-mounted device (SMD) technology. SMD is more common for LED monitors; it uses red, green, and blue diodes that are mounted as individual triads as opposed to discrete LED technology, which clusters these triads together into pixels.

LED monitors are essentially LCD monitors with a different backlight. Whereas LCD monitors use CCFL as the illumination source, LED monitors use light-emitting diodes, which release photons; this process is known as electroluminescence. These are commonly known as LED-backlit LCD displays.

OLED

OLED stands for organic light-emitting diodes. OLED displays use organic semiconductor material that is usually in the form of polymers. Organic colored molecules are held in place between electrodes. A conductive layer made up of plastic molecules allows the organic-colored molecules to emit light. The main advantage of OLED over LED is expected to be cost; OLEDs can be printed onto just about any substrate using simple printing processes. OLED can be found in televisions, computer monitors, and especially mobile devices. One example is active-matrix OLED (AMOLED), which is small, generates little heat, and is flexible. It is very common in mobile devices, digital cameras, and media players.

Plasma

Plasma displays are rarely found in computer monitors but are often found in televisions. Nowadays, computers can use many types of televisions as their display, including plasma, as long as the computer has the correct type of video port. Plasma displays use small cells that contain electrically charged ionized gases; effectively, these are fluorescent lamps. Plasma screens are known for brightness and low-luminance black level as compared to LCD screens. This makes the plasma screen a higher energy consumer than LCD. It also prompted the LCD community to release the LED-backlit LCD displays that were mentioned previously.

Projectors

Video projectors can be plugged into a computer's external video port to project the computer's video display to a projection screen. An extremely bright bulb is necessary to project this image to the screen. The light output is measured in *lumens*. A typical high-def projector might output 3000 lumens—never allow a person to look into the projector's lamp! Increased lumens are necessary for locations with a higher amount of ambient light (existing light in the room). Projectors are used for presentations and for teaching and are common in conference rooms and training centers; however, some schools and companies opt to use large flat-screen TVs instead of projectors, even though projectors can usually project a larger image. Projectors are available in LCD, LED, and Digital Light Processing (DLP) versions. The LCD type works in a similar fashion to the monitor technology of the same name, whereas DLP uses light valves with rotating color wheels. Common high-definition display resolutions used by projectors include 720p and 1080p; the price of the projector increases with the resolution standard and with other characteristics, such as the brightness, contrast, and noise. A video projector can be used with a laptop by utilizing the display toggle button, or it can be used with a computer that has a video card with dual outputs.

Video Settings and Software

So you've selected and installed a video card and the monitor is connected to the computer. What next? Now it's time to install drivers (if this wasn't done already during the installation process) and configure settings in Windows (such as the color depth, resolution, and refresh rate) plus features such as Multiple Monitor and on-screen settings.

Drivers

Device drivers (otherwise known as software drivers) are programs that enable the operating system to communicate with the actual device. For example, a video driver enables the operating system to interact with the video card. The driver simplifies the amount of work that an application needs to do by acting as a go-between for the application and the device.

Video drivers (or the lack thereof) have been known to cause headaches for technicians. However, if a couple simple rules are adhered to, several video driver issues can be avoided:

▶ Use the *manufacturer's* driver. When you install a video card, Windows attempts to use a Microsoft version of the driver. This is usually not the best option, especially for newer cards. Instead, use the driver that came on disc with the device (or, better yet, access the manufacturer's website to download the latest driver for the device). You can check the date of the driver on the website against the date listed in Device Manager to see whether you currently have the latest.

▶ Watch out for new operating systems. Newer operating systems don't always have all the kinks worked out. Sometimes new hardware will not operate properly with a new operating system until updates have been released. Before installing a new operating system, verify that the device is listed as compatible. For example, when installing Windows, visit the Windows Compatibility Center. (For more information on compatibility, see Chapter 8.) Make sure to update the operating system after the installation is complete.

To work with video drivers in Windows, open Device Manager and then expand the Display Adapters category. This shows the video card. Right-click the device, select Properties, and then select the Driver tab. This shows a lot of information, including the manufacturer of the driver. If it says Microsoft, consider downloading the latest driver from the manufacturer's website. If it says NVIDIA, ATI, or something else, then you already have a manufacturer's version of the driver (though it might not be the latest). From this window you can also see the date of the driver, you can update the driver to the latest version, you can roll back the driver if a new installation has failed, or you can uninstall the driver completely.

Sometimes, if a driver fails, the system will not display anything on the screen. If this happens, try booting into Enable Low-Resolution Video; if that doesn't work, try booting into Safe Mode. These start the computer without the normal video driver and instead use a basic VGA driver at 640×480 resolution. In some cases, the computer automatically asks you if you want to start in Safe Mode, recognizing that there is a video issue. Note that Enable Low-Resolution Video uses a basic VGA driver, but all other drivers work normally. Safe Mode, however, starts the system with a minimal set of drivers. If a driver does fail, Internet access might be required to download the latest driver. This is not available in Safe Mode, but it is available in Enable Low-Resolution Video mode. You can also attempt to fix driver issues by performing an automated repair from the Windows Recovery Environment or System Repair Options.

Color Depth

Color depth (also known as bit depth or color quality) is a term used to describe the number of bits that represent color. For example, 1-bit color is known as monochrome—those old screens with a black background and one color for the text, like in old *Six Million Dollar Man* episodes or like Neo's computer in *The Matrix*! But what is 1-bit color? 1-bit color in the binary numbering system means a binary number with one digit. This digit can be a zero or a one, for a total of two values: usually black and white. This is defined in scientific notation as 2^1 (2 to the 1st power equals 2). Another example would be 4-bit color, which is used by the ancient but awesome Commodore 64 computer. In a 4-bit color system you can have 16 colors total. In this case, $2^4 = 16$. Of course, 16 colors aren't nearly enough for today's applications; 16-bit, 24-bit, and 32-bit are the most common color depths used by Windows. Table 12.2 shows the different color depths used in Windows.

TABLE 12.2 **List of Color Depths Used in Windows**

Color Depth	Number of Colors	Calculation
8-bit	256	2^8
16-bit	65,536	2^{16}
24-bit	16,777,216	2^{24}
32-bit	4,294,967,296	2^{32}

8-bit color is used in VGA mode, which is uncommon for normal use, but you might see it if you boot into Safe Mode or other advanced modes that disable the normal video driver. 16-bit is usually enough for the average user who works with basic applications; however, many computers are configured by default to 32-bit (also known as 3 bytes and 4 bytes, respectively).

Why is all this important? Two reasons:

▶ First, backward compatibility. A user might need to use an older program that doesn't display well in 32-bit color. You might choose to reduce the color depth to 16-bit from within the monitor's properties window or run the program in compatibility mode with a lesser color depth.

▶ Second, to reduce the amount of computer resources needed. Usually a computer has enough video resources to run 32-bit, but you never know when you will work on an older computer that has a low-end video card and limited RAM. Reducing the color depth can help the system to perform better.

To modify color depth in the monitor properties window, do the following:

▶ **In Windows 8/7:** Right-click the desktop and select Screen Resolution. Click the monitor you want to modify (if there is more than one), and then click the Advanced Settings link. In the video card's Properties window, select the Adapter tab, and then click the List All Modes button. From here, you can select color depth as well as resolution options, and you can refresh frequency.

▶ **In Windows Vista:** Right-click the desktop and select Personalize. Then click the Display Settings link. A drop-down menu for color depth is located near the bottom-right part of this window.

Resolution

Display resolution is described as the number of pixels (picture elements) on a screen. It is measured horizontally by vertically (HxV). The more pixels that can be used on the screen, the bigger the desktop becomes and the more windows a user can fit on the display. The word resolution is somewhat of a misnomer and will also be referred to as pixel dimensions. Table 12.3 shows some of the typical resolutions used in Windows.

> **Note**
>
> The following table is designed to give you an idea of the history of video resolution modes and the aspect ratios they use. I don't expect you to memorize them all. As of the writing of this book (late 2015), the important ones to know for the IT field are 720p and the last four listed in the table. The rest of the resolutions will be seen less frequently, but if you do see them, you can quickly refer to this table to find out their names, dimensions, and aspect ratios.

TABLE 12.3 **List of Display Resolutions**

Resolution Type	Full Name	Pixel Dimension	Aspect Ratio
VGA*	Video Graphics Array	640×480	4:3 (1.333:1)
XGA	Extended Graphics Array	1024×768	4:3 (1.333:1)
SXGA	Super Extended Graphics Array	1280×1024	5:4 (1.25:1)
UXGA	Ultra Extended Graphics Array	1600×1200	4:3 (1.333:1)
WXGA min. (720p)	Widescreen eXtended Graphics Array minimum	1280×720	16:9 (1.78:1)
WXGA	Widescreen eXtended Graphics Array	1280×800	16:10 (1.6:1)
HD Ready	High Definition similar to WXGA (primarily used on laptops)	1366×768	16:9 (1.78:1)
WSXGA+	Widescreen Super eXtended Graphics Array Plus	1680×1050	16:10 (1.6:1)
WSXGA+ (HD)	Widescreen Super eXtended Graphics Array Plus (High Definition)	1680×945	16:9 (1.78:1)
WUXGA	Widescreen Ultra eXtended Graphics Array	1920×1200	8:5 (1.6:1)
HD 1080p and 1080i	Full High Definition	1920×1080	16:9 (1.78:1)
QHD (WQHD) 1440p	Quad High Definition	2560×1440	16:9 (1.78:1)
UHD 4K	Ultra High Definition	3840×2160	16:9 (1.78:1)

* VGA mode is usually seen only when you attempt to boot the system into Safe Mode, another advanced boot mode, or when the video driver has failed.

> **Note**
>
> It's interesting to note that during the writing of this book, some analytical websites show 1366×768 as the most commonly used desktop resolution worldwide—and by a wide margin.

Aspect ratio can be defined as an image's width divided by its height (for example, VGA's resolution is 640×480). When you divide the width (640) by the height (480), the result is 1.333. You also hear this referred to as a four-to-three ratio (4:3). This means that for every 4 pixels running horizontally, there are 3 pixels running vertically. Wider resolutions have a higher first number (for example 16:9). Most current laptops and desktop LCD screens use a widescreen format by default (16:9, 8:5, or 16:10). Take a look at your own computer's resolution setting and figure out which aspect ratio it uses.

Display resolutions continue to get larger. Keep in mind, however, that the maximum resolution of a monitor can be achieved only if the video card can support it. A video card's maximum resolution is rated in two ways: maximum digital resolution and maximum VGA resolution. The VGA number is usually less than the digital number.

ExamAlert

Know the high-def resolution modes and understand the difference between the 16:9, 16:10, 8:5, and 4:3 aspect ratios.

To modify screen resolution in Windows, do the following:

▶ **In Windows 8/7:** Right-click the desktop and select Screen Resolution. The Resolution drop-down menu is within that window.

▶ **In Windows Vista:** Right-click the desktop, select Personalize, and then click the Display Settings link. Toward the bottom-left part of the window is a Resolution box that provides a slider that enables you to configure the pixel dimensions. Drag the slider to the appropriate resolution.

Sometimes a user might set the resolution too high, resulting in a scrambled or distorted display. This can happen when video cards support higher resolution modes than the monitor supports. When this happens, reboot the computer into either Enable Low-Resolution Video or Safe Mode, and then adjust the resolution setting to a level that the monitor can support.

A video card's amount of memory dictates the highest resolution and color depth settings. You can multiply the resolution by the color depth to find out how much memory will be needed. For example, if a user wants to run a 1920×1080 resolution at 32-bit color (4 bytes of color), the equation is 1920×1080×4, which would equal approximately 8 MB—easily covered by today's video cards. But keep in mind that this is the bare minimum needed to display Windows and that more will be necessary for advanced GUIs, such as Windows Aero and other advanced display settings. Much more video memory is necessary to run games and graphics programs. Some desktop computers and laptops have integrated video, which uses shared video memory. This means that instead of the video device having its own memory, it shares the motherboard's RAM. Motherboard RAM will usually be slower than a video card's memory, and there will probably be less available. Due to this, a PCI Express video card is recommended over integrated video for computers that run resource-intensive applications and games.

Refresh Rate

Refresh rate is generally known as the number of times a display is "painted" per second. It is more specifically known as *vertical refresh rate*. On an LCD, the liquid crystal material is illuminated at a specific frequency. This is usually set to 60 Hz and is not configurable on most LCDs. (The configuration can be found in the monitor's properties window.) However, there are some computer monitors (and many televisions) that can go to 120 Hz and 240 Hz.

Don't confuse the refresh rate with frames per second (frames/s or fps). Although the two are directly related, they are not the same thing. For example, a digital video camera might record video at 30 fps. When played back or edited, this will run fine on a 60 Hz monitor. However, if a user is playing a video game that is set to run at 90 fps, the game attempts to send those frames of video data from the video card to the monitor. If the monitor is limited to a 60 Hz refresh rate, the video card will attempt to display the additional frames within the given refresh rate, causing somewhat of a blur, which might or might not be acceptable to the user. To many users in the gaming community, the higher the frames per second, the better. But to actually attain a higher frame rate (beyond 60 fps), a higher refresh rate will also be necessary.

OSD

The on-screen display (OSD) can help configure picture quality. It can aid in fixing problems of all types, including distortion, picture size, centering, and contrast and brightness. The OSD is superimposed on top of the monitor's display and can usually be accessed by pressing a Menu button or other like button on the monitor either below the display or on one of the sides of the monitor. From there, arrow buttons enable the user to make modifications to the settings. To reduce eye strain, the two most important settings are brightness and contrast. Brightness is the amount of light that the display emits. It is also known as "black level"—if you set it to zero, the screen will be black, near-black, or simply at its darkest setting. Contrast is the quality of the luminance of the picture; it's also known simply as "picture." More advanced monitors have a higher contrast ratio, which allows for greater control of the contrast setting. Manufacturers suggest configuring the brightness setting first and then configuring the contrast setting. Keep in mind that laptop displays usually have only a brightness setting.

Multiple Displays

Windows enables you to either duplicate the display onto other monitors or extend the desktop across to multiple displays. In the latter case, it enables you to spread applications over two or more monitors that effectively work together as one. This works well for applications that are wide or if a user needs to see multiple windows at the same time. To modify how the multiple displays work, do the following:

▶ **In Windows 8/7:** Right-click the desktop and select Screen Resolution. Detect and configure multiple monitors from here.

▶ **In Windows Vista:** Right-click the desktop, select Personalize, and then select Display Settings. This opens the Display Settings window.

Figure 12.4 shows the Screen Resolution window on a laptop running Windows 8. In this example, the desktop has been extended across the laptop's built-in monitor (running at 1920×1080 resolution) and over to a secondary monitor that is plugged into the laptop's HDMI port. Note that a laptop usually has a monitor toggle button (for example, the F4 function key).

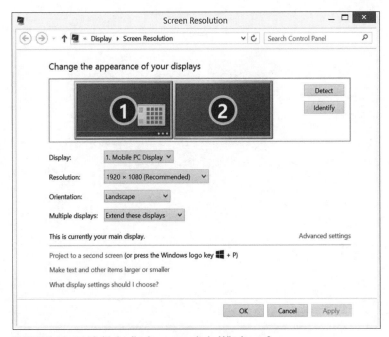

FIGURE 12.4   **Multiple display example in Windows 8**

It is possible to use multiple video cards, but keep in mind that Windows prefers identical video cards and drivers. Some applications (for example, video players) might not work perfectly on a secondary screen. This depends on the type of video played, the application, and the type of monitor used.

Newer versions of Windows find secondary monitors more easily and remember previous configurations. But if you ever find yourself trying to use a projector or other secondary display during a meeting and nothing is shown on that second device, remember to check the monitor toggle button. You can select from the following: laptop screen only, external display only, duplicate the desktop on both displays, and extend the desktop to both displays. Also, as mentioned, you can check the setting in the Screen Resolution window. And as always, be sure to check your cable connections!

Cram Quiz

Answer these questions. The answers follow the last question. If you cannot answer these questions correctly, consider reading this section again until you can.

220-901 Questions

1. Which of the following supports digital only connections?

   ○ **A.** DVI-A

   ○ **B.** DVI-D

   ○ **C.** DVI-I

   ○ **D.** VGA

2. When installing a video card, what should you do before inserting the card into the slot?

   ○ **A.** Connect cables

   ○ **B.** Install drivers

   ○ **C.** Test

   ○ **D.** Prepare the slot

3. Which of the following offers a superior viewing angle?

   ○ **A.** Active-matrix

   ○ **B.** TN

   ○ **C.** IPS

   ○ **D.** LCD

4. Where is the best place to get the latest driver for a video card?

   ○ **A.** Microsoft

   ○ **B.** CD-ROM

   ○ **C.** A friend

   ○ **D.** Manufacturer's website

5. How many colors are there if the color depth in Windows is set to 32-bit?

   ○ **A.** 16

   ○ **B.** 65,536

   ○ **C.** 16,777,216

   ○ **D.** 4 billion

6. A computer is set to 1920×1080 resolution. Which standard is it using?

   ○ **A.** VGA

   ○ **B.** Full High Definition

   ○ **C.** Quad High Definition

   ○ **D.** Ultra High Definition

7. What is a typical refresh rate for a laptop's LCD?

   ○ **A.** 30 Hz

   ○ **B.** 60 Hz

   ○ **C.** 240 Hz

   ○ **D.** 60 MHz

8. A user set the resolution in Windows too high, resulting in a scrambled, distorted display. What should you do to fix the problem? (Select the best answer.)

   ○ **A.** Upgrade the video driver.

   ○ **B.** Boot into low-resolution mode.

   ○ **C.** Press the monitor toggle key.

   ○ **D.** Check the video connections.

9. You are troubleshooting a video issue. Which utility should you use?

   ○ **A.** Regedit

   ○ **B.** Msconfig

   ○ **C.** DxDiag

   ○ **D.** Task Manager

10. You receive a computer that has a broken on-board DVI connector. What should you attempt first?

    ○ **A.** Replace the motherboard.

    ○ **B.** Replace the DVI connector.

    ○ **C.** Install a video card.

    ○ **D.** Use an adapter.

11. You just replaced a video card in a PC with another card from a different manufacturer. However, the driver installation does not complete. What should you do first?

    ○ **A.** Install the driver again.

    ○ **B.** Locate the latest version of the driver.

    ○ **C.** Roll back the driver.

    ○ **D.** Install the original video card.

Cram Quiz Answers

220-901 Answers

1. **B.** DVI-D supports digital-only connections, which are common on newer LCDs. DVI-A supports analog-only. DVI-I supports both digital and analog. VGA is an analog connection.

2. **D.** Before inserting the card into the slot, prepare the slot by manipulating any locking mechanism and removing the appropriate slot cover(s).

3. **C.** In-plane switching (IPS) is a type of active-matrix LCD that offers a wider viewing angle (and, in some cases, better color quality) than twisted nematic (TN).

4. **D.** The manufacturer's website is the best place to get the latest driver. The disc supplied with the card is usually satisfactory, but it will not be the latest driver.

5. **D.** 32-bit color is equal to approximately 4 billion colors (4,294,976,296 to be exact), otherwise known as 2^{32} power. 16 colors is 4-bit, 65,536 colors is 16-bit, and 16,777,216 colors is 24-bit.

6. **B.** 1920×1080 is Full High Definition (1080p). Video Graphics Array (VGA) is 640×480 (used by Safe Mode). Quad High Definition (QHD) is 2560×1440. Ultra High Definition (UHD) is 3840×2160.

7. **B.** A typical refresh rate for a laptop's LCD is 60 Hz.

8. **B.** Boot into a low-resolution mode. In Windows 8/7/Vista, this is called Enable Low-Resolution Video. Safe Mode is another valid option, but keep in mind that Safe Mode loads Windows with a minimal set of drivers and you can't access the Internet. Depending on the display configuration, pressing the monitor toggle key might actually fix the problem temporarily by displaying the screen on a secondary monitor, but it doesn't solve the root cause of the problem.

9. **C.** You should use DxDiag to troubleshoot video issues. The other three answers are not used to troubleshoot video.

10. **C.** Try installing a video card first to see if the system will still work. Unless it is a specialized system, the video card should be less expensive than the motherboard. (Not to mention it will take a lot less time to install.) As PC techs, we usually do not replace connectors; it is a possibility, but it should be further down your troubleshooting list. An adapter cannot help if the DVI port is broken.

11. **C.** If the driver installation doesn't complete, you should roll back the driver. It could be that you have attempted to install the incorrect driver. After you roll back the faulty installation, find the correct latest version of the video driver from the manufacturer's website. Installing the driver again can most likely have the same result. Only reinstall the original video card temporarily if you cannot find a proper solution right away.

The Audio Subsystem

In some environments, sound is not required; but more often than not, it is either wanted or is mandatory. So although troubleshooting sound is not as common as troubleshooting video (in most environments), it is still something that a technician will do fairly commonly in the field.

The audio subsystem consists of the sound card, the expansion bus used, audio ports, connectivity in the form of internal and external audio cables, speakers, sound card drivers, and any additional third-party audio software. The sound card is the basis for audio, so let's begin by discussing that device now.

Sound Cards

The sound card is responsible for generating sound from the data sent to it by the operating system. Audio devices can be integrated into the motherboard, installed to PCI and PCIe slots, and can be connected to USB and IEEE 1394 ports. However, the typical audio device known as the sound card is installed to a PCIe slot on the motherboard.

One of my computers (*Media PC*) uses a Creative Labs Sound Blaster sound card. It's a PCIe x1 card, which means that it can fit within a x1, x4, or x16 slot. It has most of the ports a user would need for outputting and inputting sound. Figure 12.5 shows the ports on the back of this card and typical integrated audio ports on the back of a motherboard.

Most sound cards are color-coded. This color scheme was originally defined by the PC System Design Guide, version PC 99 (which was finalized as version PC 2001—and the colors stuck even today). It specifies the following colors for the TRS 1/8-inch (3.5 mm) mini-jacks like the ones shown in Figure 12.5:

- ▶ **Light blue:** Line input. Sometimes this seconds as a microphone input.
- ▶ **Pink:** Microphone input.
- ▶ **Lime green:** Main output for stereo speakers or headphones. Can also act as a line out.
- ▶ **Black:** Output for surround sound speakers (rear speakers).
- ▶ **Silver/Brown:** Output for additional two speakers in a 7.1 system (middle surround speakers).
- ▶ **Orange:** Output for center speaker and subwoofer.

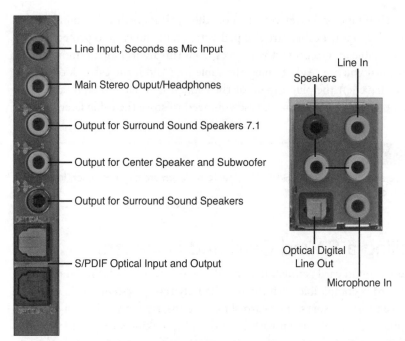

Line Input, Seconds as Mic Input

Main Stereo Ouput/Headphones

Output for Surround Sound Speakers 7.1

Output for Center Speaker and Subwoofer

Output for Surround Sound Speakers

S/PDIF Optical Input and Output

Line In

Speakers

Optical Digital Line Out

Microphone In

FIGURE 12.5 **A typical sound card's ports and integrated audio ports on a motherboard**

On the sound card shown in Figure 12.5, note an optical input and output.
This is known as a Sony/Phillips Digital Interconnect Format (S/PDIF)
port. This particular version of S/PDIF is called TOSLINK. It delivers
high-quality digital sound over fiber optic cable. It is also known as a *digital
optical port.* It is considered by some to be sonically superior to the analog
1/8-inch mini-jacks described previously. The S/PDIF output can be used
to connect to a home theater system or other receiver; this enables the user
to play CDs, MP3s, and so on, on the system of their choice. The input can
connect recording equipment, game consoles, and so on, enabling a user to
bring high-quality audio into the computer to be manipulated as the user
sees fit. The input is usually black and the output is gray. Cables connecting
TOSLINK ports can be a maximum of 10 meters but are normally found in
5-meter lengths. The optical port (when enabled in Windows) emits a red,
laser-like light. Normally, the port has a soft plastic cover that should block
this light when a cable is not plugged in. If this is missing, you can block it

with electrical tape or, better yet, turn off the optical port in the sound card software. New optical cables are shipped with small end caps to protect the ends of the cable and to protect your eyes from this light. Don't remove the end caps until you are ready to plug the cable in. (And if the cable doesn't fit, you might have left the plug cap on or the cable might need to be rotated.) Store the end caps somewhere in case you need to store the cable later.

> **Note**
>
> There are also coaxial-based S/PDIF connectors, which are more common to external audio devices.

Installing a Sound Card and Speakers

Installing a sound card is much like installing any other card. First, be sure that the card is compatible with the installed operating system. Then employ ESD prevention measures. The card should be inserted into a PCI or PCIe slot by pressing straight down with both thumbs, making sure not to wiggle the card in any direction; this way, the contacts will not get damaged. Make sure it is fully inserted; you shouldn't see any of the gold-colored edge contacts. Then screw the card in where the slot cover used to be within the case.

However, you aren't finished. Now you need to connect any front panel case connections that the card might support, hook up the optical drive (if necessary), connect the speakers, and, finally, install the driver for the card:

▶ **Make front panel connections:** One common type of front panel connection is known as Intel High Definition Audio (HD Audio). This uses a 10-pin cable that goes from a compatible sound card (or motherboard, if sound is integrated) to the front of the compatible case. It is keyed at pin 8 so that the cable cannot be connected upside down. This port enables a user to connect headphones and a microphone to the front of the case instead of having to connect them to the sound card on the back of the computer. Creative and other manufacturers also offer advanced devices that can be installed to a 5.25-inch bay so that the user can have greater access to connections, volume, and so on. The predecessor to the HD Audio connection is AC'97. You might see both connectors inside your computer case, but HD Audio is usually preferred.

▶ **Connect the speakers:** Back in the day, a pair of speakers would be connected to the sound card and you were done. But nowadays, you might be using a 5.1 or 7.1 system and, if so, you need to color coordinate! 5.1 surround sound means that the system uses five regular speakers (left, right, center, back left, and back right) and one speaker for low frequencies, which is usually a subwoofer. 7.1 builds upon this by adding two additional surround speakers. Normally, the lime-green output is for the first two speakers (or headphones), which gives standard stereo 2.1 output (two speakers + sub). The black output is for two rear speakers and the orange output is for the center channel and the subwoofer; an AC outlet will be necessary to power the subwoofer. A gray, brown, or other dark port is used for two additional speakers (middle surround) in a 7.1 system. Another option is to use the digital fiber optical output or digital coaxial output. There are a lot of options, so read the manual on the sound card and the speakers when trying to hook everything together, and pay attention to the little icons that are engraved into the back of the sound card next to the ports.

▶ **Install the driver and software:** Installing a sound card driver is usually done from the Installation disc that accompanies the sound card. It's also wise to check the manufacturer's website for any critical updates to the driver files. The disc usually comes with additional software to take control of the sound card. Keep in mind that this software might conflict with other audio software or media player software that was already installed on a PC. Consider using one or the other for things such as volume, equalization, and sound effects. Disable or uninstall any unused audio applications or media players to avoid conflicts.

ExamAlert

Know how to install sound cards, connect speakers, and connect other internal audio connections.

Troubleshooting Audio Problems

When troubleshooting an audio issue, such as no sound coming from the speakers, remember your A+ troubleshooting process and then try to break the audio subsystem down into its component parts. As we mentioned in the beginning of the audio section, the audio subsystem consists mainly of the sound card, speakers, and external audio devices, but from a less tangible point of view you have the audio software, drivers, Windows configurations, and so on. All of these should be taken into account when troubleshooting audio issues. But let's remember to look for the simple fixes first.

For example, when you don't hear any sound from the speakers, you should first check the volume, power, and connections. Are the speakers muted or was the volume turned very low in Windows? (You can modify this from the sound icon in the Notification Area.) Was the volume turned down in the audio application being used (for example, Windows Media Player)? Do the speakers have a Power button or volume knob? Are the speakers connected to the correct audio port of the sound card or to USB (as the case may be)? Are they connected at all? If the speakers are powered externally, are they plugged in?

Then you can move on to less frequent culprits. For example, the audio device might have been disabled in Device Manager or within the Sound window—which, by the way, can be accessed from the Control Panel or by right-clicking the sound icon in the Notification Area and selecting Playback devices. This becomes a bit more common on a laptop that has built-in speakers and also allows the user to connect headphones. Perhaps the incorrect driver was installed for the sound card? A rollback might fix the problem if an update failed. Or perhaps a new driver needs to be installed.

Sometimes the actual speakers of a mobile device might fail because the audio connector was jarred loose or the speakers need to be replaced. Before you open up the device, however, check the volume properties. Keep in mind that there is a master volume as well as separate volumes for individual applications, so while the master volume might be plenty loud, an individual application might be muted. Also, note that volume and mute can be configured very easily from the Function keys on a laptop—sometimes a user might mute or decrease the volume without even knowing it.

ExamAlert

Know what to do when troubleshooting a "no sound from speakers" problem. Check volume, mute, connections, and power.

Audio Quality

Audio quality is measured in several ways, but it all starts with the sampling rate and the number of bits per sample (known as bit depth). Standard audio CDs have a sampling rate of 44 kHz, sampling 16 bits at a time (known as 16-bit) per channel, using two channels (known as stereo or 2.1). This is referred to collectively as 16-bit/44 kHz and is considered CD quality. For stereo output of music, this has been the standard since CDs were first developed in the 1980s. Songs are recorded to the CD in an uncompressed format known as a .WAV file. Another measurement you might see or hear of is the total data rate (or bit rate). This is the number of bits that the CD plays per second and is calculated as sampling rate × bits × channels:

$44,100 \times 16 \times 2 = 1,411,200$ bits (or 1411 kb/s)

A standard audio CD is designed to play a maximum of 74 minutes of music at 1411 kb/s. To find the total capacity of an audio CD, multiply 1,411,200 bits × 74 (minutes) × (seconds). This comes to a total of 783 million bytes, essentially a 750 MB CD.

There are technologies that use higher data rates and technologies that use lower data rates. For example, DVD-Audio (DVD-A) can be recorded at a maximum of 24-bit/192 kHz in stereo. Given this fact, many sound cards (including the one installed during this chapter) can output at 24-bit/192 kHz. And DVD-Audio might go beyond just two speakers; it might be designed for 5.1 surround sound (however, it would be at a lesser sampling rate). At the other end of the spectrum, MP3s, which are compressed versions of audio files, generally range between 128 kb/s and 320 kb/s. Compare this to CD quality, which is 1411 kb/s. However, MP3s and other compressed audio files are done in a smart way to retain CD-quality sound.

Media players like Windows Media Player (which is built in to Windows) and iTunes can play audio CDs, DVD-Audio, and compressed files. Certain versions of these programs can also "rip" CDs, taking the song from the CD and creating a compressed file from it (if the CD is not encrypted). These compressed files are a fraction of the size of the original .WAV file on CD. They can then be transferred to just about any type of device (including portable music players, USB flash drives, SD cards, and so on) and can also be streamed to other computers and mobile devices. That is, if you aren't using a streaming service already!

Cram Quiz

Answer these questions. The answers follow the last question. If you cannot answer these questions correctly, consider reading this section again until you can.

220-901 Questions

1. What types of cables are used to connect speakers/audio devices to a sound card? (Select the two best answers.)

   ○ **A.** 1/8-inch mini-jacks

   ○ **B.** DVI

   ○ **C.** S/PDIF

   ○ **D.** RJ45

2. What standard is followed by most sound card manufacturers for the colors of the 1/8 mini-jacks?

   ○ **A.** PCI

   ○ **B.** PC 2001/99

   ○ **C.** PC 100

   ○ **D.** PCIe

3. What is the total data rate of an audio CD?

   ○ **A.** 320 kb/s

   ○ **B.** 160 kb/s

   ○ **C.** 1411 kb/s

   ○ **D.** 9.6 Mb/s

4. A customer has a PC with a sound card that is emitting a red light out of one port. What is happening?

   ○ **A.** The sound card is about to fail.

   ○ **B.** The sound card is defective.

   ○ **C.** The optical cable is not connected to the sound card.

   ○ **D.** That is the normal sound card LED.

5. A user complains that speakers are connected to the PC but are not playing audio. What should you do first?

   ○ **A.** Move the speaker cable to another jack on the sound card.

   ○ **B.** Move the speaker cable to the headphone jack on the optical drive.

   ○ **C.** Reinstall the sound drivers.

   ○ **D.** Install a new sound card.

Cram Quiz Answers

220-901 Answers

1. **A and C.** The colored connectors on the back of the sound card are known as TRS 1/8-inch mini-jacks. S/PDIF is the optical output (and possibly input) found on the back of the sound card. DVI is a video port. While RJ45 Ethernet connections can possibly be used for audio, it is much less frequent than the other two answers. By the way, RCA is another port that can be used for video and audio but it won't be found on the back of a sound card; however, RCA might be found on I/O drives that are loaded into the front of a computer in a 5.25-inch bay, enabling for greater connectivity on the computer's front panel.

2. **B.** PC 2001/99 specifies the color scheme used by all kinds of equipment, including a sound card's 1/8 mini-jacks.

3. **C.** 1411 kb/s is the total data rate (or bit rate) of an audio CD. 320 kb/s is the maximum data rate for MP3, 160 kb/s is a common data rate for WMA files, and 9.6 Mb/s is the total data rate of DVD-Audio.

4. **C.** If a red light is emitting from the sound card's port, it is because there is no cable plugged into the optical port. There is not an LED on the back of a sound card. The card is not about to fail, nor has it failed already.

5. **A.** The first thing you should check when there is no audio is whether there is volume (and if the volume is muted). Then check whether the speakers have power (if they are required to be plugged in.) But after that, the best answer is to move the speaker to another jack (the correct jack) on the sound card. Only try reinstalling sound drivers or a new card after you have eliminated the basic culprits.

CHAPTER 13

Peripherals and Custom Computing

This chapter covers the following A+ exam topics:

▶ Input/Output, Input Devices, and Peripherals

▶ Custom PC Configurations

You can find a master list of A+ exam topics in the "Introduction."

This chapter covers the CompTIA A+ 220-901 objectives 1.4, 1.7, 1.9, 1.11, 1.12, 3.1, and 3.2.

The computer is built, the OS is installed, and video is configured. Now let's discuss the devices and peripherals we add on to the computer, the ports they connect to, as well as some custom PC configurations you will undoubtedly encounter in the field.

Input/Output, Input Devices, and Peripherals

To take advantage of a computer, the appropriate input/output devices and peripherals must be connected to the proper input/output (I/O) ports. Keyboards, mice, and multimedia devices can be connected to a variety of ports. This section briefly describes those devices and the ports they connect to.

I/O Ports

I/O ports enable a user to input information by way of keyboard, mouse, or microphone; plus they enable the output of information to printers, monitors, USB devices, and so on. The CompTIA A+ exams require you to describe USB, IEEE 1394 (FireWire), and Thunderbolt ports, as well as Bluetooth technology. The most common of these by far is USB.

USB

USB ports are used by many devices, including keyboards, mice, printers, flash drives, cameras, and much more. The USB port enables data transfer between the device and the computer and usually powers the device as well. The speed of a USB device's data transfer depends on the version of the USB port, as shown in Table 13.1.

TABLE 13.1 **Comparison of USB Versions**

USB Version	Name	Data Transfer Rate
USB 1.0	Low-Speed	1.5 Mb/s
USB 1.1	Full-Speed	12 Mb/s
USB 2.0	High-Speed	480 Mb/s
USB 3.0	SuperSpeed	5.0 Gb/s
USB 3.1	SuperSpeed+	10.0 Gb/s

USB 1.0 and 1.1 are deprecated. If you encounter an older computer that has only these ports, consider installing a USB adapter card that adheres to a higher version of USB.

ExamAlert

Memorize the specifications for USB; focus on USB 2.0 and higher.

A computer can have a maximum of 127 USB devices. However, most computers are limited to a maximum of a dozen ports or so. To add devices beyond this, a USB hub can be used, but no more than five hubs can be in a series of USB devices. All cables connecting USB devices must comply with their standard's maximum length. USB version 1.1 cables are limited to 3 meters in length (a little less than 10 feet), and USB version 2.0 cables can be a maximum length of 5 meters (a little more than 16 feet). Maximum recommended USB 3.0/3.1 length is 3 meters. The standard USB cable has four pins: a +5 V pin for power, a positive data pin, a negative data pin, and a ground pin. Most USB connections are half-duplex, meaning that the device can send or receive data but cannot send and receive data simultaneously.

There are various plugs used for the different types of USB connections. The most common are Type A and Type B, which are 4-pin connectors, but there are also mini- and micro-connectors, which are 5-pin. Type A connectors are the type you see on the back of a computer or on the side of a laptop. Figure 13.1 displays an illustration of these connectors.

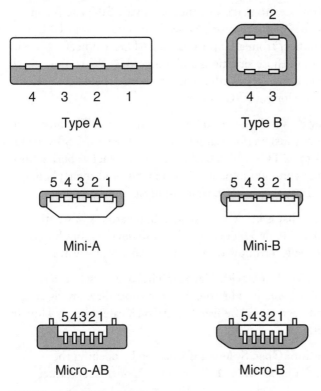

FIGURE 13.1 **USB connectors**

Type A and Type B connectors are commonly used for printers and other larger devices. Mini- and micro-connectors are often used for handheld computers, smartphones, mice, digital cameras, portable music players, and cell phones. However, some companies create proprietary cables and connectors for their devices based off of the USB specifications. These devices will not connect properly to Type A, Type B, and mini- or micro-connectors.

> **Note**
>
> As of the writing of this book, a newer USB plug (Type C) has been developed. It is about a third the size of a Type A plug and works well in conjunction with the USB 3.1 standard.

You can't put a square peg in a round hole (normally). Sometimes you need to make a connection but the devices and/or cables don't match up, so you'll need an adapter—and there are adapters for virtually everything you might want to do. Let's say you need to make a connection to a USB Type B connector from a USB Type A connector, or you need to connect from USB to RJ45, or you need to connect from a USB to the older PS/2 connector—well, there are adapters for all of those situations and more. Most PC technicians will carry a variety of adapters with them just in case the need arises. Something to think about for your PC toolkit.

Historically, a USB device was designed to be a host or a slave. The host is in charge of initiating data transfers (for example, a PC). However, USB version 2.0 introduced on-the-go (OTG), which enables a device to act as both a host and a slave. This is more common in handheld computers and smartphones (devices that connect with either mini- or micro-plugs).

USB devices connect to what is known as a root hub, regardless of whether they are USB version 1.1, 2.0, or 3.0 devices. The USB devices, root hub, and host controllers can be viewed from within Windows in a couple ways:

- ▶ **Device Manager:** Within Device Manager, click Universal Serial Bus Controllers to expand it. The root hub and controllers are listed within. Individual devices will be listed under such categories as Human Interface Devices.

- ▶ **System Information:** Open System Information by opening the Run prompt and typing **msinfo32**. Expand Components, and then select USB.

Windows offers a disk-caching component called ReadyBoost. This uses flash-based memory such as USB flash drives and SD cards to cache information for the OS at high speeds. The cache can be as much as 32 GB in size on one device or 256 GB in size if spread across multiple devices. For USB flash drives, this technology works best at USB 3.0 speeds (or higher).

When troubleshooting USB devices, keep a few things in mind:

▶ **Verify that USB is enabled in the BIOS/UEFI:** It is possible to enable/disable USB within the BIOS. Keep this in mind when troubleshooting USB devices that are not functioning whatsoever. The user might have inadvertently set this to disabled or perhaps the computer was shipped in that state.

▶ **Make sure the computer is running the correct version of USB:** For example, if the computer is USB 3.0-compliant from a hardware standpoint, make sure it is running USB 3.0 on the software side. Some versions of Windows need to be updated to communicate at the latest USB speeds. This update makes a huge difference in the speed of data transfer. Sometimes Windows informs the user that an update to USB is available and that the USB devices work faster if this update is completed. In other cases, a USB firmware update for the motherboard is needed.

▶ **Check the version of the USB port:** For example, if a device can run at USB 3.0, make sure it isn't connected to a USB 2.0 (black port), because that will cause the device to run at USB 2.0 speeds. If it is connected to a slower port, be sure to connect it to a USB 3.0 (blue) port.

▶ **Verify connectivity:** Make sure the device is plugged in and that it is using the correct cable. Some incompatible USB plugs might look similar to the correct plug and might even connect to a device.

When removing USB devices from a computer, remember to disable them in the Notification Area before disconnecting them. Do this by right-clicking on the Safely Remove Hardware and Eject Media icon and selecting Eject. This will avoid damage to a USB device (for example, corruption to the USB flash drive). If you cannot disable it in the system, power down the computer and then disconnect them. For more information about USB, visit http://www.usb.org.

One of the problems with USB is that it suffers from latency. Due to this fact, users who work with audio and video prefer a zero-latency connection, such as IEEE 1394.

IEEE 1394

The Institute of Electrical and Electronics Engineers (IEEE) is a nonprofit organization that creates standards regarding cables and connectors and other technology related to electricity. One common standard is IEEE 1394, also referred to as FireWire (a deprecated Apple standard replaced by Thunderbolt). It is a port used for devices that demand the low-latency transfer of data in real time, such as music or video devices. Up to 63 devices can be powered by a computer, with no more than 16 devices per chain. Table 13.2 describes some of the IEEE 1394/FireWire versions.

TABLE 13.2   **Comparison of IEEE 1394/FireWire Versions**

IEEE 1394 Version	Data Transfer Rate	Connector Type	Cable Length Between Devices
IEEE 1394a	400 Mb/s	4-conductor and 6-conductor	4.5 meters (15 feet)
IEEE 1394b	800 Mb/s	9-conductor	10 meters (100 meters with Category 5e cable)

ExamAlert

Know the specifications for IEEE 1394a (FireWire 400) and 1394b (FireWire 800).

Thunderbolt

Thunderbolt is a high-speed hardware interface developed by Intel. As of the writing of this book, this is used primarily by Apple computers. It combines elements of PCI Express and DisplayPort technologies. Versions 1 and 2 use the Mini DisplayPort connector and version 3 uses the USB Type-C connector. Cables used with Thunderbolt should be no more than 3 meters (copper) and 60 meters (optical).

Thunderbolt 2 gives you access to the latest 4K monitors. In fact, with the Mac Pro, you can connect up to three 4K displays at once. And because Thunderbolt is based on DisplayPort technology, it provides native support for the Apple Thunderbolt Display and Mini DisplayPort displays. DVI, HDMI, and VGA displays connect through the use of adapters.

Thunderbolt can be used to transfer data at high rates to external storage devices or to displays (or both; up to six devices can be daisychained, meaning wired together in sequence). If you look at the ports of the computer and see the thunderbolt icon next to the Mini DisplayPort port, then it is meant to be used for data transfer to peripherals. If you see a display icon, then it can be used with a monitor. While you can physically connect a Thunderbolt device to a Mac with DisplayPort, the device will not work, but if you connect a DisplayPort device to a Mac with Thunderbolt, the device will work. Table 13.3 describes the different versions of Thunderbolt.

TABLE 13.3 **Comparison of Thunderbolt Versions**

Thunderbolt Version	Data Transfer Rate	Connector Type	PCI Express Version Required
Version 1	10 Gb/s	DisplayPort	Version 2.0
Version 2	20 Gb/s	DisplayPort	Version 2.0
Version 3	40 Gb/s	USB Type-C	Version 3.0

ExamAlert

Know the Thunderbolt versions, speeds, and connection types.

If a desktop computer doesn't come with a Thunderbolt connector, you can add a Thunderbolt adapter card, which can facilitate the use of high-speed, large-capacity storage devices and other technologies. There are also adapters that connect Thunderbolt to USB 3.0 and eSATA. On the video side, there are adapters that allow Thunderbolt to be changed over to DVI or to HDMI. As mentioned before, there are adapters for everything. If you can dream it up, it probably already exists.

PS/2

The PS/2 connector is used for connecting keyboards and mice to a desktop computer or laptop. The PS/2 port was originally introduced in the late 1980s as part of IBM's Personal System/2 computer. Keyboards and mice connect via a 6-pin Mini-DIN connector. In the PC 99 color scheme, PS/2 keyboard ports are purple and PS/2 mouse ports are green.

Although PS/2 had almost a 20-year run, these connectors are less common on new computers; they were the standard until USB became popular. However, like the older DB15 VGA port, you might see them for backward compatibility. For example, the *AV Editor* computer's motherboard has a single PS/2 port.

Bluetooth

Moving on to a wireless option for peripherals: Bluetooth is a short-range, low-speed wireless network primarily designed to operate in peer-to-peer mode (known as ad hoc) between PCs and devices such as printers, projectors, smartphones, mice, keyboards, and so on. It can be used with gaming consoles and by connecting a smartphone to a car's technology system or to a smart TV.

Bluetooth runs in virtually the same 2.4 GHz frequency used by IEEE 802.11b, g, and n wireless networks, but it uses a spread-spectrum frequency-hopping signaling method to help minimize interference. Bluetooth devices connect to each other to form a personal area network (PAN).

Some systems and devices include integrated Bluetooth adapters, and others need a Bluetooth module connected to the USB port to enable Bluetooth networking. Bluetooth devices must first be paired before they can be used together.

Bluetooth version 1.2 offers a data transfer rate of 1 Mb/s. Version 2 is rated at 3 Mb/s. Version 3 has theoretical speeds of up to 24 Mb/s, but it does so by combining with 802.11 technology. Bluetooth is divided into classes, each of which has a different range. Table 13.4 shows these classes, their ranges, and the amount of power their corresponding antennae use to generate signal.

TABLE 13.4 **Bluetooth Classes**

Class	mW	Range
Class 1	100 mW	100 meters (328 ft.)
Class 2	2.5 mW	10 meters (33 ft.)
Class 3	1 mW	1 meter (3 ft.)

As you can see, Class 1 generates the most powerful signal and has the largest range. The most common Bluetooth devices are Class 2 devices, with a range of 10 meters. Examples of this include portable printers, headsets, and computer dongles that connect to USB ports and allow the PC to communicate with other Bluetooth-enabled devices.

Input, Output, and Hybrid Devices

I/O devices (also called peripherals) can be used solely to input information, to output information, or to act as a hybrid of the two. Let's start with the types of devices used to input information and the various peripherals a technician might see in the field.

The usual suspects include the keyboard, for typing information in Windows or other OS, and the mouse, for manipulating the GUI. These two are known as human interface devices (HID). Some other devices that you might not have worked with yet include touchpads, digital cameras, web cameras, microphones, biometric devices, bar code readers, and MIDI devices. Table 13.5 describes these devices.

TABLE 13.5 **Description of Various Input Devices and Peripherals**

Device	Description	Types and Connections
Keyboard	Used to type text and numbers into a word processor or other application.	101-key keyboard is standard, USB, PS/2, and wireless connections.
Mouse	Used to control the GUI; works in two dimensions. Might have two or more buttons and a scroll wheel to manipulate the OS. The Buttons tab in Mouse Properties is used to change which buttons act as the primary and alternative click buttons.	Optical mouse, USB, PS/2, and wireless connections.
Touchpad	Device used on a laptop to control the cursor on the screen.	These are often integrated to the laptop but can also be connected externally via USB or Wi-Fi.
Motion sensor	Device used with PCs, Macs, and gaming consoles to allow a user to control the computer by swiping, grabbing, pinching, and so on in mid-air.	Often connected via USB or Wi-Fi, these are controlled with infrared technology. Some devices can also be controlled with voice activation.
Digital cameras/ Camcorders	Takes still photographs and/or video using an electronic image sensor. Images are displayed on-screen and can be saved to solid-state media such as SD cards and CompactFlash.	Can be a single device or integrated into smartphones/tablets. Can connect to the PC via USB or Wi-Fi.
Web cameras (webcam)	Enables a user to monitor other areas of a home or building, communicate via video telephony, and take still images.	Can connect to a PC via USB, to a LAN via RJ45, or via Wi-Fi.
Scanner	Used to optically scan images and other objects and convert them into digital images to be stored on the computer.	Can connect via USB, and IEEE 1394, or via Wi-Fi.
Microphones	Enables users to record their voices or other sounds to the computer. Common usages are webcasts, podcasts, for voice-overs while screen capturing, and for gaming.	Can connect to a PC via 1/8-inch (3.5 mm) mini-jack (sound card) or via USB.

Device	Description	Types and Connections
Biometric devices	Provides access to systems based on a particular physical characteristic of a user. Used for authentication purposes (for example, a fingerprint reader).	Can be integrated to the PC or can be connected via USB, Wi-Fi, or connected to the network.
Barcode readers	Reads barcodes (for example, linear barcodes, 2D barcodes, Post Office barcodes, and such). After physical installation, they need to be programmed to understand these codes.	Connects to the PC via USB, Wi-Fi, PS/2, or might be integrated into handheld computers and smartphones.
Smart card reader	Device that accepts smart cards used for authentication and data storage.	Can be integrated as a slot (for, example to a laptop). Also available in USB versions.
Musical Instrument Digital Interface (MIDI) devices	Enables computers, music keyboards, synthesizers, digital recorders, samplers, and so on to control each other and exchange data.	Uses a 5-pin DIN Connector.
Gamepads and joysticks	Gamepads are game controllers made famous by Nintendo, PlayStation, and Xbox; there are also gamepads for PCs. Joysticks are often used for flight simulator games.	Connects via USB Type A connections. Older versions used the 15-pin gaming port on a sound card.

Troubleshooting any of the devices in Table 13.5 is usually quite easy. Make sure that the device is connected properly to the computer (or has a working wireless connection) and verify within the Device Manager that the latest drivers are installed for the device. Then find out if any additional software is necessary for the device to function. Portions of the software might have to be installed to the device and to the OS.

Keyboards and mice can be especially troublesome. Keyboard errors are commonly caused by jammed keys and defective cables or cable connectors. A common mouse issue is when the cursor jumps around the screen. This could be due to an incorrect mouse driver or perhaps the mouse is on an uneven or nonreflective surface. Also, you might encounter a mouse that stops working after a computer comes out of sleep mode. Make sure that Windows is updated and that the correct and latest driver is being used for the mouse. Use the associated Control Panel apps to troubleshoot the device. Calibrate the device and/or synchronize the device to the system as necessary.

The main output devices you should know for the exams are display devices and speakers (covered in Chapter 12) and printers (to be discussed in Chapter 14). Because they are covered in those chapters, we will not discuss them here.

A few of the hybrid devices you will encounter are touchscreens, KVMs, smart TVs, and set-top boxes. Table 13.6 describes those in brief.

TABLE 13.6   **Description of Hybrid I/O Devices**

Device	Description	Types and Connections
Touchscreen	A video display that detects the presence of either a finger, stylus, or light pen that enables interaction with the OS. It incorporates a digitizer (the input portion of the device) that converts the tapping on the screen into digital functions.	Used in tablet PCs, AIO PCs, smartphones, and drawing tablets.
KVM switch	Enables a user to control two or more computers from one Keyboard, Video display, and Mouse (KVM).	Passive: works off computer's USB power Active: plugs into an AC outlet.
Smart TV	Combines the functionality of a television with Internet features and streaming of media.	Users can interact with the TV by inputting information via keyboard, gamepad, or remote control.
Set-top box (STB)	Device used by cable TV and satellite-based TV providers to allow access to digital (and possibly encrypted) television stations. Also used as a hybrid device that combines conventional TV with Internet technologies.	These often manifest themselves as small computers offering two-way communications over TCP/IP networks.

Cram Quiz

Answer these questions. The answers follow the last question. If you cannot answer these questions correctly, consider reading this section again until you can.

220-901 Questions

1. What is the data transfer rate (speed) of USB 3.0?
   - ○ **A.** 12 Mb/s
   - ○ **B.** 400 Mb/s
   - ○ **C.** 480 Mb/s
   - ○ **D.** 5 Gb/s

2. What is the maximum number of USB devices a computer can support?
   - ○ **A.** 4
   - ○ **B.** 63
   - ○ **C.** 127
   - ○ **D.** 255

3. Which type of USB connector is normally found on a desktop PC or laptop?
   - ○ **A.** Type A
   - ○ **B.** Type B
   - ○ **C.** Type C
   - ○ **D.** Type D

4. What is the maximum data transfer rate of IEEE 1394a?
   - ○ **A.** 400 Mb/s
   - ○ **B.** 800 Mb/s
   - ○ **C.** 5 Gb/s
   - ○ **D.** 24 Mb/s

5. You just installed a barcode reader to a laptop. What should you do next?
   - ○ **A.** Adjust the light wavelength.
   - ○ **B.** Test the reader by reading barcodes.
   - ○ **C.** Program the reader to recognize codes.
   - ○ **D.** Point the barcode reader at someone.

6. What does a KVM do?

    ○ **A.** Connects a computer to Bluetooth-enabled devices

    ○ **B.** Allows multiple users to share a single computer

    ○ **C.** Networks multiple computers together

    ○ **D.** Connects multiple computers to save resources

7. You are installing a wireless keyboard to a PC. What does the PC require?

    ○ **A.** Bluetooth dongle

    ○ **B.** Thunderbolt connection

    ○ **C.** Ethernet connection

    ○ **D.** IEEE 1394

8. A user calls you with a complaint that none of his USB devices are working. What is the most probable cause?

    ○ **A.** The USB 3.0 controller has failed.

    ○ **B.** The root hub is not configured.

    ○ **C.** The USB is disabled in the BIOS.

    ○ **D.** The USB is disabled in Windows.

9. You plug a USB device into the front panel port of a PC but nothing happens. What is the most likely cause?

    ○ **A.** The front panel connectors are not plugged into the motherboard.

    ○ **B.** You plugged a USB 3.0 device into a USB 2.0 port.

    ○ **C.** You need to reboot the computer.

    ○ **D.** You plugged a USB 2.0 device into a USB 3.0 port.

10. Which of the following has a data transfer rate of 40 Gb/s and uses a USB Type-C connector?

    ○ **A.** USB 3.1

    ○ **B.** Thunderbolt version 3

    ○ **C.** Bluetooth version 3

    ○ **D.** Thunderbolt version 2

11. Which of the following are considered both input and output devices?

    ○ **A.** Keyboard, mouse, touchpad

    ○ **B.** Smart card reader, motion sensor, biometric device

    ○ **C.** Printer, speakers

    ○ **D.** Smart TV, touchscreen, KVM, STB

Cram Quiz Answers

220-901 Answers

1. **D.** 5 Gb/s is the data rate for USB 3.0; 12 Mb/s is the data rate for USB version 1.1; and 400 Mb/s is the data rate of IEEE 1394a (FireWire 400). USB 2.0 has a maximum data transfer rate of 480 Mb/s.

2. **C.** USB can support up to 127 devices on one computer. However, USB hubs will be necessary to go beyond the number of USB ports (usually 4 or 6) commonly found on a system. FireWire supports up to 63 devices.

3. **A.** Type A connectors are almost always included on desktop PCs and laptops.

4. **A.** IEEE 1394a (FireWire 400) specifies a maximum data transfer rate of 400 Mb/s. IEEE 1394b (FireWire 800) specifies 800 Mb/s. USB 3.0 runs at 5 Gb/s. Bluetooth version 3 runs at 24 Mb/s.

5. **C.** After installing the device as well as the driver for the device, program the reader to recognize the codes.

6. **D.** A KVM connects multiple computers to a single keyboard, mouse, and monitor. This way, fewer resources in the way of peripherals (input/output devices) are necessary to use the computers.

7. **A.** Wireless keyboards and mice often use Bluetooth to transmit to a PC or laptop. The computer must either have a built-in Bluetooth antenna or a Bluetooth dongle connected to a USB port for the keyboard to function. These types of devices do not connect to Thunderbolt, Ethernet, or IEEE 1394 ports.

8. **C.** If none of the USB devices are working, chances are that USB has been disabled in the BIOS. This might be company policy so that users can't access USB drives or boot the computer to a USB drive. If the USB 3.0 controller fails, the USB 2.0 controller should still be functioning for other ports. The USB root hub requires no configuring; it is auto-configured by Windows. Although it might be possible to disable one USB device at a time in Windows, it will be uncommon. Disabling all the devices in Windows is rare.

9. **A.** Most likely, the front panel connectors are not plugged into the motherboard. A USB 3.0 device will work fine in a USB 2.0 port but at the lower speed. A USB 2.0 device will work at USB 2.0 speed when plugged into a USB 3.0 port. Rebooting is usually not necessary when installing USB devices.

10. **B.** Thunderbolt version 3 has a data transfer rate of 40 Gb/s and uses a USB Type-C connector. Although SuperSpeed+ USB 3.1 can use the newer USB Type-C connector, it has a data transfer rate of 10 Gb/s. Bluetooth version 3 has theoretical speeds up to 24 Mb/s. Thunderbolt version 2 transfers data at 20 Gb/s and uses a DisplayPort (or Mini DisplayPort) connector.

11. **D.** Smart TVs, touchscreens, KVMs, and STBs are considered both input and output devices. Keyboards, mice, touchpads, smart card readers, motion sensors, and biometric devices are considered input devices. Printers and speakers are considered output devices.

Custom PC Configurations

There are several custom configurations that you might encounter in the IT field. You should be able to describe what each type of computer is and the hardware that is required for these custom computers to function properly.

Audio/Video Editing Workstation

Multimedia editing, processing, and rendering require a fast computer with high-capacity storage and big displays (usually more than one). Examples of audio/video workstations include

- **Video recording/editing PCs:** These run software such as Adobe Premiere Pro, Final Cut, or Sony Vegas.

- **Music recording PCs:** These run software such as Logic Pro or Pro Tools.

Note

Identify the software programs listed above and understand exactly what they are used for.

Adobe Premiere Pro: http://www.adobe.com/products/premiere.html

Apple Final Cut: http://www.apple.com/final-cut-pro/

Apple Logic Pro: http://www.apple.com/logic-pro/

Avid ProTools: http://www.avid.com/us/products/family/pro-tools

---

This just scratches the surface, but you get the idea. These computers need to be designed to easily manipulate video files and music files. So from a hardware standpoint, they need a specialized video or audio card, the fastest hard drive available with a lot of storage space (definitely SSD and perhaps SATA Express or PCI Express-based), and multiple monitors (to view all of the editing windows). Keep in mind that the video cards and specialized storage drives are going to be expensive devices; be sure to employ all antistatic measures before working with those cards.

ExamAlert

Remember that audio/video workstations need specialized A/V cards; large, fast hard drives; and multiple monitors.

CAD/CAM Workstation

Computer-aided design (CAD) and computer-aided manufacturing (CAM) workstations are common in electrical engineering, architecture, drafting, and many other engineering arenas. They run software such as AutoCAD. This software is CPU-intensive and images require a lot of space on the screen. Hardware-wise, a CAD/CAM workstation needs a powerful, multi-core CPU (or more than one if you are using advanced CAD software or if you are performing 3-D design/rendering), a high-end video card (perhaps a workstation-class video card—much more expensive), and as much RAM as possible. If a program has a minimum RAM requirement of 2 GB of RAM, you should consider quadrupling that amount; plus, the faster the RAM, the better—just make sure your motherboard (and CPU) can support it.

> **ExamAlert**
>
> Don't forget, CAD/CAM computers need powerful, multicore CPUs, high-end video cards, and as much RAM as possible.

Virtualization Workstation

A virtualization workstation is a computer that runs one or more virtual operating systems (also known as virtual machines or VMs). Did you ever wish that you had another two or three extra computers lying around so that you could test multiple versions of Windows, Linux, and possibly a Windows Server OS all at the same time? Well, with virtual software, you can do this by creating virtual machines for each OS. But if you run those at the same time on your main computer, you are probably going to bring that PC to a standstill. However, if you build a workstation specializing in virtualization, you can run whatever operating systems on it that you need. The virtualization workstation uses what is known a hypervisor, which allows multiple virtual operating systems (guests) to run at the same time on a single computer. It is also known as a virtual machine manager (VMM). But there are two different kinds:

▶ **Type 1: Native:** This means that the hypervisor runs directly on the host computer's hardware. Because of this, it is also known as *bare metal*. Examples of this include VMware vSphere and Microsoft Hyper-V.

▶ **Type 2: Hosted:** This means that the hypervisor runs within (or "on top of") the operating system. Guest operating systems run within the hypervisor. Compared to Type 1, guests are one level removed from the hardware and therefore run less efficiently. Examples of this include Microsoft Virtual PC and Oracle VirtualBox. Figure 13.2 shows an example of VirtualBox. You will note that it has a variety of virtual machines inside, such as Windows 7, Windows Server, and Linux Ubuntu.

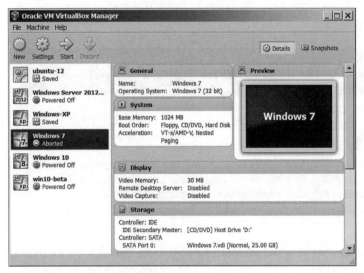

FIGURE 13.2   VirtualBox Manager window

Generally, Type 1 is a much faster and efficient solution than Type 2. Because of this, Type 1 hypervisors are the kind used for virtual servers by web-hosting companies and by companies that offer cloud-computing solutions. It makes sense, too. If you have ever run a powerful operating system such as Windows Server within a Type 2 hypervisor such as Virtual PC, you know that a ton of resources are used and those resources are taken from the hosting operating system. It is not nearly as efficient as running the hosted OS within a Type 1 environment. However, keep in mind that the hardware/software requirements for a Type 1 hypervisor are more stringent and more costly. In addition, you need to make sure your CPU supports virtualization. For example, some CPUs do not support Intel Virtualization Technology (VT). To check whether your CPU can support VT, http://ark.intel.com/Products/VirtualizationTechnology.

Intel CPUs that support x86 virtualization use the VT-x virtualization extension. Intel chipsets use the VT-d and VT-c extensions for input-output memory management and network virtualization, respectively. AMD CPUs that support x86 virtualization use the AMD-V extension. AMD chipsets use the AMD-Vi extension.

Any computer designed to run a hypervisor often has a powerful CPU (or multiple CPUs) with four cores or more and as much RAM as can fit in the system. This means a powerful, compatible motherboard as well. So in essence, the guts—the core of the system—need to be robust. Keep in mind that the motherboard BIOS/UEFI and the CPU should have virtualization support.

> **ExamAlert**
>
> Remember that virtualization systems depend on the CPU and RAM heavily. These systems require maximum RAM and CPU cores.

> **Note**
>
> For more information on how to create virtual machines with programs such as Hyper-V and VirtualBox, visit https://technet.microsoft.com/en-us/library/hh846766.aspx and https://www.virtualbox.org/manual/ch01.html.

In general, the security of a virtual machine operating system is the equivalent to that of a physical machine OS. The VM should have the latest updates, the newest AV definitions, perhaps a personal firewall, strong passwords, and so on. However, there are several things to watch out for that, if not addressed, could cause all your work compartmentalizing operating systems to go down the drain. This includes considerations for the virtual machine OS as well as the controlling virtual machine software. Keep an eye out for network shares and other connections between the virtual machine and the physical machine or connections between two VMs.

Consider disabling any unnecessary hardware from within the virtual machine, such as optical drives, USB ports, and so on. One last comment: A VM should be as secure as possible, but, in general, because the hosting computer is in a controlling position, it is likely more easily exploited. A compromise to the hosting computer probably means a compromise to any guest operating systems. Therefore, if possible, the host should be even more secure than the VMs it controls.

Thin Client

A *thin client* (also known as a slim, lean, or cloud client) is a computer that has few resources compared to a typical PC. Usually, it depends heavily on a server. It is often a small device integrated directly into the display or could be a stand-alone device using an ultra-small form factor (about the size of a cable modem or gaming console). Some thin clients are also known as diskless workstations because they have no hard drive or optical discs. They do have a CPU, RAM, and ports for the display, keyboard, mouse, and network; they can connect wirelessly as well. They are also known simply as computer terminals which might provide only a basic GUI and possibly a web browser. There is a bit of a gray area when it comes to thin clients due to the different models and types over the years, but the following gives a somewhat mainstream scenario.

Other examples of thin clients include point-of-sale (POS) systems such as the self-checkout systems used at stores or touchscreen menus used at restaurants. They serve a single purpose and require minimum hardware resources and minimum OS requirements.

When a typical thin client is turned on, it loads the OS and applications from an image stored (embedded) on flash memory or from a server. The OS and apps are loaded into RAM; when the thin client is turned off, all memory is cleared.

ExamAlert

Viruses have a hard time sticking around a thin client because the RAM is completely cleared every time it is turned off.

So, the thin client is dependent on the server for a lot of resources. Thin clients can connect to an in-house server that runs specially configured software or they can connect to a cloud infrastructure to obtain their applications (and possibly their entire operating system).

Note

Back in the day, this was how a mainframe system worked; however, back then, the terminal did virtually *no* processing, had no CPU, and was therefore referred to as a "dumb" terminal. This is an example of *centralized computing*, where the server does the bulk of the processing. Today, we still have mainframes (super-computers), but the terminal (thin client) incorporates a CPU.

The whole idea behind thin clients is to transfer a lot of the responsibilities and resources to the server. With thin-client computing, an organization purchases more powerful and expensive servers but possibly saves money overall by spending less on each thin client (for example, Lenovo thin clients) while benefitting from a secure design. The typical thin client might have one of several operating systems embedded into the flash memory, depending on the model purchased. This method of centralizing resources, data, and user profiles is considered to be a more organized and secure solution than the typical PC-based, client/server network, but it isn't nearly as common.

> **ExamAlert**
>
> A thin client runs basic, single-purpose applications, meets the minimum manufacturer's requirements for the selected operating system, and requires network connectivity to reach a server or host system where some, or even the majority, of processing takes place.

Standard Thick Client

A standard *thick client*, or fat client, is effectively a PC. Unlike a thin client, a thick client performs the bulk of data processing operations by itself and uses a drive to store the OS, files, user profile, and so on. In comparison to thin clients and the somewhat centralized computing, with a thick client, a typical local area network of PCs would be known as *distributed computing*, where the processing load is dispersed more evenly among all the computers. There are still servers, of course, but the thick client has more power and capabilities compared to the thin client. Distributed computing is by far the more common method today. When using a thick client, it's important to verify that the thick client meets the recommended requirements for the selected OS.

An example of a standard thick client is a desktop computer running Windows 8 and Microsoft Office, and offers web browsing and the ability to easily install software. This standard thick client should meet (or exceed) the recommended requirements for Window 8, including a 1 GHz 64-bit CPU, 2 GB of RAM, and 20 GB of free hard drive space.

> **ExamAlert**
>
> A standard thick client runs desktop applications such as Microsoft Office and meets the manufacturer's recommended requirements for the selected operating system. The majority of processing takes place on the thick client itself.

Home Server PC

A real server runs software such as Windows Server or Red Hat Enterprise Linux. But this software is expensive and requires a lot of know-how. For the average home user, a server OS is not usually necessary. It requires too much money and hardware resources and takes too much time to configure. However, if you want to have a home server PC, you can do so with any Windows OS that can start a HomeGroup, a Mac with OS X, or with most desktop variants of Linux. Once that computer is configured properly, information can be stored centrally on that system. Files and printers can be shared to the rest of the devices on the network, and media can be streamed to the other systems as well. To configure media streaming in Windows, go to Control Panel > HomeGroup, and then click the Change advanced sharing settings link. Open the appropriate network type and then click the Choose media streaming options link. Turn on media streaming and then click Customize for any particular device. From these last two locations, you can choose what is to be streamed, and you can select parental ratings if you want.

> **Note**
>
> Linux is another great option for powerful home server PCs, but it is unlikely that you will encounter a question about Linux media streaming on the A+ exams.

To make this server function quickly and recover from faults, we would equip it with a gigabit network adapter minimum (wired, for best results) and set up a RAID array. The RAID array could be RAID 0 (striping), but to incorporate fault tolerance, we would want RAID 1 (mirroring, 2 drives) or RAID 5 (striping with parity, 3 drives or more). To do this on a Windows system, we might need a RAID controller either embedded on the motherboard or installed as a separate adapter card. Or an external RAID array could be connected to the computer or connected to the network directly (NAS box) and controlled by the computer. Then we would need to configure file sharing and possibly print sharing, discussed in Chapters 16 and 14, respectively.

> **ExamAlert**
>
> Remember that a home server PC should have a fast network adapter and a RAID array, and needs to be part of a network (such as a HomeGroup) so that file and print sharing and media streaming can be configured.

Home Theater PC (HTPC)

A home theater PC (HTPC) can take the place of a Blu-ray player, DVD player, CD player, and various audio equipment. In some cases, it can also take the place of a set-top box (STB) as well. However, this depends on the area you live in. It has become more difficult (but not impossible) to use the HTPC for television reception due to cablecards and encryption techniques.

The requirements for an HTPC include a small form factor (micro-ATX or mini-ITX), a quiet desktop case with a silent video card, and an HDMI output for connectivity to big-screen televisions or projectors. To keep the rest of the computer quiet, a liquid-cooled CPU (instead of fan-based) and solid-state hard drive would complete the equation. Surround sound audio is desired as well, whether it comes from a sound card on the computer or from an external source. Finally, if you want to get TV reception, you would need a TV tuner and possibly an antenna.

> **ExamAlert**
>
> Know that an HTPC needs a small form factor, quiet equipment, surround sound audio, HDMI output, and possibly a TV tuner.

> **Note**
>
> *Media PC*, which I built for this book, would work well as an HTPC. However, I built another computer called *HTPC1* for exactly this purpose. You can learn more about it at http://www.davidlprowse.com/articles/?p=639.

Home entertainment enthusiasts often have computers hooked up to their home theaters. If this is the case, they might install TV tuner cards. These cards can accept the signal from a cable or satellite provider or an over-the-air (OTA) antenna and then send it back out to the TV or other devices in the home theater. Some TV tuners also act as capture cards, meaning that they can capture the signal and record TV programs. Many come with a remote control (and IR blaster) so that the computer can be controlled in the same manner as a TV.

The purpose of all this is to record shows onto the computer and basically use the computer as a digital video recorder (DVR), among other things. By using programs such as Windows Media Center (WMC) and Kodi, users can control their TV experience. However, according to Microsoft, Windows 8.1 is the last OS that will support WMC.

TV tuner cards are available with PCI Express, PCI, ExpressCard and Mini PCIe (for laptops), and USB interfaces. TV tuners often have RG-6 connectors for cable in and antenna. Make sure you connect to the right one!

An HTPC is often also used as a home server PC because most of the requirements are the same.

Gaming PC

Now we get to the core of it: Custom computing is taken to extremes when it comes to gaming. Gaming PCs require almost all the resources mentioned previously: a powerful, multicore CPU; lots of fast RAM; one or more SSDs (SATA Express or PCI Express); advanced cooling methods (liquid cooling if you want to be serious); a high-end video card and specialized GPU; an above average, high-definition sound card; a big monitor that supports high resolutions and refresh rates; plus a fast network adapter and strong Internet connection (and mad skills). This all creates a computer that is expensive and requires care and maintenance to keep it running in perfect form. For the person who is not satisfied with gaming consoles, this is the path to take.

> **ExamAlert**
>
> A gaming PC requires a multicore CPU, high-end video with specialized GPU, a high-definition sound card, and high-end cooling.

Games are some of the most powerful applications available. If even just one of these elements is missing from a gaming system, it could easily ruin the experience. The video card is a huge component of this equation. Gamers are always looking to push the envelope for video performance by increasing the number of frames per second (frames/s or fps) that the video card sends to the monitor. One of the ways to improve the video subsystem is to employ multiple video cards. It's possible to take video to the next level by incorporating Nvidia's Scalable Link Interface, known simply as SLI (previously Scan Line Interleave) or AMD's CrossFire. A computer that uses one of these technologies has two (or more) identical video cards that work together for greater performance and higher resolution. The compatible cards are bridged together to essentially work as one unit. It is important to have a compatible motherboard and ample cooling when attempting this type of configuration. Currently, this is done with two or more PCI Express video cards (x16/version 3) and is most commonly found in gaming rigs, but you might find it in other PCs as well (such as video editing or CAD/CAM workstations). Because some motherboards come with only one PCIe x16 slot for video, a gaming system needs a more advanced motherboard: one with at least two PCIe x16 slots to accomplish SLI.

Cram Quiz

Answer these questions. The answers follow the last question. If you cannot answer these questions correctly, consider reading this section again until you can.

220-901 Questions

1. Which of the following is the best type of custom computer for use with Pro Tools?

   - ○ **A.** CAD/CAM workstation
   - ○ **B.** Audio/Video Workstation
   - ○ **C.** Gaming PC
   - ○ **D.** HTPC

2. What do CAD/CAM workstations require most?

   - ○ **A.** Liquid cooling and RAM
   - ○ **B.** TV tuner and silent hard drive
   - ○ **C.** Surround sound card and specialized GPU
   - ○ **D.** Powerful CPU and RAM

3. Your organization needs to run Windows in a virtual environment. The OS is expected to require a huge amount of resources for a powerful application it will run. What should you install Windows to?

   - ○ **A.** Type 2 hypervisor
   - ○ **B.** Gaming PC
   - ○ **C.** Type 1 hypervisor
   - ○ **D.** Thin client

4. What are some of the elements of a home server PC? (Select the two best answers.)

   - ○ **A.** Liquid cooling
   - ○ **B.** Fast network adapter
   - ○ **C.** The best CPU
   - ○ **D.** RAID array
   - ○ **E.** Gamepad

5. You just set up an HTPC. However, the Windows Media Center live TV option is not working. All connections are plugged in and all the other portions of Windows Media Center work. What is the most likely cause of the problem?

- ○ **A.** The coax cable is plugged into the antenna port.
- ○ **B.** Media Center needs to be reinstalled.
- ○ **C.** Windows libraries are malfunctioning.
- ○ **D.** The computer overheated.

Cram Quiz Answers

220-901 Answers

1. **B.** The audio/video workstation is the type of custom computer that would use Pro Tools, Logic Pro, and other music and video editing programs.

2. **D.** A CAD/CAM workstation most requires a powerful CPU and RAM. Liquid cooling, a surround sound card, and a specialized GPU are required by gaming PCs. TV tuners and silent hard drives are needed by HTPCs.

3. **C.** If the virtual operating system needs a lot of resources, the best bet is a "bare metal" type 1 hypervisor. Type 2 hypervisors run on top of an operating system and therefore are not as efficient with resources. Gaming PCs have lots of resources but are not meant to run virtual environments. Thin clients have the least amount of resources.

4. **B and D.** Home server PCs require a fast network adapter for the quick transfer of files over the network and a RAID array to offer fast and reliable access to data.

5. **A.** If everything is working except for the live TV option, then the coax cable is probably plugged into the antenna port instead of the cable in port of the TV tuner card. This is also a common mistake on set-top boxes.

CHAPTER 14

Printers

This chapter covers the following A+ exam topics:

▶ Printer Types and Technologies

▶ Installing, Configuring, and Troubleshooting Printers

You can find a master list of A+ exam topics in the "Introduction."

This chapter covers CompTIA A+ 220-901 objectives 1.13, 1.14, 1.15, and 4.6.

Printers are the number two output device, behind video displays. Their main purpose is to output paper versions of what you see on the computer screen. Many printers connect via USB, but you will also encounter printers that connect directly to the network (be it wired or wirelessly)—and on the rare occasion, you might encounter printers that connect via infrared or to serial or parallel ports. Some printers also act as fax machines, copiers, and scanners; these are known as multifunction devices or multifunction printers (MFPs).

Generally, the different versions of Windows behave the same when it comes to printing. So whenever one operating system is mentioned in this chapter, the same applies to the other operating systems, unless otherwise stated.

This chapter is broken into two sections: printer types and technologies, and installing, configuring, and troubleshooting printers.

Printer Types and Technologies

Businesses utilize several types of printers. The most common business-oriented printer is the laser printer. However, inkjet printers are more prevalent in the home due to their lower cost and their capability to print in color with excellent resolution. A technician might also encounter thermal and impact printers. Some printers connect directly to a computer; others connect to the network or to a print server. This section describes the four main types of printers and how they function; it also discusses the differences between local and network printers.

Types of Printers

Each type of printer has its own characteristics that affect how a technician installs, configures, and troubleshoots them. The most common type of printer used at a business is the laser printer; this type of printer also happens to be the most complicated and difficult to troubleshoot.

Laser Printers

Laser printers can produce high-quality text and graphics on cut sheets of paper; printers that print to individual pieces of paper are known as *page printers*. The bulk of laser printers print in black, but there are also color laser printers (which, of course, are more expensive). They are called laser printers because inside the printer is a laser beam that projects an image of the item to be printed onto an electrically charged drum; this image is later transferred to the paper. Text and images that are shown on paper are created from electrically charged toner, which is a type of powder stored in a replaceable toner cartridge. The type of toner used can vary from one brand to the next, but they all work essentially the same way.

Known also as a photoelectric or photosensitive drum, the laser printer drum is at the center of the whole laser printing process, but there are a couple of other important components, including the primary corona wire, transfer corona wire, fusing assembly, and of course, the laser itself. These components are shown in Figure 14.1.

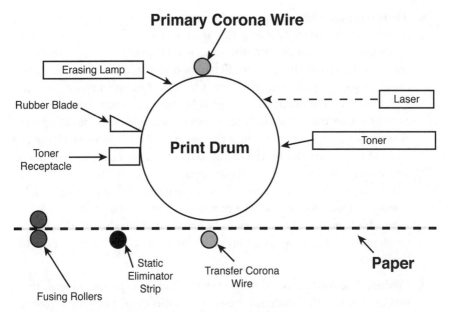

FIGURE 14.1   **Components involved in the laser printing process**

The laser printing process that a laser printer goes through is sometimes referred to as an imaging process. Knowledge of this process can help you when it comes time to troubleshoot a laser printer.

The following list describes the typical laser printing process:

1. **Processing:** The text or image to be printed is sent to the printer, where a processor recalculates it and stores it in RAM while the printer readies itself for the ordeal of laser printing! Note that additional processing may be done at the local computer that initiated the printing.

2. **Charging:** Also known as conditioning. A negative charge is applied to the drum by the primary corona wire, which is powered by a high-voltage power supply within the printer.

3. **Exposing:** Also known as writing. The laser is activated and "writes" to the drum as it spins. Where the laser hits the drum, it dissipates the negative charge toward the center of the drum that is grounded. The "exposed" areas of the drum now have a lesser negative charge. (By the way, the drum is also known as an imaging drum.)

4. **Developing:** The surface of the drum that was previously exposed to the laser is now applied with negatively charged toner. This toner has a higher charge than the areas of the drum that were written to.

5. **Transferring:** The toner, and therefore the text or image, is transferred to paper as the drum rolls over it. The movement of the paper is assisted by pickup rollers (for feeding the paper) and transfer rollers (to move it through the rest of the printer). Separation pads are used to make sure only one page is picked up at a time. On many laser printers, the paper slides between the drum and a positively charged corona wire (known as the transfer corona wire). The transfer corona wire applies the positive charge to the paper. Because the paper now has a positive charge, and the toner particles on the drum have a negative charge, the toner is attracted to the paper. (For voltages, opposites attract.) In many printers the paper passes by a static elimination device (often a strip), which removes excess charge from the paper. Some color laser printers use a transfer belt to apply the various layers of colors to the paper. Some printers use a duplexing assembly that allows the paper to be printed on both sides.

6. **Fusing:** The toner is fused to the paper. The paper passes through the fusing assembly that includes pressurized rollers and a heating element that can reach approximately 400 degrees F (or about 200 degrees C).

7. **Cleaning:** A rubber blade removes excess toner from the drum as it spins. An erasing lamp removes any leftover charge on the drum, bringing it to zero volts. The printer is now ready for another print job.

ExamAlert

Know the steps of the laser printing process (also known as an imaging process).

ExamAlert

Although specific laser printer component names differ by manufacturer, CompTIA lists the following laser printer components that you should be familiar with for the 901 exam:

Imaging drum, fuser assembly, transfer belt, transfer roller, pickup rollers, separation pads, duplexing assembly.

In some laser printers, the drum, laser, and primary corona wire are contained within the toner cartridge. Issues that are caused by these components can usually be fixed just by replacing the toner cartridge.

> **Note**
>
> Toner cartridges are replaceable; they are known as *consumables*. Whatever material it is that actually prints onto paper is usually considered a consumable, regardless of the type of printer.

Laser printers have some advantages over other printers:

► **Speed:** A laser printer can print anywhere from 10 to 100 pages per minute (ppm), depending on the model and whether it is a color or black-and-white laser printer.

► **Print quality:** The laser printer commonly prints at 600 dots per inch (DPI), which is considered letter quality, but 1,200 DPI and 2,400 DPI resolution printers are also available.

> **ExamAlert**
>
> Of all printer types, the laser printer is considered to have the lowest cost per page, making it an excellent long-term printer choice for businesses.

Inkjet Printers

Inkjet printers are common in small offices, home offices, and for personal use. They can print documents but more commonly print photographs and graphical information in color; most of the time, they connect to the computer by way of USB or Wi-Fi.

The inkjet printer works by propelling ink onto various sizes of paper. Many inkjets store ink in multiple ink cartridges that are consumable; they have to be replaced when empty. Some inkjet printers stop operating if just one of the ink cartridges is empty. Two common types of inkjet printers are the thermal inkjet and the piezoelectric inkjet:

► **Thermal inkjets:** These account for the bulk of consumer inkjets and are the more recognizable type of inkjet printer. To move the ink to the paper, heat is sent through the ink cartridge, forming a bubble (known as the thermal bubble) that pushes the ink onto the paper; immediately afterward, another charge of ink is readied. The reservoir of ink is within the ink cartridge; this is where the heat transfer occurs. HP and Canon develop many models of thermal inkjet printers. Don't confuse thermal inkjets with thermal printers.

▶ **Piezoelectric inkjets:** These account for the bulk of commercial ink-jets. The printing processes within a piezoelectric inkjet and a thermal inkjet are similar; however, the piezo inkjet applies current to the ink material, causing it to change shape and size, forcing the ink onto the paper. The reservoir of ink is in another area outside of where the current is applied. This process enables longer print head life as compared to thermal inkjets. Epson develops many models of piezoelectric ink-jet printers. Piezoelectric inkjets can also be found in manufacturing assembly lines.

The inkjet print process is fairly simple:

1. The paper or other media is pulled or moved into position by a roller and feeder mechanism or it's moved into position by an assembly line's conveyor belt (as with some piezoelectric inkjets).

2. The print head, located on a mechanical arm, moves across the paper, assisted by a carriage and belt system. The print head delivers black and colored ink from the ink cartridges as directed by the print driver.

3. At the end of the line, the paper or media is advanced and the print head either reverses direction and continues to print (often referred to as Hi-Speed mode) or returns to the left margin before printing continues. In printers that allow for duplexing, a duplexing assembly refeeds the paper back into the printer for printing on the other side.

4. After the page is completed, the paper or other media is ejected.

> **ExamAlert**
>
> Know that inkjet printer components include ink cartridge, print head, roller, feeder, duplexing assembly, carriage, and belt.

Thermal Printers

Thermal printers produce text and images by heating specially coated thermal paper. It is typical to see thermal printers used in point-of-sale (POS) systems, gas station pumps, and so on. Thermal printers consist of the following parts:

▶ **Thermal head:** This generates the heat and takes care of printing to the paper.

▶ **Platen:** This is the rubber roller that feeds the paper past the print head.

▶ **Spring:** This applies pressure to the print head, which brings the print head into contact with the paper.

▶ **Circuit board:** This controls the mechanism that moves the print head.

To print, thermal paper is inserted between the thermal head and the platen. The printer sends current to the thermal head, which, in turn, generates heat. The heat activates the thermo-sensitive coloring layer of the thermal paper, which becomes the image.

Impact Printers

Impact printers use force to transfer ink to paper (for example, a print head striking a ribbon with paper directly behind it—similar to a typewriter). This type of printer is somewhat deprecated although certain environments might still use it: auto repair centers, warehouses, accounting departments, and so on.

One type of impact printer, the daisy wheel, utilizes a wheel with many petals, each of which has a letter form (an actual letter) at the tip of the petal. These strike against the ribbon, impressing ink upon the paper that is situated behind the ribbon. But by far the most common type of impact printer is the dot matrix.

Dot-matrix printers are also known as line printers because they print text one line at a time and can keep printing over a long roll of paper, as opposed to page printers that print to cut sheets of paper. The paper is fed into the printer using a tractor-feed mechanism—many dot-matrix printers use paper that has an extra perforated space with holes on each side that allow the paper to be fed into the printer. Dot-matrix printers use a matrix of pins that work together to create characters, instead of using a form letter. The print head that contains these pins strikes the ribbon that, in turn, places the ink on the paper. Print heads come with either 9 pins or 24 pins; the 24-pin version offers better quality, known as *near letter quality* (NLQ). Dot-matrix printers are loud and slow but are cheap to maintain.

Local Versus Network Printers

A local printer is one that connects directly to a computer, normally by USB, or on rare occasions, by RS-232 serial (DB9M) or parallel (DB25F) connections. When a user works at a computer, that computer is considered to be the local computer. So, when a printer is connected to that computer, it is known as the local printer.

A network printer is one that connects directly to the network (usually Ethernet) or to a print server device. Network printers are shared by more than one user on the computer network. Usually, network printers are given an IP address and become yet another *host* on the network. If the printer connects directly to the network, it is usually by way of a built-in RJ45 port on the printer, just as a computer's network card connects to the network. A print server could be a computer or smaller black box device. Many small office/home office (SOHO) routers offer print server capabilities. In this case, the printer connects via USB to the print server/router and a special piece of software is installed on any client computers that want to print to that printer.

Network printing can also be accomplished wirelessly on most of today's printers. This can be done via Wi-Fi (802.11 a, b, g, n, and ac) or by Bluetooth. The former is more common in a wireless LAN, where everything connects to a wireless access point—this is referred to as infrastructure mode. The latter is more common with mobile devices and, in this case, no wireless access point exists—also known as ad hoc mode. Of course, there is crossover between the two.

Less commonly, printers might also connect wirelessly using infrared technology. When it comes to communications, infrared has the shortest range, Bluetooth has a better range, and Wi-Fi offers the best range.

Then there is cloud-based printing. It is altogether possible today to harness the power of the cloud to print remotely. You might have a document you need printed to a printer in a network in another city. If your organization has implemented a cloud-based solution, you can do this simply by selecting the printer in a drop-down menu. We'll discuss cloud-based technologies more in Chapter 15, "Computer Networking Part I."

Regardless of whether a printer is local, on the network, or across the cloud, it can be controlled by an operating system such as Windows, which is described in the following section.

Cram Quiz

Answer these questions. The answers follow the last question. If you cannot answer these questions correctly, consider reading this section again until you can.

220-901 Questions

1. Which type of printer uses a photoelectric drum?

    ○ **A.** Impact

    ○ **B.** Dot-matrix

    ○ **C.** Laser

    ○ **D.** Inkjet

2. During which step of the laser printing/imaging process is the transfer corona wire involved?

    ○ **A.** Developing

    ○ **B.** Transferring

    ○ **C.** Fusing

    ○ **D.** Cleaning

3. Which stage of the laser printing/imaging process involves extreme heat?

    ○ **A.** Fusing

    ○ **B.** Transferring

    ○ **C.** Exposing

    ○ **D.** Writing

4. What are the two most common types of consumer-based printers? (Select the two best answers.)

    ○ **A.** Thermal printer

    ○ **B.** Laser printer

    ○ **C.** Thermal inkjet printer

    ○ **D.** Impact printer

5. What is the rubber roller that feeds the paper past the print head in thermal printers known as?

    ○ **A.** HVPS

    ○ **B.** Cartridge

    ○ **C.** Spring

    ○ **D.** Platen

6. What is a common number of pins in a dot-matrix printer's print head?

  ○ **A.** 40

  ○ **B.** 24

  ○ **C.** 8

  ○ **D.** 84

7. Which represents the proper order of the laser printing/imaging process?

  ○ **A.** Processing, charging, developing, exposing, fusing, transferring, cleaning

  ○ **B.** Developing, processing, charging, exposing, transferring, fusing, cleaning

  ○ **C.** Charging, exposing, developing, processing, transferring, fusing, cleaning

  ○ **D.** Processing, charging, exposing, developing, transferring, fusing, cleaning

8. Which of the following are associated with inkjet printers?

  ○ **A.** Imaging drum, fuser assembly, transfer belt, transfer roller, pickup rollers, separate pads, duplexing assembly

  ○ **B.** Ink cartridge, print head, roller, feeder, duplexing assembly, carriage and belt

  ○ **C.** Feed assembly, thermal heating unit, thermal paper

  ○ **D.** Print head, ribbon, tractor feed, impact paper

Cram Quiz Answers

220-901 Answers

1. **C.** The laser printer is the only type of printer that uses a photoelectric drum.

2. **B.** The transfer corona wire gets involved in the laser printing/imaging process during the transferring step.

3. **A.** The fusing step uses heat (up to 400 degrees Fahrenheit/200 degrees Celsius) and pressure to fuse the toner permanently to the paper.

4. **B and C.** The laser printer and the thermal inkjet printer are the most common types of printers used in the consumer market today. Don't confuse a thermal inkjet printer (often simply referred to as an inkjet printer) with a thermal printer.

5. **D.** The platen is the rubber roller that feeds the paper past the print head in thermal printers. The spring applies pressure to the print head, which brings the print head into contact with the paper.

6. **B.** Dot-matrix printer print heads usually have 24 pins or 9 pins.

7. **D.** The proper order of the laser printing/imaging process is processing, charging, exposing, developing, transferring, fusing, cleaning.

8. **B.** Inkjet printer components include ink cartridge, print head, roller, feeder, duplexing assembly, carriage, and belt. Imaging drum, fuser assembly, transfer belt, transfer roller, pickup rollers, separate pads, and duplexing assembly are associated with laser printers. Feed assembly, thermal heating unit, and thermal paper are associated with thermal printers. Print head, ribbon, tractor feed, and impact paper are associated with impact printers.

Installing, Configuring, and Troubleshooting Printers

Physically installing printers and installing device drivers is usually straightforward, but the configuration of printers in Windows is more complex because so many configurable options exist. As always, troubleshooting should be approached from a logical standpoint. This section covers the installation, configuration, and troubleshooting of printers.

Printer Installation and Drivers

When installing printers, focus on several things:

▶ **Compatibility:** Make sure that the printer is compatible with the version of Windows that runs on the computer that controls the printer. Check the Windows compatibility lists to verify this. If the printer is to connect to the network, make sure that it has the right type of compatible network adapter to do so.

▶ **Installing printer drivers:** Generally, the proper procedure is to install the printer driver to Windows before physically connecting the printer. However, if the driver already exists on the computer, the printer can simply be connected. Usually, the best bet is to use the driver that came on the disc with the printer or download the latest driver from the manufacturer's website. Verify whether the driver to be installed is the right one based on the version and edition of the operating system (for example, 32-bit or 64-bit versions of Windows, and Windows 8 versus Windows 7). Printer drivers are installed in a similar fashion to other drivers described in this book; it is performed in the Devices and Printers section of the Control Panel. Any current printers should be listed. From there, right-click anywhere in the work area and select "Add..." (the text will vary according to the version of Windows you are using).

▶ **Connecting the device:** In general, devices connecting via USB can be connected without turning the computer off. (That is, they are hot-swappable.) However, devices that connect to older parallel ports or serial ports require the computer to be shut down first. Plug the USB or other connector cable into the computer first, and then connect the printer to an AC outlet. (It's recommended to use a surge protector for printers but it is *not* recommended to use a UPS for a laser printer due to the high draw of the laser printer.) Verify that the device turns on.

▶ **Calibrating the printer:** Color laser printers, inkjet printers, and multifunction printers might need to be calibrated before use. This involves aligning the printing mechanism to the paper and verifying color output. Usually the software that accompanies the printer guides a user through this process. In some cases, these calibration tests can be done via the small display on the printer.

▶ **Testing the printer:** First, test the printer by printing a test page in Windows. This is also done from the Devices and Printers window in Windows 8 and 7 (in Windows Vista, use the Printers window). Right-click the printer, select Printer Properties, and then click the Print Test Page button on the General tab. The resulting page should show the operating system the local computer runs and various other configuration and driver information. If the page can be read properly and the Windows logo is using the correct colors, the test passed. Some printers offer a test page option on the display of the printer as well. After a test page has been printed, it might be wise to try printing within the most used applications as well, just to make sure they work properly. Some applications might behave differently, and some configurations of printers in Windows might cause a particular application to have print failures.

Configuring Printers

Configuration of printers can be done in one of three places. The first is the small display that might be included on a printer; these are more common on laser printers. These menu-driven displays are usually user-friendly and intuitive. The second is within a printer's web interface (if it is a network printer); this is often accessed through a web browser. The third—and the one that I'd like to focus on in this section—is within Windows, specifically by double-clicking the printer icon within the Devices and Printers window (again, in Vista, use Printers) and by accessing the appropriate properties or preferences page of the printer. To open a printer, simply double-click it. To manage its properties and preferences, right-click the printer in question and select Printer properties or select Printer preferences. If you work with printers often, consider placing a shortcut to the printer or printers on the desktop, Quick Launch, or pin it to the taskbar. Several items can be configured by double-clicking the printer and by using the Printer Properties window, including managing print jobs, setting the priority of the printer, configuring the print spooler, and managing permissions.

Basic Printer Configuration Settings

A typical print job is simple—one printed page, printed on one side, on 8 1/2 by 11-inch paper in portrait mode, and at the standard 600 DPI resolution. For example, you might print a typical document (such as a resume) this way. However, there are many occasions where the typical settings are not enough. There are four basic printer configuration settings you should know for the exams: duplexing, collating, orientation, and print quality. They are generally found in the printing preferences section. Let's briefly describe each one now.

First is duplexing. This means printing on both sides of the paper. Some organizations require this (for most print jobs), establishing policies in their efforts to reduce paper consumption. However, most printers are not set to duplex by default. This needs to be configured in the printer's properties page in Windows. This might simply be called "print on both sides." Once enabled, you might also see this on the main print screen when you go to perform a print job—it might be called "manual duplex."

Next is collating. If you print a single job, collating is not an issue. But it's when you print multiple copies of the same job that collating might become necessary. Historically, multiple copies of the same print job would print out all of page 1, then all of page 2, then all of page 3, and so on. It was up to the user to manually arrange, or collate, these pages. However, as printers became more sophisticated, they were equipped with the processing power to collate the jobs, sorting them as page 1, page 2, page 3, and so on, and then moving on to the next copy of the entire job. This, of course, saves a lot of time for the user. Some printers are set this way by default. Others have to be configured to do so. An example of this configuration is shown in Figure 14.2. This setting is often found in the advanced section of the printing preferences. The figure shows Copy Count set to 5 and that collating is enabled. Once it is enabled, you can also select it from the main print screen when you go to print a document.

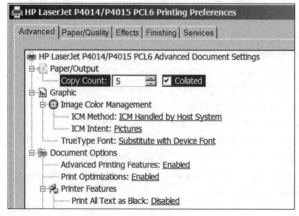

FIGURE 14.2 Collating on a typical printer

Then we have orientation. This is the method of positioning a printed page and is based on whether the page is going to be viewed vertically (portrait) or horizontally (landscape). This can be set permanently from the printer preferences page, but it can also be set manually when you go to print a single document. Often, it will be found in the "layout" section. Most documents are printed in portrait mode (such as a report or a resume done in a word processor), but sometimes you need to print a spreadsheet or a slide presentation, which is best done in landscape mode.

Finally, we have print quality. This is the print resolution, as measured in DPI. 600 DPI or higher is considered to be letter quality and acceptable as a professional document. But you might want an even better quality (1200 or 2400 DPI), especially if your document includes graphics. This can usually be configured for a default number of DPI within the advanced section of the printing preferences, but it can also be configured from the print window, often using more generic terms (such as draft, normal, and best).

Take a look at your printing preferences, printer properties pages, and the main print screen (when you go to print a document) and view the four configuration settings we just discussed. Even if you don't have a printer, you can set up a false or "faux" printer on your system by adding the printer in the Devices and Printers window in the Control Panel. Typically, I suggest selecting any one of the newer HP laser printers from the list as a faux printer. You can then access its printer properties just like you would on a printer that is actually installed to the computer or network.

ExamAlert

Know the four printer configuration settings: duplex, collate, orientation, and quality.

Managing Printers and Print Jobs

To manage a printer or an individual print job, just double-click the printer to which the job was sent. A window similar to Figure 14.3 should display on the monitor.

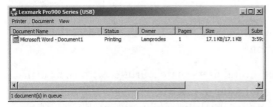

FIGURE 14.3   **A typical printer window showing one print job**

Figure 14.3 shows that one print job, called Document1, is listed. The job went to the printer properly; you can tell because it says Printing under the Status column. Any other message would mean that the job was either spooled, queued, stopped, or has failed. These jobs can be paused, restarted, or stopped completely if they are not printing properly. This can be done by right-clicking on the job in the window or by clicking the Document menu. Keep in mind that larger documents take longer to spool before they start printing. (*Spooling* is the page-by-page processing done at the local system before the print job goes to the printer. We'll discuss that topic in a little bit.) In addition to this, all documents can be paused or canceled or the entire printer can be taken offline from the Printer menu. Use these tools to troubleshoot any printing issues or *misqueues*.

Printer Priority

Printer priority can be configured within the Advanced tab of a printer's Properties page, as shown in Figure 14.4.

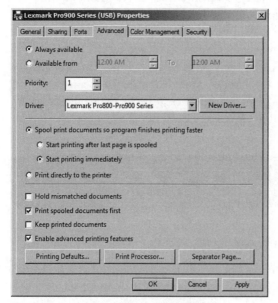

FIGURE 14.4 **Printer priority and spooling**

The priority of a printer can be configured from 1 to 99; 99 being the highest. This is useful in two situations:

▶ **Scenario 1:** Let's say that several users share a printer with their manager. Chances are, you would want to give the manager the highest priority when it comes to print jobs. It is possible to install two software printers in Windows that point to the same physical printer. The first software printer could be given a higher priority (say, 99), a share name such as "manager," and with permissions that allow access only by the manager. The second software printer could be given a lower priority (say, 50) and use a share name such as "users." After the client computers are configured properly to access the correct printers, the manager's print jobs would always get precedence over other print jobs on the shared physical printer.

▶ **Scenario 2:** Imagine that there are two or more physical printers that have been combined to create a printer pool. Each printer in the pool can be given a different priority. One printer in the pool is often set aside for managers and executives and with a higher priority than the others.

Print Spooling

Whenever a job goes to print, there are three options:

▶ **Print directly to the printer:** This means that the print job goes right to the printer without any delays. This relies solely on the amount of memory in the printer (which can be increased, just like with computers). Of course, if the print job is larger than the amount of RAM in the printer, the job will probably fail. Usually a better solution is to spool the document.

▶ **Start printing immediately:** This is the first of two spooling options. When this setting is selected, one page at a time of the document will be *spooled* to the hard drive. When an entire page has been spooled, it is sent to the printer for printing. This repeats until all the pages of the document have been spooled and ultimately printed. This is the default setting in Windows and is usually the best option because it prints faster than other spooling options. An example of this is shown in Figure 14.4.

▶ **Start printing after last page is spooled:** This means that the entire document will be spooled to the hard drive and then pages are sent to the printer for printing. This is usually slower than Start Printing Immediately but might have fewer issues, such as stalls or other printing failures.

The print spooler is controlled by the Print Spooler service. This service processes print requests and sends them to the printer. Not only can you experience issues in which print jobs or printers stop working, the Print Spooler service also can fail. This service can be started, stopped, and restarted from the GUI and from the Command Prompt:

▶ **Adjusting the Print Spooler service in Computer Management:** Open the Computer Management console window, click the + sign to expand Services and Applications, and then click Services. In the right window pane, scroll until you find the Print Spooler service. To start a stopped service, right-click it and click Start. Alternatively, you can click the Start button or other buttons on the toolbar.

▶ **Adjusting the Print Spooler service in Task Manager:** Open Task Manager, right-click the taskbar, and then click Start Task Manager (or press Ctrl+Shift+Esc). Under the Services tab, right-click the Print Spooler service and select Start, Stop, or Restart service (the options vary according to your OS version).

▶ **Adjusting the Print Spooler service in the Command Prompt:** When the Command Prompt is open (in elevated mode), you can start the Print Spooler service by typing `net start spooler`. Typing `net stop spooler` stops the service.

> **ExamAlert**
>
> Know how to configure spooling and how to start and stop the Print Spooler service within Computer Management, Task Manager, and in the Command Prompt.

Printer Pooling

Printer pooling takes multiple separate printers and combines them to form a team of printers that works together to complete print jobs as quickly as possible. This can be accomplished from the Ports tab of the printer's Properties window. Normally a printer will be shown next to the port it connects to. To add a second installed printer to the pool, click Enable printer pooling and then click the check mark next to the other printer listed, as shown in Figure 14.5.

As you can see in Figure 14.5, the printer pooling option has been selected and a second printer (HP LaserJet) has been selected, adding it to the pool along with the Lexmark Pro900 printer. At this point, any jobs sent to the first printer that can't be processed right away will be transferred to the second printer. This is a one-way printer pool; two-way printer pools are also possible but aren't used as often. Quite often, printer pools consist of all identical printers.

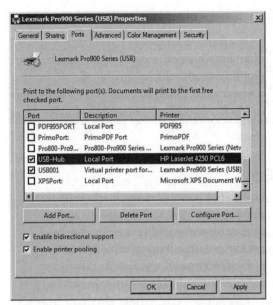

FIGURE 14.5   **Enabling the printer pooling option**

> **Note**
>
> Remote printers can be connected to and controlled from the Ports tab. This can be done by adding a port and then entering the IP address of the printer to be controlled or entering the name of the computer that the remote printer connects to.

Sharing Printers and Managing Permissions

A networked printer must first be shared before other users can send print jobs to it. There are two steps involved in sharing printers in Windows. First, printer sharing in general must be enabled. To enable Printer Sharing in Windows, go to Control Panel > All Control Panel Items > Network and Sharing Center. Then click the Change Advanced Sharing Settings link. Click the down arrow for your network type and then select the radio button labeled Turn on File and Printer Sharing.

Next, the individual printer needs to be shared. This can be done in the Sharing tab of the printer's properties window. Click the Share This Printer radio button and give the printer a share name. Note that the share name does not need to be the same as the printer name. Click OK, and the printer should show up as shared within the Printers window. We'll discuss sharing in more depth in the networking chapters (Chapters 15 and 16).

Permissions can be set for a printer in the Security tab of the printer's Properties window. Users and groups can be added in this window, and the appropriate permission can be assigned, including Print, Manage Printers, and Manage Documents. Regular users normally are assigned the Print permission, whereas administrators get all permissions, enabling them to pause the printer or cancel all documents (Manage Printers) and pause, cancel, and restart individual documents. For more information on permissions, see Chapter 17 "Security."

Selecting a Separator Page

Separator pages help users to find the start and end points of their print jobs. The separator page might be printed as a blank piece of paper or with the username and title of the document to be printed. This can be added from the Advanced tab by clicking the Separator Page button. From there, click the Browse button; this shows the System32 folder by default. Initially four separator pages are in this folder, the most common of which are pcl.sep and pscript.sep. However, some companies opt to use a custom separator page. Click the appropriate separator page, click Open, and then click OK. The separator page will be added to the appropriate documents.

> **Note**
>
> There are a lot of other settings in the printer Properties window. Spend some time looking through the various tabs and configurations to better prepare for the exam.

Virtual Printing

Let's go beyond the physical printer and briefly discuss virtual printing. Virtual printing is when a document, image, or web page is "printed" to a file format and stored on the computer instead of being printed on paper at a printer. There are several reasons to do this, including accessibility, compatibility, storage of documents to be printed later, and so on. There are four types of virtual printing you should know for the exam: print to file, print to XPS, print to PDF, and print to image. Let's begin with the oldest type—and a great fallback solution: print to file.

Print to File

Let's say that you finish creating a document at your home office on a PC but you don't have a printer to print the document to and you *do* want to print the document so you can submit it to someone at work. Let's also imagine that your organization's main office has a couple of printers but none of the computers have the application you use, and purchasing another license for that application is too expensive. One possible solution is to print to file, which stores the document as a printable file that can then be transported by flash drive or other means to a computer at the main workplace and then printed from there.

Let's say this is a Microsoft Word document. You could select Print, as you normally would, and then instead of selecting a particular printer, you could select the Print to File checkbox. This then saves the file as a .prn file to be stored as you wish and can be printed from later. When you arrive at your workplace, you can print the file from the Command Prompt using the following sample syntax:

```
copy x:\filename.prn \\computername\printersharename
```

What does that mean? Well, you need to know several bits of information. First, you need to know the drive letter of the flash drive (or other storage medium) where the file is stored. I used "x:" as a variable, but it could be any letter. We'll say it's a flash drive that is using the F: drive letter. Next, you need to know the filename—we'll say it's "printjob1." Then you need the name of the computer that the printer is connected to (or controlled by). We'll say the printer is connected to a computer named "workstation3." Finally, you need to know the share name of the printer. (See the previous section on printer sharing.) Let's say the share name is "printer1." Now we have all the information we need and the syntax in this scenario would be

```
copy f:\printjob1.prn \\workstation3\printer1
```

> **Note**
>
> If the printer is connected directly to the network, you can forgo the computername\printersharename and connect directly to the printer name or, better yet, its IP address (for example, \\192.168.1.150).

That "copies" the print job to the printer and prints it out to the best of its ability. And I say "best" because you might encounter several issues with print-to-file technology, including print failures, incorrect printing, ASCII printing, and so on. The technology is not without its quirks. That's why other, newer technologies are often selected, such as PDFing and printing to XPS.

Print to XPS

Windows incorporates the XML Paper Specification (XPS) print path. The XPS spooler is meant to replace the standard Enhanced Metafile print spooler that Windows has used for years. XPS provides improved color and graphics support, support for the CMYK colorspace, and reduces the need for color-space conversion.

This is implemented as the Microsoft XPS Document Writer that can be found in Control Panel > Devices and Printers. A document created within any application in Windows can be saved as an .xps file to be later viewed on any computer that supports XPS. It can also be printed from any computer that supports XPS but prints with proper fidelity only when the computer has an XPS-compliant printer. If you do not have an XPS printer, the functionality might need to be turned on within the Windows Features utility (a link that can be found in Control Panel > All Control Panel Items > Programs and Features).

In most cases, this solution will replace "print to file," but it is good to have print to file as a backup in case XPS fails or is not running on the computer in question.

Print to PDF

To make a document universally readable, you have several options. One of the most common is to convert it into a Portable Document Format (PDF), also known as "print to PDF." The most common PDF-making software is Adobe Acrobat (which is a paid program) and Adobe also makes the most common PDF reader software (Adobe Acrobat Reader, which is free). However, there are other versions of freely available PDF making and reading software available on the Internet.

They all work in the same manner: as a virtual printer. If you want to convert a document into a PDF, go to Print and then select the PDF converter from the printers list. That then creates a file with a .pdf extension that can be distributed how you wish. As long as the target user has a PDF reading program, he will be able to view the document without any need for the original program that the document was written on.

Print to Image

It is also possible to capture a document, web page, or even a window (or region) of the operating system as an image file. A simple example of this print-to-image technology can be found on any Windows computer simply by using the Print Screen button on the keyboard. The entire screen capture can then be pasted into the appropriate program. Going beyond this, screen capturing programs such as The Snipping Tool (included in Windows 7 and 8) and Snagit can be used to capture the entire screen, an individual window, a region of the screen, or even a scrolling web page as an image file. Programs such as this enable you to save the file as a .jpg, .gif, .tif, .png, and so on—just about any one of the commonly used graphic file extensions. These screen captures are also often referred to as screenshots. Most of the Windows screen captures you see in this book were produced with Snagit (free trial version is available on the TechSmith website). So it works great for instructional purposes and for documentation. However, you might also need to capture a particular set of data and send that final captured image to engineers, designers, marketers, and so on—anyone who does not have the program that you use installed on their computer.

ExamAlert

Know the four types of virtual printing: Print to file, print to XPS, print to PDF, and print to image. Perform each type of virtual printing on your own computer.

Troubleshooting Printers

Sometimes companies hire paid consultants to manage all their printers and copiers, and sometimes the care of these devices is the job of the in-house IT technician. Either way, it is a good idea to know some of the basic issues that can occur with printers and how to troubleshoot them. Table 14.1 describes some of these issues and possible solutions. Some of these issues (for example, paper jams and resulting error codes) might be displayed on a printer's LCD.

TABLE 14.1 **Printer Problems and Solutions**

Printer Issue	Possible Solution
Paper jams or creased paper	1. Turn the printer on and off in the hopes that the printer will clear the jam. This is known as power-cycling the printer. If that doesn't work, open the printer. Turn the printer off and unplug it before doing so.
	2. Remove paper trays and inspect them for crumpled papers that can be removed by grabbing both ends of the paper firmly and pulling or rotating the rollers to remove it. In general, clear the paper path.
	3. Verify that the right paper type is in the printer. If the paper is too thin or thick, it might cause a paper jam. Also, watch for paper that has been exposed to humidity.

Printer Issue	Possible Solution
	4. Check for dirty or cracked rollers. A temporary fix for dirty rubber rollers is to use isopropyl alcohol. A permanent fix is to replace the rollers.
	5. Check whether the fusing assembly has overheated. Sometimes the printer just needs time to cool, or perhaps the printer is not in a well enough ventilated area. In uncommon cases, the fuser might have to be replaced. Be sure to unplug the printer and let the printer sit for an hour or so before doing so due to the high temperatures of the fuser. The fusing assembly can usually be removed by removing a few screws.
	6. Finally, check the entire paper path. Duplexing printers (ones that print on both sides of the paper) will have more complicated and longer paper paths, providing more chances for paper to get jammed.
Printing blank pages	1. The toner cartridge is empty or has failed. Install a new one. Toner cartridge failures could be associated with the developing and transferring stages of the laser printing process, with the developing stage being more common.
	2. The toner cartridge was installed without the sealing tape removed.
	3. The transfer corona wire has failed. If the transfer corona wire fails, there will be no positive (opposite) voltage to pull the toner to the paper. Replace the wire.
Multiple pages are fed in at once	Check whether the separation pad is getting enough traction; it might need to be cleaned. Also check whether the paper is too thin; 20 lb or heavier paper is usually recommended.
Error codes	If a specific error is shown on the printer's LCD, read it. It might tell you exactly what the error is and how to fix it (or at least what the error is). On some printers, it displays an error number. Check your printer's documentation to find out what the error means.
Out of memory error or low memory message	Check whether the user's computer is spooling documents. The setting with the least chance of this error is the Start Printing Immediately spool setting. You might also need to restart the Print Spooling service. If a user tries to print a large image, he might need to change settings in the application in which the image was made. In some cases, the printer's RAM might need to be upgraded. Whenever installing RAM to a printer, take all the same precautions you would when working on a PC.
No image on printer display	Check whether the printer is in sleep mode (or off altogether). Verify that the printer is plugged in. In rare cases, the internal connector that powers the display might be loose.

Printer Issue	Possible Solution
Vertical lines on page, streaks, smearing, toner note fused to paper	Black lines or streaks can be caused by a scratch in the laser printer drum or a dirty primary corona wire. Usually, the toner cartridge needs to be replaced. White lines could be caused by a dirty transfer corona wire; this can be cleaned or replaced. Wide white vertical lines can occur when something is stuck to the drum. Smearing can occur if the fusing assembly has failed; in this case, you might also notice toner coming off of the paper easily. If it is an inkjet, one or more ink cartridges might need to be replaced or the printer might need to be calibrated.
Garbage printout or garbled characters on paper	This can occur due to an incorrect driver. Some technicians like to try "close" drivers. This is not a good idea. Use the exact driver for the exact model of the printer that corresponds to the appropriate version of the operating system. A bad formatter board or printer interface can also be the cause of a garbage printout. These can usually be replaced easily by removing two screws and a cover.
Ghosted image	Ghosted images or blurry marks can be a sign that the drum has some kind of imperfection or is dirty. Especially if the image reappears at equal intervals. Replace the drum (or toner cartridge). Another possibility is that the fuser assembly has been damaged and needs to be replaced.
No connectivity	If there is no connectivity, check the following: ▶ The printer is plugged in to an AC outlet and is "online." ▶ The printer is securely connected to the local computer or to the network. ▶ The computer has the correct print driver installed. ▶ The printer is shared to the network. ▶ The printer has a properly configured IP address. (This can be checked on the LCD display of most networkable laser printers.) ▶ Remote computers have a proper connection over the network to the printer. ▶ The printer is set up as the default printer if necessary.
Access denied	If an Access Denied message appears on the screen while attempting to print, the user doesn't have permission to use the printer. You (or the network administrator) will have to give the user account permissions for that particular printer. This message might also be displayed when a person attempts to install a printer without the proper administrative rights.
Backed-up print queue	If your printer window shows several documents listed in the queue, but is not currently printing anything, then a document might have stalled and needs to be restarted. Also, the print spooler might need to be restarted within the Services console window, Task Manager, or in the Command Prompt.

Printer Issue	Possible Solution
Color printouts are different color than the screen	The printout will always be *slightly* different than the screen. But if the difference is more noticeable, check the ink or toner cartridges and make sure none of the colors are empty. Verify that the printer is a PostScript-capable printer that can do raster image processing (RIP). If this functionality is not built into the printer, then it might be available as a separate software solution.

In general, when working with printers, keep them clean and use printer maintenance kits. Like changing the oil in a car, printers need maintenance also. HP and other manufacturers offer maintenance kits that include items such as fusers, rollers, separation pads, and instructions on how to replace all these items. Manufacturers recommend that this maintenance be done every once in a while (for example, every 200,000 pages printed). When you finish installing a maintenance kit, be sure to reset the maintenance count. You should also have a toner vacuum available for toner spills. A can of compressed air can be helpful when you need to clean out toner from the inside of a laser printer; remember to do this outside. Vacuum any leftover residue. Printer maintenance can be broken down into the following basic categories:

▶ **Laser:** Replace toner, apply maintenance kit, calibrate, clean.

▶ **Inkjet:** Clean heads, replace cartridges, calibrate, clear jams.

▶ **Thermal:** Replace paper, clean heating element, remove debris.

▶ **Impact:** Replace ribbon, replace print head, replace paper.

When troubleshooting printers, don't forget to RTM (Read The Manual)! Most printers come with manuals, and these manuals often provide troubleshooting sections toward the end of them. In some cases, the manual will be in PDF format on the disc that accompanied the printer. Regardless of whether a manual accompanied the printer or whether it can't be found, the manufacturer will usually have the manual on its website in addition to a support system for its customers. Use it! And keep in mind that many products come with a warranty or the customer might have purchased an extended warranty. I remember one time I was troubleshooting two color-laser printers. They were only two weeks old when they failed. When the manufacturer knew the error code that was flashing on the printer's display, it didn't want to hear anything else; it simply sent out a tech the next day because the device was under warranty. To sum up, let the manufacturer help you. If it doesn't cost the company anything, it can save you a lot of time and aggravation.

Cram Quiz

Answer these questions. The answers follow the last question. If you cannot answer these questions correctly, consider reading this section again until you can.

220-901 Questions

1. When connecting a laser printer's power cable, what type of device is not recommended?

   ○ **A.** Surge protector

   ○ **B.** Line conditioner

   ○ **C.** UPS

   ○ **D.** AC outlet

2. When finished installing a new printer and print drivers, what should you do? (Select all that apply.)

   ○ **A.** Calibrate the printer.

   ○ **B.** Install the print drivers.

   ○ **C.** Check for compatibility.

   ○ **D.** Print a test page.

3. Which is the faster option for spooling documents?

   ○ **A.** Print directly to the printer.

   ○ **B.** Start printing immediately.

   ○ **C.** Start printing after the last page is spooled.

   ○ **D.** Start printing after the separator page.

4. What command turns off the print spooler?

   ○ **A.** `net disable print spooler`

   ○ **B.** `net stop print spooler`

   ○ **C.** `net restart spooler`

   ○ **D.** `net stop spooler`

5. What is it known as when two printers are joined together so that they can work as a team?

   ○ **A.** Printer pooling

   ○ **B.** Printer spooling

   ○ **C.** pscript.sep

   ○ **D.** Printer joining

6. Where would you go in Windows to enable printer sharing?

   ○ **A.** Network Connections

   ○ **B.** Network and Sharing Center

   ○ **C.** Network

   ○ **D.** My Network Places

7. How can a paper jam be resolved? (Select all that apply.)

   ○ **A.** Clear the paper path.

   ○ **B.** Use the right type of paper.

   ○ **C.** Check for damaged rollers.

   ○ **D.** Check for a damaged primary corona wire.

8. What is a possible reason for having blank pages come out of a laser printer?

   ○ **A.** Failed transfer corona wire

   ○ **B.** Failed primary corona wire

   ○ **C.** Failed fusing assembly

   ○ **D.** Damaged roller

9. What is a possible reason for having black lines on printouts?

   ○ **A.** Scratch on the laser printer drum

   ○ **B.** Damaged roller

   ○ **C.** Damaged transfer corona wire

   ○ **D.** Scratch on the fusing assembly

10. Which of the following are usually included in a laser printer maintenance kit? (Select the two best answers.)

   ○ **A.** Rollers

   ○ **B.** Image drum

   ○ **C.** Toner

   ○ **D.** Duplexer

   ○ **E.** Fuser

11. One of your customers is connected to a stand-alone printer. The customer says there is an Out of Memory Error when printing large graphic files. What should you do?

   ○ **A.** Upgrade the hard drive on the computer.

   ○ **B.** Upgrade RAM on the printer.

   ○ **C.** Upgrade RAM on the computer.

   ○ **D.** Reinstall the printer drivers.

12. What should you do first when removing a paper jam?

   ○ **A.** Take the printer offline.

   ○ **B.** Clear the print queue.

   ○ **C.** Open all the doors of the printer.

   ○ **D.** Turn off the printer.

13. While working in Microsoft Word at a customer's site, you saved a large .prn file to a PC and copied it to a USB flash drive that you would like to print on the big laser printer at the office. What checkbox did you select to save this document?

   ○ **A.** Print to XPS

   ○ **B.** Print to Image

   ○ **C.** Print to PDF

   ○ **D.** Print to File

14. You have been called to a customer site to perform maintenance on an impact printer. Which should you consider?

   ○ **A.** Replacing paper, cleaning heating element, removing debris

   ○ **B.** Replacing toner, applying maintenance kit, calibrating, cleaning

   ○ **C.** Replacing ribbon, replacing print head, replacing paper

   ○ **D.** Cleaning heads, replacing cartridges, calibrating, clearing jams

Cram Quiz Answers

220-901 Answers

  1. C. An uninterruptible power supply (UPS) is not recommended for laser printers due to the high draw of the laser printer. When using a surge suppressor, the laser printer should be the only device connected to it.

  2. A and D. After the printer is installed (meaning it has been connected and the drivers have been installed), you should calibrate the printer (if necessary) and print a test page. Before starting the installation, you should check for compatibility with operating systems, applications, and so on.

3. **B.** Start Printing Immediately is the faster print option when spooling documents. Print Directly to the Printer doesn't use the spooling feature. There is no Start Printing After the Separator Page.

4. **D.** The command `net stop spooler` stops or turns off the print spooler service.

5. **A.** Printer pooling is when two or more printers are combined to get print jobs out faster.

6. **B.** The Network and Sharing Center in Windows is where printer sharing is enabled.

7. **A, B, and C.** There are several possible reasons why a paper jam might occur. The paper could be stuck somewhere in the paper path, the paper could be too thick, or the rollers could be damaged.

8. **A.** If the transfer corona wire has failed, there is no way for the toner to be "attracted" to the paper, resulting in blank sheets coming out of the printer. It is also possible for the toner cartridge to fail, causing blank pages to print. This would mean that blank pages could be caused by failures during the Developing and Transferring stages of the laser printing process, with failures during the Developing stage being more common.

9. **A.** A scratch on the laser printer drum can account for black lines showing up on printouts. Another culprit can be a dirty primary corona wire.

10. **A and E.** Maintenance kits usually include things like paper pickup rollers, transfer rollers, and a fuser. The duplexer, image drum, and toner are parts of the printer and/or toner cartridges. Toner cartridges are not included in maintenance kits.

11. **B.** You should upgrade the RAM on the printer. Large graphic files need a lot of memory to work with (both on the PC and the printer). But if the PC can send the file to the printer, it has enough RAM and hard drive space. Printer drivers will not cause an Out of Memory Error to display on the printer.

12. **D.** Turn off the printer before you start working inside of the printer. You want to make sure it is off (and unplugged) before you put your hands inside of it. Taking it offline is not enough in this case.

13. **D.** You likely selected Print as you normally would and then checked the Print to File checkbox. This saves the file as a .prn file that can be copied to removable media and printed later on. The other virtual printing options do not save to .prn. Printing to Microsoft XPS saves the file with an .xps extension. Printing to an image typically saves a file as a .jpg, .gif, .tif, .png, and so on. Printing to PDF saves the file with a .pdf extension.

14. **C.** Impact printer maintenance procedures include replacing ribbon, replacing print head, and replacing paper. Laser printer maintenance includes replacing toner, applying maintenance kit, calibrating, and cleaning. Thermal printer maintenance includes replacing paper, cleaning heating element, and removing debris. Inkjet printer maintenance includes cleaning heads, replacing cartridges, calibrating, and clearing jams.

CHAPTER 15

Computer Networking Part I

This chapter covers the following A+ exam topics:

▶ Types of Networks, Network Devices, and Cloud Technology

▶ Cables, Connectors, and Tools

▶ TCP/IP

You can find a master list of A+ exam topics in the "Introduction."

This chapter covers CompTIA A+ 220-901 objectives 2.1–2.4, 2.8, 2.9, and 4.1 and 220-902 objectives 2.3 and 2.4.

Virtually every business has one or more computer networks, and it seems that nowadays just about every home has a network as well. But what is a computer network? The simple answer: A computer network is two or more computers that communicate. For the more in-depth answer, read on!

We use networks so that computers can share files, access databases, collaborate on projects, browse websites, send e-mail, play games, place phone calls, research, shop, and on and on. As you can see, so much is dependent on a well-designed, quick-and-efficient, cost-effective network, making the topic of computer networking extremely important for the A+ exams.

I've broken down the networking section of this book into two chapters—this one and Chapter 16—because there is just so much content to cover. And know this: the content in these two chapters just scratches the surface of computer networking; the field is that vast.

In this chapter we'll cover the types of networks and network devices you should know for the test; the cables, connectors, and tools you might use in the field; and the protocol suite that controls everything—TCP/IP. Let's begin by discussing the different types of computer networks and the devices that connect those networks together.

Types of Networks, Network Devices, and Cloud Technology

Computer networks might inhabit one small area or larger areas; different terms—such as LAN and WAN—are used to describe these types of networks. To connect computers in these networks, we use a variety of devices, including switches and routers. How the computers physically connect to each other is known as a topology. These three concepts make up the core of networking fundamentals.

Network Types

It's important to know how networks are classified. The two most common terms are local area network (LAN) and wide area network (WAN). But you should also know what a MAN and PAN are. Let's begin with LAN and WAN.

A *LAN* is a group of computers and other devices usually located in a small area: a house, a small office, or a single building. The computers all connect to one or more switches, and a router allows the computers access to the Internet.

A *WAN* is a group of one or more LANs over a large geographic area. Let's say a company has two LANs: one in New York and one in Los Angeles. Connecting the two would result in a WAN. However, to do this, we would require the help of a telecommunications company. This company would create the high-speed connection required for the two LANs to communicate quickly. Each LAN would require a router to connect to each other.

There is a smaller version of a WAN known as a metropolitan area network (*MAN*), also known as a municipal area network. This is when a company has two offices in the same city and wants to make a high-speed connection between them. It's different from a WAN in that it is not a large geographic area, but it is similar to a WAN in that a telecommunications company is needed for the high-speed link.

On a slightly different note, a personal area network (*PAN*) is a smaller computer network used for communication by small computing devices. Take this to the next level by adding wireless standards such as Bluetooth and you get a wireless PAN (WPAN). These networks are ad hoc, meaning there is no single controlling device, server, or access point.

> **ExamAlert**
>
> Be able to define LAN, WAN, MAN, and PAN.

Network Devices

To allow communication between computers, we need to put some other devices in place. For example, hubs, switches, and access points connect computers on the LAN. Routers and firewalls enable connectivity to other networks and protect those connection points. There are many types of devices you should know for the A+ exams; let's start with basic connectivity of computers on the LAN that use the Ethernet standard.

Hub

The *hub* is the original connecting device for computers on the LAN. It creates a simple shared physical connection that all computers use to send data. It's a basic device that has multiple ports, usually in intervals of four. Internally, the hub actually has only one trunk circuit that all the ports connect to. It regenerates and passes on the electrical signals initiated by computers. This device broadcasts data out to all computers. The computer that it is meant for accepts the data; the rest drop the information. Because of this broadcasting and sharing, this device allows only two computers to communicate with each other at any given time. In the days of 10 Mb/s and 100 Mb/s networks, it was common to have a hub. It's still listed on the A+ objectives, but in most instances today, the hub has given way to the switch.

Switch

Ethernet switching was developed in 1996 and quickly took hold as the preferred method of networking. A *switch*, like a hub, is a central connecting device that all computers connect to (a design known as a star topology). Like a hub, it regenerates the signal, but that's where the similarity ends. A switch sends the signal (frames of data) to the correct computer instead of broadcasting it out to every port. It does this by identifying the MAC address of each computer. This can effectively make every port an individual entity, and it increases data throughput exponentially. Switches employ a matrix of copper wiring instead of the standard trunk circuit. They are intelligent, and they use this intelligence to pass information to the correct port. This means that each computer has its own bandwidth (for example, 1000 Mb/s). In today's networks, the switch is king and is common in 1000 Mb/s (1 Gb/s) and 10 Gb/s networks. You might also see older 100 Mb/s connections. Hubs and switches both work within the Ethernet standard, which is the most common networking standard used today; it was ratified by the IEEE and is documented in the 802.3 set of standards. For example, a typical Ethernet network running at 1000 Mb/s and using twisted-pair cable is classified as 802.3ab. 10 Gb/s Ethernet over twisted-pair cable is 802.3an.

Wireless Access Point

A *wireless access point (WAP)* enables data communications over the air when your computer is equipped with a wireless networking adapter. The WAP and the wireless networking adapter transmit data over radio waves either on the 2.4 GHz or 5 GHz frequencies. This brings mobility to a new level.

WAPs are also included in most multifunction network devices, known as SOHO routers or simply routers. This enables wireless computers to not only communicate with each other but to access the Internet. Although hubs and switches deal with wired networks, the WAP deals with wireless connections. It is also based on Ethernet but now we are talking about the IEEE 802.11 group of standards that define wireless LANs (WLANs), simply referred to as Wi-Fi. Wireless access points act as a central connecting point for Wi-Fi-equipped computers. Like the switch, a WAP identifies each computer by its MAC address.

Power over Ethernet

Power over Ethernet (PoE) is an Ethernet standard that allows for the passing of electrical power in addition to data over Ethernet cabling. The most common type is implemented as the Ethernet 802.3af standard, which can deliver approximately 12 watts maximum to a variety of devices, as long as the sending and receiving devices are both PoE 802.3af compliant.

This is an excellent solution for devices that require specific placement but where no electrical connection can be made (for example, outdoor video cameras or WAPs that need to be mounted to the ceiling). In these cases, all that needs to be run is a twisted-pair network cable, which takes care of power *and* data. No electrical connection is necessary.

The technology is broken down into the two devices:

▶ The power sourcing equipment (PSE), which could be a switch or other similar device.

▶ The powered device (PD), which as we mentioned could be an IP-based camera (or WAP) and also an IP phone, IPTV device, router, mini network switch, industrial device, lighting controller, and more.

For organizations with a group of remote devices, a 24- or 48-port PoE-enabled switch is the way to go. For a smaller organization that only has one or two remote devices that need to be powered, the *PoE injector* is a decent, cheaper PSE solution. This device is installed where the main network switch is and plugs into one of the switch's ports. It is also powered normally from an AC outlet. But the injector has a second RJ45 port used to connect out to the remote device. This port sends Ethernet data as well as power over the Ethernet connection. This way, the organization can get power and data to an 802.3af-compliant access point, IP camera, or other device that needs to be located in an area where it would be difficult (not to mention expensive) to add an electrical outlet.

Repeater/Extender

A *repeater* or extender is a device used to lengthen the signal farther than it was designed to go originally. For example, a standard wired LAN connection from a switch can transmit data 328 feet (100 meters), but a repeater could increase that distance by as much as two times. There are repeaters for wireless access points as well that can increase the range of your overall wireless network.

Router

A *router* is used to connect two or more networks to form an internetwork. They are used in LANs and WANs and on the Internet. This device routes data from one location to another, usually by way of IP address and IP network numbers. Routers are intelligent and even have their own operating systems. The router enables connections with individual high-speed interconnection points. A common example would be an all-in-one device or multifunction network device that might be used in a home or small office. These devices route signals for all the computers on the LAN out to the Internet. Larger organizations use more advanced routers that can make connections to multiple various networks as well as the Internet.

Firewall

A *firewall* is any hardware appliance or software application that protects a computer from unwanted intrusion. In the networking world, we are more concerned with hardware-based devices that protect an entire group of computers (such as a LAN). When it comes to small offices and home offices, firewall functionality is usually built into the router. In larger organizations, it is a separate device. Or it could be part of a more complex, all-in-one solution such as a unified threat management (UTM) device. The firewall stops unwanted connections from the outside and can block basic networking attacks. We'll discuss firewalls more in Chapter 17, "Security."

Bridge

The *bridge* is a device that can either connect two LANs together or separate them into two sections. There are wired bridges and wireless bridges; today they are used to increase the size of networks.

Modem

Now, let's move outside of the LAN and talk about Internet and WAN connectivity. The term *modem* is a combination of the words *mo*dulate and *dem*odulate. It is a device that allows a computer (or, in rare cases, multiple computers) to access the Internet by changing the digital signals of the computer to analog signals used by a typical land-based phone line. These are slow devices and are usually used only if no other Internet option is available. However, they might be used in server rooms as a point of remote administration or as failover Internet access in case the main Internet service goes down.

VoIP Phones

Voice over Internet Protocol (VoIP) is a collection of technologies, devices, and protocols that allows voice communication over IP-based networks. VoIP phones are the Internet telephony devices that a person uses to make telephone calls over the Internet. These devices connect directly to the Ethernet network and communicate on the network just like a computer. All the words you speak are converted and encapsulated into packets that are sent across the network. It is a cheaper method of telephony, but there can be sound quality and latency issues if they are not configured properly.

> **ExamAlert**
>
> Be able to describe typical network devices.

Cloud Technology and Server Roles

Cloud computing can be defined as a way of offering on-demand services that extend the capabilities of a person's computer or an organization's network. These might be free services, such as browser-based e-mail from providers such as Yahoo! and Gmail, and personal storage from providers such as Microsoft (OneDrive); they might also be offered on a pay-per-use basis, such as services that offer data access, data storage, infrastructure, and online gaming. A network connection of some sort is required to make the connection to the "cloud" and gain access to these services in real time.

Some of the benefits cloud-based services provide for organizations include lowered costs, less administration and maintenance, more reliability, increased scalability, and possible increased performance. A basic example of a cloud-based service would be browser-based e-mail. A small business with few employees definitely needs e-mail, but it can't afford the costs of an e-mail server and perhaps does not want to have its own hosted domain and the costs and work that go along with that. By connecting to a free browser-based service, the small business can benefit from nearly unlimited e-mail, contacts, and calendar solutions. However, with cloud computing, you lose administrative control, and there are some security concerns as well.

Servers are a huge part of the cloud. Because so many server systems have moved from an organization's LAN to the cloud, we'll discuss those in this section as well.

Cloud Computing Services

Cloud computing services are generally broken down into three categories of services:

▶ **Software as a service (SaaS):** The most commonly used and recognized of the three categories, SaaS is when users access applications over the Internet that are provided by a third party. The applications need not be installed on the local computer. In many cases, these applications are run within a web browser; in other cases, the user connects with screen-sharing programs or remote desktop programs. A common example of this is webmail.

▶ **Infrastructure as a service (IaaS):** IaaS is a service that offers computer networking, storage, load balancing, routing, and VM hosting. More and more organizations are seeing the benefits of offloading some of their networking infrastructure to the cloud.

▶ **Platform as a service (PaaS):** PaaS is a service that provides various software solutions to organizations, especially the ability to develop applications in a virtual environment without the cost or administration of a physical platform. PaaS is used for easy-to-configure operating systems and on-demand computing. Often, this utilizes IaaS as well for an underlying infrastructure to the platform.

> **ExamAlert**
>
> Know what SaaS, IaaS, and PaaS are.

Types of Clouds

There are different types of clouds used by organizations: public, private, hybrid, and community. Let's discuss each briefly.

▶ **Public cloud:** When a service provider offers applications and storage space to the general public over the Internet. A couple of examples of this include free, web-based e-mail services and pay-as-you-go business class services. The main benefits of this include low (or zero) cost and scalability. Providers of public cloud space include Google, Rackspace, and Amazon.

▶ **Private cloud:** As opposed to the public cloud, the private cloud is designed with the needs of the individual organization in mind. The security administrator has more control over the data and infrastructure. There are a limited number of people who have access to the cloud, and they are usually located behind a firewall of some sort in order to gain access to the private cloud. Resources might be provided by a third-party or could come from the security administrator's server room or data center.

▶ **Hybrid cloud:** A mixture of public and private clouds. Dedicated servers located within the organization and cloud servers from a third party are used together to form the collective network. In these hybrid scenarios, confidential data is usually kept in-house.

▶ **Community cloud:** Another mix of public and private, but one where multiple organizations can share the public portion. Community clouds appeal to organizations that usually share a common form of computing and way of storing data.

> **ExamAlert**
>
> Know what public, private, hybrid, and community clouds are.

The type of cloud an organization uses will be dictated by its budget, the level of security it requires, and the amount of manpower (or lack thereof) it has to administer its resources. While a private cloud can be very appealing, it is often beyond the ability of an organization, forcing that organization to seek the public or community-based cloud. Whatever an organization chooses, the provider will measure the services supplied. *Measured services* is when the provider monitors the services rendered so that the provider can properly bill the customer and make sure that the customer's use of services is being handled in the most efficient way.

There are some other cloud-based terms you should be familiar with for the A+ exams. For example, *rapid elasticity*, which is the ability to build your cloud-based network. Choosing a provider that can provide you with a scalable model is important for an organization's growth. You also want to have on-demand service. The cloud should be available in real time and whenever you need it (24/7). In a community cloud scenario, the provider usually implements *resource pooling*, which is the grouping of servers and infrastructure for use by multiple customers but in a way that is on-demand and scalable.

Server Roles

Servers take care of centralizing data, allowing access to the network, making connections to printers, controlling the flow of e-mail, and much more. Whatever the role, the concept of the server is to do this in a centralized fashion, reducing the burden on client computers. Regardless of whether the server is in the organization's LAN or in the cloud, they will have the same purpose. However, it is more common that servers will run in a virtual environment in the cloud. Some of the server types you should know for the A+ exams include file server, network controller/authentication server, print server, e-mail server, web server, and other servers that take care of networking services (such as DHCP, DNS, and proxy connections). Let's discuss each of these servers briefly.

File server computers store, transfer, migrate, synchronize, and archive files. Any computer can act as a file server of sorts, but examples of actual server software include Microsoft Server, OS X Server, and the various types of Linux server versions (for example, Ubuntu Server or Red Hat Server), not to mention Unix.

A network controller is a server that acts as a central repository of user accounts and computer accounts on the network. All users log in to this server. An example of this would be a Windows Server system that has been promoted to a domain controller (meaning it runs Active Directory). These servers are one type of *authentication server*—they serve to validate the user that is attempting to log on.

Print servers are basic servers that take control of multiple printers on the network. All caching of information, spooling, printer pooling, sharing, and permissions is controlled centrally by the print server. While a Windows client computer (or other client) could act as a print server, and you can also purchase a basic print server device that plugs into your network, the best print servers will run Windows Server, so that they can handle lots of simultaneous print requests from client computers.

E-mail servers are part of the message server family. When we make reference to a message server, we mean any server that deals with e-mail, faxing, texting, chatting, and so on. But for the purposes of the A+ exams, we concentrate strictly on the e-mail server. The most common of these is Microsoft Exchange. An Exchange Server might run POP3, SMTP, and IMAP, and allow for Outlook Web App (OWA) connections via a web browser. That's a lot of protocols running. So it's not surprising to hear some Exchange admins confess that running an e-mail server can be difficult at times. For the A+ exams you should know how to connect a client to an e-mail server such as Microsoft Exchange. This is done by using appropriate e-mail client software (such as Outlook) and knowing the server name, protocols and ports used, the username and password, and whether there is additional security involved.

The *web server* is the one that houses the website of an organization. Examples of web servers include Microsoft's Internet Information Services (IIS), Apache HTTP Server (Linux), lighttpd (FreeBSD), and iPlanet Web Server Sun (Oracle).

Some servers do have less tangible duties. For example, the *DHCP server* is in charge of handing out IP addresses to clients. But don't underestimate this function; if an organization has a couple thousand computers that rely on obtaining IP addresses from a DHCP server, it becomes one of the most important servers on the network. If it fails, computers will have great difficulty doing anything on the network. The *DNS server* takes care of resolving domain names to IP addresses. In smaller networks, this server is at the ISP. However, larger networks might decide to run a DNS server internally. In fact, it becomes a necessity if the company has a domain controller, because the domain relies on DNS name resolutions for just about everything that needs to be accessed. Finally, a *proxy server* is used as a go-between for the client and the website accessed. The proxy server can analyze data as it passes through and filter it accordingly; also, it can cache information so that another user accessing the same web page won't have to get it from the Internet, because it already exists on the proxy server, which increases general performance and efficiency. For a client computer to use a proxy server, the web browser needs to be configured properly. We'll show this and discuss the security concerns of that configuration in Chapter 17.

So there's a little primer on servers. The server is the home of the systems administrator/network administrator. A lot of you reading this are probably very interested in servers. The A+ exams focus more on the client side of things, but you should attempt to learn as much as you can about the various servers we just discussed. Ultimately, you will be working on them!

ExamAlert

Know the differences between file servers, authentication servers, print servers, e-mail servers, web servers, DHCP servers, DNS servers, and proxy servers.

Cram Quiz

Answer these questions. The answers follow the last question. If you cannot answer these questions correctly, consider reading this section again until you can.

220-901 Questions

1. Which of the following is a group of Windows 8 desktop computers located in a small area?

   ○ **A.** LAN

   ○ **B.** WAN

   ○ **C.** PAN

   ○ **D.** MAN

2. Which of the following are most often used to connect a group of computers in a LAN? (Select the two best answers.)

   ○ **A.** Hub

   ○ **B.** Switch

   ○ **C.** Bridge

   ○ **D.** WAP

3. What device protects a network from unwanted intrusion?

   ○ **A.** Switch

   ○ **B.** Router

   ○ **C.** Access point

   ○ **D.** Firewall

4. Which of the following allows voice communication over IP-based networks?

   ○ **A.** Firewall

   ○ **B.** Modem

   ○ **C.** Patch panel

   ○ **D.** VoIP

5. Which of the following network devices moves frames of data between a source and destination based on their MAC addresses?

   ○ **A.** Hub

   ○ **B.** Switch

   ○ **C.** Router

   ○ **D.** Modem

6. Which of the following network devices allows a remote device to obtain Ethernet data as well as electrical power?

○ **A.** PD

○ **B.** PoE injector

○ **C.** Repeater

○ **D.** Router

220-902 Questions

7. Which of the following types of cloud services offers e-mail through a web browser?

○ **A.** SaaS

○ **B.** IaaS

○ **C.** PaaS

○ **D.** Community cloud

8. Which type of server runs Microsoft Exchange?

○ **A.** File server

○ **B.** Authentication server

○ **C.** E-mail server

○ **D.** Web server

Cram Quiz Answers

220-901 Answers

1. A. A local area network (LAN) is a group of computers, such as a SOHO network located in a small area. A wide area network (WAN) is a group of one or more LANs spread over a larger geographic area. A personal area network (PAN) is a smaller computer network used by smartphones and other small computing devices. A metropolitan area network (MAN) is a group of LANs in a smaller geographic area of a city.

2. B and D. Computers in a LAN are connected by a central connecting device; the most common of these are the switch and the wireless access point (WAP). Hubs are deprecated devices; they are the predecessor of the switch. A bridge is used to connect two LANs or separate a single LAN into two sections.

3. D. A firewall is a hardware appliance or software application that protects one or more computers from unwanted intrusion. A switch is a device that connects multiple computers together on a LAN. A router is used to connect two or more networks. An access point (or wireless access point) allows Wi-Fi-enabled computers and devices to communicate on the LAN wirelessly.

4. **D.** Voice over Internet Protocol (VoIP) is a technology that allows for voice communication over IP-based networks. A firewall is a device or software that protects computers from threats on the Internet. A modem is a device that allows a computer to connect to the Internet by way of a standard phone line. A patch panel provides a connection point between network equipment, such as switches and the ports to which computers are connected.

5. **B.** A switch sends frames of data between computers by identifying the systems by their MAC addresses. A hub broadcasts data out to all computers. The computer that it is meant for accepts the data; the rest drop the information. Routers enable connections with individual high-speed interconnection points and route signals for all the computers on the LAN out to the Internet. A modem is a device that allows a computer to access the Internet by changing the digital signals of the computer to analog signals used by a typical land-based phone line.

6. **B.** A PoE injector sends Ethernet data and power over a single twisted-pair cable to a remote device. PD stands for "powered device," the 802.3af-compliant remote device that is receiving the power. A repeater extends the distance of a network connection. While a PoE injector can act as a repeater, not all repeaters are PoE injectors. A router makes connections from one network to another or from the LAN to the Internet.

220-902 Answers

7. **A.** Software as a service (SaaS) is the most commonly recognized cloud service; it allows users to use applications to access data that is stored on the Internet by a third party. Infrastructure as a service (IaaS) is a service that offers computer networking, storage, load balancing, routing, and VM hosting. Platform as a service (PaaS) is used for easy-to-configure operating systems and on-demand computing. A community cloud is mix of public and private clouds, but one where multiple organizations can share the public portion.

8. **C.** Microsoft Exchange is a type of e-mail server. While you could run multiple services on a single server—for example, you could run the web server and e-mail server on the same machine—it isn't recommended. All servers (such as file servers, authentication servers, e-mail servers, DHCP servers, and so on) should be separate entities.

Cables, Connectors, and Tools

Although wireless is becoming more and more popular, cables still provide huge amounts of data transfer over today's networks. In this section, we'll discuss twisted-pair, fiber optic, and coaxial cable types; their varying characteristics; and connectors. Plus we'll briefly go over some of the cabling tools you should be aware of.

Cable Types and Connectors

Cable types are broken down into two categories: cables that use electricity and cables that use light. Twisted-pair and coaxial cables use copper wires as their transmission media and send electricity over those wires. Fiber optic, on the other hand, uses glass or plastic as the transmission media and sends light (photons) over those.

Twisted Pair

The most common type of cable used in today's networks is *twisted pair*. It is referred to as twisted pair because the copper wires inside of the cable are twisted together into pairs throughout the entire length of the cable. Regularly, admins use UTP cable, short for unshielded twisted pair. Typical versions of twisted pair include *Category 6* and *Category 5e* (often abbreviated to just Cat 6 or Cat 5e). Table 15.1 shows the various categories of twisted pair you should know for the exam and the networks they are rated for.

TABLE 15.1 **UTP Categories and Speeds**

Category UTP	Rated For
Category 3	10 Mb/s networks
Category 5	100 Mb/s and 1 Gb/s networks (100 MHz)
Category 5e	100 Mb/s and 1 Gb/s networks (100 MHz/350 MHz)
Category 6/6a	1000 Mb/s and 10 Gb/s networks (250 MHz/500 MHz)
Category 7/7a	1000 Mb/s and 10 Gb/s networks (600 MHz/1000 MHz)

Network data transfer rates (also known as speed or bandwidth) are normally measured in bits because networks usually transfer data serially, or one bit at a time. 100 Mb/s is 100 megabits per second. 1 Gb/s is equal to 1 gigabit per second (known as a gigabit network), or 1000 Mb/s. 10 Gb/s is equal to 10 gigabits per second. Now, a cable might be rated for 10 Gb/s networks (such as Cat 6), but you probably won't attain that speed over the cable. Typically, the actual speed (known as throughput) might be 250 Mb/s, 500 Mb/s, 1 Gb/s, and possibly more. That depends on many factors, including the frequency of the cable (for example, Cat 6 is 250 MHz and Cat 6a is 500 MHz), the technology used to send data, the encoding rate, whether duplexing is involved, the length of the cable, the quality of the installation, and so on. So, it's difficult to put a specific number to each category of cable—just remember what network speeds each category of cable is rated for.

ExamAlert

Know what network speeds Cat 3, 5, 5e, 6, and 7 are rated for.

Note

As of the writing of this book, Category 8 is under development with potential frequencies between 1600 and 2000 MHz and capable of supporting 40 Gb/s over copper wire!

Most wiring standards are based on the original BOGB color group: *B*lue, *O*range, *G*reen, *B*rown. In a typical twisted-pair cable, the blue pair consists of a white wire with blue stripes (known as white/blue) and a solid blue wire. The orange pair consists of a white wire with orange stripes and a solid orange wire, and so on. The Telecommunications Industry Association/ Electronic Industries Alliance (TIA/EIA) defines standards for cabling and wiring, such as the T568A and T568B standards, which are based on the BOGB colors. Generally speaking, the most common standard you see is the T568B standard. Table 15.2 shows the color sequence for each of the wires (or pins) for the T568B and T568A standards. Figure 15.1 shows a close-up of the wires organized for a T568B connection.

TABLE 15.2 **T568B and A Wiring Standards**

T568B	T568A
White/Orange	White/Green
Orange	Green
White/Green	White/Orange

T568B	T568A
Blue	Blue
White/Blue	White/Blue
Green	Orange
White/Brown	White/Brown
Brown	Brown

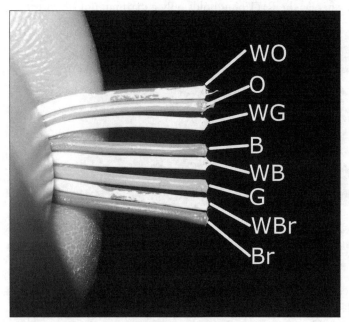

FIGURE 15.1 Wires organized for the T568B standard

> **Note**
>
> Some manufacturers and technicians might refer to white/orange as orange/white, white/blue as blue/white, and so on. However, what is shown in the table is the most common description of colors for twisted-pair cable.

Any physical cabling equipment used in the network must comply with this standard. This includes cables, patch panels, jacks, and even connectors. The connector used with twisted-pair networks is known colloquially as the RJ45 (more specifically, the 8P8C connector). RJ45 plugs connect to each end of the cable, and these cables connect to RJ45 sockets within network adapters and on network switches.

As you can see in Figure 15.2, RJ45 plugs look a lot like the plugs that connect your telephone (known as RJ11). However, the RJ45 plug is larger and contains eight wires, whereas the RJ11 plug holds only a maximum of six wires.

RJ45

RJ11

FIGURE 15.2 **RJ45 and RJ11 plugs**

A standard twisted-pair patch cable that you would use to connect a computer to a switch or RJ45 jack is wired for T568B on each end. That makes it a *straight through cable*. However, if you wanted to connect a computer directly to another computer, you would need to use a *crossover cable*. This type of cable is wired for T568B on one end and T568A on the other. You can see in Table 15.2 that certain pins are "crossed" to each other from T568B to T568A. Pin 1 on T568B crosses to pin 3 on T568A, and pin 2 crosses to 6. You can also use a crossover cable to connect one switch to another; though this is usually not necessary nowadays because most switches will auto-sense the type of cable you plug into them.

Note

The way that a crossover cable's pins are wired is the basis for a loopback—a connection made to test the local computer or system (for example, an RJ45 loopback plug described later in the book).

UTP has a couple disadvantages:

▶ It can be run only 100 meters (328 feet) before signal attenuation occurs, which is the weakening or degrading of signal.

▶ Its outer jacket is made of plastic and it has no shielding, making it susceptible to electromagnetic interference (EMI) and vulnerable to unauthorized network access in the form of wire tapping.

Because the UTP cable jacket is made of PVCs (plastics) that can be harmful to humans when they catch on fire, most municipalities require that plenum-rated cable be installed in any area that cannot be reached by a sprinkler system. A plenum is an enclosed space used for airflow. For example, if cables are run above a drop ceiling, building code requires that they are plenum-rated: This means that the cable has a special Teflon coating or is a special low-smoke variant of twisted pair, reducing the amount of PVC chemicals that are released into the air in the case of fire.

ExamAlert

To meet fire code, use plenum-rated cable above drop ceilings and anywhere else necessary.

Because UTP is susceptible to electromagnetic interference (EMI), a variant was developed known as STP or shielded twisted pair. This includes metal shielding over each pair of wires, reducing external EMI and the possibility of unauthorized network access. A couple of disadvantages of STP include higher cost of product and installation and the fact that the shielding needs to be grounded to work effectively. Keep in mind that all server room and wiring closet equipment—such as patch panels, punch blocks, and wiring racks—should be permanently grounded before use.

ExamAlert

STP cable is resistant to EMI.

Coaxial

Coaxial cable is another way to transfer data over a network. This cable has a single conductor surrounded by insulating material, which is then surrounded by a copper screen and, finally, an outer plastic sheath. Some networking technologies still use coaxial cable; for example, cable Internet connections use RG-6 coaxial cable (previously RG-59). This cable screws on to the terminal of a cable modem using an F-connector. It is the same cable and connector used with cable TV set-top boxes (STB) and DVRs.

Generally, RG-6 cable can be run as far as 500 to 1000 feet. The maximum distance varies because several factors play into how far the data can travel before attenuation (for example, the frequency used, protocol used, and so on). Its speed also varies depending on what type of transmission is sent over it. A typical RG-6 cable has a minimum bandwidth of 1 GHz, which can loosely translate to 1 Gb/s, but the data throughput will most likely be capped at some number below that. For example, cable Internet providers will often cap that at 30 Mb/s to 50 Mb/s, and some fiber optic providers (who change the cable type from fiber optic to coaxial at the house or business) might cap it at anywhere between 100 Mb/s and 500 Mb/s. This all varies according to the provider and how many services are being transmitted over the same line.

There are two derivatives of RG-6 that you should know: RG-6/U, which is double-shielded, and the more common RG-6/UQ, which is quadruple-shielded and is often referred to as "quad shield." It is a better option if you are running RG-6 in ceilings or near any electrical appliances.

> **Note**
>
> Long ago, local area networks were built using RG-58 coaxial cable and BNC screw-on connectors. It is unlikely that you will see these because of their slow speeds, but you might still see the BNC connector used in other applications (such as older video switching devices). BNC is listed in the CompTIA objectives acronym list, but because it is rare, it is unlikely you will see a question on it.

Fiber Optic

Fiber optic is fast and, when dealing with EMI, it's a better option than copper-based cables. Because fiber optic cables transmit data by way of light instead of electricity, they can send signals much faster and further than copper wires and EMI doesn't even play into the equation. Plus, fiber optic cables are difficult to splice into, unlike copper-based cables. Due to these reasons, fiber optic cable is the most secure type of cable.

You might encounter single-mode and multimode fiber; for the most part, single-mode fiber is used over longer distances, but both types are easily capable of supporting 1000 Mb/s and 10 Gb/s networks and can be run farther than twisted-pair cable. A couple types of connectors used with fiber include ST and SC, as shown in Figure 15.3. Another connector is LC, which looks quite similar to SC.

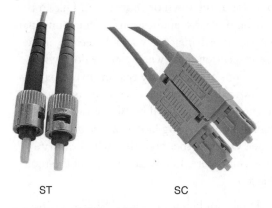

ST   SC

FIGURE 15.3   **ST and SC connectors**

Multimode cables have a larger core diameter—either 50 microns (millionths of a meter) or 62.5 microns in diameter—than single-mode cables. The 50-micron version can handle three times the bandwidth and can support longer cable runs than the 62.5-micron version. It is the more commonly used fiber optic cable in server rooms and when making backbone connections between buildings in a campus. It transmits data approximately 600 meters. Single-mode, on the other hand, is only 8 to 10 microns in diameter and is used for longer distance runs, perhaps from one city to the next (as far as thousands of kilometers). At shorter distances, single-mode cable can go beyond 10 Gb/s.

> **ExamAlert**
>
> Know the differences between multimode and single-mode, as well as the approximate speed and distance limitations.

Cabling Tools

If you plan to build a physical network, you will need to stock up on some key networking tools. These tools will aid you when running, terminating, and testing cable. For this short section, let's imagine a scenario where you are the network installer and are required to install a wired network for 12 computers.

To start, you should check with your local municipality for any rules and regulations for running networking cable. Some municipalities require an installer to have an electrician's license. But most require only an exemption of some sort that anyone can apply for at the town or county seat. Due to the low-voltage nature of network wiring (for most applications), some municipalities have no rules regarding this. But in urban areas, you will need to apply for a permit and have at least one inspection done when you are done with the installation. Permits and regulations aside, let's say that in this scenario you have been cleared to install 12 wired connections to computers (known as drops) and have diagrammed where the cables will be run and where they will terminate. All cables will come out of a wiring closet, where you will terminate them to a small patch panel. On the other end, they will terminate at in-wall RJ45 jacks near each of the computers. Let's discuss each of the tools that you will use to complete this job.

▶ **Cable cutter:** The first tool you should have is a good, sharp cutting tool. You will need to make a clean cut on the end of the network cable; scissors will not do. Either cut pliers or other cable cutting tools will be necessary.

▶ **Wire stripper:** The second tool is a wire stripper (cable stripper). This tool is used to strip a portion of the plastic jacket off the cable, exposing the individual wires. At this point, you can separate the wires and get ready to terminate them.

▶ **Punchdown tool:** The third tool is a punchdown tool. This device punches the individual wires down into the 110 IDC clips of an RJ45 jack and the patch panel. This "punching down" of the wires is the actual termination.

▶ **Cable testers:** The last tool necessary for the job is a cable testing tool. There are a few options here:

  ▶ The best option is a proper network cable tester, also known as a continuity tester or cable certifier. This device will have a LAN testing unit that you can plug into a port on the patch panel and a terminator that you plug in to the other end of the cable in the corresponding RJ45 jack (or vice versa). This tool will test for continuity and will test each wire in the cable, making sure every one is wired properly.

  ▶ Another option is the tone and probe kit (also known as a fox and hound). This kit consists of two parts: a tone-generating device, which connects to one end of the network cable and, when turned on, sends a tone along the length of the cable; and a probing device, also known as an inductive amplifier, which can detect the tone anywhere along the cable length and at the termination point. This tool is not as good as a proper network cable tester because it tests only one of the pairs of the wires. However, it is an excellent tool for finding individual phone lines and is more commonly used for that. You can also use a multimeter to do various tests of individual lines, but it is usually not necessary if you own the other tools mentioned. The cable tester mentioned previously can usually create tone as well.

At this point, the cables have been run, terminated on both ends, and tested. The only other thing you need is patch cables. The patch cables connect the various ports of the patch panel to a switch and the RJ45 jacks to the computers.

▶ **RJ45 crimper:** Usually, you would buy patch cables for $2 or $3 each and be done with it. However, you can make them, too. You would have to purchase cable as well as RJ45 plugs. The plugs are attached to the cable ends with an RJ45 crimping tool. This tool can come in especially handy when you need to make a crossover patch cable. There are other types of crimpers for coaxial cable as well.

▶ **Patch tester:** Before connecting the patch cables, you should test them with a patch tester. This device has two RJ45 jacks; you plug each end of the patch cable into the tester, and then press the button to make sure each wire on each connection makes a proper connection.

▶ **Loopback plug:** Another tool every PC tech should have is a loopback plug. It simulates a network connection and has two main functions. First, it can help find what port on a switch an RJ45 jack is wired to. You plug it into an RJ45 jack on the wall and it bounces the signal back down the cable to the switch, lighting up the port that the cable is ultimately connected to. This tells you which port on the switch a particular cable is connected to in case it wasn't labeled previously. You can also accomplish this by connecting it to the end of a patch cable because the device usually has a male and a female RJ45 connection. Second, you can test the network adapter on a PC and find out if TCP/IP is functioning properly. An easy way to do this is to plug in the loopback adapter to the RJ45 port of the PC, open the command line, and then type `ping 127.0.0.1` (or ping the actual IP address of the system). The loopback plug is essentially a really short crossover connection—the appropriate pins are crossed within the device, looping the signal and data back to where it came from.

> **Note**
>
> You could even make your own loopback plug if you really wanted to! It's essentially a crossover connection, so you could connect an individual wire on an RJ45 plug to pins 1 and 3 and a second wire to pins 2 and 6. Tedious stuff, but great to know if you are in a tight spot and only have twisted-pair wire and RJ45 plugs on you (and a crimper).

Figure 15.4 identifies some of the tools we described in this section.

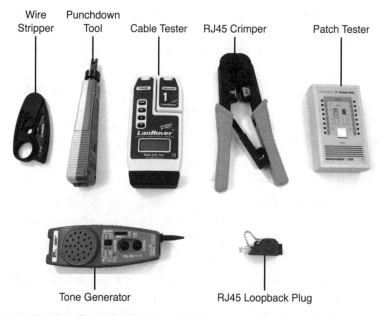

FIGURE 15.4 **Twisted-pair cabling tools**

> **ExamAlert**
>
> Know the following tools for the exam: crimper, wire/cable stripper, tone generator and probe, cable tester, punchdown tool, and loopback plug.

Cram Quiz

Answer these questions. The answers follow the last question. If you cannot answer these questions correctly, consider reading this section again until you can.

220-901 Questions

1. Which of the following would be suitable for 1000 Mb/s networks? (Select all that apply.)

   ○ **A.** Category 3

   ○ **B.** Category 5

   ○ **C.** Category 5e

   ○ **D.** Category 6

2. Which type of cable would you use if you were concerned about EMI?

   ○ **A.** Plenum-rated

   ○ **B.** UTP

   ○ **C.** STP

   ○ **D.** Coaxial

3. Which type of cable can connect a computer to another computer directly?

   ○ **A.** Straight-through

   ○ **B.** Crossover

   ○ **C.** T568A

   ○ **D.** T568B

4. Which of the following cables has a core diameter of 62.5 microns?

   ○ **A.** Single-mode

   ○ **B.** Category 6

   ○ **C.** Multimode

   ○ **D.** STP

5. Which connector is used for cable Internet?

   ○ **A.** LC

   ○ **B.** F-connector

   ○ **C.** BNC

   ○ **D.** RJ45

6. Which tool is used to test a network adapter not connected to the network?

   ○ **A.** Punchdown tool

   ○ **B.** Cable tester

   ○ **C.** Loopback plug

   ○ **D.** Tone and probe

Cram Quiz Answers

220-901 Answers

1. **C and D.** Category 5e and Category 6 are suitable for 1000 Mb/s networks (and Cat 6 is also suitable for 10 Gb/s networks). Category 3 is suitable for 10 Mb/s networks only. Category 5 is suitable for 100 Mb/s networks.

2. **C.** STP (shielded twisted pair) is the only cable listed here that can reduce electromagnetic interference. Plenum-rated cable is used where fire code requires it; it doesn't burn as fast, releasing fewer PVC chemicals into the air.

3. **B.** A crossover cable is used to connect like devices: computer to computer or switch to switch. Straight-through cables (the more common patch cable) do not connect like devices (for example, they connect from a computer to a switch). T568B is the typical wiring standard you will see in twisted-pair cables; T568A is the less common standard. A crossover cable uses the T568B wiring standard on one end and 568A on the other end.

4. **C.** Multimode cable has a core diameter of either 50 microns or 62.5 microns. Single-mode is 8 to 10 microns. Category 6 is twisted pair and uses between 22 and 24 gauge copper wire. STP is shielded twisted pair.

5. **B.** Cable Internet connections use RG-6 coaxial cable (usually) with an F-connector on the end. LC is a type of fiber optic connector. BNC is an older connector type used by coaxial networks. RJ45 is the connector used on twisted-pair patch cables.

6. **C.** To test a network adapter without a network connection, you would use a loopback plug. This simulates a network connection. It can also be used to test a switch port. Punchdown tools are used to punch individual wires to a patch panel. Cable testers such as continuity testers test the entire length of a terminated cable. The tone and probe kit also tests a cable's length but only tests one pair of wires.

TCP/IP

You all have heard of TCP/IP. It's the most famous acronym in networking; it stands for Transmission Control Protocol/Internet Protocol. Within the name are the two most-used protocols when computers send information to each other on an IP network. However, there are lots of other protocols and ports as well, and we will speak to them a little later in this section. The two versions of IP you need to know for the exam are IPv4 and the newer IPv6. Let's start with Internet Protocol version 4.

Configuring IPv4

Configuring IP works the same way in most versions of Windows. First, we navigate to the Internet Protocol (TCP/IP) Properties window, which we refer to as the IP Properties dialog box. To do this, go to Control Panel > Network and Internet > Network and Sharing Center, and then select the Change Adapter Settings link. (In Windows Vista, select the Manage My Network Connections link.) Then right-click the Ethernet icon (or Local Area Connection icon) and select Properties. Finally, highlight Internet Protocol Version 4 and then click the Properties button. (For speed, right-click the network icon in the Notification Area and select Open Network and Sharing Center.)

The first item to be configured is the IP address, which is the unique assigned number of your computer on the network. IPv4 IP addresses consist of four octets, with each octet's value ranging between 0 and 255. Each number is separated by a dot (for example, 192.168.0.100). The binary equivalent of 0–255 would be 00000000 through 11111111. For example, 192 is equal to 11000000 in binary. Because each octet contains 8 bits and there are four octets, the IP address collectively is a 32-bit number but is normally expressed in dotted-decimal notation.

There are two main types of addresses: dynamic and static. Dynamically assigned addresses are more common for a client computer; this is when the computer seeks out a DHCP server so that it can get its IP information automatically. Figure 15.5 shows a radio button labeled Obtain an IP Address Automatically. When you select this, the rest of the information becomes grayed out and the computer attempts to get that IP information from a host (such as a multifunction network device or DHCP server). This is common; in fact, it's the default configuration for Windows. Static addresses are generated when we configure the IP information manually. Figure 15.5 shows an example of statically configured IP settings. In the figure, we configured the computer to use the address 192.168.0.100, but the IP address differs from machine to machine depending on several factors. Remember that the address should be unique for each computer on the network.

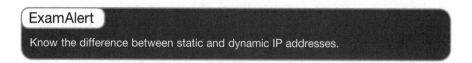

ExamAlert

Know the difference between static and dynamic IP addresses.

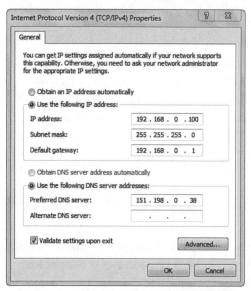

FIGURE 15.5   **IP Properties dialog box in Windows**

IP addresses can also be self-assigned by the computer. In Windows, this is known as *automatic private IP addressing (APIPA)*, and it occurs when a computer cannot contact a DHCP server to obtain an IP address. When APIPA self-assigns an address, it will be on the 169.254.0.0 network. Addresses on this network are also known as link-local addresses.

IP addresses are divided into two sections: the network portion, which is the number of the network the computer is on, and the host portion, which is the individual number of the computer. The subnet mask defines which portion of the IP address is the network number and which portion is the individual host number. In this case, the subnet mask is 255.255.255.0. The 255s indicate the network portion of the IP address. So, 192.168.0 is the network this computer is a member of. The zeros (in this case, there is only one of them) indicate the host number, so 100 is the individual number of this computer. Quite often the subnet mask will be configured automatically by Windows after you type the IP address.

The gateway address is the IP address of the host that enables access to the Internet or to other networks. The IP address of the gateway should always be on the same network as the computer(s) connecting to it. In Figure 15.5, we know it is because the first three octets are 192.168.0. If a computer is not configured with a default gateway address, it cannot connect to the Internet.

> **ExamAlert**
>
> To use the gateway, computers must be on the same network number as the gateway device.

The DNS server address is the IP address of the host that takes care of domain name translation to IP. When you use your browser to connect to a website, you might type something like www.davidlprowse.com. What you need to remember, however, is that computers actually communicate by IP address, not by name. So the DNS server takes care of translating the name davidlprowse.com to its corresponding IP address and forwarding that information back to your computer. When your computer knows the IP address of the website, it can start a session with the website and transmit and receive files. Notice in Figure 15.5 that the DNS server address is on a completely different network than our computer. This is typical; in this case, the DNS server is run by the Internet service provider (ISP) that provides me with my Internet connection. However, DNS servers can also be run internally by a company; this happens more often with larger companies.

You will also note a checkbox labeled Validate settings upon exit. If you set up a static IP address on a computer, you should select this checkbox. This way, Windows will check whether the configuration works properly and will let you know when any basic errors arise. Who knows, the IP configuration might have an incorrect DNS server, gateway address, or IP network number.

> **ExamAlert**
>
> Know where and how to configure client-side DNS and DHCP settings.

If your IP Properties dialog box is set to Obtain an IP address automatically, you will see the Alternate Configuration tab. This allows you to have a secondary IP configuration. Let's say there was a scenario in which you used a laptop at work and got your IP address from a DHCP server, but you also go on the road. The alternate configuration would kick in automatically when you are away from the office and allow you access to the Internet or to virtual private networks, depending on how you configure it. The alternate configuration can be on a wholly different IP network than the main configuration.

IPv4 Classes and CIDR

When working with classful IP addresses, the first number in the IP address dictates what class the address is part of. For example, suppose you use 192.168.0.100. In that case, the first number is 192, which means that the IP address is part of a Class C network.

Table 15.3 shows the various classes and their associated IP address ranges. Table 15.4 shows the IP classes and their associated default subnet masks, which, as we mentioned, identify which portion of the IP address is the network portion and which is the host portion.

Take a look at Table 15.3 and try to get a feel for the different IP classes available. You realize that this classification system was created to appease different organizations of different sizes. If you have a small network at home, it is simplest and most common to use Class C.

TABLE 15.3 **IP Classifications**

IP Class	Range	Number of Networks	Number of Hosts per Network	Who Uses It?
A	1–126	126	16,777,214	Large Corps, ISPs
B	128–191	16,384	65,534	Corps, Universities
C	192–223	2,097,152	254	Small offices/home offices (SOHO)

> **Note**
>
> Class D (224–239) is used for multicast testing, and Class E (240–255) is reserved for future use.
>
> APIPA addresses on the 169.254 network are part of Class B.

You probably noticed that the number 127 was skipped. That is because this network number is reserved for loopback testing. Technically, it is part of the Class A range, but it cannot be configured as an IP address within the IP Properties dialog box. As mentioned previously, the built-in loopback address is 127.0.0.1.

You might have also noticed that there are only 254 possible hosts per network in Class C (instead of 256). This is because you can never use the first or the last address in the range; the first is actually the network number and the last is the broadcast address.

The total number of hosts, for all classes combined, is just under four billion—and we have pretty much used up all those addresses. This is one of the reasons for the inception of IPv6.

> **ExamAlert**
>
> Memorize the IP ranges for Classes A, B, and C.

TABLE 15.4 **IP Class Ranges and Their Equivalent Binary Values and Subnet Masks**

IP Class	Binary Equivalent	Default Subnet Masks
A: 1–126	00000001–01111110	255.0.0.0 Net.node.node.node
B: 128–191	10000000–10111111	255.255.0.0 Net.net.node.node
C: 192–223	11000000–11011111	255.255.255.0 Net.net.net.node

Notice in Table 15.4 how the number 255 in a subnet mask coincides with the name net. Also, notice the 0 coincides with the name node. Net is the network portion of the IP address, whereas node is the host or computer portion of the address.

> **ExamAlert**
>
> Memorize the default subnet masks for Class A, B, and C.

It is also important to know the difference between private and public addresses. A private address is one that is not displayed directly to the Internet and is normally behind a firewall. Typically, these are addresses that a SOHO router would assign automatically to clients. A list of reserved private IP ranges is shown in Table 15.5. Public addresses are addresses that are displayed directly to the Internet; they are addresses that anyone could possibly connect to around the world. Most addresses, besides the private ones listed in Table 15.5, are considered public addresses.

TABLE 15.5 **Private IP Ranges (As Assigned by the IANA)**

IP Class	Assigned Range
A	10.0.0.0–10.255.255.255
B	172.16.0.0–172.31.255.255
C	192.168.0.0–192.168.255.255

ExamAlert

Memorize the private IP ranges for Classes A, B, and C.

While classful IP addresses used in Classes A, B, and C are still commonly implemented in SOHO networks, they are not quite as necessary any more in general. In fact, many corporate networks use *classless* IP addressing exclusively. This means that any network number can use *any* subnet mask. (Breaking all the rules!) For example, one of my test networks uses the 10.254.254.0 network and the 255.255.255.0 subnet mask, making the network number 10.254.254 instead of just 10. How is this done? By changing the subnet mask to 255.255.255.0 instead of the default 255.0.0.0. This method is known as Classless Inter-Domain Routing (CIDR), often pronounced as "cider."

You will frequently see CIDR notation; this specifies the individual IP address or IP network along with a routing prefix. An example of this is 192.168.1.100/24. The IP address is 192.168.1.100. The routing prefix is /24 and that defines the subnet mask. It does this by stating the number of *masked* bits in the subnet mask. In binary, a masked bit is a 1 and an unmasked bit is 0. So /24 means there are 24 masked bits (24 binary ones). Remember that an IPv4 subnet mask has 32 bits in total, so when you see /24, you know there are 24 masked bits and the remaining 8 bits are unmasked:

/24 = 11111111 11111111 11111111 00000000

This equates to a subnet mask of 255.255.255.0, which is normal in a classful network. We can identify the network portion of the address as 192.168.1 and the host portion as .100. Even though it turns out to be a classful address, it (and any other address) can still be expressed in terms of CIDR notation.

Here's another example of CIDR notation, this time for a true classless IPv4 address: 10.52.128.201/16. In this case, the routing prefix is /16, which means 16 masked bits:

/16 = 11111111 11111111 00000000 00000000

This equates to a subnet mask of 255.255.0.0. That means that the network portion of the IP address is 10.52 and the host portion of the address is 128.201.

> **Note**
>
> The binary masked bits are also known as *leading bits*.

> **ExamAlert**
>
> Know what CIDR is and understand how to read CIDR notation.

Configuring IPv6

IPv6 is the next generation of IP addressing. Used on the Internet and on many LANs and WANs, it is designed to meet the inadequacies of IPv4. One of the main reasons for the development of IPv6 was the rapidly approaching global shortage of IPv4 addresses. Where IPv4 (a 32-bit system) can have approximately 4 billion total theoretical addresses, IPv6 (128-bit) can have a total of 340 *undecillion* theoretical addresses—a far greater total. Various limitations of the system will drastically reduce that number, but the remaining result is still orders of magnitude above and beyond the IPv4 system. However, IPv6 is also known for security. IPsec is a fundamental piece of the IPv6 puzzle and if used properly, it can offer much more secure communications than IPv4. IPv6 also supports larger packet sizes, which are known as jumbograms. Table 15.6 summarizes some of the differences between IPv4 and IPv6.

TABLE 15.6 **IPv4 Versus IPv6**

IPv4	IPv6
32-bit	128-bit
4 billion addresses	340 undecillion addresses
Less secure	More secure; IPsec is embedded
65,536 byte packet size max	4 billion bytes max

IPv6 addresses are 128-bit hexadecimal numbers that are divided into eight groups of four numbers each. The most commonly used type is the unicast address, which defines a single IP address on a single interface (such as a network adapter). Windows auto-configures a unicast address when

IPv6 is installed. The address will start with FE80, FE90, FEA0, or FEB0. Collectively, this range is shown as FE80::/10 and it comprises all of the link-local addresses for IPv6. Every Windows computer with IPv6 installed also receives a loopback address that is ::1. The IPv6 address ::1 is the equivalent to IPv4's loopback address of 127.0.0.1.

> **ExamAlert**
>
> Know the loopback addresses for IPv6 and IPv4.

There are three types of IPv6 addresses, as shown in Table 15.7.

TABLE 15.7 **IPv6 Address Types**

IPv6 Type	Address Range	Description
Unicast	Global Unicast, begins at 2000	▶ Address assigned to one interface ▶ Link-Local addresses begin at FE80::/10 ▶ Loopback is ::1
Anycast	Uses the Unicast structure	▶ Address assigned to a group of interfaces ▶ Packets are delivered to the first interface only
Multicast	FF00::/8	▶ Address assigned to a group of interfaces ▶ Packets are delivered to all interfaces

Here's an example of an IPv6 address:

```
2001:7120:0000:8001:0000:0000:0000:1F10
```

IPv6 addresses are broken down into three sections: the global routing prefix (in this case, 2001:7120:0000); a subnet that is 8001; and the individual interface ID, shown as 0000:0000:0000:1F10.

This is the full address, but you will more commonly see truncated addresses. There are two ways to truncate, or shorten, an IPv6 address. The first is to remove leading zeros. Any group of 4 zeros can be truncated to a single zero; basically zero is always zero, so the additional zeros are not necessary. Also, one consecutive group of zeros can be truncated as a double colon (::). The example shows 12 consecutive zeros that can be truncated simply to a double colon. (A double colon can be used only once in an address.) The following is the end result of both of these abbreviations:

```
2001:7120:0:8001::1F10
```

> **ExamAlert**
>
> Understand how IPv6 addresses can be truncated.

IPv6 addresses can be assigned statically as well; this can be done within the Internet Protocol Version 6 Properties dialog box, which can be accessed from Local Area Connection Properties (and is listed next to IPv4).

TCP/IP Protocols and Their Ports

Network sessions on an IP network are normally either TCP or UDP. Let's briefly discuss these two.

Transmission Control Protocol (TCP) sessions are known as connection-oriented sessions. This means that every packet that is sent is checked for delivery. If the receiving computer doesn't receive a packet, it cannot assemble the message and will ask the sending computer to transmit the packet again. No one packet is left behind.

User Datagram Protocol (UDP) sessions are known as connectionless sessions. UDP is used in streaming media sessions. In these cases, if a packet is dropped, it is not asked for again. Let's say you were listening to some streaming music and you heard a break in the song or a blip of some kind. That indicates some missing packets, but you wouldn't want those packets back because by the time you get them, you would be listening to a totally different part of the music stream!

It's expected that you might lose packets in UDP streams but not when making TCP connections. Both TCP and UDP utilize protocols and ports to make connections. Let's further discuss these protocols and ports.

For two computers to communicate, they must both use the same protocol. For an application to send or receive data, it must use a particular protocol designed for that application and open up a port on the network adapter to make a connection to another computer. For example, let's say you want to

visit www.google.com. You would open up a browser and type **http://
www.google.com**. The protocol used is HTTP, short for Hypertext
Transfer Protocol. That is the protocol that makes the connection to the
google.com web server. The HTTP protocol selects an unused port on your
computer (known as an outbound port) to send and receive data to and from
google.com. On the other end, google.com's web server has a specific port
open at all times ready to accept sessions. In most cases the web server's
port is 80, which corresponds to the HTTP protocol. This is known as an
inbound port. Figure 15.6 illustrates this.

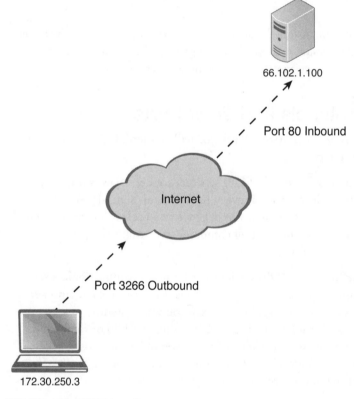

FIGURE 15.6 **HTTP in action**

The local computer on the bottom-left part of Figure 15.6 has been given the
IP address 172.30.250.3, a Class B private address. It uses port 3266 to go out
to the Internet and start a session with google.com. For security purposes,
this is a dynamically assigned port and will be different every time you connect to another web server, but it will normally be somewhere in the thousands. The session is accepted by google.com's web server, using the public

IP address 66.102.1.100, inbound port 80. Conversely, if you want to run your own web server at home and sell widgets and such, that web server would need to have port 80 open to the public at all times. If it were ever closed, you would lose sales! Computers that connect to your web server would use dynamically assigned ports.

There are 65,536 ports in total, numbered between 0 and 65,535, and almost as many protocols! Don't worry; you only need to know about a dozen for the exam, which are listed in Table 15.8.

TABLE 15.8 **Common Protocols and Their Ports**

Protocol	Port
FTP	21
SSH	22
Telnet	23
SMTP	25
DNS	53
HTTP	80
POP3	110
IMAP	143
SLP	427
HTTPS	443
SMB	445, 137–139
AFP	548
RDP	3389

ExamAlert

Memorize the protocol port numbers in Table 15.8!

The ports mentioned in Table 15.8 are the inbound ports used by the computer. Keep in mind that these are the default port numbers and that most protocols can be configured to use whatever inbound port you want. This is less common but is done sometimes as a security precaution. Let's discuss the individual protocols a little bit:

▶ **FTP:** The File Transfer Protocol allows computers to transfer files back and forth. When you connect to an FTP server, that FTP server will have port 21 open. Some type of FTP client software is necessary to connect to the FTP server; this could be done in the command line within the FTP shell or by using a GUI-based application (such as FileZilla).

▶ **SSH:** Secure Shell enables data to be exchanged between computers on a secured channel. This protocol offers a more secure replacement to FTP and Telnet. The Secure Shell server housing the data you want to access would have port 22 open. There are several other protocols that use SSH as a way of making a secure connection. One of these is Secure FTP (SFTP). Regular FTP can be insecure. SFTP combats this by providing file access over a reliable data stream, generated and protected by SSH.

▶ **Telnet:** Short for Telecommunication network, this provides remote access to other hosts using the command-line interface (CLI). It uses port 23 but is an insecure and somewhat deprecated protocol. However, because some companies *might* still use it to access routers and other hosts, you might see a question about it on the exam.

▶ **SMTP:** Simple Mail Transfer Protocol sends e-mail. When you send e-mail from home, it goes to an SMTP server (which has inbound port 25 open) at your ISP and is then sent off to its destination. A good way to remember this is by using the mnemonic device Send Mail To People. It is worth noting that another port (587) can be used with SMTP in the case that an ISP or other agency blocks port 25.

▶ **DNS:** The Domain Name System is the group of servers on the Internet that translates domain names to IP addresses. A DNS server has inbound port 53 open by default.

▶ **HTTP:** Hypertext Transfer Protocol transfers web pages and other web-based material from a web server to your web browser. It is normally done in a compressed format but not in a secured format. Web servers have port 80 open by default.

▶ **POP3:** Post Office Protocol Version 3 is used by e-mail clients to retrieve incoming e-mail from a mail server. The POP3 mail server uses port 110.

▶ **IMAP:** Internet Message Access Protocol (IMAP) is an e-mail protocol that enables messages to remain on the e-mail server so they can be retrieved from any location. IMAP also supports folders, so users can organize their messages as desired. IMAP e-mail servers use inbound port 143 open.

▶ **SLP:** The Service Location Protocol enables computers and other devices to access network services in the LAN without prior configuration. They do this with the aid of a URL; for example, service:printer:lpr://hostname or service:tftp://hostname. It works on port 427, and often uses UDP as the transport mechanism, but can also use TCP.

▶ **HTTPS:** Hypertext Transfer Protocol Secure sends and receives information like HTTP but includes the Transport Layer Security protocol (a successor of the Secure Sockets Layer [SSL] protocol) to encrypt the information, most commonly when making purchases/payments online or when logging in to a confidential website. The HTTPS server has port 443 open.

▶ **SMB:** The Server Message Block (SMB) protocol provides access to shared items such as files and printers. These are actual packets that authenticate remote computers through what are known as interprocess communication (IPC) mechanisms. They can communicate directly over TCP using port 445 or by working with the NetBIOS protocol using a port between 137 and 139. This was also referred to as the Common Internet File System (CIFS) protocol.

▶ **AFP:** Apple Filing Protocol offers file services for Mac computers running OS X allowing for the transfer of files across the network. It uses port 548 (and sometimes 427) for establishing the communication between two systems. Mac computers can also make use of SMB (and other protocols) for making connections to other systems.

▶ **RDP:** To facilitate connections to remote computers and allow full remote control, Microsoft uses the Remote Desktop program, which is based off the Remote Desktop Protocol (RDP). This works in three ways. First, users can be given limited access to a remote computer's applications (such as Word or Excel). Second, administrators can be given full access to a computer so that they can troubleshoot problems from another location. Third, another part of the program known as Remote Assistance allows users to invite a technician to view their desktops in the hopes that the technician can fix any encountered problems. These invitations can be made via e-mail or by Windows Messenger. The RDP port, 3389, is also used by Remote Desktop Services/ Microsoft Terminal Services, which is the server-based companion of Remote Desktop.

There are some additional TCP/IP protocols you should know for the exam:

▶ **DHCP:** The Dynamic Host Configuration Protocol (DHCP) is used to automatically assign IP addresses to hosts. These hosts could be computers, printers, servers, routers, and so on. In most SOHO networks, a router will use DHCP to assign IP addresses to the client computers. However, your ISP will also use DHCP to assign an IP address to you; usually your router gets this. The DHCP service makes life easier for the network administrator by automatically assigning IP addresses, subnet masks, gateway addresses, DNS servers, and so on, from a central location. If you get your address from a DHCP server, you are getting your address assigned dynamically, and it could change periodically. Computers that do obtain IP addresses from a DHCP server have the advantage of automatically getting new addressing when they are moved to a different network segment. However, some computers require a static address, one that is assigned by the network administrator manually. It is better in many situations for servers and printers to use static addresses so you know exactly what the address is and so it won't change.

▶ **SNMP:** Simple Network Management Protocol (SNMP) is used as the standard for managing and monitoring devices on your network. It manages routers, switches, and computers and is often incorporated in software known as a network management system (NMS). The NMS is the main software that controls everything SNMP-based; it is installed on a computer known as a manager. The devices to be monitored are known as managed devices. The NMS installs a small piece of software known as an agent that allows the NMS to monitor those managed devices.

▶ **LDAP:** Lightweight Directory Access Protocol (LDAP) is used to access and maintain distributed directories of information (such as the kind involved with Microsoft domains). Microsoft refers to this as directory services.

ExamAlert

I know there's a lot, but know your protocols and their functions for the exam! Write 'em down or make flash cards to commit them to memory.

Cram Quiz

Answer these questions. The answers follow the last question. If you cannot answer these questions correctly, consider reading this section again until you can.

220-901 Questions

1. Which protocol uses port 22?

   ○ **A.** FTP

   ○ **B.** TELNET

   ○ **C.** SSH

   ○ **D.** HTTP

2. Which of these addresses needs to be configured to enable a computer access to the Internet or to other networks?

   ○ **A.** Subnet mask

   ○ **B.** Gateway address

   ○ **C.** DNS address

   ○ **D.** MAC address

3. The IP address 128.0.0.1 would be part of which IPv4 class?

   ○ **A.** Class A

   ○ **B.** Class B

   ○ **C.** Class C

   ○ **D.** Class D

4. Which technology assigns addresses on the 169.254.0.0 network number?

   ○ **A.** DHCP

   ○ **B.** Static IP

   ○ **C.** APIPA

   ○ **D.** Class B

5. Which type of IPv6 address is commonly assigned to client computers?

   ○ **A.** Unicast

   ○ **B.** Anycast

   ○ **C.** Multicast

   ○ **D.** FF00

6. You want to test the local loopback IPv6 address. Which address would you use?

   ○ **A.** 127.0.0.1

   ○ **B.** ::1

   ○ **C.** FE80::/10

   ○ **D.** ::0

7. Which of these would be used for streaming media?

   ○ **A.** TCP

   ○ **B.** RDP

   ○ **C.** UDP

   ○ **D.** DHCP

8. Which port is used by the IMAP protocol?

   ○ **A.** 53

   ○ **B.** 80

   ○ **C.** 110

   ○ **D.** 143

9. Which protocol sends and receives information in an encrypted manner by default?

   ○ **A.** FTP

   ○ **B.** HTTP

   ○ **C.** HTTPS

   ○ **D.** POP3

10. Which IP address can be a gateway for a computer using the IP address 10.58.64.192 and a subnet mask of 255.255.255.0?

   ○ **A.** 10.58.64.255

   ○ **B.** 10.58.64.1

   ○ **C.** 10.58.64.0

   ○ **D.** 10.59.64.1

11. A user can receive e-mail but cannot send any. Which protocol is not configured properly?

   ○ **A.** POP3

   ○ **B.** FTP

   ○ **C.** SMTP

   ○ **D.** SNMP

Cram Quiz Answers

220-901 Answers

1. **C.** SSH (Secure Shell) uses port 22, FTP uses port 21, Telnet uses port 23, and HTTP uses port 80.

2. **B.** The gateway address must be configured to enable a computer access to the Internet through the gateway device. By default, the subnet mask defines the IP address's network and host portions. The DNS server takes care of name resolution. The MAC address is the address that is burned into the network adapter; it is configured at the manufacturer.

3. **B.** The IP address 128.0.0.1 is part of the Class B range that encompasses 128–191. Class A is 1–126. Class C is 192–223. Class D is 224–239.

4. **C.** If you see an address with 169.254 as the first two octets, then it is Automatic Private IP Addressing (APIPA). This is also the link-local range for IPv4. The Dynamic Host Configuration Protocol (DHCP) assigns IP addresses automatically to clients but by default does not use the 169.254 network number. Static IP addresses are configured manually by the user in the IP Properties window. Class B is a range of IP networks from 128 through 191.

5. **A.** Unicast addresses beginning with FE80::/10 are commonly assigned to client computers automatically. Anycast and multicast addresses are assigned to a group of interfaces; the difference is that anycast packets are delivered to the first interface only and multicast packets are delivered to all interfaces. FF00::/8 is the address range of multicast packets.

6. **B.** You would use the ::1 address. That is the local loopback address for IPv6. 127.0.0.1 is the local loopback for IPv4. FE80::/10 is the range of unicast auto-configured addresses. ::0 is not valid but looks similar to how multiple zeros can be truncated with a double colon.

7. **C.** User Datagram Protocol (UDP) is used for streaming media. It is connection-less, whereas TCP is connection-oriented and not a good choice for streaming media. RDP is the Remote Desktop Protocol used to make connections to other computers. DHCP is the Dynamic Host Configuration Protocol used to assign IP addresses to clients automatically.

8. **D.** The Internet Message Access Protocol (IMAP) uses port 143. DNS uses port 53. HTTP uses port 80. POP3 uses port 110. Know those ports!

9. **C.** Hypertext Transfer Protocol Secure (HTTPS) sends information like HTTP but over a secure channel via SSL or TLS. The other three protocols do not encrypt the data by default.

10. **B.** The gateway address should be 10.58.64.1. It is a classless network; the network number is 10.58.64 because we are using the 255.255.255.0 subnet mask. So the gateway cannot be on the 10.59.64 network; the gateway needs to be on the same network number as the client IP addresses. We cannot use 255 or 0 as the last digit of the IP address because 255 is the broadcast and 0 is the network number. Keep in mind that this is not a Class A network we are dealing with in the question; it is classless. The gateway address can be defined with CIDR notation as 10.58.64.1/24.

11. **C.** The Simple Mail Transfer Protocol (SMTP) is probably not configured properly. It deals with sending mail. POP3 receives mail. FTP sends files to remote computers. SNMP is used to manage networks.

CHAPTER 16

Computer Networking Part II

This chapter covers the following A+ exam topics:

▶ SOHO and Windows Networking

▶ Troubleshooting Networks

You can find a master list of A+ exam topics in the "Introduction."

This chapter covers CompTIA A+ 220-901 objectives 2.5–2.7 and 4.4 and 220-902 objective 1.6.

In this second chapter on computer networking, we'll delve into Windows networking, focusing on small office/home office (SOHO) environments as well as the troubleshooting of networks.

I urge you to review your A+ troubleshooting theory from Chapter 1 before beginning this chapter. I will assume that you know it like the back of your hand. I also recommend briefly reviewing the Windows chapters (especially Chapters 9 and 11) to keep your Windows configuring and troubleshooting skills sharp.

We discussed a lot of concepts in the first computer networking chapter (Chapter 15). Now let's build on those concepts. Know that CompTIA wants you to be aware of the most organized, budget-friendly, approaches to SOHO networking, and be prepared to implement efficient solutions to problems.

SOHO and Windows Networking

In this section, we'll discuss what it takes to set up a small Windows network and connect it to the Internet. We'll assume that your Windows operating systems are all installed but not yet quite configured for networking. Before we can connect the Windows computers to the network and the Internet, we need to create a network. We'll need a multifunction network device, which I will refer to as a router for simplicity. And the router must be compatible with the Internet service we want to use. So first, we'll talk about the types of Internet connections available. Then we'll discuss the router and its various configurations. Finally, we'll configure and connect the computers' network adapters and Windows operating systems so that they can connect to the network and out to the Internet. Let's go!

Internet Services

There are a lot of different options for connecting to the Internet, including fiber-based systems, DSL, cable Internet, the venerable dial-up, and more. The type of Internet connection dictates download speeds to the clients on a SOHO network.

Dial-Up

Strange as it might seem, dial-up Internet is still used by many people around the world, and in some areas of the United States, it is the only Internet connectivity available. Dial-up connections are inexpensive but at the cost of slow data throughput and dropped connections. To connect to a dial-up service, a user needs four things: a working phone line (with an RJ11 connection), an account with an Internet service provider (ISP), a modem to dial up to the ISP's networks, and some type of software to control the dial-up connection (for example, dial-up networking). The modem serves to modulate and demodulate signals that travel between the computer and the phone line. It sends and receives data in a serial fashion, meaning one bit at a time. Today, the dial-up modem is usually a USB-based device, but on older laptops it could be integrated, and on older desktops it could act as an internal adapter card or an external device that connects to a DE-9 serial port that utilizes the RS-232 data transmission standard. The modem uses a universal asynchronous receiver transmitter (UART)—this converts the serial information coming in from the phone line into parallel data to be sent to the processor. The UART is commonly integrated into a microcontroller either within the computer's motherboard or within the modem itself. Dial-up utilizes the plain old telephone service/public switched telephone network (POTS/PSTN). POTS is that simple landline that comes into a home, allowing a person to make phone calls. PSTN is the entire set of hardware and technologies at a telephone company's central office that controls POTS connections. Be careful when connecting a phone line to a computer. Make sure that it is connected to a modem (RJ11) and not to the network card (RJ45). The phone company sends a strong voltage through the line, which can damage a network adapter.

> **Note**
>
> Because dial-up connections are typically limited to 56 Kb/s, they should be avoided unless there is absolutely no other option for connecting to the Internet.

ISDN

Integrated Services Digital Network (ISDN) is a digital technology developed to combat the limitations of PSTN. Users can send data, talk on the phone, fax—and all from one line. It is broken down into two types of services:

▶ **BRI:** Basic Rate ISDN: 128 Kb/s. Two equal B channels at 64 Kb/s each for data and one separate 16 Kb/s D channel for timing.

▶ **PRI: Primary Rate ISDN:** 1.536 Mb/s, runs on a T-1 circuit; 23 equal 64 Kb/s B channels for data and one 64 Kb/s D channel for timing.

ISDN is not used as often as cable Internet or fiber optic services, but some companies still use ISDN for video conferencing or as a fault-tolerant secondary Internet access connection. Data commuters use this if DSL or cable is not available.

DSL

Digital subscriber line (DSL) builds on dial-up by providing full digital data transmissions over phone lines but at high speeds. DSL modems connect to the phone line and to the PC's network adapter or to a SOHO router enabling sharing among multiple computers. One of the benefits of DSL is that you can talk on the phone line and transmit data at the same time. There are several derivatives of DSL, for example:

▶ **ADSL (Asymmetrical Digital Subscriber Line):** ADSL enables transmission over copper wires that is faster than dial-up. It is generally geared toward the consumer that requires more downstream bandwidth than upstream. Because the downloading and uploading speeds are different, it is known as an asymmetric technology. There is a group of ADSL technologies offering data transfer rates of anywhere from 8 Mb/s down/1 Mb/s up to 52 Mb/s down/16 Mb/s up, with newer, faster technologies being developed as of the writing of this book. ADSL is often offered to consumers who cannot get cable Internet.

▶ **SDSL (Symmetrical Digital Subscriber Line):** SDSL is installed (usually to companies) as a separate line and is usually more expensive. Unlike ADSL, SDSL upload and download speeds are the same, or symmetrical. Maximum data transfer rates for typical versions of SDSL are 1.5 Mb/s and 5 Mb/s (depending on the version).

Cable Internet

Broadband cable, used for cable Internet and cable TV, has download transfer rates from 5 Mb/s to 150 Mb/s or more (depending on the ISP). Uploading speeds are almost always slower, often 10 times slower than download speeds. Like most Internet connectivity options, cable Internet is shared by the customer base. The more users who are on the Internet, the slower it becomes for everyone. Cable Internet is a common option for home use and for SOHO networks that use a router to allow multiple computers access to the Internet via a cable. An RG-6 cable is run into the office and connected to the cable modem by way of a screw-on F-connector. The cable modem also has an RJ45 connection for patching to the router or to an individual computer's network adapter.

> **ExamAlert**
>
> Understand how cable Internet connections are made.

Fiber Optic

Instead of using a copper connection to the home or business the way dial-up, DSL, or cable Internet do, some companies offer fiber optic connections direct to the customer. This is known as fiber to the premises (FTTP)—it is the installation and use of optical fiber from a central point directly to individual buildings, such as residences, apartment buildings, and businesses.

Most FTTP services run over a fiber optic line to a network interface device in the home or office (specifically an optical network terminal); from there, it changes over to copper, which then makes the connection to the customer's SOHO router or individual computer. This copper connection could be a twisted-pair patch cable (for example, a Cat 6 cable) or a coaxial cable using the Multimedia over Coax Alliance (MoCA) protocol. Examples of companies that offer FTTP include Verizon (FIOS) and Google (Google Fiber).

However, there are other varieties of fiber available to the customer, and these varieties are defined by the point where the fiber ends and the copper begins. Collectively, these are referred to as "fiber to the x," where x equals the end-point for the fiber run. For example, FTTN is fiber to the neighborhood, where the fiber is terminated at a street enclosure that could be up to miles away from the customer's premises. Another example is FTTC (fiber to the cabinet), which generally means that the wiring cabinet is within 1000 feet of the premises. FTTdp (fiber to the distribution point) brings the connection within meters of the customer's premises.

Again, the service we first mentioned, FTTP, is the most common and it's broken down into FTTB (fiber to the building or business) and FTTH (fiber to the home). But it's possible to get the fiber optic connection even closer to the individual user by acquiring the FTTD (fiber to the desktop) service. This could terminate at a fiber media converter near the user's computer or even connect directly to a fiber optic network adapter in the computer. However, a service such as FTTD is much more expensive and therefore is used much less frequently—that is, if the service is even available in your area.

Fiber optic cables can run at much higher data transfer rates than copper-based cables. Home-based fiber optic Internet connections can typically download data at 100 Mb/s and even 1000 Mb/s. Upload speeds are typically less, as they are in most Internet services.

WiMAX

The Worldwide Interoperability for Microwave Access (WiMAX) is an IEEE 802.16 wireless technology that offers high-speed connections (up to a gigabit) but over much larger distances than a standard Wi-Fi access point reaches—on average, 50 kilometers. So if your organization is within 50 km of an urban area, it might be able to connect its LAN to the Internet at high speed in a completely wireless fashion. There are individual WiMAX modems for laptops and PCs and gateway devices for entire LANs. For an optimal connection, these gateways (or routers) will usually be placed on a window sill facing where the signal is coming from. As of the writing of this book, it has been all but overtaken by 4G LTE and is only used in specific niche markets.

Satellite

Satellite connectivity uses a parabolic antenna (satellite dish) to connect via line of sight to a satellite; it is used in places where standard landline Internet access is not available. The satellite is in geosynchronous orbit, at 22,000 miles (35,406 km) above the Earth. This is the farthest distance of any Internet technology. The "dish" connects to coax cable that runs to a switching/channeling device for your computers. Today's satellite connections offer speeds close to traditional broadband access (similar to cable Internet access). One of the issues with satellite is electrical and natural interference. Another problem is latency. Due to the distance (44,000 miles total) of the data transfer, there can be a delay of .5 seconds to 5 seconds. That's the highest latency of any Internet technology. Latency goes hand-in-hand with distance. In the past, satellite-based Internet connections offered high-speed downloads, but uploads were slow due to the fact the service would use a dial-up line to upload information. Newer satellite Internet technologies allow for the upload of data to the satellite as well, and while this is often still slower than the download speed, it is much faster than uploading via dial-up.

Another technology similar to this is *line-of-sight* microwave links. These are often made between wireless towers (such as WiMAX) but can also be installed at a campus. Parabolic antennae are positioned on different buildings so they can see each other and send information at high speed without the need for a cabled connection. There are also line-of-sight wireless Internet services for customers who are within eyeshot of the radio tower providing the service.

Cellular

The term *cellular* has grown to encompass several different technologies, such as GSM, CDMA, GPRS, EDGE, 4G, LTE, and more. Cellular data connections are also referred to as wireless WAN or WWAN connections. Use of cellular on a smartphone, tablet, or with a WAN card requires a subscription with a cellular provider. For more information on cellular technologies, see Chapter 18, "Android, iOS, OS X, and Linux."

Router Setup and Wireless

Okay! Now that we have Internet connectivity out of the way, let's talk about the setup and configuration of our SOHO router. These devices have been called a plethora of different names—router, switch, firewall, access point, or multifunction network device—because they usually incorporate all of those functions into one device. Again, for simplicity, we'll refer to this as a router.

SOHO Router Setup

First, the router needs to be physically connected, which is very easy. It requires power from an AC outlet and a connection to the Internet, which is done with a twisted-pair patch cable using RJ45 plugs on each end; one end connects to the Internet (or WAN) port of the router, and the other end connects to the cable modem or other network interface device.

Most SOHO routers are set up to be plug-and-play, meaning that computers can be plugged in to the routers' switch ports (often 4 or 8 of them) and they can communicate with each other and access the Internet right out of the box. But a word of caution: You don't want to use the default settings that the manufacturer gives you; they might be insecure. So the first thing we want to do is to log in to the router so that we can make some changes. (We'll assume that your computers are already cabled to the router.) To do this, open a browser window and type the IP address of the router. For example, different manufacturers use different default IP addresses (such as 192.168.0.1 or 192.168.1.1) or they allow a connection via a URL (such as http://routername). Check your documentation to find out what the address or link is. Sometimes the login information is very basic (for example, "admin" is the username) and there is no password or there is a very basic password (possibly the same as the username). That will depend on the age of the router. Newer routers usually offer more security. Again, the documentation that came with the router will tell you the defaults.

Once you have gained access to the router, the first thing you want to do is change the password to something more complex. Consider changing the username also, if possible. Next, update the firmware so that it gets the latest functionality, options, and security available. Now the device has some basic security and is updated; it is ready to be configured.

SOHO routers normally obtain an IP address from the Internet service provider; it is dynamically assigned and is known as the WAN address. It is a public address that is visible on the Internet. The router also has a LAN address, which is a private address visible only to the computers on your network. That is the address you used to log in to the router (192.168.0.1 or 192.168.1.1, and so on) and also acts as the gateway address for the clients on your network. Figure 16.1 shows the LAN and WAN settings on a typical SOHO router.

LAN	
MAC Address:	30-B5-C2-B2-59-E6
IP Address:	192.168.0.1
Subnet Mask:	255.255.255.0

WAN	
MAC Address:	30-B5-C2-B2-59-E7
IP Address:	64.121.138.225
Subnet Mask:	255.255.240.0
Default Gateway:	64.121.128.1
DNS Server:	208.59.247.45 , 208.59.247.46

FIGURE 16.1   **LAN and WAN connections on a typical SOHO router**

As you can see from the figure, the router's LAN address is 192.168.0.1. This device makes use of DHCP, which can be turned on or off. When on, it automatically assigns IP addresses to most of the clients on this network starting with 192.168.0.100 and ascending from there—192.168.0.101, 192.168.0.102, and so on. The router and all of the clients are on the same local area network number (192.168.0.0) using the same subnet mask (255.255.255.0), so they can all communicate with each other.

The WAN address, however, is 64.121.138.225. This was obtained automatically from the ISP and allows connectivity to the ISP's network infrastructure and out to the Internet. The subnet mask (255.255.240.0) is not a default subnet mask, so we know that subnetting (the subdividing of an IP network) has been implemented. The default gateway (64.121.128.1) is the address that our router looks for to get into (and beyond) the ISP network and out to the Internet; just as the LAN clients look for the 192.168.0.1 gateway to go beyond the LAN. Finally, the DNS server addresses (starting with 208) are on a completely different network altogether, as they usually are. These resolve domain names to IP addresses when the router tries to access a server on the Internet.

If you have one, take a look at your SOHO router and identify the LAN and WAN addresses. The numbers will often be different, but the concepts remain the same. If you don't have a SOHO router, you can easily find an emulator of a router online. Try companies such as ASUS, D-Link, and other manufacturers of SOHO routers—they often provide emulators that simulate their actual routers.

> **ExamAlert**
>
> Understand the concept of the LAN and WAN address of a SOHO router. It is the basis for all routing!

In some cases, you need to use a static IP address for your WAN connection, or perhaps you need to configure a secure connection to the Internet with Point to Point Tunneling Protocol (PPTP) or Layer 2 Tunneling Protocol (L2TP). If that is the case, you would have to input the correct information, including IP address, username, and so forth. This information should be provided to you by the ISP you connect to.

802.11 Wireless

Until now, we have been talking about wired network connectivity. Now I'd like to shift gears for a moment and move over to wireless options for the LAN. This type of wireless connectivity is known as Wi-Fi or wireless LAN (WLAN). The Institute of Electrical and Electronics Engineers (IEEE) developed the 802.11 series of protocols. These define the various speeds, frequencies, and protocols used to transmit data over radio waves in small geographic areas using unlicensed spectrums.

There are several different 802.11 derivatives you need to know for the exam: 802.11a, 802.11b, 802.11g, 802.11n, and 802.11ac. Table 16.1 shows these technologies and the characteristics that differentiate them.

TABLE 16.1 **802.11 Standards**

802.11 Version	Maximum Data Rate	Frequency
802.11a	54 Mb/s	5 GHz
802.11b	11 Mb/s	2.4 GHz
802.11g	54 Mb/s*	2.4 GHz
802.11n	300/600 Mb/s	5 and/or 2.4 GHz
802.11ac	1.7 Gb/s	5 GHz

* 802.11g network throughput can be doubled to 108 Mb/s using Super G technology.

> **ExamAlert**
>
> Know the data rates, and frequencies used, for each of the 802.11 versions!

One thing I left out of the table is coverage or distance. It is difficult to put an exact number on the maximum wireless transmission distances for each standard because it depends on the signal strength of the WAP's antenna, the use of additional features, and environmental factors such as obstructions and interference. But generally, the wireless range from WAP to client increases with each standard listed on the table, with 802.11n and 802.11ac providing similar ranges.

> **Note**
>
> New technologies are being developed as of the writing of this book that use higher frequency ranges and can transmit much more data per second. Always be on the alert for emerging networking technologies!

The data transfer rates of newer wireless network technologies are increased using a concept known as *multipath propagation*. This is when an antenna (or antennas) receive radio signals on two or more paths. A common example of this is multiple-input and multiple-output (MIMO) technology, which is incorporated into 802.11n and 802.11ac wireless networks (as well as 4G LTE). As of the writing of this book, typical 802.11ac wireless devices use three or four antennas; the 802.11ac standard complies with multiuser MIMO (or MU-MIMO), which can have four simultaneous downlinks.

Now let's take a look at the actual wireless settings of a typical router. Examine Figure 16.2.

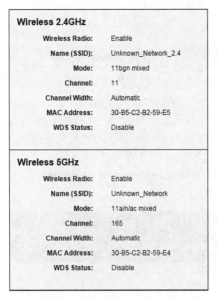

FIGURE 16.2   Wireless configuration on a typical SOHO router

We can see that this device is running two wireless networks: one on the 2.4 GHz frequency and one on 5 GHz. Each has its own network name, also known as a Service Set Identifier (SSID). For example, the 5 GHz network's SSID is "Unknown_Network." (A bit of a quirky name, but you'll find that peculiar names are somewhat common when it comes to SSIDs.) That's the name that users would need to know in order to make a wireless connection to the LAN. It's currently running on channel 165. If using the 5 GHz frequency range in the United States, a wireless access point can be set up on any channel between 48 and 165. Other countries may have slightly different ranges. The wireless network shown in the figure is currently configured to run in mixed mode, meaning that it can accept connections from wireless clients running the 802.11a, 802.11n, or 802.11ac protocols. This allows for greater compatibility. However, some organizations will require only a single type of connection for all clients (for example, 802.11ac). This can result in greater WAP efficiency and, of course, greater speed for all clients involved—but at greater expense.

The other wireless network on the 2.4 GHz frequency is set to channel 11. In the United States, the 2.4 GHz frequency range consists of channel 1 through 11. (Again, other countries may differ slightly.) For noninterference with other wireless devices, choose channel 1, 6, or 11. That's because the 2.4 GHz spectrum is divided into three sections: channels 1–5, channels 6–10, and channel 11. This network is also running in mixed mode; it allows connections from 802.11b, 802.11g, and 802.11n (2.4 GHz) wireless clients.

ExamAlert

Know the difference between the wireless frequencies 5 GHz and 2.4 GHz and the channel ranges for each.

It's important to encrypt the wireless connection. The accepted standard for SOHO networks (as of the writing of this book) is to use the protocols WPA2 and AES. We'll discuss these more in Chapter 17, "Security."

More SOHO Router Tidbits

Most people are wireless crazy nowadays, but don't forget that these SOHO routers normally come with four wired LAN ports that are rated for 100BASE-T and 1000BASE-T. That means that it can auto-negotiate connections at 100 Mb/s and 1000 Mb/s (1 Gb/s). The BASE applies to any speed, and it is short for baseband, meaning every computer on the network shares the same channel or frequency. The T is short for twisted pair. By default, unshielded twisted-pair cables can send data 328 feet (100 meters) before the electronic signal attenuates to such a point where it is useless.

The physical ports make up the switching portion of our SOHO router. But these devices work with TCP/IP ports as well, such as FTP port 21 or HTTP port 80. There are several things you might be called on to configure regarding ports:

▶ **NAT:** Network address translation (NAT) is the process of modifying IP addresses as information crosses a router. Generally, this functionality is built into a router. It hides an entire IP address space on the LAN (for example, 192.168.0.1 through 192.168.0.255). Whenever an IP address on the LAN wants to communicate with the Internet, the IP is converted to the public IP of the router (for example, 68.54.127.95) but it will be whatever IP address was assigned to the router by the ISP. This way, it looks like the router is the only device making the connection to remote computers on the Internet, providing safety for the computers on the LAN. It also allows a single IP to do the work for many IP addresses in the LAN.

▶ **Port forwarding:** This forwards an external network port to an internal IP address and port. This enables you to have a web server, FTP server, and other servers, but you need to have only one port for each open on the WAN side of the router. It can be any port you like; of course, you would need to tell people which port they need to connect to if it is not a standard one. Some devices use what are called virtual servers, making the process a lot more user-friendly. So, for example, you might have an FTP server running internally on your LAN; its IP address and port might be 192.168.0.100:21 (notice how the colon separates the IP address from the port), but you would have users on the Internet connect to your router's WAN address (for example, 65.43.18.1) and any port you want. The router takes care of the rest, and the forwarding won't be noticed by the typical user. Port forwarding is also referred to as destination NAT (DNAT).

▶ **Port triggering:** This enables you to specify outgoing ports that your computer uses for special applications, and their corresponding inbound ports will be opened automatically when the sessions are established. This is helpful for things like bit torrents.

▶ **DMZ:** A demilitarized zone (DMZ) is an area that is not quite on the Internet and not quite part of your LAN. It's a sort of middle ground that is for the most part protected by a firewall, but particular traffic will be let through. It's a good place for web servers, e-mail servers, and FTP servers because these are services required by users on the Internet. The beauty of this is that the users will not have access to your LAN—if it is configured correctly, of course. Quite often, the DMZ is set up as the third leg of a firewall. The first leg connects to the LAN, the second leg connects to the Internet, and the third connects to the DMZ. You need to know the ports that your servers will use and create rules within the firewall (or an all-in-one device, such as a SOHO router) to allow only the required traffic into the DMZ.

There are some other router technologies and functions you should be aware of and know how to configure, including QoS and UPnP:

▶ **QoS:** Quality of service is a feature that attempts to prioritize streaming media, such as VoIP phone calls and audio or video playback, over other types of network traffic.

▶ **UPnP:** Universal Plug and Play is a group of networking protocols that allows computers, printers, and other Internet-ready devices to discover each other on the network. It is a consumer-level technology designed to make networking easier for the user.

ExamAlert

Know the terms NAT, DNAT, port forwarding, port triggering, DMZ, QoS, and UPnP. Practice working with these technologies on your own SOHO router or with an online emulator.

Usually, QoS and UPnP can be enabled by simply selecting the appropriate checkbox in the router configuration screen. Finally, when configuration is complete, we need to place our SOHO router. It is important to keep the device away from any electrical sources (such as outlets, UPSes, or microwaves) and any large amounts of metal to avoid interference (EMI). The basement is probably not the best place for a router due to the thick walls, copper pipes, and electrical panels causing wireless interference. The device should be placed in the physical center of the office or the home for best reception. The more centralized the router is, the better the wireless access your computers will get. The antennas should be either at a 90-degree angle from each other or pointing toward where the computers are. And that pretty much wraps up the basic configuration of a SOHO router. Let's move on to the Windows computers!

Windows Configurations

For the exam, you need to know how to configure network adapter settings, become a member of a network, and make networking connections. Let's begin with network card properties.

Network Card Properties

When configuring and analyzing the network adapter, we can use several status indicators; some are hardware-based and some are software-oriented.

Note

Technicians use several terms when referring to a network card: network adapter, network interface controller (NIC), Ethernet card, and so on. Be ready for different terminology on the exam and in the field. For this chapter, I usually refer to it as network adapter because it won't always be in "card" format.

The first types of indicators are physical; they show up as LED lights on the network adapter itself. Different network adapters have different LED lights, but typically you have a connectivity LED and an activity LED. The connectivity LED tells you if you have a good connection to a router or switch by displaying a solid color (for example, solid green), which would mean connectivity at 1000 Mb/s. However, if the connectivity LED is blinking, then you know there is an intermittent connection that should be troubleshot. The activity LED blinks when data is passing through the network adapter. The functionality of both might be combined into one LED on some network adapters.

The second group of indicators is logical and shows up in the operating system. These indicators normally manifest themselves in the Notification Area and can be put there by Windows or by the manufacturer of the network adapter, depending on whether you let Windows install the card or whether you used the additional software that came with the network adapter. However, you can add a shortcut to network adapters and place them on the desktop or on the taskbar.

Let's check out the status of a wired network connection and a wireless network connection. Right-click the Network icon in the Notification Area and select Open Network and Sharing Center. If wireless is your primary method of connecting to the network, you will see a wireless icon; if your primary connection is wired, you will see a little icon displaying a monitor and network cable.

In the Network and Sharing Center window, click the Change adapter settings link. This opens the Network Connections window. Double-click the desired connection to bring up its status window. This is named "Wi-Fi" for the wireless adapter or "Ethernet" ("Local Area Connection" in Windows 7/Vista) for the wired adapter. Figure 16.3 shows both types of connections.

> **Note**
>
> You can change the name of the network connection. Know the different names and the default settings.

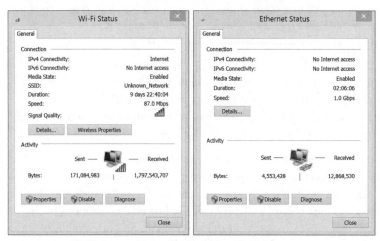

FIGURE 16.3   **Wireless and wired network adapter status**

From here, we can see what our "speed" is, how long we have been connected, and how many bytes have been sent and received. For example, the Wi-Fi connection is connected at 87 Mb/s, even though it is a strong signal on an 802.11ac network (you can imagine the data that flies through my airwaves). On less frequently used wireless networks, you might see connections of up to 300 Mb/s, 600 Mb/s, or even 1 Gb/s. As you can see, the speed indicator can be very telling about a wireless connection. If you suspect a slow wireless speed, make sure that the latest driver is installed, verify placement of the wireless antennas, check for interference, and even check for unauthorized usage of the wireless network. Consider using a Wi-Fi analyzer to investigate your wireless network and the wireless networks around you. You might find that there is some frequency and channel overlap.

In the second window in Figure 16.3, we see that the Ethernet connection has a 1 Gb/s connection. Remember that these connection speeds are the maximum at which the network adapter will transfer data. In addition, to get this speed, every link in the networking chain must operate at 1 Gb/s, including the network adapter, patch cables, and the SOHO router itself. If any one of those links runs at less than 1000 Mb/s, the entire connection would be brought down to that lesser number.

> **Note**
>
> In the computer networking world, "speed" is also referred to as "bandwidth," though both terms might not be quite accurate technically. If you purchase a gigabit network adapter for your computer, its maximum data transfer rate will be 1 Gb/s. However, the *actual* data transferred is known as data throughput.

If we click the Properties button, it brings us to the Properties window for that specific connection—a nice shortcut to the TCP/IP settings and plenty of other networking settings, some of which can be accessed from the Configure button. Let's discuss a few of those now.

How well your network adapter operates depends on several factors (for example, the duplex setting it is configured for). There are two duplex settings that a network adapter can be set for: half-duplex and full-duplex. Half-duplex means that your network adapter can send or receive data but not at the same time; full-duplex means that the adapter can do both simultaneously, thus doubling the maximum data throughput. This can be configured by navigating to Device Manager and then going to the properties of the network adapter (also accessible from the aforementioned Configure button in the network adapter's Status window). Either way, access the Advanced tab and the Link Speed & Duplex setting (or like name). This is normally set to auto-negotiation, but you can modify the speed or duplexing settings to take full advantage of your network. Of course, this depends on the type of device your network adapter connects to and how that device is configured. If your router is capable of 1000 Mb/s in full duplex mode, by all means select this on the network adapter! That will enable it to send *and* receive 1000 Mb/s at the same time.

> **ExamAlert**
>
> Know the difference between half-duplex and full-duplex.

You might also decide to configure other settings, such as Wake-on-LAN (WoL), Power over Ethernet (PoE), and quality of service (QoS)—if your network adapter supports them. WOL is used so that the computer can be woken up by a remote computer when that remote system sends data to the network adapter. (This can be a special packet known as a magic packet.) This is great for small networks when you store data on one computer that is set to sleep after, say, 15 minutes. The data sent to the network adapter will wake up the computer, allowing the remote user to get the data required. (I have a video showing how to implement WOL on my website if you are interested.) As mentioned in Chapter 15, PoE is when a device is supplied power by the Ethernet networking connection. The power travels along the network cable along with the data. It is standardized as Ethernet 802.3af. This is common for IP-based devices, such as WAPs, IP cameras, VoIP phones, and so on. As mentioned before, QoS attempts to prioritize streaming media and other types of data.

Workgroup, HomeGroup, and Domain

After you have configured your network adapter, you are ready to join a network. There are a few choices; in the business world, it's either workgroup or domain. A home or home office that is inhabited by Windows 7 or newer computers can be configured for HomeGroup, which is another type of workgroup.

Workgroups and domains are more logical groupings of computers. A workgroup (sometimes also referred to as peer-to-peer) is usually a small group of computers that share the same network name. No one computer controls the network and all systems are considered equal. One of the disadvantages is that a computer storing data can be accessed only by a maximum of 20 other systems simultaneously. A domain builds on this by having one or more computers that are in control of the network and enabling for more computers, more simultaneous access, and centralized administration. Domains also get a name and are sometimes also referred to as client/server networks. You can select whether your computers will be part of a workgroup or a domain by opening the System Properties dialog box and selecting the Computer Name tab. (Or go to Run and type **SystemPropertiesComputerName**.) Then click the Change button. This displays the Computer Name/Domain Changes dialog box, as shown in Figure 16.4.

FIGURE 16.4 **Computer Name/Domain Changes dialog box**

From here, you can join a workgroup (which is the default, by the way) or attempt to join a domain. Your SOHO network will probably not have a domain, but who knows. If you are anything like me, you might end up running multiple domains, which is entirely possible even in a small SOHO network. However, most SOHO networks in the field will not use domains; they are more commonly found in larger organizations. The domain is controlled by a Microsoft server known as a domain controller. To connect to the domain from a client computer, you need to know the domain name (for example, supernetwork.com) and the DNS server IP address for that domain. You also need an account on the domain and need to log on to that domain with a username and password assigned to you by the systems administrator or network administrator. At this point, it gets beyond the scope of the A+ exams and into the realm of Microsoft certifications.

Windows can help you select your computer's location and optimize the system for that location. To change the location, open the Network and Sharing Center and click the View Your Active Networks link. From here, you can select whether the computer is part of a Home network, a Work network, or a Public network. (This is also asked of you when you complete a Windows installation.) The most common and default option is the Home network. When part of a Home network, you can create or join HomeGroups.

The HomeGroup element of Windows 7 and newer offers SOHO users a quick-and-dirty way to accomplish networking. It is aimed at sharing files, multimedia, printers, and so on. To configure HomeGroup, go to Start > Control Panel > All Control Panel Items > HomeGroup. From here, you can leave and join HomeGroups, view the password (an alphanumeric code created by the OS automatically), and configure advanced settings (for example, enabling/disabling network discovery, enabling/disabling file and printer sharing, configuring media streaming, and configuring file sharing encryption). Take a look at the options available to you. You will find the same settings listed in the Network and Sharing Center > Advanced Sharing Settings.

> **ExamAlert**
>
> Be able to define the differences between a HomeGroup, workgroup, and domain.

Sharing Resources and Making Network Connections

Before anyone can view the amazing things you have to offer on your computer, you need to *share* them. As mentioned previously, sharing needs to be turned on in the Network and Sharing Center or the HomeGroup Advanced Settings. Then it can be enabled for individual resources. For example, let's say we had a folder named "data" and we wanted to share the contents of that folder to other users and computers. We would need to locate the folder, right-click it, and either select Share with or select Properties and then click the Sharing tab. Figures 16.5 and 16.6 show both of these.

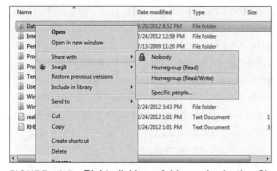

FIGURE 16.5 **Right-clicking a folder and selecting Share with**

FIGURE 16.6   The Sharing tab of the Data folder Properties window

In Figure 16.5, you can see that folders are locked by default and are shared with no one. However, you can opt to have other users in the HomeGroup read the data or be able to read and modify the data. Figure 16.6 shows that we can share here as well; plus we can enable Advanced Sharing and set custom permissions for users. Now, in some cases you might find that HomeGroup doesn't do exactly what you want. For example, when you share a folder, it might add to the network path in a way that doesn't allow third-party devices to connect. If that is the case, use the Advanced Sharing button within the Sharing tab of the folder's Properties sheet. That will eliminate any additions to the network path. And for whatever reason, in the future you might not want to be a member of a HomeGroup any more. To exit the HomeGroup, open the HomeGroup window again and select Leave. Then you can also stop and disable the services HomeGroup Listener and HomeGroup Provider. Later, if the computer becomes a member of a domain, it can still access shared resources on other computers in the HomeGroup, but the computer will not be able to share its own resources to other systems. You can also create administrative shares, which can be seen by administrators but not by typical users. To do this, add a dollar sign ($) to the end of the share name. Drive letters are automatically shared as administrative shares (for example, C$).

Now, if you want to access shares on another computer, you can do it in myriad ways. First, if you are part of a HomeGroup, go to Windows Explorer/ File Explorer and click HomeGroup on the left window pane. Any shares on other computers should show up there. You can also browse the network through the Network component in Windows Explorer/File Explorer.

Another way to access shares is to map a network drive. This makes a permanent connection to a shared folder using Explorer and assigns it a drive letter. These network drives are mapped according to the universal naming convention (UNC), which is \\computername\sharename.

To map a drive, do the following:

1. Locate the Map Network Drive window.

   ▶ In Windows 8: Open File Explorer, click Computer on the Menu bar, and then click Map network drive.

   ▶ In Windows 7/Vista: Open Windows Explorer, click Tools on the Menu bar, and then click Map Network Drive. (If the Menu bar is not visible, press Alt+T on the keyboard.)

2. Select a drive letter (for example, F:).

3. Type the entire path to the share you want to map to. Use the naming convention mentioned previously or connect by \\IPaddress\sharename.

4. Click Finish.

An example is shown in Figure 16.7. You'll note the computer name is Music-Box and the share name is Data.

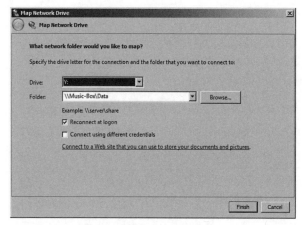

FIGURE 16.7   **Map Network Drive window**

Mapping network drives can also be done in the Command Prompt with the Net Use command. For example, to map the same drive as shown in Figure 16.7, the syntax would be `net use y: \\Music-Box\data`.

> **ExamAlert**
>
> Know how to map network drives in the GUI and in the Command Prompt.

Let's say you want to connect to your network but you are at a remote location. Enter the VPN. Virtual private networks (VPNs) were developed so that telecommuters, salespeople, and others could connect to the office from a remote location. If set up properly, the remote logon connection is seamless and appears as if you are actually at the LAN in the office. You log on just as you would if you were at your desk at headquarters. VPNs give the user access to all the resources that they get when logging on locally. VPNs take advantage of the infrastructure of the Internet and fast connections (such as cable, fiber, DSL, and so on). A VPN connection can be identified by an additional network connection in the Notification Area, as an additional network connection when using the `ipconfig` command, or as a pop-up window that comes up during the logon process (for example, the kind used by Cisco VPN software). Connections to VPNs can be initiated by navigating to the Network and Sharing Center and selecting the Set Up a New Connection or Network link. From there, you would opt for Connect to a Workplace and then select VPN. You would need to know the IP address or name of the VPN server you are connecting to as well as a username and password to get in. Alternate IP configurations are sometimes used with VPN connections.

Cram Quiz

Answer these questions. The answers follow the last question. If you cannot answer these questions correctly, consider reading this section again until you can.

220-901 Questions

1. Which Internet service makes use of PSTN?

   ○ **A.** Dial-up

   ○ **B.** ISDN

   ○ **C.** DSL

   ○ **D.** Cable Internet

2. Which 802.11 version has a maximum data rate of 54 Mb/s and uses the 2.4 GHz frequency range?

   ○ **A.** 802.11a

   ○ **B.** 802.11b

   ○ **C.** 802.11g

   ○ **D.** 802.11n

3. Which of the following forwards an external network port to an internal IP address/port on a computer on the LAN?

   ○ **A.** Port triggering

   ○ **B.** Port forwarding

   ○ **C.** DMZ

   ○ **D.** DHCP

4. Which of the following is described as the simultaneous sending and receiving of network data?

   ○ **A.** Half-duplex

   ○ **B.** Latency

   ○ **C.** PoE

   ○ **D.** Full-duplex

5. Which of the following requires a Windows-created password to gain access to?

   ○ **A.** Workgroup

   ○ **B.** Client/server

   ○ **C.** HomeGroup

   ○ **D.** Domain

6. You want to connect to a share on \\server1\data-share. Which of the following should be used to accomplish this?

   ○ **A.** HomeGroup

   ○ **B.** Right-click the folder and select Share with

   ○ **C.** `ipconfig`

   ○ **D.** `net use`

Cram Quiz Answers

220-901 Answers

1. **A.** Dial-up Internet connections make use of the public switched telephone network (PSTN) and POTS phone lines. ISDN was developed to meet the limitations of PSTN. DSL provides faster data transmissions over phone lines (or separate data lines). Cable Internet is a broadband service that offers higher speeds than DSL; it is provided by cable TV companies.

2. **C.** 802.11g uses the 2.4 GHz range and has a maximum rate of 54 Mb/s. 802.11a also has a rate of 54 Mb/s but uses the 5 GHz range. 802.11b is 11 Mb/s. 802.11n is 600 Mb/s max.

3. **B.** Port forwarding is used to forward external network ports to an internal IP and port. This is done so a person can host services such as FTP internally. Port triggering allows you to specify outgoing ports that a computer on the LAN uses for special applications. The DMZ is an area that is protected by the firewall but separate from the LAN. Servers are often placed here. DHCP is the protocol that governs the automatic assignment of IP addresses to clients by a server.

4. **D.** Full-duplex is when a network adapter (or other device) can send and receive information at the same time. Half-duplex is when only sending or receiving can be done at one time. Latency is the delay it takes for data to reach a computer from a remote location. PoE is Power over Ethernet, a technology that allows devices to receive data and power over an Ethernet network cable.

5. **C.** HomeGroup connections require an alphanumeric password that was created by Windows automatically. Joining or creating a workgroup does not require a password. Client/server networks such as Microsoft Active Directory domains require a username and password, but these are created by the administrator of the network or selected by the user.

6. **D.** The `net use` command can connect to shares such as \\server1\data-share or any other share on the network. Of course, you could also do this by mapping a network drive in Explorer. HomeGroup uses a more user-friendly approach to sharing and connecting to shares. Right-clicking the folder and selecting Share with will share the folder but won't make a connection to the share. `Ipconfig` is used to find out the IP configuration of the network adapter in the Command Prompt.

Troubleshooting Networks

Okay, now that we've shown some of the basics of networking, let's get into a little bit of network troubleshooting. To troubleshoot client connectivity properly, we need to know a little bit more about command-line interface (CLI) tools and be able to identify some of the common symptoms you will encounter when networking computers together.

Command-Line Interface Tools

There are many command-line tools that we can use in Windows to help us troubleshoot situations; in this section, we delve into seven of them. I recommend that you try all the variations of these on your computer. Some commands require that you open the Command Prompt as an administrator (elevated mode). I suggest simply running the Command Prompt as an administrator all the time (because that's what you want to be, an administrator, right?). For more information on how to open the Command Prompt as an administrator in your version of Windows, see Chapter 9, "Configuring Windows." The most commonly used command for analyzing a computer's networking configuration is ipconfig. Let's start with that.

Ipconfig

The Internet protocol configuration command or ipconfig displays current TCP/IP network configuration values. This is one of the first tools you should use when troubleshooting network connectivity. When you type **ipconfig**, you get results similar to the following:

```
Windows IP Configuration
Ethernet adapter Local Area Connection:
Connection-specific DNS Suffix . :
Link-Local IPv6 Address. . . . . : fe80::404b:e781:b150:b91a%11
IPv4 Address. . . . . . . . . . . : 192.168.0.100
Subnet Mask . . . . . . . . . . . : 255.255.255.0
Default Gateway . . . . . . . . . : 192.168.0.1
```

Ipconfig combined with the /all switch shows more information, including whether or not DHCP is being used, the DNS server address, and the MAC address. The MAC address is the hexadecimal address that is burned into the ROM of the network adapter. This is a set of six hexadecimal numbers (for example, 00-03-FF-A0-55-16).

> **ExamAlert**
>
> To view additional IP configuration information, such as DNS servers and MAC addresses, use the `ipconfig /all` command.

This command can offer a lot of information about a problem. For example, if a user cannot connect to any Internet resources, it could be because the gateway address is improperly configured. Remember that the gateway address must be on the same network number as the IP address of the client computer. If a user can't connect to any websites but can connect to other computers on the LAN, it could be that the DNS server address is incorrectly configured. Ipconfig also tells you whether the client computer's IP address is obtained from a DHCP server or assigned via APIPA and whether it is a private or public address.

`Ipconfig` can also be used to release and renew IP addresses. Sometimes this needs to be done if a computer's IP address is not working properly and you want to obtain a new address from a DHCP server. To release the current IP address, type **ipconfig/release**; to renew, type **ipconfig/renew**.

Finally, if you are having DNS issues (for example, problems connecting to websites), you can erase the DNS cache by typing **ipconfig/flushdns**. Check out the various `ipconfig` switches by opening the Command Prompt and typing **ipconfig /?**. You should try this with every command in this section.

> **Note**
>
> `ifconfig` is the equivalent command in Linux and OS X. We discuss this command in Chapter 18, "Android, iOS, OS X, and Linux."

Ping

`Ping` tests whether another host is available over the network. It's the easy way to see if another host is "alive." Let's say your gateway's IP address is 192.168.0.1. To ping that computer, you would type **ping 192.168.0.1** as an example and hopefully get the following output:

```
Pinging 192.168.0.1: with 32 bytes of data:
Reply from 192.168.0.1: bytes=32 time<1ms TTL=64
Reply from 192.168.0.1: bytes=32 time<1ms TTL=64
Reply from 192.168.0.1: bytes=32 time<1ms TTL=64
Reply from 192.168.0.1: bytes=32 time<1ms TTL=64
```

```
Ping statistics for 192.168.0.1:
Packets: Sent = 4, Received = 4, Lost = 0 (0% loss),
Approximate round trip times in milli-seconds:
Minimum = 0ms, Maximum = 0ms, Average = 0ms
```

The replies indicate that the host is alive and can be communicated with on the network. Any other message would indicate a problem (for example, the Request Timed Out or Destination Host Unreachable messages would require further troubleshooting). Keep in mind that if it's the local computer that is configured incorrectly, you might not be able to ping anything! Also watch for the amount of time the ping took to reply back. A longer latency time could indicate network congestion.

> **Note**
>
> Latency is the time it takes for sent data packets to be received by a remote computer. Latency increases with distance, type of network connection used, and network congestion. For example, a ping to a computer on the LAN should have very low latency, perhaps less than 1 millisecond (ms). But a ping initiated from a computer in New York City to a computer in Los Angeles, over a cable Internet connection, might have a latency of 25 ms. This can be a very enlightening piece of the ping results.

You can also use `ping` to test whether a computer has TCP/IP installed properly, even if it isn't wired to the network! To do this, use the `ping 127.0.0.1` command for IPv4 and `ping ::1` for IPv6. These IP addresses are known as loopback addresses; they are used for testing and are available on every host that has TCP/IP installed. They differ from the IP addresses we talked about previously (for example, 192.168.0.100) in that they work internally. Loopback ping commands essentially enable you to ping yourself, meaning you can test the local computer's network connection without a valid IP configuration and without a physical connection to the network. Replies are simulated within the local computer; they prove if the network adapter and TCP/IP have been installed properly. However, it does not prove if TCP/IP has been *configured* properly for your particular network.

> **Note**
>
> You can also use the `ping loopback` and `ping localhost` commands, but for testing, pinging the IP address is usually recommended.

> **ExamAlert**
>
> Know how to ping the local loopback IPv4 and IPv6 addresses.

You can also modify the way that ping works with switches. There are several, but three you should know for the exam are -t, -n, and -l:

▶ **ping -t:** This pings the host until the command is stopped. Remember, a host is any device or computer with an IP address. An example of this would be ping -t 192.168.0.1; the switch can go before or after the IP address. You will keep getting replies (or timeouts) until you stop the command by pressing Ctrl+C or by closing the Command Prompt. This is a great way to test cable connections. After running the command, you can plug and unplug cables and watch the screen to see which cables or ports are live. You can also use it to monitor a connection over a period of time, discerning whether there are many packet drops or whether the connection slows down at certain times.

▶ **ping -n:** This pings a host a specific number of times. For example, the syntax ping -n 20 192.168.0.1 would ping that host 20 times and then display the results. This can be a good baselining tool if you run it every day against a router or server and compare the results. (You would probably want to do a higher quantity than 20.)

▶ **ping -l:** This pings the host but you can specify the number of bytes per packet to be sent. If you look at the previous ping results, you can see that the default number of bytes is 32, but this can be increased to simulate real data. For example, ping -l 1500 192.168.0.1 would send four 1500-byte packets to the other host. This can also be beneficial when testing how a server, router, or other device reacts to larger packet sizes.

▶ **ping -a:** This resolves addresses to hostname. When pinging an IP address with -a, you also see the hostname associated with the IP address.

▶ **ping -4:** This forces the use of IPv4 and results in IPv4-based data. For example, in Windows, if you are running both IPv4 and IPv6 and type a command such as ping loopback, your results will by default be IPv6-based and might read Reply from ::1 (that is, if your system is working properly). But by adding the -4 option, you force the use of IPv4, so the command ping -4 loopback can result in Reply from 127.0.0.1.

▶ **ping -6:** This forces the use of IPv6 and results in IPv6-based data.

ExamAlert

Know how to use the -t, -n, -l, -a, -4, and -6 switches with ping.

These switches can be combined as well, for example, `ping -n 450 -l 1500 192.168.0.1` would send 450 pings, each 1500 bytes in size. To create a baseline, you could do this at a specific time every month, store the results, and then compare them to find possible deficiencies in performance of a server, router, and so on.

Tracert

`Tracert`, short for trace route, builds on `ping` in that it send packets to destinations beyond the local computer's network. It pings each router along the way between you and the final destination. Let's say we ran the command `tracert davidlprowse.com`. An example of the `tracert` output follows:

```
Tracing route to davidlprowse.com [216.97.236.245] over a maximum of
30 hops:
1 6 ms 5 ms 5 ms bdl1.eas-ubr16.atweas.pa.cable.rcn.net [10.21.80.1]
2 10 ms 9 ms 9 ms vl4.aggr1.phdl.pa.rcn.net [208.59.252.1]
```

The `tracert` would continue for a dozen or more lines and end in the following:

```
18 86 ms 86 ms 86 ms unused-240-180-214.ixpres.com [216.240.180.214]
19 98 ms 96 ms 97 ms lwdc.dbo2.gi9-4.host1.23680.americanis.net
   [38.96.20.2]
20 97 ms 96 ms 96 ms zosma.lunarpages.com [216.97.236.245]
Trace complete.
```

Note that there are three pings per line item measured in milliseconds (ms). Also note that every line item contains a router name and IP address. It starts by sailing through the various routers in our ISP, RCN.net. It ends at a server named zosma.lunarpages.com that hosts www.davidlprowse.com (as of the writing of this book). If you saw any asterisks in the place of the millisecond amounts, you might question whether the router is functioning properly. If the `tracert` stops altogether before saying Trace Complete, you would want to check your network documentation to find out which router it stopped at and/or make sure that the router is troubleshot by the appropriate personnel. As with `ping`, the -4 and the -6 options will force IPv4 and IPv6, respectively.

`Tracert /d` will not resolve IP addresses to hostnames. So instead of seeing zosma.lunarpages.com on the last line, you would see only the IP address 216.97.236.245. Running numerical versions of commands can be faster because there is no name resolution to get in the way. Connecting directly by IP will always be faster than connecting by name.

Netstat

Moving on to another concept, netstat shows the network statistics for the local computer. The default command displays sessions to remote computers. In the following example, I connected to www.google.com and ran the netstat command. Output follows:

```
Active Connections
TCP Music-Box:1395 8.15.228.165:http ESTABLISHED
TCP Music-Box:1396 he-in-f101.google.com:http ESTABLISHED
```

This output shows that there are two established TCP sessions (they're actually both to the same website) to google.com. In the local address column, we see our computer (Music-Box) and the outbound ports it uses to access the website (1395 and 1396). In the foreign address column, we see an IP address and the protocol used (http); in the second session, we see a hostname followed by the protocol (again http). The protocol used by google.com corresponds to port 80. This command can tell us a lot about our sessions (for example, whether a session times out or whether it closes completely). To see this information numerically, try using the -n switch. To see TCP and UDP sessions, use the -a switch. To see TCP *and* UDP in numeric format, use the -an switch.

Nbtstat

Nbtstat displays network protocol statistics that use NetBIOS over TCP/IP connections. Nbtstat can be used to show the services running on the local computer or a remote computer. It calls this the name table. For example, you could find out what services are running, what the computer's name is, and what network it is a part of by typing **nbtstat -A 192.168.0.100** (or whatever your local IP is). The results would be similar to the following:

```
Computer1    <00>    Unique    Registered
Workgroup    <00>    Group     Registered
Computer1    <20>    Unique    Registered
```

The computer and network names are easy to see: Computer1 and Workgroup. But also notice that there are numbers in alligators, such as <00> and <20>. These are the services mentioned previously. <00> is the workstation service, which is the service that allows your computer to redirect out to other systems to view shared resources. <20> is the server service that allows your computer to share resources with other systems.

The -a switch (lowercase a) shows the same name table but you invoke this information using the computer name instead of the IP address. Nbtstat has a variety of other switches that can display, purge, and reload name tables and sessions. Check out the other various switches by typing **nbtstat /?**.

Nslookup

Nslookup queries DNS servers to discover DNS details, including the IP address of hosts. For example, to find the IP address of davidlprowse.com, I would type **nslookup davidlprowse.com**. The resulting output should look something like this:

```
Non-authoritative answer:
Name: davidlprowse.com
Address: 216.97.236.245
```

So from the output, we now know the IP address that corresponds to the domain name davidlprowse.com. Nslookup means name server lookup and can aid in finding DNS servers and DNS records in a domain as well. If the command nslookup is typed by itself, it brings the user into the nslookup shell. From here, several commands can be utilized; to find out more about these, type **?**. To exit the nslookup shell, type **exit**, press Ctrl+C, or press Ctrl+Break.

Net

The net command is actually a collection of commands. In Chapter 14, "Printers," we used the net stop command to stop the print spooler. In networking, you might use the net view command to see which computers are currently available on the network or the net share command to share folders and for other users to view. For the exam, you should know the types of net commands that enable you to view or create mapped network drives. To view any currently mapped network drives, simply type **net use**. To create a mapped network drive, use the following syntax:

```
net use x: \\computername\sharename
```

X: is the drive letter (in this case, X is a variable; you can use whatever drive letter you want if it's available). Computername is the name of the remote host you want to connect to and sharename is the share that was created on that remote host.

There is a network share on another computer on my network called C$. The following syntax shows the command to connect to it and the resulting output:

```
net use f: \\Music-Box\c$
The command completed successfully.
```

In this example, we used F: as our drive letter; the computer we connected to is called Music-Box and the share is C$ (the default hidden share). For more information on the `net` command, type **net /?**. For more information on the `net use` command, type **net use /?**.

Netdom

`Netdom` is a command-line tool that is built into Windows Server. It is designed to manage Active Directory domains from the command line. It is available if you have the Active Directory Domain Services server role installed, meaning if you are running a domain controller. It is also available if you install the Active Directory Domain Services Tools that are part of the Remote Server Administration Tools (RSAT). This way, it can be used from client computers, such as Windows 8. Otherwise, if you are running a Windows client OS without RSAT, the command will not function.

With this command, you can join computers to a domain, manage computer accounts, establish trust relationships between multiple domains, and so on. Because this gets into more in-depth Microsoft systems administration, I don't go into any further detail here, but if you are interested in learning more, visit https://technet.microsoft.com/en-us/library/cc772217.aspx.

Troubleshooting Common Symptoms

Network troubleshooting? Oh yes, it could be the best way to learn. First, I recommend reviewing the CompTIA troubleshooting theory in Chapter 1, "Introduction to Troubleshooting." Second, for successful troubleshooting, remember to check the simple and obvious first. Power connections, network connections, and so on are common culprits for network problems.

Let's discuss some symptoms you might encounter and how to troubleshoot the underlying problems.

▶ **No connectivity:** If a user complains of a problem connecting to the network and you verify that there is indeed a problem, check that patch cable first and verify there is a link light. Make sure the user's computer is actually connected to the network. If it appears to be a cable issue, use a cable tester to solve the problem. If it isn't a cable problem, make sure the network adapter is enabled. If it's a laptop and the user has wireless, check the Wi-Fi switch or button. Next, run an `ipconfig /all` and check the settings. Afterward, ping the local computer to see if TCP/IP works. If you haven't resolved the problem by now (and you probably will), access the Network and Sharing Center in Windows and view the graphical connections to see if there is a red x anywhere denoting a problem. Use the network troubleshooter if necessary. You can also right-click the Network icon in the Notification Area and select Troubleshoot problems (in Vista, select Diagnose and Repair). This brings up the Windows Network Diagnostics program; follow the steps for a possible resolution. Check for the latest drivers for the network adapter. You can also try rebooting the computer to find out from the user if any programs were recently installed or updated. Sometimes antivirus software or firewall updates can cause connectivity issues. Some switches and routers have the capability to enable/disable specific ports; make sure the port in question is enabled in the firmware. If a network-wide problem, power down the network equipment (SOHO routers, cable modems, and so on); then disconnect the network and power cables and wait 10 seconds. Finally, reboot the network equipment. If users cannot find the wireless network that they need to connect to using Windows or the wireless adapter's software, there are third-party Wi-Fi locator programs that can be downloaded for free. These will locate all wireless networks in the vicinity and display SSID, signal quality, distance, and channel used (as long as the wireless network adapter is functional). If an SSID does not show up in Windows or in third-party software, you should enter the SSID manually.

▶ **Limited and intermittent connectivity:** If the problem is limited connectivity, attempt some pings. First, ping the localhost to see if TCP/IP is functioning. If that works, ping the router or another system on the network. If that fails, then the user only has local connectivity. Run an `ipconfig /all` and check the rest of the IP settings. If pinging the router *did* work, try pinging a website by domain name. If that fails, then the DNS server address is probably not configured properly. Check it with an `ipconfig /all` and modify in the IP Properties dialog box if necessary. Run an `ipconfig /release` and `/renew` if you suspect an issue with obtaining an address from a DHCP server. Intermittent connectivity could be caused by a faulty patch cable, wireless network adapter that is too far away from the WAP, or a router that needs to be reset. In a larger environment, if a person can access some networks but not others, you might want to try a `tracert` to inaccessible networks to see where the problem lies. This type of network troubleshooting gets a bit more in depth, but the `tracert` program will basically show which router between you and the final destination has failed.

▶ **Slow transfer speeds:** The type of Internet connection is going to be the biggest contributor to this. If a user has dial-up and complains about slow transfer speeds, it's time to upgrade! Even though dial-up can be tweaked for speed, it's simply easier to move up to DSL, cable, or fiber-based services. Slow transfer speeds could also be caused by the network equipment, patch cables, and network adapter. The newer and faster the equipment and cables, the better the data transfer rate. Of course, slow speeds could also be caused by network congestion. Run a `netstat -a` to see which types of connections the local computer has to the Internet currently. If you see dozens of connections, the computer might be compromised by malware or be part of a botnet. Or perhaps the user runs torrent software or just goes to a lot of websites for various reasons. Check the router as well. See what kind of traffic is passing through it. Update everything, clear all cache, power cycle all equipment, and you just might see an improvement.

▶ **Low RF signal:** A low radio frequency signal spells doom for wireless users. The first thing to check is the distance of the computer from the WAP. Make sure the computer is within the appropriate range. If the WAP uses 802.11ac and the wireless adapter is 802.11g, consider upgrading to an 802.11ac adapter. Update the software on the wireless adapter and WAP as well. Placement of the router is important; it should be central to all users and away from sources of EMI. Try different antenna placement on the router and the wireless adapter. Normally, the 90-degree angle is best, but a little tweaking can go a long way. Also, some routers can boost their wireless signals. Check for this setting in the firmware.

▶ **IP conflict:** An IP conflict message will pop up on the displays of both Windows computers that are causing the conflict. Usually, the first computer that used the IP address will continue to function, whereas the second computer will not be able to access the network. The second computer will have to be reconfigured to a different IP address and rebooted. Reboot the first computer for good measure. IP conflicts usually happen only when static IP addresses are being used. If this is the case, consider using DHCP for all client computers.

▶ **APIPA address:** If a computer is showing an APIPA address (such as 169.254.49.26) when you type `ipconfig /all`, it means that the computer is attempting to obtain an IP address from a DHCP server but is failing to do so. APIPA addresses always start with 169.254. APIPA is assigned internally, so the real problem could be that the computer is not getting connectivity to the network. Check everything in the first bullet point. Also, consider using `ipconfig /release` and `/renew`. Finally, if these do not work, check the DHCP server to make sure it is functional.

ExamAlert

Double-study your troubleshooting techniques! It's all about troubleshooting!

Cram Quiz

Answer these questions. The answers follow the last question. If you cannot answer these questions correctly, consider reading this section again until you can.

220-901 Questions

1. Which of the following commands will display the MAC address of a computer?
    - ○ **A.** ping
    - ○ **B.** netstat
    - ○ **C.** ipconfig /all
    - ○ **D.** ipconfig /renew

2. Which command will ping continuously?
    - ○ **A.** ping /?
    - ○ **B.** ping -t
    - ○ **C.** ping -l
    - ○ **D.** ping -n

3. Which command will show the path of routers between your computer and a web server?
    - ○ **A.** ping
    - ○ **B.** ipconfig
    - ○ **C.** tracert
    - ○ **D.** nbtstat

4. You need to map a network drive to a share named data1 on a computer named Jupiter-Server. You want to use the J: drive letter. Which syntax should you use if you were to do this in the Command Prompt?
    - ○ **A.** net use J: \\Jupiter-Server\data1
    - ○ **B.** net use J \Jupiter-Server\data1
    - ○ **C.** net use Jupiter-Server\J\data1
    - ○ **D.** net use J: \Jupiter-Server\data1

5. A user complains that the computer is not connecting to the network. Which of the following should be done first?
    - ○ **A.** Use ipconfig /all.
    - ○ **B.** Ping the router.
    - ○ **C.** Check the patch cable.
    - ○ **D.** Check the network drivers.

6. One computer loses connectivity. All connectors and settings appear to be correct. Which tool should be used to fix the problem?

   ○ **A.** Multimeter

   ○ **B.** PSU tester

   ○ **C.** Loopback plug

   ○ **D.** Cable tester

7. One of your customers no longer has access to a frequently accessed website. You ping another computer and the router on the network successfully. Which of the following should be done next?

   ○ **A.** Check the IP configuration.

   ○ **B.** Ping the website.

   ○ **C.** Update the OS.

   ○ **D.** Update the AV software.

8. A user moves a laptop from one office to another. The patch cable and the network adapter do not appear to be working properly at the new office. The cable is plugged in correctly and tests okay when checked with a patch tester. Which of the following should be done first?

   ○ **A.** Check whether the port on the switch is enabled.

   ○ **B.** Update the network adapter driver.

   ○ **C.** Replace the patch cable with a crossover cable.

   ○ **D.** Make sure the network adapter is compatible with the OS.

Cram Quiz Answers

220-902 Answers

1. **C.** `Ipconfig /all` will display the MAC address of a computer. `Ping` is used to test whether other computers are available on the network. `Netstat` displays all the network sessions to remote computers. `Ipconfig /renew` is used with `/release` to reissue DHCP-obtained IP addresses.

2. **B.** `Ping -t` is a continuous ping. It can be stopped by pressing Ctrl+C. `Ping /?` will display the help file. `Ping -l` allows you to specify the number of bytes per ping. `Ping -n` specifies the exact number of pings to send.

3. **C.** `Tracert` is used to run a trace between the local system and a remote destination. It shows all routers along the way. `Ping` is used to test connectivity to another system directly. `Ipconfig` will display the Internet Protocol configuration of the local computer. `Nbtstat` shows the name table cache and services running on the system.

4. **A.** You should use this syntax: `net use J: \\Jupiter-Server\` `Data1`. All other answers are incorrect. The UNC is \\computername\ sharename.

5. **C.** Check the super-obvious first. Make sure the computer has a physical cabled connection to the network. Then attempt things such as `ipconfig`, `ping`, and network driver updates.

6. **D.** Use a patch cable tester to check the patch cable and possibly use a continuity tester to test longer network cable runs. Multimeters are great for testing wires inside the computer or AC outlets but they are not used for network troubleshooting. A PSU tester tests power supplies. The loopback plug will verify whether the local computer's network adapter is functional.

7. **B.** This is the concept of pinging outward. Start by pinging the localhost, then a computer, and then the router on the network. Then ping a domain name or website. If you can ping the website but the browser cannot get through, the browser might have been compromised. If you cannot ping the website, you should check the IP configuration; the DNS server address might be incorrectly configured. Updating the OS and AV software should be done right away if you guess that the browser has been compromised.

8. **A.** Some routers and switches can disable physical ports (a smart security measure). Check that first. Later, you can check whether the network adapter is compatible with the OS and update it if necessary. Do not replace the cable with a crossover; those are used to connect one computer to another.

CHAPTER 17

Security

This chapter covers the following A+ exam topics:

▶ Security Threats and Prevention

▶ Desktop Operating System Security

▶ SOHO Security

You can find a master list of A+ exam topics in the "Introduction."

This chapter covers CompTIA A+ 220-901 objectives 1.1 and 1.6, and 220-902 objectives 2.4, 3.1 through 3.7, and 4.2.

Everyone should have some basic knowledge of security. Computers and computer networks are constantly at risk, and new risks are always rearing their ugly heads.

This chapter concentrates on demonstrating how to secure an individual computer system as well as a basic SOHO network. But you must ask yourself some questions: What kind of computers and network devices am I trying to secure? What operating systems are in use, and what applications are loaded? How will the files be protected? What type of computer hardware is employed, and what BIOS/UEFI security is in place? What kind of networking hardware is being utilized? What kind of threats should I be prepared for? And how can I prevent security breaches and troubleshoot security issues if they do occur? We'll answer all these questions in the hope that you end up with a secure computer and network.

Security Threats and Prevention

This section covers common security threats, prevention techniques, and physical and digital security methods. From the entrance to your building to the most hidden confidential file, you should have a security focus to your mindset. Let's start with a most dangerous foe: malicious software.

Malicious Software

Malicious software, or *malware*, is software designed to infiltrate a computer system and possibly damage it without the user's knowledge or consent. Malware is a broad term used by computer professionals to include viruses, worms, Trojan horses, spyware, rootkits, adware, and other types of undesirable software.

Of course, we don't want malware to infect our computer systems, but to defend against it, we first need to define it and categorize it. Then we can put preventative measures into place. It's also important to locate and remove/quarantine malware from a computer system in case it does manifest itself. Table 17.1 summarizes the various malware threats you should know for the exam. Most examples are of well-documented malware that have antimalware solutions.

TABLE 17.1 **Malware Types**

Malware Threat	Definition	Example
Virus	Code that runs on a computer without the user's knowledge; it infects the computer when the code is accessed and executed.	Love Bug virus Example: love-letter-for-you.txt.vbs
Worm	Similar to viruses except that it self-replicates, whereas a virus does not.	Nimda Propagated through network shares and mass e-mailing
Trojan horse	Appears to perform desired functions but is actually performing malicious functions behind the scenes.	Remote access Trojan Example: Plugx
Spyware	Malicious software either downloaded unwittingly from a website or installed along with some other third-party software.	Internet Optimizer (aka DyFuCA)
Rootkit	Software designed to gain administrator-level control over a computer system without being detected.	Boot loader rootkits Example: Evil Maid Attack

Malware Threat	Definition	Example
Spam	The abuse of electronic messaging systems such as e-mail, broadcast media, and instant messaging.	Phishing identity theft e-mails Lottery scam e-mails
Ransomware	Restricts access to a computer system or locks the system until a ransom is paid. Often propagated by a Trojan.	CryptoLocker

Preventing and Troubleshooting Malicious Software

Now that we know the types of malware, let's talk about how to stop them before they happen and how to troubleshoot them if they do happen. If a system is affected by malware, it might be sluggish in its response time, it might display unwanted pop-ups and incorrect home pages, or applications (and maybe even the whole system) could lock up or shut down unexpectedly. Quite often, malware uses CPU and memory resources directly or behind the scenes, causing the system to run slower than usual. A technician should look for erratic behavior from the computer, as if it had a mind of its own! Let's go over how to prevent malware and how to troubleshoot it when it does occur.

Preventing and Troubleshooting Viruses

We can do several things to protect a computer system from viruses. First, every computer should have antivirus (AV) software running on it. McAfee and Symantec are examples of manufacturers of AV software, but there are many others. Second, the AV software should be updated, which means that the software will require a current license; this is renewed yearly with most providers. When updating, be sure to update the AV engine *and* the definitions if you are doing it manually. Otherwise, set the AV software to automatically update at periodic intervals (for example, every day or every week). It's a good idea to schedule regular full scans of the system within the AV software.

As long as the definitions have been updated, antivirus systems will usually locate viruses along with worms and Trojans. However, these systems will usually not locate rootkit activity. Keep in mind that AV software is important but it is not a cure-all.

Next, we want to make sure that the computer has the latest updates available. This goes for the operating system and applications such as Microsoft Office.

Backdoors into operating systems and other applications are not uncommon, and the OS manufacturers often release fixes for these breaches of security. Windows offers the Windows Update program. This should be enabled, and you should either manually check for updates periodically or set the system to check for updates automatically. It might be that your organization has rules governing how Windows Update will function. If so, configure Automatic Updates according to your company's policy. You can check whether your computer is up to date by going to Control Panel > Windows Update.

It's also important to make sure that a firewall is available, enabled, and updated. A firewall closes all the inbound ports to your computer (or network) in an attempt to block intruders. The Windows Firewall is a built-in feature of Windows, and you might also have a SOHO router with a built-in firewall. By using both, you have two layers of protection from viruses and other attacks. You can access the Windows Firewall by navigating to the Control Panel. Keep in mind that you might need to set exceptions for programs that need to access the Internet. This can be done by the program or the port used by the protocol and can be configured in the Exceptions tab, enabling specific applications to communicate through the firewall while keeping the rest of the ports closed.

Another good technique when trying to prevent viruses (and just about any malware) is to disable Autoplay/Autorun for optical drives and USB-connected devices. If you disable Autoplay, an optical disc won't automatically start its Autorun application (if it has one), and any embedded malware won't have a chance to infect the system before you scan the media. To disable Autoplay/Autorun in Windows, complete the following steps:

Step 1. Go to the search field (or Run prompt) and type `gpedit.msc`. This opens the Local Group Policy Editor. (This is not available in some editions of Windows.)

Step 2. Navigate to Computer Configuration > Administrative Templates > Windows Components > AutoPlay Policies.

Step 3. Double-click the Turn Off Autoplay setting. This displays the Turn Off Autoplay configuration window.

Step 4. Click the Enabled radio button, and then click OK. You are actually enabling the policy named Turn Off Autoplay.

> **Note**
>
> The previous steps turn off all AutoPlay and Autorun features. Use this sparingly on laptops that are used for presentations because these computers might require AutoPlay.

Finally, educate users as to how viruses can infect a system. Instruct them on how to screen (or filter) their e-mails and tell them not to open unknown attachments. Show them how to scan removable media before copying files to their computers or set up the computer to scan removable media automatically. Sometimes user education works; sometimes it doesn't. One way to make user education more effective is to have a technical trainer educate your users instead of doing it yourself. This can provide for a more engaging learning environment. During this training you might opt to define an organization's acceptable use policy (AUP). This is a document stipulating constraints and practices that a user must agree to before being granted access to a corporate network or the Internet. Sometimes, the AUP can be a bit difficult for the average nontechie to understand. However, the document is usually designed to not only stipulate constraints but to educate the user, so it is in the user's best interest to learn what policies are within the AUP.

By using these methods, virus infection can be severely reduced. However, if a computer is infected by a virus, you want to know what to look for so that you can "cure" the computer.

Here are some typical symptoms of viruses:

- ▶ Computer runs slower than usual
- ▶ Computer locks up frequently or stops responding altogether
- ▶ Computer restarts on its own or crashes frequently
- ▶ Hard drives and applications are not accessible or don't work properly
- ▶ Windows Update fails
- ▶ Permission to specific files and folders is denied
- ▶ Strange sounds occur
- ▶ You receive unusual error messages or security alerts (which are most likely false)
- ▶ Display or print distortion occurs
- ▶ New icons appear or old icons (and applications) disappear

▶ There is a double extension on a file attached to an e-mail that was opened (for example, .txt.vbs or .txt.exe)

▶ Antivirus programs will not run, can't be installed, or can't be updated

▶ Files disappear, have been renamed or corrupted, or folders are created automatically

You don't want it to happen, but it does; viruses infect computers all the time. So you need to know what to do if an infection occurs. Here is the CompTIA recommended procedure for the removal of malware in general:

1. Identify malware symptoms.

2. Quarantine infected systems.

3. Disable system restore (in Windows).

4. Remediate infected systems.

   a. Update antimalware software.

   b. Use scan and removal techniques (for example, Safe Mode and preinstallation environment).

5. Schedule scans and run updates.

6. Enable system restore and create restore point (in Windows).

7. Educate end users.

ExamAlert

Know the CompTIA malware removal procedure.

Let's discuss some of these steps in a little more detail, using the virus as the example.

When a system is infected, disconnect the network cable from the computer to stop the virus from spreading to any other systems on the network. Before making any changes to the computer, make sure that you back up critical data. If necessary, remove the hard drive and copy critical data to another system using an external connection.

ExamAlert

Know what to do first when troubleshooting a virus.

Now the technician should attempt to identify the virus or viruses. To do this, perform a thorough scan of the system using the AV software's scan utility; if allowed by the software, run the scan in Safe Mode or use Msconfig to configure Safe boot from the Boot tab. (You might also need to disable System Restore before starting a scan.) Another option is to move the affected drive to a "clean machine," which is a computer that is used solely for the purpose of scanning for malware and does not connect to the Internet. This can be done by slaving the affected drive to an SATA or eSATA port of the other computer and running the AV software on the clean machine to scan that drive. PC repair shops have this kind of isolated clean machine.

Hopefully, the AV software will find and quarantine the virus on the system. If the AV software's scan does not find the issue, or if the AV software has been infected and won't run, you can try using an online scanner such as Trend Micro's HouseCall (http://housecall.trendmicro.com/) or download Microsoft's Malicious Software Removal Tool at http://www.microsoft.com/security/pc-security/malware-removal.aspx.

If it is a new virus, you might have to download an individual antivirus definition. To make sure the definition is authentic, check the hash key. The key you saw on the website should match the hash key of the downloaded file on your computer.

If viruses are removed yet reappear on the computer after reboot, consider reverting the computer to an older restore point.

In rare cases, you might need to delete individual files and remove Registry entries. This might be the only solution when a new virus has infected a system and there is no antivirus definition released. Instructions on how to remove viruses in this manner can be found on AV software manufacturers' websites.

When it comes to boot sector viruses, your AV software is still the best bet. The AV software might use removable media (optical discs or USB flash drives) to accomplish scanning of the boot sector, or it might have boot shielding built in.

> **Note**
>
> Watch out for rogue antivirus programs. These are actually malicious programs that appear to be antivirus programs, using similar names and logos as the real thing. Keep a sharp eye out for programs masquerading as other programs!

Windows offers the `bootrec /fixmbr` command from within the System Recovery Options Command Prompt. Keep in mind that System Recovery Options methods might not fix the problem; they might render the hard drive inoperable, depending on the type of virus. It is best to use the AV software's various utilities that you have purchased for the system.

The hardware in a computer can also help to avoid viruses and other malware. Some BIOS programs can scan the boot sector of the hard drive at startup; this might need to be enabled in the BIOS setup first. Newer UEFI systems use Secure Boot technology, which adds to this the ability to prevent operating systems from booting unless they're signed by a key loaded into the UEFI.

Going further, most CPUs use NX bit technology (*No-eXecute*), a security feature that allows the processor to classify areas in memory where application code can or cannot execute. This helps to stop viruses (and worms) from inserting code. For this to work, the CPU must be compliant and the operating system must support it as well, though most do at this point in one form or another. Finally, it needs to be enabled in the BIOS/UEFI. Intel's version of this is called XD bit (*eXecute Disable bit*), AMD refers to it as Enhanced Virus Protection, and ARM-based CPUs (for mobile devices) call this XN (eXecute Never).

After viruses have been deleted and/or quarantined, go to Control Panel > Action Center in Windows 8/7 (or go to Security Center in Vista) and make sure there are no security messages that need your attention. Check for any updates to Windows and the AV software, run a full scan of the system, and if everything checks out, create a new restore point. Then explain to the user what happened and how the user can avoid viruses in the future.

> **Note**
>
> Many organizations use corporate-level, centrally managed antivirus solutions. These can push out updates to all the computers on the network at once.

Preventing and Troubleshooting Worms and Trojans

Worms and Trojans can be prevented and troubleshot in the same manner as viruses. There are scanners for Trojans as well (for example, Microsoft's

Malicious Software Removal Tool). In some cases, AV software scans for worms and Trojans in addition to viruses. Both of these tools can easily detect Trojans, regardless of whether it is the actual attacker's application or any .exe files that are part of the application and are used at the victim computer.

Preventing and Troubleshooting Spyware

Preventing spyware works in much the same manner as preventing viruses in that spyware prevention includes updating the operating system and using a firewall. Also, because spyware has become much more common, antivirus companies have begun adding antispyware components to their software. Here are a few more things you can do to protect your computer in the hopes of preventing spyware:

▶ Download and install antispyware protection software. Your system might already have a program (for example, Windows Defender or Microsoft Security Essentials); if not, there are plenty of third-party programs available on the Internet. Be sure to keep the antispyware software updated.

▶ Adjust web browser security settings. Enable a phishing filter if you have one and turn on automatic website checking. This attempts to filter out fraudulent online requests for usernames, passwords, and credit card information, which is also known as web-page spoofing. Enable checking of certificates. If a certificate (a secure encrypted connection on the web) has been revoked or is otherwise invalid, you want to know about it—a message such as "invalid certificate (trusted root CA)" will only be received when the browser is checking for it. If not, you could inadvertently stumble on to a disreputable website. Additional security settings can also help to fend off session *hijacking*; that is, the act of taking control of a user session after obtaining or generating an authentication ID. Another attack similar to session hijacking is browser redirection. This is when a user's web browser is automatically redirected to one or more malicious websites. It can be done when a user inadvertently accesses a malicious website from a search; it can be caused by a Trojan that modifies a computer's DNS entries (for example, DNSChanger); or it can be caused by spyware or a virus that configures a proxy server address within the browser and/or modifies the HOSTS.txt file. Figure 17.1 shows a web browser configured to use a proxy server. As you can see, the IP address of the proxy server is 192.168.0.15 and uses port 80, just like a web server would. If this proxy server is not authorized, then it should be removed—after which you should restart the computer and verify that it is still disabled. This can be avoided by increasing a browser's security settings, updating antivirus programs, and by educating users. It can be fixed by scanning the system with antivirus software, removing the proxy server address from the browser's settings, and deleting and rewriting the HOSTS.txt file.

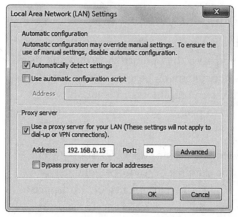

FIGURE 17.1   **Proxy server configuration in a web browser**

▶ Uninstall unnecessary applications and turn off superfluous services (for example, turn off Telnet and FTP if they are not used).

▶ Educate users on how to surf the Web safely. User education is actually the number one method of preventing malware! Access only sites believed to be safe, and download only programs from reputable websites. Don't click OK or Agree to close a pop-up window; instead, press Alt+F4 on the keyboard to close that window. Be wary of file-sharing websites and the content stored on those sites. Be careful of e-mails with links to downloadable software that could be malicious.

▶ Consider technologies that discourage spyware. For example, use a browser that is less susceptible to spyware. Consider running a browser within a virtual machine, or recommend a tablet or basic Internet appliances to users who use a computer to access the Internet only.

Here are some common symptoms of spyware:

▶ The web browser's default home page has been modified.

▶ A particular website comes up every time you perform a search.

▶ Excessive pop-up windows appear. Rogue antivirus applications seem to appear out of nowhere, supposedly scanning the system.

▶ The network adapter's activity LED blinks frequently when the computer shouldn't be transmitting data.

▶ The firewall and antivirus programs turn off automatically.

▶ New programs, icons, and favorites appear.

▶ Odd problems occur within Windows (the system is slow, applications behave strangely, and so on).

▶ The Java console appears randomly.

To troubleshoot and repair systems infected with spyware, first disconnect the system from the Internet. Then try uninstalling the program from Control Panel > Programs and Features in Windows. Some of the less malicious spyware programs can be fully uninstalled without any residual damage. Be sure to reboot the computer afterward and verify that the spyware was actually uninstalled! Next, scan your system with the AV software to remove any viruses that might have infested the system and might get in the way of a successful spyware removal. Again, do this in Safe Mode if the AV software offers that option.

Next, scan the computer with the antispyware software of your choice in an attempt to quarantine and remove the spyware. You can use other programs, such as HijackThis, in an attempt to remove malware, but be careful with these programs because you will probably need to modify the Registry. Remove only that which is part of the infection.

Finally, you need to make sure that the malware will not reemerge on your system. To do this, check your home page setting in your browser, verify that your host's file hasn't been hijacked (located in C:\WINDOWS\system32\ drivers\etc), and make sure unwanted websites haven't been added to Trusted Sites within the browser.

564
CHAPTER 17: Security

Preventing and Troubleshooting Rootkits

A successfully installed rootkit enables unauthorized users to gain access to a system, acting as the root or administrator user. Rootkits are copied to a computer as a binary file; this binary file can be detected by signature-based and heuristic-based antivirus programs. However, after the rootkit is executed, it can be difficult to detect. This is because most rootkits are collections of programs working together that can make many modifications to the system. When subversion of the operating system takes place, the OS can't be trusted and it is difficult to tell whether your antivirus programs run properly or any of your other efforts have any effect. Although security software manufacturers attempt to detect running rootkits, they are not always successful. One program that can be used to detect rootkits is Microsoft Sysinternals Rootkit Revealer (http://technet.microsoft.com/en-us/sysinternals/bb897445.aspx).

One good way to identify a rootkit is to use removable media (a USB flash drive or a special rescue CD-ROM) to boot the computer. This way, the operating system is not running, which means the rootkit is not running, making it much easier to detect by the external media.

Unfortunately, because of the difficulty involved in removing a rootkit, sometimes the best way to combat rootkits is to reinstall all software. Generally, upon detecting a rootkit, a PC technician will do this because it usually is quicker than attempting to fix all the rootkit issues and it can verify that the rootkit has been removed completely.

However, software isn't the only method of defense and repair when it comes to rootkits. Newer motherboards equipped with a UEFI/BIOS take advantage of Secure Boot technology, which can help to protect the preboot process against rootkit attacks. This way, a rootkit can potentially be stopped *before* it actually causes any damage.

Preventing and Troubleshooting Spam

The key is to block as much spam as possible, report those who do it, and train your users. Here are several ways that spam can be reduced:

▶ **Use a strong password:** E-mail accounts can be hijacked if they have weak passwords. This is especially common with web-based e-mail accounts, such as Gmail or Yahoo! Mail. After he gets access, the hijacker sends spam to everyone on the user's contact list. Use a complex password and change it often to prevent e-mail hijacking.

▶ **Use a spam filter:** This can be purchased for the server-side as software or as an appliance. One example of an appliance is the Barracuda

Networks Spam Firewall (www.barracudanetworks.com). Barracuda monitors spam activity and creates and updates whitelists and blacklists, all of which can be downloaded to the appliance automatically. On the client side, you can configure Outlook and other mail programs to a higher level of security against spam; this is usually in the Junk E-mail Options area. Many popular antivirus suites have built-in spam filtering. Make sure it is enabled!

▶ **Use whitelists and blacklists:** Whitelists are lists of e-mail addresses or entire e-mail domains that are trusted, whereas blacklists are not trusted. These can be set up on e-mail servers, e-mail appliances, and within mail client programs such as Outlook.

▶ **Train your users:** Instruct users to create and use free e-mail addresses whenever they post to forums and newsgroups; they should not use their company e-mail addresses for anything except company-related purposes. Make sure that they screen their e-mail carefully; this is also known as e-mail vetting. E-mail with attachments should be considered volatile unless the user knows exactly who sent the email. Train your users and customers never to make a purchase from an unsolicited e-mail.

Unauthorized Access

Unauthorized access is access to an organization's premises, computer resources, and data without consent of the owner. It might include approaching the system, trespassing, communicating, storing and retrieving data, intercepting data, or any other methods that would interfere with a computer's normal work. To ensure privacy, access to data must be controlled. Improper administrative access would fall into this category as well.

Unauthorized access can be prevented through the use of authentication, which is the verification of a person's identity. It is a preventative measure that can be broken down into four categories:

▶ Something the user knows (for example, a password or PIN)

▶ Something the user has (for example, a smart card or other security token)

▶ Something the user is (for example, the biometric reading of a fingerprint or retina scan)

▶ Something the user does (for example, a signature or speaking words)

We'll talk about various methods of operating system authentication in the Windows Security section. For now, let's talk about some ways to enforce physical security and how to protect the entire network using Internet security appliances.

Physical Locks

The physical lock and key is one of the oldest security methods used as a deterrent against unlawful entry. In addition to main entrances, you should always lock server rooms, wiring closets, labs, and other technical rooms when not in use. It should be documented who has the keys to server rooms and wiring closets. Locks should be changed out and rotated with other locks every so often. This keeps things dynamic and harder to guess at. Another type of lock is the cipher lock, which uses a punch code to unlock the door. These physical methods might be used by themselves or combined with an electronic system.

Special cable locks can also be installed for PCs and laptops. Some PC cases come with built-in locks. Configure the BIOS to log when someone opens the case of the computer. This is logged as a chassis intrusion notification. Some computers (mainly laptops) can even be outfitted with the LoJack service, which can locate computers when they have been stolen or misplaced.

Entry Systems

The most common electronic entry system is the cardkey system. These use proximity-based door access cards that you simply press against a transmitter next to the door handle. Although these are common, they are not the most secure option (smart cards can be more secure, as we will discuss in a moment). But because they are less expensive than other systems, you will see them quite often. Other electronic systems use key cards that incorporate a photo ID (a worker's badge), a magnetic stripe, a barcode, or a radio frequency identification (RFID) chip. Each of these can contain information about the identity of the user. These don't have to be cards; they can come in smaller form factors, such as key fobs, which can be attached right to a user's keychain. These systems will sometimes offer entry control, which will limit someone's ability to enter or exit during certain times of the day and identify and check names against an authenticated roster or an entry control roster.

Moving on to the next level of security, let's talk briefly about the smart card. These are cards that have a nano-processor and can actually communicate with the authentication system. Examples of these include the Personal Identity Verification (PIV) card used by U.S. government employees and contractors and the Common Access Card (CAC) used by DoD personnel. These cards identify the owner, authenticate them to areas of the building and to computers, and can digitally sign and encrypt files and e-mail with the RSA encryption algorithm (using an RSA token). Because these are physical items a user carries with him to gain access to specific systems, they are known as tokens. A token might also display a code that changes, say, every minute or so. When a person wants access to a particular system, such as the accounting system or other confidential system, that person would have to type the current code that is shown on the token into the computer. This is a powerful method of authentication but can be expensive as well.

Some organizations will design what is known as a mantrap, which is an area with two locking doors. A person might get past a first door by way of tailgating but might have difficulty getting past the second door, especially if there is a guard in between the two doors. If the person doesn't have proper authentication, he will be stranded in the mantrap until authorities arrive.

Biometrics

Biometrics is the science of recognizing humans based on one or more physical characteristics. Biometrics is used as a form of authentication and access control. It is also used to identify persons who might be under surveillance.

Biometrics falls into the category of "something a person is." Examples of bodily characteristics that are measured include fingerprints, retinal patterns, iris patterns, and even bone structure. Biometric readers (for example, fingerprint scanners) are becoming more common in door-access systems and can be found integrated with mobile devices or used as external USB devices that connect to the computer. Biometric information can also be combined with smart card technology. An example of a biometric door-access system is Suprema, which has various levels of access systems, including some that incorporate smart cards and biometrics, together forming a multifactor authentication system. One example of biometric hardware for a local computer is the Microsoft Fingerprint Scanner, which is USB-based.

Biometrics can be seen in many movies and TV shows. However, many biometric systems over the past decade have been easily compromised. It has only been of late that readily available biometric systems have started to live up to their hype. Thorough investigation and testing of a biometric system is necessary before purchase and installation. In addition, it should be used in a multifactor authentication scheme. The more factors, the better, as long as your users can handle it. (You would be surprised what a little bit of training can do.) Voice recognition software has made great leaps and bounds since the turn of the millennium. A combination of biometrics, voice recognition, and pin access would make for an excellent three-factor authentication system. But, as always, only if you can get it through budgeting!

Protecting Data Physically

Confidential documents should never be left sitting out in the open. They should either be properly filed in a locking cabinet or shredded and disposed of when they are no longer needed. Passwords should not be written down and definitely not left on a desk or taped to a monitor where they can be seen. Many organizations implement a clean desk policy that states each user must remove all papers from her desk before leaving for lunch, breaks, or at the end of the day. Anything that shows on the computer screen can be protected in a variety of ways. To protect data while the person is working, you can install a privacy filter, which is a transparent cover for PC monitors and laptop displays. It reduces the cone of vision, usually to about 30 degrees, so that only the person in front of the screen can see the content shown on the screen. Many of these are also antiglare, helping to reduce eye stress of the user. Also, users should lock their computers whenever they leave their workstations. Windows can also be automatically set to lock after a certain amount of time, even if users forget to do so manually.

Internet Security Appliances

There are a variety of security devices that can be used to block unauthorized access, including firewalls, UTMs, and IDS and IPS solutions.

The network firewall is first and foremost; every organization has one protecting its network. These are usually rackmountable devices that connect to the LAN on one side and to the Internet on the other (and possibly to a DMZ or other secondary network using a third connection). Their primary function is to close ports (such as HTTP port 80) so that unwanted intrusion can be prevented. A typical firewall implementation closes all inbound ports so that external users are blocked from access to the LAN of an organization. However, in some cases, you will find that a port on a firewall was opened previously to allow communication by a service or application that is no longer in use. If that happens, you need to disable (or close) that port or delete the rule that was created for that type of communication. These rules are also known as access control lists.

A firewall can be part of a unified threat management (UTM) gateway solution as well. UTM is the evolution of the firewall, incorporating the features of the firewall along with antivirus, antispam, content filtering, and intrusion prevention for the entire network. It might also incorporate data loss prevention (DLP) by way of content inspection. The idea behind UTM is that it can take the place of several units doing separate tasks and consolidate them into one easily administered system. The drawback to this is that it can act as a single point of failure. So many organizations will consider secondary UTM units or fallback firewalls.

The A+ objectives also require that you understand two other terms, IDS and IPS, and that you know the difference between them. An *intrusion detection system (IDS)* can determine whether an unauthorized person has attempted to access the network and then alert the systems administrator of its findings. In this case, an admin is alerted to the problem but the unauthorized user might actually gain access to the network; the damage might be done before the admin has a chance to rectify the situation. Building on this concept, an *intrusion prevention system (IPS)* will not only detect unauthorized access to the network, it will attempt to thwart it, making the admin's job somewhat easier. IDS and IPS solutions are available as security appliances for the entire network and, in this case, are also referred to as network-based IDS (NIDS) and network-based IPS (NIPS), respectively. They are often incorporated into UTM devices, most commonly NIPS. However, IDS and IPS solutions are also available for individual hosts. In this case, they are referred to as host-based IDS (HIDS) and host-based IPS (HIPS).

> **ExamAlert**
>
> Know the differences between a firewall, UTM, IDS, and IPS.

Social Engineering

Social engineering is the act of manipulating users into revealing confidential information or performing other actions that are detrimental to users. Almost everyone gets e-mails nowadays from unknown entities making false claims or asking for personal information (or money!); this is one example of social engineering. Here are the social engineering techniques you should know for the exam.

Phishing

Phishing is the attempt at fraudulently obtaining private information. A phisher usually masquerades as someone else, perhaps another entity. Phishing is usually done by electronic communication/phone. Little information about the target is necessary. A phisher may target thousands of individuals without much concern as to their backgrounds. An example of phishing would be an e-mail that requests verification of private information.

The e-mail will probably lead to a malicious website that is designed to lure individuals into a false sense of security to fraudulently obtain information. The website will often look like a legitimate website. A common phishing technique is to pose as a vendor (such as an online retailer or domain registrar) and send individuals e-mail confirmations of orders that they supposedly placed.

Specific groups of people might be targeted with more streamlined phishing campaigns; this is known as *spear phishing*. A campaign can even target specific individuals. This is common when targeting senior executives of corporations, a concept known as whaling.

As you can imagine, several different types of social engineering are often lumped into what is referred to as phishing, but actual phishing for private information is normally limited to e-mail and websites. To defend against this, a phishing filter or add-on should be installed and enabled on the web browser. Also, individuals should be trained to realize that institutions will not call or e-mail requesting private information. If individuals are not sure whether they're being targeted, they should hang up the phone or simply delete the e-mail. A quick way to find out if an e-mail is phishing for information is to hover over a link (but don't click it!). You will see a URL domain name that is far different from the institution that the phisher is claiming to be—probably a URL located in a distant country.

Shoulder Surfing

Shoulder surfing is when a person uses direct observation to find out a target's password, PIN, or other such authentication information. The simple resolution for this is for the user to shield the screen, keypad, or other authentication requesting devices. A more aggressive approach is to courteously ask the assumed shoulder surfer to move along. Also, private information should never be left on a desk or out in the open. Computers should be locked or logged off when the user is not in the immediate area. Shoulder surfing and the following two sections are examples of no-tech hacking.

Piggybacking/Tailgating

Piggybacking is when an unauthorized person tags along with an authorized person to gain entry to a restricted area—usually with the person's consent. Tailgating is essentially the same, yet with one difference: It is usually without the authorized person's consent. Both of these can be defeated through the use of mantraps. A mantrap is a small space that can usually fit only one person. It has two sets of interlocking doors; the first set must be closed before the other will open, creating somewhat of a waiting room where people are identified (and cannot escape).

Multifactor authentication is often used in conjunction with a mantrap. Multifactor authentication is when two or more types of authentication are used when dealing with user access control (for example, using a proximity card and PIN at the first door and then using a biometric scan at the second). A mantrap is an example of a preventive security control. Turnstiles, double entry doors, and employing security guards are other less expensive solutions to the problem of piggybacking and tailgating and help address confidentiality in general.

Hard Drive Recycling and Disposal

Hard drives that contain an organization's data can also be a security threat. When a hard drive is removed from a computer, it needs to be recycled or disposed of in a proper manner. Sanitizing the hard drive is a common way of removing data, but it's not the only way. The manner in which data is removed might vary depending on its proposed final destination. Proper data removal goes far beyond file deletion or the formatting of digital media. The problem with high-level formats done in the operating system and low-level formats done by the BIOS is the data remanence (or the residue) that is left behind; with the help of third-party software, that residue can be used to re-create files. Organizations typically employ one of three options when they remove data:

▶ **Clearing:** This is the removal of data with a certain amount of assurance that it cannot be reconstructed. The data is actually recoverable with special techniques. In this case, the media is recycled and used within the company again. The data-wiping technique (also known as shredding) is used to clear data from media by overwriting new data to that media or by performing low-level formats. A regular format within the operating system is not enough because it can leave data behind (known as data remanence). The low-level format is initiated through third-party software (or, in some cases, in the BIOS), which formats the drive in a way that is similar to when the drive first came from the manufacturer. In some cases, patterns of ones and zeros are written to the entire drive. Several software programs are available to accomplish this.

▶ **Purging:** Also known as sanitizing, this is again the removal of data, but this time, it's done in such a way so that it cannot be reconstructed by any known technique (in this case, the media is released outside the company). Special bit-level erasure software (or other means) is employed to completely destroy all data on the media. This type of software will comply with the U.S. Department of Defense (DoD) 5220.22-M standard, which requires seven full passes of rewrites. It is also possible to degauss the disk, which will render the data unreadable but might also cause physical damage to the drive. Tools such as electromagnetic degaussers and permanent magnet degaussers can be used to permanently purge information from a disk.

▶ **Destruction:** This is when the storage media is physically destroyed through pulverizing (with a hammer or other similar tool), drilling holes through the platters, electromagnetic degaussing, shredding, incineration, and so on. At this point—if there is anything left of the drive—the media can be disposed of in accordance with municipal guidelines. Some organizations require a certificate of destruction to show that a drive has indeed been destroyed. This is obtained from the third-party that performs the drive destruction.

> **ExamAlert**
>
> Know the differences between clearing, purging, and destruction.

The type of data removal used will be dictated by the data stored on the drive. If there is no personally identifiable information or other sensitive information, it might simply be cleared and released outside the company. But in many cases, organizations will specify purging of data if the drive is to leave the building. In cases where a drive previously contained confidential or top-secret data, the drive will usually be destroyed.

Additional Attacks and Security Vulnerabilities

Because there are so many types of threats and vulnerabilities in today's computers and networks, there are many types of attacks as well. Let's briefly describe a couple more types of attacks and common vulnerabilities that a typical organization might have to face.

A *spoofing* attack is when an attacker masquerades as another person by falsifying information. This can be done as a social engineering attack, such as in the previously mentioned phishing method, or it can be performed as a more technical attack, such as the *man-in-the-middle (MITM) attack*. This is when an attacker intercepts all data between a client and a server. It is a type of active interception. If successful, all communications are diverted to the MITM computer. The attacking computer can at this point modify the data, insert code, and send it to the receiving computer. This type of eavesdropping is only successful when the attacker can properly impersonate each endpoint.

Then there are attacks that exploit vulnerabilities that haven't even been discovered yet or have been discovered but have not been disclosed through the proper channels so that security administrators can be aware of them. These are known as *zero-day attacks*. An attacker will exploit a vulnerability in an operating system or a network security device in such a way that makes it almost impossible to defend against. Because of this, zero-day attacks are a severe threat. Actually, most vulnerabilities are discovered through zero-day attacks, and the first group of systems that are attacked have very little defense. But once the attack is detected, the development of a solution is not far behind (it could be days or even hours); the vulnerability (and attack) becomes known and is no longer zero-day.

Most of the attacks and malware we have described so far can be initiated by *zombies*: computers that distribute the malware or participate in an attack without the knowledge of the owner. These zombies (or robots) can be grouped together by a central attacker to form a *botnet*. This is done to perpetuate large-scale attacks against particular servers. The distributed denial-of-service (DDoS) is an example of an attack committed by a botnet; it is designed to bring down a server or website.

Most organizations have policies regarding security best practices. The biggest vulnerability to an organization is the violation of those best practices (namely, noncompliant systems). For example, an organization might have rules stating that all systems must be updated at particular intervals: operating systems, antimalware applications, and so on. If a single computer fails to be updated, it is no longer in compliance with policy. This one computer could be used by a hacker or malicious insider to cause all kinds of harm, even on systems that are updated, simply because the nonupdated system is behind the firewall (on the LAN) with the rest of the computers. When updating systems, double-check that everything has indeed been updated. Use scanning software to find all systems on the network, and review network documentation to make sure no systems have "fallen through the cracks."

Cram Quiz

Answer these questions. The answers follow the last question. If you cannot answer these questions correctly, consider reading this section again until you can.

220-902 Questions

1. Which of the following types of malware self-replicates?

   - ○ **A.** Virus
   - ○ **B.** Worm
   - ○ **C.** Trojan
   - ○ **D.** Rootkit

2. Which type of malware is the abuse of electronic messaging systems?

   - ○ **A.** Virus
   - ○ **B.** Spyware
   - ○ **C.** Spam
   - ○ **D.** Worm

3. Which of the following are symptoms of viruses? (Select the three best answers.)

   - ○ **A.** A computer runs slowly.
   - ○ **B.** A computer locks up.
   - ○ **C.** Excessive pop-up windows appear.
   - ○ **D.** A strange website is displayed whenever a search is done.
   - ○ **E.** Unusual error messages are displayed.

4. Which of the following is the science of recognizing humans based on physical characteristics?

   - ○ **A.** Mantraps
   - ○ **B.** Biometrics
   - ○ **C.** Tailgating
   - ○ **D.** Something a person is

5. A hard drive needs to be disposed of in a way so that no one can access the data. Which method should be used?

   - ○ **A.** Phishing
   - ○ **B.** Clearing
   - ○ **C.** Shoulder Surfing
   - ○ **D.** Destruction

6. Which of the following is the best mode to use when scanning for viruses?

○ **A.** Safe Mode

○ **B.** Last Known Good Configuration

○ **C.** Command Prompt only

○ **D.** Boot into Windows normally

7. One of your customers tells you that a bank employee called and asked her for her bank balance and telephone number. What is this an example of?

○ **A.** Spam

○ **B.** Virus

○ **C.** Social Engineering

○ **D.** Trojan

Cram Quiz Answers

220-902 Answers

1. **B.** A worm will self-replicate, whereas a virus will not; otherwise, the two are very much the same. Trojans perform malicious functions behind the scenes and allow remote access to systems. Rootkits are designed to gain administrator (or root) level access to the computer.

2. **C.** Spam is the abuse of electronic messaging systems (such as e-mail). Viruses and worms are code that run on a system, infecting its files. Spyware is malicious software downloaded from the Internet that spies on a user's web activities.

3. **A, B, and E.** Some symptoms of viruses are a computer running slowly, a computer locking up, and unusual errors. Excessive pop-ups and strange websites displaying after searches are symptoms of spyware.

4. **B.** Biometrics is the science of recognizing humans based on physical characteristics. It falls into the category of "something a person is." Mantraps are areas of a building implemented in an effort to stop tailgating.

5. **D.** You should destroy the hard drive, sanitize it with special bit-level erasure software, or degauss it. Phishing is a type of social engineering in which a person attempts to gain confidential information from unwitting users by e-mail. Clearing is the removal of data from a drive that is to be recycled and used again within the organization. Shoulder surfing is when a person attempts to find out passwords or other information by viewing another user's display without that user's knowledge.

6. **A.** Safe Mode should be used (if your AV software supports it) when scanning for viruses. Safe Mode is found in the Advanced Boot Options menu (Startup settings in Windows 8). Other tools found there include the Last Known Good

Configuration, which is used to revert a system back to how it operated the last time the user logged in; Command Prompt only, which offers command-line access only; and the option to boot into Windows normally.

7. **C.** A bank employee will never ask for this information. This is someone masquerading as a bank employee and is a type of social engineering known as phishing. (More to the point, vishing, because it was done by phone.) Spam is the abuse of e-mail. A virus infects files on a computer. Trojans are used to gain access to the computer system, usually through back doors.

Desktop Operating System Security

Windows security is all about authenticating users and protecting files. Proper usage of usernames and passwords, user accounts, permissions, encryption, and firewalls can lead to a secure Windows computer.

User Accounts

Users are what it's all about when it comes to Windows security. There are three types of user accounts you should know for the exam:

▶ The Administrator account has full (or near full) control of an operating system. It is usually the most powerful account in Windows and has access to everything.

▶ The Standard User account (also simply referred to as the User) is the normal account for a person on a network. The user has access to (owns) his data but cannot access the data of any other user and by default cannot perform administrative tasks (such as installing software).

▶ The Guest account has limited access to the system. A Guest cannot install software or hardware, cannot change settings or access any data, and cannot change the password.

> **Note**
>
> Another type of account in previous editions of Windows, the power user, was given specific administrative permissions. However, if you see that account type in Windows Vista or newer, it will simply be considered a Standard User account.

You need to make sure that users' data is secured and that no one else can masquerade as a legitimate user. Windows user accounts can be secured through a combination of a strong username/password, user policies, and User Account Control.

Usernames and Passwords

The username/password combination is the most common type of authentication for gaining access to computers. The username is known to all parties involved and can be seen as plain text when typed. In some cases, the user has no control over what his username will be; in other cases, his username might be his name or e-mail address (and the username could be selected by the user). For example, you might use the Live sign-in to access the Windows Store for apps; in this case, it is typical to use your e-mail address as your username. You can see it, it shows up on the screen, and you can be identified by it. The password is either set by the user or created automatically for the user. This password, however, is not something we want anyone else to know or see.

It is common knowledge that a strong password is important for protecting a user account, whether the account is with a bank, at work, or elsewhere. But what is a strong password? Many organizations define a strong password as a password with at least 8 characters, including at least one uppercase letter, one number, and one special character. The best passwords have similar requirements but are 15 characters or more. Many password-checker programs are on the Web (for example, Microsoft's password checker and The Password Meter). Table 17.2 shows a strong password and a "best" password.

TABLE 17.2 **Strong and Stronger Passwords**

Password	Strength of Password
|Ocrian7	Strong
This1sV#ryS3cure	Very strong or "best"

Notice the first password is using the | pipe symbol instead of the letter L. This is a special character that shares the \ backslash key on the keyboard. The second password uses 16 characters, including three capital letters, two numbers, and a partridge in a pear tree, um, I mean one special character ☺. (Just checking whether you are still with me!) Of course, a partridge wouldn't help your password security, but the other methods make for an extremely strong password that would take a super computer a long time to crack.

ExamAlert

Understand what is required for a complex password.

Note

As mentioned in Chapter 2, BIOS/UEFI passwords are also very important, especially the supervisory/administrative password. The same basic rules we mentioned here apply to BIOS passwords as well.

Changing your password at regular intervals is important as well. The general rule of thumb is to change your password as often as you change your toothbrush. However, because this is a subjective concept (to put it nicely!), many organizations have policies concerning your password. It might need to meet certain requirements, or it might need be changed at regular intervals, among other policies. Figure 17.2 shows an example of the default password policy on a Windows 7 Ultimate computer. This can be accessed by navigating to Control Panel > Administrative Tools > Local Security Policy. When in the Local Security Settings window, continue to Security Settings > Account Policies > Password Policy.

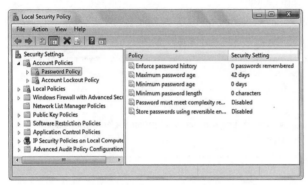

FIGURE 17.2   Default password policy in Windows 7

As shown in the figure, there are several items that we can configure (or can be configured by the network administrator centrally if the computer is part of a domain). The four important ones for the exam include

▶ **Enforce password history:** When this is defined, users cannot use any of the passwords that are remembered in the history. If you set the history to 3, the last three passwords cannot be used again when it is time to change the password.

▶ **Maximum password age and Minimum password age:** These settings define exactly how long a password can be used. The maximum is initially set to 42 days but does not affect the default Administrator account. To enforce an effective password history, the minimum must be higher than zero.

▶ **Minimum password length:** This requires that the password must be at least the specified number of characters. For a strong password policy, set this to between 8 and 14.

▶ **Password must meet complexity requirements:** This means that passwords must meet three of these four criteria: uppercase characters, lowercase characters, digits between 0 and 9, and nonalphabetic characters (special characters).

Note

You can display the various operating system policy settings in the Windows Command Prompt by using the `gpresult` command. You can refresh those policy settings using the `gpupdate` command. Visit the following links for more information on those two commands:

https://technet.microsoft.com/en-us/library/bb490915.aspx

https://technet.microsoft.com/en-us/library/bb490983.aspx

Note

For more information on password best practices, visit http://technet.microsoft.com/en-us/library/cc784090.aspx.

Now that we have a secure password and a password policy in place, let's talk about securing the user accounts for Windows. There are a few things we can do to secure these:

1. **Rename and password protect the Administrator account:** It's nice that Windows has incorporated a separate administrator account. The problem is that, by default, the account has no password. To configure this account, navigate to Computer Management > System Tools > Local Users and Groups > Users and locate the Administrator account. By right-clicking the account, you see a drop-down menu in which you can rename it and/or give it a password. (Just remember the new username and password!) It's great to have this additional administrator account on the shelf just in case the primary account fails, but Windows disables this account by default. (A down arrow indicates a disabled account, just as a down arrow in the Device Manager indicates a disabled device.) To enable it, right-click the account and select Properties. In the General tab, deselect the Account is disabled checkbox. Alternatively, open the command line and type `net user administrator /active:yes`.

2. **Verify that the Guest account (and other unnecessary accounts) are disabled:** This can be done by navigating again to Local Users and Groups > Users, right-clicking the account in question, selecting Properties, and then selecting the checkbox named Account Is Disabled. (It is disabled by default in most version of Windows.) It is also possible to delete accounts (aside from built-in accounts, such as the Guest account); however, companies usually opt to have them disabled so that the company can retain information linking to the account.

3. **Set the Account lockout threshold:** If a user attempts to log on to a system and is unsuccessful (after a specified number of attempts), the user will be locked out of the system. The settings and thresholds for this can be configured in the Local Security Settings window. Navigate to Security Settings > Account Policies > Account Lockout Policy. From here, you can set the threshold to a certain number of invalid logons, set how long the user will be locked out, and set how long until the lockout counter is reset. If an account is locked out and you need to unlock it immediately, follow one of the options at the end of step 1.

It's important to note that when logging on to a Microsoft network, the logon process is secured by the Kerberos protocol, which is run by the Active Directory domain controller. This adds a layer of protection for the username and password as they are being authenticated across the network.

Regardless of whether a user is part of a domain or not, when the user takes a break or leaves for lunch, the computer should be locked. This can be done by pressing Windows+L. When doing so, the operating system goes into a locked state, and the only way to unlock the computer is to enter the username and password of the person who is logged in to the computer. The difference between this and logging out is that a locked computer leaves all the session's applications and files open; logging out closes all open applications and files.

Aside from locking the computer manually, the user can opt to put the computer to sleep after a certain period of time or enable a password-protected screensaver, both of which will force the user to log on when returning to the computer. Sleep settings can be accessed at Control Panel > Power Options (for more information on that, see Chapter 9, "Configuring Windows"). To password-protect the screensaver in Windows, go to Control Panel > Personalization and click the Screen Saver link on the bottom right. Then pick a screensaver, select the timeout, and select the On Resume, Display Logo Screen checkbox.

Password Cracking

One way that attackers attempt to gain access to systems is by way of password cracking. This is usually done with the aid of password-cracking software. Two common methods of password cracking are the dictionary attack and the brute-force attack.

A dictionary attack uses a prearranged list of likely words, trying each of them one at a time. It can be used for cracking passwords, passphrases, and keys. It works best with weak passwords and when targeting multiple systems. The power of the dictionary attack depends on the strength of the dictionary used by the password-cracking program.

A brute-force attack is when every possible password instance is attempted. This is often a last resort because of the amount of CPU resources it might require. It works best on shorter passwords but can theoretically break any password, if given enough time and CPU power.

Once again, a complex and long password is the best way to prevent these types of attacks from succeeding. But a system and its network should also be protected with the Internet security appliances mentioned previously.

> **ExamAlert**
>
> Know the differences between dictionary and brute-force attacks.

User Account Control (UAC)

User Account Control (UAC) is a security component of Windows that keeps every user (besides the actual Administrator account) in standard user mode instead of as an administrator with full administrative rights—even if the user is a member of the administrators group. It is meant to prevent unauthorized access and avoid user error in the form of accidental changes. With UAC enabled, users perform common tasks as nonadministrators and, when necessary, as administrators, without having to switch users, log off, or use Run As.

UAC is partially based on the *principle of least privilege*. This principle says that a user should have access to only what is required. If a user needs to update Excel files and browse the Internet, that user should not be given administrative access. You might think of this as common sense, but it should not be taken lightly. When user accounts are created locally on a computer and especially on a domain, great care should be taken when assigning users to groups. Also, as many programs are installed, they request who can use and make modifications to the program; quite often, the default is All Users. Some technicians just click Next when hastily installing programs, without realizing that the user now has full control of the program—control that you might not want to provide them. Just remember, keep users on a need-to-know basis; give them access only to what they specifically need.

Basically, UAC was created with two goals in mind: first, to eliminate unnecessary requests for excessive administrative-level access to Windows resources. And second, to reduce the risk of malicious software using the administrator's access control to infect operating system files. When a standard end user requires administrator privileges to perform certain tasks (such as installing an application), a small pop-up UAC window appears, notifying the user that an administrator credential is necessary. If the user has administrative rights and clicks Continue, the task will be carried out; if the user does *not* have sufficient rights (and can't provide an administrative password), the attempt fails. Note that these pop-up UAC windows do not appear if the person is logged on with the actual Administrator account.

In Windows 8/7, you can turn off UAC by going to Control Panel > User Accounts and Family Safety. Then select User Accounts and click the Change User Account Control settings link. Unlike Windows Vista, where you can only turn UAC on or off, Windows 8/7 displays a slider that enables you to select from four settings:

▶ **Always Notify:** This configures the OS to notify the user whenever software installations are started or whenever any changes to Windows settings are attempted by the user.

▶ **Default: Notify Me Only When Programs Try to Make Changes to My Computer:** This configures the OS to notify the user when a program attempts to make a change but does *not* notify the user when the user attempts to make a change to settings.

▶ **Notify Me Only When Programs Try to Make Changes to My Computer (Do Not Dim My Desktop):** This is essentially the same as the last item, but the desktop is not dimmed when the notifications appear.

▶ **Never Notify:** This effectively turns UAC off; UAC will not notify the user regardless of the program or user change.

So UAC, by default, notifies a user before changes are made to a computer that requires administrator-level permission. In Windows Vista, this can be turned off altogether only; in Windows 8/7, it can be controlled with a little bit more definition. Of course, a user will need administrative rights to make changes to UAC settings.

ExamAlert

Be sure to know how to turn UAC on and off for the exam!

File Security

To start, files can be assigned four different attributes in Windows: Read-Only, Hidden, Compression, and Encryption. To access these, right-click any file and select Properties. On the General tab you will see the Read-Only checkbox; this makes it so no one can save modifications to the file, but a new file can be saved with the changes. The Hidden checkbox makes the file invisible to all users except the user who created the file. Admins can unhide files individually or for the entire system, as I will explain in a moment. When you click the Advanced button, you see Compression, which allows you to convert the file to a smaller size that takes up less space on the drive, and you see Encryption, which scrambles the file content so only the user who created the file can read it. We'll discuss encryption later in this chapter.

> **Note**
>
> The `attrib` command in the Command Prompt can modify the Read-Only, Archive, System, and Hidden attributes for files and display the attributes for each file. This older command is still available in Windows but is not used often. For more information about this command, see the document on my website (http://www.davidlprowse.com).

System files and folders are hidden from view by the OS to protect the system. In some cases, you can simply click the Show the Contents of This Folder link, but to permanently configure the system to show hidden files and folders, navigate to the Folder Options window in Windows Explorer/File Explorer. Then select the View tab and, under Hidden Files and Folders, select the Show hidden files, folders and drives radio button. To configure the system to show protected system files, deselect the Hide protected operating system files checkbox, located shortly below Show hidden files and folders. This enables you to view files such as bootmgr, pagefile.sys, and hiberfil.sys.

> **ExamAlert**
>
> To view files such as bootmgr, pagefile.sys, and hiberfil.sys, deselect the Hide protected operating system files checkbox.

Administrative Shares

Folders and files need to be shared so that other users on the local computer and on the network can gain access to them. Windows operating systems use an Access Control Model for securable objects like folders. This model takes care of rights and permissions, usually through discretionary access control lists (DACLs) that contain individual access control entries (ACEs). All the shared folders can be found by navigating to Computer Management > System Tools > Shared Folders > Shares, as shown in Figure 17.3. You can see that I have shared a folder named Data.

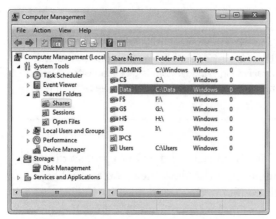

FIGURE 17.3   **Windows Shares**

Here we also see the hidden *administrative shares* that can be identified by the $ on the end of the share name. These shares cannot be seen by standard users when browsing to the computer over the network; they are meant for administrative use. Note that every volume (C: or F:, for example) has an administrative share. Although it is possible to remove these by editing the Registry, it is not recommended because it might cause other networking issues. You should be aware that only administrators should have access to these shares. Administrative shares can be created by simply adding a $ to the end of the share name when enabling the share. Administrative shares can be accessed only if the user knows the exact network path to the folder and has permissions to access it.

Permissions

Folders are shared by accessing the Sharing tab of the folder's Properties window. There are two levels of permissions:

▶ Share permissions can be accessed from the Sharing tab. By default, the Everyone group has read-only access by default. The other two permissions available to us are Change and Full Control. Only administrators should have Full Control.

▶ NTFS permissions are accessed from the Security tab. Here we have six default levels of permissions, from Read to Write to Full Control, as shown in Figure 17.4. NTFS permissions take precedence over share permissions. So for example, if a user was given Full Control access in the Share permissions and only Read in the NTFS permissions, the user would ultimately have only the Read permission.

ExamAlert

NTFS permissions are modified in the Security tab of the folder's Properties window.

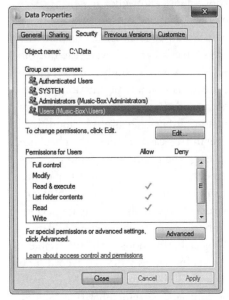

FIGURE 17.4   Security tab of a folder's Properties window

The weakest of the NTFS permissions is Read and the strongest, of course, is Full Control. Administrators have Full Control by default. However, typical users have only Read, List Folder Contents, and Read & Execute by default. You also note that we have the option to Allow access or Deny access and that this can be done by the user or by their user group, thus the term user-level security. Generally, when you want users to have access to the folder, you add them to the list and select Allow for the appropriate permission. When you don't want to allow them access, normally you simply don't add them. But in some cases, an explicit Deny is necessary. This could be because the user is part of a larger group that already has access to a parent folder but you don't want the specific user to have access to this particular subfolder.

Of course, permissions can get very in-depth; for more information on NTFS file and folder permissions, visit http://technet.microsoft.com/en-us/library/bb727008.aspx. (This is an older document, but most of it applies to today's versions of Windows.)

Permission Inheritance and Propagation

If you create a folder, the default action it takes is to inherit permissions from the parent folder. So any permissions that you set in the parent will be inherited by the subfolder. To view an example of this, locate any folder within an NTFS volume (besides the root folder), right-click it, select Properties, access the Security tab, click the Advanced button, and then click the Change Permissions button. Here you see an enabled checkbox named Include Inheritable Permissions from the Object's Parent toward the bottom of the window, as shown in Figure 17.5. (Names will be slightly different in other versions of Windows.) What this means is that any permissions added or removed in the parent folder will also be added or removed in the current folder. In addition, those permissions that are inherited cannot be modified in the current folder. To make modifications in this case, deselect the checkbox. When you do so, you have the option to copy the permissions from the parent to the current folder or remove them entirely. So by default, the parent is automatically propagating permissions to the subfolder and the subfolder is inheriting its permissions from the parent. You can also propagate permission changes to subfolders that are not inheriting from the current folder. To do so, select the Replace All Child Object Permissions with Inheritable Permissions from this Object checkbox. (Again, names will vary according to the version of Windows.) This might all seem a bit confusing; you will probably not be asked many questions on the subject. Just remember that folders automatically inherit from the parent unless you turn inheriting off—and you can propagate permission entries to subfolders at any time by selecting the Replace option.

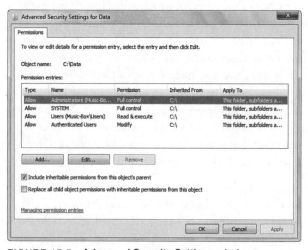

FIGURE 17.5 Advanced Security Settings window

Moving and Copying Folders and Files

This subject (and the previous one) is actually an advanced Microsoft Windows concept, so we'll try to keep this simple. Moving and copying folders have different results when it comes to permissions. Basically, it breaks down like this:

▶ When you copy a folder on the same or to a different volume, the folder inherits the permissions of the parent folder it was copied to (target directory).

▶ When you move a folder to a different location on the same volume, the folder retains its original permissions.

> **Note**
>
> Keep in mind that when you move data, the data isn't actually relocated; instead, the pointer to the file or folder is modified.

Encryption

Encryption is the process of converting information with the use of a cipher (algorithm), making it unreadable by other users unless they have the correct "key" to the information. Cryptography is the practice of hiding information. In a cryptosystem, information is protected by disguising it.

Encrypting File System

There are a few different encryption technologies used in Windows. For example, whenever you log on to a Windows network, that authentication is secured with the Kerberos protocol. Another example is when you want to encrypt one or more files or folders. In this case, Windows uses the Encrypting File System (EFS), a component of NTFS. Follow these steps to encrypt a file in Windows:

1. Locate the file, right-click it, and select Properties. This brings up the General tab within the file's Properties window.

2. At the bottom of the General tab, click the Advanced button. This brings up the Advanced Attributes window.

3. Check the box labeled Encrypt Contents to Secure Data.

4. Click OK for both windows. (When you do so, the system should ask whether you want to encrypt the parent folder and the file or just the file. It's recommended that the file's parent folder be encrypted as well.)

The file should now appear green within Windows Explorer/File Explorer. To unencrypt the file and return it to normal, simply deselect the checkbox.

> **Note**
>
> By the way, green is not the only filename color you might see. Black is the standard file color, blue indicates a compressed file, and red files can be accessed only by Windows.

If a file needs to be decrypted and the original user (owner of the key or certificate) isn't available, an EFS recovery agent will need to be used. In many cases, the default recovery agent is the built-in Administrator account. It is important to note a couple more items: One is that EFS isn't designed to protect data while it is transferred from one computer to another; the other is that it is not designed to encrypt an entire drive.

> **Note**
>
> File-sharing connections are also encrypted in Windows 7 and higher. You can modify this setting within Network and Sharing Center > Advanced Sharing Settings or in HomeGroup > Advanced Sharing Settings. 128-bit encryption is the recommended default.

BitLocker Encryption

To encrypt an entire disk, you need some kind of full disk encryption software. There are several currently available on the market. One developed by Microsoft is called BitLocker, which is available only on Windows 8 Pro, 7/Vista Ultimate, and 8/7/Vista Enterprise. This software can encrypt the entire disk, which, after it's completed, is transparent to the user. However, there are some requirements for this, including

- ▶ A Trusted Platform Module (TPM): A chip residing on the motherboard that actually stores the encrypted keys.

  or

- ▶ An external USB key to store the encrypted keys.

  and

- ▶ A hard drive with two volumes, preferably created during the installation of Windows. One volume is for the operating system (most likely

C:) that will be encrypted; the other is the active volume that remains unencrypted so that the computer can boot. If a second volume needs to be created, the BitLocker Drive Preparation Tool can be of assistance and can be downloaded from Windows Update or from http://www.microsoft.com/en-us/download/details.aspx?id=7806.

ExamAlert

Know the components necessary for BitLocker.

BitLocker software is based on the Advanced Encryption Standard (AES) and uses a 128-bit key. Keep in mind that a drive encrypted with BitLocker usually suffers in performance compared to a nonencrypted drive and could have a shorter shelf life as well.

By default, BitLocker is used to encrypt the internal drive of a system. However, you can also encrypt USB drives and other removable devices by using BitLocker To Go.

S/MIME

Originally developed by RSA Security, Secure/Multipurpose Internet Mail Extensions (S/MIME) is an IETF standard that provides cryptographic security for electronic messaging, such as e-mail. It is used for authentication, message integrity, and nonrepudiation of origin. Most e-mail clients have S/MIME functionality built-in. S/MIME uses a separate session key for each e-mail message.

S/MIME relies on a public key infrastructure (PKI) and the obtaining and validating of certificates from a certificate authority (CA), namely X.509v3 certificates. Is also relies on digital signatures when attempting to establish nonrepudiation. S/MIME enables users to send both encrypted and digitally signed e-mail messages.

S/MIME can be implemented in Outlook by first obtaining a certificate known as a Digital ID, publishing the certificate within Outlook, and then modifying the settings for Outlook.

One of the issues with S/MIME is that it encrypts not only messages but any malware that found its way into the message. This could compromise systems between the sender and receiver. To defeat this, consider scanning messages at a network gateway that has a copy of the private keys used with S/MIME. Do this after decryption. If an e-mail program stores an S/MIME-encrypted message and the private key used for encryption/decryption is lost, deleted, or corrupted, the message cannot be decrypted.

Windows Firewall

The Windows Firewall is meant to protect client computers from malicious attacks and intrusions, but sometimes it can be the culprit when it comes to certain applications failing. You can access the firewall in Windows by going to Control Panel > Windows Firewall or by accessing the Run prompt and typing `firewall.cpl`. When you turn on the firewall, the default setting is to shield all inbound ports (effectively closing them). This means that certain applications that need to communicate with a remote host might not work properly. Or if the client computer wanted to host some services (such as FTP or a web server), the firewall would block them. That's where exceptions come in. You can still use the firewall, but you can specify applications that are exceptions to the rule. Figure 17.6 shows an example of exceptions. To create exceptions, click the Allow a Program or Feature Through Windows Firewall link.

> **Note**
>
> Older versions of Windows store the firewall settings within the Properties sheet of the network adapter.

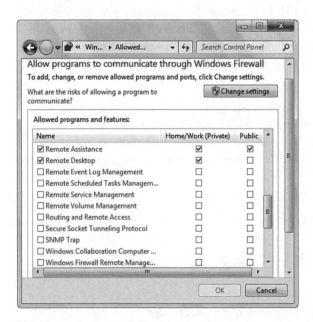

FIGURE 17.6   **Firewall exceptions**

In this example, we have two applications that are not blocked from incoming connections. Remote Assistance is not blocked at all, not on the LAN nor on the Internet. However, Remote Desktop is allowed only on the LAN (listed as Home/Work Private Network). So as long as the firewall is enabled, this computer can make remote assistance calls to other users on the Internet. But if a person wanted to connect to this system through Remote Desktop without an invitation, that person would have to be on the LAN. This way, we aren't sacrificing the entire security of the system. All other incoming connections will be blocked.

We can get more in-depth with the firewall settings. By clicking the Advanced Settings link, we can make use of the Windows Firewall with Advanced Security (also available in Administrative Tools and as a snap-in in the MMC). You can also get to this by opening the Run prompt and typing **wf.msc**. From here, you can create inbound and outbound rules for individual applications based on the private network, the public network, or both. For more information on the Windows Firewall with Advanced Security, visit https://technet.microsoft.com/en-us/library/cc754274.aspx.

If the firewall gives you errors when attempting to either update the firewall settings, add exceptions, or access the advanced settings, make sure the Windows Firewall service is enabled and running.

Cram Quiz

Answer these questions. The answers follow the last question. If you cannot answer these questions correctly, consider reading this section again until you can.

220-902 Questions

1. Which of the following is the strongest password?

   ○ **A.** |ocrian#

   ○ **B.** Marqu1sD3S0d

   ○ **C.** This1sV#ryS3cure

   ○ **D.** Thisisverysecure

2. Which of the following is a security component of Windows?

   ○ **A.** UAC

   ○ **B.** UPS

   ○ **C.** Gadgets

   ○ **D.** Control Panel

3. A customer complains that while he was away at lunch, someone used his computer to send e-mails to other co-workers without his knowledge. Which of the following should you recommend?

   ○ **A.** Enable a screensaver.

   ○ **B.** Unplug the network cable before leaving for lunch.

   ○ **C.** Use the Windows lock feature.

   ○ **D.** Enable the out-of-office message in e-mail when leaving for lunch.

4. Which of the following best describes encryption?

   ○ **A.** Prevents unauthorized users from viewing or reading data

   ○ **B.** Prevents unauthorized users from deleting data

   ○ **C.** Prevents unauthorized users from posing as the original source sending data

   ○ **D.** Prevents unauthorized users from decompressing files

5. One of the users on your network is trying to access files shared on a remote computer. The file's share permissions allow the user full control but the NTFS permissions allow the user Read access. Which of the following will be the resulting access for the user?

○ **A.** Full Control

○ **B.** Modify

○ **C.** Read

○ **D.** Write

6. You are the administrator for your network and you set up an administrative share called Data$. Which of the following is necessary in order for another user to access this share? (Select the two best answers.)

○ **A.** The user must be part of a HomeGroup.

○ **B.** The user must have permissions to access the share.

○ **C.** The user must know the decryption key.

○ **D.** The user must know the exact network path to the share.

○ **E.** The user must enable File Sharing in the Network and Sharing Center.

Cram Quiz Answers

220-902 Answers

1. **C.** Answer C incorporates case-sensitive letters, numbers, and special characters and is 16 characters long. That makes it the strongest password of the listed answers. |ocrian# has special characters but is missing uppercase letters and numerals—plus it is only 8 characters long. Marqu1sD3S0d does not have any special characters. Thisisverysecure is 16 characters long and has one capital letter but does not have any numerals or special characters.

2. **A.** User Account Control (UAC) adds a layer of security to Windows to protect against malware and user error and conserve resources. A UPS is an uninterruptible power supply used to provide power to computers during a blackout or brownout. Gadgets are a function of older Windows desktops and in fact are very insecure and have been deprecated. The Control Panel is simply the master list of utilities in Windows. You can get to UAC by accessing the Control Panel > User Accounts, and then clicking the Change User Account Control settings link.

3. **C.** Tell the customer to lock the computer (by pressing Windows+L or by using the Start menu) before leaving for lunch. As long as there is a strong password, other co-workers should not be able to access the system. Screensavers by themselves do not secure the system, but a user can enable the password-protected screensaver feature (be aware that there is a delay before the screen-saver turns on). Unplugging the network cable is not a legitimate answer; plus it can always be plugged back in. The out-of-office message will reply only to people e-mailing the user; it won't stop outgoing e-mails.

4. **A.** Encryption prevents unauthorized users from viewing or reading data. Properly configured permissions prevent unauthorized users from deleting data or attempting to decompress files. A strong logon password prevents unauthor-ized users from posing as the original source sending data.

5. **C.** The user will get only Read access. Remember that NTFS-level permissions take precedence over Share-level permissions.

6. **B and D.** The user needs to have permissions to the share and must know the exact path to the network share because it is an administrative share. HomeGroup does not play into this scenario. Also, the question does not men-tion whether the file is encrypted. The user doesn't need to enable sharing; the person is trying to access a share.

SOHO Security

In the previous chapter, we discussed the setup of a small office/home office (SOHO) network. But without securing the network, we may as well just call up a hacker and ask him to invade the network. The core of the SOHO network is the multifunction network device. This device acts as a switch, router, firewall, and wireless access point. For the rest of this section, we'll talk about how to secure this device and we'll refer to it simply as a router.

> **Note**
>
> As mentioned in the previous chapter, you can access online emulators for several different kinds of routers. It's good to run through these configurations on your own router or an emulator of some sort.

Changing Default Passwords

The first thing we should do to secure the router is to change the password. Most routers come with a blank password. Connect to the router by opening up your favorite browser (your favorite should be the most secure one), typing the IP address of the router (for example, 192.168.0.1), and logging in. Some routers allow you to change the username; if so, do it, just like you would for a Windows computer. But no matter what the router, you will definitely be able to change the password (and you should change it). Make it something complex, based on the rules we discussed in the Windows Security section. Save the settings (which will log you out) and then log in with the new password to make sure it took effect.

> **ExamAlert**
>
> Remember to change the admin password first before anything else!

Some routers also have a user password. Change this as well but change it to a different password than the admin password.

Changing and Disabling the SSID

The Service Set Identifier (SSID) is used to name a wireless network. Default SSIDs are usually basic; it is wise to change the name of the wireless network before enabling wireless on the router. Names that include uppercase letters, lowercase letters, and numbers will be more challenging for casual wireless passersby to memorize.

After all wireless clients are connected to the network, consider disabling the SSID. Though it is not a perfect solution, it will mask part of the SSID broadcast, making it impossible to see with normal wireless locating software. Figure 17.7 shows a modified SSID named Saturn6Network and that it is set to Invisible.

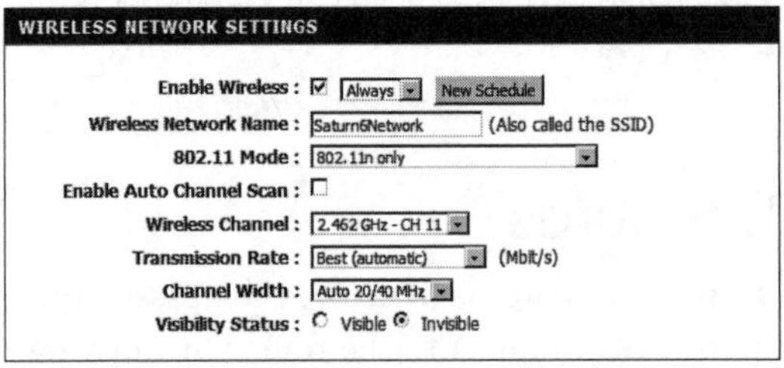

FIGURE 17.7   **Renamed and disabled SSID**

When the SSID is disabled, wireless clients won't be able to scan for it. If you need to connect additional wireless clients, you will either have to enable the SSID broadcast or enter the wireless SSID manually when connecting. To connect manually, open the Network and Sharing Center and select the Connect to a network link. Then select Manually connect to a wireless network. (The wireless adapter must be installed with correct drivers to see this link.) You will have to type the SSID, the type of wireless, and the security key to get in the network.

Configuring Wireless Encryption

Windows supports wireless networking protocols such as WPA2 and encryption methods such as AES to provide data confidentiality. Figure 17.8 displays a common secure wireless encryption technique on a typical router. Table 17.3 shows the characteristics of the various wireless protocols and encryption methods.

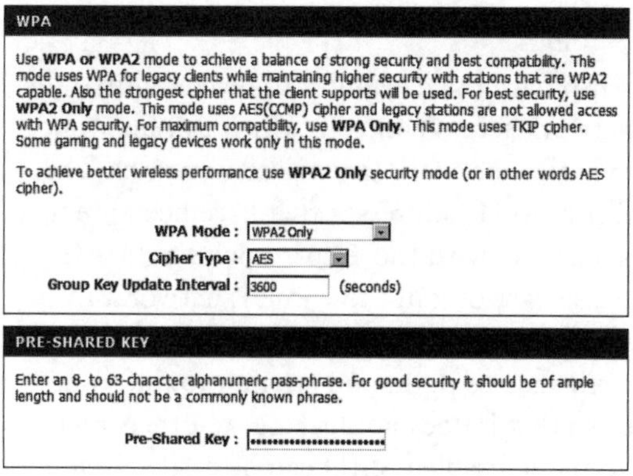

FIGURE 17.8 Wireless network settings on a common router

TABLE 17.3 **Wireless Encryption Methods**

Wireless Protocol	Description	Encryption Level
WEP	Wired Equivalent Privacy (Deprecated)	64-bit
WPA	Wi-Fi Protected Access	128-bit
WPA2	Version 2	256-bit
TKIP	Temporal Key Integrity Protocol	128-bit
	Deprecated encryption protocol used with WEP or WPA	
AES	Advanced Encryption Standard Encryption protocol used with WPA/WPA2	128-, 192-, and 256-bit
	Strongest encryption method in this table	

Figure 17.8 shows router is using WPA2 only and AES as the encryption protocol. It also has a 16-character key for accessing the wireless network. Aside from using external servers for authentication, this is the best method on this router and similar routers as well. This is the best line of defense against war drivers—attackers who attempt to gain access to unprotected wireless networks. They drive around and use a laptop looking for wireless networks in range.

WEP is the weakest type of encryption; WPA is stronger and WPA2 is the strongest of the three. However, it is better to have WEP as opposed to nothing. If this is the case, use encryption keys that are difficult to guess and consider changing those keys often. Some devices can be updated to support WPA, whether it is through a firmware upgrade or through the use of a software add-on.

Enabling MAC Filtering

The wireless access point might also have the capability to be configured for MAC filtering (a basic form of network access control), which can filter out which computers can access the wireless network (and wired network). The WAP does this by consulting a list of MAC addresses that have been previously entered. Only the network adapters with those corresponding MAC addresses can connect; everyone else cannot join the wireless network. In some cases, a device might broadcast this MAC table. If this is the case, look for an update for the firmware of the access point and attempt to fine-tune the broadcast range of the device so that it does not leak out to other organizations. Because MAC filtering and a disabled SSID can be easily circumvented using a network sniffer, it is important to also use strong encryption and possibly consider other types of network access control (such as 802.1X) and external authentication methods (such as RADIUS).

Disabling WPS

Wi-Fi Protected Setup was originally intended to make connecting to a wireless access point easier for the average user. However, anything that is made more simple is often less secure as well. Case in point, WPS is vulnerable to brute-force attacks, which can lead to intrusions on the network. Brute-force attacks are used to guess passwords and codes by trying combinations of letters, numbers, and symbols. The WPS code is usually 8 to 10 digits long, which is not very difficult to crack. So your best bet is to disable WPS on the router to help secure the network. Figure 17.9 shows WPS as disabled. You can also see the basic 8-digit PIN code that is used.

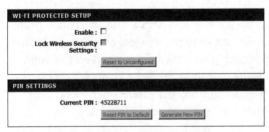

FIGURE 17.9 Disabled Wi-Fi Protected Setup on a common router

Assigning Static IP Addresses

A SOHO router can be set to limit the number of dynamic addresses it hands out. If there are not enough to go around, you might find that certain hosts (such as servers or printers) lose connectivity when there are more client computers on the network. First, consider increasing the scope of addresses that the router is configured to hand out to clients. Second, try assigning static IP addresses to the servers and printers—essentially, any hosts that share information or services. If more clients obtaining dynamic addresses are added in the future, the servers and printers will not be affected.

Disabling Physical Ports

Many routers come with the capability to disable the physical ports on the switch portion of the device. This is a wise precaution. If you disable unused physical ports, a rogue computer can be plugged in to the router physically but won't have any hopes of accessing the network. This concept is a policy in most organizations. Unused router or switch ports are disabled so that a person can't connect a laptop to any old RJ45 jack on the premises.

ExamAlert

Know the various ways to secure a SOHO router.

A Final Word on SOHO Routers

To round out this section, make sure that the router's firmware is up to date. Also, always make sure the built-in firewall is enabled. This firewall is going to be much more important than the Windows firewalls on the individual computers, though both are recommended. Most routers' firewalls are on by default, but you should always check. If you do any kind of port forwarding, port triggering, DMZ configurations, or remote connections of any kind, make sure the firewall is allowing traffic only through the specific port or ports you require and that everything else is blocked. Check for updates every month or so, and while you are at it, change the administrator password for good measure.

Cram Quiz

Answer these questions. The answers follow the last question. If you cannot answer these questions correctly, consider reading this section again until you can.

220-902 Questions

1. Which of the following describes an attempt to guess a password by using a combination of letters and numbers?

   ○ **A.** Brute force

   ○ **B.** Social engineering

   ○ **C.** WPS

   ○ **D.** War driving

2. Which of the following helps to secure a SOHO router? (Select the three best answers.)

   ○ **A.** Change default passwords.

   ○ **B.** Enable SSID.

   ○ **C.** Enable MAC filtering.

   ○ **D.** Enable WPS.

   ○ **E.** Enable WPA2.

3. Which of the following is the strongest form of wireless encryption?

   ○ **A.** WPA

   ○ **B.** WEP

   ○ **C.** AES

   ○ **D.** TKIP

4. You want to prevent rogue employees from connecting a laptop to the SOHO router and accessing the network. How can you accomplish this? (Select the two best answers.)

   ○ **A.** Enable MAC filtering.

   ○ **B.** Create a DMZ.

   ○ **C.** Configure a complex SSID.

   ○ **D.** Disable physical ports.

Cram Quiz Answers

220-902 Answers

1. **A.** Brute-force attacks use a combination of letters, numbers, and symbols to guess passwords, PINs, and passcodes. Social engineering is an attempt to manipulate people into providing confidential information. WPS stands for Wi-Fi Protected Setup; it uses a code that attackers might try to crack with a brute-force attack. War driving is the act of attempting to intrude on wireless networks with a laptop from within a vehicle.

2. **A, C, and E.** Changing default passwords, enabling MAC filtering, and enabling WPA2 can all increase the security of a SOHO router. Enabling the SSID makes it visible. Enabling WPS makes it easier to connect to but has security implications.

3. **C.** Advanced Encryption Standard (AES) is the strongest form of wireless encryption (given the listed answers). WPA is a wireless encryption protocol that is not bad, but WPA2 is recommended. WEP and TKIP are deprecated, have been compromised, and should be avoided.

4. **A and D.** By enabling MAC filtering, you can create a list of MAC addresses that the SOHO router will accept. Any other computers with different MAC addresses will not be allowed access to the network. This works for wired and wireless connections. You can also disable physical ports on the router; this blocks any physical signal from being sent to those unused ports. A DMZ is used to host servers and acts as a separate area between the LAN and the Internet. A complex SSID is great but won't matter to a user connecting a laptop physically to the router because the SSID affects only wireless access.

CHAPTER 18

Android, iOS, OS X, and Linux

This chapter covers the following A+ exam topics:

▶ Android and iOS Basics

▶ Android/iOS Networking and Synchronization

▶ Android/iOS Security and Additional Troubleshooting

▶ OS X and Linux

You can find a master list of A+ exam topics in the "Introduction."

This chapter covers CompTIA A+ 220-902 objectives 2.1, 2.2, 2.5, 2.7, 4.3, and 4.4.

Mobile devices have simply exploded onto the mainstream scene, and the number of mobile devices in use has been growing exponentially. Now it seems that everywhere you look, there is someone tapping away on a tablet computer, smartphone, or other mobile device. Because of this, CompTIA has an entire mobile devices section listed in the A+ 220-902 objectives. We discussed mobile device hardware in Chapter 7, "Mobile Device Hardware," but it's not even close—it's the software that holds the most importance. As an A+ technician, you need to know the differences between the two main mobile operating systems (Android and iOS), how to network and synchronize the devices that run those operating systems, and how to secure them.

In this chapter, we'll pay the most attention to Android-based devices and Apple devices, but we'll also briefly discuss some of the other players in the market. I refer to typical tablets and smartphones but you need to remember the speedy rate at which new devices are released. What I talk about in this book might work in generally the same way on future devices, but quite often the names of particular settings and the navigation to those settings will vary slightly. Be ready for a small learning curve with each new version of mobile device and each new software update.

This chapter is power-packed. Not only do we cover iOS and Android, but I also incorporate the secondary desktop operating systems: OS X and Linux. It might seem a strange place to cover these, but the segue between Apple's iOS and OS X was irresistible. Plus, Android is actually a type of Linux, and OS X, while not a variant of Linux, is similar in functionality, especially in the command line. So it all just seemed to fit. You probably won't see many questions on the 220-902 exam pertaining to OS X and Linux, mainly because their business-based market share is extremely low compared to Windows. So the content on those two OSes will be very concise.

So enough banter, let's dig into Android and iOS now.

Android and iOS Basics

Without a doubt, Android and iOS are the two most commonly used operating systems loaded on smartphones and tablets—and by a wide margin. As of the writing of this book (2015), other mobile operating systems only have an estimated 5 to 10 percent of the market. You never know with technology, but that is not expected to change in the near future. Because of that, Android and iOS are covered the most, and I only briefly mention other mobile operating systems.

Open-Source and Closed-Source Operating Systems

Currently, mobile device software comes in one of two forms: open source, which is effectively free to download and modify; and closed source, otherwise known as *vendor-specific*, which cannot be modified without express permission and licensing. There are benefits and drawbacks to each type of system. Because you will see both in the field, you should know each one equally. Let's go over these two systems.

Open Source: Android

Android is an example of open-source software. It is a Linux-based operating system used mostly on smartphones and tablet computers and is developed by the Open Handset Alliance, a group directed by Google. Google releases Android code as open source, allowing developers to modify it and freely create applications for it. Google also commissioned the Android Open-Source Project (AOSP); its mission is to maintain and further develop Android. You'll know when you are dealing with the Android open-source OS and related applications when you see the little robot caricature, usually in green.

Android versions are referred to as Cupcake, Gingerbread, Honeycomb (version 3), Ice Cream Sandwich (version 4.0), Jelly Bean (version 4.1–4.3), KitKat (version 4.4), Lollipop (version 5), and the list continues. To find out the version you are currently running, start at the Home screen; this is the main screen that boots up by default. Access the Settings screen (often by swiping down from the top). Scroll to the About section and then tap it. The version should be listed there. For example, Figure 18.1 shows a smartphone using Android version 4.4.4 (KitKat).

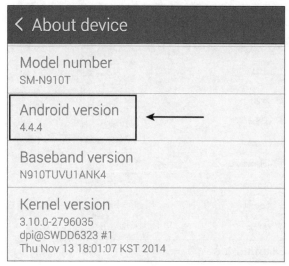

< About device

Model number
SM-N910T

Android version
4.4.4

Baseband version
N910TUVU1ANK4

Kernel version
3.10.0-2796035
dpi@SWDD6323 #1
Thu Nov 13 18:01:07 KST 2014

FIGURE 18.1 **Typical smartphone using Android version 4.4.4**

Suppose a company wanted to create a custom version of Android for a hand-held computer that it was developing. According to the license, the company would be allowed to do this and customize the OS to its specific hardware and applications. This is exactly what companies such as Samsung, HTC, and a host of others do, and it's what differentiates those devices' software packages from each other. These companies will all design their own type of launcher software. The launcher is the part of the graphical user interface (GUI) in Android where a user can customize the Home screen.

Manufacturers of Android-based devices (as well as the general public) can create their own applications for Android as well. To do this, a developer would download the Android application package (APK), which is a package file format used by the Android operating system for distribution and installation of application software and middleware.

Closed Source: iOS

Apple's iOS is an example of closed-source software. It is found on iPhones and iPads. It is based off of Apple's OS X (used on Mac desktops and laptops) and is Unix-based.

To find out the version of iOS you are running, go to the Home screen and then tap Settings. Tap General and then tap About. You'll see the Version number. For example, Figure 18.2 shows an iPad running Version 8.4.1 (12H321). 12H321 is the build number, 8 is the version, and .4.1 is the point release.

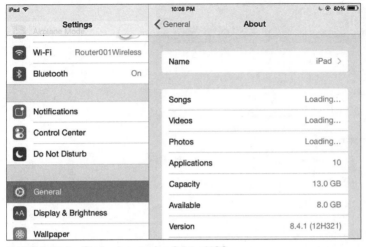

FIGURE 18.2 **iPad using version 8.4.1 of iOS**

Unlike Android, iOS is not open source and is not available for download
to developers. Only Apple hardware uses this operating system. This is an
example of vendor-specific software. However, if developers want to create
an application for iOS, they can download the iOS software development kit
(SDK). Apple license fees are required when a developer is ready to go live
with the application.

> **ExamAlert**
>
> Understand the difference between open source and closed source.

Obtaining Applications

Mobile devices are nothing without applications. To this end, both Android
and iOS have application sources where you can download free and paid
applications (also known as *apps*).

Android users download applications from Google Play. This can be done
directly from the mobile device. Or if a mobile device is connected via USB
to a computer (tethered), the user can browse apps on the Google Play website while working on the computer and download directly from the site to
the device, passing through the computer.

iOS users download applications from the App Store. Apps can also be downloaded to a Mac or PC through the iTunes application.

ExamAlert

Know where to obtain applications for Android and iOS devices.

Regardless of the OS, users would search for the name of the application they want, download it, start the installation process, agree to a license, agree to usage of other apps and components of the device (such as GPS or the camera), and then finally make use of the app.

Some applications don't work unless a user were to hack the OS and gain "superuser" privileges. In the Android world, this is known as *rooting* the phone or other mobile device. In the iOS world, it is known as *jailbreaking*. Note that performing either of these could be a breach of the user license agreement. It can also be dangerous. These types of hacks often require a user to wipe out the device completely and install a special application that may or may not be trustworthy. Many phones are rendered useless or are compromised when attempting this procedure. Applications that have anything to do with rooting or jailbreaking should generally be avoided.

Screen Configurations

Mobile device displays rotate by default if the user turns the device, allowing the screen to be viewed vertically or horizontally. This aids when looking at pictures, movies, or viewing websites. But in some cases, a user might want to lock the rotation of the device so that it stays as either vertical or horizontal, without moving. On an Android device, this can be done by accessing Settings, tapping Display, and then deselecting Screen Rotation (or similar name). On an iOS device (such as an iPhone), this can be done within the status bar by tapping the lock button (orientation lock). iPads have a side switch that can be configured to enable/disable rotation lock; this feature can be turned on in Settings > General > Use side switch to: Lock Rotation.

Screen orientation is a simple concept to understand and use. But it can be more complicated when it comes to applications. For example, Android and iOS-based mobile devices make use of the *accelerometer*, which is a combination of hardware and software that measure velocity. Accelerometers detect rotation, shaking of the device, and so on. It's the accelerometer that enables a mobile device to automatically adjust from portrait (vertical) to landscape (horizontal) mode using the three axes: the X-axis (left to right), the Y-axis (up and down), and the Z-axis (back to front). These are manipulated by developers for applications and games so that the program can recognize particular movements of the device and translate them to specific application functions. Newer devices include a *gyroscope*, which adds the measurements of pitch, roll, and yaw, just like in the concept of flight dynamics. You won't need a pilot's license to use a mobile device, but this additional measurement of movement has a great impact on the development of newer applications and especially games. Of course, if the accelerometers or gyroscope of the mobile device fail and a reset of the device doesn't fix the problem, it must be repaired at an authorized service center.

> **ExamAlert**
>
> Understand the concepts of *accelerometer* and *gyroscope*.

Some mobile devices (especially older ones) make use of a screen calibration utility. To make sure that the three axes are calibrated properly, this program is run while the mobile device is laid on a flat surface. You can tell whether the surface is level by the horizontal and vertical leveling bubbles or by a crosshair or similar image in the center of the screen. You need to tap with a stylus as close to the center of the display as possible. If a stylus is not available, use the pointed end of a pen cap. However, many new devices auto-calibrate, and if there is actually a problem with the calibration, the device must be brought to an authorized service center for repair. A reset can also fix problems with calibration, which we will discuss later in this chapter.

Sometimes, issues that appear to be calibration problems are actually something else that have an easy fix. For example, cheaper screen protectors can bubble and otherwise cause problems when tapping on the screen. Removing the protector and properly installing a new one can fix this problem. When installing a screen protector, use a long, flat surface to squeeze all the bubbles out; there are shims that can be purchased for just this purpose. Use a decent screen protector, and be sure to clean the screen beforehand and make sure it is dry before the installation. Good quality screen protectors (glass-based) will not only protect the display, they will also reduce glare, smudging, and fingerprints without reducing sensitivity. Dirty screens can also be a culprit when a user is having difficulty tapping on icons or smaller items. Clean the display with a lint-free cloth. If the screen is very dirty, create a mixture that is 50 percent isopropyl alcohol and 50 percent water, apply it conservatively to the cloth, and then clean the display with the cloth. Make sure all traces of liquid are removed when you are done. If none of these steps work, the device needs to be taken to an authorized service center for repair.

Virtual Assistants

A virtual assistant is an intelligent application installed on a mobile device that helps users send messages, place phone calls, search for restaurants, search the Web, find directions, and lots more. Virtual assistants are usually voice activated. For example, iOS-based devices use Siri, which allows a user to ask questions and make further conversation, all of which helps the assistant to adapt to the user over time. To access the assistant, press and hold the Home button. Microsoft has a similar personal assistant called Cortana. Other device manufacturers might offer comparable voice-activated software (such as Samsung's S Voice, which has a special key word to bring the device out of sleep), or they might make use of third-party voice recognition software such as Dragon NaturallySpeaking. This technology is constantly changing, expanding, and improving. Take a look at your device now and see if it supports a virtual assistant. If not, go to your store for applications and look at the current virtual assistant downloads available to you.

GPS and Geotracking

The Global Positioning System (GPS), developed by the U.S. DoD, is a worldwide system of satellites that provide location information for anything with a GPS receiver. Any mobile device with a GPS receiver can use this system to identify its location and utilize mapping programs and any other applications that rely on GPS. Some mobile devices do not have a GPS receiver; they instead use cell tower triangulation to locate them, or Location Services, which uses crowd-sourced Wi-Fi locations to determine the approximate location of the device.

GPS (Location Services, also known simply as *Location*) can be enabled in Settings. Many applications require the use of GPS, as do emergency notification systems and mobile payment systems (such as Samsung Pay or Square), so be sure to know where to enable that on your particular mobile device.

> **ExamAlert**
>
> Know that GPS or Location Services needs to be enabled in Settings for many applications to work.

Geotracking is the practice of tracking and recording the location of a mobile device over time. This location tracking is done by Apple and Google as well as other organizations and governments. Privacy issues aside, this practice is being done, so if a user doesn't want his location known, simply disable the GPS or Location setting.

ExamAlert

Understand the definition of geotracking.

Microsoft Mobile Operating Systems

The two operating systems the CompTIA objectives are concerned with the most are Android and iOS, due to their giant market share. However, these are not the only players on the field! Let's not forget about Microsoft mobile operating systems, such as Windows RT and Windows Phone. As of the writing of this book, these operating systems are in a state of flux; they are being replaced by mobile versions of Windows 10 (which is not covered in the CompTIA A+ objectives). So let's briefly describe Windows RT and Windows Phone.

Windows RT

Windows RT, launched in 2012, is a derivative of Windows 8 used on some mobile devices—specifically, the Microsoft Surface tablet computer. It is a leaner version of Windows 8 meant for ARM-based CPUs. Windows RT (and all versions of Windows) is closed source, so Microsoft has pretty tight control over which devices can use the operating system. Besides the Microsoft Surface, other manufacturers that developed Windows RT–based tablets include ASUS, Dell, Samsung, and Lenovo.

Note

Know that some versions of the Microsoft Surface (such as the Surface Pro and other newer versions) use a more powerful CPU, such as the Intel Core i5 and i7 CPU, and use Windows 8 (or Windows 10) instead of Windows RT.

Microsoft includes a special version of Microsoft Office within Windows RT that has Word, Excel, PowerPoint, and OneNote. Tools such as OneNote have been around for a while, and although they work decently on a PC, they can really shine if the computer provides a touchscreen. Also included is a variant of Windows 8's File Explorer and Internet Explorer. If a user wanted additional applications, that person would have to go to the Windows Store to download them. One of the original goals of Windows RT was to have increased USB support in comparison to iOS and Android. Now, however, Windows RT has been phased out so that devices such as the Microsoft Surface can run operating systems such as Windows 8.1 and Windows 10.

Windows Phone

Windows Phone, originally launched as Windows Phone 7 in 2010, is a series of operating systems used by smartphones developed by manufacturers such as HTC and Nokia. It is the successor to Windows Mobile and is not compatible with it. It replaced Symbian as Nokia's default mobile phone OS. Windows Phone 7 (and all previous versions of Microsoft phone software) is based on Windows CE, also known as Windows Embedded. Windows CE acts as the core for Windows Phone 7. CE is licensed by Microsoft to original equipment manufacturers (OEMs) and device makers, who then modify it as they see fit to modify the user interface and to ensure it works efficiently with their devices and software. However, Windows Phone 8 (released in 2012) moved from the Windows CE–based architecture to a variant of the Windows NT architecture. This was done in an attempt to offer better hardware support. Just as with Windows 8, the initial screen, known as the Start screen, is filled with tiles, some of which are known as "live tiles." These live tiles are dynamic, real-time links to applications and games that give information and show pictures even when the user has not clicked on them.

As of the writing of this book, Windows Phone has a very small market share when compared to iOS and Android. In 2015, the name changed slightly again with the release of Windows 10 Mobile.

Cram Quiz

Answer these questions. The answers follow the last question. If you cannot answer these questions correctly, consider reading this section again until you can.

220-902 Questions

1. A user is having difficulty tapping on icons. Which of the following are the best ways to help the user? (Select the two best answers.)

   ○ **A.** Clean the display.

   ○ **B.** Tap the home button.

   ○ **C.** Install a screen protector.

   ○ **D.** Initiate a soft reset.

   ○ **E.** Initiate a hard reset.

2. Which of the following can aid a mobile user in finding the nearest coffee shop? (Select the best answer.)

   ○ **A.** Geotracking

   ○ **B.** iOS

   ○ **C.** GPS

   ○ **D.** GSM

3. A user wants to stop his tablet from shifting horizontally when he turns it. Which of the following should you enable?

   ○ **A.** Lock rotation

   ○ **B.** Accelerometer

   ○ **C.** Gyroscope

   ○ **D.** Screen calibration

4. Which of the following are the two most common operating systems used by mobile devices?

   ○ **A.** Windows Phone

   ○ **B.** iOS

   ○ **C.** Windows Vista

   ○ **D.** Android

5. Which OS is considered to be closed source?

  ○ **A.** Android

  ○ **B.** Bluetooth

  ○ **C.** Linux

  ○ **D.** iOS

Cram Quiz Answers

220-902 Answers

1. **A and D.** A dirty display can cause issues when trying to manipulate a multi-touch touchscreen. By cleaning it, the user might find it easier to use. A soft reset (turning the device off and on) can sometimes fix the problem as well. Tapping the Home button simply brings the user to the Home screen. Screen protectors are a good idea, but if installed incorrectly, they could actually be the reason that a user has issues tapping icons. After the screen is cleaned, a decent quality screen protector should be installed. Hard resets often initiate a complete wipe of the system. Use this only as a last resort.

2. **C.** GPS is used to locate the mobile user. From that information, one of several programs can locate that all-important nearest coffee shop. Geotracking is the practice of tracking and recording the location of a mobile device. However, geotracking is done by organizations, whereas GPS is something installed to the mobile device. iOS is the operating system used by Apple mobile devices. GSM is a cellular standard that we will cover in more depth in the next section.

3. **A.** Enable Lock rotation on Apple devices. On Android devices, disable screen rotation (or auto-rotate or similar terminology). The Accelerometer is a term used by Apple to describe the hardware/software that controls the three axes of movement. The Gyroscope is another term used by Apple to describe the device that measures the additional three movements (pitch, roll, and yaw) of newer Apple devices. Screen calibration is used to reset the device that measures the three axes.

4. **B and D.** The two most common operating systems used by mobile devices are iOS and Android. Windows Phone trails far behind; while still supported for the time being, it is being phased out by newer OSes. Windows Vista is a desktop OS, not a mobile OS.

5. **D.** Apple iOS is a closed-source, vendor-specific operating system. Android is a type of Linux that is open source. Bluetooth is a wireless standard, not an operating system.

Android/iOS Networking and Synchronization

Now that we've discussed mobile device software, let's go ahead and harness their power through networking and synchronization.

From cellular GSM connections to Wi-Fi and Bluetooth, a mobile device can create connections to computers and networks, download e-mail, and work with headsets and remote printers.

Synchronization is the matching up of files, e-mail, and other types of data between one computer and another. We use synchronization to bring files in line with each other and to force devices to coordinate their data. When dealing with synchronization, a mobile device can connect to a PC via USB (the most common), RS-232 serial connections (less common), and, of course, Wi-Fi and Bluetooth.

Cellular Radio Technologies

Cellular phones originally used the Global System for Mobile Communications (GSM) to make voice calls and use GSM or the general packet radio service (GPRS) to send data at 2G speeds through the cellular network. Extensions of these standards—the Universal Mobile Telecommunications System (UMTS) and Enhanced Data rates for GSM Evolution (EDGE)—are used to attain 3G speeds. 4G and 4G LTE speeds can be attained only when a mobile device complies with the International Mobile Telecommunications Advanced (IMT-Advanced) requirements, has a 4G antenna, and is in range of a 4G transmitter. Devices manufactured during the writing of this book most commonly use 4G and LTE (which builds on 4G by using an updated radio interface/antenna in the mobile device and by utilizing core network infrastructure improvements).

Most devices cannot shut off the cellular antenna by itself (unless you shut down the device itself). However, every device manufactured now is required to have an "airplane mode," which turns off any wireless antenna in the device, including disabling the connection to the cellular network (such as GSM, CDMA, 4G, and so on), and disabling Wi-Fi, GPS, and Bluetooth. This can be accomplished by either going to Settings > Airplane Mode or by holding the Power button down and selecting Airplane Mode. You will find that some airlines don't consider this to be acceptable and for security purposes will still ask you to turn off your device altogether, either for the duration of the flight or at least during takeoff and landing.

ExamAlert

Know what airplane mode is and how to configure it on Android and Apple devices.

Let's get a little more into it and briefly discuss some additional mobile technology and acronyms, such as PRL updates, baseband updates, radio firmware, IMEI versus IMSI and VPN.

PRL stands for preferred roaming list. It is used by cellular providers (such as Sprint, Verizon, and U.S. Cellular) that utilize code division multiple access (CDMA) technology instead of GSM. It's a database that contains information about the provider's radio bands, sub-bands, and service provider IDs. Ultimately, it allows a phone to connect to the correct tower; without the database, the phone might not be able to roam outside the provider's network. When necessary, PRL information is sent as an update over the air. However, you can also update it manually by dialing a number that is unique to each provider. You can find out the version you are using within the About section on most phones.

By the way, the other major providers (AT&T and T-Mobile) use GSM. They also use UMTS and LTE, which were mentioned previously. This is one of the reasons you can't bring a phone from one provider to another—well, that and the fact that most phones are locked by the provider!

When a phone uses GSM, that technology and its radio functions are controlled by a chip and software package that is collectively referred to as "baseband." Baseband updates are necessary to communicate properly with GSM cell towers. If an older phone won't update properly, it must be taken to the provider for a wired, manual update. Baseband is also referred to as radio firmware in that it controls network connectivity for GSM. Other wireless antennas such as Wi-Fi and GPS are controlled by the operating system's drivers.

Warning

Do not attempt a radio firmware (baseband) update if your phone does not require it. A faulty update can easily make the phone inoperable.

Now onto IMEI and IMSI—these are both identification technologies. IMEI stands for International Mobile Station Equipment Identity and it identifies phones used on 3GPP-based networks (GSM, UMTS, and LTE). You can find this ID number printed inside the phone either on or near the battery. It is used only to identify the device. However, International Mobile Subscriber Identity (IMSI) is used to identify the user. For GSM, UMTS, and LTE networks, this ID is loaded into the subscriber identity module (SIM) card. For CDMA networks, the ID is loaded directly into the phone or to a removable user identity module (R-UIM), which is similar to a SIM card.

> **ExamAlert**
>
> Know that the IMEI ID identifies the device and the IMSI ID identifies the user of the device.

Today's mobile devices can also use virtual private networking (VPN) technology to make secure connections—tunneling though the provider's radio network. The VPN data is also updated frequently as updates to mobile operating systems are released, as well as for security purposes. For more information about VPNs, see Chapter 16, "Computer Networking Part II."

You can find the versions of all these technologies (and the types of radio technology used) within the About (or About device) section and you can learn more information by going to the About > Status section. Refer to Figure 18.1 for an example of the baseband version used. Take a look at your own mobile device's settings and see which radio technologies you are connecting to and which versions of firmware you are running. Also, if you have a removable battery, take a look at the IMEI ID as well.

> **Note**
>
> Sometimes, finding the information you are looking for can be a bit of a chore; the level of difficulty varies according to the device and the version of OS installed to it. Plus, the various IDs, signal levels, types of technologies used, and so on can be dispersed among different areas of the phone. Consider using a cell tower analyzer, radio signal analyzer, or network signal information app to see this data in a more visual and centralized manner.

All of these radio network technologies can be affected by a mobile phone update, such as a version update. To prevent network connectivity issues, consider waiting until a new mobile OS version has been thoroughly tested before you update your phone.

Wi-Fi Network Connectivity

Using a cellular connection can be slow when transmitting data (even if you happen to have a strong 4G signal). That's why all mobile devices are equipped with an embedded wireless antenna to connect to wireless LANs. This Wi-Fi antenna can allow access to 802.11a, b, g, n, and ac networks. The wireless configuration works similar to a wireless connection on a PC or laptop. See Chapter 16 for a detailed description of connecting to wireless networks.

In general, the mobile device must first search for wireless networks before connecting. On a typical mobile device, this is done in Settings > Wi-Fi, which displays the screen shown in Figure 18.3.

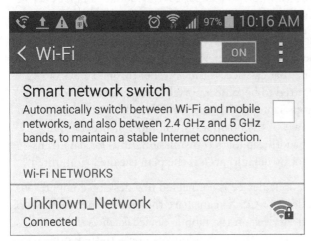

FIGURE 18.3 **Android Wi-Fi screen**

In the Wi-Fi settings screen, perform the following general steps:

1. Most devices usually scan for wireless networks automatically, or you can tap Add Wi-Fi Network (or similar name) to add one manually.

2. When adding a network manually, enter the SSID of the wireless access point in the Add Wi-Fi Network window.

3. Enter the passcode for the network. If the code is correct, then the wireless adapter in the mobile device gets an IP address, allowing it to communicate with the network. If a wireless network uses WPA2 and the mobile device isn't compatible, you should search for an update to the operating system to make it WPA2-compliant.

> **ExamAlert**
>
> Understand how to connect to a Wi-Fi network in Android and iOS.

Almost all types of devices display the universal wireless icon when connected to a wireless network, as shown in Figure 18.4. This icon not only lets you know when you are connected, it tells you how strong the connection is. The more curved lines you see, the better the connection.

FIGURE 18.4   **Universal wireless symbol**

Some mobile devices can initiate *tethering*. This is when the mobile device shares its Internet connection with one or more other mobile devices and computers. It is broken down into two categories: the mobile hotspot (Wi-Fi tethering) and USB tethering.

A *mobile hotspot*, also known as *Wi-Fi tethering*, is when the mobile device shares its Internet connection with other Wi-Fi capable devices. For example, if a user has a smartphone that can access the Internet through a 3G or 4G network, it can be configured to become a portable Wi-Fi hotspot for other mobile devices (or desktops/laptops) that are Wi-Fi capable but have no cellular or GPRS option. Beware of the hotspot option; most providers have a fairly low consumer bandwidth cap (data transmission limit) for data transferred through the hotspot by default, even if the plan is called "unlimited."

USB tethering is when a mobile device is connected to a desktop computer via USB; that desktop (Windows or OS X) can share the phone's mobile network. Quite often, Wi-Fi-based services on the mobile device (such as Wi-Fi calling) need to be shut down before this technology can be activated; otherwise, they will be shut down automatically.

> **ExamAlert**
>
> *Wi-Fi Calling* is the ability to place and receive phone calls over the Wi-Fi network (using a type of VoIP). It takes advantage of the user's Internet connection but must be supported by the cellular provider, by the mobile device, and the user must be within fairly close range of the WAP to avoid call drops.

Some devices can also be configured for *Internet pass-through* as well. This means that the phone or other device connects to a PC via USB and accesses the Internet using the PC's Internet connection. So it is effectively the reverse of tethering. This can be very handy when the mobile device doesn't have a Wi-Fi option, the Wi-Fi/4G is slow, or there is no Wi-Fi network available.

ExamAlert

Know the terms *mobile hotspot* and *USB tethering* and how they operate.

Wi-Fi Troubleshooting

When troubleshooting mobile device wireless connections, always make sure of the following basic wireless troubleshooting techniques:

▶ The device is within range.

▶ The correct SSID was entered (if manually connecting).

▶ The device supports the encryption protocol of the wireless network.

▶ Tethering is not conflicting with the wireless connection.

If you still have trouble, here are a few more methods that can help to connect or reconnect to a wireless network:

▶ Power cycle the mobile device.

▶ Power cycle Wi-Fi.

▶ Remove or "forget" the particular wireless network and then attempt to connect to it again.

▶ Consider using a Wi-Fi analyzer app to locate the wireless network in question. Sometimes these analysis apps can give you more information that can help to solve the connectivity problem. They're also a great security tool to check your own WAP. Just be careful because some can use up a good deal of system resources and possibly cause the battery to run hot.

▶ Access the advanced settings and check whether there is a Wi-Fi sleep policy, whether Wi-Fi scanning has been turned off, whether there is a proxy configuration, or whether a static IP is used. Any of these could possibly cause a conflict. You might also try renewing the lease of an IP address, if the device is obtaining one from a DHCP server (which it most likely will be.) Some devices also have an option for Best Wi-Fi Performance, which uses more power but might help when connecting to distant WAPs. Another possibility is that the mobile device needs to have an encryption certificate installed, which is usually done from here as well. The advanced settings will vary from device to device, but they can usually be found by going to Settings > Wi-Fi > Advanced (or something similar). An example of this is shown in Figure 18.5. Note the IP address at the bottom of the figure; if you ever need to know that address, this is a good place to go.

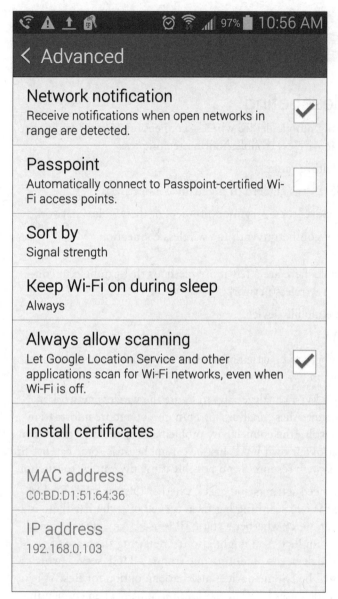

FIGURE 18.5 **Advanced wireless settings**

One of these methods usually works when troubleshooting a wireless connection, but if all else fails, a hard reset can bring the device back to factory settings. (Always back up all data and settings before performing a hard reset.) And if the mobile device still can't connect to any of several known good wireless networks, take the device to an authorized service center.

ExamAlert

Know your Wi-Fi troubleshooting techniques!

Bluetooth Configuration

Bluetooth is a wireless standard for transmitting data over short distances. It is commonly implemented in the form of a headset or printer connection. It is also used to create a wireless personal area network (WPAN) consisting of multiple Bluetooth-enabled mobile devices.

To connect a Bluetooth device to a mobile device, Bluetooth first needs to be enabled. Then the Bluetooth device needs to be synchronized to the mobile device. This is known as *pairing* or linking. It sometimes requires a pin code. Once synchronized, the device should automatically connect and should function at that point. Finally, the Bluetooth connection should be tested. Following are the steps involved in connecting a Bluetooth device to a typical mobile device. Before you begin, make sure the Bluetooth device is charged (if applicable). Here is a typical procedure for making a Bluetooth connection:

1. Go to Settings > Bluetooth and turn on Bluetooth. This enables Bluetooth on the mobile device.

2. Prepare the device. For example, on a typical Bluetooth headset, press and hold the button while opening the microphone. Keep holding the button.

3. Scan for devices on the mobile device.

4. Once the desired device is found, connect to it and pair it to the mobile device.

5. Enter a pin code if necessary. Some devices come with a default pin of 0000.

When finished, the screen will look similar to Figure 18.6. Note the Bluetooth icon at the top of the screen. This icon indicates whether Bluetooth is running on the device. It will remain there even after you disconnect the Bluetooth device. To disconnect the Bluetooth device, simply tap the device on the screen and tap OK. It will remain paired but nonfunctional until a connection is made again.

FIGURE 18.6   Installed Bluetooth device

Mobile devices can also connect to other Bluetooth-enabled devices (forming a WPAN) or to a computer equipped with a Bluetooth dongle. To do this, you must set the mobile device to discoverable (a mode that generally lasts for only 2 minutes). In the same fashion that the headset was discovered by the mobile device in the previous procedure, a mobile device can be discovered by a computer or other mobile device. When connecting a mobile device to another mobile device or PC, it can be identified by its name. You can modify this name if you want. It is authenticated by a pin code chosen at the PC or on another mobile device. You can test these types of connections by sending data or by initiating communications.

Bluetooth devices can be connected to only one mobile device at a time. If you need to switch the Bluetooth device from one mobile device to another, be sure to disconnect it or "forget" it from the current connection before making a new one.

ExamAlert

Know how to configure Bluetooth devices in Android and iOS.

Bluetooth Troubleshooting

If you have trouble pairing a Bluetooth device and connecting or reconnecting to Bluetooth devices or PANs, try some of the following methods:

- ▶ Make sure the phone or other mobile device is Bluetooth-capable.

- ▶ Verify whether Bluetooth is enabled on the mobile device. Also, if applicable, verify whether it is enabled on the target device (for example, an automobile sound system).

- ▶ Verify whether your devices are fully charged, especially Bluetooth headsets.

- ▶ Check whether you are within range. For example, Class 2 Bluetooth devices have a range of 10 meters.

- ▶ Restart the mobile device and attempt to reconnect.

- ▶ Check for conflicting Wi-Fi frequencies. Consider changing the channel used by the Wi-Fi network.

- ▶ Use a known good Bluetooth device with the mobile device to make sure that the mobile device's Bluetooth is functional.

- ▶ Remove or "forget" the particular Bluetooth device, turn off Bluetooth in general, restart the mobile device, and then attempt to reconnect.

> **ExamAlert**
>
> Know your Bluetooth troubleshooting techniques!

E-Mail Configurations

Although there are many other types of communication available to mobile users, e-mail still accounts for an important percentage. You should know how to configure a mobile device for web-based e-mail services such as Gmail, Yahoo!, and so on. You should also know how to configure POP3, IMAP, and connections to Microsoft Exchange Servers.

Web-Based E-Mail for Mobile Devices

Mobile devices can access web-based e-mail through a browser, but this is not necessary nowadays due to the "app." For example, most Android-based devices come with a Gmail application built in, allowing a user to access Gmail directly without having to use the browser. Devices also might have a proprietary e-mail application. Apple iOS devices allow connectivity to Gmail, Yahoo!, and a host of other e-mail providers as well. Apple users might also connect to the iCloud for mail features. Users of other devices might use Microsoft's Outlook.com. As you can see, there are a lot of options when it comes to mail services for mobile devices.

Connecting to these services is simple and works in a fashion that is similar to working on a desktop or laptop computer. Choose the type of provider you use, enter a username (the e-mail address) and password (on Apple devices, an Apple ID is also required), and the user will have access to web-based e-mail.

When troubleshooting issues with e-mail, make sure that the username and password are typed correctly. Using onscreen keyboards often leads to mis-typed passwords. Also make sure that the mobile device is currently connected to the Internet.

POP3, IMAP, and Exchange

When you need to connect your mobile device to a specific organization's e-mail system, it gets a little bit more complicated. You need to know the server that you want to connect to, the port you need to use, and whether security is employed.

Here's the typical step-by-step process for connecting a smartphone or tablet to a POP3 account.

1. Go to Settings > E-mail and then configure or otherwise manage the account.

2. Add an account by pressing the + sign or by clicking "add account" or similar name.

3. Select whether you want POP3, IMAP, or Exchange. (For this exercise, select POP3.)

4. Type the e-mail address and the password of the account.

5. Configure the incoming settings. If you want, change the username to something different than the e-mail address. Then type the POP3 server name. By default, it will be the domain name portion of the e-mail address, which is usually correct. If security is used, select SSL or TLS. This information should be supplied by the network administrator. Type the port number. For POP3, this is 110 by default. If port numbers are different, they will also be supplied to you by the network administrator.

6. Configure the outgoing settings. Type the SMTP server. Organizations will often use the same server name as the POP3 server. However, small office and home users might have to use their ISP's SMTP server. If security is used, select SSL or TLS (or S/MIME, which is covered in Chapter 18). Type the port number for SMTP, which is 25. (Again, this is a default.) Then tap Next.

7. Configure account options. From here, you can tell the mobile device how often to check for mail and whether to notify you when it arrives. At this point, new e-mail should start downloading.

8. Finally, you can give the account an easier name for you to remember it by.

> **ExamAlert**
>
> Know how to add web-based and POP3 e-mail accounts in Android and iOS.

Now, if you instead have to connect an IMAP account, you have to type the IMAP server (for downloading mail), which uses port 143 by default, and you have to type the outgoing SMTP server (for sending mail). If you connect to a Microsoft Exchange mail server, that server name often takes care of both downloading and uploading of e-mail. You might need to know the domain that the Exchange server is a member of. Secure e-mail sessions require the use of SSL or TLS on port 443. Check with the network administrator to find out which protocol to use. POP3 also has a secure derivative known as APOP, a challenge/response protocol that uses a hashing function to prevent replay attacks during an e-mail session.

Troubleshooting E-mail Connections

If you have trouble connecting an e-mail account, try some of the following methods:

▶ Make sure the mobile device has Internet access. If connecting through the cellular network, make sure there is a decent reception.

▶ Verify that the username, password, and server names are typed correctly. Remember that the username is often the e-mail address itself.

▶ Check the port numbers. By default, POP3 is 110, SMTP is 25, and IMAP is 143. However, network administrators might decide to use nondefault port numbers!

> **Note**
>
> There is another SMTP mail submission port that can be used by e-mail clients for increased security—port 587.

▶ Double-check whether security is required in the form of SSL or TLS. For nonstandard port numbers and security configurations, check with your network administrator.

> **ExamAlert**
>
> When troubleshooting e-mail connections on mobile devices, double-check all settings such as username, password, server name, and port number.

Synchronizing Android and iOS-based Devices to a PC

In the past, synchronization was a bit of a hassle, but today's mobile devices synchronize much more seamlessly. And, in fact, synchronization is not nearly as necessary today due to users storing much of their data on the cloud. However, you might opt to synchronize a variety of data to a desktop computer, including contacts, programs, e-mail, pictures, music, videos, calendars, web browser bookmarks, documents, location data, e-books, and social media data.

When you connect mobile devices to a PC via a USB connection, they are typically seen automatically and are represented as a drive letter in Windows Explorer/File Explorer. On older devices, you might have to select an option on the mobile device screen (such as "Disk Drive") when the device is first connected via USB.

Many mobile devices come with synchronization software (which can also be downloaded from the manufacturer website) that can synchronize music, pictures, videos, the calendar, contacts, bookmarks and more. This synchronization can be initiated from the mobile device or from the program on the PC. Documents, music, pictures, and video will often be synchronized by default to the Windows Libraries of the same names.

If you use the mobile device's built-in contacts and e-mail programs, the information within those programs can be transferred to the PC's corresponding programs. For example, the calendar and contacts can be synchronized with Microsoft Outlook.

However, not everyone uses synchronization software. Some people exclusively use Gmail on the Android platform. Google automatically synchronizes mail, contacts, and the calendar so that you can view the information on the mobile device or on the PC (when connected to the Gmail website). However, because the data is stored on a Google server, security can be compromised. If you choose to do this, you should use an extremely strong password, change it every month or so, and use a secure browser when connecting to Gmail from your PC. The same users who use Gmail usually transfer data by simply mounting the mobile device as a drive in Windows (usually by just connecting the device by USB). This effectively renders the synchronization software unnecessary for those users.

There are third-party tools available when a user wants to synchronize an Android device with a PC or Mac via Bluetooth or Wi-Fi. On another note, Google Sync (using Exchange ActiveSync) can be used to synchronize e-mail, contacts, and calendars between an Android 2.0 mobile device and higher with an Exchange Server.

ExamAlert

Know the various ways to synchronize data between an Android and a PC.

When you plug in an iPad/iPhone to a PC via USB, Windows should automatically recognize it and install the driver for it. At that point, you can move files between the PC and the device's memory card. The device shows up in Windows Explorer/File Explorer as Apple iPad or Apple iPhone directly inside of the Computer location of Explorer.

To synchronize data such as contacts, calendars, and so on, PC users need to use iTunes for Windows. From iTunes, a user would select Sync Contacts or Sync Calendars, for example. This information can be synchronized to Microsoft Outlook 2003 or higher and Windows Contacts (in Windows 8/7/ Vista). Mac users benefit from the simplicity of synchronization across all Apple products. They can use iTunes or they can use the iCloud to store, back up, and synchronize information across all Apple devices. This can be done by USB or via Wi-Fi (when the various Apple devices are on the same wireless network). Calendar items can also be synced from the Apple-based device (such as an iPad) by going to Settings > Mail, Contacts, Calendars. Then scroll down and select Sync.

> **ExamAlert**
>
> Know the various ways to synchronize data between an Apple mobile device and a PC or Mac.

Synchronizing Other Devices

One of the benefits of Windows Phone and Windows RT (and Windows 10 mobile OS solutions) is that they can seamlessly synchronize with Windows PCs. These programs can synchronize data between the mobile device and the PC via USB, Bluetooth, or Wi-Fi connections. The concept behind newer versions of Windows mobile operating systems is that they can exist on a LAN just like any other Windows computer. Microsoft emulates web-based synchronization (similar to Google and Apple) through the use of the all-inclusive "Microsoft Account," web-based applications such as Office 365, Outlook.com, and cloud storage such as OneDrive.

> **Note**
>
> The predecessors to Windows Phone, Windows Mobile and Windows CE, are still sometimes found in the transportation, medical, and surveying fields as well as other niche markets that require rugged, waterproof devices. These devices synchronize to the PC by way of the Windows Mobile Device Center (Windows Vista or newer) or other third-party solutions.

Remote management of mobile devices is becoming more important for companies of all sizes. Some companies embrace a "Bring Your Own Device" (BYOD) policy and, in many cases, a network admin might see Android, iOS, or Windows mobile devices. The need to centrally administer these becomes paramount. Microsoft offers the server-based System Center Configuration Manager (SCCM) software to help with management of these mobile devices.

> **Note**
>
> In addition to Microsoft, there are several other companies that offer mobile device management platforms, including Citrix, Xerox, HP, SOTI, and many others.

Cram Quiz

Answer these questions. The answers follow the last question. If you cannot answer these questions correctly, consider reading this section again until you can.

220-902 Questions

1. Which of the following are valid Wi-Fi troubleshooting methods? (Select the two best answers.)

   ○ **A.** Power cycle the device.

   ○ **B.** Restart Bluetooth.

   ○ **C.** Use a static IP.

   ○ **D.** Make sure the device is within range.

   ○ **E.** Rename the SSID.

2. Which of the following connections require a username, password, and SMTP server? (Select the two best answers.)

   ○ **A.** Bluetooth connection

   ○ **B.** Wi-Fi connection

   ○ **C.** POP3 connection

   ○ **D.** Exchange connection

   ○ **E.** IMAP connection

3. Which of the following is the most common connection method when synchronizing data from a mobile device to a PC?

   ○ **A.** Wi-Fi

   ○ **B.** Bluetooth

   ○ **C.** USB

   ○ **D.** FireWire

4. When configuring a Wi-Fi connection, which step occurs after successfully entering the SSID?

   ○ **A.** Select POP3.

   ○ **B.** Check whether the device is within range of the WAP.

   ○ **C.** Enter a passcode for the network.

   ○ **D.** Scan for networks.

5. Which technology should be used to connect a headset to your mobile phone?

   - ○ **A.** Bluetooth
   - ○ **B.** GSM
   - ○ **C.** Wi-Fi
   - ○ **D.** Exchange

6. Which of the following allows other mobile devices to share your mobile device's Internet connection?

   - ○ **A.** Internet pass-through
   - ○ **B.** Locator application
   - ○ **C.** IMAP
   - ○ **D.** Wi-Fi tethering

7. Which of the following is used to synchronize contacts from an iPad to a PC? (Select the best answer.)

   - ○ **A.** Gmail
   - ○ **B.** Google Play
   - ○ **C.** iTunes
   - ○ **D.** System Center Configuration Manager

Cram Quiz Answers

220-902 Answers

1. **A and D.** Valid Wi-Fi troubleshooting methods include power cycling the device and making sure that the mobile device is within range of the wireless access point. Bluetooth could possibly cause a conflict with Wi-Fi. If you suspect this, Bluetooth should simply be turned off. Static IP addresses are one thing you can check for when troubleshooting. Normally, the mobile device should obtain an IP address dynamically from a DHCP server. Renaming the SSID of the access point could cause problems for all clients trying to connect. However, you should make sure that the correct SSID was typed (if the connection were made manually).

2. **C and E.** POP3 and IMAP e-mail connections require an incoming mail server (either POP3 or IMAP) and an outgoing mail server (SMTP). Bluetooth and Wi-Fi connections do not require a username or SMTP server. Exchange connections require a username and password, but no SMTP server. The Exchange server acts as the incoming and outgoing mail server.

3. **C.** USB is the most common connection method used when synchronizing data from a mobile device to a PC. Though Wi-Fi and Bluetooth are also possible, they are less common. Few mobile devices have FireWire connections.

4. **C.** After you enter the SSID (if it's correct) you would enter the passcode for the network. POP3 has to do with configuring an e-mail account. If you have already entered the SSID, then you should be within range of the wireless access point (WAP). Scanning for networks is the first thing you do when setting up a Wi-Fi connection.

5. **A.** The Bluetooth standard is used to connect a headset and other similar devices over short range to a mobile device. GSM is used to make voice calls over cellular networks. Wi-Fi is used to connect mobile devices to the Internet. Exchange is a Microsoft e-mail server; some mobile devices have the capability to connect to e-mail accounts stored on an Exchange server.

6. **D.** Wi-Fi tethering (mobile hotspot technology) allows a mobile device to share its Internet connection with other Wi-Fi capable devices. Internet pass-through is when the mobile device connects to a PC to share the PC's Internet connection. Locator applications are used to find lost or stolen mobile devices through GPS. IMAP is another e-mail protocol similar to POP3.

7. **C.** PC users need iTunes to synchronize contacts and other data from an iPad to a PC. While Gmail can work to synchronize contacts, it is all based on web storage; nothing is actually stored on the iPad. Google Play is a place to get applications and other items for Android. System Center Configuration Manager (SCCM) is a Microsoft server program that enables the management of multiple mobile devices.

Android/iOS Security and Additional Troubleshooting

Mobile devices need to be secure just like any other computing devices. But due to their transportable nature, some of the security techniques will be a bit different. I recommend that you prepare for the possibility of a stolen, lost, damaged, or compromised device. The following methods can help you to recover from these problems and also aid you in preventing them from happening.

Stolen and Lost Devices

Because mobile devices are expensive and could contain confidential data, they become a target for thieves. Plus, they are small and easy to conceal, making them easier to steal. But there are some things you can do to protect your data and attempt to get the mobile device back.

The first thing a user should do when receiving a mobile device is to set a passcode, which is a set of numbers. This is one of several types of *screenlocks*. Locking the device makes it inaccessible to everyone except experienced hackers. The screen lock can be a pattern that is drawn on the display, a PIN (passcode), a password, or it can be based on fingerprint or facial recognition technology. A complex password will usually be the strongest form of screen lock. This is typically accessed from the lock screen option in Settings. You can also select how long the phone will wait after inactivity to lock (part of the screen timeout). Generally, this is set to 1 or 2 minutes or so, but in a confidential environment, you might set this to less.

Speaking of passwords, some devices have the option to make passwords visible. This is almost never recommended because it makes the mobile device vulnerable to shoulder surfers (people looking over your shoulder to find out your password); it should be deselected. When deselected, only asterisks (*) are shown when the user types a password.

> **ExamAlert**
>
> Know how to configure a screen lock using a passcode or password and how to disable visible passwords.

Aside from the default timeout, devices can also be locked by pressing the Power button quickly. If configured, the passcode must be supplied whenever a mobile device comes out of a sleep or lock state and whenever it is first booted.

If a user fails to enter the correct passcode after a certain number of attempts (typically three or five), the device locks temporarily (30 seconds typically) and the user has to wait a certain amount of time before attempting the passcode again. If the user fails to enter the correct passcode again, the timeout increases on most devices. After a certain number of attempts, the device either needs to be connected to the computer it was last synced to or it must be restored to factory condition with a hard reset (which can wipe the data).

ExamAlert

Understand the consequences of entering an incorrect passcode too many times.

Some devices have a setting where the device will be erased automatically after a certain number of incorrect password attempts. There are also third-party apps available for download for most mobile devices that can wipe the data after x number of attempts. Some apps configure the device to automatically take a picture after three failed attempts and e-mail the picture to the owner.

There's an app for virtually everything. For example, say the device was lost or stolen. If the user had previously installed a locator application and the GPS/Location Services was enabled on the device, the user could track where the device is. At that point, the organization would decide whether to get the police involved.

ExamAlert

Know what locator applications are.

Even if you track your mobile device and find it, it might be too late. A hacker can get past passcodes and other screen locks. It's just a matter of time before the hacker has access to the data. So, an organization with confidential information should consider a remote wipe program. As long as the mobile device still has access to the Internet, the remote wipe program can be initiated from a desktop computer, which will delete all the contents of the remote mobile device. In some cases, the command that starts the remote wipe must be issued from an Exchange server or Mobile Device Management server.

> **ExamAlert**
>
> Know the remote wipe programs available for mobile devices.

You should also have a backup plan in place as well so that data on the mobile device is backed up to a secure location at regular intervals. This way, if the data needs to be wiped, you are secure in the fact that most of the data can be recovered. The type of remote wipe program, backup program, and policies regarding how these are implemented will vary from one organization to the next. Be sure to read up on your organization's policies to see exactly what is allowed from a mobile security standpoint.

Compromised and Damaged Devices

Theft and loss aren't the only risks a mobile device faces. We should protect against the chance that a mobile device is damaged or if the device's security is compromised. The device could be the victim of unauthorized account access, root access, leaked files, location tracking, camera/microphone activation, and so on. These could be due to a rogue application, malware installation, or other hijacking of the mobile device. You need to be prepared before these things happen.

Many organizations implement backup and remote backup policies. iOS devices can be backed up to a PC via USB connection and by using iTunes. Also, they can be backed up remotely to the iCloud. In addition, you can use third-party apps for remote backup. Information can even be restored to newer, upgraded iOS devices. Android (as of the writing of this book) doesn't allow a complete backup without rooting the phone (which I don't recommend). However, almost all the data and settings can be backed up in a collection of ways. First, the Google Cloud can be used to back up e-mail, contacts, and other information. If you use Gmail, then e-mail, contacts, and calendars are backed up (and synchronized) to Google servers automatically. If a mobile device is lost, the information can be quickly accessed from a desktop computer or other mobile device. Android applications can be backed up as long as they are not copy-protected. Typically, Android settings and apps can be backed up and restored from Settings > Backup and Reset. If you choose not to use the Google cloud to back up files or not to use the synchronization program that came with the device, there are plenty of third-party apps that can be used to back up via USB to a PC or to back up to the cloud.

One way to protect mobile devices from compromise is to patch or update the operating system. By default, you will be notified automatically about available updates on Android and iOS-based devices. However, you should know where to go to manually update these devices as well. For Android, go to Settings > About Device > Software Updates (or a similar path, such as Settings > System Updates > Software Updates). From here, tap Check Now, or tap Software Updates to begin downloading. You are also notified of updates in the notification panel/status screen.

If you find that there are system updates or security updates available for download, they should probably be installed right away. Security patches are a large percentage of system updates because there are a lot of attackers around the world who want to compromise the Android operating system. But let's be real—attackers will go for any OS if it catches their fancy, be it Android or iOS or any other operating system! Updates for iOS can be located at Settings > General > Software Update (or similar path).

> **Note**
>
> Remember that the exact path to the update feature in a mobile OS can be different from one device to the next and from one manufacturer to the next. In addition, new versions of the software are constantly being released, resulting in changed paths and modified settings names. However, you can find out the path you need by consulting the software manufacturer's website (visit the following links), by going to the device manufacturer's website, or even by going to your cellular provider's website.
>
> ▶ Android: https://support.google.com/android/?hl=en
>
> ▶ iOS: https://www.apple.com/support/ios/

> **ExamAlert**
>
> Know how to check for, and perform, Android and iOS updates.

Updates are great, but they are not created to specifically battle viruses and other malware. So, just like there is antivirus software for PCs, there is also AV software for mobile devices. These are third-party applications that need to be paid for, downloaded, and installed to the mobile device. Some examples for Android include Lookout (built into many devices), McAfee, Trend Micro, 360 Security, and the list goes on.

iOS, on the other hand, is a tightly controlled operating system. One of the benefits of being a closed-source OS is that it can be more difficult to write viruses for. But there is no OS that can't be compromised. For the longest time, there was no antivirus software for iOS. That is, until 2011, when a type of jailbreaking software called jailbreakme used a simple PDF to move insecure code to the root of the device, causing a jailbreak. Ever since, AV software became a reality for iOS-based devices.

iOS *jailbreaking* is the process of removing the limitations that Apple imposes on its devices that run iOS. This enables users to gain root access to the system and allows the download of previously unavailable applications and software not authorized by Apple.

> **ExamAlert**
>
> Understand the term *jailbreaking*.

Any AV software for Android or iOS should be checked regularly for updates—if the device is not configured to automatically download updates, that is. Also, as previously mentioned, for large organizations that have many mobile devices, a *Mobile Device Management* (*MDM*) suite can be implemented. An MDM can take care of pushing updates and configuring hundreds of mobile devices from a central location. Decent quality MDM software will secure, monitor, manage, and support multiple different types of mobile devices across the enterprise.

> **Note**
>
> One of the lesser-used MDM solutions mentioned on the A+ objectives is the Apple Configurator. It is an application that allows administrators to remotely configure and manage mass quantities of iOS devices, such as iPhones, iPads, and more.

Stopping Applications

Applications that are opened on a mobile device will continue to run in the background unless they are specifically turned off within the app or within the OS, or the device is restarted.

To turn off apps (or services) that are running on a typical Android-based system, go to Settings > Application Manager (or similar path). That displays all the currently running applications and services, though the services portion might be within a different tab of that screen. As with PCs, mobile device apps use RAM. The more RAM that is used by the mobile device, the worse it will perform; it will slow it down and eat up battery power. So, to close an app, you would simply tap it and on the next screen tap Stop (or

Force stop). Figure 18.7 shows an example of an app info screen with the Force stop option. You can also stop services or processes in this manner. If you are not absolutely sure what the service is, do not initiate a Stop because it can possibly cause system instability. In the past, due to that instability, force stops were reserved only for services; they are now an option on many devices for applications as well. Just remember that force stops can cause the OS to behave erratically.

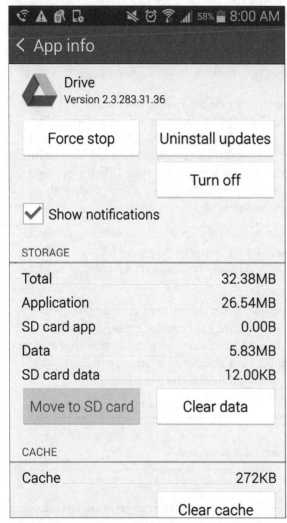

FIGURE 18.7   **The Force Stop option in Android**

To force quit an app on an iOS-based device, press and hold the Sleep/Wake button for a few seconds until a red slider appears. Then press and hold the home button until the app quits.

> **ExamAlert**
>
> Understand how to stop apps on Android and Apple devices.

There are third-party apps that can close down all of the apps in one shot if you need to save time. However, these can cause erratic behavior as well. Finally, if an application is causing the device to lock up and you can't stop the app normally or through a force stop, then a soft reset or a hard reset will be necessary.

Initiating Resets

A *soft reset* is done by simply powering off the mobile device and powering it back on. This resets the drivers and the OS. Soft resets are similar to shutting down a PC and powering it back up. Some technicians will also call this a power cycle. The soft reset can help when certain applications are not functioning properly or when network connectivity is failing. When a smartphone is still locked up when it is restarted, try pulling the battery (if applicable), replacing it, and restarting the phone again.

iOS-based devices can do a variety of more advanced software resets beyond a simple power cycle, such as Reset All Settings, Erase All Content and Settings, Reset Network Settings, and so on. These are available by tapping Settings > General > Reset.

A *hard reset* should be initiated only when things have gone terribly wrong; for example, when hardware or software has been compromised or has failed and a soft reset does not fix the problem. You want to make sure that all data is backed up before performing a hard reset because some hard resets will reset the mobile device back to the original factory condition.

> **Warning**
>
> All data will be wiped when a hard reset is initiated!

Hard resets vary from one device to the next. They can be initiated from within the OS (for example, within the Backup and Reset settings screen). Or they can be initiated by pressing a special combination of buttons, possibly while restarting the device. For example, you might press and hold the Power button, Volume Up button, and Home button until you access Recovery

Mode. Or you might have to press the Volume Down button and press and release the Power button at the same time to access reset options such as Clear Storage and Recovery.

> **Note**
>
> On some devices, pressing and holding the Volume Down button and the Power buttons simultaneously will bring up Safe Mode. This turns off user-installed apps and can be very helpful when troubleshooting.

At the recovery location, follow the prompts to initiate a hard reset. Again, all data should be backed up prior to starting a reset—I can't say it enough! At this point, the device will be reset and you will have to restore data and settings from backup.

> **ExamAlert**
>
> Know how to perform soft and hard resets on Android devices.

Unlike many other mobile devices, hard resets on iOS-based devices do not delete data. They instead stop all apps and reset the OS and drivers. This can be accomplished with the following steps:

1. Make sure that the device has at least 20 percent battery life remaining. (This process could take some time, and you don't want the battery to discharge completely in the middle of it.)

2. Press the Sleep/Wake button and the Home button simultaneously for 10 seconds or until the Apple logo appears. (Ignore the red slider.)

3. When the logo appears, the hard reset has been initiated. It may take several minutes to complete.

To fully reset an iOS-based device such as an iPad to factory condition, you need to go to Settings > General > Reset > Erase all Content and Settings. Another way to do this is to connect the iOS device to a computer via USB and open iTunes on the computer. Then select the iPad option, click Summary, and then click Restore. Regardless of the method you choose, initiate a hard reset to complete the procedure.

> **ExamAlert**
>
> Remember how to reset settings and erase all content on iOS devices.

As you have seen with Android and Apple, the types of resets vary from one device to the next, so be sure to go to the manufacturer's website to find out exactly what the various resets do for your mobile device and how you can perform them—and one more time, back up your data!

Additional Mobile Device Troubleshooting

Let's discuss a little more about troubleshooting mobile devices, namely display issues, application issues, overheating, and radio connectivity issues. We previously discussed some touchscreen and battery issues in Chapter 7, "Mobile Device Hardware," so we won't repeat those things here.

Mobile Device Display Troubleshooting

The display is the cause of many a user's headache. Lots of things can go wrong with it; sometimes they are a failure of the device, but more often than not, they are due to user error or more accurately user ignorance.

For example, the display might look dim. This could be because the brightness level is too low in the display settings. Or it could be that automatic brightness was enabled and perhaps it doesn't react well in highly lit areas. Or perhaps auto-brightness isn't calibrated properly; perhaps it was initially enabled in a very bright (or very dark) environment. To recalibrate the device's light sensor, turn off auto-brightness and then go to an unlit room and set the brightness to the lowest setting. Finally, turn auto-brightness back on and leave the unlit room. The device should now make better use of its light sensors and auto-brightness should function better.

You might also encounter a situation in which there is no display whatsoever or what appears to be no display. This could simply be that the device is in sleep mode (or off). Always check the simple solutions first; as a tech, you'll find they happen more often than you would like! But it could also be that the brightness (once again) is at the lowest setting and the user is working in a bright area. When taking the device out of sleep mode, the user can't tell that the display is working (though it may be barely visible). Take the device to a dark area to fix it or hold it under a desk or table to be able to see the screen until it is fixed. The brightness might have been turned down by accident, the user might have turned it down the night before (because it was dark out), or a virus could affect the slider that controls the brightness. Brightness is definitely a common culprit—let's just thank our lucky stars that there is no contrast setting on the bulk of mobile devices! However, no display could also mean that the device is indeed off or that the battery has been discharged.

Mobile Device Application and OS Troubleshooting

The operating system and the loaded applications can give users some heartache, too—especially given how some people truly *love* their smartphones and tablets.

We talked about keeping the device updated; in general, this is true, especially for antimalware applications. But sometimes, an update is not a good idea. For example, the latest version of a mobile OS might not work well on your device (even if the experts say it will). The older the device, the slower the CPU, and therefore the worse the new version of the OS will function. The same goes for the latest versions of apps, though not to such an extent. In the case that a device is updated and it starts to work sluggishly, a downgrade may be necessary. This means going back to the original factory image for the phone and usually requires a USB connection to a desktop computer, with USB debugging enabled. In order to enable USB debugging, some devices require you to "become a developer," which can be done, for example, by tapping the build number (in About) seven times or some other similar technique. Once you are in developer mode, you can enable USB debugging from Settings. Other devices allow you to select USB debugging when you first plug in the device via USB. You'll need to have a full battery before initiating a downgrade. Check your device documentation for more information, or go to the manufacturer's website to find out how to enable USB debugging for your specific device.

Applications can also cause a mobile device OS to perform slowly or freeze the system altogether. If this happens, first restart the device. If that does not work, consider force-stopping the application in question, uninstalling unnecessary apps, and possibly resetting the device. See the previous sections "Stopping Applications" and "Initiating Resets" for more information.

Apps might also fail to load or might load very slowly. This could be a sign that there is no space left on the device. Remove and/or relocate apps to see if it fixes the problem. On most Android devices, you can also clear the cache memory for the system and for individual apps. To clear the system cache, reboot the device into recovery mode (usually with a simultaneous button combination, such as Power, Volume Up, and Home), and then select "wipe cache partition" or similar name. Just be very careful not to select the factory reset option! It is often very close in proximity on the menu. Individual app cache (and app data) can be cleared on the same screen where force stops are performed.

Mobile Device Overheating

How many times have you heard a user say that his mobile device is running hot? How many times has your own device run hot? It's common. Overheating can be caused by a number of things: poorly written applications, excessive use of applications, excessive browsing, old batteries, damaged batteries, and, of course, the simple fact that the device is very small and that there is an inherent lack of ventilation.

Some applications use a lot of power (CPU-wise, and battery-wise). It's these applications that tend to slow down the mobile device, eat up battery reserves, cause a power drain, and make the device run hot. Certain GPS programs, games, and streaming media apps are among the top contenders for this, but just about any app could cause this. And then you have the aging effect; newer apps don't run so well on older devices because of the lack of resources, and as a result, they can overheat the device. Unfortunately, there isn't too much the user can do about this other than self-policing, removing apps suspected to be the cause of the problem, and disabling unnecessary functionality on the device. Does the user need that live wallpaper? Has that user collected enough "coins" in that game? You know what I mean.

But the battery can get hot simply because it is old (or damaged). Battery manufacturers use the term "charging cycle." That is when you take a mobile device that is completely discharged and charge it up to 100 percent. Most battery manufacturers say that a typical battery can handle several hundred charge cycles maximum. That essentially means that a typical smartphone battery has a shelf life of about two to three years, because most people charge them every day. Tablets usually last much longer because of the greater battery capacity and the fact that they aren't charged as often. So it's the mobile phone that we are most concerned with. Aside from buying a new battery every couple of years, a user can do the following:

▶ **Avoid draining the battery:** Charge the device often, before it gets too low. The more the battery is discharged below 50 percent, and especially below 10 percent, the less shelf life it will have in general.

▶ **Conserve power:** Set sleep mode to 1 minute or less. Disable or remove unnecessary functions and apps. Restart the phone at least once a day to stop any running apps (this is a big power saver). Consider putting the device into airplane mode at night.

▶ **Keep the device away from heat sources:** For example, if the device is mounted near a vehicle's air vent during the dead of winter, it's bound to run hot. Sarcasm aside, this can actually cause battery wear and damage over time. Keep it out of direct sunlight, too, if at all possible.

▶ **Turn off the mobile device when not in use:** Some people simply cannot do this, but I thought I'd mention it anyway!

▶ **Don't bang or throw the device:** Sounds crazy that I would have to say this, but it's good advice. Not only can a user break the device completely, but dropping, throwing, or banging the device can damage the battery, which can cause it to overheat, reduce the lifespan of the battery, and, in the worst case scenario, cause a battery leak, which is a toxic mess that you don't want to be a part of.

▶ **Select protective cases carefully:** A protective case is a very good idea (especially if you are prone to actions in the previous bullet), but make sure it has good airflow. Sometimes these cases can envelop the battery, causing it to overheat.

▶ **Clean your device:** Every month or so, turn off the device, take it out of the case, remove the battery, and clean it (and the inside of the case) with a mix that is half isopropyl alcohol and half water (applied to a dry, lint-free cloth). This really works. Use that solution sparingly though; a little goes a long way. This is especially true if you clean the battery contacts (with a cotton swab); also, always make sure that the contacts are completely dry before reinstalling the battery.

Cram Quiz

Answer these questions. The answers follow the last question. If you cannot answer these questions correctly, consider reading this section again until you can.

220-902 Questions

1. You want to prevent a user from accessing your phone while you step away from your desk. What should you do?

    ○ **A.** Implement remote backup.

    ○ **B.** Set up a remote wipe program.

    ○ **C.** Configure a screen lock.

    ○ **D.** Install a locator application.

2. Which of the following can be described as removing limitations on iOS?

    ○ **A.** Rooting

    ○ **B.** Jailbreaking

    ○ **C.** Geotracking

    ○ **D.** AV software

3. An application won't close on an Android smartphone. You've tried to force-stop it, to no avail. What should you do?

    ○ **A.** Hard reset the device.

    ○ **B.** Stop the service in Running Services.

    ○ **C.** Soft reset the device.

    ○ **D.** Take the device to an authorized service center.

4. Your organization is concerned about a potential scenario where a mobile device with confidential data is stolen. Which of the following should be recommended first? (Select the best answer.)

    ○ **A.** Remote backup application

    ○ **B.** Remote wipe program

    ○ **C.** Passcode locks

    ○ **D.** Locator application

5. You are concerned with the possibility of jailbreaks on your organization's iPhones and viruses on the Android-based devices. Which of the following should you implement? (Select the two best answers.)

    ○ **A.** AV software

    ○ **B.** Firewall

    ○ **C.** Mobile Device Management

    ○ **D.** Device reset

6. A user's mobile device is overheating. Which of the following could be the problem? (Select the two best answers.)

    ○ **A.** A damaged battery.

    ○ **B.** The brightness setting is too low.

    ○ **C.** Excessive gaming.

    ○ **D.** The device is not in a case.

    ○ **E.** The charging cable is defective.

Cram Quiz Answers

220-902 Answers

1. **C.** You should configure a screen lock (either a pattern drawn on the screen, a PIN, or a password). Remote backup, remote wipe, and locator applications will not prevent a user from accessing the phone.

2. **B.** Jailbreaking is the process of removing the limitations of an iOS-based device so that the user gets super-user abilities. Rooting is a similar technique used on Android mobile devices. Geotracking is the practice of tracking a device over time. AV software is antivirus software, which is used to combat malware.

3. **C.** If you've already tried to stop the application within Running Services, attempt a soft reset. Pull the battery if the application is frozen. Hard resets on Android devices should be used only as a last resort because they will return the device to factory condition—wiping all the data. The question indicated that the application won't close, not that a service won't stop, though you could try finding an underlying service that might be the culprit. But try resetting the device before doing this or taking it to an authorized service center.

4. **B.** The remote wipe application is the most important one listed. This will prevent a thief from accessing the data on the device. Afterward, you might recommend a backup program (in case the data needs to be wiped), as well as passcode locks and a locator application.

5. **A and C.** You should implement antivirus (AV) software on the local mobile device and consider MDM for deploying antivirus updates to multiple mobile devices remotely. This can protect against viruses and other malware as well as jailbreaks on Apple devices. As of the writing of this book, firewalls for mobile devices are not common, but that could change in the future. Device resets are used to restart the mobile device or to reset it to factory condition, depending on the type of reset and the manufacturer of the device.

6. **A and C.** The best answers listed are a damaged battery and excessive gaming. If the brightness setting is low, the device should use less power and run cooler. If the device is not in a case, it should not overheat; however, a poorly manufactured case could cause it to overheat. A defective charging cable will usually not cause the device to overheat; if it is defective, it likely is not even charging the device.

OS X and Linux

Although Windows dominates the desktop and laptop market, there are other operating systems you can choose from as well. In this book, we focus on Apple's OS X and Linux. OS X is a favorite with users who need to manipulate audio and video media. Also, some people just prefer OS X to Windows. On the desktop side, Linux is used mostly by enthusiasts and techies. Both have a very small business market share, even smaller than the home consumer share. But even a small share of the market is still a substantial number of computers. As of the writing of this book (2015), various analytics show that OS X is installed on 15 to 17 percent of desktops/laptops in North America and about 10 percent worldwide. That's a 2 to 3 percent increase over the past year or two, which is an interesting trend to keep an eye on. Linux, on the other hand, is loaded on only about 3 percent of desktops. That includes all known desktop-based distributions of Linux. To put it into perspective, there are more computers with Windows Vista installed on them than all the Linux desktop versions combined. However, Linux has a big presence in the server market, so we will discuss both the Linux client and server platforms briefly. Because OS X has a larger market share, we'll begin with that.

OS X

OS X (pronounced "OS 10") is the proprietary operating system used by Apple for its Macintosh desktop computers and MacBook Pro and Air laptop computers. This operating system (and the Mac computer in general) has been a favorite of multimedia designers, graphic artists, and musicians since the 1990s.

OS X has used version numbers since its inception. Originally, it was simply named "System," but as of version 7.6, it's officially known as Mac OS. During the early versions, the operating system could be run only on Macintosh computers that had Motorola processors. However, in 2002, Apple introduced Mac OS X, which could be run on Macintosh computers with PowerPC or Intel processors. Since version 10.6 (known as Snow Leopard), the OS has run only on Macintosh computers with Intel platforms. Since version 10.8 (Mountain Lion), the operating system has simply been referred to as OS X. Apple also updates the operating system with what are known as point releases. For example, in August of 2015, Apple released the (10.10.5) point release, updating the Yosemite version of OS X and making it more secure.

Although Macintosh computers have Intel processors, they are not PCs. Likewise, OS X is not compatible with PC hardware. Conversely, PC-based operating systems, such as Windows and Linux, do not normally run on Macintosh computers—though it can be done in the case of Windows (for example, with Boot Camp, which is described later).

Apple is credited with making the graphical user interface that people manipulate with a mouse and keyboard—the mainstream way of working with the computer. Today's OS X takes this to a new level by using antialiasing, ColorSync, and drop-shadow technologies to create a more exciting and fluid interface. OS X uses control panels (windows with icons) to configure, troubleshoot, and maintain the computer. This is similar to the Microsoft Windows Control Panel, though different functions have varying names and locations. Some applications are ported for OS X (for example, Microsoft Office for Mac); however, OS X uses its own web browser (Safari) as opposed to Internet Explorer. Web browsers such as Chrome and Firefox can be run on OS X as well. Figure 18.8 shows an example of the OS X desktop with Safari running.

FIGURE 18.8 **OS X desktop**

OS X's desktop has a user-friendly design that includes a basic menu bar at the top, which includes the Apple menu (on the far left), the currently opened application (Safari in the figure), and standard options (such as File, Edit, and so on). There are icons on the bottom (in the "Dock") used for commonly used applications, such as Safari, Mission Control, Mail, and FaceTime. On the desktop you can see that the Safari web browser is open to the OS X support page. The link to this is https://www.apple.com/support/osx/.

OS X Features

There are many, many features in OS X that make it a user-friendly environment. The CompTIA exams focus on a few of those; let's discuss them now.

The best way to open applications or files is to use *Finder*, a program similar to Windows Explorer/File Explorer but designed in such a way as to make finding applications easy. This is available on the menu bar as well as within the Dock. Applications and files can also be stored on the Dock and anywhere on the desktop, but if you don't see the application or file you want, use the Finder program. If you still can't find what you are looking for or you aren't even sure if it is on your computer, use the *Spotlight* search tool. This is displayed as a spyglass in the menu bar on the top right of the desktop and can also be accessed by pressing and holding the Command and space bar keys simultaneously on the keyboard. This search tool searches through files, e-mails, apps, songs, printers, and so on. It can also search other computers on the network (which it discovers using Bonjour—a networking technology used by OS X to locate networked computers and devices). Plus, it looks through external sources such as Wikipedia, Bing, and iTunes, to name a few. The goal is to receive a media-rich, definitive set of results to your query.

> **ExamAlert**
>
> Understand what the Finder and Spotlight programs are in OS X.

Let's get into what you see on a Mac and how it is displayed. First, you can modify how the desktop is displayed or you can set up multiple desktops. This is done within *Mission Control*. Mission Control zooms away from the desktop, giving you a larger perspective of apps, "spaces," and virtual desktops. It acts as an application switcher and window manager. Mission Control can be launched in a variety of ways, including swiping up on the Trackpad with three fingers, double-tapping the Magic Mouse (which is an Apple mouse that allows for special clicking and gesturing, making it easier to navigate through OS X), clicking the Mission Control icon on the Dock, or pressing the Mission Control key on the keyboard. Now you can have multiple desktops by dragging windows to the upper-right corner or you can add windows to already existing desktops by dragging them to the appropriate desktop at the top of the window. The Dashboard is available here as well; it has some default functions, such as the clock, calendar, and calculator. You can also add special programs to the Dashboard by clicking the + sign. This technology has great implications for the researcher, student, programmer, A/V editor, and so on. It allows a user to highly customize the user interface. But be careful, too many desktops and too many open applications will cause the system to run sluggishly. Also, users will sometimes forget that they have applications open in other desktops; a quick, three-finger swipe up will reveal anything that is currently running.

Speaking of three-finger swipes, there are all kinds of gestures and multitouch gestures that can make you a more efficient OS X user. If you have the supporting hardware (such as a Magic Trackpad or Magic Mouse), you can make use of things such as tapping, scrolling, pinching, and swiping, similar to the same functions on a mobile device. For example, a two-finger swipe up or down will scroll content; a two-finger double tap will perform a smart zoom, and you can do it again to return; and, of course, there is the pinch out to zoom. The list goes on and on. For a complete list of these multitouch gestures, visit https://support.apple.com/en-us/HT204895.

You can also allow users on other Macs to view your screen and even take control of your computer with a tool called *Screen Sharing* (similar to Windows Remote Desktop). To enable this, go to the Apple menu > System Preferences and then click Sharing. For a step-by-step procedure on how to do this, visit https://support.apple.com/kb/PH18686?locale=en_US. It gets a little more complicated when you want a Windows computer to control (or just see) a Mac. Third-party VNC software (such as RealVNC) can help with this. VNC works cross-platform between Windows, OS X, Linux, and mobile OS versions. VNC can also be used to view a Mac that has Screen Sharing enabled.

Sometimes you might need to share the screen with a second display or to a projector. Many Mac computers come with a secondary DisplayPort (DP) port to enable duplication of the screen. This works in a fashion similar to that which was described previously in the book in the laptops and video sections.

ExamAlert

Know how to configure multiple desktops, Screen Sharing, and the replication of the display to a secondary monitor.

Ah, the dual-booters! It's amazing how many people want to run Windows on their Mac. Apple offers a utility called *Boot Camp* that allows you to do just this with Windows 7 and higher (64-bit versions). After the Windows OS is installed, you can reboot the computer to switch from one OS to the other. Boot Camp can be found in Finder > Applications > Utilities and then select Boot Camp Assistant. You then need to download the supporting software, create a partition (to be used by Windows), and preferably install the OS from a disk image (ISO). This image can be created with third-party programs such as PowerISO. Then follow the Boot Camp prompts, complete the installation of Windows, and reboot the system. You can switch from OS X to Windows by making use of the Startup Disk preference pane or you can switch from Windows to OS X by accessing the Boot Camp icon in the Notification Area.

As you can imagine, there are some security concerns when it comes to dual-booting. Now the computer is potentially open to attacks on the OS X *and* the Windows side. Both OSes (especially Windows) should be carefully secured if you are a Mac owner with a dual-boot system.

Speaking of security, passwords need to be protected in OS X just as they are in any other OS. Apple provides the *Keychain* utility, a password management system that can contain not only passwords but private keys and certificates. It can be accessed from Finder > Applications > Keychain Access.

Managing and Maintaining OS X

Once again, for the locating and managing of files and running applications, OS X uses Finder. The program will open up automatically whenever you access a drive or file listing. From here, you can create files, copy and paste files, access "Favorites" (such as Applications, Downloads, and so on), access removable drives, and tag files/applications with various colors. Files can also be manipulated in the command line. OS X possesses a shell utility called *Terminal* that allows you to manipulate data and make configuration changes similar to the Command Prompt in Windows. However, the syntax is different and is based off of Linux. (We'll cover several commands you can use in the upcoming Linux section.) To open the Terminal, go to Finder > Applications > Utilities > Terminal. You can also open up applications such as this by using the Spotlight tool and simply typing the name of the application.

> **Note**
>
> If finding and launching applications become a bit difficult over time, consider a third-party program such as Quicksilver to create a more flexible interface and to increase productivity.

Aside from locally stored data, you can view remote discs on other Mac computers by sharing them in the System Preferences, and you can view them from the local computer by selecting the Remote Disc option in Finder > Devices. This is required sometimes, especially when the user is working at a MacBook that does not have an optical drive. Data can also be stored on the cloud—Apple's version is called the *iCloud*. To back up data to the iCloud, go to the Apple menu > System Preferences and click iCloud, click Manage, and then select Backups.

For backing up the state of the computer, OS X utilizes the *Time Machine* backup program. To enable this, go to the Apple menu and select System Preferences. Then select the Time Machine icon and turn it on to enable automatic backing up of any drive. From here, you can back up drives locally or to the iCloud. Restoring data also happens from this program. Essentially, you can select the point to which you want to restore the drive—be it a day ago or a year ago—to restore the drive, simply select this "snapshot" from a timeline in the program. This is similar to Windows System Restore. Because the program saves multiple states of files over time, a separate backup method (such as a USB flash drive or other external media) is also recommended for important files.

Although Macs are known for their resilience, their drives should still be maintained. The built-in *Disk Utility* is used for verifying and repairing the hard drive, repairing drive permissions, and possibly booting from the recovery partition (which all Macs have). Disk Utility can also be used to create an image or to recover a system from that image.

Sometimes you might encounter the spinning pinwheel. This is a variation of the mouse pointer arrow; it appears when an application either becomes temporarily unresponsive or enters an infinite loop and cannot recover. If an application freezes or is otherwise not responding properly, you can force that app to close by using the Force Quit application. This is located on the Apple menu; once you open Force Quit, you can select the application you want to force to close. This is similar to using Task Manager in Windows. You can also use the keyboard combination Command+Option+Esc, which is similar to Ctrl+Alt+Del on a Windows PC.

> **ExamAlert**
>
> Know how to use the Time Machine, Disk Utility, and Force Quit tools in OS X.

General system maintenance includes system updates, antimalware updates, driver updates, and firmware updates. OS X can be updated by going to the Apple menu and selecting Software Update. It can also be updated from the

App Store. Antimalware updates should of course be done within the third-party application you are using; we discuss malware in more depth in Chapter 17, "Security." The video driver is built into OS X so it can only be updated by upgrading to a new version of the operating system. Keyboards, mice, and many other devices need to be approved for use with Mac computers, so if you can buy it, it should work with OS X. Unfortunately, if the device requires a higher version of OS X, you'll have to upgrade. Most printers work with OS X also, but if a printer driver needs to be downloaded, OS X will automatically run the AirPrint program to locate and download the driver. In general, OS X is designed to simplify the process of installing devices. Finally, firmware updates are usually done automatically when you upgrade to a newer version of OS X. If you are unsure if a firmware update is necessary, you can find out the current version by going to Finder > Applications > Utilities and opening the System Information app. The boot ROM version and SMC firmware version are listed toward the bottom of the hardware overview, as shown in Figure 18.9.

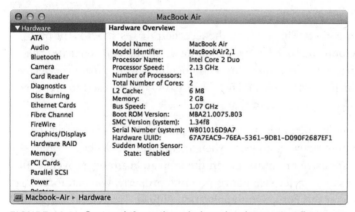

FIGURE 18.9   System Information window showing current firmware

Firmware downloads for all types of Macs can be found at https://support.apple.com/en-us/HT201518.

Although OS X is not a derivative of Linux, it is definitely similar in many ways. The two are certainly linked, from their architectural structure to their respective command lines. Let's move into the world of Linux now.

Linux

Linux is an ever-expanding group of operating systems that are designed to run on PCs, gaming consoles, DVRs, mobile phones, and many other devices. Originally, Linux was designed as an alternative operating system to Windows. But again, currently it is estimated that no more than 3 percent of the U.S. market uses Linux on PCs. However, Linux has a much larger market share when it comes to servers and other computer devices, and in those markets, the percentage is growing rapidly.

Linux was originally written by Linus Torvalds (thus the name) and can be freely downloaded by anyone. Several companies emerged, developing this free code (or a variant of the free code) into their own versions of Linux, which are referred to as distributions. Some examples of these distributions include Ubuntu, SUSE, Red Hat, and Knoppix. Although Linux is free to download, it is licensed under a General Public License (GPL). This states that derived works can be distributed only under the same license terms as the software itself.

Linux users have the option of using one of a few GUIs that are similar to the OS X GUI. The two most popular GUI environments are GNOME and KDE; however, there are others (such as Enlightenment, Unity, and Cinnamon) that are gaining in popularity. Most of these are based on either GNOME or KDE, so we'll focus on those in this section.

GNOME stands for GNU Network Object Model Environment. A graphical user interface that runs on top of the Linux operating system, it consists solely of free and open-source software. Its emphasis is on simplicity and accessibility while endeavoring to use a low amount of resources.

KDE previously stood for K Desktop Environment but has since been renamed KDE Software Compilation. The applications within the environment are meant to run on various Linux platforms but can also be compiled to run in Windows and OS X. KDE is considered by some to be a more powerful environment. It includes a web browser called Konqueror, but many of the distributions of Linux use Mozilla Firefox. There are programs for Linux available that are just about the equivalent of Microsoft applications. For example, OpenOffice and LibreOffice are free software applications that can be used to create word processing documents, spreadsheets, and so on. Newer versions of Microsoft Office are offering a limited amount of compatibility with these documents.

The command-line functionality in most Linux distributions is in depth and well documented, allowing a user to configure, and troubleshoot, just about anything from within the "shell" or command line. To help you learn more about any commands, the operating system usually has built-in manual (MAN) pages that are also accessible online.

Linux Desktop Distributions

Overall, the most common types of Linux by far include Android (for mobile devices), Google Chrome OS, and various derivatives of Linux used by gaming consoles. However, this section concentrates on desktop computers and the types of Linux that can be loaded on them.

There are literally hundreds of Linux desktop distributions. Most are used by PC enthusiasts and gamers, as well as some programmers. You'll hear of all kinds of distributions of Linux, including SUSE, Debian, FreeBSD, Fedora, Mint, and many more. There are so many Linux distributions that we could fill a book with them, and many more are being released every week. That's the beauty of the license for Linux. It is free to use and develop. People at home can make their very own version of Linux if they so desired. One popular distribution (or "distro" as they are called) is Ubuntu. As far as Linux goes, it is commonly used for a variety of purposes. Some manufacturers (such as gaming system designers) even offer it as the loaded OS of choice on some of their desktop systems. Figure 18.10 shows an example of the Ubuntu GUI.

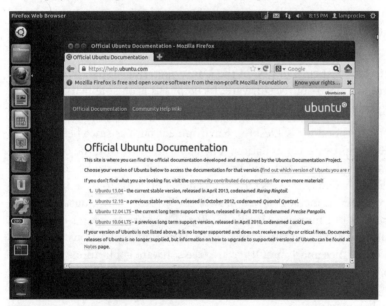

FIGURE 18.10   **Ubuntu desktop**

Figure 18.10 shows a basic information bar on the top that shows the active window that is running—in this case, the Firefox web browser. It also displays the time, the user that is logged in, and icons such as messages, volume, and so on. On the left side of the screen we see various standard icons used for exploring and opening folders and files, creating documents and spreadsheets (with LibreOffice), configuring System Settings, and managing updates. Finally, we see that the Firefox application is open and is currently at the Ubuntu help and documentation web page.

> **Note**
>
> For practice with Ubuntu, consider creating a Ubuntu bootable USB stick within Windows. For details, visit http://www.ubuntu.com/download/desktop/create-a-usb-stick-on-windows. This enables you to practice Linux commands using the built-in Terminal application. Or consider downloading the latest version of Ubuntu and installing it to a virtual machine. For details, visit http://www.ubuntu.com/download/desktop.

> **Note**
>
> There are also self-booting versions of Linux, such as Linux Live CDs (Knoppix and others) and Hiren's Boot CD. These are generally run from an optical disc and are very handy when troubleshooting a desktop system that has failed; they include excellent repair tools.

Linux Server Distributions

Linux desktop distributions can also work quite nicely as servers if need be, but there are several types of distributions that are designed specifically to be servers. SUSE Enterprise Linux and Red Hat Enterprise Linux are commonly used corporate and enterprise platforms. Also, Ubuntu Server, Debian, CentOS, and ClearOS are found in small- to mid-sized businesses. Often these systems are manipulated directly from a command-line with no GUI (by default), as is the case in Red Hat Enterprise. Figure 18.11 shows an example of this.

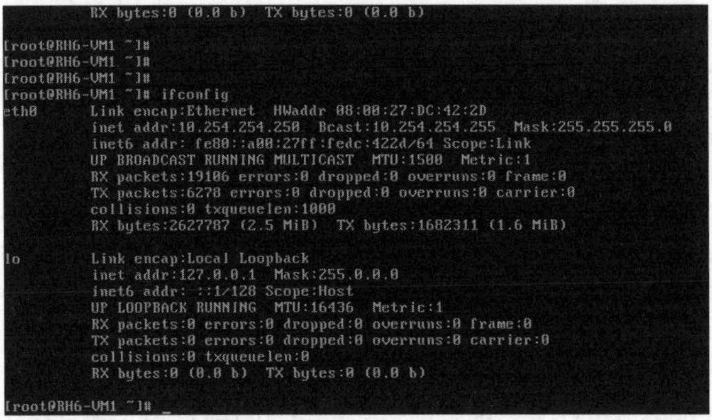

```
                RX bytes:0 (0.0 b)  TX bytes:0 (0.0 b)
[root@RH6-VM1 ~]#
[root@RH6-VM1 ~]#
[root@RH6-VM1 ~]#
[root@RH6-VM1 ~]# ifconfig
eth0      Link encap:Ethernet  HWaddr 08:00:27:DC:42:2D
          inet addr:10.254.254.250  Bcast:10.254.254.255  Mask:255.255.255.0
          inet6 addr: fe80::a00:27ff:fedc:422d/64 Scope:Link
          UP BROADCAST RUNNING MULTICAST  MTU:1500  Metric:1
          RX packets:19106 errors:0 dropped:0 overruns:0 frame:0
          TX packets:6270 errors:0 dropped:0 overruns:0 carrier:0
          collisions:0 txqueuelen:1000
          RX bytes:2627787 (2.5 MiB)  TX bytes:1682311 (1.6 MiB)

lo        Link encap:Local Loopback
          inet addr:127.0.0.1  Mask:255.0.0.0
          inet6 addr: ::1/128 Scope:Host
          UP LOOPBACK RUNNING  MTU:16436  Metric:1
          RX packets:0 errors:0 dropped:0 overruns:0 frame:0
          TX packets:0 errors:0 dropped:0 overruns:0 carrier:0
          collisions:0 txqueuelen:0
          RX bytes:0 (0.0 b)  TX bytes:0 (0.0 b)

[root@RH6-VM1 ~]# _
```

FIGURE 18.11   **Red Hat command line**

As you can see in Figure 18.11, it is all text. A user who works on Linux should have a strong foundation in the Linux command line. The beauty of Linux is that the command line functions essentially the same way across the various distributions. In fact, given the displayed information in Figure 18.11, even a practiced IT technician would be hard-pressed to know exactly what distribution was being worked on.

In Figure 18.11, the command ifconfig has been issued, displaying the network configuration of the network adapter. For example, the IP address (shown as inet addr) is displayed for the primary network adapter (known as eth0). The last line shows the prompt. "Root" is the default administrative user in Linux. RH6-VM1 just happens to be the name of this Linux computer. This command-line information is accessible and available in all versions of Linux. Let's discuss it a bit further and talk about some of the common commands you will use.

Linux File Systems

Linux uses the GUID Partition Table (GPT)—as defined in Chapter 9, "Configuring Windows"—to list and control the partitions on the systems. GPT supports UEFI, 128 partitions, partition sizes beyond 2 TB, and is stored in multiple locations, making it superior to master boot record (MBR) technology.

> **Note**
>
> By the way, Apple's OS X version 10.4 and higher require GPT. In this respect (and many others), it is similar to Linux. Older versions of OS X used the Apple Partition Map, though it is unlikely that you will see that today.

Linux supports many file systems, including the ext family, FAT32, and NTFS. It also supports the Network File System (NFS), a distributed file system that allows a client computer to access files over the network; it was designed especially for Linux and Unix systems but other systems such as Windows can use it as well.

However, the most common file systems used on the local system are ext3 and ext4. ext4 is the Fourth Extended file system, which can support volume sizes of up to 1 exabyte (EB). You can discern the type of file system used in Linux by typing the df -T command. On systems commonly used during the writing of this book (2015), the /dev/sda1 (or /dev/hda1) partition (where the Linux OS is installed) is usually ext4.

The /dev refers to the file system representation of devices. There can be more than one hard drive within the /dev path. Originally, "sd" stood for SCSI devices, but now also includes SATA drives. (You might also see "hd," which refers to older IDE drives and other drives that Linux sees.) Instead of calling each disk "disk 0," "disk 1," and so on (as Windows does), Linux refers to them as "a," "b," "c," and so on. The number at the end of the path is the number of the partition. Linux is normally installed to partition 1, the full path being either /dev/sda1 or /dev/hda1; this is known as the boot partition. The second partition listed is an extended partition, similar to the Windows extended partition in that it can be used to create additional partitions for data, such as /dev/sda3 or /dev/sda4 and beyond. Often /dev/sda5 is used by the OS as a swap file (paging file) between the memory and the hard drive. You can find a list of the partitions available on most Linux systems by opening the command line (or terminal) and typing the `fdisk -l` command.

The `fdisk` command can also be used to make modifications to the partition table. To find out more information about the `fdisk` command, simply type `fdisk -?` in the command line or locate the online manual (MAN) page for the command. That's a great lead-in for the next section about Linux.

Linux Command Line

The command line is also referred to as a "terminal" (and as the "shell"). In some versions of Linux, the terminal is available by navigating the menu system. In others, it is accessed by using the Search tool and searching for "terminal." And in still others, it runs automatically, as is the case in versions of Linux that don't use a GUI.

Table 18.1 describes several commands you should know for the exam. Know that when working in the Linux directory structure, you always use a slash (/) to separate directory levels. (In Windows, a backslash [\] is used.) So you might have a path such as /downloads/music/mp3s. If there is ever any confusion as to which is the slash and which is the backslash on the keyboard, remember this: the back*slash* (\) is the one near the back*space* key. Use the slash / for Linux, which usually shares the key with the question mark.

TABLE 18.1 **List of Linux-based Commands**

Command	Description
ls	Lists directory contents. Similar to `dir` in Windows.
cd	Changes directory. Same as Windows command.
mv	Moves files. Similar to Windows `move` command.
cp	Copies files and directories. Similar to the Windows `copy` command.

Command	Description
rm	Removes files or directories. Similar to Windows del and rd commands.
dd	Converts and copies a file (for example, from ASCII to EBCDIC).
chmod	Modifies the read and write permissions for a file or folder.
chown	Changes the file owner and group.
ps	Displays information about a process.
apt-get	Used to handle packages (installing, updating, or upgrading).
sudo	Allows a user to execute a command as another user (such as an administrator). su lets you run the shell as another user altogether.
vi	Opens the text editor shell. Normally followed by a filename. Press q or q! to exit. You may have to press the colon (:) key first.
passwd	Used to update a user's password.
pwd	Displays the full path/filename of the working directory. Don't confuse with passwd!
grep	Searches for matching information in specified files and displays that information.
ifconfig	Shows the TCP/IP properties of the network connections. Similar to Windows ipconfig command but can also be used to configure network interfaces.
iwconfig	Shows the TCP/IP properties of the wireless network connections and can configure them. (Not available in OS X.)
shutdown	Brings the system down but can be modified in a variety of ways to gracefully shut down the system, notify users, and many more options.

ExamAlert

Know your Linux commands! Practice them on a distribution such as Ubuntu or in OS X—or both!

Remember, you can learn more about any of these commands by typing man and then the command; for example, man cd. You can also learn about them online at http://www.die.net/ and http://linuxconfig.org/linux-commands.

Basic Linux Troubleshooting

Let's discuss a couple of common issues that can occur in Linux. Let's say you boot the OS, and instead of booting normally, the graphical user interface (GUI) fails to load. Instead you see a basic command-line prompt. This could mean a couple of things. It could be that the GUI shell has failed and needs to be reinstalled or updated. It could be that the system booted to a special mode or an application made it boot to the command line. Or perhaps the video driver failed.

The first thing you should try is one of the many start commands. This will vary according to your version of Linux. For example, you might use the `startx` command in an attempt to bring up the GUI. Or, if you're using Ubuntu or a similar distro, you might use the command `sudo service lightdm start`. If you suspect that the driver has failed, you will need to install the appropriate package with the `apt-get` command. Of course, we are assuming that you have already ruled out a hardware or connectivity issue. You might also find that a recently installed application is causing the failure. Again, the `apt-get` command will be instrumental in removing undesirable applications.

Of course, you might boot the system and see a worse error, such as the kernel panic error. This is akin to the Windows BSOD, and the system won't be able to boot properly. Similar to this, but less disastrous, is the kernel oops, which is when a particular process causes a problem but the kernel kills (terminates) the process successfully. However, watch for these errors, as they might lead to full-blown kernel panic errors. One possible solution to kernel panic is to reboot to rescue media from an optical disc or USB flash drive. You might opt to use Knoppix or other third-party, bootable repair tools. The `apt-get --reinstall` command might be instrumental in the solution as well.

Bootloader files such as GRUB and LILO can fail as well and the system won't boot. (These are similar to bootmgr in Windows.) Once again, third-party bootable utilities can help with the problem, or in the case of Ubuntu, the specially designed Boot Repair utility can help. That would have to be installed from the command line of an externally running Linux OS, and then it will require some configuration. Be ready to have an extra flash drive just for booting special Linux-based repair OSes, such as Knoppix.

One of the great things about Linux is that many of the distributions are incredibly well documented on the Internet—and by very talented people. For example, Ubuntu support can be found officially and nonofficially at the following links:

http://www.ubuntu.com/support

http://ubuntuforums.org/

Use these resources; chances are, the error you are encountering has been seen before, described online, and solved.

Cram Quiz

Answer these questions. The answers follow the last question. If you cannot answer these questions correctly, consider reading this section again until you can.

220-902 Questions

1. Which of the following is the built-in web browser for OS X?

   ○ **A.** Safari

   ○ **B.** Chrome

   ○ **C.** Firefox

   ○ **D.** Internet Explorer

2. Which program should you use to access Utilities in OS X? (Select the two best answers.)

   ○ **A.** Mission Control

   ○ **B.** Finder

   ○ **C.** Spotlight

   ○ **D.** Safari

3. Which of the following should be enabled when you want a user at another Mac to take control of your computer?

   ○ **A.** Remote Desktop

   ○ **B.** Remote Assistance

   ○ **C.** Screen Sharing

   ○ **D.** Screen Mirroring

4. Which utility allows a Mac user to dual-boot OS X and Windows?

   ○ **A.** Ubuntu

   ○ **B.** Knoppix

   ○ **C.** bootrec

   ○ **D.** Boot Camp

5. You want to save the state of the Mac running OS X. Which tool should be used?

   ○ **A.** System Restore

   ○ **B.** Time Machine

   ○ **C.** Force Quit

   ○ **D.** Disk Utility

6. Which program handles installing a printer's driver automatically in OS X?

- ○ **A.** Bonjour
- ○ **B.** Magic Mouse
- ○ **C.** AirPrint
- ○ **D.** iCloud

7. Which command in Linux will show the directory contents?

- ○ **A.** ls
- ○ **B.** dir
- ○ **C.** cd
- ○ **D.** mv

8. Which command should be used to change the permissions of a file?

- ○ **A.** ps
- ○ **B.** chown
- ○ **C.** NTFS
- ○ **D.** chmod

9. Which command will show the configuration details of a wireless connection in Linux?

- ○ **A.** ifconfig
- ○ **B.** ipconfig
- ○ **C.** iwconfig
- ○ **D.** grep

Cram Quiz Answers

220-902 Answers

1. **A.** Safari is Apple's web browser. It is used in OS X and iOS. Chrome is developed by Google and can be added on to OS X. Firefox (Mozilla) can also be added to OS X. Internet Explorer is the built-in browser that Windows uses.

2. **B and C.** Finder is the application to use when looking for applications and files. Utilities is located in Finder > Applications. Spotlight can be used to locate just about anything on the Mac, including Utilities. Mission Control allows you to modify the desktop (and run multiple desktops). Safari is Apple's web browser.

3. **C.** Use Screen Sharing in OS X to allow another user to view and take control of your Mac. (The remote user could also use VNC.) Remote Desktop and Remote Assistance are similar programs used in Windows. Screen mirroring is a technology (common in mobile devices) that allows the display to be mirrored to a TV or to another computer.

4. **D.** Use the Boot Camp Assistant to dual-boot OS X and Windows on a Mac. Ubuntu is a distribution of Linux. Knoppix is a bootable version of Linux used for troubleshooting. Bootrec is a command used in Windows to troubleshoot boot manager and data store issues.

5. **B.** Use the Time Machine to save the state of the computer or to restore to that computer's earlier state. This is similar to the Windows System Restore utility. Force Quit is a utility in OS X that will close a nonresponsive application. Disk Utility is used to verify and repair OS X drives.

6. **C.** AirPrint is the technology used to install printers automatically into OS X (as long as the printer is compatible with OS X). Bonjour is a networking technology used by OS X to locate networked computers and devices. The Magic Mouse is an Apple mouse that allows for special clicking and gesturing, making it easier to navigate through OS X. iCloud is Apple's cloud infrastructure, where a Mac user can store and back up data. While AirPrint might locate the printer driver on iCloud, iCloud is not the best answer.

7. **A.** `ls` will list the directory contents in Linux and OS X. It is similar to the `dir` command in Windows. `cd` is used to change directories. It is very similar to the Windows command of the same name. `mv` is used to move files.

8. **D.** Use the `chmod` command to change permissions in Linux and OS X. `ps` displays information about a given process. `chown` changes ownership of a file. NTFS is the file system used by Windows that allows for file-level security assigned by the user or group.

9. **C.** `iwconfig` is used to display the configuration settings of a wireless adapter in Linux (but not in OS X). It can also be used to configure that adapter. `ifconfig` shows the configuration details for wired connections. `ipconfig` shows the configuration details of network connections in Windows. `grep` is used to search for matching information in specified files.

CHAPTER 19

Safety, Procedures, and Professionalism

This chapter covers the following A+ exam topics:

▶ Safety

▶ Procedures and Environmental Controls

▶ Professionalism and Communication Skills

You can find a master list of A+ exam topics in the "Introduction."

This chapter covers CompTIA A+ 220-902 objectives 5.1 through 5.5.

Now we come to the crux of it all. Everything you have learned so far could be for naught if you do not make use of the crucial information in this chapter.

Safety should always be on your mind. Protect yourself and protect your computer. Electrical safety, physical safety, and fire prevention are the keys to a happy and healthy career. And by using electrostatic discharge (ESD) prevention methods, you protect your computer's components and keep it safe as well.

Pay attention to the environment, and use your wisdom to control it when possible. Try to eliminate interference from electrical and radio devices. Understand what *material safety data sheets* (*MSDSs*) are, how to access them, and what to do when a particular material gives you trouble. Understand how to address prohibited content, and know how to explain privacy, licensing, and policy concepts.

Finally, mind your customer service skills. You might be a super-tech, but without people skills, your job market will be limited. By being professional and utilizing good communication skills, you increase the chances of receiving a good customer reaction. Also, these skills help you to get to the heart of the issue and can help to make you more efficient, saving time as you repair computer problems. Throughout the rest of the book, you learned how to repair the computer. Now put those abilities together with a professional demeanor and good communication skills and there should be no lack of new customers in the future.

Safety

Safety first! Remember to put safety on the top of your priority list when dealing with computers, power, networking, and anything else in IT. Let's talk about some of the things to watch out for when working on computers, how to keep yourself and the computer safe, and how to be environmentally conscious.

Electrical Safety

Electricity is a great energy that should be treated as such. Before working on any computer component, turn off the power and disconnect the device from the AC outlet. If a device such as a power supply or video monitor has a label that reads No Serviceable Components Inside, take the manufacturer's word for it and send the component to the proper repair facility, or simply replace the component. The message on the device is intended to keep a person out, usually because the internal components might hold an electrical charge.

Be sure to use your multimeter and power supply tester properly. If you do not know how to use these, refer to Chapter 5, "Power," or escalate the issue to another person in your company. If you find issues with AC outlets or other AC equipment, refer this to your manager or building supervisor. Do not try to fix these issues. If you find an issue like this in a customer's home, tell him about the problem and recommend that he have the AC outlet repaired before going any further.

Do not open power supplies. As far as the A+ exam is concerned, if a power supply goes bad, replace it, even if you think it is just the fan and would be an easy repair. It is known as a *field replaceable unit (FRU)* for a reason. Although it is possible to repair power supplies, it should be done only by trained technicians. Remember that the power supply holds a charge; this alone should be enough to keep you away from the internals of the power supply. But in addition to that, the amount of time it would take a person to repair a power supply would cost more to a company than just buying a new one and installing it.

LCD monitors can also be dangerous. I can't actually tell you *not* to work on them, especially because laptops integrate them. Regardless, it is again recommended that the failed monitor (or laptop) be sent to the proper repair organization or to the manufacturer if the device is within warranty. However, if a technician does decide to work on the LCD, one thing to be careful of is capacitors; these are normally near the LCD power supply and hold a charge. Also, make sure that the device is turned off and unplugged; if it is a laptop, make sure the battery has been removed. One of the items that can fail on an LCD monitor is the backlight inverter. The inverter is usually mounted on a circuit board, and if it fails, either a fuse needs to be replaced or the entire inverter board needs to be replaced. The inverter is a high-voltage device; try not to touch it, and be especially sure not to touch it when the LCD device is on. A lot of this is common sense, but it is worthwhile to always be sure—like measuring twice before you cut.

> **ExamAlert**
>
> Do not touch an LCD's inverter if the device is on!

> **Note**
>
> In the uncommon scenario that you come across a CRT monitor, don't open it. These carry a lethal charge. Instead, refer these monitors to a company that specializes in monitor repair. If you need to dispose of CRTs, there are some monitor repair companies that will buy them or simply accept them without charge. Otherwise, they need to be recycled in compliance with local government regulations and/or municipal ordinances.

Another device that you need to make sure you turn off and unplug is the laser printer. Extremely dangerous high voltages are inside a laser printer. On a related note, if the printer was recently used, watch out for the fuser; the fuser runs hot!

Finally, it is important to match the power requirement of your computer equipment with the surge protector or uninterruptible power supply (UPS) that it connects to. Verify that the number of watts your computer's power supply requires is not greater than the amount of power your surge protector can provide; the same goes for the watts (or volt-amps) that the UPS can provide. In addition, be sure that you do not overload the circuit that you connect to. For more information regarding electricity used by your computer, see Chapter 5. For additional information about electrical safety, see the electrical safety and health topics at the Occupational Safety & Health Administration (OSHA) website:

http://www.osha.gov/SLTC/electrical/index.html

Electrical Fire Safety

Let's talk a little about electrical fire safety. The safest measures are preventative ones. Buildings should be outfitted with smoke detectors and fire extinguishers. The proper type of fire extinguisher for an electrical fire is a Class C extinguisher. For example, CO_2-based BC fire extinguishers are common and relatively safe to humans, but they can cause damage to computers. If equipment needs to be protected by more than a CO_2-based BC fire extinguisher, an ABC Halotron extinguisher should be used. Server rooms and data centers will often be protected by a larger special hazard protection system that uses the FM-200 clean agent system. This clean agent won't cause damage to servers and other expensive equipment.

If you see an electrical fire, use the proper extinguisher to attempt to put it out. If the fire is too big for you to handle, then the number one thing to do is dial 911. Then evacuate the building. Afterward, you can notify building management, your supervisor, or other facilities people.

Hopefully, you will never come near a live electrical wire. But if you do, you want to attempt to shut off the source. Do not attempt to do this with your bare hands, and make sure that your feet are dry and that you are not standing in any water. Use a wooden stick, board, or rope. If this is not possible, you need to contact your supervisor or building management so that they can shut down power at another junction. If you find an apparently unconscious person underneath a live wire, do not touch the person! Again, attempt to move the live wire with a wooden stick or similar object. Never use anything metal, and do not touch anything metal while you are doing it. After moving the wire, call 911 and contact your superiors immediately. While waiting, attempt to administer first aid to the person.

ESD

Electrostatic discharge (ESD) occurs when two objects of different voltages come into contact with each other. The human body is always gathering static electricity, more than enough to damage a computer component (for example, that $500 video card you just purchased!). ESD is a silent killer. When you touch a component without proper protection, the static electricity could discharge from you to the component, most likely damaging it, but with no discernable signs of damage. Worse yet, it is possible to discharge a small amount of voltage to the device and damage it to the point at which it works intermittently, making it tough to troubleshoot. It takes only 30 volts or so to damage a component. On a dry winter day, you could gather as much as 20,000 volts when walking across a carpeted area! You can equalize the electrical potentials in several ways, allowing you to protect components from ESD, including the following:

▶ **Use an antistatic wrist strap:** The more common kind is inexpensive and takes only a moment to put on and connect to the chassis of the computer. (The chassis is an unpainted portion of the frame inside the case.) By doing so, you constantly discharge to the case's metal frame instead of to the components that you handle. Of course, the chassis of the computer can absorb only so much ESD, so consider another earth-bonding point to connect to or try to implement as many other antistatic methods as possible. Most wrist straps come equipped with a resistor (often 1 megaohm) that protects the user from shock hazards when working with low-voltage components.

More advanced types of wrist straps are meant to connect to an actual ground (such as a ground strip or the ground plug of a special dedicated AC outlet). These are used in more-sophisticated repair labs. Do *not* attempt to connect the alligator clip of a basic wrist strap (purchased at an office store) to the ground plug of an outlet in your home.

▶ **Touch the chassis of the computer:** To further discharge yourself, do this before handling any components. This is also a good habit to get into when an antistatic strap is not available.

▶ **Use antistatic bags:** Adapter cards, motherboards, and the like are normally shipped in antistatic bags; hold on to them! When installing or removing components, keep them inside the bag until you are ready to work with them.

Note

Remember to keep the computer unplugged—disconnect the power or hit the kill switch on the back of the computer (if there is one) before working on the system. You might not know whether the AC outlet is wired properly. Regardless, by simply disconnecting the power, you eliminate any chance of a shock.

ExamAlert

Remember the three main ways to avoid ESD: wearing an antistatic strap, touching the computer case, and using antistatic bags.

▶ **Handle components properly:** If you are sitting at your desk without any ESD protection, there is no reason to be handling components, so don't. Handle components only when you are fully protected. When you do handle components, try to hold them at the edge. For example, when installing RAM, hold the module at the sides. This will inhibit any direct handling of the chips, contacts, and other circuitry. Adapter cards should be held by the metal plate (bracket) or by the edge of the fiberglass board but never by the contacts.

▶ **Use an antistatic mat:** Place the computer on top of the antistatic mat and connect the alligator clip of the mat to the computer's chassis in the same manner that you did with the wrist strap. (Some technicians stand on the mat and connect its alligator clip to the computer.)

▶ **Use antistatic wipes:** Use products such as Endust to clean the outside of monitors, computer cases, and keyboards; these wipes apply a certain amount of ESD protection.

▶ **Use antistatic sprays:** These can be sprayed on clothing or on the floor or table in which a technician works.

A few less direct ways to reduce ESD are as follows:

▶ **Keep your feet stationary:** When working on the computer and touching components, keep your feet stationary to reduce friction.

▶ **Work in an uncarpeted area:** Carpeting creates additional friction that leads to ESD. Some computer labs have special tiling with antistatic properties, but if you work for a company that doesn't have a proper lab or repair room, consider using an uncarpeted warehouse space or uncarpeted cafeteria. If you work at home, consider uncarpeted areas such as the kitchen, basement, or garage.

▶ **Raise the humidity:** By increasing the humidity to 50 percent (if possible), you decrease the chance of friction and ultimately decrease the chance of ESD. Did you ever notice that electrostatic discharges happen more readily during the winter? This is because of the lower humidity during that season.

▶ **Remove jewelry and wear protective clothing:** Remove any jewelry before working on a computer. You don't want this to come into contact with any components. Consider wearing clothes that are tighter fitting so that there is no chance of anything contacting the computer components. In some labs, you might see technicians wearing antistatic nylon jumpsuits. For the average person, rubber-soled shoes can also help to prevent ESD.

▶ **Keep away from devices that use electricity:** Try to steer clear of mechanized tools, such as battery-operated screw guns. Watch out for vacuums as well. Keep anything that is AC powered far away from the computer. Keep battery-operated devices away as well unless it's your trusty multimeter.

▶ **Don't use a vacuum cleaner:** Vacuum cleaners can be a deadly source of ESD. When cleaning those dust bunnies out of the computer, do it outside and consider using compressed air or other specialized cleaning kits. Use Stabilant 22a or a similar cleaner to enhance any contact's connectivity when you finish.

Remember, ESD needs to happen only once and that $500 video card you try to install is toast!

Physical Safety

Physical safety considerations include the following:

▶ Securing cables

▶ Using caution with heavy items

▶ Not touching hot components

▶ Use safety equipment

▶ Considering workplace ergonomics

Cables can be a trip hazard. Employ proper cable management by routing cables away from high-traffic areas and keeping computer cables stowed away and tie-wrapped. Network cables should have been installed permanently within the walls and ceiling, but sometimes you might find a rogue cable. If you discover a cable on the floor or hanging from the ceiling, alert your network administrator or your manager. Do not attempt to reroute the network cable. You don't know what data is transferred on the cable. Because network cabling is monitored by municipalities the same way other electrical work is done, only qualified, trained technicians should take care of network wiring.

Lifting heavy items incorrectly can cause many types of injuries. As a general rule, if an item is heavier than one quarter of your body weight, you should ask someone else to help. When lifting items, stand close to the item, squat down to the item by bending the knees, grasp the item firmly, keep the back straight, and slowly lift with the legs, not the back. Be sure not to twist the body; keep the item close to the body. This helps to prevent back injuries. When moving items, it is best to have them stored at waist level so that minimal lifting is necessary. OSHA has plenty of guidelines and recommendations for physical safety at the workplace. Its website is http://www.osha.gov/.

Be careful when handling components that might be hot. The best method when dealing with hot items (such as a laser printer's fuser, a burned-out power supply, or a CPU or hard drive that needs to be replaced) is to wait until they have cooled. To be safe, before replacing items, wait 15 minutes for them to cool. Servers and networking equipment can get quite hot as well, even when they are stored in a climate-controlled room. Take great care when working with these devices. Also, be careful with items that hold a charge. For the A+ certification, know that if a device has the possibility of holding a charge, you should not open it. This includes power supplies and CRT monitors. These types of electronics can be recycled in most municipalities. Programs might include curb-side pickup, drop-off centers, or recycling events. Usually these are free. There are also many donation programs for equipment that still functions.

Use safety equipment whenever necessary. This includes safety goggles, hard hats, air filter masks, fluorescent clothing, and so on. Whenever you enter a work area, lab, construction site, and any other nonoffice environments in the field, be sure to follow safety instructions.

You probably won't get any questions on the exam about this, but ergonomics are important when operating the computer. Ergonomics can affect the long-term health of the computer operator. It is important to keep the wrists and hands in-line with the forearms and to use proper typing technique. Keep the elbows close to the body and supported if possible. The lower back should be supported, your head and neck should be straight and in-line with your back, and your shoulders should be relaxed. Keep the top of the monitor at or just below eye level. Take breaks at least every two hours to avoid muscle cramps and eyestrain. To further reduce eyestrain, increase the refresh rate of the monitor if possible. For more information on ergonomics, see OSHA's information on computer workstations at http://www.osha.gov/SLTC/etools/computerworkstations/index.html.

Cram Quiz

Answer these questions. The answers follow the last question. If you cannot answer these questions correctly, consider reading this section again until you can.

220-902 Questions

1. If a power supply fails, what should you do?

   ○ **A.** Replace it.

   ○ **B.** Repair it.

   ○ **C.** Use a different computer.

   ○ **D.** Switch it to a different voltage setting.

2. Which of the following are ways to avoid ESD? (Select three.)

   ○ **A.** Use an antistatic wrist strap.

   ○ **B.** Use a vacuum cleaner.

   ○ **C.** Use an antistatic mat.

   ○ **D.** Touch the chassis of the computer.

3. You walk into the server room and see a person lying on the floor with a live electrical wire draped over. What should you do first?

   ○ **A.** Run out and call 911.

   ○ **B.** Grab the wire and fling it off the person.

   ○ **C.** Grab the person and drag him out from under the wire.

   ○ **D.** Grab a piece of wood and use it to move the wire off the person.

Cram Quiz Answers

220-902 Answers

1. **A.** Replace the power supply. It can be dangerous to try to repair it and is not cost-effective to the company.

2. **A, C, and D.** Antistatic wrist straps, mats, and touching the chassis of the computer are all ways to stop ESD. Vacuum cleaners can cause damage to components.

3. **D.** The first thing you should do is get a wooden stick, rope, or something similar (every server room should have one) and use it to CAREFULLY move the wire off of the person. In reality, the first thing you should do is breathe and not make any rash decisions because in the heat of the moment, you might think a bit less clearly than you are right now. Anyways, after the wire is removed, you should call 911 and then attempt to offer first aid to the victim. DO NOT ever touch a live wire or anything that the live wire is coming into contact with.

Procedures and Environmental Controls

Environmental factors vary from one organization to the next. For the exam, you need to know how and why to control temperature and humidity, what an MSDS is and how to use it, and how to deal with dust and debris when it comes to computers. You should also have a basic understanding of some of the procedures that a typical organization puts into practice.

Temperature, Humidity, and Air

You should be aware of the temperature and humidity measurements in your building. You should also be thinking about airborne particles and proper ventilation. Collectively, OSHA refers to this as "air treatment," which is the removal of air contaminants and/or the control of room temperature and humidity. Though there is no specific government policy regarding this, there are recommendations, including a temperature range of 68 to 76 degrees Fahrenheit (20 to 24 degrees Celsius) and a humidity range of between 20 percent and 60 percent. Remember, the higher the humidity, the less chance of ESD, but it might get a bit uncomfortable for your co-workers; they might not want to work in a rainforest, so a compromise will have to be sought. If your organization uses air handlers to heat, cool, and move the air, it will be somewhat difficult to keep the humidity any higher than 25 to 30 percent. That brings us to ventilation. An organization should employ the use of local exhaust (to remove contaminants generated by the organization's processes) and the introduction of an adequate supply of fresh outdoor air through natural or mechanical ventilation.

For air treatment, organizations should make use of filtration devices, electronic cleaners, and possibly chemical treatments activated with charcoal or other sorbents (materials used to absorb unwanted gases). Most filtration systems make use of charcoal and HEPA filters. These filters should be replaced at regular intervals. Air ducts and dampers should be cleaned regularly. And ductwork insulation should be inspected now and again. If there still is a considerable amount of airborne particles, portable air filtration enclosures can be purchased that also use charcoal and HEPA filters; you can also utilize ultraviolet light to eliminate particles. These are commonly found in PC repair facilities due to the amount of dust and dirt sitting in PCs that are waiting for repair. Some organizations even foot the bill for masks or even respirators for their employees. Many PC workbenches will be equipped with compressed air systems and vacuum systems. This way, the PC tech can blow out the dust and dirt from a computer and vacuum it up at the same time. Otherwise, it is usually best to take the computer outside (unless it is windy).

EMI and RFI

Electromagnetic interference (EMI) is an unwanted disturbance that affects electrical circuits. Network interference could be caused by EMI. For example, if an unshielded network cable were inadvertently draped over a fluorescent light above the drop ceiling, the light's EMI could cause data loss on that cable. Keep network cables away from lights, junction boxes, and any other AC electrical sources. Anything with magnets (speakers, CRTs, and UPSes) should be kept away from the computer and cables should be routed away from these devices. It's possible that lightning can cause EMI line noise to occur within the power cable. A good surge protector or line-conditioning device should deflect this.

Radio frequency interference (RFI) is closely related to EMI. For the A+ exam, some things to consider include cordless phone and microwave usage. Because these devices can also inhabit the 2.4 GHz frequency range used by 802.11b, g, and n networks, they can interfere with the network signal. Be sure that all devices are on different channels (1, 6, and 11 are the nonoverlapping ones) and that the microwave is not physically near any wireless devices.

Cables can act as antennas for radiated energy and should be shielded if possible.

MSDS and Disposal

Products that use chemicals require material safety data sheets (MSDSs). These are documents that give information about particular substances (for example, the ink in inkjet cartridges). Information in the MSDS includes

▶ Proper treatment if the substance is ingested or comes into contact with the skin

▶ How to deal with spills and other hazards

▶ How to dispose of the substance

▶ How to store the substance

It's easy to find MSDSs; most companies have them online. You can search for them at the manufacturer's website or with a search engine. An MSDS identifies the chemical substance, possible hazards, fire-fighting measures, handling and storage, and so on. Make sure you have Adobe Acrobat Reader installed because most MSDSs are in PDF format.

It's important to know what to do if someone is adversely affected by a product that has chemicals. A person might have skin irritation due to coming into contact with toner particles or with a cleaner that was used on a keyboard or mouse. As a technician, your job is to find out how to help the person. If you do not have direct access to the MSDS, you should contact your facilities department or building management. Perhaps the cleaning crew uses a particular cleaning agent that you are not familiar with and only the facilities department has been given the MSDS for this. It's better to review all MSDS documents and be proactive, but in this case, you probably won't have access to the document. Collaborate with the facilities department to get the person who was affected the proper first aid and, if necessary, take the person to the emergency room. Finally, remove the affected device (such as a keyboard or mouse). Replace it with a similar device until you can get the original device cleaned properly.

ExamAlert

Know that an MSDS contains information about chemical substances and hazards.

Generally, substances that contain chemicals should be stored in a cool, dry place, away from sunlight. "Cool" means the lower end of the OSHA guideline, approximately 68 degrees F (20 degrees C). Often, this will be in a storage closet away from the general work area and outside of the air filtration system. This also allows the items to be stored in a less humid area.

Recycling and proper disposal are also important. Batteries should not be thrown away with normal trash because they contain chemicals. First, you should check your local municipal or EPA guidelines for proper disposal of batteries and, in some cases, you will find that there are drop-off areas for these—either at the town municipal center or sometimes at office and computer supply stores. This applies to alkaline, lithium (for example, CR2032), lithium-ion, and NiCd batteries.

ExamAlert

Check your local municipal and EPA guidelines for disposal of batteries and other equipment.

Ink and toner cartridges can usually be sent back to the manufacturer, or office supply stores and printer repair outfits often will take them for later recycling. Some municipalities have a method for recycling electrical devices in general.

Incident Response and Documentation

How you follow up on an incident is a good measure of your ability to an organization. Incident response is the set of procedures that any investigator follows when examining a technology incident. How you first respond, how you document the situation, and your ability to establish a chain of custody are all important to your investigating skills.

First Response

When you first respond to an incident, your first task will be to identify exactly what happened. You must first recognize whether this is a simple problem that needs to be troubleshot or whether it is an incident that needs to be escalated. For example, if you encounter a person who has prohibited content on a computer, this can be considered an incident and you will be expected to escalate the issue to your supervisor, reporting on exactly what you have found. Copyrighted information, malware, inappropriate content, and stolen information could all be considered prohibited. So before you do anything, you should report your findings to the proper channels and then make sure that the data and affected devices are preserved. This often means making a backup of the computer's image. However, this will depend on your organization's policies. You might be told to leave everything as is and wait for a computer forensics expert or a security analyst; it will depend on the scenario. The idea here is that the scene will be preserved for that other person so that he can collect evidence.

Documentation

You want to document everything that you find and anything that happens after that. If your organization doesn't have any other methodology, write it down! When you leave the scene, you will be required to divulge all information to your supervisor. If you fixed the problem and no other specialists were required, the documentation process will continue through to the completion of the task and beyond when you monitor the system. You should also document any processes, procedures, and user training that might be necessary for the future.

Documentation might also include things that you collect, such as licenses for software. For example, Microsoft has used the certificate of authenticity (COA) and the client-access license (CAL) for ages. These commercial licenses come with software that is purchased and they prove that the organization paid for the software or the additional client licenses to connect to that software (as is the case with Windows Server products). Many types of software use a standard end-user licensing agreement (EULA), a personal license which might be on paper or stored on the computer (or online) and might be a personal single license or commercial multiple licenses. In addition, some media is encrypted with digital rights management (DRM) software. You might also need to collect personally identifiable information (PII) as well. This will all depend on the policies of the company you work for and the organization that you are dealing with at the time. Be sure to follow those policies and apply security best practices when doing so.

Chain of Custody

If you are required to preserve evidence, one way to do this is to set up a chain of custody. This is the chronological documentation or paper trail of evidence. It should be initiated at the start of any investigation. It documents who had custody of the evidence all the way up to litigation (if necessary). It also verifies that the evidence has not been modified or tampered with.

As a PC tech, you will usually not get too involved with investigations. But you should know the basic concepts of first response, documentation, and chain of custody for the exam as well as if you find yourself in a situation where you have found prohibited content or illegal activities.

CompTIA A+ Troubleshooting Theory

The most important procedure for the CompTIA A+ exams is the six-step troubleshooting theory. I can't stress enough how vital this is. We discussed this in Chapter 1 (and used it throughout the book), but let's just review the steps here one more time.

Step 1. Identify the problem.

Step 2. Establish a theory of probable cause. (Question the obvious.)

Step 3. Test the theory to determine cause.

Step 4. Establish a plan of action to resolve the problem and implement the solution.

Step 5. Verify full system functionality and, if applicable, implement preventative measures.

Step 6. Document findings, actions, and outcomes.

> **ExamAlert**
>
> Be sure to memorize the A+ six-step troubleshooting theory!

Cram Quiz

Answer these questions. The answers follow the last question. If you cannot answer these questions correctly, consider reading this section again until you can.

220-902 Questions

1. What document can aid you if a chemical spill occurs?

   ○ **A.** MSKB

   ○ **B.** MSDS

   ○ **C.** MCSE

   ○ **D.** DSS

2. A co-worker complains that after the cleaning crew has come through, the keyboard irritates his hands and leaves some green residue. What should you do?

   ○ **A.** Call the fire department.

   ○ **B.** Contact the facilities department.

   ○ **C.** Contact the manufacturer of the keyboard.

   ○ **D.** Call OSHA and complain.

3. You find illegal materials on a customer's computer. Your boss commands you to preserve computer evidence until he gets to the scene. What is your boss asking you to begin?

   ○ **A.** Documentation

   ○ **B.** Chain of custody

   ○ **C.** First response

   ○ **D.** EMI prevention

4. During what step of the A+ troubleshooting theory might you collect a CAL?

   ○ **A.** Establish a theory of probable cause.

   ○ **B.** Test the theory to determine cause.

   ○ **C.** Verify full system functionality.

   ○ **D.** Document findings.

Cram Quiz Answers

220-902 Answers

1. **B.** The material safety data sheet (MSDS) defines exactly what a chemical is, what the potential hazards are, and how to deal with them.

2. **B.** Contact the facilities department to see if they have the MSDS for the cleaner. You and/or the facilities department should then treat the irritation according to the MSDS. If this does not work and the problem gets worse, take the co-worker to the emergency room. Remove the keyboard from the work environment.

3. **B.** Your boss is asking you to begin the process of a chain of custody: the chronological paper trail of evidence. It is a form of documentation, but a specific one. You were the first responder. These cases will be rare, but you should understand the terminology and what to do if you find illegal materials.

4. **D.** You would collect information such as client access licenses (CALs), COAs, EULAs, and PII during the last step of the A+ troubleshooting theory—document findings, actions, and outcomes. You might also do this during the first step—identify the problem—but that answer wasn't listed.

Professionalism and Communication Skills

For the A+ exams, professionalism and communication consist of 10 categories:

▶ **Punctuality:** Be on time! If a customer has to wait, the situation might become difficult before you even begin. If you are running late, contact the customer, apologize, and let him know that you will be late.

▶ **Listen to the customer:** Actively listen to the customer (taking notes). Don't interrupt the customer, even if you think you know what the problem is before she has fully explained the situation. Be respectful and allow her to complete her explanation. Her tale just might give you clues as to what the *real* problem is. Listen carefully but be assertive when eliciting answers.

▶ **Clarify the problem:** Ask concise questions to the customer to further identify what the issue is and narrow the scope of the problem. After you think you understand what the problem is, you should always clarify by repeating the problem back to the customer. Restate the issue to verify everyone understands the problem.

▶ **Be positive:** Try to maintain a positive attitude and project confidence, even if the customer thinks the situation is hopeless or the customer is frustrated. Sometimes problems that appear to be the worst have the easiest solutions! And there is *always* a solution. It's just a matter of finding it. Also, as part of being positive, try to project confidence. Be calm and assure your customer that the problem will be solved.

▶ **Speak clearly:** Speak slowly and clearly so the customer can fully understand what you tell her. Refrain from slang and profanity. Avoid computer jargon and acronyms (for example, WPA or TCP/IP). If you use computer jargon, the customer might think that you are insecure and cannot clearly explain things. Stay away from the techno-babble. The customer expects you to know these things technically but to explain them in a simple manner.

▶ **Set and meet expectations:** When you have a clear idea of what the customer's trouble is, set a timeline; offer a reasonable assessment of how long it will take to fix the issue and what will be involved. Stay in contact with the customer, giving him updates at certain intervals— every half hour for smaller jobs and perhaps two or three times a day for larger jobs. If applicable, offer different repair or replacement options as the job progresses. At first, you might inform a customer that it appears a power supply needs to be changed. Later, you might find that an optical drive also needs to be replaced. Keep the customer up to date and offer options. Whatever the service, be clear as to the policies of your company and provide the proper documentation about the services you will be performing. After you finish the job, follow up with the customer to verify that the computer runs smoothly and that he is satisfied.

▶ **Avoid distractions:** Cell phone calls should be screened and left to go to voicemail unless it is an emergency. The same goes for e-mails that arrive on your smartphone and text messages on the phone. If other customers call, explain to them that you are with a customer and will call them back shortly (or have your manager or co-worker take care of them if they are available). Avoid talking to co-workers when dealing with customers. The customer wants to feel valued and wants to get her problem fixed in a timely manner. Try to avoid personal interruptions in general. And avoid using those social media sites.

▶ **Do not look at or touch confidential information:** Ask the customer to move the confidential items to another area where you cannot see them. Do not look at or touch the confidential materials located on a computer, desktop, printer, and so on. This could include bank statements, accounting information, legal documents, and other top-secret company information. Going beyond this, don't disclose any work experiences you had with an organization on social media outlets.

▶ **Do the right thing:** If a customer asks you to do something that you think is inappropriate, be sure to verify exactly what it is the customer wants you to do. Then take appropriate action. For example, if a customer asks you to install company software on his personal laptop, you should verify that the installation is allowed under the company's licensing agreements. If so, no harm is done. If not, you will have to politely refuse the customer. This type of customer behavior, while rare, should be reported to your manager.

▶ **Deal with customers professionally:** Understand that customers can come from all walks of life. By being patient, understanding, and respectful, you show customers that you are a professional and serious about fixing their computer problems. Never argue with customers or take a defensive or offensive stance. This is another one of those times in which I like to think of Mr. Spock. Approach customers' computer problems and complaints from a scientific point of view. Try not to make light of a customer's computer issues, no matter how simple they might seem, and avoid being judgmental of any possible user error. Never ask things such as "What did you do?" or "Who was working on this?" because these questions can come across as accusations. Ask computer-oriented, open-ended questions when eliciting answers from the customers (for example, ask "What is wrong with the computer?" or "What can you tell me about this computer?"). Stick with the senses; questions such as "What type of strange behavior did you see from the computer?" keeps customers more relaxed and can help you to narrow down the cause of the problem. Again, if a customer doesn't come across clearly, restate what you believe to be the issue or repeat your question so that you can verify your understanding so both of you will be on the same page.

ExamAlert

Be professional, punctual, positive, and practice all the other skills mentioned in this section. They are important for the exam—and much more important in the computer field.

Cram Quiz

Answer these questions. The answers follow the last question. If you cannot answer these questions correctly, consider reading this section again until you can.

220-902 Questions

1. How will speaking with a lot of jargon make a technician sound?

   ○ **A.** Competent

   ○ **B.** Insecure

   ○ **C.** Smart

   ○ **D.** Powerful

2. A customer experiences a server crash. When you arrive, the manager is upset about this problem. What do you need to remember in this scenario?

   ○ **A.** Stay calm and do the job as efficiently as possible.

   ○ **B.** Imagine the customer in his underwear.

   ○ **C.** Avoid the customer and get the job done quickly.

   ○ **D.** Refer the customer to your supervisor.

3. Which of the following are good ideas when dealing with customers? (Select two.)

   ○ **A.** Speak clearly.

   ○ **B.** Ignore them.

   ○ **C.** Avoid distractions.

   ○ **D.** Explain to them what they did wrong.

4. You are a field technician working at a customer's site. One of the workers asks you to load a copy of an organization's purchased software on a personal laptop. What should you do first?

   ○ **A.** Verify that the installation is allowed under the company's licensing agreement.

   ○ **B.** Act as though you are distracted and ignore the user.

   ○ **C.** Leave the premises and inform the police.

   ○ **D.** Tell the worker that installing unlicensed software is illegal.

   ○ **E.** Notify the worker's manager of a security breach.

Cram Quiz Answers

220-902 Answers

1. **B.** Too much computer jargon can make an end user think that you do not have the qualifications needed and are masking it with techno-babble.

2. **A.** There isn't much you can do when a customer is upset except stay calm and fix the problem!

3. **A and C.** Speak clearly so that customers understand you, and avoid distractions so that the customers know they have your complete attention.

4. **A.** You should first check whether the company allows installations of paid software on personal computers or laptops. If it is allowed, go ahead and do the installation. If not, then you should refuse and notify your manager of the occurrence.

CHAPTER 20

Taking the Real Exams

This chapter provides the following tools and information to help you be successful when preparing for and taking the CompTIA A+ 220-901 and 220-902 exams:

▶ Getting Ready and the Exam Preparation Checklist

▶ Tips for Taking the Real Exam

▶ Beyond the CompTIA A+ Certification

ExamAlert

Warning! Don't skip this chapter!

I impart some of the most vital things you need to know about taking the real exams here.

Getting Ready and the Exam Preparation Checklist

The CompTIA A+ certification exams can be taken by anyone; there are no prerequisites, but CompTIA recommends one year of prior lab or field experience working with computers. For more information on CompTIA and the A+ certification, visit http://certification.comptia.org/.

Also visit my A+ page at www.davidlprowse.com for information, additions, and updated errata.

To acquire your A+ certification, you need to pass two exams: 220-901 and 220-902. These exams are administered by Pearson Vue (www.pearsonvue.com). You need to register with Pearson Vue to take the exams.

> **ExamAlert**
>
> I strongly suggest that you *do not* take both exams on the same day. Instead, take them a week or so apart (at least). Trust me on this.

Each exam consists of two types of questions:

▶ **Multiple-choice:** These pose a question to you and ask you to select the correct answer (or answers) from a group of four or more choices. They are quite similar to the questions you've seen throughout this book.

▶ **Performance-based:** These ask you to answer a question, complete a configuration, or solve a problem in a hands-on fashion. The questions might ask you to drag and drop information to the correct location or complete a simulation in a virtual system.

To master both types of questions, you will need to have a deep understanding of the theory, but you will also need to know the hands-on. So practice on your actual computers as much as possible. This is, of course, imperative for the exams, but it is even more important for the real world. The more you install, configure, and troubleshoot real systems, the more you will be prepared for the job interview, as well as whatever comes your way once you have acquired a position within an organization.

ExamAlert

You've been warned! Practice as much as possible on the following:

▶ Real desktop/laptop computer hardware and software

▶ A SOHO router

▶ Smartphones and tablets

▶ Printers, displays, and other peripherals

An Important Note Regarding Exam Questions

This book does not offer the exact questions that are on the exam. There are two reasons for this:

1. CompTIA reserves the right to change the questions at any time. Any changes, however, will still reflect the content within the current A+ objectives.

2. The contents of the CompTIA A+ exams are protected by a nondisclosure agreement (NDA); anyone who sits an exam has to agree to this before beginning a test. The NDA states that the questions within the exams are not to be discussed with anyone.

So I cannot tell you exactly what is on the exams, but I do cover all of the objectives within this book in order to give you the best chance of passing the exams.

You must be fully prepared for the exam, so I created a checklist (see Table 20.1) that you can use to make sure you have covered all the bases. Go through the checklist twice, once for each exam. For each exam, place a check in the status column as each item is completed. Do this first with the 220-901 exam and then again with the 220-902 exam. I highly recommend completing each step in order and taking the 220-901 exam first. Historically, my readers and students have benefited greatly from this type of checklist.

TABLE 20.1 **Exam Preparation Checklist**

Step	Item	Details	220-901 Status	220-902 Status
1.	Review the Exam Alerts	The little boxes with Exam Alerts are interspersed throughout the book. Review these and make sure you understand every one.		

Step	Item	Details	220-901 Status	220-902 Status
2.	Review the Cram Quizzes	Cram Quizzes are categorized by exam. You can review them in the text or on the disc. On the first run-through of this checklist, start with the 220-901 questions. On the second run-through, use the 220-902 questions.		
3.	Complete the Practice Exams in the book	Directly after this chapter are two practice exams, one for 220-901 and 220-902. They are also available on the disc. Your goal should be to get at least 90 percent correct on each exam on the first try. (100 percent would be preferable!) If you score less than 90 percent, go back and study more! Also, consider getting my *A+ Exam Cram Practice Questions* book. It comes with hundreds of additional questions and in-depth explanations.		
4.	Study the Real-World Scenarios	These can be found directly after the practice exams. They are broken down by the 220-901 and 220-902 exams. Complete these by answering them and accessing the corresponding videos and simulations on the disc.		
5.	Create your own cheat sheet	Although there is a Cram Sheet in the beginning of this book, you should also create your own. See Table 20.2 for an example. The act of writing down important details helps commit them to memory. Keep in mind that you will not be allowed to take this or the Cram Sheet into the actual testing room.		

Step	Item	Details	220-901 Status	220-902 Status
6.	Register for the exam	Do not register until you have completed the previous steps; you shouldn't register until you are fully prepared. When you are ready, schedule the exam to commence within a couple days so that you won't forget what you learned! Registration can be done online. Register at Pearson Vue (www.pearsonvue.com). It accepts payment by major credit cards for the exam fee. You need to create an account to sign up for exams.		
7.	Study the Cram Sheet and cheat sheet	The Cram Sheet is a fold-out in the beginning of this book. It is also on the disc. Study from this and your cheat sheet during the last 24 hours before the exam. (If your exam is delayed for any reason, go back to step 2 and retake the cram quizzes and practice exams 24 hours prior to your test date.)		
8.	Take the exam!	Check mark each exam to the right as you pass the exam. Good luck!		

ExamAlert

Do not register for the exam until you are thoroughly prepared. Meticulously complete items 1 through 5 in Table 20.1 before you register.

Table 20.2 provides a partial example of a cheat sheet that you can create to aid in your studies. Fill in the appropriate information in the right column. For example, the first step of the six-step troubleshooting process is "Identify the problem."

TABLE 20.2 **Example Cheat Sheet**

Concept	Fill in the Appropriate Information Here
The six-step troubleshooting theory	1.
	2.
	3.
	4.
	5.
	6.
The motherboard form factors you should know	
The types of DDR and their typical data transfer rates	
The laser imaging process	
The malware removal process	
Windows startup files	
Commands and descriptions	
(For example, `ping` tests to see whether other systems on the network are live.)	
* Etc.	

* Continue Table 20.2 in this fashion on paper. The key is to write down various technologies, processes, step-by-steps, and so on to commit them to memory.

Tips for Taking the Real Exam

Some of you will be new to exams. This section is for you. For other readers who have taken exams before, feel free to skip this section or use it as a review.

The exam is conducted on a computer and is multiple-choice and performance-based. You have the option to skip questions. If you do so, be sure to "flag" them for review before moving on. Feel free to flag any other questions that you have answered but are not completely sure about. This is especially recommended for the performance-based questions. In fact, you might choose to leave all of the performance-based questions until the end. That, of course, is up to you.

When you get to the end of the exam, there will be an item review section, which shows you any questions that you did not answer and any that you flagged for review. Be sure to answer any questions that were not completed.

The following list includes tips and tricks that I have developed over the years. I've taken at least 20 certification exams in the past decade and the following points have served me well.

General Practices for Taking Exams

▶ **Pick a good time for the exam:** It would appear that the fewest number of people are at test centers on Monday and Friday mornings. Consider scheduling during these times. Otherwise, schedule a time that works well for you, when you don't have to worry about anything else. Keep in mind that Saturdays can be busy. Oh, and don't schedule the exam until you are ready. I understand that sometimes deadlines have to be set, but in general, don't register for the exam until you feel confident you can pass. Things come up in life that can sometimes get in the way of your study time. Keep in mind that most exams can be canceled as long as you give 48 hours' notice. (To be sure, check that time frame when registering.)

▶ **Don't overstudy the day before the exam:** Some people like to study hard the day before; some don't. My recommendations are to study off the Cram Sheet and your own cheat sheets, but in general, don't overdo it. It's not a good idea to go into overload mode the day before the exam.

▶ **Get a good night's rest:** A good night's sleep (7 to 9 hours) before the day of the exam is probably the best way to get your mind ready for an exam.

▶ **Eat a decent breakfast:** Eating is good! Breakfast is number two when it comes to getting your mind ready for an exam, especially if it is a morning exam. Just watch out for the coffee and tea. Too much caffeine for a person who is not used to it can be detrimental to the thinking process.

▶ **Show up early:** The testing agency recommends that you show up 30 minutes prior to your scheduled exam time. This is important; give yourself plenty of time and make sure you know where you are going.

Know exactly how long it takes to get to a testing center and account for potential traffic and construction. You don't want to have to worry about getting lost or being late. Stress and fear are the mind killers. Work on reducing any types of stress the day of and the day before the exam. By the way, you do need extra time because when you get to the testing center, you need to show ID, sign forms, get your personal belongings situated, and be escorted to your seat. Have two forms of ID (signed) ready for the administrator of the test center. Turn your cell phone or smartphone off when you get to the test center; they'll check that, too.

▶ **Bring ear plugs:** You never know when you will get a loud testing center or, worse yet, a loud test taker next to you. Ear plugs help to block out any unwanted noise that might show up. Just be ready to show your ear plugs to the test administrator.

▶ **Brainstorm before starting the exam:** Write down as much as you can remember from the Cram and cheat sheets before starting the exam. The testing center is obligated to give you something to write on; make use of it! By getting all the memorization out of your head and on "paper" first, it clears the brain somewhat so that it can tackle the questions. I put paper in quotation marks because it might not be paper; it could be a mini dry-erase board or something similar.

▶ **Take small breaks while taking the exam:** Exams can be brutal. You have to answer a lot of questions (typically anywhere from 65 to 90) while staring at a screen for an hour or more. Sometimes these screens are old and have seen better days; these older flickering monitors can cause a strain on your eyes. I recommend small breaks and breathing techniques. For example, after going through every 25 questions or so, close your eyes and slowly take a few deep breaths, holding each one for five seconds and then releasing each one slowly. Think about nothing while doing so. Remove the test from your mind during these breaks. It takes only about half a minute but can help to get your brain refocused. It's almost a Zen type of thing; but for me, when I have applied this technique properly, I have gotten a few perfect scores. It's amazing how the mindset can make or break you.

▶ **Be confident:** You have studied hard, gone through the practice exams, created your cheat sheet—you've done everything you can to prep. These things alone should build confidence. But actually, you just have to be confident for no reason whatsoever. Think of it this way: You are great...I am great...(to quote Dr. Daystrom). But truly, there is no disputing this! That's the mentality you must have. You are not being pretentious about this if you think it to yourself. Acting that way to others…well, that's another matter. So build that inner confidence and your mindset should be complete.

Smart Methods for Difficult Questions

▶ **Use the process of elimination:** If you are not sure about an answer, first eliminate any answers that are definitely incorrect. You might be surprised how often this works. This is one of the reasons why it is recommended that you not only know the correct answers to the practice exam questions, you also know why the wrong answers are wrong. The testing center should give you something to write on; use it by writing down the letters of the answers that are incorrect to keep track. Even if you aren't sure about the correct answer, if you can logically eliminate anything that is incorrect, the answer will become apparent. To sum it up, the character Sherlock Holmes said it best: "When you have eliminated the impossible, whatever remains, however improbable, must be the truth." There's more to it, of course, but from a scientific standpoint, this method can be invaluable.

▶ **Be logical in the face of adversity:** The most difficult questions are when two answers appear to be correct, even though the test question requires you to select only one answer. Real exams do not rely on "trick" questions. Sometimes you need to slow down, think logically, and compare the two possible correct answers. Also, you must imagine the scenario that the question is a part of. Think through step-by-step what is happening in the scenario. Write out as much as you can. The more you can visualize the scenario, the better you can figure out which of the two answers is the best one.

▶ **Use your gut instinct:** Sometimes a person taking a test just doesn't know the answer; it happens to everyone. If you have read through the question and all the answers and used the process of elimination, sometimes this is all you have left. In some scenarios, you might read a question and instinctively know the answer, even if you can't explain why. Tap into this ability. Some test takers write down their gut instinct answers before delving into the question and then compare their thoughtful answers with their gut instinct answers.

▶ **Don't let one question beat you!:** Don't let yourself get stuck on one question, especially the performance-based questions. Skip it and return to it later. When you spend too much time on one question, the brain gets sluggish. The thing with these exams is that you either know it or you don't. And don't worry too much about it; chances are you are not going to get a perfect score. Remember that the goal is only to pass the exams; how many answers you get right after that is irrelevant. If you have gone through this book thoroughly, you should be well prepared. You should have plenty of time to go through all the exam questions with time to spare to return to the ones you skipped and marked.

▶ **If all else fails, guess:** Remember that the exams might not be perfect. A question might seem confusing or appear not to make sense. Leave questions like this until the end. When you have gone through all the other techniques mentioned, make an educated, logical guess. Try to imagine what the test is after and why it would be bringing up this topic, as vague or as strange as it might appear.

Wrapping Up the Exam

▶ **Review all your answers:** If you finish early, use the time allotted to you to review the answers. Chances are you will have time left over at the end, so use it wisely! Make sure that everything you have marked has a proper answer that makes sense to you. But try not to overthink! Give it your best shot and be confident in your answers. You don't want to second-guess yourself!

Beyond the CompTIA A+ Certification

CompTIA started a policy on January 1, 2011. A person who passes the A+ exams will be certified for 3 years. To maintain the certification beyond that time, you must either pass the new version of the exams (before the three years is up), pass a higher level CompTIA exam (such as the Network+ or Security+), or enroll in the CompTIA Continuing Education Program. This program has an annual fee and requires that you obtain Continuing Education Units (CEUs) that count toward the recertification. There are a variety of ways to accumulate CEUs. See CompTIA's website for more information.

After you pass the exams, consider thinking about your technical future. Not only is it important to keep up with new technology and keep your technical skills sharp, but technical growth is important as well; consider expanding your technical horizons by learning different technologies.

Usually, companies wait at least six months before implementing new operating systems and other applications on any large scale, but you will have to deal with it sooner or later—most likely sooner. Windows, OS X, Linux, Android, and iOS are always coming out with new versions. Consider keeping up with the newest versions and obtaining access to the latest software and operating systems. Practice installing, configuring, testing, securing, maintaining, and troubleshooting them.

To keep on top of the various computer technologies, think about subscribing to technology websites, RSS feeds, and periodicals, and read them on a regular basis. Check out streaming video tech channels on the Internet. Join computer Internet forums and attend technology conventions. After all, a technician's skills need to be constantly honed and kept up to date. Feel free to contact me for specific and current recommendations.

Information Technology (IT) technicians need to keep learning to foster good growth in the field. Consider taking other certification exams after you complete the A+. The CompTIA A+ certification acts as a springboard to other certifications. For example, the CompTIA Network+ certification is designed to identify a technician's knowledge of network operating systems, equipment, and networking technologies. The CompTIA Security+ certification takes this to another level, evaluating the technician's knowledge of how to secure networks, computers, and their applications. Now that you know exactly how to go about passing a certification exam, consider more certifications to bolster your resume.

The best advice I can give is for you to do what you love. From an IT perspective, I usually break it down by technology, as opposed to by the vendor or certification. For example, you might want to learn more about e-mail systems, or securing internetworks, or you might prefer to work on databases, build websites, develop apps—who knows! You are limited only by your desire. Whatever the field, learn as much as you can about that field and all its vendors to stay ahead.

Final Note: I wish you the best of luck on your exams and in your IT career endeavors. Please let me know when you pass your exams. I would love to hear from you! Also, remember that I am available to answer any of your questions about this book via my website:

 http://www.davidlprowse.com.

Sincerely,

David L. Prowse

Practice Exam 1

CompTIA A+ 220-901

The 80 multiple-choice questions provided here help you to determine how prepared you are for the actual exam and which topics you need to review further. Write down your answers on a separate sheet of paper so that you can take this exam again if necessary. Compare your answers against the answer key that follows this exam.

Exam Questions

1. You are attempting to load an operating system DVD at computer startup. Which of the following settings should you modify in the BIOS/UEFI?

   ○ **A.** Enable a BIOS password

   ○ **B.** Boot sequence

   ○ **C.** Enable TPM

   ○ **D.** Disable TPM

2. Which of the following devices should be configured to block specific ports on the network?

   ○ **A.** Firewall

   ○ **B.** Gateway

   ○ **C.** Router

   ○ **D.** Bridge

   ○ **E.** Access point

3. Which connector is necessary to supply power to a graphics expansion card? (Select the best answer.)

   ○ **A.** 8-pin 12 V

   ○ **B.** PCIe 6-pin

   ○ **C.** 20-pin

   ○ **D.** SATA

4. Which of the following describes the use of DNS as it relates to TCP/IP networks?

   ○ **A.** Provides automated addressing to computers on the network

   ○ **B.** Provides mapping of user-friendly names to network resources

   ○ **C.** Provides separate control and data connections between network resources

   ○ **D.** Provides remote connectivity to resources on the network

5. Which of the following is the best option for storing 6,153 MB of data on one disc?

   ○ **A.** DVD-9 DL

   ○ **B.** CD-R 48x

   ○ **C.** DVD-5 SL

   ○ **D.** RAID 5

6. Which of the following memory technologies enables protection against random inconsistencies when storing data?

   ◯ **A.** Quad-channel

   ◯ **B.** Unbuffered

   ◯ **C.** Dual-channel

   ◯ **D.** ECC

7. A laptop's volume buttons do not function. Which of the following should be downloaded and installed to make the volume button function properly?

   ◯ **A.** ACPI driver from the manufacturer's website

   ◯ **B.** Special keys driver from the manufacturer's website

   ◯ **C.** AHCI driver from the manufacturer's website

   ◯ **D.** Bluetooth stack/driver from the manufacturer's website

8. Of the following lists, which is the best group of configurations for a Home Theater PC, a Thick Client, and a Gaming PC?

   ◯ **A.** Home Theater PC

        Dual core CPU, 4 GB RAM, 250 watt HTPC, TV Tuner, 250 GB SSD

        Thick Client

        Quad core CPU, 16 GB RAM, 800 watt Full ATX, Liquid Cooling, 250 GB SSD

        Gaming PC

        Dual core CPU, 8 GB RAM, 400 watt ATX, Windows 7 32-bit, 1 TB SATA

   ◯ **B.** Home Theater PC

        Dual core CPU, 12 GB RAM, 250 watt HTPC, TV Tuner, 250 GB SSD

        Thick Client

        Dual core CPU, 4 GB RAM, 250 watt ATX, Windows 7 32-bit, 250 GB SATA

        Gaming PC

        Quad core CPU, 16 GB RAM, 800 watt Full-ATX, Liquid Cooling, 1 TB SATA

   ◯ **C.** Home Theater PC

        Single core CPU, 4 GB RAM, 250 watt HTPC, TV Tuner, 250 GB SATA

        Thick Client

        Hex core CPU, 32 GB RAM, 800 watt Full ATX, Video Capture Card, 250 GB SSD

        Gaming PC

        Dual core CPU, 32 GB RAM, 800 watt mini-ATX, Windows Vista 32-bit, 3 TB SATA

   ○ **D.** Home Theater PC

   Quad core CPU, 32 GB RAM, 1000 watt HTPC, Virtualization software, 1 TB SATA

   Thick Client

   Dual core CPU, 4 GB RAM, 250 watt Full ATX, Dual NICs, No hard drive

   Gaming PC

   Pentium IV CPU, 16 GB RAM, 400 watt ATX, Specialized audio card, RAID array

9. A computer you are working on randomly reboots. Which of the following should be checked first when troubleshooting the computer? (Select the two best answers.)

   ○ **A.** Memory integrity

   ○ **B.** Video card integrity

   ○ **C.** CMOS battery

   ○ **D.** PSU integrity

   ○ **E.** Optical drive integrity

10. Which of the following scenarios can be described as memory modules divided into two banks, only one of which can be seen by the computer at any time?

   ○ **A.** Single-sided

   ○ **B.** Double-sided

   ○ **C.** ECC

   ○ **D.** Non-ECC

11. Which of the following cooling methods will an integrated GPU in a common desktop most likely use?

   ○ **A.** Heat sink and fan

   ○ **B.** Heat sink

   ○ **C.** Liquid cooling

   ○ **D.** Video card cooling fan

12. Which of the following connection types is used to "beam" information between two devices over very short distances?

   ○ **A.** 802.11n

   ○ **B.** Parabolic antenna

   ○ **C.** IR

   ○ **D.** Bluetooth

13. Which type of memory will a smartphone typically use for storage of videos and music?

- ○ **A.** SD
- ○ **B.** eMMC
- ○ **C.** microSD
- ○ **D.** SODIMM

14. You have been tasked with configuring two drives for maximum performance. Which of the following RAID types should you select?

- ○ **A.** RAID 0
- ○ **B.** RAID 1
- ○ **C.** RAID 5
- ○ **D.** RAID 10

15. Which of the following are input devices that you might use with video games? (Select the three best answers.)

- ○ **A.** Microphone
- ○ **B.** Webcam
- ○ **C.** Gamepad
- ○ **D.** Joystick
- ○ **E.** Digitizer
- ○ **F.** Camcorder

16. Which of the following is the most common type of networking connector?

- ○ **A.** RJ11
- ○ **B.** F-connector
- ○ **C.** BNC
- ○ **D.** RJ45

17. Which protocol is relied upon most by Active Directory? (Select the best answer.)

- ○ **A.** SMB
- ○ **B.** HTTP
- ○ **C.** LDAP
- ○ **D.** WINS

18. Which of the following printer technologies uses piezoelectric pressure pads to produce small bubbles that are moved to the paper?

   ○ **A.** Laser

   ○ **B.** Inkjet

   ○ **C.** Thermal

   ○ **D.** Impact

19. You are working on a laptop. Which of the following devices requires you to remove the CPU to replace it?

   ○ **A.** Backlight

   ○ **B.** Keyboard backlight

   ○ **C.** Function key

   ○ **D.** System board

20. Which of the following environmental impacts can cause the customer to lose data?

   ○ **A.** Blackout

   ○ **B.** Air filters

   ○ **C.** Being on time

   ○ **D.** Backup battery

21. Which of the following video ports can send purely digital signals?

   ○ **A.** HDMI and DVI

   ○ **B.** VGA and DVI

   ○ **C.** VGA and HDMI

   ○ **D.** DVI and S-Video

22. Which of the following types of cables uses a 9-pin connector?

   ○ **A.** USB

   ○ **B.** Ethernet

   ○ **C.** Serial

   ○ **D.** RJ11

23. You need to describe RAID to a nontechnical customer. Which of the following represents the best way to describe RAID?

- ○ **A.** RAID stands for Redundant Array of Independent Disks.
- ○ **B.** RAID utilizes multiple disks to increase performance and/or enable protection from data loss.
- ○ **C.** RAID is a dynamic disk management system.
- ○ **D.** RAID uses striping to reduce the amount of hard drive write time and utilizes parity bits to reconstruct the data from a failed hard drive.

24. A customer of yours is opening an Internet Café and wants to offer computers for the patrons to access the Internet. Which type of computer system should you recommend?

- ○ **A.** Thin client
- ○ **B.** Thick client
- ○ **C.** HTPC
- ○ **D.** Gaming PC

25. You replaced a bad internal WLAN card in a Windows 7 laptop. You complete the installation and verify that the new WLAN card is listed in the Device Manager as enabled. What should you do next to actually use the card?

- ○ **A.** Type the security passphrase
- ○ **B.** Update the firmware of the WLAN card
- ○ **C.** Configure encryption on the router
- ○ **D.** Add the SSID of the network to the connection

26. Which of the following lists the correct nonoverlapping channels in the 2.4 GHz wireless spectrum?

- ○ **A.** 2, 4, 6, 8, 10
- ○ **B.** 1, 5, 10
- ○ **C.** 1, 6, 11
- ○ **D.** 3, 6, 10

27. Which of the following is the module format used by a laptop's DDR4 SODIMMs?

- ○ **A.** 200-pin
- ○ **B.** 204-pin
- ○ **C.** 240-pin
- ○ **D.** 260-pin

28. Which of the following is the correct pinout for T568B?

    ○ **A.** Orange/white, orange, green/white, blue, blue/white, green, brown/white, brown

    ○ **B.** Blue, blue/white, orange/white, orange, brown/white, brown, green/white, green

    ○ **C.** Green/white, green, orange/white, blue, blue/white, orange, brown/white, brown

    ○ **D.** Orange/white, orange, brown/white, brown, green/white, green, blue, blue/white

29. A customer wants to share a local USB printer with other users in the office. Which of the following is the best method to accomplish this?

    ○ **A.** Install a print server

    ○ **B.** Enable print sharing

    ○ **C.** Install a USB hub

    ○ **D.** Install shared PCL drivers

30. Your co-worker's laptop screen is extremely dim. You attempt to alter the brightness with the function keys but the display never gets brighter. Which of the following is the most likely cause?

    ○ **A.** Backlight failure

    ○ **B.** Bulb failure

    ○ **C.** Battery failure

    ○ **D.** The display driver is corrupted

31. Which of the following has the shortest wireless range for printing?

    ○ **A.** Bluetooth

    ○ **B.** Infrared

    ○ **C.** 802.11g

    ○ **D.** 802.11a

32. Which of the following should be reset during normal printer maintenance?

    ○ **A.** Page count

    ○ **B.** Job queue

    ○ **C.** Print job cache

    ○ **D.** Tray settings

33. Which of the following is the best protocol to use when securely transferring large files?

   ○ **A.** FTP

   ○ **B.** SSH

   ○ **C.** TELNET

   ○ **D.** SFTP

34. A laptop's battery fails to charge. Which of the following should be checked first?

   ○ **A.** DC-in jack

   ○ **B.** AC-in jack

   ○ **C.** CMOS battery

   ○ **D.** AC circuit breaker

35. You are replacing a PSU for a computer that requires power connections for two SATA hard drives, an older fan that uses Molex power connectors and two video cards configured for SLI with their own power connections. How many *unique* power connectors will the PSU need to accommodate the listed devices?

   ○ **A.** 2

   ○ **B.** 3

   ○ **C.** 4

   ○ **D.** 5

36. You need to make a patch cable to connect a computer to an RJ45 wall jack. Which tool of the following tools should be used to attach the RJ45 plugs to the patch cable?

   ○ **A.** Crimper

   ○ **B.** Punchdown tool

   ○ **C.** Loopback plug

   ○ **D.** Cable tester

37. A user with an inkjet printer states that all color printouts are missing red ink. The printer has cartridges for each of the CMYK colors, and the user has recently replaced the magenta cartridge. Which of the following steps should be performed next?

   ○ **A.** Verify that the printer cables are connected

   ○ **B.** Perform printer head cleaning

   ○ **C.** Purchase a maintenance kit

   ○ **D.** Use different weighted paper

38. Which of the following cable types might be used in POTS connections?

   ○ **A.** Cat 3

   ○ **B.** RG-6

   ○ **C.** RG-59

   ○ **D.** Multimode

39. Which of the following should be placed on a DMZ?

   ○ **A.** Smartphones

   ○ **B.** Wireless printers

   ○ **C.** Gaming servers

   ○ **D.** Backup servers

40. One of your customers runs Windows 7 on a laptop. A new security flaw and fix has been published regarding Windows 7. Which of the following can prevent exploitation?

   ○ **A.** Encrypting the hard drive

   ○ **B.** Training the customer

   ○ **C.** Implementing a patching policy

   ○ **D.** Configuring screen locks

41. Which of the following is one of the main hardware differences between a tablet computer and a laptop computer?

   ○ **A.** The laptop always has a multitouch touchscreen.

   ○ **B.** Tablets are typically not upgradeable.

   ○ **C.** Laptops are typically not upgradeable.

   ○ **D.** Laptops typically use ARM processors.

42. Which of the following resolution modes by design provides the best possible visual quality on an LCD monitor?

   ○ **A.** Digital

   ○ **B.** Native

   ○ **C.** SVGA

   ○ **D.** XGA

43. Which of the following is the main purpose of cleaning a printer during the imaging process?

- ○ **A.** It increases the speed of the print process.
- ○ **B.** It keeps the printer clean and prolongs its shelf life.
- ○ **C.** It prolongs the toner cartridge's lifecycle.
- ○ **D.** It takes off any residual toner left after development.

44. You need to use the correct version of PING that will resolve an IP address to a hostname. Which switch should you use?

- ○ **A.** -a
- ○ **B.** -f
- ○ **C.** -n
- ○ **D.** -t

45. A workgroup of five PCs uses a shared printer. A customer says she cannot print to the printer but can access shares on another PC used for common files. The printer appears to be powered on. Which of the following would be the most likely cause?

- ○ **A.** PC is off the network
- ○ **B.** Printer needs to be restarted
- ○ **C.** Printer is low on toner
- ○ **D.** Device drivers are corrupted

46. A user boots a computer and a message is displayed that reads "Alert! Cover previously removed." Which of the following was configured in the UEFI/BIOS to cause this alert?

- ○ **A.** Date and time settings
- ○ **B.** Boot sequence
- ○ **C.** Intrusion detection
- ○ **D.** Virtualization support

47. One of the users on your network states that a laser printer has a smudge that repeats itself every few inches down the center of every printed page. Which of the following most likely needs replacing?

- ○ **A.** Fuser
- ○ **B.** Pickup assembly
- ○ **C.** Rollers
- ○ **D.** Toner drum

48. Which of the following features makes logical processor cores appear as physical cores to the operating system?

   O **A.** 64-bit

   O **B.** MMU virtualization

   O **C.** Hyper-Threading

   O **D.** XD bit

49. Which of the following RAM types is compatible with PC3-8500 and will maintain the same performance as PC3-8500?

   O **A.** PC-2700

   O **B.** PC3-10600

   O **C.** PC3-6400

   O **D.** PC2-5300

50. Which of the following describes the function of a switch in a network?

   O **A.** Converts a packet for transmission from one network to another network

   O **B.** Transmits packets it receives to specific connections

   O **C.** Broadcasts packets it receives to all connections

   O **D.** Determines whether a packet belongs on an internal or an external network

51. Of the following, which components are the most important in a virtualization server? (Select the two best answers.)

   O **A.** Maximum memory

   O **B.** High-end sound card

   O **C.** High-end video card

   O **D.** Dual-rail 1000w PSU

   O **E.** Quad-core CPU

52. The power supply fan and case fans spin but there is no power to other devices. Which of the following is the most likely cause of this?

   O **A.** Failed hard drive

   O **B.** Improper connectivity

   O **C.** Drive not recognized

   O **D.** Failed RAM

53. When installing a printer in Windows, which of the following is the purpose of the Additional Drivers button within the Sharing tab of a printer's Properties window?

   ○ **A.** To add additional drivers to emulate a different printer

   ○ **B.** To add additional drivers for other printers on the computer

   ○ **C.** To add additional drivers for other operating systems

   ○ **D.** To add additional drivers for different printing modes

54. Which of the following cables is prone to EMI?

   ○ **A.** Fiber optic

   ○ **B.** STP

   ○ **C.** UTP

   ○ **D.** Multimode

55. Which of the following wireless standards can operate at two different channel widths within the same spectrum at the same time?

   ○ **A.** 802.11a

   ○ **B.** 802.11b

   ○ **C.** 802.11g

   ○ **D.** 802.11n

56. Which of the following would benefit the most from the use of dual monitors?

   ○ **A.** Gaming PC

   ○ **B.** HTPC

   ○ **C.** A/V editing workstation

   ○ **D.** Thin client

57. A user tells you that a printer is not printing as clearly as it used to. Which of the following should be your first step to fixing this?

   ○ **A.** Calibrate the printer.

   ○ **B.** Replace the ink cartridges.

   ○ **C.** Replace the USB cable.

   ○ **D.** Use a different type of paper.

58. You are required to install a printer on a Windows 7 Professional x86 workstation. Which print driver do you need to complete the installation?

    ○ **A.** 86-bit

    ○ **B.** 16-bit

    ○ **C.** 32-bit

    ○ **D.** 64-bit

59. You just installed a barcode reader. Which of the following should you do to configure the reader?

    ○ **A.** Use the Device Manager to enable the IR port.

    ○ **B.** Adjust jumper switches.

    ○ **C.** Enable the reader in the BIOS.

    ○ **D.** Scan in program codes.

60. Which of the following ports is used by DNS traffic by default?

    ○ **A.** 25

    ○ **B.** 53

    ○ **C.** 143

    ○ **D.** 3389

61. Which of the following is a possible symptom of a damaged video display?

    ○ **A.** Disconnected punchdown

    ○ **B.** Low RF signal

    ○ **C.** Dead pixel

    ○ **D.** Computer repeatedly boots to Safe Mode

62. Which of the following voltages are normally supplied by a PSU's rails? (Select the two best answers.)

    ○ **A.** 1.5 V

    ○ **B.** 3.3 V

    ○ **C.** 5 V

    ○ **D.** 9 V

63. You previously installed a biometric device using the supplied manufacturer driver. You confirmed that the device works properly. Afterward, you update the laptop's Windows and AV updates. Which of the following statements best explains why the biometric device has stopped functioning?

   ○ **A.** A virus that specifically targets retinal scanning software infected the laptop because the user was late applying new definitions.

   ○ **B.** The recently updated AV software is interfering with the proper operation of the biometric device.

   ○ **C.** The biometric device needs to be recalibrated.

   ○ **D.** The recently installed Windows updates overwrote the manufacturer driver.

64. Which type of display uses the most power?

   ○ **A.** LCD

   ○ **B.** LED

   ○ **C.** LED with backlight

   ○ **D.** Plasma

65. You are troubleshooting a printer. Which of the following are common symptoms of printer failure or other printer issues? (Select the two best answers.)

   ○ **A.** Vertical lines on the page

   ○ **B.** Num lock indicator lights are on

   ○ **C.** Unable to install the printer

   ○ **D.** Failure to document cable and screw locations

   ○ **E.** Failure to organize parts

66. Which of the following cable types carries analog video signal across three separate physical channels?

   ○ **A.** RCA

   ○ **B.** Component

   ○ **C.** DVI-analog (DVI-A)

   ○ **D.** VGA

67. Which of the following should be used when building a high-end graphics workstation for CAD applications? (Select the two best answers.)

   ○ **A.** An eSATA drive

   ○ **B.** More than four accessible USB 3.0 ports

   ○ **C.** Main memory of 16 GB or more

   ○ **D.** A 32-bit OS for the large amount of expected drive I/O

   ○ **E.** A PCIe video card with a large amount of memory

68. Which of the following computer components are located on the northbridge? (Select the two best answers.)

    ○ **A.** CPU

    ○ **B.** Hard drive

    ○ **C.** Audio

    ○ **D.** Fan

    ○ **E.** RAM

69. Which of the following socket types is used by an AMD CPU?

    ○ **A.** 775

    ○ **B.** FM1

    ○ **C.** 1155

    ○ **D.** 1366

70. Which of the following is an example of a MAC address?

    ○ **A.** 10.1.1.255

    ○ **B.** 4410:FF11:AAB3::0012

    ○ **C.** http://www.davidlprowse.com

    ○ **D.** 00-1C-C0-A1-55-21

71. Which of the following is enabled in the BIOS/UEFI that will prompt a user to enter her password every time the laptop performs a POST?

    ○ **A.** Administrative password

    ○ **B.** Windows password

    ○ **C.** Power-on password

    ○ **D.** Supervisory password

72. When placing a mobile device into airplane mode, which of the following features are typically disabled? (Select the two best answers.)

    ○ **A.** Wireless

    ○ **B.** Cellular data

    ○ **C.** Multitouch capability

    ○ **D.** Data encryption

73. A fully functional touchscreen LCD monitor requires a DVI connection and a power connection. Which of the following is also required?

- ○ **A.** SCSI connection
- ○ **B.** USB connection
- ○ **C.** Ethernet connection
- ○ **D.** Parallel connection

74. Which of the following are common hardware requirements in a home server? (Select the two best answers.)

- ○ **A.** RAID array
- ○ **B.** Virtualization support
- ○ **C.** Gigabit Ethernet
- ○ **D.** Touchscreen
- ○ **E.** Dual monitors

75. You have been tasked with resolving a shadowy image that is being printed from a network printer. What should you do?

- ○ **A.** Replace the drum
- ○ **B.** Replace the fuser
- ○ **C.** Run a calibration
- ○ **D.** Replace the network cable

76. You are tasked with upgrading memory from 2 GB to 4 GB on 10 Windows 7 laptops. Some of the laptops have DDR2 memory and some have DDR3 memory. The memory that was purchased for the upgrade is DDR3. Which of the following is the most likely outcome?

- ○ **A.** The DDR3 memory will not work properly within the laptops unless the CL rating is compatible.
- ○ **B.** The DDR2 laptops will work with the DDR3 RAM as long as the DDR2 stick is installed in the first slot.
- ○ **C.** The DDR3 laptops are the only computers that will accept the purchased memory.
- ○ **D.** The DDR2 memory will work fine with the DDR3 memory.

77. Which of the following cable types would most likely experience degraded video signal quality over long distances?

- ○ **A.** VGA
- ○ **B.** HDMI
- ○ **C.** DVI
- ○ **D.** DisplayPort

78. Which of the following is a private class B IP address?

   ○ **A.** 10.0.36.144

   ○ **B.** 172.16.22.108

   ○ **C.** 172.37.1.1

   ○ **D.** 192.168.1.1

79. A desktop computer (named workstation22) can't connect to the network. A network card was purchased without documentation or driver discs. Which of the following is the best way to install the network card driver?

   ○ **A.** Purchase the disc online and install.

   ○ **B.** Run Windows Update to install the drivers.

   ○ **C.** From the desktop computer (workstation22), download and install the drivers.

   ○ **D.** Copy the driver to a flash drive and install.

80. John is a PC technician for an organization that has a computer network with 12 computers. Each contains vital information, so each uses static IP addresses (on the 192.168.50.0 network). John just finished troubleshooting a Windows 8.1 computer that could not access the network. He ascertained (correctly) that the computer needed a new network card. He purchased a Plug and Play card and physically installed the card. He then turned on the computer, noting that the network card's LED link was lit and that there was activity. He then rebooted the computer to Windows and then documented the whole process. Later, his boss tells him that the user is complaining that she cannot access the Internet. Which step of the A+ troubleshooting theory did John forget to perform?

   ○ **A.** Identify the problem.

   ○ **B.** Establish a theory of probable cause.

   ○ **C.** Test the theory to determine cause.

   ○ **D.** Establish a plan of action to resolve the problem.

   ○ **E.** Verify full system functionality.

   ○ **F.** Document findings, actions, and outcomes.

Answers at a Glance

1.	B	**28.**	A	**55.**	D
2.	A	**29.**	B	**56.**	C
3.	B	**30.**	A	**57.**	A
4.	B	**31.**	B	**58.**	C
5.	A	**32.**	A	**59.**	D
6.	D	**33.**	D	**60.**	B
7.	B	**34.**	A	**61.**	C
8.	B	**35.**	B	**62.**	B and C
9.	A and D	**36.**	A	**63.**	D
10.	B	**37.**	B	**64.**	D
11.	A	**38.**	A	**65.**	A and C
12.	C	**39.**	C	**66.**	B
13.	C	**40.**	C	**67.**	C and E
14.	A	**41.**	B	**68.**	A and E
15.	A, C, and D	**42.**	B	**69.**	B
16.	D	**43.**	D	**70.**	D
17.	C	**44.**	A	**71.**	C
18.	B	**45.**	A	**72.**	A and B
19.	D	**46.**	C	**73.**	B
20.	A	**47.**	D	**74.**	A and C
21.	A	**48.**	C	**75.**	A
22.	C	**49.**	B	**76.**	C
23.	B	**50.**	B	**77.**	A
24.	A	**51.**	A and E	**78.**	B
25.	D	**52.**	B	**79.**	D
26.	C	**53.**	C	**80.**	E
27.	D	**54.**	C		

Practice Exam 2

CompTIA A+ 220-902

The 80 multiple-choice questions provided here help you to determine how prepared you are for the actual exam and which topics you need to review further. Write down your answers on a separate sheet of paper so that you can take this exam again if necessary. Compare your answers against the answer key that follows this exam.

Exam Questions

1. You are working on a Windows 7 Ultimate computer. An application called DLP 2.0 is failing to start properly. You are required to disable two of its components in `msconfig`. Which two tabs should you access? (Select the two best answers.)

   ○ **A.** General

   ○ **B.** Boot

   ○ **C.** Services

   ○ **D.** Startup

   ○ **E.** Tools

2. Which of the following applications can be scheduled to delete unwanted, compressed, older files?

   ○ **A.** Disk Defragmenter

   ○ **B.** Disk Cleanup

   ○ **C.** CHKDSK

   ○ **D.** Disk Management

3. Which of the following usually incorporates an 8-digit code that can be found on the bottom of a SOHO router?

   ○ **A.** Port forwarding

   ○ **B.** WPS

   ○ **C.** Wireless encryption

   ○ **D.** Port triggering

4. Which of the following commands might need to be run after a virus removal if a computer won't boot?

   ○ **A.** DXDIAG

   ○ **B.** BOOTREC /FIXMBR

   ○ **C.** Msconfig

   ○ **D.** Safe Mode

5. Which operating system feature will show a hard drive's status?

   ○ **A.** Tasklist

   ○ **B.** Administrative tools

   ○ **C.** Disk Management

   ○ **D.** Ping

6. You have been asked to set up a new networking closet and you notice that the humidity level in the room is very low. Which of the following tasks should be done before rack-mounting any networking equipment?

    ○ **A.** Install grounding bars.

    ○ **B.** Set up a dehumidifier.

    ○ **C.** Use an ESD strap.

    ○ **D.** Implement a fire suppression system.

7. You have been testing a financial software program by printing several test documents. Which of the following statements describes how to handle the confidential test documents when you are finished testing?

    ○ **A.** Give the printouts to the manager at the office.

    ○ **B.** Throw the documents out.

    ○ **C.** Leave the documents exactly where they are.

    ○ **D.** Shred the documents.

8. One of your customers has not received any e-mails on his smartphone in the past few days. However, he's able to access the Internet. Which of the following should be your first troubleshooting step?

    ○ **A.** Reconfigure the e-mail account.

    ○ **B.** Update the mobile OS.

    ○ **C.** Restart the smartphone.

    ○ **D.** Resynchronize the phone.

9. By default, a file or folder will receive its NTFS permissions from the parent folder. This process is known as which of the following terms?

    ○ **A.** Permission propagation

    ○ **B.** Single sign-on (SSO)

    ○ **C.** Client-side virtualization

    ○ **D.** Proxy settings

    ○ **E.** Recovery image

    ○ **F.** Inheritance

10. You come across prohibited materials on a computer located in a common area. Which of the following statements describes what you should do *first*?

    ○ **A.** Copy the items to the intranet.

    ○ **B.** Show the items to others so that they can be witnesses.

    ○ **C.** Report the incident to management.

    ○ **D.** Remove the items from the computer.

11. Which of the following are examples of physical security? (Select the two best answers.)

- ○ **A.** Directory permissions
- ○ **B.** RSA tokens
- ○ **C.** Principle of least privilege
- ○ **D.** Privacy filters

12. A user is reporting that his web browser is not going to the site he is trying to access. Which of the following statements describes the best way to resolve this?

- ○ **A.** Ensure the user is not utilizing a proxy server.
- ○ **B.** Remove all Internet shortcuts.
- ○ **C.** Delete all Internet cookies.
- ○ **D.** Clear all Internet cache.

13. Which of the following options is the best way to secure a Windows workstation?

- ○ **A.** Screensaver
- ○ **B.** User education
- ○ **C.** Disable Autorun
- ○ **D.** Complex password
- ○ **E.** ID badge
- ○ **F.** Key fob
- ○ **G.** Retinal scan

14. Which of the following terms best describes the Apple utility used with iOS devices for synchronizing and upgrading?

- ○ **A.** Safari
- ○ **B.** iMac
- ○ **C.** iTunes
- ○ **D.** Bluetooth

15. Which of the following is a way to remove data from a hard drive through destruction? (Select the two best answers.)

- ○ **A.** Disabling ports
- ○ **B.** Shredding
- ○ **C.** Drilling
- ○ **D.** Using low-level formatting
- ○ **E.** Purging

16. Which of the following statements describes the proper lifting technique?

   ○ **A.** Squat and lift from the legs.

   ○ **B.** Use gloves to pick up an item.

   ○ **C.** Bend down and pick the item up.

   ○ **D.** Have two people bend down and pick up the item.

17. Which type of technology is used when pairing devices such as headsets to a smartphone?

   ○ **A.** Bluetooth

   ○ **B.** Exchange

   ○ **C.** Locator application

   ○ **D.** Remote wipe

18. Your organization's network consists of 25 computers. Your boss is interested in employing a file server with network shares and a print server. Which of the following Windows network setups should you recommend?

   ○ **A.** Workgroup

   ○ **B.** Ad hoc

   ○ **C.** Star

   ○ **D.** Domain

19. Which of the following is the best example of the use of chain of custody?

   ○ **A.** The technician notes the date, time, and who was given the computer.

   ○ **B.** The technician remembers when and who he or she gave the computer to.

   ○ **C.** The technician uses a third-party to hand over the computer to the proper authorities.

   ○ **D.** The technician calls the supervisor after the computer has been transferred.

20. Which Windows utility can be used to see which users are currently logged on?

   ○ **A.** `Msconfig`

   ○ **B.** Disk Management

   ○ **C.** Task Manager

   ○ **D.** Administrative Tools

21. Which of the following tools are commonly used to remove dust from the inside of a computer? (Select the two best answers.)

   - ○ **A.** Compressed air
   - ○ **B.** Cotton and alcohol
   - ○ **C.** Feather duster
   - ○ **D.** Antibacterial surface cleaner
   - ○ **E.** Vacuum

22. A user wishes to access contacts from an Android phone. Which of the following solutions will provide the most up-to-date contact information on the user's phone on a daily basis?

   - ○ **A.** Enabling Bluetooth and transferring the contacts from a laptop to the cell phone
   - ○ **B.** Enabling contact synchronization by setting up the e-mail account on the phone
   - ○ **C.** Enabling e-mail synchronization and e-mailing the contacts to the user account for download
   - ○ **D.** Downloading all contacts to a .csv file and importing them via USB

23. You are servicing a computer and notice a lot of icons linking to inappropriate websites. Which of the following statements describes your first course of action?

   - ○ **A.** Report your findings through proper channels.
   - ○ **B.** Track the evidence.
   - ○ **C.** Document all changes to the computer.
   - ○ **D.** Preserve the data on the computer.

24. When it comes to sanitizing drives, which of the following statements best describes the difference between overwriting a drive and formatting a drive?

   - ○ **A.** Overwriting writes 1s and 0s to the drive, replacing only the user's data but not the OS data; formatting destroys the hard drive.
   - ○ **B.** They both destroy the data so no one can recover it.
   - ○ **C.** Overwriting replaces all the data with a single file that fills the hard drive, destroying the data; formatting erases all the data.
   - ○ **D.** Overwriting writes 1s and 0s to the drive, replacing the data; formatting only clears the reference to the data and only overwrites as space is used.

25. Which of the following is a common symptom of a problem that can occur while starting up the Windows operating system?

- ○ **A.** Spontaneous shutdown/restart
- ○ **B.** Invalid boot disk
- ○ **C.** WinRE won't start
- ○ **D.** The optical disc failed
- ○ **E.** The emergency repair disk doesn't boot
- ○ **F.** REGSVR32 has failed

26. A user tries to connect to the Internet using a dial-up modem and receives a message that says "no dial tone detected." Which of the following should be checked first?

- ○ **A.** Cable is connected to the modem's line RJ11 port
- ○ **B.** Cable is connected to the modem's phone RJ11 port
- ○ **C.** Cable is connected to the modem's line RJ45 port
- ○ **D.** Cable is connected to the modem's phone RJ45 port

27. Which of the following are possible symptoms of malware? (Select all that apply.)

- ○ **A.** Security alerts
- ○ **B.** Windows Update failures
- ○ **C.** Preinstallation environment
- ○ **D.** Renamed system files
- ○ **E.** Rogue antivirus
- ○ **F.** User error

28. What is the correct path to determine the IP address of an iOS device?

- ○ **A.** General > Settings > SSID Name > Network > IP Address
- ○ **B.** Wi-Fi > SSID Name > Network > IP Address
- ○ **C.** Location Services > Settings > Wi-Fi > IP Address
- ○ **D.** Settings > Wi-Fi > SSID Name > IP Address

29. Which type of fire extinguishing technology should be used during an electrical fire?

- ○ **A.** Overhead sprinkler systems
- ○ **B.** Water-based fire extinguishers
- ○ **C.** Class B fire extinguishers
- ○ **D.** Non-water-based fire extinguishers

30. You attempt to install a legacy application on a computer running Windows 8. You receive an error that says the application cannot be installed because the OS is not supported. Which of the following describes the first step you should take to continue installing the application?

    ○ **A.** Install the latest SP.

    ○ **B.** Install the application in Safe Mode.

    ○ **C.** Install the application in compatibility mode.

    ○ **D.** Install the latest security updates.

31. A customer calls to report that when she walks away from her laptop for an extended period of time, she has to reconnect to wireless upon her return. Which of the following will most likely correct this issue?

    ○ **A.** Replace the wireless card.

    ○ **B.** Install a higher capacity battery.

    ○ **C.** Adjust the power settings.

    ○ **D.** Disable the screensaver.

32. Which of the following identifies the best utilization for a virtual machine running locally on a PC?

    ○ **A.** Using the virtual machine for patch testing before rollout

    ○ **B.** Using the virtual machine in a thick client configuration

    ○ **C.** Using the virtual machine in a gaming workstation configuration

    ○ **D.** Using the virtual machine on a PC with minimal RAM

33. You are required to remove the ability for standard users to shut down or restart a shared computer. Which command should be used to accomplish this task?

    ○ **A.** `shutdown.exe`

    ○ **B.** `bootrec.exe`

    ○ **C.** `gpedit.msc`

    ○ **D.** `services.msc`

34. You are required to replace a desktop power supply. Which of the following tasks should be performed first?

    ○ **A.** Remove your watch and jewelry.

    ○ **B.** Review local regulations for disposal procedures.

    ○ **C.** Read the MSDS.

    ○ **D.** Check for environmental concerns.

35. You are helping a customer with an Internet connectivity problem. The customer tells you that the computer cannot connect to her favorite website. After quickly analyzing the computer, you note that it cannot connect to *any* websites. Which of the following tasks should be performed next?

- ○ **A.** Identify the problem.
- ○ **B.** Establish a theory of probable cause.
- ○ **C.** Test your theory to determine cause.
- ○ **D.** Establish a plan of action.

36. Your customer has a computer (named comp112) that has been infected by a worm. The worm has propagated to at least 30 other computers on the network. Which of the following tasks should be performed before attempting to remove the worm from the comp112 computer?

- ○ **A.** Log the user off the system.
- ○ **B.** Boot the system in Safe Mode.
- ○ **C.** Run a full virus scan.
- ○ **D.** Disconnect the network cable from the computer.

37. One of your co-workers is attempting to access a file on a share located on a remote computer. The file's share permissions are set to allow the user full control; however, the NTFS permissions allow the user to have read access. Which of the following will be the user's resulting access level for the file?

- ○ **A.** Read
- ○ **B.** Write
- ○ **C.** Modify
- ○ **D.** Full Control

38. You are installing a 32-bit program on a 64-bit version of Windows 8. Where does the program get installed to?

- ○ **A.** C:\
- ○ **B.** C:\Program Files
- ○ **C.** C:\Windows
- ○ **D.** C:\Program Files (x86)

39. Which type of user account should be disabled to adhere to security best practices?

- ○ **A.** Guest
- ○ **B.** Administrator
- ○ **C.** Standard user
- ○ **D.** Power user

40. You are working on a client computer and receive a message that says the trust relationship to the domain has been broken. Which of the following steps should be taken to resolve this problem from the client computer?

- ○ **A.** Update the BIOS using the latest version.
- ○ **B.** Run CHKDSK.
- ○ **C.** Rejoin the computer to the domain.
- ○ **D.** Reboot the PC as the domain will automatically rebuild the relationship.

41. At one of your customer's locations, two users share the same Windows 7 computer. The first user creates a document intended to be used by both users and then logs off the computer. The second user logs on and types the name of the document in the Start menu but the document cannot be found. Which of the following statements describes the problem?

- ○ **A.** The document is locked.
- ○ **B.** The document is set to hidden.
- ○ **C.** The document is owned by the first user.
- ○ **D.** The document is encrypted.

42. You are working with a virtual machine (VM) when you discover that it has been infected with malware. Which of the following will apply?

- ○ **A.** The host computer will quarantine the VM automatically.
- ○ **B.** The VM will crash and cause damage to the host PC.
- ○ **C.** The host computer will delete the VM automatically.
- ○ **D.** The VM can be shut down with no harm to the host PC.

43. You have been tasked with diagnosing a laptop that is experiencing heavy artifact corruption along with random loss of video during operation. Which of the following are the most likely causes to the problem? (Select the two best answers.)

- ○ **A.** The integrated system video chip is failing.
- ○ **B.** Video drivers were not installed directly from Windows Update.
- ○ **C.** Incompatible or untested video drivers were installed.
- ○ **D.** The BIOS is not set for proper video chipset temperature.
- ○ **E.** The BIOS is underclocking the video card.

44. You are configuring a friend's iPad. He needs to access his work e-mail. To do this, you require information from his IT department. Which information should you ask for?

- ○ **A.** Server and gateway
- ○ **B.** IP address and domain
- ○ **C.** IP address and DNS
- ○ **D.** Server and domain

45. You are installing Windows to a PC with a RAID card. All cables are connected properly, but the install DVD does not detect any hard drives. Which of the following tasks should be performed next?

- ○ **A.** Enable PATA in the BIOS.
- ○ **B.** Hit the refresh button to auto-detect the drives.
- ○ **C.** Select the load driver.
- ○ **D.** Press F8 when prompted.

46. A customer tells you that it takes a long time to load the Windows desktop after logon. Which tool can help with this problem?

- ○ **A.** Msconfig
- ○ **B.** System File Checker (SFC)
- ○ **C.** bootrec /fixmbr
- ○ **D.** Disk Management

47. Which of the following statements best describes how to secure only physically unused network ports on a switch?

- ○ **A.** Disable DNS on the network.
- ○ **B.** Use DHCP addressing on the network.
- ○ **C.** Power down the router when it is not being used.
- ○ **D.** Disable the ports in the firmware.

48. Which command in Windows can initiate CHKDSK at boot time?

- ○ **A.** CONVERT
- ○ **B.** IPCONFIG
- ○ **C.** CHKNTFS
- ○ **D.** NETDOM

49. A customer reports to you that a file shared on her computer for another user is not accessible to that third party. The customer says that the third party was given Allow rights for Read and Write access to the file. Which of the following could be a reason as to why the third party cannot access the file?

    ○ **A.** The parent folder has explicit Allow rights set for the third-party user.

    ○ **B.** The parent folder has explicit Deny rights set for the third-party user.

    ○ **C.** The user forgot to share the parent folder and only shared the specific file.

    ○ **D.** The parent folder likely has the archive attribute enabled.

50. By default, EFS files display in which of the following colors?

    ○ **A.** Blue

    ○ **B.** Black

    ○ **C.** Green

    ○ **D.** Red

51. Which Windows command can stop a single process from the command line?

    ○ **A.** Taskkill

    ○ **B.** Shutdown

    ○ **C.** Tasklist

    ○ **D.** DEL

52. When dealing with Bluetooth, which of the following statements best describes the purpose of discovery mode?

    ○ **A.** Disconnects all devices and connects the closest powered-on device

    ○ **B.** Allows a peripheral to be contacted by the mobile device

    ○ **C.** Instructs the phone to seek out all nearby devices and connect to them

    ○ **D.** Allows two Bluetooth devices to connect to each other without a mobile device

53. Of the following ways to manipulate a file, which can retain the file's NTFS permissions?

    ○ **A.** Moving the file to another NTFS volume

    ○ **B.** Copying the file to another FAT32 volume

    ○ **C.** Moving the file to a new location on the same volume

    ○ **D.** Copying the file to a new location on the same volume

54. In a SOHO wireless network, which of the following prevents unauthorized users from accessing confidential data?

- ○ **A.** Enabling MAC filtering
- ○ **B.** Changing the SSID name
- ○ **C.** Setting encryption
- ○ **D.** Reducing broadcast power

55. Which CP utility is best used to remove a Windows application?

- ○ **A.** Disk Cleanup
- ○ **B.** Administrative Tools
- ○ **C.** Folder Options
- ○ **D.** Programs and Features

56. A user can no longer print from his computer to the default printer. While troubleshooting this issue, you learn that you can print a test page from the printer, and the printer's queue shows that the job is ready to print. Which of the following tasks should be performed next to resolve the situation?

- ○ **A.** Delete the job and resubmit it.
- ○ **B.** Reinstall the print drivers.
- ○ **C.** Reset the printer.
- ○ **D.** Restart the Print Spooler service.

57. A customer reports to you that he cannot access the company FTP site. He says that he is using the IP address given to him: 86200.43.118. What is most likely the problem?

- ○ **A.** Port 21 is blocked.
- ○ **B.** This is an invalid IP address.
- ○ **C.** The FTP site is down.
- ○ **D.** The FTP program is not working.

58. Which of the following allows you to make phone calls and transfer data from your smartphone without the need for additional programs?

- ○ **A.** Wi-Fi
- ○ **B.** Bluetooth
- ○ **C.** Cable Internet
- ○ **D.** GSM

59. Which command would display the contents of C:\Windows\System32\?

   O **A.** NET
   O **B.** CD
   O **C.** System Information Tool
   O **D.** DIR

60. Which of the following is the most commonly used file system in Windows?

   O **A.** exFAT
   O **B.** FAT32
   O **C.** CDFS
   O **D.** NTFS

61. Which of the following is an Apple smartphone feature that enables data to be backed up to a remote location?

   O **A.** iCloud
   O **B.** iOS
   O **C.** App Market
   O **D.** Google Play

62. When setting up a Microsoft Exchange mail account to synchronize with an iPhone, which of the following items can be configured to synchronize besides e-mail? (Select the two best answers.)

   O **A.** Shared calendars
   O **B.** Archives
   O **C.** Global address list
   O **D.** Calendar
   O **E.** Address book

63. A computer has been infected with multiple viruses and spyware. Which of the following tasks should be performed before removing this malware?

   O **A.** Disable System Restore
   O **B.** Disable network cards
   O **C.** Run Windows Update
   O **D.** Run the CHKDSK /R command

64. One of your customers has set up a perimeter firewall and has implemented up-to-date AV software. She asks you what else she can do to improve security. Which of the following will have the greatest impact on her network security? (Select the two best answers.)

- ○ **A.** Conduct a daily security audit.
- ○ **B.** Use strong passwords.
- ○ **C.** Install additional antivirus software.
- ○ **D.** Assign security rights based on job roles.
- ○ **E.** Disable screensavers.

65. You have been tasked with limiting computer access to certain users. Which of the following should be configured?

- ○ **A.** System Configuration
- ○ **B.** Local Security Policy
- ○ **C.** BCD
- ○ **D.** Advanced Security

66. You need to set up an alert that will be sent to an administrator when the CPU stays above 90 percent for an extended period of time. Which tool enables you to accomplish this?

- ○ **A.** Task Scheduler
- ○ **B.** Task Manager
- ○ **C.** Performance Monitor
- ○ **D.** System Configuration

67. Which of the following enables a user to reset his password with a series of security questions that only he should know?

- ○ **A.** Permission propagation
- ○ **B.** Administration
- ○ **C.** Verification
- ○ **D.** Authentication

68. You need to find out which Windows OS is running on a computer. Which command should be used?

- ○ **A.** SET
- ○ **B.** VER
- ○ **C.** Device Manager
- ○ **D.** CMD

69. Which of the following can allow a hidden backdoor to be used by remote workstations on the Internet?

   ○ **A.** XSS

   ○ **B.** Rootkit

   ○ **C.** Firmware

   ○ **D.** SQL injection

70. Which of the following statements describe how to demonstrate professionalism when dealing with a customer? (Select the three best answers.)

   ○ **A.** Avoid distractions.

   ○ **B.** Retain a chain of custody.

   ○ **C.** Avoid being judgmental.

   ○ **D.** Leave documentation to the customer.

   ○ **E.** Meet expectations that the customer sets for you.

71. Which of the following is an advantage of a PC-hosted virtual machine?

   ○ **A.** It reduces the amount of physical hardware required.

   ○ **B.** It reduces the amount of CPU required on the host PC.

   ○ **C.** It reduces the amount of RAM required on the host PC.

   ○ **D.** It reduces the amount of training required for employees.

72. A frustrated customer calls you about a PC that is not functioning properly. Which of the following questions should you ask of the user?

   ○ **A.** "What were you doing when the computer crashed?"

   ○ **B.** "Don't use that computer until it's fixed."

   ○ **C.** "What was the last thing that occurred before the computer stopped functioning properly?"

   ○ **D.** "What was the last thing you did before the computer stopped functioning properly?"

73. You are configuring a SOHO wireless network for a customer. The customer wants only five authorized computers to connect to the network within a defined IP range. Which of the following should be configured on the router? (Select the two best answers.)

   ○ **A.** SSID

   ○ **B.** DMZ

   ○ **C.** DHCP

   ○ **D.** MAC filtering

   ○ **E.** ARP

74. You previously installed a new application for a customer, adding three new services. Today, the customer informs you that the application will not start. You find out that one of the three new services has failed to start and manual attempts to start it fail. Where should you look next for information? (Select the two best answers.)

- ○ **A.** Registry
- ○ **B.** Event Viewer
- ○ **C.** %systemroot%\System32\Drivers
- ○ **D.** Log files for the new application
- ○ **E.** Task Manager

75. A computer you are troubleshooting keeps showing a message that says "low virtual memory." Where should you go to increase virtual memory?

- ○ **A.** System > Advanced
- ○ **B.** System > Remote
- ○ **C.** System > System Restore
- ○ **D.** System > Hardware

76. You are placing a computer back into service that has not been turned on in several months. It was healthy when taken out of service and boots quickly without any problems. Which of the following actions would be best practices to begin computer maintenance? (Select the two best answers.)

- ○ **A.** Defragment the hard drive.
- ○ **B.** Run AV updates.
- ○ **C.** Run an AV scan.
- ○ **D.** Run Windows updates.
- ○ **E.** Configure the firewall.

77. A user launches an application on an Android device. Once the software loads, the user reports that when turning the tablet to work the application in landscape mode, the software does not automatically adjust to landscape mode. Which of the following is the cause of the issue?

- ○ **A.** The auto-adjust setting is not enabled in the operating system.
- ○ **B.** The tablet is running low on power and disabled landscape mode.
- ○ **C.** The application was not developed to react to changes to the gyroscope.
- ○ **D.** The user did not switch the tablet to landscape mode.

78. Which of the following OSes supports full usage of 8 GB of RAM? (Select the two best answers.)

- ○ **A.** Windows 8.1 Pro 64-bit
- ○ **B.** Windows Vista Home Premium x86
- ○ **C.** Windows 7 Professional x86
- ○ **D.** Windows 7 Home Premium x64
- ○ **E.** Windows 8 32-bit

79. Which of the following is the best way to maintain data security for a mobile device that has been lost or stolen?

- ○ **A.** Passcode lock
- ○ **B.** GPS
- ○ **C.** Remote wipe
- ○ **D.** Login attempt restrictions

80. Which of the following is part of the second step of the CompTIA A+ trouble-shooting process: Establish a theory of probable cause?

- ○ **A.** Question the user.
- ○ **B.** Question the obvious.
- ○ **C.** Test the theory to determine cause.
- ○ **D.** Establish a plan of action.

Answers at a Glance

1. C and D	**28.** D	**55.** D
2. B	**29.** D	**56.** D
3. B	**30.** C	**57.** B
4. B	**31.** C	**58.** D
5. C	**32.** A	**59.** D
6. A	**33.** C	**60.** D
7. D	**34.** A	**61.** A
8. C	**35.** B	**62.** D and E
9. F	**36.** D	**63.** A
10. C	**37.** A	**64.** B and D
11. B and D	**38.** D	**65.** B
12. A	**39.** A	**66.** C
13. D	**40.** C	**67.** D
14. C	**41.** C	**68.** B
15. B and C	**42.** D	**69.** B
16. A	**43.** A and C	**70.** A, C, and E
17. A	**44.** D	**71.** A
18. D	**45.** C	**72.** C
19. A	**46.** A	**73.** C and D
20. C	**47.** D	**74.** B and D
21. A and E	**48.** C	**75.** A
22. B	**49.** B	**76.** B and D
23. A	**50.** C	**77.** C
24. D	**51.** A	**78.** A and D
25. B	**52.** B	**79.** C
26. A	**53.** C	**80.** B
27. A, B, and D	**54.** C	

Real-World Scenarios

The purpose of this section is to help prepare you for the performance-based questions on the CompTIA A+ Exams as well as prepare you for the real world of computer configuration and troubleshooting.

While these questions will not be exact representations of the questions on the CompTIA exams, they will give you an idea of the typical kinds of things you will be called on to answer. CompTIA can ask you anything that was covered in the book; plus, they can change the questions at any time. The goal of this section is to get you into the habit of practicing everything in a hands-on manner. Do this for any of the concepts I discuss in the book. The more you practice this way, the better you will do on the exams and the more prepared you will be for the IT field.

220-901 Scenarios

Let's go through some hands-on scenarios based on the 220-901 objectives. Read through each scenario and answer the following items on paper. Afterward, watch the video solution and perform the simulation.

Scenario 1: Design a CAD Workstation Computer

You have been tasked with building a computer that will be used for computer-aided design. It needs to be powerful enough to run CAD software programs. Remember! That means a high-end multicore CPU, lots of fast RAM, and a professional video card. Think about the type of software that it will be running and answer the following questions, providing as many specifications as possible. Then watch the corresponding video and complete the simulation.

1. Which type of CPU will you select? Research the manufacturer (Intel or AMD) on the Internet and specify the exact model of CPU you want to use.

   _____

   _____

   _____

2. Which type of RAM will you use, and how much?

   _____

   _____

   _____

3. Which type of video card will you install?

   _____

   _____

   _____

4. Think about the rest of the devices and connections to the motherboard that are required. Which type of motherboard and power/data connections will you use?

_____

_____

_____

Watch the corresponding video: "Video-01."

Complete the corresponding simulation: "Simulation-01."

Scenario 2: Select the Best Components for Three Computers

You are a technician working on a PC bench. Your job today is to build three computers: a Gaming PC, an HTPC, and a typical thick client. Write down the types of components you think should go into each type of computer. Then watch the corresponding video and complete the simulation.

1. Gaming PC

_____

_____

_____

2. HTPC

_____

_____

_____

3. Thick Client

_____

_____

_____

Watch the corresponding video: "Video-02."

Complete the corresponding simulation: "Simulation-02."

Scenario 3: Identify Video Ports

Your organization needs you to purchase several types of video cards to be used with various computers, monitors, and external video equipment.

Do the following for each of the ports listed in the table below:

1. Identify the port visually by researching each port on the Internet.

2. Write out the complete name of the port and any other identifying characteristics that you think are important.

3. Research actual video cards from manufacturers that have the ports.

4. Identify monitors, projectors, or other equipment online that might use each port.

Video Port	Full Name	Usage
HDMI		
DVI		
DisplayPort		
Thunderbolt		
S-Video		
VGA		

Watch the corresponding video: "Video-03."

Complete the corresponding simulation: "Simulation-03."

Scenario 4: Configure Wi-Fi on a SOHO Router

Now you've been tasked with configuring Wi-Fi settings on a typical SOHO router. The default settings on these devices leave a lot to be desired. You are in charge of making the device more secure. Answer the following questions and then watch the corresponding video.

1. What should you do first on a SOHO router?

_____

2. What is the SSID?

_____

3. What is the best encryption to use?

_____

4. What are the different channel ranges for the 2.4 GHz and the 5 GHz frequencies?

_____

5. What is MAC filtering?

_____

6. Why would you disable the SSID?

_____

Watch the corresponding video: "Video-04."

Scenario 5: Identify Various Wireless Ranges

Your boss wants to implement all kinds of different wireless technologies, but she isn't sure about the maximum ranges for each of them. Explain to your boss what the different technologies are used for and what their respective ranges are (providing the distance in feet and meters).

1. What is Bluetooth used for?

_____

2. What are the ranges for Bluetooth Class 1, 2, and 3 devices?

_____

3. What is NFC used for?

_____

4. What is the range for NFC?

_____

5. What is Infrared used for?

_____

6. What is the range for Infrared?

_____

7. What is WLAN (Wi-Fi) used for?

_____

8. What are the ranges for 802.11a, b, g, n, and ac?

_____

_____

_____

Complete the corresponding simulation: "Simulation-05."

Scenario 6: Identify IP Addresses

You will be interviewing for a junior network administrator position at your organization. To get the job, you will need to know TCP/IP very well, especially the different types of IP addresses that exist. Answer the following questions, and then complete the corresponding video and simulation.

1. What is the difference between a private and a public IP address?

_____

2. What is an example of a public IP address?

_____

3. What are the private IP ranges for Classes A, B, and C?

_____

_____

_____

4. What is the definition of a loopback address?

_____

5. What are the loopback addresses for IPv4 and IPv6?

_____

_____

6. What is an example of an APIPA/link-local address?

7. What is CIDR?

8. Define the parts of the CIDR address below:

10.10.251.189/24

Watch the corresponding video: "Video-06."

Complete the corresponding simulation: "Simulation-06."

220-902 Scenarios

Let's move onto the 220-902 scenarios. Here are some more hands-on scenarios based on the 220-902 objectives. Read through each scenario and answer the following questions on paper. Afterward, watch the video solution and perform the simulation.

Scenario 7: Troubleshoot an IP Issue with Ipconfig

You are troubleshooting a computer that cannot connect to the network. Use the `ipconfig` command in the Windows Command Prompt to help identify and solve the problem. Also use the command to test your solution.

Answer the following questions and then complete the video and simulation.

1. What does the `ipconfig` command do?

2. Which option can be used with `ipconfig` to find out advanced information, such as the DNS server and whether DHCP is enabled?

3. Which option can be used to discharge an IP address that was obtained automatically from a DHCP server?

_____

4. Which option can be used to *apply* an IP address automatically from a DHCP server?

_____

5. Which commands should be used to verify and test the connection?

_____

_____

Watch the corresponding video: "Video-07."

Complete the corresponding simulation: "Simulation-07."

Scenario 8: Sharing and Mapping in the Command Prompt

Your next task: Share a folder on one computer and map to it from another. But do it in the Command Prompt. Why? As you increase in speed in the Command Prompt (or any command line, for that matter) you will find that you can accomplish what you need to do faster than in the GUI.

Answer the following questions and then complete the video and simulation.

1. Which command enables you to share data on a computer?

_____

2. Write the syntax for sharing a folder as data1 on a computer named workstationA.

_____

3. Which command enables you to map to a share on a computer?

_____

4. Write the syntax for mapping to the folder mentioned in question #2 using drive letter F:.

_____

Watch the corresponding video: "Video-08."

Complete the corresponding simulation: "Simulation-08."

Scenario 9: Troubleshooting a System with Msconfig

One of the applications loaded on a Windows 7 computer is causing the system to behave erratically, sometimes locking up. Your task is to disable the application and its underlying service using the `Msconfig` command. Answer the following questions, and then watch the corresponding video.

1. What is the proper name for the msconfig application?

   _____

2. How do you open the msconfig application?

   _____

3. Which tab is used to disable the application?

   _____

   (Note that this is done in Task Manager in Windows 8/8.1.)

4. Which tab is used to disable the application's underlying service? (This is an easy one.)

   _____

5. What do you need to do after the configuration is complete?

   _____

Watch the corresponding video: "Video-09."

Scenario 10: Fixing a Computer That Won't Boot

One of your customer's computers can't boot into Windows. You need to fix the problem using the Windows Recovery Environment (Windows RE) and the Boot Recovery command. Answer the following items, and then complete the corresponding video and simulation.

1. How can you access the Windows Recovery Environment?

   _____

   _____

2. How do you get to the Command Prompt in Windows RE?

_____

_____

3. Write the syntax you would type to rewrite the boot sector of the hard drive.

_____

4. Write the syntax you would type to rewrite the master boot record of the hard drive.

_____

5. Bonus: Write the syntax you would type to rebuild the Boot Configuration Data store.

_____

Watch the corresponding video: "Video-10."

Complete the corresponding simulation: "Simulation-10."

> **Note**
>
> That's the end of this section, but make sure you watch the brief wrap-up video as well. If you have any questions, feel free to contact me at www.davidlprowse.com.

Index

756
Disk Cleanup

P

To receive your 10% off
Exam Voucher, register
your product at:

www.pearsonitcertification.com/register

and follow the instructions.